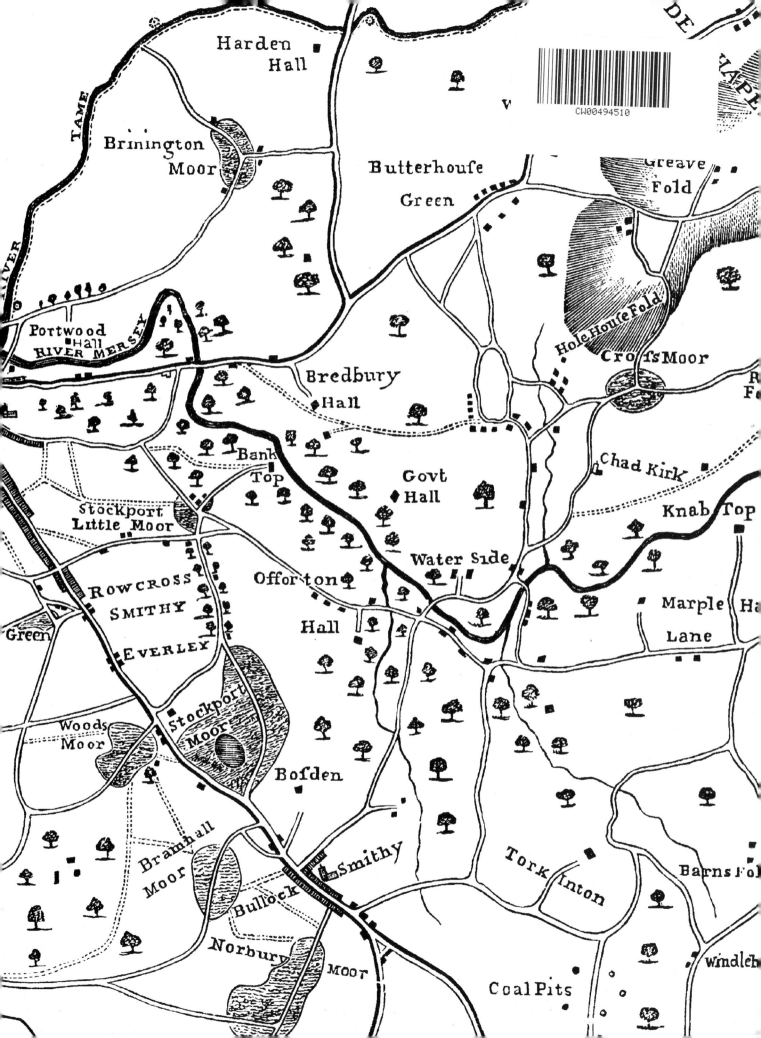

STOCKPORT

A HISTORY

Peter Arrowsmith

1997

STOCKPORT METROPOLITAN BOROUGH COUNCIL

Published by
Stockport MBC Community Services Division, and Stockport Libraries,
in association with
The University of Manchester Archaeological Unit.

ISBN 0 905164 99 7

Printed and bound in England by
Deanprint Ltd, Stockport, Cheadle Heath Works, Stockport Road, SK3 0PR.

FOREWORD

TELEPHONE:
0161 - 480 4949

TOWN HALL,
STOCKPORT,
SKI 3XE

November 1997

As Mayor of Stockport in 1997/98 I am honoured to have the opportunity to welcome this new and official history of the Metropolitan Borough of Stockport.

Stockport: A History, commissioned by Stockport Council and written by Peter Arrowsmith, is the first detailed book on the borough since Henry Heginbotham published the final part of his history of the town over a century ago in 1892.

Although much has been written and published in the twentieth century, this book is the first to provide a comprehensive study of the history, evolution and traditions of the borough. Like the very best of English local history writing, the author builds on the past rather than completely replacing what has gone before. It is both scholarly and immensely readable.

As Stockport's 'first citizen', a Councillor and local resident, I am pleased that the book treats the borough as a unified area. It was, after all, in 1974 that Stockport Metropolitan Borough was created by joining the county borough and four surrounding urban district councils.

I also welcome this book for another important reason; the history and heritage of a local authority are one of the ways in which local government can support the borough and its economy. Any book which encourages enthusiasm for local knowledge by residents, historians, tourists, businesses and visitors is to be supported.

I would recommend *Stockport: A History* to you all. Stockport is an exciting, living borough with a fascinating past and between the pages of the book there is something for everyone to appreciate – and perhaps remember but above all to enjoy.

Malcolm Lowe

Councillor Malcolm Lowe
Mayor of Stockport

ACKNOWLEDGEMENTS

This volume has been produced by the University of Manchester Archaeological Unit on behalf of Stockport Metropolitan Borough Council. Thanks are due to John Walker, Unit Director; to Tom Burke, Photographer, Graham Eyre-Morgan, Chris Howarth, Mike Nevell, John Roberts and Sue Mitchell, Unit Administrator; and to Dave Power for the skill and dedication with which he carried out the line drawings. Information from the Greater Manchester Sites and Monuments Record was provided by Norman Redhead of the Greater Manchester Archaeological Unit. The assistance of Chris Perkins, University of Manchester Map Curator, is also gratefully acknowledged. Judith Kent of the John Rylands University Library of Manchester carried out the proofreading of the volume, freely giving much of her own time and enduring the author's continual edits with remarkable good humour.

Acknowledgement is also given to staff members of Stockport MBC: Sean Baggaley, Collections Assistant, Stockport Heritage Services; John Baker, Head of Stockport Heritage Services; Collette Curry, Schools and Community Education Officer, Stockport Heritage Services; Robert Durn, Library Photographer; Jean Fricker, Planning Officer, Technical Services Division; Frank Galvin, Section Head Curatorial and Design Services, Stockport Heritage Services; Norman Hudson, Manager, Land Management and Development; David Isaac, Central Library Manager; Rosalind A Lathbury, Senior Library Assistant, Stockport Local Heritage Library; Gillian A Lund, International Liaison Officer; Margaret J Myerscough, Archivist, Stockport Local Heritage Library; T D W Reid, Local Heritage Librarian; Angela Stead, Manager, Bramall Hall; and the staff of Stockport Local Heritage Library for their continuous assistance in locating, processing and copying material.

A number of private individuals very kindly gave their time, answering queries, providing photographs and allowing access to property. Their help, interest and hospitality have been a constant source of encouragement. For these reasons, thanks are due to Tony and Joan Abrams, Bottoms Hall, Mellor; Donald Allister, Rector of St Mary's parish church, Cheadle, and Rod Macaulay, Verger; P J Bardsley, Marple Local History Society; Heather Coutie, Stockport Historical Society; Morris Garratt, Stockport Historical Society; David George; Anne Hearle, Marple Local History Society; Peter Jenner, Rector of St Thomas's parish church, Mellor, and Parish Secretary Jenny Butterworth; Shirley McKenna, Stockport Historical Society; Tom Oldham, Marple Local History Society; Ray Preston; Alan Richardson; Derek and Pat Seddon; and Peter Wroe.

Professor Robert Glen of the University of New Haven kindly read draft chapters of the volume. I am very grateful for his comments and for those of Frank Galvin, David Isaac, T D W Reid and John Walker. Their own expertise has led to a reconsideration of a number of issues, and the finished volume is much improved as a consequence.

Finally, I would like to give my special thanks to Adele for her continuous support.

Dr Peter Arrowsmith
University of Manchester Archaeological Unit

ABBREVIATIONS

CRO	Cheshire Record Office
LRO	Lancashire Record Office
GMAU	Greater Manchester Archaeological Unit
GMSMR	Greater Manchester Sites and Monuments Record (held by GMAU at the University of Manchester)
MCL	Manchester Central Library, Local Studies Unit
SLHL	Stockport Local Heritage Library
UMAU	University of Manchester Archaeological Unit
CN&Q	Cheshire Notes and Queries
DAJ	Derbyshire Archaeological Journal
DKR	Annual Report of the Deputy Keeper of the Public Records, HMSO
GMAJ	Greater Manchester Archaeological Journal
JCAS	Journal of the Chester Archaeological Society
JHC	Journal of the House of Commons
MM	Manchester Mercury
PP	Parliamentary Papers
RSLC	The Record Society of Lancashire and Cheshire
SA	Stockport Advertiser
SH	Stockport Heritage
THSLC	Transactions of the Historical Society of Lancashire and Cheshire
TLCAS	Transactions of the Lancashire and Cheshire Antiquarian Society
mf	microfilm

CONTENTS

List of Illustrations

List of Plates

CHAPTER ONE

INTRODUCTION

'The glorious epic of Stockport'

It may seem strange to the people of modern Stockport that at times in the past the town was the subject of some highly unfavourable criticism. Engels in the 1840s considered it to be 'one of the darkest and smokiest holes in the whole industrial area'.[1] Two centuries earlier there was a saying which was even less complimentary: 'When the world was made the rubbish was sent to Stockport'.[2] It may be surprising that the town also received glowing praise. An early eighteenth-century rector of Stockport compared, in verse, the setting of the town with the finest landscape of classical Greece.[3] In the twentieth century Stockport has been described as 'a city of balance, proportion and harmony'.[4] Beauty, of course, is in the eye of the beholder. The industrial scene which Engels viewed with disgust was to others an object of admiration.[5] The diversity of opinions expressed about Stockport, however, also reflects a historical truth: the continual and at times momentous changes which have taken place within the town during its long history (Ill 1.1).

There have been many Stockports in another sense, that of the extent of the area to which the very name has been applied. Place-names have long been flexible. The name of Stockport has been associated with a variety of administrative districts, among them a manor, a township, a parish, a poor law union, a municipal borough, a county borough and most recently a

Ill 1.1 Stockport, from the Stockport Sunday School, in 1910.
The face of Stockport has changed continually over the centuries. This early twentieth-century view is the very epitome of an industrial scene, with the chimneys of cotton mills and other works crowding the skyline. In the centre is the parish church of St Mary, the oldest part of which dates from the medieval period when Stockport was a small market town.

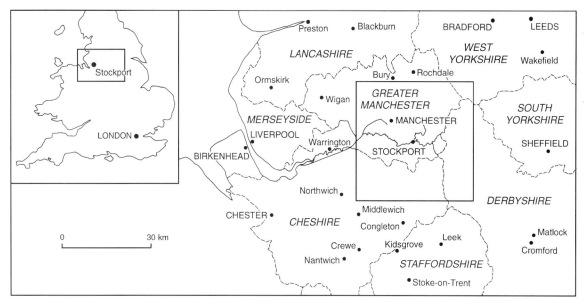

Ill 1.2 The Borough in its wider setting, showing the location of places mentioned in the text.

metropolitan borough. It is this last area, the modern Borough, as well as the town itself, which is considered within this volume *(Ills 1.2 & 1.3)*.

The history of Stockport has been described as a 'glorious epic'.[6] It is the story of a town which rose from national obscurity to become one of the earliest, and one of the leading, textile centres of the Industrial Revolution, and which by broadening its economic base successfully weathered the decline of that traditional industry. It is also a story of continuity as well as change. Alongside industry, trade has been the major driving force in Stockport's development. At the heart of the modern commercial town is its Market Place. One of the earliest documents relating to Stockport is a charter of 1260 granting its manorial lord the right to hold a market. The very place-name of Stockport, to which we will later return, shows that a market was held here even before that date. There is still a thriving market in the town.

A NEW BOROUGH AND A NEW COUNTY

The Metropolitan Borough of Stockport is a relatively new creation. It came into being in 1974 as part of a major reorganization of local government across the country authorized by Parliament in 1972. The Borough replaced five existing local authorities: the county borough of Stockport and the urban district councils of Bredbury and Romiley, Cheadle and Gatley, Hazel Grove and Bramhall, and Marple. They were themselves the product of a continual reshaping of local government which had begun in the nineteenth century. The basic building blocks of that process were the ancient administrative units known as the townships *(Ill 1.4)*. The area of the new Borough encompassed all, or virtually all, of eighteen townships and roughly half of one other, Werneth (the remainder of which lies within

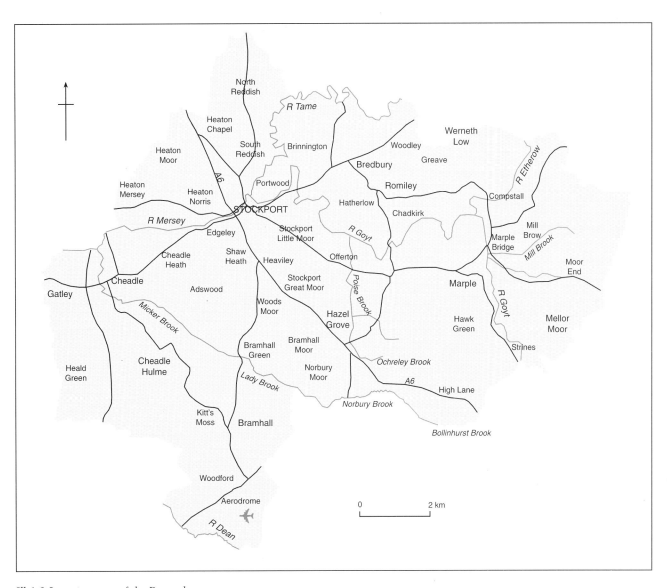

Ill 1.3 Location map of the Borough.

3

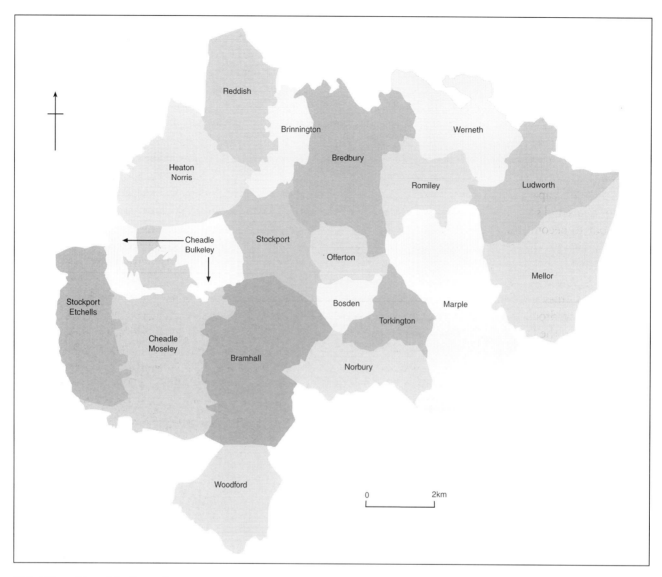

Ill 1.4 Townships of the Borough.

Prior to reorganization in the nineteenth century the basic units of local government were the townships. These were divisions within the ecclesiastical parishes to which administrative responsibilities were given in the sixteenth century. In most cases the areas of the townships corresponded with local manors, areas under the feudal control of a lord. The township boundaries shown above are derived from nineteenth-century maps. It should be noted that, for simplification, small 'detached' portions (parts of one township lying within the boundaries of another) have been omitted.

the neighbouring Metropolitan Borough of Tameside). The Borough at present also includes much smaller parts of several other townships, added as the result of boundary adjustments since the Local Government Act of 1972. Most of the township names are still familiar as local place-names, but some may be less well-known. Gatley and Heald Green once lay within the township of Stockport Etchells. Cheadle village formed part of Cheadle Bulkeley, while Cheadle Hulme lay within a township more usually known as Cheadle Moseley. One name, Heaton Norris, is now used for only a part of the ancient township, which also included Heaton Mersey, Heaton Chapel and Heaton Moor.

The ancient townships of the Borough lay within three separate counties: Heaton Norris and Reddish in Lancashire; Mellor and Ludworth in Derbyshire; and the rest in Cheshire, whose boundary followed the Mersey and the Tame on the north, and the Goyt on the east. A boundary change in 1889 transferred the Heaton Norris part of Stockport County Borough to Cheshire, to which Mellor and Ludworth were also added in 1936 when they became part of Marple Urban District. The Local Government Act of 1972 brought a more sweeping change. Under its provisions, in 1974 the Metropolitan Borough of Stockport, with nine other districts, became part of a new county, Greater Manchester.

4

THE LANDSCAPE

The natural landscape of the Borough is one of contrasts, for its area straddles two of the North-West's main geographical features: the Cheshire plain and the Pennine hills. In the east the high ridge of Werneth Low, the uplands of Mellor and Ludworth and, somewhat lower than these, the ridge at Marple all form part of the Pennines' western foothills. Below these the overall lie of the land slopes more gradually to the west, but this central landscape of the Borough is also cut by the valleys of rivers and streams. In the west the landscape flattens out to become part of the plain. The highest point of the Borough lies on Mellor Moor at 327 metres above sea level. By its western boundary the land alongside the Mersey falls below 30 metres.

Four rivers cross the Borough. The Mersey has its starting point in Stockport, formed by the confluence of the Tame and the Goyt. To the east of the town the Goyt is joined by the Etherow whose steep-sided valley divides Werneth Low from the uplands of Ludworth. The valley of the Goyt itself separates the ridge at Marple from the uplands of Mellor. A fifth river, the Dean, forms the southernmost boundary of the Borough at Woodford.

Of the tributary streams of these rivers, the longest in the Borough flows south-east to north-west to join the Mersey at Cheadle. It is known by various names along its length: the Bollinhurst Brook at High Lane, the Norbury Brook at Hazel Grove, the Lady Brook at Bramhall and the Micker Brook at Cheadle. The hillslopes of Mellor and Ludworth are punctuated by valleys through which small tributary streams flow down to the Goyt. Rivers and streams have played an important part in the Borough's history. In the medieval period and later they powered local cornmills. In the eighteenth century they were put to new purposes, powering the Borough's earliest textile mills and supplying water to bleaching and printing works (Ill 1.5).

In the early nineteenth century it was said of Stockport that 'There is not in England a more irregular spot of ground than that on which this town stands'.[7] Here the Mersey flows through a steep-sided valley, cut through a sandstone ridge. To the east of the town that ridge slopes to the valleys of the Tame and the Goyt. To the west of the town centre the Mersey valley continues to be flanked by steep valley sides, at Brinksway on the south and Heaton Mersey on the north, but that valley also widens as the ridge itself falls

Ill 1.5 Moor End, Mellor.
The hills in the east of the Borough are cut by the valleys of streams flowing down to the River Goyt. In the late eighteenth and early nineteenth centuries small water-powered cotton mills were built along their banks. Several such factories existed at Moor End.

5

away to the Cheshire plain. The town of Stockport first developed on the south side of the river valley. Its historic core, the Market Place, occupies a roughly triangular promontory of land (Ill 1.6). From here the ground falls away on the west to the Mersey, on the north to the Goyt, and on the south to a ravine cut by a tributary stream of the Mersey. This stream, now culverted, is here known as the Tin Brook but higher up its short course as the Carr Brook and Hempshaw Brook. The ravine of the Tin Brook is more familiar today as the street known as Little Underbank (Ill 8.16). At the north-west corner of the Market Place is a further, smaller triangular promontory. Historically this has been known as Castle Hill and its summit as Castle Yard. Traditionally, and almost certainly correctly, it has been identified as the site of Stockport's medieval castle. Immediately below Castle Hill the Mersey valley is at its narrowest, as is the river itself. This is the site of an ancient bridging point, known since at least the sixteenth century as Lancashire Bridge, from where a road led to Manchester. Upstream of this bridge, towards the confluence of the Tame and Goyt, there was also a ford. Stockport's role as a crossing place on the Mersey must be considered to be one of the key factors behind the town's origins. Another contributing factor may have been its position on the approach to an important trans-Pennine route, for to the north-east, beyond Werneth Low, lies the entrance to the pass of Longdendale. (Prior to the 1974 boundary changes this pass formed the projecting arm or 'panhandle' of the county of Cheshire.)

The local river system played a major role in Stockport's later development. During the Industrial Revolution the town was one of the North-West's premier locations for the siting of water-powered factories. Twentieth-century engineering has ensured that the Mersey continues to contribute to Stockport's

Ill 1.6 Stockport's historic centre, detail of an Ordnance Survey map of 1895.
The historic core of Stockport is the Market Place. It lies on a triangular sandstone promontory, from which the ground falls in steep cliffs on the west and south, to Great and Little Underbank, and more gently on the north. Little Underbank and Royal Oak Yard lie within a natural ravine cut by the Tin Brook, a tributary stream of the Mersey. At the north-west corner of the Market Place is a further steep-sided sandstone outcrop, known historically as Castle Hill. It overlooks the site of Lancashire Bridge, an ancient crossing point on the Mersey.

economy, albeit in a more indirect fashion. In the centre of the town the river was covered over in the 1930s to provide a new relief road, Merseyway, and in the 1960s the corridor of this road was in turn incorporated within a new pedestrianized shopping precinct *(Ill 9.4)*. While this section of the river is now hidden from view, the slopes of the Mersey valley are still very much in evidence. To enter the town from the north (along Wellington Road North or Lancashire Hill) or from the south (along Wellington Road South or Hillgate) involves a steep descent towards the valley bottom. That valley and the ravine of the Tin Brook still give rise to an irregular townscape, characterized by sharp variations in ground level, public steps and rising streets.

To the west of Stockport, where the Mersey valley widens out and shallows, the once broad flow of the river has left an ancient terrace of sands and gravels. This rises above the narrower valley bottom through which the river presently flows, and over which, despite the modern precaution of defensive dykes, it occasionally floods. It is this high terrace which is the location of the villages of Gatley and Cheadle *(Ill 1.7)*. At Cheadle the ancient river terrace is bordered by one of the Borough's more sizeable areas of glacially deposited sands and gravels. Other large glacial deposits of this type are found at Hazel Grove along the course of the

Ochreley Brook and Poise Brook and, most extensively of all, on either side of the Mersey valley at Stockport, Heaton Mersey and Heaton Norris. The predominant 'drift', or overlying, geology of the Borough, however, is glacial boulder clay. This has long been dug locally for the manufacture of bricks and tiles.[8]

The 'solid', or underlying, geology has also given rise to local industries.[9] In the east this geology comprises coal-bearing rocks of the Carboniferous period, which form part of the extensive Lancashire coalfield. These rocks shelve towards the west where they are overlain by later deposits of the Permo-Triassic period. The Carboniferous deposits resulted in a local mining industry, while the Permo-Triassic overlay effectively defined that industry's westernmost limits as being at Bredbury, Offerton, Marple and Norbury. Outcropping rocks have also been quarried for building purposes. The Permo-Triassic deposits contain sandstones which are easily worked and also easily eroded, but the Carboniferous rocks include harder Millstone Grit.

A now vanished landscape feature were the mosslands, or peat bogs, which once dotted the Borough's lowlands. They provided their own natural resource, turves of peat which were dried for use as fuel. The Borough's mosslands have all been drained but many are still recalled in local place-names. Kitt's Moss in

Ill 1.7 The parish church of St Mary and the White Hart, Cheadle village, about 1910.
Cheadle is one of the most ancient places of settlement in the Borough. It lies on a terrace of land rising above the flood plain of the River Mersey and close to an ancient crossing point on that river. At the time of Domesday Cheadle was one of the most important manors in north-east Cheshire and was probably also already the centre of a parish. The present parish church dates from the sixteenth century.

Bramhall and Hall Moss in Woodford provide the most obvious examples, but former mosslands lie behind such local 'moor' names as Heaton Moor, Stockport Great Moor and Little Moor, Woods Moor, Bramhall Moor and Norbury Moor.[10]

THE PRESENT VOLUME

Previous work

Mention of Stockport in antiquarian or descriptive accounts dates back to about 1540, when John Leland referred to the town and its 'maner place' or manor house.[11] In about 1620 William Webb briefly described the town in his Itinerary of Cheshire, and also noted the halls of the gentry and churches in the neighbourhood. In the eighteenth century the growth of industry and the advent of factories added new topics of interest. The earliest known description of Stockport as a place of industry is found in the 1769 edition of Daniel Defoe's *Tour through the whole island of Great Britain*.[12] John Aikin in 1795 and James Butterworth in 1827 provided increasingly more detailed accounts of the town and the surrounding area.

It was Henry Heginbotham, a doctor, a member of the town's council and for two years its mayor, who compiled the first major history of the town, *Stockport Ancient and Modern*, published in two volumes in 1882 and 1892. This work dealt in considerable detail with the administrative and religious development of the town, but placed far less emphasis on its economic and industrial progress. It remains nonetheless an indispensable source for many details of Stockport's history. It also contains brief accounts of each of the townships within the Stockport poor law union, an administrative area which included much of the modern Borough.

The 1890s and 1900s saw the publication of shorter accounts of Cheadle, Marple and Hazel Grove compiled by other local figures.[13] The number of works on individual localities within the Borough remained modest, however, until the early 1970s. Partly in response to the imminent demise of long-established local authorities, those years saw a growing interest in local history and marked the beginning of a steady stream of new works by amateur local historians, which has continued into the 1990s. These publications include histories of individual local places, studies of particular industries, institutions and public services, and personal reminiscences.

The twentieth century has also seen the appearance of a number of works by professional historians and research students on particular aspects of the history of Stockport and its neighbourhood. The first of these was a pioneering study by George Unwin and others on Samuel Oldknow.[14] A number of its conclusions have been revised by more recent research by Phyllis Giles, whose thorough and admirable studies of Stockport's history include a monumental dissertation on the economic, social and political development of the town between 1815 and 1836.[15] Robert Glen has used Stockport for a case study of urban working-class organization and unrest in the Industrial Revolution of the late eighteenth and early nineteenth centuries. Naomi Reid has effectively picked up the story where Phyllis Giles's dissertation ended, by examining the development of Chartism in the town.[16] Other academic studies include examinations of aspects of Stockport's local government and the local provision of education.

The aims of the book

By 1995 it was felt appropriate by Stockport MBC to commission a history of the area of the Borough, which would bring together the findings of this growing body of work in a single, unified volume. The present book is the result of that initiative, but its compilation has required an additional element. While the existing body of local histories and studies is wide-ranging, it is not comprehensive. Some parts of the Borough are considerably better covered by the available works than others. The same is also true of the different periods of its history, and of specific local themes.

In part these gaps have been filled by casting the net at a wider body of studies which touch upon the Borough. At the same time the problem has also been addressed through new research undertaken for the volume. This has involved the use of a variety of sources. Among these have been early newspapers (including the *Stockport Advertiser*, first published in 1822), trade directories and parliamentary papers. Use has also been made of a range of documentary evidence. Some of this has been published (most notably the probate records from Stockport township transcribed by members of the Stockport Historical Society);[17] some of it has not. Within the constraints of the project this research has of necessity been extremely selective.

The present volume is not an all-embracing study of the area of the Borough as a whole or of the individual places within its boundaries. The principal intention has rather been to consider and highlight some of the key aspects of its development and major episodes within its history. In doing so, it is hoped that the work not only informs but also serves as a stimulus for future research.

CHAPTER TWO

ORIGINS

'Gamel holds Cedde [Cheadle] of the earl. His father held it as a free man.'

INTRODUCTION

It is not possible to construct a detailed or continuous account of the history of the Borough prior to the medieval period (by which is meant the period following the Norman takeover in the late eleventh century AD). The necessary information is simply lacking. The available material for the earlier periods comprises three main sources of information: archaeological evidence, place-names and, for the Anglo-Saxon period, the Domesday survey.

For the prehistoric and Roman periods in particular, archaeology, the study of the physical remains of the past, provides by far the majority of evidence. To date, however, only three pre-medieval sites in the Borough have been investigated using modern methods of archaeological recording: a prehistoric burial site on Mellor Moor, the earthwork known as Nico Ditch in North Reddish and a Roman road in Woodford. Burial mounds in Ludworth have also been excavated, but according to the standards of a less scientific age.

The bulk of archaeological material from the Borough consists of artefacts unearthed by chance during day-to-day activities such as ploughing, digging foundations and gardening. Most are single finds from which we can often only surmise their original context. A prehistoric tool might, for example, be an indication of an early settlement site, but it could equally well have been dropped and lost in transit. However, even the most unpromising artefact when considered as part of a wider body of evidence may be informative. The distribution patterns of finds can indicate areas of more intensive human activity. More particularly they may suggest the presence of an individual site or feature, such as a settlement or the line of a Roman road. Many archaeological finds made over the years in the Borough have no doubt gone unrecorded. New finds continue to be made and, if reported, will add to the existing body of information on its past.

The study of place-names has its own strengths and weaknesses. Although there are exceptions, most of the names by which the major localities within the Borough are known can be traced back several centuries. Because of changes of language, their original meaning is now generally forgotten, but invariably this meaning was descriptive. Names were coined which referred to some natural or manmade characteristic of a place, to its use, or to some person or persons with a close association. Most of the major local place-names are derived from Old English, the language of the Anglo-Saxons, although some originated with their British predecessors. Such names can provide us with an invaluable snapshot of a locality at an early point in its past. However, place-names can involve an element of geographical flexibility, with the name coming to be used of a wider area than the specific locality to which it originally referred. This is particularly troublesome in the case of settlement sites, whose existence may be evident from a place-name but whose precise location is now lost. A further difficulty is the question of when a particular place-name came into use, which usually can only be answered in terms of a fairly broad date-range. It is only at the very end of the Anglo-Saxon period, with the Domesday account of local estates or manors in 1066, that we have the first picture of places across a wide proportion of the Borough at a fixed point in time.

The following chapter is very much in the nature of a review of the evidence for these early periods of the Borough's history. Several main points will be considered: the distribution of archaeological finds and sites and their implication for patterns of settlement and other human activity; the problem of the courses of the Borough's Roman roads; the significance of the place-name evidence and the Domesday account for the identification of the major local places in the Anglo-Saxon period; and the possible date and function of the earthwork known as Nico Ditch. Future discoveries will hopefully add to the evidence presented here, and may confirm or even amend the conclusions drawn from the body of material presently available.

PREHISTORY

Hunter-gatherers of the Mesolithic

It seems likely that the Borough has been the scene of human activity since the Mesolithic period or Middle Stone Age. The people of that era, which lasted approximately from 8000 to 3500 BC, were hunter-gatherers, living off the wildlife and natural fruits of the land. They first made inroads into the North-West at a time when the climate was becoming warmer after the last Ice Age and woodland was replacing a barren tundra. Flint arrow points and barbs (known as 'microliths'), tools and waste flints left by these people have been found on the Pennine uplands to the east and north-east of the Borough, particularly along the Longdendale valley. They are believed to indicate the sites of temporary camps, used by Mesolithic hunters in the summer months as they followed the seasonal migration of game. Few lowland camps, which would have been used at other times of the year, have been identified in the North-West. This imbalance may partly be a result of the more favourable conditions in the uplands for the discovery of such sites. Most have been found on the high moors. Here the growth of blanket peat covered the flints until erosion in recent times began to bring them to light again.

A possible microlith was found in Cheadle Hulme in the early 1990s, but the previous use of this site as a market garden leaves open the possibility that it was brought here in soil from elsewhere.[1] Although Mesolithic activity in the Borough awaits to be confirmed, it seems likely that the Mersey valley was used during this period both for hunting and fishing and as a communications route to the hunting grounds in the uplands.

The Neolithic and Bronze Age

The earliest firm evidence for human activity in the Borough dates from the Neolithic period or New Stone

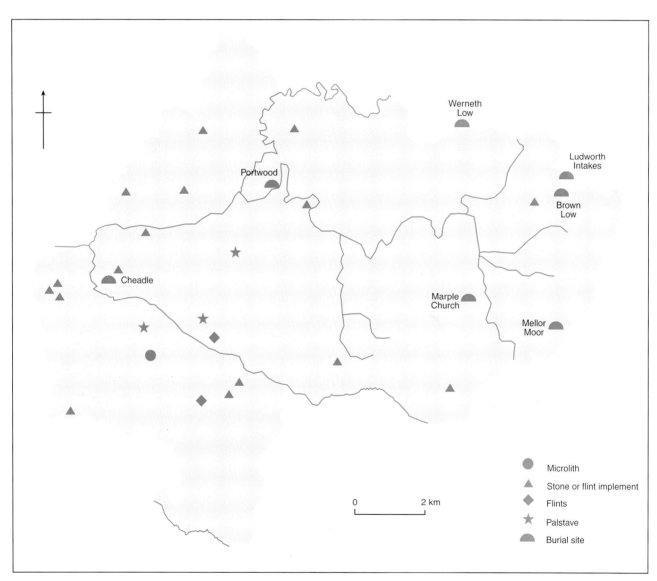

Ill 2.1 Prehistoric sites and finds in the Borough.
The local evidence for prehistoric peoples largely consists of chance finds, most probably dating from the Bronze Age. Their distribution suggests that activity was concentrated along the lowland valleys of the rivers and their tributaries.

Age, approximately 3500 to 2000 BC, or the Early Bronze Age, approximately 2000 to 1200 BC. The Neolithic was marked by a revolutionary change, the introduction of farming. With it came the establishment of more permanent places of settlement. The people of the Neolithic and Early Bronze Age were also the first to build lasting structures, in the form of ceremonial sites and funerary monuments. In the North-West the most common types are burial mounds, typically of earth in the lowlands and stone in the uplands, raised over the remains of the dead.

Activity along the river valleys

Within the Borough the prehistoric evidence from the Neolithic period onwards largely consists of chance finds, mostly flint and stone tools and weapons. The exact locations at which these finds were made is often unknown, but their general distribution suggests a concentration of activity along, or close to, the valleys of the Mersey, the Tame and the Goyt (*Ill 2.1*). These river valleys provided a natural communications route and a plentiful supply of water both for men and livestock. The valley bottoms themselves would be liable to flooding, but the river terraces which rise from these contain sands and gravels, which in places are also found on the higher ground flanking the valley sides. These are light and well-drained soils and were probably preferable locations for prehistoric settlement than the heavier, more impermeable boulder clay which predominates across much of the Borough.

Among the earliest of the chance finds are two polished stone axes, one unearthed at Gatley,[2] the other at Cheadle (*Ill 2.2*).[3] Their date probably falls in the Neolithic period or the beginning of the Early Bronze Age. A flint axe, polished at the cutting edge, was found in 1975 at a market garden at the very south-west corner of the Borough, near Heald Green. There is a strong possibility that this particular artefact had been recently carried to the site in a load of soil brought from Wilmslow.[4] In addition to the stone axe, at least two other prehistoric finds have been discovered at Gatley. One is a stone 'axe-hammer'. This is a common implement of the Early Bronze Age, with a flattened butt at one end, a point at the other and, between these, a drilled hole through which a wooden handle would have been inserted.[5] The other is a perforated 'mace head', a circular stone implement with a hole for a shaft, also possibly of an Early Bronze Age date.[6]

Not all the prehistoric finds from along the Mersey valley are stone implements. In Cheadle village three Bronze Age urns were discovered in 1872 during the digging of the foundations of new houses off Massie

Street. It is reported that 'owing to the ignorance and stupidity of the workmen, they were broken to pieces'.[7] Although no further finds are reported from this location, these urns are indicative of a burial site, with at least one of the urns probably containing the ashes of the dead.

To the north-east, during construction work at the sewage works in Cheadle Heath, a perforated mace head was found buried below nearly 4 metres of gravel which had been presumably deposited by the river.[8] This same site revealed a 'wooden oar'. It had evidently been preserved in water-logged deposits which also contained the remains of tree trunks, but a supposed prehistoric date for this object is no more than conjecture.[9]

Three finds of possible Early Bronze Age date are known from the high ground on the north side of the Mersey, an area of extensive sands and gravels. In Heaton Mersey, at the brickworks behind St John's Church, a broken perforated stone implement described as a 'stone hammer' was discovered in a sandy soil.[10] To the east, a flint knife has been found at Norris Hill,[11] while further inland an object described as a 'perforated stone hammer' was discovered at Heaton Chapel.[12]

No finds of prehistoric date are known from the town centre of Stockport, despite the likelihood that in prehistory, as later, there was a fording point across the river here.[13] East of the town, however, the occurrence of Bronze Age finds continues along the Tame and the Goyt. At Portwood, on the tongue of land between these rivers, three urns were unearthed in 1896.[14] As at Cheadle, they signify a burial site, although again no further remains were noted. One of these vessels was salvaged from the site. It is now the only known

Ill 2.2 Stone axe found at Cheadle (left) and axe-hammer found at Woodbank (right).

surviving example of at least seven Bronze Age funerary vessels discovered in the Borough (*Plate I*). In this same general locality, 'at Brinnington', an axe-hammer was found in 1889, not in the earth but in the thatch of a cottage, where it had possibly been reused as a weight.[15] Along the Goyt an axe-hammer has also been discovered at Woodbank (*Ill 2.2*).[16]

'Inland' finds

Other prehistoric artefacts have been found further inland to the south and east of the river valleys. It may be significant that some of these lay near to another watercourse, the Micker or Lady Brook, a tributary of the Mersey. These finds included three pieces of Bronze Age metalwork. All are 'palstaves', a type of bronze axe, and approximately date from 1500 to 1200 BC. One was discovered in 1901 during the digging of a sewer trench at Cheadle Road, to the south of Cheadle village.[17] A second was uncovered in 1892 during a similar operation at a location variously described as Adswood or Shaw Heath.[18] The third was found in 1932

in a clay pit in Adswood, presumably at the brickworks on the north side of the Lady Brook.[19]

Close to that last site, in a garden in Bramhall, an Early Bronze Age 'barbed and tanged' arrowhead was found with twelve other flints, mostly waste pieces but also including a scraper and a broken blade. These finds, discovered in a sandy soil, may indicate the existence of a site at this locality. This may have been small-scale and temporary in nature – the flints could be the tool-kit of an Early Bronze Age hunter.[20] Again in Bramhall, but to the south of the Lady Brook, a 'stone hammer head' was discovered in 1857 near what is now Seal Road.[21] A 'hammerstone' or stone 'pounder' was found, in approximately this same locality, 'near Pownall Green' during road repairs in 1906.[22]

The Lady Brook may not have been the only focus of prehistoric activity in Bramhall. Two flint arrowheads are reported to have been discovered in Ack Lane.[23] The eastern end of this road is known to have roughly followed the edge of Kitt's Moss, one of the Borough's many former peat bogs.[24] It is possible that these arrowheads, which might be of Neolithic

Ill 2.3 Brown Low burial mound, Ludworth.
This Bronze Age site was excavated in 1809, when fragments of bone were discovered. It is one of at least three burial sites of this period in the eastern uplands of the Borough.

or later date, are evidence of hunting on the mossland's fringe.

Hazel Grove has its own local watercourses, the Poise Brook and the Ochreley Brook, which are flanked by light well-drained sands and gravels. A flint knife of a possible Early Bronze Age date has been discovered in this locality.[25] Further to the east, a perforated stone artefact was discovered at High Lane. Its function is unclear, although a use as a hoe or a loom weight have both been suggested.[26]

Burial sites in the uplands

This last find brings us close to the uplands in the eastern extremity of the Borough. It is this area which after the river valleys provides the main evidence of prehistoric activity. Unlike the lowlands, where the evidence largely comprises tools and other implements, that in the uplands is largely concerned with the burial of the dead. It includes not only chance finds but also standing funerary monuments, among which are two of the most impressive archaeological sites in the Borough. These are the Bronze Age burial mound of Brown Low and the neighbouring burial mound on Ludworth Intakes.

Brown Low lies in woodland below the crest of Ludworth Intakes. The mound is approximately 25 metres in diameter and 2 metres high (*Ill 2.3*). It was opened in 1809 by the local antiquarian the Reverend William Marriott with the aid of four workmen. After digging through successive layers of 'small stones, boulders, and flat slabs', they came upon an inner earthen mound which in the centre 'lay near three feet above the natural surface; and declining thence on all sides, was in no place less than two'. This inner mound contained fragments of bone and possible evidence of a funeral fire. According to Marriott, 'the materials of the barrow were restored to their original order', but two hollows on its summit may be a legacy of this investigation.[27]

Approximately 400 metres to the north of Brown Low and straddling the boundary between the Borough and Derbyshire lies the burial mound on the summit of Ludworth Intakes. It is slightly smaller than its neighbour. In 1809 Marriott had also planned to excavate this mound. Word of his intention spread and he was pre-empted by a sizeable gathering of local people, who succeeded in breaking into the mound before being stopped by a representative of the landowner. The results of that episode can still be seen in the form of a great gash which cuts into the mound from its western side. Marriott, drawing on an eye-witness account and his own observations of the

despoiled mound, reported that its composition was similar to that of Brown Low to as far as a level of slabs. Below these, however, were three concentric circles of 'loose stones, piled together without cement, about two feet in height, and half of one in breadth. The vacuum, left between each wall, admeasured a yard and a half, and was paved or overspread with slabs, similar to those which formed its covering'. This base contained cremated bones, and possible evidence of a funeral fire was again noted. Placed within the centre of the mound, reportedly above the covering of stone slabs and 'about a yard and a half or two yards from the surface', was an urn. Unfortunately this was broken by the act of its discovery and its contents lost.[28]

To the south of the Ludworth burial mounds, on the summit of Mellor Moor and at the highest point in the Borough, is a third burial site. This comprises a low mound, barely discernible above the surrounding heather. Limited archaeological excavation in 1976 revealed a spread of cobbles, which seemed to be contained within a kerb of larger stones. The same survey team identified a second possible burial cairn a short distance to the north.[29]

A now destroyed burial mound once stood on the highest point of Werneth Low, just beyond the Borough boundary. In 1810 Marriott reported that the bulk of the mound had already been dismantled for its stone, but a surrounding kerb of large stones still defined its extent, which was 'perfectly circular' and measured 'ninety paces in circumference'. Marriott also believed that features on the northern and eastern sides of the Low were further burial mounds, but the few descriptive details which he gives of these sites do not allow this to be confirmed. He may, however, provide evidence of one other Bronze Age burial site in the east of the Borough. In 1808, he recalled, during the digging of the foundations of the church of All Saints at Marple a 'very ancient urn' was uncovered.[30] No further details are given, but the likelihood that this had been originally covered by a Bronze Age burial mound is strengthened by the location of the site on the crest of a ridge. Although the outlook from the site is now partially obscured by buildings, at one time it would have commanded extensive views on three sides, across the valley of the Goyt to the north and east and over the lowlands to the west. A commanding location on or, as in the case of Brown Low, one just below a hilltop is common to all the known upland burial mounds in the Borough and is a frequently encountered feature of such upland sites in general.

With the exception of the burial mounds, the evidence for prehistoric activity in the uplands of the Borough is extremely limited. A stone mace head has been found on Werneth Low. The exact place of discovery is unknown, but it is not impossible that it was recovered from the dismantled cairn on the Low's summit.[31] On the hillside to the west of the Ludworth burial mounds a hammer-stone was found in a stream bed. It is reported to resemble a distinctive type of implement found in large numbers at Alderley Edge in Cheshire. There they have long been seen as evidence for the prehistoric mining of the local copper deposits, but it is only recently that Bronze Age mining on the Edge has been effectively proved. If the Ludworth hammer-stone is indeed Bronze Age in date, its presence in this locality is something of a puzzle.[32]

Late prehistoric

With the end of the Early Bronze Age, in about 1200 BC, the datable prehistoric evidence from the Borough comes to a close. There are neither artefacts nor sites which we can associate with either the Late Bronze Age or the Iron Age, that is between approximately 1200 BC and AD 70. In part this apparent lack of evidence may reflect a deterioration in the climate from the late second millennium BC onwards. This is likely to have reduced agricultural yields, and perhaps also the level of population, on the Pennine fringe before conditions improved in the late first millennium BC.[33]

It is possible that evidence of occupation during that final period of local prehistory awaits to be found at a site beyond the Borough boundary, on the north-western edge of Werneth Low. Here, at Hangingbank, two lines of ditches define a small enclosure, now the site of a war memorial. A small-scale archaeological excavation in 1991 produced a single piece of Romano-British pottery from the backfill of the ditches. The double-ditched form of this enclosure suggests that it was a native farmstead, and it is also a form which is found in farmsteads of the Iron Age as well as the Romano-British period.[34] Similar sites may yet be discovered in the Borough itself.

THE BOROUGH UNDER THE ROMANS

The North-West came under Roman rule in the AD 70s and remained so until Britain was abandoned by the Empire in the early fifth century. The establishment of that rule made the region part of a frontier zone dotted with forts housing Roman auxiliaries. Two such sites lay close to the Borough. To the north-west was Manchester, situated at a major junction of Roman roads. To the north-east, near Glossop, was the fort now commonly known as Melandra, guarding the entrance

to the Longdendale pass. Outside the walls of both these forts civilian settlements or 'vici' developed. At Manchester there is evidence that both the fort and vicus were occupied well into the fourth century. At Melandra the abandonment of the fort and vicus occurred as early as the mid-second century, a period which saw the removal of troops from a number of forts in the region.

Beyond these new local, and in the case of Melandra relatively short-lived, centres of population the impact of Rome is thought to have been far more limited. In the region in general the native British population living in the countryside appears to have been both sparser and less affluent than its counterparts in the south and east of the country. While native farmers might buy Roman pottery and other minor trappings of Roman culture, their way of living remained otherwise largely unchanged. It is a picture that we need to bear in mind when considering the fragmentary and often uncertain evidence for the Roman period in the Borough. That evidence falls into two main categories. The first is concerned with the question of Roman roads in the Borough, the second with possible places of settlement.

The evidence for Roman roads

Manchester to Buxton

The observation that Roman roads in Cheshire are 'elusive and as unsatisfactory as a will of the wisp'[35] is particularly true of the Borough. Its position between the Roman fort at Manchester and Buxton, the Roman Aquae Arnemetiae, makes it probable that a road linking those two places crossed the Borough. Since the eighteenth century it has generally been supposed that from Manchester this road headed for Stockport where it crossed the Mersey. According to the traditional view, the line of much of this first section of the Roman road may lie beneath the present main Manchester to Stockport road, the A6. It should be noted that the straight course which this modern road follows through the centre of Stockport, crossing the valley of the Mersey by Wellington Bridge, is deceptive. This particular section of road alignment dates from only the 1820s, when it was built as a means of avoiding the existing more congested route through the historic centre of the town. On the south side of the town that earlier route followed Hillgate; on the north side it crossed the Mersey by Lancashire Bridge and followed Tiviot Dale, Lancashire Hill and Manchester Road, which joins the A6 at Heaton Chapel. Lancashire Hill, part of that northerly route, was itself of a relatively

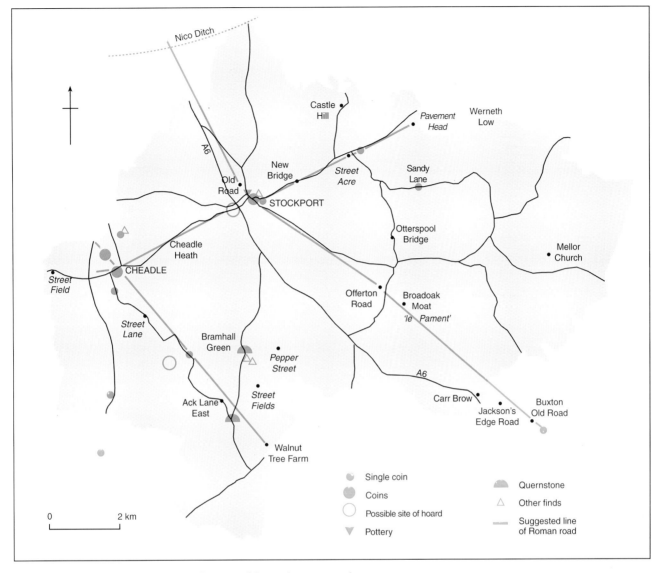

Ill 2.4 Roman finds in the Borough and suggested lines of Roman roads.
The local evidence for Roman roads is for the most part slight and inconclusive, but suggests that the Borough was crossed by two separate roads running between Manchester and Buxton. At Stockport and Cheadle these may have been crossed by a road running south of the Mersey, perhaps linking with the Manchester to Chester road. Other roads have been postulated. Finds from Stockport are believed to be related to a Roman site there, and a site may also have existed at Cheadle. In each case its nature is unknown.

modern date. It was built in 1794 and replaced Old Road, which followed a more westerly course of ascent up the side of the Mersey valley *(Ill 5.9)*.[36]

The long-standing belief that the pre-1794 route into Stockport from the north followed the line of the Roman road may be supported by its early name of 'High Street'. This name, along with a 'Street House Lane' in Heaton Norris, is documented in the early seventeenth century.[37] The original meaning of 'street' is a road with evidence of a made surface, and early occurrences of the term may, although not exclusively, refer to a Roman road.[38] This traditional alignment for the presumed Roman road between Manchester and Stockport may, however, include too many deviations

over a relatively short distance to be the actual line. An alternative suggestion is that the lines of the Roman road and the modern road part company at the old northern boundary of Levenshulme, by the Midway Hotel, and interestingly where the modern road crosses the line of the ancient earthwork known as Nico Ditch. From there the Roman road may have continued on a straight alignment to join Old Road at the edge of the Mersey valley *(Ill 2.4)*.[39]

Having descended Old Road, the Roman road is generally assumed to have crossed the Mersey by a ford upstream from the later Lancashire Bridge. In the late nineteenth century this ford was still visible, when the water was low, as a paved surface on either side of the

15

river. However, the ford itself is said to have still been used as late as about 1790, some five centuries after the bridge is first documented. During times when the bridge was being repaired or rebuilt, it may have provided the only local crossing point of the river. The date of this paving can, therefore, only be conjectured.[40]

The course which the Roman road may have followed through the Borough after crossing the Mersey has long been a matter of debate. Modern opinion tends to the view that to the south-east of the Borough the road passed through Disley and Higher Disley on a south-eastwards alignment now largely followed by Buxton Old Road. At Higher Disley the line of the road is reported to have been confirmed by excavation, and a coin of Valentinian I (364-75) has been discovered in that same locality, on Buxton Old Road.[41] If the alignment of the road suggested at Disley is projected north-westwards, it provides a course which heads almost directly for Stockport, passing Broadoak Moat in Torkington, Hazel Grove. Although this moated site has sometimes been supposed to be Roman in date, it is now firmly recognized as being medieval. However, in the fifteenth century a parcel of land adjacent to this site was known as 'le Pament' ('the pavement'), a name which may be a reference to a Roman road.[42] In 1996 a geophysical survey outside the moat revealed possible evidence for a road along the suggested north-west to south-east alignment.[43] Further to the north-west, builders digging foundations on the west side of Offerton Road in the 1970s uncovered, about 1.5 metres below the ground, 'a very solid layer of stones and packed gravels' which they assumed to be an early road.[44]

The north-western alignment from Disley is not the only course which has been suggested for the Roman road from Buxton to Stockport. An alternative view takes the road along a more southerly route from Disley, as represented today by Jackson's Edge Road and Carr Brow as far as High Lane and then by the A6.[45] This route may have existed as early as the thirteenth century, when there is a reference to a 'great highway' in the vicinity of the present High Lane.[46] However, its meandering route is unlikely to follow an actual Roman course, and there is little other evidence to indicate the presence of a Roman road from which this later road may have deviated.

Antiquarians of the eighteenth and nineteenth centuries proposed a third and very different route for the Roman road between Stockport and Buxton. They took as their cue two place-names in Bramhall: 'Pepper Street', which is documented in the seventeenth century and lay to the north of the junction of Bridge Lane and Bramhall Moor Lane; and 'Street Fields', which lay to the south of the site of Bramhall High School.[47] These place-names, it was supposed, indicated that from Stockport the road had followed a south-westerly course through Bramhall. After that point a change in direction to the south-east brought it eventually to the high ground separating the Cheshire plain from the Goyt valley, where its course was inferred from further place-name evidence.[48] The diversion through Bramhall which this route would have involved is not persuasive. In 1888 a section of a road which possibly gave rise to the two Bramhall place-names was uncovered at a fairly shallow depth, about 0.25 metres, during the digging of drains in a meadow near Pepper Street. Its width was not recorded but its construction was described as a paving of 'blue boulders' above a fine layer of gravel.[49] The date and function of this road must at present be considered uncertain.

Melandra to Cheadle

The Manchester to Buxton road was not the only road which antiquarians believed to have passed through Stockport. From here, it was supposed, a road ran eastwards to the Roman fort of Melandra, near Glossop.[50] A possible course for such a route might have been along Millgate and New Bridge Lane. After crossing the River Goyt, its line might have been later roughly followed by the gently winding Stockport Road West and Stockport Road East. Place-names and the evidence of chance finds lend weight to this suggested route. In Bredbury, immediately south of Stockport Road West at its junction with Bents Lane, was a field known as 'Street Acre'. Further to the north-east at Woodley was a field named 'Pavement Head', situated a little distance to the south of Hyde Road.[51] These field-names provide a temptingly straight alignment with the river crossing of the Goyt at New Bridge. Two coins have been found along this alignment. One, an issue of the emperor Trajan (98-117), was discovered at Stockport Road East near Bredbury station.[52] The other, possibly a coin of Severus Alexander (222-35), was recently found at the western end of New Bridge Lane.[53]

There is evidence which suggests a possible continuation of this road to the west of Stockport. In the nineteenth century the local historian Fletcher Moss was told 'by those who had seen it, that several feet below the present highroad across Cheadle Heath there is an old paved road, that they supposed to have been Roman'.[54] Its line may also be indicated to the west of Cheadle by 'street' field-names in the former townships of Northen Etchells and Northenden, suggesting that the road ultimately joined with the Roman road between Manchester and Chester.[55]

Cheadle to Buxton

Cheadle may have been the site of a junction of Roman roads, for there is also evidence of a road running south-eastwards from here. The existence of this road was inferred in the nineteenth century from Street Lane, the former name of Cheadle Road.[56] To the south-east, and on the same approximate alignment as Cheadle Road, an early road was discovered in the 1880s by workmen lowering Ack Lane East in Bramhall. This road, which skirted the edge of the peat bog of Kitt's Moss, was described as being made of compacted gravel approximately 0.5 metres deep. While this composition is consistent with a Roman construction, its kerbs of single 'large boulders' and its relatively narrow width of roughly 4.5 metres are perhaps less so.[57] Further to the south-east, however, recent excavation at Walnut Tree Farm in Woodford has revealed a gravel road, whose width of 7.5 metres and cambered surface, designed to help drainage, are both in keeping with Roman methods of construction. This road may well be the 'alta strata' ('High Street') which in the thirteenth century was recorded within this same locality.[58] Beyond Walnut Tree Farm, the course of this same road has been associated with small sections of earthworks on a straight alignment which continues to a pass through the uplands near Pott Shrigley. Here excavation near Harropfold Farm has revealed a further section of road, again 7.5 metres in width. These finds would appear to confirm the antiquarians' Roman road from Bramhall to Buxton, but not their supposition that from Bramhall this road headed to Stockport. A continuation of the same straight alignment to the north-west of the exposed road section at Walnut Tree Farm would have taken the road on a direct course to Cheadle village. This alignment lies slightly to the east of both Street Lane and Ack Lane, near which the road may again be evident as an earthwork.[59] Support for this straight alignment may be provided by the discovery in 1887 of a coin of Postumus (260-9) at Millington Old Hall, on Station Road in Cheadle Hulme, a site which lies directly on this line.[60] Fletcher Moss was told of a number of Roman coins found with a gold bracelet 'on or in' a mound in Cheadle Hulme, opposite Hulme Hall.[61] If the report is authentic, this may have been a Roman hoard, buried for safekeeping but for some reason never retrieved. The site lies to the west of the proposed road alignment, but is perhaps not too distant for there to have been a possible connection.

That the road from Buxton continued beyond Cheadle has yet to be confirmed, but a continuation of its straight alignment would have meant that it forded the Mersey where the river is now crossed by Kingsway.

From here its presumed destination would have been Manchester. Such a continuation may be supported by the discovery of Roman coins on the north side of the river in Didsbury.[62]

Cheadle to Alderley Edge

It is possible that a further Roman road passed through Cheadle, leading northwards from Alderley Edge and joining with the putative road to Manchester. That mining was carried out at Alderley Edge during the Roman period has been shown by the recent discovery of a coin hoard, hidden in the upper part of a back-filled shaft. Firm evidence for the suggested road is as yet lacking, but a possible line is suggested by a mid-fourth-century coin found in Heald Green near the junction of Wilmslow Road and Outwood Road (*Ill 2.5*), and by an issue of Gallienus (253-68) discovered in 1986 in Handforth.[63]

Ill 2.5 Roman coins found at Cheadle (left) and Heald Green (right).
Coins form by far the majority of known Roman finds from the Borough. They may provide evidence of roads or sites of this period.

The Werneth Low road

It has been argued in recent years that a Roman road crossed the Borough along a roughly north-south alignment, to the east of Stockport. Its northern destination has been suggested as the Roman fort at Castleshaw, near Oldham, its southern destination as a possible Roman military site at Astbury, near Congleton.[64]

Much of the case for this road rests on two early descriptions of the boundaries of the medieval forest of Macclesfield. One of these was compiled in 1619, the other possibly in the late thirteenth century.[65] The two appear to provide essentially the same account and to differ only in a few minor details. According to these documents, the forest's western boundary for much of its length followed a series of roadways. Beginning at Rodegreen, a place to the north of Congleton, these passed through Gawsworth, Prestbury and Norbury Low to the 'stream of Bosden' (*Ill 3.7*). The precise location of Norbury Low is uncertain, but Norbury itself was part of what is now Hazel Grove. The 'stream of Bosden' is the present Ochreley Brook and Poise Brook. From a bridge over that stream, known as 'Salter's Bridge', the forest boundary was then followed by a further roadway to Otterspool Bridge on the Goyt, at which point the river became the boundary. The forest of Macclesfield was established by the mid-twelfth century. It is the early date of its creation which largely underlies the supposition that the roadways followed by its western boundary represent the course of a Roman road.

Further to the north this suggested Roman road is believed to have climbed Werneth Low, having crossed the Goyt either at the present Otterspool Bridge or, further to the east, near Compstall. To the south of Otterspool Bridge the line has been linked with the possible early road found to the west of Offerton Road in the 1970s. To the north of the bridge it has been associated with the discovery of a coin of Augustus, issued in 23 BC. This was found lodged in the side of a disused stone culvert buried roughly a metre below the surface alongside Sandy Lane in Romiley.[66]

A suggested context for the establishment of such a road between Astbury and Castleshaw is the Roman campaigning in the North-West in the AD 70s. Proof of the existence of this road and of its proposed early date would represent a significant contribution to our understanding of the Roman annexation of the region. However, some observations must be made about this postulated Roman route. Firstly, there is documentary evidence that the road which runs along the summit of Werneth Low, once known as the Ridgeway, was in existence by the late thirteenth century.[67] This road was probably a continuation of that mentioned in the earliest account of the forest boundary as crossing first Salter's Bridge and then Otterspool Bridge. Bridges appear to have been something of a rarity in the locality in the thirteenth century, the only other one documented at this date being that over the Mersey at Stockport. Their presence on the road to Werneth Low implies that this was a route of some importance. So too does the very name of Salter's Bridge. This is one of a series of place-names which suggest a medieval routeway from the salt-producing area of central Cheshire to the Longdendale valley and on into Yorkshire.[68]

The second observation concerns the forest boundary. The fact that beyond Norbury it followed other features implies that the sequence of roads from Rodegreen ended at that point. This may have been at the junction with the present Stockport to Buxton road (the A6) which, as we have seen, was possibly in existence in the thirteenth century. While the boundary roads from Rodegreen to Norbury presumably predate the creation of Macclesfield forest, it may be significant that this route passed through Prestbury, the probable centre of an extensive Anglo-Saxon and Norman parish.

In short, the evidence appears to point to two separate routeways, rather than one, each of which is explicable in terms of an origin later than the Roman period. It should be stressed that the only Roman evidence along the line of these roads is the coin found at Sandy Lane. A Roman date is most unlikely for the culvert in which it was found, making the provenance of this coin itself a matter of uncertainty. On Werneth Low, beyond the Borough boundary, two lengths of embankment have been tentatively identified as the rampart of a Roman marching camp. However, limited excavation has failed to prove a Roman origin for these features which may be no more than much later field boundaries.[69]

Roman Stockport and other sites

Stockport

Antiquarians of the late eighteenth and nineteenth centuries were in little doubt that a Roman military station had existed at Stockport.[70] Its supposed location was on Castle Hill, the Roman station being viewed as a forerunner of the medieval castle which stood on this site. Castle Hill, now occupied by Castle Yard, is a small triangular sandstone outcrop projecting from the north-west corner of the larger promontory occupied by the Market Place. It stands above the Mersey, a short distance upstream from the site of the early ford (*Ill 1.6*).

The antiquarians' argument for a Roman military site at Stockport was based mainly on its location at a junction of several supposed Roman roads and on the natural defensive qualities of Castle Hill. It is not a supposition that is readily supported by the archaeological evidence. Two early sources report the discovery of Roman finds at Stockport. The Reverend John Stone, rector of the Cheshire parish of Coddington in the early eighteenth century, recorded that 'coins, paterae, and Roman implements were found at Stockport at the close of the last century'.[71] By 'paterae' bowls of either pottery or bronze are probably meant.

In 1751 William Stukeley, the most famous antiquarian of his time, mentioned in his diary a coin of the emperor Honorius (393-423) sent to him by Mr Peel, an excise officer, which had been found 'on removal of some rubbish, called the Castle, at Stockport', presumably a reference to Castle Hill.[72] There is no reason to doubt the authenticity of these early reports of finds. Later accounts may be more dubious.

In the 1770s Stockport's first water-powered cotton mill was erected on Castle Hill. A century later Henry Heginbotham reported that during the levelling of the site for the construction of that mill 'strong works were discovered, very firm and exceedingly substantial, and also some remains of a tesselated pavement evidently Roman'. No earlier antiquarians, however, refer to the finding of Roman material on Castle Hill at this time. Heginbotham himself, who took the report from a local paper 'published some years since', believed it to be 'founded on tradition only'.[73] In the mid-nineteenth century the mill was demolished and Castle Yard was levelled to become an extension to the Market Place. During the levelling operations, remains were uncovered which were again believed to be Roman, but no details are given which could verify this conclusion.[74] Bricks, and flooring and roofing tiles discovered in the late nineteenth century during the digging of foundations for a building on Shawcross Fold (below the north side of the Market Place) were claimed by some to be Roman, perhaps even the remains of a bath house. Others believed them to indicate a much later kiln site.[75] It is possible that during the nineteenth century the antiquarians' supposition that Stockport was a site of some importance in the Roman period led to any unearthed remains which could not otherwise be identified being pronounced as Roman.[76] The same may be said of 'some Roman remains' reported to have been discovered along the road from Stockport to Marple or the supposed Roman 'tesselated pavement' said to have been found below the base of a cross, itself presumably medieval or later, to the south-east of the town at Mile End (by the A6).[77] One report from the late nineteenth century, however, may well refer to Roman finds. During the digging of foundations for a new police parade room on Castle Yard, pottery was uncovered which was said to be Roman. It included one piece described as 'earthenware' bearing the letters 'LM', which strongly suggests a piece of stamped Roman coarseware.[78]

In the early twentieth century a coin of Gallienus (253-68) was discovered 'in the sand on the bank of the Mersey near Stockport'. This was presumably in a location to the west of the town, but the exact find spot is uncertain.[79] In the 1970s local collectors were offered coins which appear to have come from a single hoard. All date from 375-8 and had been struck at the same mint. The location at which they were found is uncertain, but was rumoured to be Daw Bank, where the town's new bus station was then under construction.[80] If this was indeed the case, the burial of these coins for safekeeping may have had as much to do with the proximity of this site to the suggested road to Cheadle as with any Roman site in Stockport itself.

Even with this final, questionable addition, the catalogue of known Roman finds from Stockport is slim. That some form of site existed here, probably centred on Castle Hill, seems likely but its nature remains elusive.

Cheadle

Equally problematic is the question of Roman Cheadle, where over the years a surprisingly large number of Roman coins have been unearthed in or close to Cheadle village. Fletcher Moss was told of 'many coins continually found on a certain farm' here, four of which he was able to purchase. These were an issue of Augustus, of 16 BC, and coins of Philip I (244-9), Diocletian (284-305) and Constantius I (293-306). The wide date-range suggests that these did not simply come from a single hoard.[81] More recently at least five coins have been found between the village and the river. One, an issue of Galerius (305-11), was discovered in 1948 to the south-west of Barnes Hospital (*Ill 2.5*).[82] Four others have been found to the east of the hospital, at a location on the Micker Brook known as Red Rocks. Two of these, discovered in 1981, were an issue of Faustina II (d 176) and a coin of the fourth century; the others, found in 1972, were also fourth-century issues, possibly of Constantius II (337-61).[83] Further to the north-east, a coin of Valentinian I (364-75) or Valens (364-78) has been found near Cheadle Wood Farm, off Manchester Road.[84] A Roman gaming counter, made from a broken piece of Samian pottery, has also been discovered in this locality.[85] Within Cheadle village itself three coins, of Postumus (260-9), Claudius II (268-70) and Constantine I (307-37), were unearthed on a site at the corner of Massie Street and High Street.[86] On the south side of the village a coin of Gallienus (253-68) was discovered in the bank of the Micker Brook near Broadway.[87]

The significance of these finds from Cheadle is uncertain. Some may have been simply dropped and lost. Others may represent one or more deliberately buried coin hoards. Some, perhaps all, of the finds may be explicable in terms of the Roman roads which other evidence suggests passed through Cheadle and to which this concentration of finds itself gives considerable support. If the Roman road from Buxton continued beyond Cheadle and crossed the Mersey by a ford, it may not be over fanciful to suppose that at least one individual in antiquity chose to bury his coins here rather than risk their loss during the river crossing. Another possibility is that at least some of these finds were related to an actual site, although its nature, as at Stockport, is unknown.

Possible native settlements

Other possible sites of the Roman period may be tentatively identified within the Borough. In the late nineteenth century the upper part of a stone rotary quern, used for grinding corn, was found at Siddall House, in Bramhall, a farm which stood on Woodford Road close to the junction with Moss Lane in the present Bramhall village. The quern was of a type with twin holes for feeding in the grain and was probably Romano-British in date (*Ill 2.6*). Siddall House stood close to the south-east corner of Kitt's Moss, and the find raises the possibility that a native British settlement existed on this mossland fringe. Interestingly a quernstone of this same type has been recovered from Red Moss, near Bolton. However, the Siddall House stone was not found in situ but had been

Ill 2.6 Quernstone found at Bramhall.
This find suggests the existence of a local settlement of the Roman period. Grain was fed into the twin holes in the quernstone. It was turned using a handle inserted in the socket in the side, grinding the grain against a stone base, now lost.

reused as part of a makeshift seat at the roadside. John Owen, the antiquarian who spotted the object in this position and identified its true function, was shortly afterwards shown the lower part of a quernstone by a farmer at Bramhall Green, nearly 2 kilometres to the north. This base fitted the upper part of the Siddall House quernstone so well that Owen believed that the two had originally belonged together. The present whereabouts of the base are unknown, but if Owen was correct, it is possible that both originated from Bramhall Green.[88] A settlement here would have had the advantage of being located close to the Lady Brook. The possibility of such a site may be supported by two other finds from this locality. One is a lead spindle whorl found on Fir Road near the junction with Bramhall Lane South. This might be Romano-British, although a medieval date is also possible. The other is also a spindle whorl, this time of stone, found close by on Waterloo Road.[89] Such native settlements, as noted above in connection with Werneth Low, might have their origins in the Iron Age.

Two other locations may also be tentatively suggested as the sites of Romano-British or Iron Age farmsteads. One, in the eastern uplands of the Borough, is the projecting tongue of high ground occupied by Mellor's parish church of St Thomas. This site, from which the ground slopes away steeply on all sides but the east, and which commands extensive views across the valley of the Goyt, would have been an obvious choice for such an early settlement. In the early nineteenth century the Reverend Marriott recorded that 'some years ago' digging in the churchyard for the construction of a vault revealed what appears to have been the remains of an infilled ditch. He also reports that 'many years before' the same feature was found during the sinking of the foundations of the adjacent house now known as the Old Vicarage.[90]

The other possible location is a hilltop above the River Tame in Bredbury, known as Castle Hill. The origins of this name are unknown. There are no reasons to suppose that a medieval castle stood here, but the name might suggest the existence of defensive ditches of an earlier period.[91]

Two sites which early antiquarians supposed to be Roman, the moated sites at Peel Moat in Heaton Moor and Broadoak Moat in Torkington, already referred to, are now recognized by archaeologists as belonging to the medieval period. A Roman origin has also sometimes been proposed for the earthwork known as Nico Ditch, the line of which is followed by part of the Borough boundary in North Reddish. We shall return to this enigmatic earthwork later.

THE ANGLO-SAXON PERIOD

Between the end of Roman rule in the early fifth century and the Norman takeover in the late eleventh, the history of the Borough was dominated by one central occurrence, the change from a British to an Anglo-Saxon society. This may have involved Anglo-Saxon settlers moving into the locality from elsewhere, or it may have been achieved by the native British adopting the language and culture of their new Anglo-Saxon overlords.[92] In either case the process must have begun no later than the mid- to late seventh century, when the people of the North-West came under the rule of two expanding rival Anglo-Saxon kingdoms, Mercia to the south and Northumbria to the north.

The boundary between these two kingdoms is likely to have been the Mersey and its tributary the Tame. The name Mersey is itself Old English in origin and means 'the river at the boundary'. The name Tame is British in origin but its meaning is uncertain. The use of these rivers as boundaries would have meant that the Borough was divided between these two kingdoms. It may also have been the case that the rivers fulfilled a similar role prior to that date, as the demarcation between two British petty kingdoms which had emerged after the Roman withdrawal and which now lost their independence to these larger Anglo-Saxon powers.[93]

Place-names and settlement

Pre-English place-names

The most widespread evidence for the Anglo-Saxon domination of the Borough is provided by its place-names (*Ill 2.7*). Of the 'major' place-names (those of the later townships), most are Old English in origin and were therefore probably coined in the seventh century or later. Only three have an earlier derivation. These are Werneth (meaning 'the place where alders grow'),[94] Mellor ('bare hill')[95] and Cheadle. The last name originated as a pre-English word meaning 'wood'. At a later date the Old English **leah** ('wood' or 'clearing in a wood') was added, possibly at a time when the meaning of the original name had been forgotten.[96] Like many pre-English place-names, these particular instances all describe natural features in the landscape. However, it is now recognized that such topographical terms could also be used as the names of settlements. The three localities within the Borough may have had a long history of settlement since each, as has already been noted, was possibly occupied during the Roman period.

It is unlikely that Cheadle, Mellor and Werneth were the only places of settlement in the Borough in the early seventh century. Others can be assumed to have existed, possibly also with a long history behind them, but to have been subsequently given new Anglo-Saxon names.

Old English place-names

Among the earliest of the Old English major place-names of the Borough is probably that of Bosden, now part of Hazel Grove. The first component is 'Bosa', a person's name. The second is the Old English **dun**, meaning 'a hill', hence 'Bosa's hill'. **Dun**, like pre-English topographical names, may have been used of a settlement situated on such a feature. It is also believed to have been only rarely applied to a place after the eighth century.[97] **Dun** is also found, again in conjunction with a personal name, in the minor place-name Cobden (Edge) in Mellor, meaning 'Cobba's hill'.[98]

Two other possible early Old English place-names are Bredbury and Norbury, each of which contains the word **burh**. This is not only an explicit term for a settlement but also implies that this was of some importance. It can be translated as a 'fortified place' and appears to have been a well-established element of English place-names by the eighth century.[99] Bredbury means 'at the **burh** built of planks'.[100] The description provides the earliest evidence for the form of construction of any dwelling or settlement within the Borough. Why this should have been so named is uncertain, but possibly the reference is to an extensive use of timber which distinguished it from other less important settlements. Its location can only be conjectured, but the Anglo-Saxon fortified site might provide another explanation for the place-name Castle Hill in Bredbury. The second **burh** name is Norbury, 'at the north **burh**'. The geographical significance of the name and the location of the site are both unknown.[101] The pre-Norman origin of both Bredbury and Norbury is firmly shown by their mention in Domesday.

Other Old English place-names may be perhaps no earlier than the eighth century. Among these are names which include the words **tun** and **leah**, two of the most common of Old English place-name elements. Some place-names with these later elements may postdate the Norman takeover.[102]

Tun, like **burh**, is an explicit term for a settlement and can be translated as 'a farm'. In the Borough it is found in four major place-names: Brinnington, Heaton, Offerton and Torkington. Brinnington, which was once supposed to mean the 'burnt **tun**', is now recognized

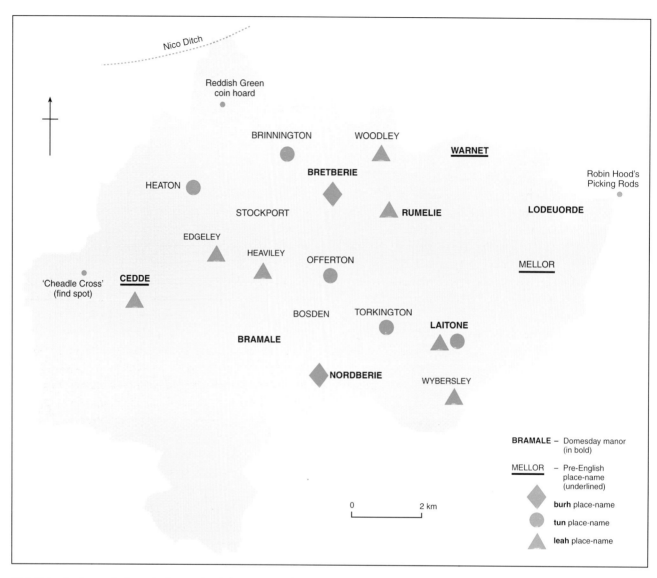

Ill 2.7 Anglo-Saxon finds in the Borough, place-names and Domesday manors.
Cheadle, Norbury and Bredbury appear to have been settlements of particular local importance in the Anglo-Saxon period. Lesser settlements may have included Heaton, Brinnington, Offerton, Torkington and Stockport itself, whose main significance was perhaps as a central trading place.

as 'the farm called after Bryni'.[103] Heaton, meaning the 'farm on high land', is presumably derived from the elevated position of the place above the Mersey valley.[104] In the twelfth century Heaton was granted to the le Norreys family. Their name was added to the original place-name to give Heaton Norris. Offerton is of uncertain derivation. It may be 'the farm at Offa's ford', presumably a reference to a crossing point on the River Goyt. Another possibility is that the name is a combination of 'ford' and a word meaning 'way up, an ascent'.[105] Torkington is perhaps 'the farm called after Turec'.[106] There is also probably a fifth **tun** name. This is 'Laitone', which is named in the Domesday survey as a manor in north-east Cheshire. It has been plausibly linked with Leighton, a place near Hawk Green in

Marple.[107] The name 'Laitone' is a combination of **tun** and **leah**. 'Laitone' is the only **tun** place-name in the Borough mentioned in Domesday, but a pre-Norman origin for the others is probable. It is noteworthy that Brinnington, Offerton and Torkington, together with Bosden, Bredbury and Norbury, form a block of places extending from the Tame in the north to the Norbury Brook in the south. This is an area with a mixture of a plentiful water-supply, some good soils and a relatively low-lying landscape, all favourable conditions for settlement.

Although seemingly referring to the landscape, **leah**, a 'wood' or 'clearing in a wood', is another example of a term which could also be used to describe the location of a settlement. Within the Borough **leah** place-names are found in two main geographical groups. These suggest belts of woodland in which the settlements were established. One comprises a group of place-names running north to south from Woodley ('**leah** in a wood'), through Romiley ('roomy **leah**') and Leighton ('farm at the **leah**') to Wybersley ('Wigbeorht's **leah**').[108] These places lie on the more hilly ground to the east of the favourable area for settlement which we have just noted. The other group lies in the west of the Borough and includes Cheadle, Edgeley ('**leah** at an enclosed park') and Heaviley ('heathy **leah**'), although not Gatley which is a corruption of an Old English name meaning 'goats' bank'.[109] With the exception of Cheadle, all of these **leah** places were of fairly minor importance in the medieval (post-Anglo-Saxon) period. While Cheadle, 'Laitone' and Romiley, which is also mentioned in Domesday, were the locations of settlements in the Anglo-Saxon period, other **leah** places may represent later clearances of these woodland belts.

Only two other major place-names in the Borough can be securely dated to the pre-Norman period, by virtue of their mention in Domesday. One is Bramhall, the second part of which is the Old English **halh**, which here probably means 'a small valley' and refers to the valley of the Lady Brook; the first component of the place-name is the shrub broom, presumably a common or distinguishing feature of the locality.[110] The other is Ludworth, meaning 'Luda's enclosure'. The place-name element **worth** or 'enclosure', like **tun** and **leah**, may be no earlier than the eighth century. It is used of places or settlements which were originally only of minor importance, as part of a larger Anglo-Saxon estate. It is possible that the particular original use of Ludworth, and of other upland **worth** places in the region, was as grazing land for livestock during the summer months.[111]

The remaining major place-names in the Borough are Reddish, Marple, Woodford, Etchells (the township which included Gatley) and Stockport. Reddish means 'the ditch where reeds grow', perhaps a reference to Nico Ditch which formed its northern boundary.[112] The existence of an Anglo-Saxon settlement here is suggested by the discovery at Reddish Green in 1789 of a hoard of six silver coins. These were issues of the Anglo-Saxon king Eadred (946-55) and probably of his predecessor Edmund (939-46).[113] Apart from the fragments of one or more crosses discovered near Cheadle, these appear to be the only chance finds of Anglo-Saxon date known from the Borough.

The derivation of the place-name Marple is uncertain, but one suggested meaning is '(at) the stream at the boundary', with the name perhaps originally being that of the River Goyt.[114] The place-name Woodford

means 'ford at the wood', possibly a reference to a crossing of the River Dean at Deanwater Bridge.[115] Etchells means 'land added to an estate', apparently in the sense of agricultural land reclaimed from waste land.[116] The later history of Etchells suggests that the estate in question was the Anglo-Saxon manor of Northenden, a place which lies immediately to the west and is mentioned in Domesday. Following the Norman takeover Etchells was divided into two, with the boundary along Gatley Brook. The eastern of these two halves, which probably in the twelfth century was given to the lord of Stockport, lies within the Borough.[117]

The place-name of Stockport has long been the subject of debate, fuelled by the diversity of early spellings which include 'Stopport', 'Stockford' and 'Stopford'. However, the name is first documented in the twelfth century as 'Stokeport', derived from the Old English **stoc** and **port**. The second of these words means 'a market place'. The first, like **worth**, is now understood to refer to a minor settlement within a larger estate and is sometimes translated as 'a hamlet'.[118]

This early market, like its better known medieval successor, can be supposed to have served as a central meeting place to which people from other places came to trade mostly agricultural produce. That this particular place should have been chosen for this role may be evidence that at this date, as during the Roman period, Stockport stood on one or more important routeways. It would, of course, be very useful to know when the place-name came into being, but firm evidence on this is lacking. **Stoc** is believed to be among those place-name elements which are unlikely to predate the eighth century.[119] We cannot be certain that Stockport, 'the market place at the hamlet', had received its name before the Norman takeover. However, the relatively early (twelfth-century) documentary evidence for the name, coupled with the destruction wreaked on many of the surrounding farming communities during the Norman takeover, makes an Anglo-Saxon date for this early trading centre highly probable.

While the British and Anglo-Saxon major place-names of the Borough highlight the extent of pre-Norman settlement, they also show a distinct lack of influence from one other ethnic group, the Vikings. Both Northumbria and eastern Mercia came under Viking rule by conquest in the late ninth century. Mercia was recovered by the Anglo-Saxons in the early tenth century. One consequence of that reconquest was the creation of the county of Cheshire, its original purpose being to provide the manpower to garrison Chester as a defence against any future Viking aggression.[120] It was possibly at that same date that the territory north of the Mersey and south of the Ribble was also regained from Viking control.

The ninth-century conquests marked the beginning of extensive Viking settlement in northern and eastern England, but in what is now Greater Manchester firm evidence for this is slight. Scandinavian place-name elements are found in the county, although mostly in minor place-names or field-names. In the Borough examples include Chadkirk (**kirkja**, 'church') and Cheadle Hulme (**hulm**, 'water-meadow').[121] Such local place-names might have been coined by Viking settlers, but they can be explained equally well in terms of Scandinavian words being adopted by the English. Many of these 'Scandinavian' names are in fact likely to be medieval in date.[122] Antiquarian accounts give the Vikings a more dramatic role in the Borough's history. The place-name 'Stopport', in fact a modification of the earlier 'Stokeport', was supposed to show that a battle had been fought here in which the Anglo-Saxons halted the advance of a Viking army.[123] The Vikings also provided the traditional explanation for Nico Ditch, which was said to have been built as a defence against them by the people of Manchester in a single night.[124]

The Domesday manors

The earliest documentary references to any places within the Borough occur in the Domesday survey. Although compiled in 1086 on the order of William I, this also gives some details of places in the time of King Edward the Confessor, in 1066. As a list of settlements in the Borough at that date, this evidence is far from complete. Domesday was an administrative record and the places recorded for the Borough are the units of local administration, manors or estates held by individual lords. Only the names of these estates are given, not those of their component places.

Unfortunately for the part of the Borough north of the Mersey and Tame even the names of estates are lacking from Domesday. This area was part of the Salford hundred, an administrative division of the land 'between the Ribble and the Mersey'. In 1066 two manors in this hundred (Salford and Radcliffe) were held by King Edward. The remainder of the hundred was divided into twenty-one manors, each held by a 'thane' or tenant of the king, but of these manors only Rochdale, held by Gamel, is mentioned by name.[125]

The Cheshire part of the Borough lay within the Hamestan hundred in that county, later known as the Macclesfield hundred after its administrative centre. Seven places in this part of the Borough are named: 'Bramale' (Bramhall),[126] 'Bretberie' (Bredbury),[127] 'Nordberie' (Norbury),[128] 'Rumelie' (Romiley), 'Warnet' (Werneth), 'Laitone'[129] and 'Cedde'.[130] 'Cedde' has sometimes been identified with Chadkirk in Romiley, but is now generally recognized as being Cheadle.[131] The name 'Laitone', we have already seen, is very probably to be connected with Leighton in Marple. It may have been that the Domesday manor, recalled in this minor place-name, was of roughly the same extent as the later Marple township. Even so, several other later townships in the Cheshire part of the Borough appear to be unaccounted for in Domesday. In the Derbyshire part only 'Lodeuorde' (Ludworth) is named.[132] Mellor, despite its early place-name, is not.

The absence of some later township names from Domesday might be accidental. An alternative explanation is that these places were at that date only part of larger estates whose names do appear in the Domesday accounts. This is best illustrated by the cases of 'Nordberie' and 'Bretberie'. According to Domesday the Anglo-Saxon lord of 'Nordberie' in 1066 had been replaced by 1086 by Bigot de Losges. His extensive Cheshire estates also included the manor of Aldford, near Chester. By the thirteenth century there is documentary evidence to show that the lords of Aldford controlled not only the manor of Norbury but also the neighbouring manors of Offerton and Torkington. Similarly, by the late twelfth century Brinnington and Bredbury, also neighbouring manors, were both held by the same overlord, in this case Hamo de Massey.

The great nineteenth-century historian of Cheshire, George Ormerod, inferred from the common ownership of Norbury, Torkington and Offerton by the lords of Aldford that in 1086 these were all components of 'Nordberie'.[133] A similar inference can be made for the relationship between the Domesday 'Bretberie' and the townships of Bredbury and Brinnington. This interpretation is consistent with the place-name evidence, since the **burh** element in the place-names Norbury and Bredbury suggests that both were of a high social status. It is likely, therefore, that by 1066 Bredbury and Norbury were the most important settlements within larger manors or estates to which they gave their names but which also contained the less important settlements of Brinnington, Torkington and Offerton.

The most striking absence from the Domesday list, given its later history, is Stockport itself. To local antiquarians in the nineteenth century, who believed that Stockport had been a place of importance since the Roman period, this omission required a special explanation. Stockport, they supposed, had suffered devastation to such a degree during the Norman campaigning in Cheshire in 1069-70 that in 1086 nothing remained to be recorded. Support for this supposed destruction was found in the place-name of neighbouring Brinnington, which the antiquarians believed to mean 'the burnt town' but which is now recognized as having the less dramatic meaning of the 'farm called after Bryni'. Stockport's own place-name may offer the true explanation for its Domesday omission. It was still 'the market place at the hamlet', not only by name but also by nature. It had an economic importance as a central trading place, but as a settlement it was a dependent part of a larger estate.

The geographical position of Stockport suggests four possible candidates for that larger manor: 'Cedde', 'Bramale', 'Bretberie' and 'Nordberie'. 'Cedde' has recently been proposed as a likely candidate.[134] However, there are two factors which may favour the inclusion of Stockport within 'Bretberie'. The first is that Portwood (which has been interpreted as 'the wood belonging to the port', presumably Stockport) lay within the later township of Brinnington.[135] The second is that the boundary of the township of Bredbury with Stockport extended across the Goyt to include Woodbank. Both factors imply a certain looseness in the early demarcation between Stockport on the one hand and Bredbury and Brinnington on the other. If these places had originally been divided between two separate estates we might expect the boundary to have been firmly fixed along the Goyt.

The early church

The history of the church in the Borough is obscure until more than a century after the Norman takeover when we first have documentary evidence for the medieval parish churches of Stockport and Cheadle. Unlike for other parts of Cheshire, Domesday mentions not a single Anglo-Saxon church or priest in the Hamestan hundred. This undoubtedly represents an omission of information rather than a reflection of the reality. Both Stockport and Cheadle parish churches have been supposed to be Anglo-Saxon foundations, as has a third religious building in the Borough, Chadkirk Chapel in Romiley.

Chadkirk, a medieval foundation?

The place-name Chadkirk means 'the church of Chad'. There is still a chapel building here, nestling against the hillslope which rises like a natural theatre from the flood plain of the Goyt (Ill 3.19). The chapel is first explicitly mentioned in the 1530s, and the oldest fabric of the present building is of approximately this same date. When the place-name came into being is, as we noted earlier, a matter of uncertainty. It is first documented in the early fourteenth century, implying that a church was standing here either at or before that time. Among the earliest occurrences of the place-name is a reference in the 1340s to William de Chadkirk, chaplain, but it is not known whether Chadkirk here is merely a surname or refers to the place of his chaplaincy.[136]

An archaeological excavation carried out within the interior of Chadkirk Chapel in 1994 produced no evidence of a pre-sixteenth-century building. However, given the degree of ground disturbance which had taken place from the sixteenth century onwards, the existence of such an earlier building on this site cannot be discounted. It is also possible that the earlier chapel building had in fact stood on a different site close by, its remains perhaps still waiting to be discovered.[137]

Chad himself was a seventh-century cleric who played a prominent role in the conversion of the Mercians to Christianity and who from 669 to his death in 672 was bishop of the Mercian diocese of Lichfield. Local tradition makes him the founder of the first chapel at Chadkirk as part of that missionary work. However, the place-name is perhaps more likely to have arisen in another manner. After his death Chad was elevated to the position of patron saint of the diocese of Lichfield. As a consequence many churches in the diocese, of which Cheshire was itself a part until the 1540s, were dedicated to him.

In the sixteenth century Chadkirk was part of the estates in Romiley and Bredbury owned by the Davenport family of Henbury. They cannot have built the first chapel here, since they only acquired these lands in the late fourteenth century, some time after the name Chadkirk is first documented.[138] The Davenports received these estates from the lord of Stockport, and it may have been an earlier holder of that lordship who was responsible for the construction of the first chapel at Chadkirk. This would place the foundation of the chapel after 1248, since the lords of Stockport only obtained lands in Romiley after that date.[139] If the chapel was a medieval foundation, its likely purpose was as a 'chapel of ease'. Such buildings served the more outlying areas of medieval parishes, in this case the parish of Stockport.

The choice of location for the chapel is as great a mystery as the date of its foundation. One possibility is raised by the presence, across the lane from the chapel, of a stone-built wellhouse fed by a natural spring. It has been known since at least the late nineteenth century as St Chad's Well or Holy Well. The wellhouse itself is of a relatively recent date, probably eighteenth- or nineteenth-century, but 'holy wells' dedicated to saints can be sites of pagan worship which were later Christianized. This may be the case of the well at Chadkirk, with the first chapel being built next to a site which already had an ancient religious significance. It is equally possible that a religious connotation was attached to the spring only after the chapel was built, and it cannot be entirely discounted that its name was no more than a piece of late romanticism.[140] A more prosaic explanation for the siting of the chapel may be one of convenience for the local community which it was intended to serve. There was a ford across the Goyt at Chadkirk, and a bridge across the river at Otterspool is known to have been in existence in the medieval period, perhaps by the end of the thirteenth century.[141] Whether or not a Roman road ran through Chadkirk linking Otterspool with Werneth Low, the place was probably readily accessible by local roads by that later date.

Cheadle and Stockport

In the 1870s during the construction of Barnes Hospital to the north-west of Cheadle village, men working in a nearby brickfield uncovered the broken remains of what contemporary accounts suggest may have been as many as three stone crosses. Probably, at some unknown date, these had been dumped in an old marl pit. The only remains from this site whose whereabouts are now known comprise a cross head with fan-shaped arms and a central boss, rising from a crudely carved shaft. This sculptured cross, now in Cheadle parish church, stands to a height of about a metre but is only the upper part of the original monument. Its style suggests a date in the late tenth or eleventh century (*Ill 2.8*). Found with it were said to be the remains of another and 'much older' cross and the upper part of a stone shaft. The last piece was described as being 'exactly similar in character to some upright stones from 6 to 7 feet in height which were found in various parts of Macclesfield Forest'.[142] The reference appears to be to a distinctive type of Anglo-Saxon cross shaft, found in east Cheshire, Derbyshire and Staffordshire, which is characterized by being round in section but squared off at the top. Examples of this type are found both singly or in pairs set side by side on a common base. They include the twin shafts known as Robin Hood's Picking Rods, which are located immediately beyond the Borough boundary at Ludworth (*Ill 2.9*).[143] Many Anglo-Saxon crosses are known to have been removed from their original position. However, the remote location of the Picking Rods was perhaps typical of many such round-shafted crosses which may have been originally set up on waysides. Sculptured crosses on the other hand appear to have been more usually associated with church sites.[144] There, they may have served as a focus for worship, predating the building of a church itself.

Within the Hamestan hundred, despite the silence of Domesday, an Anglo-Saxon church almost certainly existed at Prestbury ('the priests' burh'). By 1066 this probably had already become the centre of an extensive parish which in the north included Woodford and Poynton.[145] In the north-east of the hundred it is possible that by this same date a parish centre existed at Mottram, but it seems unlikely that this would have served more than the population of Longdendale. This would leave the north-west of the hundred unaccounted for, and here the most likely site for such a centre is undoubtedly Cheadle. Of the handful of places mentioned in Domesday in this part of Hamestan hundred, Cheadle is the only one to have had a church

Ill 2.8 The Cheadle Cross.
This upper part of a cross is dated to the late tenth or eleventh century. It was found in the 1870s near Cheadle village and suggests that Cheadle may have been the centre of a parish by the late Anglo-Saxon period. The cross is now in the parish church of St Mary.

Ill 2.9 Robin Hood's Picking Rods, Ludworth Moor.
These twin cylindrical cross shafts, set within a stone base, are believed to date from the late Anglo-Saxon period. Similar cross shafts are found elsewhere in east Cheshire, Derbyshire and Staffordshire.

in the medieval period. Its Anglo-Saxon lord in 1066 was the father of Gamel, who himself held the manor in 1086 after the Norman takeover. Other Domesday entries suggest that these men were important landowners, with estates in Cheshire, Staffordshire, Derbyshire, Yorkshire and Lancashire, where Gamel was lord of Rochdale. More will be said about this family's links with Cheadle in the following chapter. For the moment, it is sufficient to note that the family's apparent high status adds further weight to the likelihood of Cheadle being the centre of a pre-Norman parish, served by its own priest and perhaps with its own church.[146]

By contrast there is little evidence to support the existence of an Anglo-Saxon church or parish centre at Stockport. In 1066 this was probably the site of a local market, but otherwise of little importance, merely a minor settlement within a larger manor, possibly that of 'Bretberie'. Stockport's day was yet to come.

NICO DITCH

There is one major local archaeological feature which is still surrounded with uncertainty despite over a century of speculation and recent excavations. This is the linear earthwork known as Nico Ditch. It ran on a gently curving line between two large mosslands, Ashton Moss on the east and Hough Moss on the west, a distance of 7 kilometres.[147] Hough Moss has long been drained but is still recalled by the name of Moss Side, originally a township on its northern edge. Much of the length of Nico Ditch was still visible in the late nineteenth century when it carried an open watercourse. Subsequent urban development has meant that it has largely been covered over or destroyed. The section followed by the northern boundary of Reddish is itself no longer visible but surviving sections can still be seen at Denton golf course, Melland playing field in Levenshulme, and at the Unitarian chapel by Platt Fields Park in Fallowfield. Several archaeological excavations have been carried out along the line of the ditch, including two at Reddish.[148] The results suggest that it was originally 3-4 metres wide but in no case has evidence been found for the date of its construction.

Nico Ditch may in fact represent only one half of a larger system. Nineteenth-century maps show that on the west side of Hough Moss the line of Nico Ditch continued as a series of field boundaries for roughly 4.5 kilometres. This strongly suggests a second ditch. It would have run between Hough Moss and a further area of mossland at Urmston, itself part of a group of mosses which once presented a formidable barrier along the Irwell and the Mersey.[149]

Documentary evidence shows that Nico Ditch was already in existence by about 1200, when part was used as the boundary of land in Audenshaw near Ashton Moss. It was then known as the 'Mykelldiche', meaning 'the great ditch'.[150] The modern name is a corruption of this early form. Not surprisingly, such an existing convenient feature in the landscape was adopted as a boundary along other parts of its length, both in the medieval period and later. The section of the ditch in Reddish is recorded in 1322, when it formed the northern boundary of that township with the barony of Manchester.[151]

While it is generally agreed that Nico Ditch is earlier than the Norman takeover of the region, opinions differ as to its date and function. One suggestion is that it was intended for mossland drainage, but a single ditch would have been of only limited effect in achieving that end. At Ashton Moss the ditch did in fact continue into the actual mossland. However, this was achieved by a sharp shift in its alignment and was probably a later extension of the original line which ended at the moss's edge. Despite the traditional account that it was built by the people of Manchester as a protection against the Vikings, the defensive qualities of the earthwork are questionable. Early accounts supposed that a bank had run along the north side of the ditch, but confirmation of this is lacking. It has sometimes been supposed that the purpose of the ditch was to delineate agricultural land associated with the Roman fort at Manchester.[152] Others tend to the view that the ditch was post-Roman in date and was constructed to mark the southern boundary of either Northumbria or an earlier British kingdom.[153] A further possibility is raised by comparison with the linear earthwork known as Grey Ditch in Derbyshire. The relationship between that ditch and local Roman roads and the broken line of the earthwork, which is absent on slopes too steep for traffic, have led to the suggestion that it marked the boundary between two late Roman provinces, since customs were collected at such points.[154] Nico Ditch and its possible continuation to the west of Hough Moss might similarly have served to regulate traffic along the several Roman roads which converge on Manchester to the north.

CHAPTER THREE

THE MEDIEVAL TOWN AND COUNTRYSIDE, 1069-1540

'Every burgess shall have one perch of land to his house and one acre in the fields'

INTRODUCTION

The medieval period was a formative era for the Borough. During its course the handful of places of settlement which had existed in the Anglo-Saxon period multiplied. The number of manors increased to create a pattern of local government which remained unchanged until the nineteenth century. It is in the medieval period that we have the first evidence for a local textile trade. Cornmills were erected on rivers and streams, in some cases on sites which would be utilized by the textile mills of a later age. Perhaps most significant of all for the Borough's future development was the rise of Stockport itself. This was transformed into by far the

Ill 3.1 Bramall Hall, the 'de Bromhale' arms.
The hall is one of the oldest standing buildings in the Borough, with parts dating back to the fourteenth century. The 'de Bromhale' family were lords of the manor of Bramhall until the 1370s and this carving, below a window in the south wing of the hall, is believed to date from their time.

largest of the Borough's medieval communities, no longer 'the market place at the hamlet' but a market town.

Most of the information concerning the Borough in the medieval period is contained within documentary sources, but there is also an important body of physical evidence. The oldest standing buildings in the Borough date from this period *(Ill 3.1)*. Other sites now survive as earthworks. Archaeological excavations have also added to our understanding of this time.

The medieval period was one of great social and economic changes nationally. Between the time of the Domesday survey and the end of the thirteenth century the population of England increased dramatically, settlements grew in both size and number and included many new towns, and more and more land was brought under the plough. In the fourteenth century, which saw the outbreak of famine in 1315 and the Black Death in 1348-9, the population was greatly reduced. The resulting shortage of manpower helped to weaken traditional feudal ties between manorial lords and their tenants, and encouraged a move away from arable to greater pastoral farming. Many of these national developments can be seen mirrored in the Borough. However, while the evidence for Stockport and other local places in this period is perhaps greater than might be anticipated, it is far from comprehensive. Much documentary material which might shed further light on the area's medieval history is also unpublished.

A word must be said on the extent of the period considered in this chapter. From a national perspective the medieval period in England is traditionally considered to have ended in 1485 with the death of Richard III and the succession of Henry VII. The definition used in this work of the period ending in about 1540 is in line with some recent regional studies. In general terms it reflects the comparatively minor changes to the life of local people between the mid-fifteenth century and the early sixteenth. The beginning of the English Reformation in the 1530s on the other hand signals a watershed for the Stockport area, as elsewhere. The starting point for the medieval period has been derived from a regional event, the devastation of 1069-70 which marked the beginning of the Norman takeover of the North-West.

THE NORMAN TAKEOVER

The transition of the North-West from an Anglo-Saxon society to one dominated by new Norman overlords was harsh in the extreme. In the winter of 1069-70 William I led an army westwards across the Pennines. Behind him, as punishment for rebellion, much of north-east England lay wasted. The North-West, which had also risen in revolt against the Norman king, was to experience the same. Once punishment had been meted out, a new regime followed. An earl of Chester was appointed, the first in a succession of such men who ruled Cheshire until 1237. Most of the estates in the county were taken from their Anglo-Saxon lords and either retained by the earl or, in the majority of cases, granted to his own men. To the north of Cheshire the land 'between the Ribble and the Mersey' (later to become southern Lancashire) was given its own overlord, under whom its various estates were similarly reallocated.

The evidence of the effect of the Norman takeover on the Borough is to be found in Domesday. Of the manors listed in the Cheshire part of the Borough, 'Bramale' was valued at 32 shillings in 1066 but at only 5 shillings in 1086. The value of 'Nordberie' had decreased from 10 shillings to 3. In both places their Anglo-Saxon lords had been replaced by Normans; Brun and Hacon at 'Bramale' by Hamo de Massey, Brun at 'Nordberie' by Bigot de Losges.[1] In each case Domesday notes that 'he found it waste'. This very probably refers to the condition of the manors when they were taken over by their new lords.[2] Taken in conjunction with the decline in value, it indicates the devastation which these places had suffered in 1069-70 and from which they had not yet recovered some sixteen years later. No individual valuations are given for 'Warnet' (Werneth), 'Rumelie' (Romiley) or 'Laitone' (Leighton in Marple) but the group of eight east Cheshire manors in which these are listed had decreased in value from 40 shillings in 1066 to 10 in 1086.[3] It is also reported that the whole group 'was and is waste'. These manors had been held by eight separate lords in 1066; by 1086 they had been dispossessed, but the earl of Chester had not yet given these lands to his own followers. In Derbyshire the manors of 'Langedenedele' (Longdendale) had all lost their Anglo-Saxon lords, including Brun in 'Lodeuorde' (Ludworth), and were held by the king. In 1066 these manors are said to have been collectively worth 40 shillings. No value is given for 1086 but it is reported that all 'Langedenedele' was then waste, with 'woodland, unpastured, fit for hunting'.[4] It was subsequently to become part of the royal hunting forest of the Peak.

The economic effects of the Norman takeover on the Lancashire part of the Borough are obscure. This area lay within the Salford hundred, a division of the land 'between the Ribble and the Mersey', for which Domesday provides only a summary account. However, here also there is evidence of widespread devastation in the form of a reduction in the value of the hundred, from £37 4s in 1066 to £12 twenty years later.[5]

Two local manors, 'Cedde' (Cheadle) and 'Bretberie', were each valued at 10 shillings in 1066 and were of the same value in 1086. Furthermore, they were both still held by Anglo-Saxons. Gamel, the son of the lord of 'Cedde' in 1066, held the manor in 1086 as the tenant of the earl of Chester. 'Bretberie' in 1086 formed part of the Cheshire estates of Richard de Vernon, but under him was held by Wulfric, the same man who had been its lord in 1066.[6] Gamel and Wulfric may have been figures of some importance before the Norman takeover. In 1066 it is possible that this same Gamel was also lord of Rochdale (where he still held land in 1086) and of estates in Yorkshire, Staffordshire and Derbyshire. Wulfric was probably the person of that name who in 1066 and 1086 was the lord of Butley. It lay immediately between the manors of Macclesfield and Adlington which in 1066 were held by Edwin, earl of Mercia and, after the Norman takeover, by the earl of Chester. It has been suggested that Wulfric, as lord of Butley, was the steward of the successive earls and effectively in control of the Hamestan hundred, the division comprising north-east Cheshire with Macclesfield as its administrative centre.[7] Possibly the continuing control of 'Cedde' and 'Bretberie' by their Anglo-Saxon lords enabled these manors to recover relatively quickly from the Norman devastation of 1069-70. That they were deliberately spared by William's army seems a less likely scenario.

The four most detailed Domesday entries for places within the Borough, for 'Cedde', 'Bramale', 'Bretberie' and 'Nordberie', include the number of various classes of people living there in 1086. The most numerous of these were 'bordars', found in all four manors, and 'villeins', found in all except 'Nordberie'. The distinction between the two may have been one of economic status, with the villeins being the more important. It is also possible that the bordars occupied more marginal land within these places. Both groups, however, belonged to the peasant class, who worked the land to support themselves and their families and, when required, provided labour for their lord. 'Demesne', land which the lord reserved for his own use, is listed only in 'Cedde'. There, the demesne was tilled by two 'oxmen' who worked this land with one plough, one man presumably guiding it, the other leading the team of oxen which pulled it along. The three other manors also differ from 'Cedde' in that each was home to one 'radman'. These were members of a class of freemen, above the peasantry in the social order, and were the most important individuals living within those manors.[8]

In the case of both 'Cedde' and 'Bretberie' the total number of individuals listed in 1086 is ten. That the totals for 'Bramale' and 'Nordberie' should be only five and four respectively is probably a further indication that those manors had only partly recovered from the effects of the devastation of 1069-70. The Domesday figures are not for the total number of people in these manors. However, if we allow both for the members of the family and household of the people who are listed and for those manors where no figures are given at all, it seems unlikely that in 1086 the total population of the Borough was more than a few hundred.

The human cost of the Norman takeover probably meant little to the new lords. Bigot de Losges who was given 'Nordberie', Hamo de Massey who was given 'Bramale', and Richard de Vernon who became the overlord of Wulfric in 'Bretberie' all had extensive estates in Cheshire. By the twelfth century the head manors of these estates were respectively Aldford near Chester, Dunham near Altrincham, and Shipbrook near Northwich. These places were all part of the same estates at the time of Domesday and probably already played that leading role. We can only speculate as to what extent the position of 'Bramale' and particularly 'Nordberie' as outlying manors of those estates prejudiced the rate of their economic recovery.[9]

THE STOCKPORT BARONY AND THE MEDIEVAL MANORS

The Stockport barony and the castle

In 1086 Stockport was probably only a minor settlement within a larger manor, its only significance being its use as a central trading place for the surrounding communities. By the late twelfth century the situation had radically changed. Stockport had not only become a manor in its own right but was also the site of a castle. By this date its lord probably also controlled a sizeable group of other manors, collectively known as a barony, making him one of the most important figures in Cheshire.

The castle of Geoffrey de Costentin, 1173

The earliest reference to the castle, and indeed probably the earliest reference to Stockport itself, occurs in a chronicle of the reign of Henry II, written close in time to the events which it describes. Included in its account of the rebellion against the king in 1173 by his son Henry is a list of rebels and the castles in their possession. Three of these rebels were associated with Cheshire: the earl of Chester who held the castle of Chester, Hamo de Massey who held the castles of Dunham and Ullerswood, and Geoffrey de Costentin who held the castle of Stockport. These details are repeated in a later chronicle compiled in the thirteenth century, where the holder of Stockport castle is named as Geoffrey de Constantin.[10]

Local tradition has it that the rebel who held Stockport castle was none other than the king's own son Geoffrey, who was born in 1158 and died in 1186, and who is known to have joined his brothers Henry and Richard in the revolt. This tradition, however, is mistaken. It can be traced back to the late nineteenth-century Stockport historian Henry Heginbotham who supposed that the surname of the rebel was derived from the name of Constance, the daughter of the duke of Brittany. She was betrothed to the prince Geoffrey in 1166, with the couple marrying in 1181. However, as was pointed out even in Heginbotham's own time, the true derivation of the name is from Cotentin in Normandy. The name of Geoffrey de Costentin is found as early as 1154. From the evidence of the Pipe Rolls, the accounts of the royal exchequer, he appears to have died in 1179-80. As well as holding the manor of Stockport, he owned land in Staffordshire and Ireland. De Costentin's role in the revolt of 1173 evidently cost him dearly. In 1177 his Irish estate, which had been confiscated by the king, was handed over to another.[11]

Precisely what role, if indeed any, Stockport castle actually played in the revolt of 1173 is not recorded. Nor do we know of its fate following the suppression of the rebellion. Possibly, like Chester, it was held for a while by the king. Alternatively, as in the case of some other castles belonging to the rebels, he may have ordered its demolition, although this need not have prevented the castle being later rebuilt.[12] After 1173 there is no mention of Stockport as a 'working' castle but this may simply reflect the infrequency with which castles in general, with the exception of those of the king and the most powerful lords, appear in the documentary record. On the other hand, with a few important exceptions, the majority of castles in the North-West appear to have gone out of use by the fourteenth century at the latest. That this was the case at Stockport may be suggested by a reference in 1336 to 'Castle Hill' rather than to the castle itself.[13]

Castle Hill and its walls

Castle Hill, which almost certainly took its name from the medieval castle on this site, lay at the north-west corner of the Market Place promontory. It is known today as Castle Yard. What form the twelfth-century castle took is unknown. It has been suggested that a conical earthen mound or 'motte' surmounted by a wooden tower stood on Castle Hill. A motte is the most common component of castles of this period, but these did not exclusively take this form. In the late seventeenth century a circuit of stone walls stood on

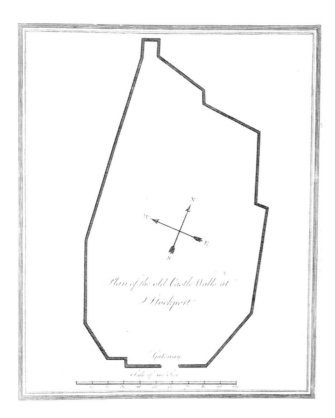

Ill 3.2 The Reverend John Watson's plan of the 'old Castle Walls' on Castle Hill.

A castle at Stockport is mentioned in 1173 but then disappears from the documentary record. Although it almost certainly stood on Castle Hill, its form is a matter of uncertainty. The stone walls recorded by Watson were demolished by the late 1770s and their date is unknown. The very existence of the castle, however, is significant. Along with the creation of the Stockport barony, with which it was probably linked, the building of the castle marked a considerable leap in Stockport's importance.

Castle Hill, with a gateway onto the Market Place. These walls are depicted in a roughly circular form on the earliest plan of the town, believed to date from about 1680 (Ill 4.2). A century later the Reverend John Watson, the rector of Stockport parish, published a plan, said to have been drawn from accurate measurements, of a more angular arrangement of walls on Castle Hill (Ill 3.2). The existence of walls on this site is also implied in 1537 when there is a mention of a parcel of land in the Market Place called 'the Bastile Room or place', the word 'bastile' at this date meaning a fortified tower. It is uncertain, however, whether the known Castle Hill walls were part of the castle or represent a later use of the site. They were levelled by the late 1770s when Sir George Warren, the lord of the manor, built an early cotton mill here. Itself known as the 'Castle', its unusual oval plan and battlemented walls recalled the spirit, if not necessarily the substance, of its medieval predecessor (Ills 5.2 & 5.3).[14] Sections of stone walling which lie against the sandstone cliffs on the west and south sides of the Market Place promontory have also been suggested as belonging to the medieval castle. We shall return to this matter later, in connection with the early development of the town.

The barony of the de Stokeports

Geoffrey de Costentin's tenure of the lordship of Stockport probably came to an end as a consequence of his part in the revolt of 1173, after which neither he nor (as far as we can tell) any subsequent member of his family is heard of in connection with Stockport again. By the late 1180s the lordship was held by Robert de Stokeport, who died in or shortly before 1206.[15] Somewhat confusingly for historians, he was the first of three successive holders of the lordship to have this name. The last of these, Robert de Stokeport III, died in the 1270s.[16] It is in connection with Robert de Stokeport II that we have the fullest evidence for the extent of the Stockport barony. This dates from 1248 and 1249 and takes the form of two versions of an 'inquisition post mortem', a record drawn up after his death of the estates which he held.[17] The core of these landholdings was a solid block of manors, comprising Stockport, Brinnington, Bredbury, Offerton, Bosden, Torkington, Norbury, Marple, Wybersley, Poynton and Woodford (Ill 3.3). Separated from this group by the manor of Cheadle were Stockport Etchells and two places in Northen Etchells, namely Sharston and 'Ragel' (much later known as Royalthorn).[18] Hattersley to the east and Mottram St Andrew to the south were similarly each

Ill 3.3 Manors of the Stockport barony in 1248.

The barony, a group of manors held by a single overlord, was probably in existence by the late twelfth century. In 1248 it was made up of a continuous block of manors and other outlying estates. (The latter included Mottram St Andrew, Old Withington and half of the manor of Marton, not shown here but all lying to the south of the main block.) Later in the thirteenth century the barony came to include lands in Romiley and Werneth. The manors of Cheadle and Bramhall lay outside the barony and were held by their own lords.

separated from the main group by only a single township. Further to the south lay two other outlying components of the barony: Marton, where Robert de Stokeport was lord of half the manor, and Old Withington. Subsequent to the death of Robert de Stokeport II, the lords of Stockport also acquired lands in Romiley and Werneth.[19]

The possible origins of the barony and castle

The origins of the Stockport barony are obscure. By the late sixteenth century the tradition had arisen that Stockport was one of eight baronies created in the earldom of Chester by Hugh Lupus, earl from the 1070s to 1101. However, while other of these baronies appear in Domesday in the form of a sizeable number of manors held by a single lord, the Stockport barony does not. Moreover, while the traditional account could put a name to the other seven barons allegedly created by earl Hugh, that of the baron of Stockport was unknown. It seems clear that, despite the lack of any documentary evidence in his support, the originator of the tradition could not resist the temptation of pushing the creation of the Stockport barony back to the earliest years of the Norman earldom.[20]

In extent the Stockport barony was comparable to the other baronies in Cheshire, but it also differed from these in one important respect. The majority of manors which made up the other baronies were held by the barons directly under the earl of Chester (in other words, in the feudal chain he was the immediate overlord). The Stockport barony was the reverse of that situation. Of all the estates listed in 1248-9, only Marple and Wybersley had been granted to the lord of Stockport by the earl. The remainder were held directly under other lords. These included Stockport itself, which was held under the de Spensers. Furthermore, in a number of cases, again including Stockport, the manors held by these overlords were probably carved from larger, Domesday, estates.[21] Compared with the other Cheshire baronies, the Stockport barony was probably a relatively late creation, superimposed on a pattern of manors which had already changed significantly since the time of Domesday.

The key to the creation of the barony may lie with Stockport's castle. Medieval castles in Cheshire can be divided into two categories. The first were those belonging to the earl himself. The second group belonged to the men who after the earl were the most powerful lords within the county, each with a number of manors in his possession.[22] Whatever other reasons may have determined who could build a castle in Cheshire, one was undoubtedly economic. The county at this period was among the poorest and least densely populated in England, and to build, maintain and man a castle was probably beyond the resources of most single Cheshire manors. Consequently it may be the very existence of a castle at Stockport in 1173 which provides the earliest evidence for the place as the head manor of a barony.

Why it was created is a further matter of uncertainty, but the castle again suggests a possible explanation. Perhaps the barony not only provided the resources necessary to construct and sustain the castle but was also established for that very purpose. Certainly the castle's intended role need not have been confined to safeguarding the persons of the lord and his household. It stood on the border of Cheshire at the meeting place of two important communication routes into the county. Only a bow shot from its walls was the ford across the Mersey and beyond that Lancashire, while to the north-east was the approach to Longdendale and the 'panhandle' of the county. As for the date of its construction, that heyday of castle building, the Anarchy of the 1140s and 1150s, in which the earl of Chester was a key player, might be suggested as a suitable context.

The ancestry of the de Stokeports

Robert de Stokeport I may not have been Geoffrey de Costentin's immediate successor as head of the Stockport barony. In the late twelfth century Hamo de Massey, then overlord of Bredbury, Brinnington and Stockport Etchells, confirmed the succession of Robert, the son of Waltheof, to those manors, previously held by Waltheof himself. There can be little doubt that the recipient of this grant was Robert de Stokeport I. Other documentary evidence suggests that the same Waltheof was also lord of Marton (attested in 1248-9 as part of the Stockport barony), and that he himself was the son of a man named Wulfric.[23] Their names show Waltheof and Wulfric to have been of Anglo-Saxon descent. Wulfric, it may be remembered, was also the name of the lord who after the Norman takeover was allowed to retain 'Bretberie', an estate which probably included the later manors of Bredbury and Brinnington.

The implication may be that when the Stockport barony was first created, Bredbury and Brinnington were still held by the family of Wulfric and were not included within its component manors. As a consequence of the part played by Geoffrey de Costentin in the revolt of 1173, the head of that family, Waltheof, was granted the barony and in turn passed this on to his son Robert de Stokeport I. It has already been noted that the Wulfric who held 'Bretberie' at the time of Domesday may well have been a figure of considerable importance in north-east Cheshire. It has also been suggested that Stockport was itself once part of 'Bretberie'.[24] Such circumstances would, of course, make the succession of Waltheof to the Stockport barony all the more appropriate.

Other early manorial lords

Cheadle and Bramhall

Although the Stockport barony was the largest landholding in the Borough in the twelfth and thirteenth centuries, it should not be overlooked that there were other manorial lords. At Cheadle, as at 'Bretberie', the Anglo-Saxon ruling family survived the Norman takeover and still held the lordship in 1086. How long they remained in power is uncertain and a connection cannot be proved with the later known lords. The earliest evidence for these is provided by the occurrence of one Robert de Chedle in a charter of the earl of Chester dating from 1162-3. (This is also possibly the earliest source relating directly to the Borough since Domesday.)[25] Bramhall by the late twelfth century was held under the de Masseys by a family named 'de Bromale', which appears to have acquired the manor at the latest by the 1180s.[26] That neither Cheadle nor Bramhall was included within the Stockport barony may indicate that they were already under the control of their own lords at the time when the barony came into being.

Manorial lords under the Stockport barony

Several of the manors of the Stockport barony were granted by the barons to other individuals who became their direct lords. Two such grants made by Robert de Stokeport II were to men already in possession of manorial estates. One of these grants involved Bosden, which he gave in the 1230s to the lord of Handforth. It was subsequently administered as part of that manor, although physically the two lay separated by Bramhall.[27] Between 1208 and 1223 the same Robert de Stokeport gave Marple and Wybersley to his sister Margaret and her husband William de Vernon. He was lord of an estate in Staffordshire and the ancestor of the Vernons of Haddon Hall in Derbyshire.[28] Other grants were made to individuals who had perhaps not previously been manorial lords. By the early thirteenth century Bredbury, Norbury, Torkington, Offerton and possibly Brinnington all appear to have been held either wholly or partly by families which each took their name from the manor which they held.[29] Between 1209 and 1228 Norbury passed by marriage from the de Norburies to the de Hyde family. They were lords of half of Hyde and by 1225 had also acquired the manor of Haughton, opposite Hyde on the Lancashire side of the Tame. Their status as major local landowners is reflected in the marriage of Robert de Hyde II to the daughter of Robert de Stokeport II.[30]

Heaton Norris and Reddish

In the Lancashire part of the Borough, Heaton Norris, which was part of the Manchester barony of the Grelley family, was given to William le Norreys by Albert Grelley between 1162 and 1180. The Norreys's ownership of the manor ended in about 1280 when it was reclaimed by Robert Grelley, but the addition of their family name to the original place-name remained.[31] Reddish was held by a family which took its name from the place and is first documented as owning the manor in 1212.[32]

Basingwerk Abbey and the manor of Glossop

In Derbyshire, Ludworth, uniquely among the places of the Borough, was held by a monastic house. The abbey of Basingwerk, near Flint in North Wales, was founded in 1131 by the earl of Chester. Its monks originally belonged to the Savignac order, but after this was dissolved in 1147 Basingwerk was transferred to the Cistercians. The granting of land to monastic houses was a particularly common occurrence in the mid-twelfth century. In 1157 it was the king himself, Henry II, who gave to Basingwerk the manor of Glossop, which included Ludworth. (Mellor, immediately to the south, lay outside the manor but was part of the much larger parish of Glossop, whose rectorship was also given to Basingwerk at this same date.) The abbot of Basingwerk was not the first lord of Glossop under the king. By the early twelfth century the manor was part of the extensive estate in north-west Derbyshire controlled by the Peverels from their fortress of Peveril Castle at Castleton. Shortly before Henry II's grant of the manor to Basingwerk, however, the Peverel estates had been forfeited to the crown.[33]

The abbot and monks of Basingwerk retained direct control of the manor of Glossop for nearly 300 years. During this period the abbey had an important impact on the manor's economic development, which will be discussed further below. By the fifteenth century monastic houses preferred to rent out control of their more distant estates. In 1433 the manor of Glossop was leased to John Talbot, later created earl of Shrewsbury. Following the dissolution of Basingwerk in 1537, the earls were granted full ownership.[34]

Later medieval manorial lords

The Stockport barony and the Warrens

It is probably in some measure a reflection of the troubled nature of the fourteenth century that during its course several local manors passed into new hands. The new owners were families which were often to retain possession through many generations and to play significant roles in the Borough's history. Foremost among these were the Warrens. They inherited the Stockport barony in the late fourteenth century. John Warren was the heir to the Etons who had themselves succeeded the Stokeports following the death of Richard de Stokeport in 1292. The barony continued through the Warren line until the death of Sir George Warren in 1801.[35] As we have already seen, a number of the manors of the Stockport barony had already been granted out by the mid-thirteenth century. By the end of the fourteenth century the barons had relinquished more of their estates, reducing the barony to the manors of Stockport and Poynton and part of the manor of Offerton.[36]

The Dokenfelds, the Ardernes and the Davenports

By the late 1320s Brinnington was acquired by the Dokenfeld family, the lords of Dukinfield.[37] Their ancestral home was Dukinfield Hall but by the late fifteenth century the family had evidently established a second home at Portwood Hall, at the southern end of their manor of Brinnington.[38] The family's relationship with the lords of neighbouring Stockport appears to have been sometimes stormy. In 1437 Robert de Dokenfeld was ordered to keep the peace with Laurence Warren. In 1525 a later Laurence Warren was alleged to have incited an armed company of over sixty persons to waylay and murder John Dokenfeld as he went from his house at Portwood to attend the parish church at Stockport.[39]

In Bredbury and Romiley in the mid-fourteenth century the Arderne family acquired manorial estates through the marriage of Peter de Arderne to Cecily, the heiress of Adam de Bredbury. The Ardernes established a family residence at Arden (or Harden) Hall in Bredbury and retained lands in these townships until they were auctioned in the early nineteenth century.[40] Much of the remainder of these same manors, together with lands in Werneth, was acquired later in the fourteenth century by John Davenport of Henbury, near Macclesfield, from John Warren. This same John Davenport also obtained the manor of Woodford which became the seat of a further branch of the Davenport family.[41] His younger brother, also named John, in about 1375 acquired his own estate in the Borough. He was the husband of Alice de Bromhale, heiress to the manor of Bramhall, which remained in this branch of the Davenport family until the nineteenth century.[42]

Cheadle and Etchells

In two instances changes of manorial ownership in the fourteenth century altered the geography of local government in the Borough. One of these cases concerned Cheadle, the other neighbouring Etchells. In or shortly before 1321 Sir Roger de Chedle, lord of the manor, died leaving no male heirs. The manor passed to his wife but after her death in 1326 was divided between their two daughters. The younger, Agnes, was married to Richard de Bulkelegh. Their share, which came to be known as Cheadle Bulkeley, descended

through the Bulkeley family until the 1750s when it was sold off to pay the family's debts. The elder daughter, Clemence, was married to William de Bagylegh. In the mid-seventeenth century this second share of the manor was acquired by the Moseley family whose tenure, though brief, gave it the name of Cheadle Moseley.[43] The two shares of the manor were not equal in size, with Clemence's being the larger. Agnes's included two main blocks of land; one was in the north-east corner of the old Cheadle manor and included Edgeley, the other was in the north-west corner and included the present Cheadle village (*Ill 1.4*). Nineteenth-century maps show that there were also a number of much smaller areas of land belonging to Cheadle Bulkeley within the boundary of Cheadle Moseley, and vice versa. Some of this complex pattern may have resulted from exchanges of land following the fourteenth-century partition. Much, however, may have resulted from the need for each of the two portions to contain a share of the various resources within the original manor, its arable land, pasture, meadow, woodland and mossland. To complicate matters even further, perhaps shortly after the partition of the manor Cheadle Moseley was itself divided by the creation of a submanor known as Hulme. This was held by a branch of the Vernon family until 1476, when the family line died out and control of the estate returned to the lord of Cheadle Moseley.[44]

The situation in Etchells was the reverse of that in Cheadle. In the thirteenth century Etchells contained two separate manors, Northen Etchells and Stockport Etchells which was part of the Stockport barony. In the 1340s, by agreement with the Etons, the two were united under the common lordship of the Ardernes.[45] The fourteenth-century division of Cheadle and unification of Etchells were not to be reversed until local government changes in the late nineteenth century.

THE MEDIEVAL TOWN OF STOCKPORT

Of all the local medieval lordships, the most important in terms of the development of the Borough was undoubtedly the Stockport barony. Its creation, arguably hand-in-hand with the construction of the castle, marked the effective beginning of Stockport as a place of significance. As we shall see, that importance is also likely to have included the foundation of a parish church here, probably prior to the end of the twelfth century. The next stage of Stockport's development, in which the baron played a key role, was the establishment of the market town.

The market

The market charter, 1260

There are perhaps few better indicators of expansion in the population and economy in the twelfth and thirteenth centuries, both nationally and regionally, than the rise of the market and fair. Medieval markets were held on a weekly basis and provided a place in which people could buy and sell foodstuffs, livestock and, to a lesser extent, manufactured goods, all usually produced locally. Fairs were held annually, usually lasting several days, and brought in traders from further afield, with more exotic products on offer. Both also provided revenue for the local lord, who could charge a toll (a tax on goods sold) and stallage (a charge for the use of a market stall). Although markets and fairs could be held simply by custom, it became increasingly common for them to be given the stamp of higher approval in the form of a royal charter. This was a policy vigorously pursued by the crown itself, not least because the recipient of the charter was required to pay for the privilege. The granting of such charters reached its peak in the third quarter of the thirteenth century.[46] It is to this period that Stockport's own market charter belongs, being granted, for an unknown fee, to Robert de Stokeport III on the 6th of September 1260. In this case the grantor was not the king but his son Edward, who in 1254 had assumed the estates and authority of the former earls of Chester and in 1272 succeeded to the crown as Edward I. The charter allowed a market to be held at Stockport every Thursday (the market was later moved to Friday) and a yearly fair to be held on eight days beginning on St Wilfred's day. This feast day then fell on the 12th of October, but following the amendment of the calendar in 1752 was moved to the 23rd.[47] This charter did not mark the beginning of a market being held at Stockport. Its very place-name is evidence of a market being held here at an earlier date, certainly by the twelfth century and probably during the Anglo-Saxon period.[48] The charter did, however, provide the market with a legitimacy which may not only have helped its future success but also, both in 1260 and later, allowed its very existence.

The catchment area and local competition

Given that many people no doubt travelled to and from a medieval market on foot and sometimes driving livestock, the distance which might be travelled can seem surprising to modern eyes. According to one thirteenth-century source a round journey of 20 miles (32 kilometres) was considered reasonable, with travel to and from the market all being accomplished in a single day. Many people of course must have travelled much shorter distances.[49] In the case of the market at Stockport the catchment area probably included all of the modern Borough and much beyond. In the 1280s it is recorded that among the traders attending the market were men from the town of Macclesfield, a distance of about 10 miles as the crow flies.[50] The market at Stockport did not enjoy a local monopoly. Even within its own likely catchment area there were other markets. In Lancashire market charters were granted to Manchester and Salford in 1227 and 1228 respectively and much later, in 1413, to Ashton-under-Lyne.[51] In Derbyshire the abbey of Basingwerk established a market at Glossop by a royal charter in 1290; in 1329 this was either supplemented or replaced by a market at Charlesworth.[52] In Cheshire the market at Macclesfield was probably established no later than the 1230s, when the place also became a borough; the market at Altrincham was established in 1290.[53] All of these places also had fairs. There is also evidence of small, if short-lived, unofficial markets. In 1288 the abbot of Chester was called before the court of the Macclesfield hundred to explain why he had established an unofficial market at Northenden, a charge which he denied. The same court session saw the appearance of Richard de Vernon to explain why he claimed toll and stallage in Marple and Wybersley, of which he was lord. These cases also highlight the eagerness of the higher authorities that markets should be held on an approved, legitimate basis.[54]

Within the restriction of travel, people could offer their goods for sale at whichever market or markets they chose. In the 1280s men from Macclesfield were trading at Stockport, and men from Stockport, Marple and Wybersley appear to have traded at Macclesfield. Although these rights were not always acknowledged, traders from both Stockport and Macclesfield were legally exempt from toll and stallage in each other's market.[55] Indeed, under the terms of their thirteenth-century borough charters, the burgesses of both places were free from such payments throughout Cheshire with the exception of the toll on salt bought at the three 'wiches', the salt-producing towns of Nantwich, Middlewich and Northwich.[56]

Despite the availability of other local markets, that at Stockport clearly flourished. By 1286 the hundred court was hearing that because of competition from Stockport's market and fair the town of Macclesfield was 'sorely damaged'. Richard de Stokeport was subsequently summoned before the court and justified his holding of a market and fair by producing the charter granted in 1260 to his father. The men of Macclesfield had the satisfaction of seeing Richard admit that he had been wrong to charge them toll and stallage, but beyond this there was perhaps little that they could do.[57]

Commodities

The published sources appear to provide only slight evidence of the range of goods bought and sold at Stockport's medieval market. The sale of livestock is represented by a report in 1285 that Robert del Wode of Marple had stolen 'a beast' and sold it at Stockport.[58] Produce from local orchards is mentioned in 1358-9, when the expense account of a serjeant of the Macclesfield hundred included one penny's worth of apples bought 'at Stockport'.[59] At a much later date Stockport was noted for its importance as a corn market. The importation of corn into the town is mentioned in the thirteenth-century borough charter, but the earliest explicit reference to its sale within the market may not occur until more than two centuries later, when in 1518 Ottiwell Booth was stabbed to death as he sold his corn in the Market Place.[60]

The Borough

The borough charter

The known history of Stockport as a town begins with its borough charter. A defining feature of a medieval borough was a class of privileged individuals known as burgesses, who were granted specific rights by their manorial lord. Membership of this class was based on possession of a plot of land, or burgage, for which each burgess paid his lord a fixed rent. Burgages were concentrated in a specific place within a manor and usually consisted of a narrow elongated plot of land extending back from a roadway. They were intended primarily as housing plots, the usual practice being for the burgess to build a house on the street front of his burgage. A borough was in effect an urban settlement. This was reflected in the very appearance of the borough and the occupations of its inhabitants. Although they farmed the land, they were also likely to earn a wage from some specialized craft. Not surprisingly, boroughs were places which usually also had a market (in the vicinity of Stockport, these included Manchester, Salford, Altrincham and Macclesfield) but not every place which had a market was also a borough.

The majority of charters by which a place was given borough status by its lord belong to the thirteenth century. Stockport's own borough charter was granted by Robert de Stokeport and was based, according to its preamble, on a charter which he himself had received from 'the lord of Cheshire' (Ill 3.4). Robert de Stokeport's charter is not dated but the internal evidence makes it likely that it is roughly contemporary with the market charter of 1260, in which case this Robert de Stokeport would have been the third of that name. The close resemblance between Stockport's borough charter and that granted by the earl of Chester to Salford between 1229 and 1232 (probably in 1231) suggests that this earlier charter served as a model.[61]

The Stockport charter is in effect a list of the rights and obligations of the burgesses.[62] Under its terms a burgage was to consist of 'one perch of land for a house'. A standard perch was 16.5 feet (5 metres) but there were local variations. In the context of the charter, the reference is probably to the width of the street frontage of the burgage. For each burgage, a burgess also received an acre of land in Stockport's common fields. In return for these two parcels of land he paid the lord a fixed sum of a shilling a year, a figure found in many other boroughs. The burgesses could freely graze cattle on the common pasture land of the manor. They were allowed to feed their pigs, again free of charge, in the manor's woodland, in which they could also collect timber as fuel or as building material. A further local source of fuel were the mosslands of the manor. Here the burgesses were given the right of 'turbary', that is freely to cut peat which was then dried and burnt. The burgesses were also free to mortgage, sell and bequeath their burgages, although where a burgage changed hands a payment was to be made to the lord. Mention has already been made of the burgesses' exemption from paying toll and stallage in the markets and fairs of Cheshire, with the exception of the toll on salt from the 'wiches'. They also had a monopoly of trades within the manor of Stockport, where under the terms of the charter no-one was to work 'as a shoemaker, a leather-worker, a fuller, or any other such person' unless he was a burgess.

Such rights set the burgesses apart from the majority of people living in the neighbouring countryside, who would have been peasants with no rights of ownership over the land which they worked and none of the economic freedoms enjoyed by the burgess. The burgesses did, however, share some common manorial obligations. Under the terms of the charter they were required to have their corn ground at his mill or mills, 'should he have one'. Bread which was made for sale was to be baked in the lord's oven, with the same proviso.

Ill 3.4 Detail of Stockport's borough charter.
The charter was granted by the lord of the manor, Robert de Stokeport, whose name can be read on the first line. The original document is lost, and this is a copy made in 1530. The granting of the charter, probably in about 1260, marks the beginning of the history of Stockport as a town.

Like other medieval lords, the barons of Stockport had their own court of law, with a jury composed of members of their free tenants, in which they were allowed to try cases which fell below the jurisdiction of higher courts in the county. Under the terms of the borough charter, cases involving burgesses were to be heard by a separate court, the 'portmoot', whose jury was composed of fellow burgesses. Responsibility for bringing offenders before this court was entrusted to an officer with the title of 'praepositus', who was to be appointed each year by the burgesses from within their ranks, with the approval of the lord or his steward. From the outset it was probably the steward who presided over the court and appointed the jury.[63] Later the portmoot appears to have been amalgamated with the main sessions of the baronial court, to form a single court for Stockport manor, known as the court leet.[64] The portmoot is still mentioned in the 1470s (records of sessions of this court survive from 1464 and 1479), while the court leet is documented from the sixteenth century.[65]

By the end of the thirteenth century the title of 'praepositus' appears to have been replaced by that of mayor. The first of Stockport's mayors to be known by

name is William de Baggilegh in 1296. The names of the borough's mayors are recorded for less than a quarter of the subsequent years up to 1540, but those names which have survived suggest that the mayors were drawn from among the more socially important and wealthy burgesses.[66]

The cases heard by the portmoot included such matters as theft, assault and the 'breaking of the assize of bread and ale', that is overcharging or providing less than the prescribed measures. According to the borough charter, those guilty of the last offence were to be fined a shilling on the first three occasions. The fourth offence brought a stricter punishment. In the late fifteenth century this was specified as being the pillory for a baker, and the tumbrel, or cart, for a brewer.[67] It was also at the portmoot that new burgesses were officially enrolled and exchanges of burgages were recorded.[68]

The early burgages

While the borough charter lists the rights and obligations of its burgesses, it gives no hint of how the borough was to be actually physically established. Given the combination of the castle, the parish church and the early market, we might speculate that a cluster of dwellings was already in existence here prior to the granting of the charter. However, we have as yet no evidence as to the extent of that possible settlement, nor to what degree any existing properties were integrated within, or disrupted by, the new burgages. If Stockport followed the pattern attested elsewhere, an appropriate number of burgages were first laid out before recruitment began of the burgesses themselves. The number of these burgages is a matter on which the charter is again silent, but other evidence may provide a figure. By the late fifteenth century the burgesses' right of turbary was organized by dividing the mosslands into allotments or 'moss rooms', with each burgage having one such plot. A total of ninety-three burgages and moss rooms was recorded in 1483, with the moss rooms being listed in two distinct groups, one of sixty-four, the other of twenty-nine.[69] This may represent more than a purely geographical division. In the late thirteenth century Hugh de Spenser, the overlord of the manor of Stockport, attempted to withhold property from the widow of Richard de Stokeport. The dispute is reported to have involved sixty houses and as many acres of land,[70] and the coincidence of numbers suggests that these were burgages and their acres in Stockport's common fields. It is possible that sixty was the original number of burgages granted out in 1260 and that the figure of ninety-three given in 1483 represents the creation of additional burgages on one or more subsequent occasions. These figures may be compared with the 120 burgages which the earl of Chester is said to have created at Macclesfield at some time prior to 1233, and the 143 or so burgages implied at Manchester in 1282.[71] At Stockport sixty burgages, if each occupied by a single household, suggest a population of about 300. This figure does not include a possible minority of individuals who held property in the town by some other form of tenure.

The burgesses

Although the burgesses all had equal rights as laid down by the terms of the charter, there were differences in terms of their wealth, occupation, social status and even place of origin. Some no doubt were former peasants, who were able to exchange their servile status for the greater economic freedom of the burgess. Some who were enrolled as burgesses were either already or later became the owners of land outside the borough. Among these is likely to have been Roger de Shotswell, mayor in 1352, who was probably a free tenant in the manor of Bramhall.[72] Some may have come to the borough

from much further afield, attracted by its economic prospects. A burgage of William de Rossindale is mentioned in 1336, his name implying that his family's origins lay in Rossendale in Lancashire.[73] Some burgesses were local manorial lords. In 1483 Robert Legh, lord of Adlington, owned ten burgages in Stockport, the largest number held by any individual in the town at this date.[74] Closely following him, with eight burgages, was John Arderne, the possessor of estates in Bredbury and Romiley.[75] In the same year Robert Dokenfeld, lord of the manors of Brinnington and Dukinfield, owned two burgages, and John Dokenfeld, probably his brother, three.[76] John Savage, lord of the manor of Cheadle Moseley, owned one burgage in the town.[77] These wealthy local landowners appear to have valued their burgages primarily as a source of income through rents. In 1483 the overwhelming majority were leased to tenants. One possible exception is a burgage owned by John Arderne on Millgate, where no tenant is named, and which he may have reserved for his own use.

For others the borough was the place in which they not only lived but also carried out a trade or craft, although documentary evidence for such activities may be limited. The records of the court of the Macclesfield hundred in 1285 and 1286 list at least sixteen individuals, including two married couples, at Stockport who were making and selling bread or ale.[78] These were universal trades, found in the countryside as well as the town, and in the case of brewing mostly carried out by women as a means of supplementing the main family income. Typically the majority of those named at Stockport were female brewers. That so many individuals were involved in this trade in the town (and the list may not give the full number) may be a reflection of the influx of outsiders attending the weekly market. The names of the people listed in 1285 and 1286 are clearly those of individuals towards the lower end of the social spectrum of the townsfolk and include 'the wife of Hiche son of Magge', 'the wife of Dobbe Mol' and 'Agnes daughter of Nalle'. Two of the names also refer to occupations, 'the wife of Simon the Weaver' and 'Cecily wife of the Tailor'. Unless their occupational names were inherited, these two individuals provide the first evidence for these trades within the town. Business may have been good, since from a later dispute it seems that Henry the Tailor and his wife were in possession of at least two burgages.[79] A third individual who may have been involved in an early textile trade in Stockport was William 'le Walker', mentioned in 1289.[80] A 'walker' was a fuller, who cleaned newly woven cloth or raw wool by treading it in a vat of diluted cow's urine and fuller's earth.

Other specialist trades in the town are suggested by the names of 'Thomas le Bowler' ('bowl maker or seller'), granted a burgage in 1336, and 'Richard le Barber of Stockport', mentioned posthumously in 1361.[81] No doubt, however, surrounds the occupations of 'Roger le Bower' and 'John le Smith' of Stockport who in 1359-60 supplied forty-two bows and twenty-four lance heads respectively for the Black Prince's castles of Chester, Flint and Rhuddlan.[82]

By the fifteenth century small tradesmen in the town had been joined by wealthy merchants. The best known of these are the Dodge family. They had property in Stockport by the 1390s, although it may not be until the 1420s, when 'William Dogge, mercer, of Stockport' is mentioned, that their mercantile interests are first attested. The name of William Dodge appears in the list of known mayors of the borough on no fewer than six occasions between 1434 and 1486 (presumably representing at least two generations of the family) and an Oliver Dodge was mayor in 1500.[83] In 1483 William Dodge was the owner of six burgages in the borough, the third highest number for an individual at that time. The prosperity of the Dodges was almost certainly based on a trade in textiles. The clearest evidence may occur in 1478, when 'Oliver Dogge of Stockport, merchant' is mentioned as buying three packs of woollen cloth, worth £40, in Chester and there hiring a ship to carry these to Ireland.[84] It is likely that by this date Stockport merchants were also dealing in cloth which had been produced locally. Although sheep do not appear to have been plentiful around Manchester and Stockport, wool could be imported from elsewhere, including the Lake District and Ireland.[85]

A web of trading links between Stockport and distant markets may already have been in place in the late fourteenth century. A John de Wakefield, William de Wakefield and William de Chester all held the position of mayor of Stockport in the 1380s and 1390s, men whose names imply a family origin in two of the most important commercial centres in the north of England.[86] In 1483 a Roger Wakefield owned six burgages in the borough, an equal number to that of William Dodge.

Edmund Shaa and the grammar school

Not all merchants with an association with Stockport lived in the town itself. The mercer John Shaa or Shaw, who died between 1441 and 1444, resided at Dukinfield, in Stockport parish. He is likely to be the individual of that name who exported cloth from the port of Hull in the early 1390s, suggesting another possible trade

link for the merchants of Stockport town. The extent of John Shaa's more local business connections may be reflected in the bequests made in the will of his eldest son Edmund in 1488. These included donations to the parish church not only at Stockport, where his mother and father were buried, but also at Ashton-under-Lyne and Cheadle; the will also provided for clothing and money to be distributed among 200 of the poor in these parishes and the parishes of Mottram-in-Longdendale, Manchester, Oldham and Saddleworth. Shaa also left money for the appointment of a priest to serve a chapel which he had built at Woodhead in the Longdendale pass. This chapel, though set in an isolated spot, lay on a main route into Yorkshire and one which may have been regularly followed by both John Shaa and Edmund in his younger days.[87] The later career of Edmund Shaa lay elsewhere. He became a London goldsmith, and was showered with the highest honours both by the Goldsmiths Company, to which he belonged, and by the city of London, of which he was elected mayor. He is perhaps best remembered for his involvement, while holding that office, in the usurpation of the throne by the duke of Gloucester, crowned Richard III.

The will of Edmund Shaa, drawn up a month before his death in April 1488, contains one other legacy to his native North-West. As well as the priest at Woodhead, a priest was to be appointed to the parish church of Stockport. Both priests were to be paid a fixed annual income from a bequest of property which was to be managed by the Goldsmiths Company. Both were entrusted with the saying of mass for the souls of Edmund and his parents, but the appointee at Stockport had an important additional role. He was also to serve as a schoolmaster, teaching grammar (by which at this date Latin and Greek were meant) free of charge to any pupil from Stockport and the surrounding district who came to him to learn. In return, twice a week the pupils were to accompany the priest to the grave of Edmund's parents in the church to say prayers for the souls of the Shaas 'and for all cristen soules'. The first appointment may have been made shortly after Shaa's death, although the involvement of the Goldsmiths Company was not to begin until 1491. In 1496 the schoolmaster is first mentioned by name, John Randall.[88] Prior to Shaa's bequest only one grammar school is known to have been founded in Cheshire, at Chester by 1368, although beginning with Macclesfield in 1502 other places in the county received similar foundations in the sixteenth century.[89] Shaa's wish to found a school in his native region may have arisen from his own relatively humble beginnings, while his choice of location for that school, at Stockport, was clearly linked with the church being the burial place of his parents. The foundation did, however, add a further dimension to the local importance of the town.

The layout of the town

The heart of the medieval town of Stockport was the Market Place, situated on its steep-sided triangular promontory above the valley of the Mersey and the Goyt and the ravine of the Tin Brook which is now Little Underbank. At the west of the Market Place was the site of the castle on Castle Hill; at the east end was Stockport's parish church of St Mary (*Ills 1.6 & 4.2*). In the 1970s it was suggested that the Market Place had formed the bailey or outer courtyard of the castle, and that until the early sixteenth century the town had comprised only the streets below these outer defences. This conclusion was based mainly on the result of excavations carried out to the rear of property on the north side of the Market Place in 1974. These revealed evidence of medieval activity but not the deep build-up of levels which had been discovered in other towns. However, at the time of this excavation the only comparable evidence available was from much larger urban centres such as Chester. Since that date, excavations have been carried out in other small medieval towns in the region. They have shown a paucity of evidence to be the norm at the rear of burgages, areas which typically in these smaller towns appear to have been given over to a horticultural or agricultural use.[90]

The 'town walls'

The exclusion of the medieval town from the Market Place is not the only questionable claim which has been made for the town's early development. Situated along the sandstone cliffs which flank the west and south sides of the Market Place are two lengths of stone walling. Both are now hidden behind private property, one on Great Underbank, the other on Mealhouse Brow (*Ill 3.5*). It has commonly been supposed that these formed part of a continuous line of walling and that this defended either the supposed castle bailey or, according to a more traditional view, the medieval town.[91] Medieval town walls, however, were a rarity in the North-West. In Cheshire only Chester is known for certain to have had such defences, which in part made use of the walls of the old Roman legionary fortress. Chester was not only the largest medieval town by far in the county but was also situated dangerously close

to the border with often hostile Wales. That the town of Stockport, which was tiny by comparison and lay far from the enemy border, should have also had town walls seems most unlikely. Several archaeological excavations have failed to find evidence to show that the known sections of wall continued on the north, more gently sloping, side of the Market Place. Nor does the purpose of the extant walls at Stockport seem defensive. From their situation, not on top of the cliffs on the west and south sides of the Market Place but against them, they appear to have been retaining walls, designed to prevent the soft sandstone from eroding onto the properties below. The walls might be medieval, and that at Great Underbank includes a carved water-spout or gargoyle which might favour this, but they could equally well have been built at a later date.[92]

The streets

As well as the Market Place the medieval town included several streets. Millgate ('the road to the mill'), Hillgate ('the road up a hill') and Underbank ('under the bank', presumably a reference to the cliffs flanking the Market Place) are all mentioned by name as the site of burgages in the fifteenth century. Churchgate is documented, again as the site of a burgage, in 1541.[93] All of these may have existed as routeways before the borough was established. If the layout of the town took into account such existing factors as the Market Place, the castle, the church and the pattern of roads, it was also constrained by the natural topography which did not always lend itself to the traditional long narrow burgage plots.

Housing

All the houses which fronted the burgages are likely to have been timber-framed, with the gaps between the timbers infilled with wattle and daub. Elements of one such medieval house still remain in the building now known as Staircase House, on the north side of the Market Place. It was built using four timber A-frames known as crucks, which created a rectangular building with three internal divisions or 'bays'. It is likely that the two end bays each contained an upper and lower floor, but the central bay appears to have been open to the roof; this would have been the 'hall' or main living area and would have been heated by a hearth on the floor, the only source of heat within the building. This medieval house has been substantially altered but the two central crucks survive. Tree-ring dating has shown that the timbers of one of these crucks were felled

Ill 3.5 The 'town wall', Mealhouse Brow.
This is one of two lengths of stone walling built against the steep cliffs below Stockport's Market Place. They have variously been supposed to have been part of a medieval town wall or to have belonged to Stockport's castle. There is no evidence, however, that these walls formed part of a complete circuit and their purpose appears to have been to revet the soft sandstone cliffs.

in 1459-60. The building itself would have been constructed soon afterwards. Apart from the fourteenth-century, and much restored, chancel of the parish church, this is the oldest known surviving building in the town and one of the earliest in the Borough. Later evidence indicates that it occupied the width of one of several rectangular plots of land which ran back from this side of the Market Place and which are likely to have been medieval burgages. However, the plot occupied by Staircase House, at approximately 45 feet (13.7 metres), was half as wide again as some of its neighbours. The building may, therefore, have been one of the larger in the town. Others may not only have been smaller but also of less sturdy construction. It has been suggested that the medieval Staircase House was the home of William Dodge, who in 1483 appears to have occupied a burgage on the Market Place.[94] Lesser dwellings will have included the cottages mentioned in that same year, including one on Hillgate.

Among the other large houses of the medieval town is likely to have been the rectory, the home of the rector or parish priest. This building is mentioned in 1366 and possibly stood on the same site, the elevated ground to the east of the parish church, as the later, sixteenth- or seventeenth-century timber-framed rectory which in the 1740s was in turn replaced by the present brick Georgian building *(Ill 5.2).*[95]

Stockport's 'maner place'

A building for which there is scant evidence in the documentary sources for the medieval town is a house of the lord of the manor. Evidently such a residence had existed, for the antiquarian John Leland in about 1540 reported that Edward Warren was then living in Prestbury because 'Stoppord maner place is decayid'.[96] The reference is unlikely to be to the twelfth-century castle, since it suggests a structure which was more obviously domestic than military in nature. However, it might be to a manor house on the former castle site, a situation which evidently occurred at Manchester, where the site of the little-known castle and later manor house is now Chetham's School.[97] It is also possible that the circuit of stone walls recorded on Castle Hill in the seventeenth and eighteenth centuries surrounded such a manor house rather than the earlier castle. If such a building had existed here, it had been totally swept away by the late seventeenth century when a map of the town shows an empty plot within the walls.[98]

Wherever Stockport's 'maner place' was, the lords themselves may have used it only infrequently. As early as the late twelfth or the thirteenth century, one of the three Robert de Stokeports appointed Robert de Rumley (Romiley) as his serjeant in the manor of Stockport. Among the privileges which came with this post was the right to graze cattle in the lord's park at Stockport, unless the lord 'should wish to reside in the manor'.[99] The implication is that at this date the lord's principal residence lay elsewhere. This may have been at Poynton, where a manor house of the lord of Stockport is attested by the early fourteenth century.[100]

The bridge over the Mersey

Two other important buildings in the medieval town, the parish church and the cornmill or mills, will be discussed below, but one further structure deserves mention here. This is the medieval bridge over the River Mersey. It was rebuilt on several occasions, most notably in the eighteenth century after having been broken to prevent the forces of Bonnie Prince Charlie from crossing the river here on their march south. By the seventeenth century the location of the bridge is firmly attested as being at the foot of the present Bridge Street on the south side of Castle Hill *(Ill 3.6).* Here the river passed through what William Stukeley in the early eighteenth century described as 'a rocky channel'. William Webb, writing a century earlier and seemingly referring to the same location, noted that the river ran

Ill 3.6 Lancashire Bridge, about 1787.

A bridge across the Mersey at Stockport was probably in existence by the 1280s, but was rebuilt on several occasions. It was sited at a point where the Mersey narrowed to flow through a sandstone ravine, enabling the river to be crossed by a single span. In the medieval period this was one of only three bridges along the entire course of the Mersey, a factor which must have helped the commercial success of the town.

'with great force or rather fury under a great stone bridge'. A bridge had probably been built here by the late thirteenth century, for this is likely to have given its name to the Bridge family of Stockport and later of Bridge Hall, Adswood. (The family's name first occurs in 1282 in the Latinized form of 'de Ponte', literally 'of the bridge'.) By the early sixteenth century it had been given the name of Lancashire Bridge.[101] At one end of the medieval bridge was a chapel known as the 'Hermitage'. In the 1360s and 1370s this was occupied by a succession of minor clerics, each holding the property for one or two years by a licence from the bishop of Lichfield. Within this chapel prayers were said for the safety of travellers passing over the bridge, who in return made a payment to the priest. Similar chapels were found on other bridges over major rivers in the region, including the bridge over the Dee at Chester and that over the Irwell between Manchester and Salford.[102] The medieval bridge over the Mersey may not have entirely replaced the ford a short distance upstream, since this was still in use as a crossing point in the late eighteenth century.[103] However, it was one

of only three bridging points over the Mersey in the medieval period, the others being the bridge at Warrington, built by the early fourteenth century, and Crossford Bridge near Stretford, built by the 1530s.[104] For one late seventeenth-century commentator the importance of Stockport could be summed up by reference to only two attributes, its bridge and its market.[105] The construction of the first undoubtedly helped the success of the second.

AGRICULTURE AND THE COUNTRYSIDE

The town of Stockport was by far the largest medieval settlement in the Borough, although to modern eyes it would have seemed no bigger than a village. Other settlements would have been little more than hamlets. Even at Cheadle there is likely to have been only a small group of dwellings clustered around the parish church and the adjoining manor house.[106] The majority of settlement sites would have comprised isolated halls, farmhouses or cottages.

Farming and land tenure

Open fields and early arable farming

Despite the growth of the town of Stockport, the medieval economy of the Borough was predominantly based on agriculture. Even the townsfolk themselves, for all their involvement in trades and crafts, were engaged to some degree in farming. It will be recalled that, under the terms of the borough charter, possession of a burgage gave its owner an acre of land in Stockport's common fields. Indeed, of all the places in the Borough, it is Stockport which appears to provide the best evidence for the archetypal form of medieval arable farming, an open field divided into narrow strips which were allocated among the tenants of the manor who farmed these in common. Stockport's open-field system included land on either side of Higher Hillgate. Here the strips were later enclosed as separate fields which influenced the street pattern laid out in the late eighteenth and nineteenth centuries.[107] The name Longshut Lane off Higher Hillgate is a legacy of the earlier land use. The 'Longshote' itself is mentioned in the 1430s, and the lane in the 1570s.[108]

The earliest evidence of an open-field system in the Borough may relate to Cheadle, where there is a reference in about 1185-1200 to 'selions', a term used for the strip divisions.[109] From later, seventeenth-century evidence, an open-field system also existed around Gatley.[110] Elsewhere, the presence of such common fields may be suspected, but unequivocal evidence is not always forthcoming. The names 'Common Field', found in Werneth, and 'Town Field' or its corruption 'Tom Field', found in Bredbury, Stockport Etchells and Marple, are an important guide. Other terms which may be indicative of the divisions of open fields are found in the published field-names of every township in the Cheshire and Derbyshire parts of the Borough. These include 'acre', 'butt', 'dole', 'land', 'flat', 'furlong' and, as noted above in the case of Stockport, 'shut' or 'shoot'.[111] None of these terms, however, was used exclusively of open fields and in only a few instances is a medieval origin certain.[112] Not all local open fields may have been used for arable farming. The field-name Towns Meadow in Bramhall may indicate an alternative use to which such land could be put, as meadowland in which grass was grown for animal fodder.[113]

Further indication of local open-field systems may survive in the form of earthworks. In the Midlands in particular, such fields have left physical evidence in the shape of long strips of raised ploughland separated by narrower furrows. Earthworks of this form, known as 'ridge and furrow', survive or have been recorded in a number of locations in the Borough, from Cheadle to the slopes of Werneth Low.[114] Their origin need not, however, be medieval; some may have resulted from much later ploughing or drainage.

Domesday provides the earliest evidence for medieval arable farming in the Borough. At 'Bretberie', 'Bramale' and 'Nordberie' the occupants of each place had one team of oxen with which they ploughed the land. The villeins and bordars of 'Cedde' had two plough teams, with a third being worked by the two oxmen of Gamel's demesne. At each of the four places Domesday estimates that there was the potential for considerably more land to be brought under the plough. At 'Bramale' and 'Nordberie' only a sixth and a quarter respectively of the potential ploughland was reckoned to be in use. These were manors which were still in the process of recovering from the Norman devastation of 1069-70, but even in the manors of 'Bretberie' and 'Cedde' the figures were as low as a third and a half. In all four of these manors Domesday records areas of woodland.[115]

Population increase

In the twelfth and thirteenth centuries the population of the Borough increased considerably. Figures illustrating the rise in population in the countryside are difficult to come by but two examples may suffice to show the general trend. In 1286 Gatley, a hamlet within the manor of Stockport Etchells, contained at least six households, implying a total of about thirty individuals.[116] In Heaton Norris thirty-two 'messuages' or dwellings are recorded in 1322, suggesting a total population of roughly 150.[117] By modern standards the figures may seem risible, but they probably represent an increase by several fold from levels in the late eleventh century.

The increase in the rural population was accompanied by the creation of new farmland and, in no doubt many cases, development of new settlements. To achieve this, 'waste', land in its natural state, was cleared and brought under cultivation. Manorial lords or wealthy free tenants might make substantial clearances, but peasants might also reclaim smaller plots for their own use. The clearance of land is recorded in Woodford in the late thirteenth century,[118] but the fullest evidence for such improvements in the Borough relates to those areas lying within the boundaries of the hunting forests of Macclesfield and the Peak, and will be considered below.

Changes in land tenure

Concurrent with the rise in population and expansion of agricultural land was an increasingly complex picture of landownership. Central to this was the growing importance of the free tenant. These were individuals to whom a manorial lord had granted land in perpetuity, in return for a fixed and often nominal rent. A free tenant might range in social scale from being the lord of another manor to some lesser person, elevated from the peasantry. He might also lease out the land to others or farm it himself. Some freeholdings were no more than a few acres. Others were sizeable estates. Among the earliest references to a free tenant in the Borough is a grant of about 1185-1200, in which the lord of Cheadle gave two areas of land in the north of his manor as a wedding present to his brother-in-law, the chaplain of Bowdon. The lands in question were interestingly named 'Gomellehs' ('Gamel's clearings'), perhaps after the Domesday lord of the manor.[119] Some of the larger freeholdings were the seats of their wealthy landowners. One such estate existed at Hulme in Reddish in the reign of Henry III (1216-72). Its owners, a family who took their own name from the place, lived at Hulme Hall, later known as Broadstone Hall. By the mid-fourteenth century the Bridge family had their own large estate in Adswood in Cheadle Bulkeley, centred on the hall named after them.[120] Freeholdings, large and small, appear to have become increasingly numerous in the Borough in the fourteenth century. This has a parallel in the relinquishing of manorial estates in this period by the Stockport barons and lords of Cheadle Moseley. Both phenomena suggest the growing difficulty of larger landowners to manage directly their estates in the face of the century's changing economic and social conditions.

The fullest illustration of the variety of tenancies in a single manor within the Borough relates to Heaton Norris. The return of this manor in about 1280 from the le Norreys family to the lords of Manchester resulted in it being described in some detail in two surveys of the Manchester manor, the first in 1282, the second in 1322.[121] These surveys are especially valuable in that their comparison indicates some of the changes in estate management already under way in the early fourteenth century.

The surveys show four main classes of landholder or occupier. The first was the lord of the manor himself. In 1282 he held the demesne or home farm which contained the 'chief messuage', the manorial hall, and which altogether provided a revenue of 40 shillings a year. Perhaps significantly the demesne is not mentioned in 1322. The second group were the free tenants. Between 1282 and 1322 (when eight separate free tenants were named) the monetary rent which they paid nearly doubled, suggesting that more land had been granted out to this group in the interim. The third group were the 'bondi' or villeins, identified only in 1282. At that date, in return for the right to farm their land, they paid a total monetary rent of 20 shillings together with twenty-four hens at Christmas and 160 eggs at Easter. Although this is not specified in the valuation of the manor, it may be assumed that they were also obliged to provide labour for the lord's demesne. In 1322 there is reference to a fourth and evidently new class, the 'terminarii' or leaseholders. They appear to have been the former villeins, who had been given a more secure tenure over their homes and lands in the form of a lease for a fixed number of years. From the fourteenth century leaseholders were probably to become increasingly common throughout the manors of the Borough. There was clearly an economic advantage in this to the lord. In 1322 the leasing of land brought in £9 3s 10¼d out of a total revenue recorded for the manor of £10 10s 6¼d.[122]

Livestock and mixed farming

At Heaton Norris in 1322 farming was mixed, involving the rearing of pigs and cattle, as well as cereal production. In the twelfth and thirteenth centuries this same mixed regime is envisaged in the grants of manors and freeholdings made across the Borough, from Cheadle to Mellor, as well as in the provisions of Stockport's borough charter.[123] Pigs were perhaps the most ubiquitous of medieval livestock. Their first appearance in the documentary evidence for the Borough is as early as 1162-73, when the earl of Chester released the lord of Cheadle from his obligation to provide him with four pigs every year, presumably as rent for the manor.[124] Cattle rearing may be implicit in Domesday if, as seems likely, meadowland recorded at 'Bramale', 'Nordberie' and 'Bretberie' provided fodder for other beasts as well as the plough-oxen.[125]

The one significant variation from this pattern in the thirteenth century appears to have been in the eastern uplands of the Borough, where horses were also bred in some number. The abbot of Basingwerk is known to have kept a stable of at least twenty mares in his manor of Glossop in the 1250s, and was also the recipient of a gift of land in Mellor known by the telling name of Marefold.[126]

A mixed regime continued to the end of the medieval period and beyond. In the late fifteenth and early sixteenth centuries, for example, the growing of cereals and keeping of cattle and pigs is evident in the Brinnington estate of the Dokenfelds.[127] In Cheadle Bulkeley in the 1520s or 1530s oats belonging to the lord of the manor and his tenants, and evidently grown in the manor, were reported to have been carried off at night, with the perpetrators also threatening that they would return to drive away all the cattle.[128] In Mellor in the late fifteenth century the keeping of cattle and growing of corn are mentioned in the records of a dispute between the Ainsworth and Pilkington families over lands in the township; among those embroiled in this conflict was William Roubothom of Wyndleybothum (Windybottom) whose possessions in 1496 included a plough, four oxen and four cows.[129]

It may be suspected that from the fourteenth century onwards within this mixed regime animal husbandry grew in importance, with crops perhaps being increasingly produced as animal feed as well as for human consumption. This has not, however, been confirmed. In the published sources at least, there is a lack of good evidence on which we might make a comparative assessment of the arable and pastoral branches of farming in the Borough in the earlier and later medieval periods. There will, of course, have also been variations from one place to another. There must always have been a mixture of good and, particularly in the uplands, bad soils for crop production. The success of the medieval market at Stockport itself suggests varying degrees of local specialization.

One possible development is suggested by evidence from the very end of the medieval period. In 1541, after the death of William Davenport of Bramall Hall, an inventory was drawn up of his property. This included corn estimated to be worth £40, a herd of 159 cattle, valued at £62 16s, and some fifty-six pigs. It also included over 600 sheep. This was sheep farming on a grand scale, but of this number only twelve were kept at Bramhall, the remainder grazing the uplands of Derbyshire.[130] Earlier documentary evidence for sheep rearing in the Borough may be slight, although there is mention of 'the lamb's enclosure' in Cheadle in 1364.[131] It is probable that by this date sheep had long been kept in the Borough, but that as later at Bramhall these early flocks were small in number, with the wool being used for the needs of the household. Davenport's own sheep-rearing enterprise may be a further indication of the growing importance of the local wool trade. It is possible that by the fifteenth century smaller farmers within the Borough were also keeping sheep for the commercial value of their wool. The importance of such a change should not,

however, be exaggerated. Even in the late sixteenth and seventeenth centuries, when the keeping of sheep is widely documented in the Borough, flocks were modest in size.

Significant changes to the agricultural landscape did occur in the later medieval period. The clearances of the thirteenth century and the growing number of freeholdings (the two no doubt often being closely connected) will have resulted in an increasing number of irregular, enclosed fields. It was possibly in this century that the first enclosures of open fields occurred in the Borough.[132] As is perhaps implied at Heaton Norris, demesne land itself might have been divided between manorial tenants.

Mossland exploitation

The countryside of the Borough was not merely used for crops and livestock. An important natural resource of several of the Borough's townships were its mosslands. In dry weather these might serve as pasture but their particular value lay in the cutting of peat as a source of fuel. Among the earliest evidence for this is the provision of Stockport's borough charter giving the burgesses the right of turbary. The manor of Stockport contained two areas of mossland. One was the extensive Stockport Great Moor, which occupied the south-east corner of the manor and was bordered by the Stockport to Buxton road (the present A6). The other was the much smaller Stockport Little Moor, which lay to the east of the town (near the junction of Hall Street and Banks Lane). The moss rooms first attested in 1483 and also noted in lists of the sixteenth century were divided between the 'Black Turfs' and 'Offerton Side', both apparently parts of the Great Moor. In the sixteenth century they were described as being long strips, each 16.5 feet (5 metres) in width.[133]

Other mosses were also being dug for their peat by the late thirteenth and early fourteenth centuries. In Woodford in 1289 there is mention of 'les Turfputtes' ('the turf pits') and 'les Neweputtes' ('the new pits'), each probably being an area of peat digging on Woodford Moss.[134] Turf pits are also mentioned in 1322 on the boundary between Heaton Norris and Reddish at the south end of the 'Peyfyngate' (later known as Pinkbank Lane and now as Nelstrop Road).[135] The main mossland of Heaton Norris was Heaton Moor. By 1322 enough peat had already been dug from this moss to raise concern about its long-term value, but in other townships peat digging continued into at least the eighteenth century.

The hunting forests and parks

The hunting of deer in the Borough may be attested as early as Domesday, in which 'hays' or enclosures are mentioned in connection with the woodlands of 'Bretberie', 'Bramale', 'Nordberie' and 'Cedde'. Although their use is not specified, it has been inferred that deer were driven into these, allowing inspection of the herd. At both 'Cedde' and 'Bretberie' an eyrie was also noted in the woodland and would have provided falconers with hunting birds.[136]

Ullerswood

Among Norman kings and nobles hunting was a favourite pastime, and one which they jealously guarded. In the twelfth century the de Masseys, the barons of Dunham, hunted in Ullerswood. This area of woodland extended from what is now Manchester International Airport towards Wilmslow. It included the castle of Ullerswood, which like Stockport castle is mentioned in connection with the rebellion of 1173. The site of that castle probably lay above the River Bollin to the south of the airport, where a low mound occupied by a modern house may be the remains of the castle motte. The north-eastern part of Ullerswood encroached into the southern part of the manor of Stockport Etchells, now Heald Green. When in the twelfth century the barons of Dunham granted that manor to the new barony of Stockport, they were careful to reserve for themselves the right to hunt deer and boar there.[137]

The Peak and Macclesfield forests

In other parts of the Borough hunting was the preserve of an even higher authority, and was protected by laws which governed the lives of the local inhabitants. The places in question lay in the medieval forests of Macclesfield and the Peak. These expansive tracts of land, which together straddled the uplands of eastern Cheshire and north-west Derbyshire, were not forests in the modern sense, although both contained areas of woodland. Medieval forests were areas in which a powerful individual, usually the king, claimed for himself the right to hunt deer and protected that right through 'forest law', a set of regulations aimed at protecting both the game and its habitat. The heyday of these hunting forests was in the reign of Henry II (1154-89), when it has been estimated that forest law applied to a third of the kingdom.[138] Forests were not solely used for hunting. Forest law was imposed on areas which already included agricultural land and which continued to be farmed after this change of status. However, once an area had been designated a forest, any local landholder intending to carry out further agricultural expansion or improvement had to take forest law into account. Under its provisions, to destroy the trees or vegetation on which the game depended or to restrict the animals' movement in any way was, unless exemption had been given, punishable by a fine. Officially this meant that land was not allowed to be cleared for agricultural use or even fields fenced to protect crops from grazing animals. In reality, as the surviving judicial records of the forests show, individuals often chose to risk the penalty for such actions.

The Peak Forest was a royal forest, in which hunting was the preserve of the king, or those authorized by him. By the reign of Henry I (1100-35) its northern and western boundaries lay along the Etherow and the Goyt, so that within the Borough both Ludworth and Mellor fell within its bounds (Ill 3.7).[139] Macclesfield Forest was a hunting preserve of the Norman earls of Chester and was established by 1160.[140] According to a possibly late thirteenth-century account, the northern and eastern boundaries of the forest were the River Goyt, its southern boundary the River Dane. As we have seen in the previous chapter, the western boundary for much of its length followed the line of a series of roadways northwards as far as the present Hazel Grove. Within the Borough the forest included all of the township of Marple and also much of Norbury and Bosden and the greater part of Torkington, since these townships were crossed by this western boundary.[141]

Each forest had its own officials responsible for enforcing forest law. The day-to-day task of protecting the game fell to the 'foresters'. In the Peak Forest these were men who in return for performing this service were each granted a freeholding to provide them with a means of support. One such forester's estate existed in Mellor, and was held in the late thirteenth century by a family named 'de Meleur' after the place. Their dwelling was perhaps on the site of either the present Mellor Hall or Bottoms Hall.[142] In Macclesfield Forest the barons of Stockport were given Marple and Wybersley by the earl of Chester in return for providing a forester. When in the early thirteenth century Robert de Stokeport II in turn granted these places to his sister Margaret and her husband William de Vernon, this obligation of 'forest service' was also passed on to them.[143]

Clearance and enclosure

The individuals entrusted with upholding forest law

were themselves subject to its restrictions. In confirming the succession of Robert de Stokeport II as lord of Marple and Wybersley in or shortly after 1206, the earl stipulated that the new lord was not to undertake any action which would cause the destruction of woodland.[144] Such men, however, were also at the forefront of the piecemeal clearance and enclosure of land in the forests for agricultural use. In Mellor from the 1220s onwards the local foresters were busily adding to their existing farmland in this manner.[145] Richard de Vernon is reported to have reclaimed for his own use in 1249 'a large piece of land and wood' in Torkington just beyond Torkington Brook, which formed the boundary with Marple.[146] Other landholders were also involved in this process. In Ludworth tenants of the abbey of Basingwerk were clearing land in the early thirteenth century.[147] In Macclesfield Forest in the 1280s small parcels of land

Ill 3.7 Macclesfield and Peak forests.
These medieval hunting forests encompassed much of eastern Cheshire and north-west Derbyshire, including parts of the Borough. Within their boundaries regulations known as 'forest law' were in operation, intended to protect the game and its habitat. Peak Forest was a hunting preserve of the king, Macclesfield Forest of the earl of Chester.

were reported to have been enclosed in Hephals in Torkington, by men named as Hugh de Hephals, Thomas de Worth and Hugh de Bosden, in Bosden by Richard de Bosden, and in Norbury by Robert 'the cook'. The involvement of this last individual underlines the fact that such clearances were often carried out by men relatively low down in the social scale. In some of these cases, houses or other buildings had been erected within the new enclosures.[148] Usually, once a fine had been imposed, these improvements were allowed to remain.

During the course of the thirteenth century in two substantial areas of the Borough the clearance of forest land was conceded as a right. The first of these two instances concerned Marple and Wybersley. In 1221-3 the earl of Chester granted Richard de Vernon an additional piece of land here, described as the 'wood as far as the Bluntesbroc', a stream identified as the Bollinhurst Brook. By this same charter de Vernon was given the freedom to clear land in the woods of Marple and Wybersley 'wherever he so wished'.[149]

The second area to receive such a concession was Ludworth, as part of the manor of Glossop. The granting of that manor to the Cistercian abbey of Basingwerk by the king in 1157 placed it in the hands of a religious order highly adept at the profitable exploitation of even the most unpromising land. Under the abbey's management, clearances were made and the trees in the woodland of the manor steadily felled. In 1253 it was reported that the woodland of Ludworth had been 'wasted' by the abbot. In 1285 such actions resulted in an official enquiry, at which the abbot claimed unsuccessfully that his manor of Glossop lay outside the forest's bounds. The ultimate decision in this matter was, however, in Basingwerk's favour. By a charter of 1290 the king gave the abbot and monks the right to clear for cultivation the woods and wastes within the manor of Glossop as they so wished.[150] The charters granted to de Vernon and the abbot did not give them a complete licence. Both at Marple and Wybersley and at Glossop the earl and king reserved the right of 'venison', under which any action which might impede the movement of deer was still an offence. Nevertheless, the concession that the natural habitat of the deer might be freely swept away was an important turning point for these places.

The clearance of forest land in the Borough after the thirteenth century is less well documented in the published sources. One of the largest known clearances occurred in the mid-fourteenth century when John de Legh removed 60 acres of woodland in Torkington. The scale of this clearance was matched by the imposing

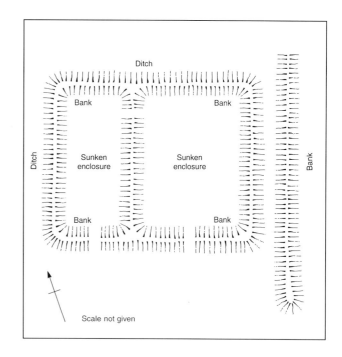

Ill 3.8 Deer hay in Bramhall.
This double enclosure is believed to have been used for the management of herds within the deer park of Bramall Hall. It still survives as an impressive earthwork.

setting of the house which de Legh built for himself on his new farmland. This was the moated site now known as Broadoak Moat, to which we will return below.

Parks

While the forests of Macclesfield and the Peak were established for the use of the Norman earls and kings, in the later medieval period it became fashionable among lesser nobles to create their own hunting grounds in the form of enclosed areas or parks, usually surrounding their manorial seat. At Stockport the name of the Park was associated by the late twelfth or thirteenth century with the low ground in the bend of the river below Castle Hill. This relatively small area, though presumably enclosed, appears to have been originally used as pasture for the cattle of the lord of the manor or, in his absence, his serjeant. By 1541 it had been divided into two separate fields.[151] In Cheadle, 'Chedlpark' and 'le Overparke' ('the higher park'), mentioned in 1345 and 1431 respectively, may have been one or more similar enclosures.[152] The lord of Stockport did have a deer park, by the mid-fifteenth century, but this was at his manor house at Poynton.[153]

Two deer parks are known to have existed in the Borough, each associated with a locally important

Ill 3.9 Old Manor Farm, Marple.
This house was once a medieval hall. The oldest part of the building (right) was a great hall, open to the roof. The timber-framed wing (left) is dated to the early sixteenth century.

manorial family *(Ill 3.13)*. One was at the Dokenfelds' estate in Portwood. This was in existence by the 1540s when it was mentioned in connection with Portwood Hall. Possibly, like the hall itself, it had been established in the fifteenth century or earlier.[154] The other park surrounded the Davenports' manor house of Bramall Hall. It was in existence by 1577 when it was shown on Saxton's map of Cheshire, but again may have originated at a somewhat earlier period. It was possibly within this park that William Davenport kept his herd of 159 cattle recorded in 1541. The park at Bramhall has left one important and rare feature, now preserved in woodland on a local golf course. This is a substantial earthwork, rectangular in plan, which comprises an outer bank and ditch enclosing a sunken interior divided into two unequal compartments by a further embankment *(Ill 3.8)*. The earthwork has been identified as a deer hay, with the two compartments allowing the separation of different animals.[155]

Rural dwellings

Halls

Of the dwellings which dotted the rural landscape of the medieval Borough, the largest were the halls. These were the homes of manorial lords and wealthy free tenants, from where they also farmed and managed their estates. The name 'hall' derives from the principal feature of these buildings, a spacious room open to the roof and heated by a central hearth; it was here that the household took its meals and many of them slept. Cross-wings at one or both ends of this open hall provided private accommodation for the owner and his family, and storage for household provisions. Cooking was carried out on the hearth in the open hall or in a kitchen, which as a fire precaution was commonly a separate building. From the documented details of landownership it can be assumed that at least one medieval hall had existed in most of the townships of the Borough. All were probably timber-framed, with stone only being used as a plinth which provided a damp-proof foundation for the timberwork. Most of the Borough's medieval halls have been lost through later demolition or rebuilding, but there are important exceptions.

One of these is Old Manor Farm or Higher Danbank, which overlooks Stockport Road in Marple, close to the township's western boundary. It occupies a position of some natural strength, on a spur of land above the confluence of Marple Brook and Torkington Brook. At the heart of this building, which is still inhabited, is an open hall, believed to date from the fifteenth century. This is cruck-framed, the same method of construction found in the mid-fifteenth-century Staircase House in the Market Place at Stockport. Flanking this open hall are two later cross-wings, one timber-framed and one built of stone,

believed to date from the early sixteenth and seventeenth centuries respectively (Ill 3.9).[156] The resulting overall plan of the building is H-shaped, a common form among halls.

The remains of a hall belonging to one of the major free tenant families of the Borough were excavated in 1992. This was Bridge Hall, in Adswood, the home of the Bridge family, the last surviving part of which was demolished in the 1930s. By 1600 the building comprised a central cruck-framed open hall with a cross-wing at each end, as at Old Manor Farm forming an H-shaped plan. The excavation uncovered the footings of one of these cross-wings and showed that while this wing had been rebuilt in the late sixteenth century it had originally been constructed as part of the medieval hall.[157]

In terms of their scale, Old Manor Farm and Bridge Hall were probably typical of most halls in the Borough. However, they are modest in comparison with one other

Ill 3.10 Bramall Hall, the 'Ballroom'.
Bramall Hall was undoubtedly one of the largest medieval halls in the Borough. This late medieval room, open to the roof, probably served as part of the private accommodation of the lord and his family. Its decoration included wall paintings dating from the early sixteenth century. Other paintings, in the gable of the end wall, were added about a century later.

hall which, though substantially altered in later years, still preserves much that is medieval. Bramall Hall, the former home of the lords of the manor of Bramhall, has been described as 'one of the four best timber-framed mansions of England'. As at Marple and Adswood, the building contains a central hall and two cross-wings. Here, however, this hall forms only part of a longer range, and the cross-wings project to create two sides of an open courtyard. Surviving early timberwork suggests that this U-shaped arrangement dates back to the fourteenth century (Ill 3.1). The fourth side of the courtyard was once enclosed by a gatehouse wing, now demolished but mentioned in the will of William Davenport in 1541. The medieval open hall also no longer remains. It was rebuilt in the late sixteenth century as a ground-floor entrance hall with a withdrawing room above. The upper floor of the south wing, however, still contains a large late medieval room open to the roof. Now known as the Ballroom, originally this probably formed part of the family's private accommodation. Its walls are painted with depictions of scrolling foliage and real and fantastic figures. These wall paintings are believed to date from the early sixteenth century. They are a rare and important survival of a form of decoration which may have been not uncommon in the homes of the wealthy at this period (Ills 3.10 & 3.11). A chapel, which also survives in the south wing, is documented in 1493. It contains the remains of a wall painting of the crucifixion, which had been whitewashed over at the time of the Reformation.[158]

Moated sites

At least three of the halls within the Borough are known to have been surrounded by a water-filled moat (Ill 3.13). The provision of a hall with a moat was an essentially medieval phenomenon. Nationally the practice is believed to have begun in the late twelfth century, with the construction of such moats reaching a peak in the thirteenth and early fourteenth centuries. In Greater Manchester the evidence for their dating is slight but suggests a broad date-range from the late thirteenth century to the early fourteenth. Opinions differ on the primary function of such moats, which have been seen as a status symbol as well as fulfilling a defensive role. The moated sites of Stockport all take, or appear to have taken, a form typical in the county, that is with a single moat surrounding a square or slightly rectangular interior area or 'platform'. They also all lie on boulder clay, which provided these moats with a natural impermeable lining.[159]

The construction of Broadoak Moat in Torkington can be dated, thanks to documentary evidence, with some precision. It was built in about 1354 by John de Legh on the land from which he had cleared 60 acres of woodland within the forest of Macclesfield. The moat is reported to have surrounded a manor house which included two 'chambers' and a kitchen; outside the moat were a barn, stables and associated fields. No buildings now stand within the moat but a small archaeological excavation in 1976 found evidence of at least one fourteenth- or fifteenth-century building on the edge of the moat platform (Ill 3.12). By a series of grants in the late 1340s and early 1350s, John de Legh, who also possessed a moated hall at Booths near Knutsford, had become the largest landholder in Torkington. By 1354 he was also the steward of the duke of Lancaster's lands in Cheshire. His earlier career had been one of violence, theft and murder, activities which were common to a number of other landowners in the region during this period. The moat at Torkington, whose ditches were among the widest in the region, may well have been his own precautionary measure.[160]

The dates of two other moats in the Borough, at Reddish Hall, where the moat no longer survives, and at Arden Hall in Bredbury, where much of the moat is still intact, are unknown. Potentially a manor house may have stood on the site of Reddish Hall by 1212, when there is a reference to Matthew de Reddish, the first known lord of the manor.[161] The present Arden Hall dates from the late sixteenth century (Ill 4.1) but presumably an earlier hall had stood on this site, either built or inherited by the Ardernes when they acquired their estates in Bredbury and Romiley in the early fourteenth century.

A fourth moated site in the Borough is something of a puzzle. This is Peel Moat, which now lies preserved on a golf course in Heaton Moor, in the former township of Heaton Norris. The name Peel is common to a number of moated sites and refers to a timber palisade which must have once surrounded them. (Beyond the western boundary of the Borough was the moated Peel Hall, now demolished but once the manor house of Etchells.)[162] The moat at Heaton Moor survives intact and in places still holds some water. Although there is no firm physical or documentary evidence for a building ever having stood on the platform, tradition held that this had been the case, and bricks and sandstone blocks are reported to have been found here.[163] The early ownership of this site is also uncertain, but it is possible that Peel Moat was the 'chief messuage', or manor house, which was recorded in Heaton Norris in 1282.[164] If so, it would be the earliest known moated site in

Ill 3.11 Bramall Hall, detail of a wall painting in the 'Ballroom'.
This early sixteenth-century painting shows two musicians in contemporary dress.

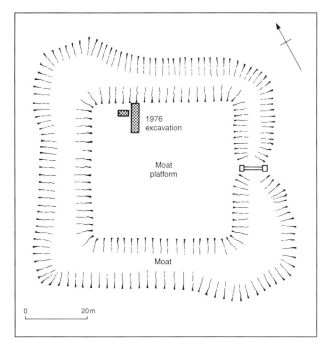

Ill 3.12 Broadoak Moat, Torkington.
This moat, which is still water-filled, was constructed in about 1354 by John de Legh. The manor house which it once surrounded no longer stands but excavations in 1976 found evidence of at least one late medieval building by the moat's edge.

Greater Manchester. Such an early date might explain the size of its platform which, at less than 1000 square metres, is among the smallest in the county.

Longhouses and cottages

The hall, whether moated or not, was the residence of the most privileged members of medieval society in the Borough. Below them, the dwelling of the most wealthy peasants and lesser free tenants may have been a longhouse. This was a rectangular building which housed the human occupants at one end and their livestock at the other. According to one account, this remained the dwelling of many Cheshire farmers until the late sixteenth century.[165] An example of a medieval longhouse is Apethorn Fold, immediately to the north of the Borough and formerly in the township of Werneth.[166] This building is a rare survival in the region and may have been more strongly built than most others of its type. For poorer peasants home would have been even less substantial, a cottage of one or two rooms, built of whatever materials were available. Even documentary evidence of such buildings is slight, but includes the 'Karlcotes' ('peasants' huts') mentioned in Romiley in the 1340s.[167]

Cornmills

Under a custom known as 'mill soke' it was the right of any manorial lord to oblige his tenants to have their corn ground at his mill. A proportion of the grain, known as a multure, was kept as payment by the miller, who leased the mill from the lord. Multures could vary from place to place according to the stipulation laid down by the lord and, it might be added, according to the honesty of the miller. At Stockport the borough charter fixed this proportion at one sixteenth and specified that this was to be levied both on corn grown within the township and imported from elsewhere.[168] The mill soke could be a useful source of income to a lord. In 1282 the lord of Manchester received revenue of £4 6s 4¼d from his manor of Heaton Norris, of which 13s 4d was derived from the mill. By 1322 this revenue had risen to £10 10s 6¼d of which 16s 8d came from the mill. At this same date it was reported that in times past the mill soke had been worth £2 a year.[169]

In manors where the local lord felt that the initial outlay was justified by the future revenues and where a suitable stream or river could be harnessed to provide power, it was common to find a cornmill. At the time of Domesday only one mill was recorded in the whole of the Hamestan hundred, at Macclesfield.[170] That many of the Borough's cornmills should have been established by the end of the thirteenth century is a measure of the growth of the local population and the increase of arable land which had occurred in the interim. It should be noted that in most cases the earliest reference to a particular mill is to a building already in existence. Its construction may have occurred at some considerable time before that date.

The earliest reference is to a mill at Cheadle, in about 1185-1200.[171] That Cheadle should head the chronological list may not be coincidental but reflect its position among the most economically important manors in the Borough at that time. At a later date Cheadle was served by two separate cornmills (*Ill 3.13*). The Higher Mill, on a bend of the Micker Brook to the south of Cheadle village, lay within Cheadle Moseley. The Lower Mill, on the same stream but on the north side of the village, was in Cheadle Bulkeley. Both probably originated as manorial mills, mirroring the division of Cheadle into two separate manors in about 1326. The location of the twelfth-century mill is uncertain but it is believed to have stood on the same site as the later Higher Mill. If this is correct, it is a token of the economic value of such sites that a mill in Cheadle Bulkeley was in existence before 1349,

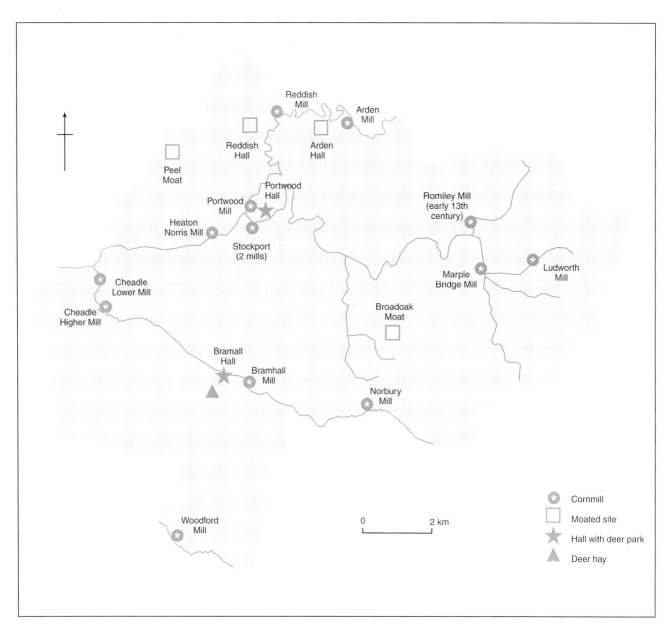

Ill 3.13 Cornmills, moated sites and deer parks in the Borough, from the twelfth century to the early seventeenth.
Water-powered cornmills were a valuable source of income to manorial lords. Deer parks provided those lords with sport but were a luxury which only the wealthiest local landowners could afford. The construction of a moat around a hall may have been prompted by the desire for protection, but some believe that moats were themselves primarily symbols of status.

during the time of its first lord, Richard de Bulkelegh.[172]

The provision in the borough charter of Stockport that the burgesses were to grind their corn at the lord's mill or mills, 'should he have one', has been taken to mean that at this date (probably about 1260) a mill had not yet been built here. The presence of a mill is documented by other evidence of the time of one of the three Robert de Stokeports, so that its construction took place no later than the 1270s. By the early seventeenth century there were two cornmills in Stockport, one on Millgate, the other in the Park below

Castle Hill. The Millgate mill was in existence by 1457, when the street itself is mentioned by name. This is likely to have been the earlier of the two mill sites, the second presumably being added to meet the increasing requirements of the growing town.[173]

Cheadle and Stockport might be expected to have a cornmill at a relatively early date, but early mills may have existed in some less obvious places. When in 1229 one Jordan de Tretune and Sibil his wife granted their lands in Ludworth and Ernocroft to Basingwerk Abbey, they excluded the water rights to the River Etherow above their mill 'at Rumelegh' (Romiley).[174] This provides evidence for an unexpected early mill, evidently downstream from Compstall.

The upland township of Ludworth had a mill by the reign of Henry III (1216-72). Its location is believed to be the site of the later Ludworth cornmill, on the Mill Brow stream which formed the boundary between Ludworth and Mellor.[175] A mill in Marple is mentioned in 1354 and is implied at an earlier date by the name of Robert the Miller, a tenant of Richard de Vernon in Marple and Wybersley in 1296. The location of this mill is not certain, but it may have been on the site of the later cornmill on the Goyt at Marple Bridge (*Ill 3.14*).[176] A mill was operating in Mellor in 1391. At some point after 1448 it fell into disuse and in 1475 it was described as being in ruins. Its location is unknown.[177]

At least two other mills are attested in the Borough by the late thirteenth century. A mill at Heaton Norris is first mentioned in 1282. In 1322 it was reported that it had originally been powered by the Mersey but was then fed by the 'Hertwellesiche'. This has been identified as the stream later known as Travis Brook. The shift to the smaller, less reliable stream, presumably necessitated by some change to the local condition of the river, was given as the reason for the decline in revenue from the mill. Despite these difficulties, it was still stipulated that 'all the tenants of Heton ought to grind at it'.[178] Woodford had a mill by 1296, possibly situated on the River Dean.[179] A mill at Reddish is first mentioned in a charter which is believed also to be late thirteenth-century in date. The site of this mill was probably that of the later Reddish cornmill next to which were built the Reddish printworks.[180]

A mill is mentioned in 1315 within the estates in Bredbury, Werneth, Romiley and Hattersley previously held by Richard de Stokeport. Its location is uncertain, but was perhaps in Bredbury.[181] Two mills are later found in that township, reflecting its division between the Ardernes and the Davenports. The mill of the Ardernes was situated on the Tame near Arden Hall. It is named in 1419 as 'Bight Milne' (after the 'bight' or bend of the river at this point) but was later known as Arden (or

Ill 3.14 Marple Bridge cornmill, about 1910.
This cornmill on the River Goyt may have stood on the same site as the mill in Marple mentioned in 1354. The Marple Bridge mill continued in operation until 1926. It was later demolished.

Ill 3.15 Stockport and Cheadle parishes.
Stockport parish (shaded) was probably created in the twelfth century, as a result of the establishment
of the Stockport barony. At least some of its component townships are likely to have been taken from the
parish of Cheadle; others may have been formerly part of the parish of Mottram-in-Longdendale.

Harden) Mill.[182] The Davenports' mill in Bredbury was on the Goyt, immediately below Otterspool Bridge, but no reference to this has been found prior to the early seventeenth century.[183]

In neighbouring Brinnington there is evidence that works associated with a mill were being planned in the late fifteenth century. In the 1480s Robert Dokenfeld was given permission by Edward Botham to build a mill weir across the Goyt between Brinnington and Botham's land in Stockport. In return Edward and his tenants were to be free from paying multure at Dokenfeld's mill.

Whether the mill was actually built is not known, but the Dokenfelds certainly had a mill in Brinnington by 1549 and by the early seventeenth century were described as having 'two water grain mills there called Portewood Mills'. Possibly both of these last mills were situated next to the Tame just above the confluence with the Goyt, where a mill is shown on a map of the Portwood estate drawn in 1696.[184]

Not every township within the Borough is known to have had a cornmill in the medieval period. Two surprising omissions are Norbury and Bramhall. Although both manors later had a mill on the Norbury and Lady Brook, no evidence has been found for this prior to 1571 in the case of Norbury[185] and the 1620s in the case of Bramhall.[186] This may be a result of the general infrequency with which early mills are documented, but another factor should also be considered. The known early mills of the Borough were all situated either on the rivers, on fast-flowing upland streams or on more low-lying streams close to their confluence with the rivers. The absence of early references to mills at Bramhall and Norbury might indicate the less favourable nature of the potential mill sites in those townships.

PARISHES, CHURCHES AND CHAPELS

In the medieval period the Borough was divided between four parishes, Cheadle and Stockport in Cheshire, Manchester in Lancashire, and Glossop in Derbyshire. The two parish churches within the Borough, at Cheadle

and Stockport, have both sometimes been claimed to have been founded before the Norman takeover. As we have seen in the previous chapter, while it seems likely that Cheadle was the centre of a late Anglo-Saxon parish, there is little reason to believe that this was also true of Stockport. In all probability the establishment of a parish of Stockport only came about when 'the market place at the hamlet' was elevated to a position of administrative importance. It was, in other words, a result of the creation of the Stockport barony.

Stockport and Cheadle

The earliest evidence for a church at Stockport is provided by mention not of the building itself but of its priest, the rector or parson. The oldest reference traditionally believed to be to a holder of that position is to Matthew the 'cleric of Stockport', whose name appears in a charter granted to Robert de Stokeport I

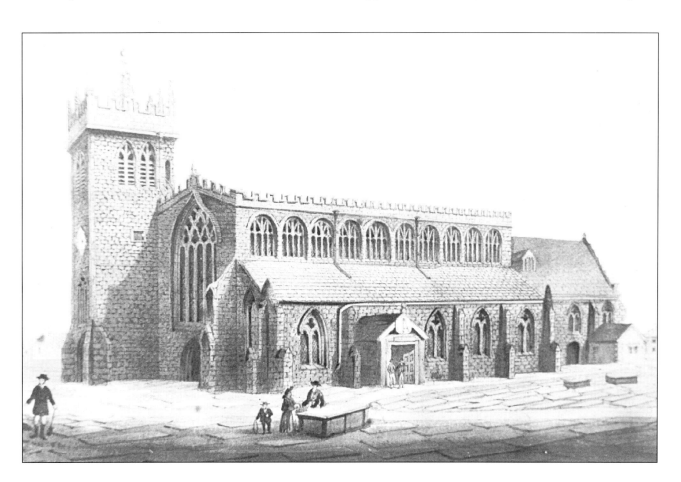

Ill 3.16 Stockport parish church, before rebuilding in the early nineteenth century.
This church was the largest in the Borough during the medieval period. From its architectural style it was built in the late thirteenth or early fourteenth century, presumably replacing an earlier and smaller church. Alterations are known to have been made in the 1530s, and the tower was not added until the early seventeenth century. In 1810 the soft local sandstone of which the church was built had so deteriorated that work began on the demolition of the tower and nave. The church was rebuilt between 1813 and 1817, leaving only the chancel from the medieval building.

at or shortly after his succession to the barony in the 1180s. The first person recorded with a title which we can unreservedly equate with the rectorship is Richard 'parson of Stockport', who is documented in about 1230.[187]

Stockport was a large parish comprising fourteen townships, the eighth greatest number in Cheshire (Ill 3.15). The majority of these townships occupied a block of land extending in the south from Bramhall to Disley Stanley and in the north from Stockport to Werneth and Hyde. It also included two outlying townships: Stockport Etchells, which was separated from the main group by Cheadle; and Dukinfield, separated from Hyde by the small township of Newton in the parish of Mottram-in-Longdendale. Although the barony and parish were not identical in area, it is likely that reasons of common manorial ownership underlie much of the parish's makeup. The inclusion of Stockport Etchells within the

Ill 3.17 Mellor Church, the font.
Dating from the eleventh or twelfth century, the font is carved with human and animal figures. Their meaning is uncertain, but one suggestion is that the mounted figure shown here represents Christ entering Jerusalem.

parish was almost certainly a consequence of its inclusion within the barony. Dukinfield may have been included because its manorial lords by the 1180s were the 'de Bromale' family, the lords of Bramhall.[188] Hyde may have been perhaps added to the parish in the early thirteenth century when the de Hydes obtained the manor of Norbury. This process could also work the other way. Bosden, though surrounded by townships within Stockport parish, was part of the parish of Cheadle. There can be little doubt that this was a result of the granting of Bosden in the thirteenth century by Robert de Stokeport II to the lord of Handforth, a township which was itself a component of Cheadle parish.

If Stockport parish was a late creation, in which parish or parishes were its townships previously? One, Stockport Etchells, had probably belonged to the Domesday parish of Northenden. The parish of Mottram-in-Longdendale may also have been a pre-Norman foundation, in which case it may have originally included Dukinfield and perhaps also one or more of the other townships later found in this north-easterly part of Stockport parish.[189] The greatest losses were probably suffered by the parish of Cheadle, which was reduced to Cheadle itself, the township of Handforth immediately to the south and its later appendage of Bosden.

Rectors were dependent for their incomes on the revenues provided by their parishioners, mainly in the form of the tithe, the tax on agricultural produce. The loss of many of the townships of his parish to Stockport did not impoverish Cheadle's rector. Cheadle itself was among the most prosperous of the manors of the Borough at the time of Domesday. Much of what was to become the parish of Stockport was in a far worse condition. By the mid- to late twelfth century the process of improvement was probably under way but may not yet have been that far advanced to provide the rector of this large new parish with a particularly wealthy living. However, in the thirteenth century the foundation of the borough of Stockport and an expanding population in the other manors of the parish must have increased his income considerably. In 1291 the revenues received by the rector of Stockport, at £18 13s 4d, were already more than double those of the rector of Cheadle, at £8. Less than a century later, in 1379, the figure given for Cheadle was £26 13s 4d, but that for Stockport was more than three times this, at £90. In 1535 the respective figures were both lower but the relative difference had now increased so that the revenue reported for Stockport parish was over five times greater than that for Cheadle, £71 3s 4d compared with £13 13s 5d. In 1379 Stockport was

Ill 3.18 Mellor Church, the pulpit.
The pulpit is carved from a single oak trunk and is believed to date from the fourteenth century. It is possibly the oldest surviving wooden pulpit in England.

already one of the wealthiest benefices in either Lancashire or Cheshire.[190]

At both Cheadle and Stockport the patronage or advowson, that is the right to appoint the rector, rested with the manorial lord. In the case of Cheadle, when the manor was divided in 1326 the advowson was given to the lords of Cheadle Bulkeley. In both parishes the rectors were themselves often the sons of wealthy families. Perhaps the best known of these was Richard de Vernon, the rector of Stockport between 1306 and 1334, and a son of the baron of Shipbrook.[191] It is a sign of his family's importance that a carved effigy was set over his grave in Stockport's parish church. No other member of the medieval clergy in Stockport is known to have been given such a monument.

By the late fourteenth century at both Stockport and Cheadle the lords sometimes appointed their own relatives to the rectorship. In the case of Henry Warren, appointed to Stockport in 1473, and Richard Bulkeley, appointed to Cheadle in 1486, these were the lords' own sons. In the appointment of members of the wealthy landowning classes, including members of the patron's own family, Stockport and Cheadle differed significantly neither from each other nor from many other churches in the region. Where Stockport may have been unusual is in the degree of competition for the rectorship, prompted by the highly profitable revenues which awaited the successful candidate. On a number of occasions the rectorship appears to have gone to the highest bidder.[192]

The differences in size and wealth of the two parishes may also be reflected in the scale and building history of their parish churches. If the first church at Stockport was indeed built in the mid- to late twelfth century, within 200 years it had been replaced by a new and almost certainly larger building. The present parish church of St Mary, for all its Gothic appearance, is itself largely the result of a rebuilding programme in 1813-17. Only the chancel was retained from the medieval church, although this itself was later much restored. The chancel is built in the Decorated style of English architecture, which flourished in the last quarter of the thirteenth century and the first half of the fourteenth. From illustrations of the church made prior to the early nineteenth-century rebuilding, it appears that the nave and the low aisles which flanked it, one on either side, were also built in that style (Ill 3.16). This evidence also shows the windows of the clerestory, that is the part of the nave walls which rose above the side aisles, were of a later date. These were in the Perpendicular style, which spanned the period from the second half of the fourteenth century to the early sixteenth. They may possibly date from about 1536, when Nicholas Elcock of the town bequeathed money towards 'the building of two aisles now in hand'. The tower, which stood at the north-west corner of the nave, dated from the early seventeenth century.[193]

The parish church of St Mary at Cheadle has a very different history of building. Here the nineteenth century saw restoration and replacement rather than rebuilding, with the result that the church has remained largely intact. It dates from the sixteenth century. Thanks to good documentary evidence, the progress of its construction can be traced with some accuracy. Work had begun by 1523, since in that year the church was described as 'lately in great ruin and decay and now a-building'. The first parts to be built appear to have been the nave and its two side aisles. As was common in parish churches, the east ends of the aisles were screened off to form private chapels belonging to important local families. The chapel in the north aisle belonged to the lord of Cheadle Moseley. At the time of the church's construction this was Sir John Savage, and the chapel itself is now known as the

Savage Chapel. The chapel in the south aisle belonged to the lord of Handforth, who at this date was Sir John Stanley. His successor to the lordship was Urian Brereton and it is after his family that the chapel is now known. A date inscribed on the wooden screen of the Savage Chapel and other dates, now removed, in the windows of the aisles imply that the nave and aisles were roofed over by the end of the 1520s. The tower at the west end of the nave may have been completed at a somewhat later date, as in 1540 Robert Arderne left a contribution to the building or repairing of Cheadle church or 'steeple'. The chancel was not completed until 1556, by Lady Katherine Bulkeley who in 1560 was buried before its great east window.[194]

Placed within the Brereton Chapel are three recumbent effigies of armoured figures (Plate II). One is of Sir Thomas Brereton who died in 1674. The others, now lying side by side, are earlier. It has been suggested these represent Richard Bulkeley, who died in 1454, and Sir John Honford who distinguished himself in the Hundred Years War against France and who died in about 1460. Alternatively, both may be members of the Honford family, the medieval lords of Handforth. In this case, other suggested candidates are Sir John's son and successor to the lordship, John Honford, who died in 1473, and William Hondford, the last of the family's male line, who was killed at the battle of Flodden Field in 1513. What does seem probable is that at least one of these effigies predates the rebuilding of the church in the sixteenth century. As such they imply the existence of a private chapel of the lords of Handforth within the earlier church.[195] Beyond this, little else is known of that building.

At Stockport, as at Cheadle, the east ends of the side aisles contained the private chapels of important families of the parish. In this case the end of each aisle was divided into not one but two such chapels. In the south aisle were the Lady Chapel, belonging to the Davenports of Bramhall, and St Peter's Chapel, belonging to the Ardernes of Bredbury. In the north aisle All Hallows Chapel belonged to the Dokenfelds of Dukinfield and Brinnington, and St Anthony's Chapel to the Hydes of Norbury. It was in these chapels that family members were buried. (As at Cheadle, members of the family of the lords of the manor, and patrons of the church, were buried in the chancel.) These four families were also collectively known as the 'principales praepositi', or later 'the Posts of the Parish'. Under this title they were entrusted with the financial affairs of the church. The Lady Chapel is documented in 1493 and the other chapels in the early sixteenth century. The 'principales praepositi' themselves are mentioned in 1464, when together with John Warren, the lord of the manor, and William Tabley, the rector, they leased out a piece of church land near Shaw Heath. How the office of praepositi, which in Cheshire was also found in the parish of Astbury, had come about at Stockport is uncertain. Possibly it was a recognition of the fact that by the fifteenth century the four families were the most important landowners within the parish, after the lord of Stockport, and perhaps also the greatest benefactors to its church.[196]

Mellor

The parish churches at Stockport and Cheadle were not the only places of public worship in the Borough during the medieval period. In the more outlying parts of large medieval parishes, a separate chapel was often built. Known as a 'chapel of ease', this was served by a clergyman who was provided by the rector of the parish church. The one medieval chapel of ease which we know for certain to have existed in the Borough

Ill 3.19 Chadkirk Chapel, Romiley, from the south-east.
The first church on this site is sometimes claimed to have been an Anglo-Saxon foundation. It may in fact have been built in the medieval period as a chapel of ease serving this part of the parish of Stockport. The present chapel is dated to the early sixteenth century. Its fabric is a record of its often troubled history. The building was originally all of timber framing on a stone plinth, but this framing survives only in the north and east walls of the chancel. Successive periods of neglect and re-use necessitated the reconstruction of the other walls in stone. The south wall visible here dates from 1747.

was that at Mellor, now the parish church of St Thomas. This was one of three such chapels in the parish of Glossop, the others being established at Charlesworth in the early fourteenth century and at Hayfield in about 1386.

The church at Mellor was rebuilt in the nineteenth century, leaving only the tower from the earlier building. This is built in the Perpendicular style, and probably dates from either the fourteenth or fifteenth century, although the foundations are said to be earlier than the main fabric. The church font, carved with curious figures which include a horse and rider, is certainly much older, either eleventh- or twelfth-century (*Ill 3.17*). It is sometimes inferred that the church itself was founded at so early a date. However, the font could have been brought here from elsewhere, and it seems more likely that the foundation of the chapel occurred at a similar time to its sister chapels of Hayfield and Charlesworth. The chapel contains one other medieval feature of note. This is its pulpit, which is carved from a single trunk of oak with decorative tracery on the exterior. It is believed to date from the fourteenth century and is claimed to be the oldest wooden pulpit in England (*Ill 3.18*).[197]

Chadkirk

There may possibly have been one other chapel of ease in the Borough, in the parish of Stockport. In the previous chapter it was noted that Chadkirk Chapel in Romiley may have been originally founded for this purpose. If this was the case, by the mid-sixteenth century it appears to have become more of a private chapel of the Davenports of Henbury, who owned Chadkirk as part of their estates in Bredbury and Romiley. The chapel itself is first mentioned in 1535 when it was served by a priest, named as Ralph Green, who received an income from land evidently given to him by the Davenports. The present chapel was probably built not long before that date. It is simple in plan, consisting of a rectangular aisleless nave and a slightly narrower chancel. It was originally constructed of timber framing on a stone plinth (*Ill 3.19*). Later rebuilding has removed the timber framing from all but two walls of the chancel, but what remains is likely to be early sixteenth-century. From its date, it was probably built by the Davenports.

The primary duty of Ralph Green seems to have been as a chantry priest, that is to say mass for the souls of members of the Davenport family. In 1548 chantries were dissolved by the crown and the lands attached to them confiscated. When Chadkirk suffered this fate, the Davenports protested, seemingly arguing that the main function of the chapel was for family baptisms, weddings and funerals. The claim may have been dubious. At this date the main seat of the family appears to have been still Henbury near Macclesfield, with family members being buried in the parish church of Prestbury. Under William Davenport the family moved to Bredbury, where they lived at the newly built Goyt Hall, but this was not until towards the end of the sixteenth century, with family members then being buried at the parish church in Stockport. In the 1550s two members of the Davenport family were perhaps living at Chadkirk, but they were younger sons, and are the only family members known to have had such a connection. In 1560 the revenues from the chantry lands at Chadkirk were still passing to the crown. It has been supposed that the Davenports subsequently recovered these lands but this has not been confirmed. What does seem to have been the case is that for perhaps over half a century the building effectively went out of use. In the seventeenth century it found new life, but the voices which then echoed around its walls preached the sermons of a very different age.[198]

CHAPTER FOUR

BUILDING A NEW WORLD, 1540-1700

'Peers Swindels purchest this land and built this house in the yeare 1694'

INTRODUCTION

The late sixteenth and seventeenth centuries saw diverse, and at times turbulent, changes in the lives of local people. Although farming continued to be the basis of the economy of the Borough, manufacture and trade were growing in importance. At the heart of this activity was the production of textiles, but other industries were also beginning to emerge. For some this was an era of rising prosperity. Houses were rebuilt in more 'modern' styles *(Ill 4.1)*, not only by rich landowners but also by tradesmen and farmers. Money

was also spent on buying land. Tenants might become landowners. The very wealthy might aspire to be manorial lords. Not everyone, however, shared in this prosperity. The poor presented a continual problem to local government. This was also an era in which men were divided by their religious beliefs and, in the mid-seventeenth century, by civil war. Local people played a part in that conflict, which in 1644 saw a military engagement at Stockport itself.

In tracing developments and events from 1540 to 1700, we have the advantage that our sources are more full and varied than for the medieval period. The oldest

Ill 4.1 Arden Hall, Bredbury, in 1794.
From the late sixteenth century houses were built in new styles. These reflected the wealth of their occupants as well as providing them with greater space, comfort and privacy. The great central block of Arden Hall was erected at the close of the sixteenth century by the Arderne family, who were among the wealthiest landowners in the Borough. This building, which probably replaced an earlier hall, is the earliest known dwelling in the Borough built of stone. The material was probably chosen as a symbol of the family's status, at a time when other local houses were timber-framed.

known maps showing places within the Borough date from this period. They include the earliest plan of Stockport town (Ill 4.2).[1] People have left details of their lives in written accounts. In the seventeenth century William Davenport of Bramall Hall recorded his experiences during the Civil War. Henry Bradshaw of Marple, better known for his own involvement in that conflict as a Parliamentarian officer, kept an account of his daily expenditure. Two generations of the Ryle family jotted down details relating to their farm at High

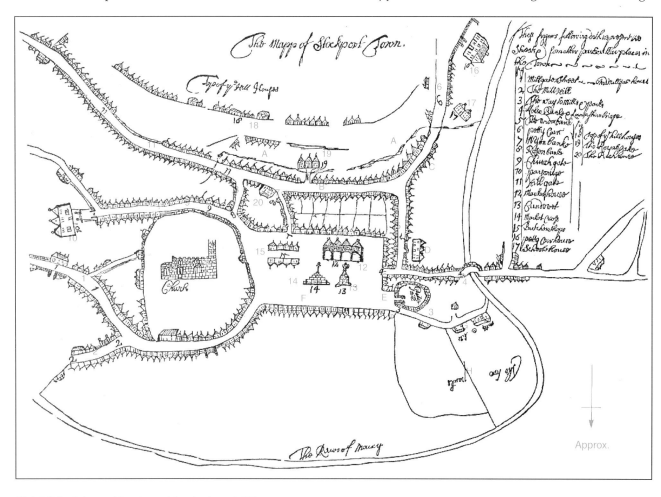

Ill 4.2 'The Mapp of Stockport Town', about 1680.
Drawn by an unknown hand, this is the earliest plan of the town. Although many of the buildings are shown in a stylized form, some effort has been made to depict the town's more distinctive structures. Of the streets in the town, the Underbanks, Millgate, Hillgate and Churchgate are all documented in the medieval period.

Key:

1. Millgate Street and Millgate House (Millgate and Millgate Hall)
2. The Mill Hill
3. The Way to Mills & Parks
4. Kelso Banke (Bridge Street) & Lancashire Bridge
5. The Underbank (Great Underbank)
6. Petty Carr (Chestergate)
7. Wynn Banke (Mealhouse Brow)
8. Rosen Banke (Rostron Bank)
9. Churchgate
10. Parsonage (Rectory)
11. Hillgate
12. Market House
13. Cundeuet (Conduit)
14. Market Cross
15. Butcher Shops
16. Petty Carr House
17. School House (Grammar school)
18. Top of the Hill Houses (High Street)
19. The Royal Oake
20. The Rackhouse (Bakehouse)

A. Tin Brook
B. Little Underbank
C. The Three Shires (approximate position)
D. Underbank Hall
E. Castle Hill
F. Staircase House (approximate position)
G. Cornmill
H. The Park

Greaves (later High Grove), near Gatley.[2] Letters of the period also survive. Probate records, in particular wills and inventories (documents listing and valuing the movable property of the deceased), provide evidence on such matters as local occupations, housing and general living standards. Those from the township of Stockport between 1578 and 1650 have been published, and summary accounts exist for Stockport in the 1660s and for Etchells, Mellor and Ludworth.[3] However, probate records survive for only a small proportion of people, making it often unclear how representative they are of the rest. Some limited additional information on occupations is provided by local parish registers, which begin in the late sixteenth century. These also provide evidence for outbreaks of disease and famine. It is also possible, with the help of tax returns, to estimate the local population.

In this chapter we will use these and other sources to trace the main themes of this period. These include the changes in the town and the countryside, the evolution of local government, the Civil War and the religious divide. We begin, however, with the industry which in future centuries would become the single most dominant force in the development of local communities.

TEXTILES

The weaving of cloth was among the oldest of the Borough's industrial occupations, perhaps dating back to the early days of the medieval borough of Stockport in the thirteenth century. Initially the industry must have been a very small-scale affair, but by the fifteenth century the local presence of cloth and wool merchants such as the Dodges and Shaas suggests that production was expanding. Growth in the manufacture of textiles towards the end of the medieval period was not confined to the town of Stockport or other communities in the Borough. This was a regional phenomenon, affecting Lancashire in particular. Its principal centre was Manchester, which by 1540 may already have become the most populous of Lancashire's towns.[4]

In the sixteenth century this regional textile industry was producing woollens and linens. Cotton does not appear to have been imported into the North-West in any significant quantity until the early seventeenth century. Until the late eighteenth century it was used mainly in cloths in combination with a linen yarn. There were local variations in the industry. In the Borough linens and woollens appear to have remained the dominant branches throughout the seventeenth century. Of the two, woollens seem to have been the more important in the uplands of the east of the Borough; elsewhere, probably by the end of the sixteenth century, the more common form of manufacture was linens.[5] By 1610 Stockport had even given its name to a type of linen called 'Stopport cloth', possibly superior to some other linens produced in the region.[6]

The weavers

The mainstay of this early textile industry was the self-employed weaver, working a handloom in his own home. He was supported by other workers, often the women and children of the family, who prepared the raw materials and spun these into yarn. In some cases weaving was itself a family business. On Hillgate in Stockport, Alexander Daniell in the late sixteenth century owned five looms which he worked with his four sons, producing both linens and woollens. The linen 'webster' (weaver) William Harrison, also of Hillgate, at the beginning of the seventeenth century had three looms, one of which was worked by his daughter.[7] The typical handloom weaver at this time was also likely to be a small farmer, for whom the industry supplemented the income which he drew from the land. In Stockport an early mention of a weaver's loom occurs in 1578 in the inventory of Robert Ryle. Although he was the owner of the freehold farm known as the Bothams, his wealth appears to have been fairly modest.[8] Some local weavers may have relied entirely on this craft for their livelihood.[9]

Supply and distribution

The means by which yarn came into the hands of a weaver and cloth passed from him to the customer were varied. The raw materials of wool, flax and hemp (which was also used in linens) were all produced within the Borough in the sixteenth and seventeenth centuries. The growing of hemp in Stockport is documented in 1577 in a survey of land owned in the township by the Legh family of Adlington.[10] Inventories of the seventeenth century provide evidence for the cultivation of hemp and flax in Etchells.[11] However, only a relatively small amount of such materials may have been produced by weavers themselves, and even local supplies provided by others were probably outstripped by the demand. Some materials may have been brought from elsewhere within the region. Much needed to be imported into the North-West itself, with Ireland being an important source of both raw wool and ready-spun linen yarn. Cotton was always an imported material.

Part of the custom of the region's weavers came from their neighbours. Spinning was a common activity among the women of a household.[12] The yarn was passed to a local weaver and returned as cloth for the family's use. An early recorded instance is provided by the inventory of William Davenport of Bramall Hall in 1541 which includes spun yarn 'at the webster'.[13]

Cloth was also produced for the open market. In this case the weaver usually had dealings with one or more traders. In those branches of the region's textile industry which involved cotton, a 'putting-out' system was in operation from an early date. This meant that a dealer provided a weaver with materials, paid him to produce cloth, and then saw to its marketing. By the late seventeenth century this system was also being adopted in the linen and woollen branches of the industry, where previously weavers had greater independence.[14] Under that earlier system, the weavers themselves had bought materials from a supplier, often on credit. The cloth which the weaver then produced was his own property, which he was free to sell to whom he wished. This might be to another trader, or perhaps even to the original supplier. Under whichever system cloth was woven, it might eventually be sold at some distant market. By the second half of the sixteenth century this was often London. Packhorses provided the means of transport until the advent of the turnpikes in the eighteenth century.

Trade in raw materials, yarn and, above all, finished cloth could prove a lucrative business. The greatest concentration of such traders in the region was probably to be found in and around Manchester. In the 1580s William Birch, a small farmer and weaver of Heaton Norris, appears to have bought flax or linen yarn on credit from one Manchester linen draper, Robert Birch.[15] Presumably other weavers in the Borough also had dealings with Manchester men. In 1610 'Stopport cloth' was sent to London by the Manchester clothier, or cloth merchant, George Tipping.[16]

The Elcocks, a Stockport merchant family

The Borough itself was home to a number of textile traders. In the sixteenth century the most important of these may have been the Elcocks of Stockport. They were living in the town in the fifteenth century, but appear to have risen to particular prominence in the first half of the sixteenth. Between 1514 and 1550 the names of Stockport's mayors are recorded for a total of thirteen years, and for eight of these the holder of that office was an Elcock. The wealth of the family during this period is evident from the will of Nicholas Elcock in 1536. This included monetary bequests totalling over £168, a substantial amount by local standards of the time. His eldest son Alexander Elcock

added to the family's property by marrying the heiress to an estate at Poole near Nantwich. He is described in 1544 as a 'merchant', perhaps the earliest evidence for the family's involvement in trade.[17]

The inheritance of the Poole estate established the main line of the family as country squires, but evidence points to at least two members having an interest in the late sixteenth-century textile trade. Nicholas Elcock, a younger son of Alexander, is said to have moved to London.[18] In doing so he was perhaps following the example of his cousin Francis Moseley. In the late sixteenth and early seventeenth centuries the Moseleys rose to be among the leading families of clothiers in Manchester. The role of Francis, and later of his brother Nicholas Moseley, in the capital is believed to have been to manage this end of the family business. Nicholas Moseley made his fortune in London, becoming lord mayor of the city. In 1596 he bought the manor of Manchester and in 1602 retired to Hough End Hall, an imposing mansion built by him on land which his family had previously tenanted. His acquisitions also included the manor of Heaton Norris.[19] Francis Moseley, in his will drawn up in London in 1568, named Nicholas Elcock as a beneficiary and also noted that he owed him 4s 4d for sackcloth, £22 5s for satin and £20 which he had loaned.[20] It is tempting to suppose that Elcock was in London to sell cloth sent down from his native Stockport, but was he also sending back materials such as this satin? If he was in London as a cloth merchant, this may not have been his first involvement in the textile trade. In 1563 a Nicholas Elcock was importing yarn through Chester from Ireland.[21]

Further evidence of the Elcocks' involvement in the sixteenth-century textile industry in Stockport is suggested by the 1577 Adlington Survey. This mentions two yarn crofts in the town rented by an Alexander Elcock. (His precise position in the Elcock family-tree is unfortunately unknown.) Yarn crofts were areas in which linen yarn, after being soaked in an alkaline solution, was bleached by exposure to sunlight, a process which took up to six months. One of these two yarn crofts was bounded on the north by the Mersey and on the west by the Tin Brook, an area perhaps chosen to minimize the possibility of theft. It included a 'yarn house', presumably used for storage. The other yarn croft was also situated next to the river, by the area of common land known as the Paddock Carr which lay beyond the western edge of the town. Adjoining this yarn croft, and also rented by Alexander Elcock, was a 'hemp garden'.[22] It should be added that such sites need not always have involved a commercial use. In 1569 John Reddish, the lord of the manor of Reddish, bequeathed a yarn croft to his wife, presumably in connection with the production of linens for her household.[23] Nor need hemp have been grown locally solely for the textile industry, since it was also the raw material of rope making.

Linen drapers and a supplier of hemp and flax

The Dickinsons were a wealthy Stockport family whose role in the textile trade is somewhat better understood. From the inventories of the linen draper Thomas 'Diconson' in 1591 and his son William Dickinson in 1619, it appears that they bought cloth, presumably from local weavers, which they then marketed. Their burgage at Stockport included a 'cloth house', presumably used for storage. Both inventories list cloth as yet unsold at places outside the town, with Manchester and Congleton being named. This buying and selling may have represented the full extent of their business, although William's inventory also included yarn 'at the bleachinge', and some flax was evidently prepared and spun within their household.[24]

The speciality of John Robinson, a prosperous yeoman of Heaviley, was the provision of raw materials. His will of 1617 shows that he was owed money by fourteen people for flax, often for small amounts of this material, and by more than forty for hemp.[25] This second group included individuals spread across a wide area in north-east Cheshire; among them were men in Woodley, Compstall and Bramhall, as well as Stockport. Some of these materials may have been for domestic use, but one of Robinson's customers, Robert Daniell of Shaw Heath (one of three individuals who owed money for both hemp and flax), was probably a son of the weaver Alexander Daniell of Hillgate. How Robinson acquired these materials is not specified, but in the 1577 Adlington Survey 'hemp yards' are mentioned in the vicinity of Heaviley Lane (now Mile End Lane). A second area in which the survey indicates that hemp was grown, the Paddock Carr, has already been noted. A third was to the east of the town, along Turncroft Lane, where a 'hemp yard' and a 'hemp croft' are mentioned. It may have been in this last area, possibly on glebe land (land rented from the parish church), that in 1621 a Thomas Burdsell was also growing a crop of hemp.[26]

Suppliers and distributors with the wealth of the Elcocks, the Dickinsons and John Robinson were probably few in the Borough, but below them were other men who sought to profit from these sides of the textile business. The linen draper James Chorlton of Stockport, who died in 1606, was a man of fairly modest means. The list of debts owing to him shows that he had

dealings in Staffordshire. It may be supposed that he personally travelled the country roads to sell cloth carried on the two packhorses recorded in his inventory.[27] William Colliare (Collier) of Stockport, who died in 1637, seems to have been a weaver who also engaged in trade. Although described as a 'chapman', or small trader, he also owned a loom and an inckle frame, used for weaving linen tape. His inventory included linen yarn, which as well as being for his personal use may have included his commercial stock.[28]

Finishing the cloth

In addition to the weavers and traders, there were local men who were engaged in the finishing side of the textile industry. Shearmen, whose job was to trim the nap of woollen cloth, the final stage in its production, appear in the probate records for Stockport and Mellor in the 1600s.[29] In the same decade the Stockport records mention cloth sent to Francis Hutchinson for dyeing, although where he carried out this business is not stated.[30]

The preliminary process in the finishing of woollen cloth was fulling. By the sixteenth and seventeenth centuries in the woollen-producing parts of the region the old process of treading the cloth with fuller's earth had been largely superseded by the fulling mill, in which the cloth was beaten by water-powered hammers.[31] In the fourteenth century a fulling mill is said to have stood somewhere on the Goyt. Primrose Mill near Mill Brow in Mellor was used for fulling in the eighteenth century, before it was adapted for cotton spinning. A possible origin as a fulling mill has been suggested for a small water-powered mill which still stands in Marple Bridge and which by 1776 was in use as a spade forge.[32] In 1569 two fulling mills were listed among the property of John Reddish of Reddish Hall, but both may have been located among his other south-east Lancashire estates.[33]

OTHER INDUSTRIES

The production of textiles was in all probability the single most important industrial activity in the Borough during this period, but it did not stand alone. The Borough had its share of other craftsmen including tailors, tanners, coopers, smiths and carpenters, occupations which were found not only in the town but also in the surrounding countryside.[34] Besides the manufacture of textiles, a number of such lesser crafts were already present in the medieval period. New industries were also becoming established. Although by 1700 these were still small in scale, in time they would develop into significant elements of the local economy.

Button making and the early silk industry

One, perhaps surprisingly, was the making of buttons, using silk, hair or linen needlework to cover a wooden base. Button making in north-east Cheshire is perhaps best documented in Macclesfield, where buttons of some description were being produced by 1574 and silk buttons by 1617. The industry was operated through a putting-out system. Women and children made the buttons in their own homes, with raw materials provided by merchants who paid them for the finished product.[35] Buttons are said to have been made in Stockport in the early seventeenth century, and a 'button man', or merchant, is recorded in Gatley in the 1660s.[36]

Silk, as well as being used for button making, was also woven locally. By about 1660 silk lace is said to have been woven in and around Stockport, Macclesfield, Congleton, Leek and Buxton. Thread, produced from raw silk, is recorded as being produced in the Macclesfield area in the late seventeenth century. Raw silk, like cotton, was an imported material. The various branches of the local silk industry, button making, weaving and the production of thread, were all dependent for their supplies on merchants from London. This was the only legal point of entry for raw silk in the country, as well as being the principal manufacturing centre of the early silk industry.[37] In the mid-eighteenth century, as we shall see in the following chapter, silk became Stockport's dominant industry.

Hatting

The second new industry was the making of felt hats, which is documented in Stockport from the 1650s.[38] Manufacture at this time was carried out in domestic workshops by felt makers using tools and processes which would have been recognizable 200 years later. A hatter's bow was used to mix the raw materials of wool and fur in an even layer (Ill 4.3), which was then formed into a large conical hood. This was alternately immersed in a boiler, or 'kettle', and rolled with a pin on a wooden board, or 'plank', to create a rough, felt hat body, which was then shaped on a wooden block. Stockport was one of a number of towns in the region with a hat-making industry by the mid-seventeenth century. The principal and longest-established hatting centre in the North-West was Chester, to where the trade had spread from London a century earlier.

Ill 4.3 A hatter's workshop.
Hatting was introduced into Stockport by the 1650s and developed into one of the town's major industries. In the initial process of hat making, shown here, the raw materials of fur and wool were mixed in an even layer, using a 'bow'. This had a catgut string, which was vibrated by being struck with a wooden 'pin'. This reconstruction is based on a later hatter's workshop at Haughton Green near Denton. The various processes of hatting were carried out by hand well into the nineteenth century.

Chester's hatting industry was in decline by the 1750s, but Stockport's expanded, making the town one of the major centres of hatting in the country.[39]

Coal mining

One other industry which was to grow in importance in later years was coal mining. It is likely that the local seams were already being exploited in the medieval period. The earliest evidence, however, may date from the late sixteenth century, a time when mining across the region seems to have been on the increase. Coal appears as a fuel in Stockport inventories from the early

1590s onwards, often alongside firewood and peat.[40] The high cost of transportation before the age of the canals means that this coal was almost certainly produced locally. In 1598 the Stockport parish register described one Bredbury man, Thomas Spooner, as a collier. Precisely where he was working as a miner is not known, but by 1606 coal was being dug on the Goyt Hall estate.[41] A coal pit at Compstall is mentioned in 1660, and mining at Norbury was probably taking place by the end of the seventeenth century.[42] The earliest workings in the Borough were presumably where the seams outcropped at the surface, or were exposed in river banks. They would have been followed by bell pits. These were shafts dug to shallow seams which were then worked outwards until the danger of collapse forced the pit to be abandoned. (The name of such workings is derived from their bell-shaped profile.) A group of pits shown in a field alongside Stockport Road East in Bredbury on a plan of 1710 may have been of this type.[43] However, in Poynton to the south of the Borough deeper shafts, with more extensive underground workings, were already being dug in the first half of the seventeenth century.[44]

Before the eighteenth century most of the coal mined in the Borough would have been burnt on household fires, but there is one notable local example of an early industrial use. Just to the north of the Borough, across the Tame, glass was made in Haughton Green from about 1616 until perhaps the 1650s, using coal as fuel. Excavation of this furnace site has shown that it was producing window panes and high-quality glassware, items which may have graced the homes of some of the Borough's more prosperous inhabitants.[45]

'A POPULOUS AND GREAT MARKETT TOWNE'

The market

While the town of Stockport was growing in importance as a place of manufacture, it also continued to flourish in its long-established role as a centre of trade. Part of this business was carried out through the weekly market, and part through what must have been an increasing number of shops. As in the medieval period, the market served traders from a wide locality. In the 1660s these included people from Werneth, Poynton and Manchester, itself a thriving market town.[46] Traders from the Borough also continued to attend other markets. In the late 1590s at least one Stockport butcher rented a stall at Manchester. In 1672 stall holders at Macclesfield included nine men from Stockport, and others from Cheadle Hulme, Offerton and Reddish.[47]

Many of the customers of Stockport's market and shops no doubt came from within the town and its close vicinity. However, when William Webb wrote in about 1620 that Stockport was 'a great market, and much frequented by dwellers far remote' he may have had more than visiting traders in mind.[48] Outside the town, people could buy from their neighbours or from itinerant traders, but the range of goods on offer might be limited. The account book of Henry Bradshaw of Marple in 1640 suggests that he bought some items locally, but he also made regular visits to Stockport, often on market day.[49] The town must have been at its busiest during the time of the fair, or rather fairs. In the 1630s the king gave permission for two such gatherings to be held in April and July, in addition to the ancient fair held in September.[50]

The weekly market dealt principally in grain, other basic foodstuffs and goods, and livestock. As one commentator summed it up in the 1670s, 'the town hath a considerable market for corn and provisions on Friday'.[51] (At an unknown date, the market had been shifted from Thursday, the day specified in the market charter of 1260.) Among local farmers selling or buying surplus crops at Stockport market in the seventeenth century were John Ryle of High Greaves and his son Reginald, who recorded in their diary variations in the price of oats, barley, wheat and beans.[52] Bread, meat and cheese were also sold here. So too were livestock – a number of people were fined for allowing their pigs to stray through the Market Place.[53] A detailed list of the types of traders, stipulating what each was to pay for renting a stall or other space in the market, was compiled in 1752. As well as foodstuffs and livestock (in this case cattle, sheep and horses are named), people could buy pots and hardware, shoes, breeches, hosiery, hats and leather. Comparison with a description of Preston market in the 1680s suggests that a list for Stockport in the late seventeenth century would not have read very differently.[54]

To help regulate the market, different types of traders were allocated different areas in the Market Place. In the 1660s the space immediately round the market cross, on the north side of the Market Place, was set aside for traders from outside the township, although it was known for some locals to try to claim this for themselves.[55] In 1752 bread was sold from the Market House. This building, which occupied part of the western end of the Market Place, was in existence by about 1680 and had a ground-floor colonnade which supported an upper chamber (*Ill 4.2*). It was in this room that the official weights and measures used to ensure fair trading were kept. Similar colonnaded public buildings existed at Liverpool, Wigan and possibly

Macclesfield. By the 1640s at the opposite end of the Market Place, in front of the parish church, were two rows of low buildings known as the Shambles, in which butchers conducted their trade.[56]

Shops

Shops are frequently mentioned in the sources for Stockport in the late sixteenth and seventeenth centuries. At this date the term carried a range of meanings. A shop might, as in the modern sense, be simply a place from which goods were sold, or a place in which they were also made; in some cases the reference appears to be solely to a workshop. Retailing shops might sell some goods which were also available at the weekly market, but they also specialized in luxury items. In the early seventeenth century a man might, for example, buy a new sword or dagger from James Tellier (Taylor), the cutler, or in the 1640s visit the shop of the bookseller, stationer and bookbinder Edward Harpur.[57]

Among the most lucrative retail shops were those of the woollen drapers, men who specialized in the sale of fabrics, such as Nicholas Elcock in the 1620s and Robert Newton in the 1660s. Both men stocked a wide variety of fabrics, some evidently aimed at the more fashionable end of the market.[58] Elcock's will shows that he was owed money by over 160 individuals, including people from almost every township in the Borough. Many, perhaps the majority, of these debts may represent goods sold on credit.

Other Stockport shopkeepers had an often bewildering combination of stock. The mercer Henry Hulme in 1609 sold both textiles and groceries.[59] The stock of the haberdasher James Boland in 1639 included more than 300 hats, suggesting that he was a wholesaler as well as a retailer, but he also sold textiles and groceries, including soap, starch, spices and honey.[60] The shop of the apothecary William Simkin in 1623 was a mixture of a chemist's, a grocer's and a tobacconist's. Similarly the grocer Edward Mosse in 1660 sold apothecary's 'stuff and drugs' as well as groceries.[61]

Inns and leisure

The seventeenth-century town was well served by places providing liquid refreshment. Its inns in this period included the Flying Horse, the Crown, the Red Lion, the White Lion (probably on the site of the present public house of this name on Great Underbank) and the Royal Oak (situated in what is now Royal Oak Yard, opposite the entrance from Little Underbank).[62]

There were other forms of diversion. In the early seventeenth century 'players' and minstrels are reported in the town, along with the spectacle of bear baiting. There was a bear pit at the foot of the sandstone cliffs on Chestergate and the 'sport' continued in the town into at least the late eighteenth century.[63] Other communities in the Borough organized their own animal baitings. At Cheadle in 1658, at the time of the local wakes, one of the churchwardens hired a bull 'to be baited from alehouse to alehouse'.[64]

The population

Helped by a combination of industry and trade, the population of the town was expanding. In 1637 Stockport could be described as 'A populous and great Markett Towne', but precisely how populous it was during the period from 1540 to 1700 is very difficult to say.[65] The hearth tax returns of 1664 allow perhaps the best estimate. Under this national tax, introduced in 1662 and abolished in 1689, each household was charged 2 shillings for every hearth; the underlying premise was that the number of hearths in a man's home could be approximately equated with the size of his wealth. There were exemptions, including some hearths used for industrial purposes but mostly involving the very poor. The returns of 1664, considered to be the most complete, list 308 households in Stockport township, suggesting a total population of about 1400 or 1500.[66] Most of these people would have lived within the town itself, although it should be noted that the township included a number of outlying cottages and farms. In 1664 Stockport seems to have been the fifth largest town in Cheshire, behind Congleton (with a population of about 1700), Macclesfield (about 2600), Nantwich (about 2900) and Chester (about 7500). Below Stockport were several other Cheshire towns with estimated populations of less than 1000.[67] The population of Manchester is believed to have been nearly 4000.[68]

Earlier figures for the population of the Borough must be even more of an estimate. A count of households conducted by the Church of England in 1563 is said to be confused in the case of Stockport. If the town experienced a similar growth as has been suggested for neighbouring Manchester (and here too the figure for 1563 poses a problem), in the century before 1664 its population would have roughly doubled.[69]

Disease and famine

The rise in population may not have been constant, not least because there were sporadic periods when the number of deaths increased significantly. Between October 1605 and August 1606 the Stockport parish register records fifty-one people whose death was attributed to the plague, beginning with a woman known as 'Madd Marye'. The vast majority, if not all, of the deceased lived within Stockport itself.[70] The town escaped lightly compared with Manchester. Here the plague began in April 1605 and subsided in November, but within this short period killed perhaps as many as a quarter of the town's population.[71]

Other, lesser outbreaks of disease may also have claimed lives.[72] It is difficult to assess the general level of hygiene in the town in this period. In addition to the apothecaries, there were doctors or 'practitioners in physicke and chirurgery' living in the seventeenth-century town.[73] Perhaps more was achieved for local health by the efforts of Stockport's manorial court, the court leet, which fined those guilty of dumping rubbish and waste in the streets and selling putrid meat.[74] Like some other communities, the town may have had its own 'plague stone', in which coins were 'disinfected' by being dipped in vinegar (Ill 4.4).

Famine caused by failed harvests could also dramatically increase the number of deaths. To it may be attributed the years of high mortality visible in the parish registers of Stockport, Cheadle and Manchester in the late 1580s and early 1590s. Worse was to follow in 1623, a year of widespread famine, when the Stockport parish register recorded as many as 256 deaths, the highest figure for any year in the late sixteenth and seventeenth centuries. A further crisis

Ill 4.4 'Plague stone' from Stockport.
This stone, said to have been found in the Market Place, is believed to have been used to contain vinegar in which coins were 'disinfected' to prevent the spread of plague. During an outbreak of the plague in 1605-6 the Stockport parish register records the burials of fifty-one people whose deaths were attributed to the disease.

occurred in 1657-8, when the Cheadle parish register shows a one-third increase from the average number of deaths in that decade. It must have been with thoughts of their own past sufferings that the congregation of Stockport parish church in 1665 and 1666 made collections on behalf of the plague-stricken people of London.[75]

The changing town

It is from the late seventeenth century that we have the earliest known map of the town. Believed to have been drawn in about 1680, it shows not only the street pattern but also the town's buildings in a pictorial form (Ill 4.2). Some sixty years earlier William Webb had written that 'Upon one round hill hath this town of Stockport been built, the summit, or top whereof, affords the market-place, and convenient room for the church, and parsonage...the skirt of the hill beautified with many fair buildings'. When the map was drawn, the centre of the town was still the Market Place, and its principal streets were those documented in the medieval period: Millgate, Hillgate and the Underbanks. Since that time, however, the number of properties had undoubtedly grown. Increasingly the edge of the town must have been pushed further outwards. This process may not only have been taking place along existing thoroughfares. By the early seventeenth century there were houses along the ridge of the Tin Brook valley, on the opposite side to the Market Place. Now known as High Street, at this earlier period this thoroughfare carried the more descriptive name of Top of the Hill.[76]

Expansion of the town could take another form. The medieval arrangement of houses occupying the street frontages of burgages offered scope for these buildings to be extended to the rear. This process, as we shall see, can still be traced at Staircase House. In some cases, a rearward expansion may have involved the division of a burgage into front and back properties. In 1619 one Stockport man bequeathed the house at the front of his burgage to one of his sons, but left the garden at the rear to a younger son to build on for his own use.[77]

The Great Rebuilding

From the late sixteenth century the houses in the town were also changing in appearance, as new ones were built, and old ones were reshaped, in a new style. These alterations were part of a national revolution in house design which has been called the Great Rebuilding and which affected houses across the Borough. As an important part of this process, the central hall of the medieval house, which had been open to the roof, now became a single storey in height. This created additional accommodation on the floor above. The hall remained a key room in the life of the household, but the central hearth of the open hall gave way to a fireplace set against one wall. Other rooms might also be heated in this fashion, a point highlighted by the hearth tax returns. Methods of construction also changed. In timber-framed buildings the use of the A-frames known as crucks had been ideal in the days of an open hall, but was far less so for a building which was divided into two storeys throughout. Accordingly it was often abandoned in favour of an alternative method of construction. Already found in the medieval period, this used the vertical and horizontal timbers of the walls to support separate roof trusses.

Timber was not the only material used in the new buildings of the Borough. The use of stone in houses had previously been confined to the footings supporting the timber-framed walls. In the seventeenth century

Ill 4.5 Underbank Hall, Great Underbank.
This fine town house probably dates from the end of the sixteenth century. It was constructed for the Arderne family of Arden Hall, with which it is roughly contemporary. Its ornate facade reflects the Ardernes' wealth and status. Since 1824 the building has been used as a bank.

Ill 4.6 The Three Shires, Great Underbank, about 1920.
This timber-framed house was built in the late sixteenth or early seventeenth century. Although the scale of the building is more modest than that of Underbank Hall, here too the facade includes decorative timberwork.

it became common for houses to be built with walls entirely of stone. The same century also saw the introduction of brick, although its use remained rare until the eighteenth century. Because of high costs of transportation, these new building materials were used close to where they were obtained. Stone buildings were most plentiful in the eastern uplands of the Borough, while the few buildings which were constructed of brick in this period were found on the central and western claylands.

In the town of Stockport timber remained the most common building material for housing throughout the

seventeenth century. Some buildings were constructed from the local sandstone, but these were probably few in number. Known examples are a wing to the rear of Staircase House, and two 'stone houses' mentioned in the 1640s.[78] The probate evidence indicates that there were at least two masons living in Stockport in the 1610s, but we may suspect that in the town itself their work was centred on the parish church, and in particular the construction of its new tower.[79]

The effects of the Great Rebuilding in Stockport can partly be traced from the documentary sources. More than one inventory from the town from the late sixteenth century to the mid-seventeenth refers, for example, to a chamber over the hall or 'house' (a term also used for the hall).[80] Some early buildings are known from pictorial evidence. Stockport is also fortunate in that three houses of this period are still standing in the town. One is Underbank Hall on Great Underbank. This was a town house of the Arderne family of Arden Hall in Bredbury. It was probably built towards the end of the sixteenth century, perhaps to replace an earlier house of the Ardernes on Millgate (Ill 4.5).[81] A second surviving timber-framed town house, also on Great Underbank, is now the Three Shires. It was built on

Ill 4.7 Staircase House, the staircase.
Staircase House, on the north side of the Market Place, is the oldest known surviving town house in Stockport. It was built in about 1460 and in the seventeenth century was remodelled and progressively enlarged. It was during that later period that the carved staircase was inserted which gives the building its present name. This feature, which was damaged by fire in 1995, was possibly the finest surviving example of its type in the North-West. The occupants of the house in the seventeenth century are unknown. However, two timber-framed buildings erected at this time at the rear of the house are believed to have been warehouses or workshops and suggest that the family's wealth was based on commerce.

land belonging to the Leghs of Adlington and has sometimes been claimed to have been part of a town house of this family (Ill 4.6).[82]

A feature of the Great Rebuilding was the increasing extent to which the external appearance of a building reflected the wealth of its occupants. The facades of both Underbank Hall and the Three Shires have decorative timberwork and are crowned with gables, with each of the upper levels projecting slightly from the floor below. These were elements which from the late sixteenth century would have been found in other fashionable buildings in the town. At Underbank Hall, the status of the Ardernes is also emphasized by additional features: the long lines of continuous windows, the entrance porch and the very position of the building. It is set back from the street from which in the late seventeenth century it was separated by a wall and gateway. The windows of this building were presumably glazed from the beginning. Window glass was an expensive commodity at this time, found only in the houses of the wealthy, although in the early seventeenth century there was evidently a sufficient demand in the locality for Stockport to be home to at least one glazier.[83]

From the rooms recorded in 1619 in the inventory of Mary Arderne, it seems likely that Underbank Hall then extended to the rear of the timber-framed building which stands today.[84] The rearward expansion of property is still evident at the third early town house surviving in Stockport, Staircase House, in the Market Place. Here the cruck-framed building erected in about 1460 was converted to a two-storey building with a triple-gabled facade. (This was replaced by successive brick frontages in the eighteenth and nineteenth centuries.) A stone inscribed with the date '1618' set within a fireplace may well commemorate this initial alteration. As part of that rebuilding, additional accommodation was provided by a wing to the rear. It was into this wing a few years later that the carved staircase which gives the building its present name was inserted. This feature, sadly damaged in a fire in 1995, was an exceptionally fine example of its period and the clearest indication of the wealth of the building's occupants (Ill 4.7). In many lesser houses of this period access to the upper floors would have been by no more than a ladder. To the rear of the staircase wing is a further extension, already mentioned as being built in stone. The identity of the occupants who carried out these various alterations is unknown, but the basis of their wealth is suggested by two other, detached timber-framed buildings built to the rear of the property in the early seventeenth century. Their likely purpose was as warehousing, although workshops have been suggested as another possibility. From what we know of the economy of the town in this period, a connection with the textile trade may be strongly suspected but cannot as yet be proved.[85]

Staircase House and Underbank Hall were both substantial buildings but there were other houses of comparable size in the seventeenth-century town. Probate records provide evidence for large houses of the Dickinsons, the linen drapers, and William Skelhorne, a flax dealer, both on Underbank, and of the mercer Roger Harpur, on or next to Millgate.[86] That same street appears to have contained at least two houses owned by members of the landowning gentry, one of which, Millgate Hall, was bought in the late seventeenth century by the Warrens, the lords of Stockport manor.[87] The map of about 1680 shows that the rectors of Stockport lived in a house whose size was in keeping with the wealth of their parish, with a triple-gabled facade looking out over the town. By this same date, standing at the western approach to the town, along what is now Chestergate, was the sizeable Petty Carr House.

Most houses, however, must have been more modest affairs. The hearth tax returns provide a rough indication of the relative sizes of people's accommodation. In 1664 of the 308 households listed, twenty-six were charged for four hearths or more. Among these were William Skelhorne (four), Sir John Arderne of Underbank Hall (six) and the rector Henry Warren (seven). Two individuals, William Beeley and John Shallcross, a member of the landowning gentry, were assessed at as many as twelve. The majority of households, 226, were reported to have had only one hearth.[88]

The hearth tax figures also have a bearing on the social composition of the town. That there were considerable variations in wealth is evident from the probate records. In the 1660s the values of surviving inventories range from nearly £600 for woollen draper Robert Newton to £5 4s 4d for the shoemaker John Daniell and £4 10s 10d for the widow Anne Clarke.[89] In 1664 just over half of the households listed were exempt from paying tax, while many of those who were charged were probably living a hand-to-mouth existence.

AGRICULTURE AND THE COUNTRYSIDE

In the countryside, as in the town, the population was growing. According to one estimate, the population of the parishes of Cheadle and Prestbury (which in the Borough included Woodford) may have been three times as great in 1664 as in 1563.[90] In the mid-1660s the hearth tax returns suggest that the total population of the Borough, excluding Stockport township, was in the order of 3500-4000.[91] Most of the people in the countryside were still living in scattered farms and cottages. A number of these may be documented for the first time between the mid-sixteenth century and the late seventeenth. Although it is likely that some such places have a much longer history, the total of rural dwellings was undoubtedly rising. Clusters of dwellings may also have been growing in size and number, but for the most part these could still be described by modern standards as no more than hamlets.[92]

Changes in landownership

Despite the growing importance of textiles and the beginnings of other new industries, the majority of people in the Borough still derived at least part of their income from agriculture, either by farming the land themselves or leasing it out to others. Much of the land remained in the possession of the lords of the various manors, a number of whom were absentee landlords. Between the mid-sixteenth century and the end of the seventeenth many of the manors changed hands, as the old families died out or their estates were sold off. Norbury was sold in about 1690 by the Hydes to the Legh family of Lyme Park, to help pay off family debts.[93] In another transaction, in or shortly after 1672, the Ardernes of Arden Hall substantially added to their lands in Bredbury by buying up the former estate of the Davenports of Goyt Hall.[94]

The most far-reaching change in ownership involved Marple. In 1606 the lord of the manor, Sir Edward Stanley, sold off his Marple estate as freeholdings to his tenants. One was Henry Bradshaw, who by this date was probably already living at Marple Hall. By his purchase in 1606 he also acquired land in Wybersley, and by 1621 had also bought from his fellow freeholders in the township the farm known as The Place.[95] He was the grandfather of Henry Bradshaw, the Parliamentarian officer and author of the account book, and also of John Bradshaw, whose services to Parliament were to lie in a very different direction.

Although no other manor could match the wholesale disposal of lands in Marple, other local lords were willing to sell off at least some of their estates. From about 1700 William Tatton allowed a large number of his tenants in Etchells to buy their lands.[96] In Bredbury in 1672 there were eleven freeholders; at least one of their estates, in Woodley, seems to have been purchased from the Ardernes earlier in the century.[97] In 1671 a total of twenty-one freeholders were listed in the parish of Cheadle. Among these were the Kelsall family of Bradshaw Hall, an estate which had been bought from the lord of Cheadle Moseley in about 1550.[98]

By the late sixteenth and early seventeenth centuries wealthy freeholders as well as the manorial lords were considered to be part of the local 'gentry'. Below them in the social scale were the 'yeomen', a term used both for other freeholders and for some individuals holding land by other forms of tenure. The dividing line between a prosperous freeholding yeoman and a gentleman could be very blurred, and as the seventeenth century progressed the term gentleman came to be used increasingly widely. At the lower end of the social scale were 'husbandmen', who farmed land as tenants of a larger landowner, and labourers. From the account book of Henry Bradshaw, in about 1640 a general labourer might be paid 3d or 4d a day, a mower or ploughman twice that amount.[99] For comparison the income of William Davenport of Bramall Hall at about this time has been estimated to have been 'probably no more than £400 a year'.[100]

Farming

Farming in the Borough, for which the bulk of the evidence is provided by probate records, was still mixed, combining the growing of crops with the rearing of animals. Cattle were the most common type of livestock. They were kept not only for their meat but also for their milk, used to produce cheese for which Cheshire was already famous in the seventeenth century. By the middle of that century oxen, the principal draught animal in the medieval period, had been effectively replaced in that role by the horse. Sheep were kept for their wool and were perhaps most common in the upland townships of the east of the Borough, where they were grazed on the open moors. (It was in this area that the woollen branch of the textile industry was also probably strongest.) Crops, principally oats, wheat, barley and hay, provided food for the household and livestock, and where possible a surplus for the market. In the seventeenth century pasture for cattle was improved by the introduction of a system of rotation. Land was planted for several years in succession with arable crops, followed by a period, double the length of that time, during which it was kept under grass. Improvement could also be made by spreading the fields with marl, a limey clay. Its use as a fertilizer can be traced back in the Borough to the medieval period and continued into the nineteenth century.[101]

Enclosure

Enclosed fields, owned or rented by individual farmers, had existed in the Borough since the medieval period. Common, open fields were to be found in at least some manors but their days were numbered. The Adlington Survey of 1577 shows that an open-field system was still being worked at Stockport. References to 'doles', divisions within the township's open fields, continue into the late eighteenth century. However, the large-scale enclosure of common land in Stockport in the early eighteenth century was confined to pasture and waste. By that date, with the possible exception of the glebe land, it is questionable whether arable land was being farmed in common in the township to any significant degree.[102] The diary of John Ryle indicates an open-field system around Gatley in Etchells in the late seventeenth century, but when William Tatton's tenants were allowed to buy their land the practice of common farming seems to have fallen into disuse.[103]

In a continuation of a process which had begun in the medieval period, piecemeal enclosure was taking place on common uncultivated land. At Torkington in the 1630s and 1650s recent enclosures are mentioned on the common pasture land of Torkington Green and on waste near the main road to Stockport.[104] Some reclamation of common land provided room for the building of new dwellings. Such instances included a cottage erected on waste land in Marple in about 1641 by the son of one of the township's freeholders, and a house recorded in 1612 as having been erected on the eastern edge of Stockport Great Moor. Adjoining this last property were three enclosed fields.[105]

Large-scale enclosure of waste land was perhaps rare in the Borough before the eighteenth century. An early recorded example is the enclosure between 1699 and 1710 by William Tatton of a large part of the waste of Bolshaw Outwood, near Heald Green.[106] A proposed but unfulfilled scheme in the seventeenth century involved the enclosure of waste land in Mellor. The township was part of the king's lordship of the High Peak. It also lay within the bounds of the royal Peak Forest. In the 1630s Charles I agreed to a petition that this should be 'disafforested' (that is that the ancient 'forest law' should no longer apply) and its wastes be enclosed. In Mellor, along with other places in the forest, the waste was divided into three grades, best, middle and worst. One half of these was allocated to the freeholders, who were also given the option of buying the half reserved by the crown. The king's share in Mellor lay in the north-east of the township, that of the tenants in the south-east on Mellor Moor. Proceedings were interrupted, however, by the Civil War.

After the Restoration the question of the ownership of the king's share became the subject of a lengthy dispute. In Mellor what had been the king's share was not enclosed until the early eighteenth century, while the final enclosure of Mellor Moor did not occur until 1779.[107]

Rural dwellings

The homes of the gentry

In the countryside, as well as in the town, the appearance of houses was changing. Here the first dwellings to be affected by the Great Rebuilding were probably the halls of manorial lords and the wealthiest freeholders. These dwellings saw a spate of building activity towards the end of the sixteenth century and the beginning of the seventeenth. At this date new or remodelled halls in the region often still followed the medieval plan of a central block with a wing at one or both ends. Their facades might now, however, include a porch, either placed centrally (giving an E-shaped plan), or tucked in the angle of one of the wings, with a similar projection against the other wing preserving the symmetry of the building. Their facades generally showed the new fashion for greater decoration, while internally fireplaces now heated many of the rooms. In the Cheshire part of the Borough at least two new halls were built during this initial stage of the Great Rebuilding, both in Bredbury. Goyt Hall was built on his Bredbury estate by Randall Davenport of Henbury, whose initials were set over two of its gables. It probably dates from not long before 1590 and was the residence of Randall's son and heir, William.[108] The other great landowning family in Bredbury, the Ardernes, were rebuilding their manor house at Arden Hall by 1597, with the work probably being finished by 1602. Perhaps uniquely among the halls of the Borough in this early period, it was built of stone, possibly in an attempt to outdo the residences of other members of the local gentry (Ill 4.1).[109] It also included a large great hall, a feature common to a number of the more stately homes of this period. In the Lancashire part of the Borough, Reddish Hall also appears to have been rebuilt in the late sixteenth century or early seventeenth. The building was demolished in 1780 but it is known to have been timber-framed, with a richly decorated facade.[110]

Other wealthy landowners made substantial alterations to their existing properties. Wings might be rebuilt or added, as at Bridge Hall in Adswood, and Woodford Old Hall, the manor house of the local branch of the Davenports.[111] At Bramall Hall in the early 1590s the very heart of the medieval building, the great hall open to the roof, was remodelled by William and Dorothy Davenport. The result was a ground-floor entrance hall and a first-floor withdrawing room with decorative plasterwork on the ceiling and over the fireplace (Plate III). Above this range the Davenports built another fashionable feature of the day, a long gallery. Here family members could take indoor exercise, perhaps under the gaze of family portraits which were often displayed in these rooms.[112]

The development of other manorial halls in the Borough during this formative period is less well understood. Among these is Norbury Hall, the principal residence of the Hydes. This timber-framed hall, described as in ruins by the early nineteenth century, no longer survives, although its name is recalled by that of a local farmhouse. In 1664 the hall was one of the largest dwellings in the Borough, being charged for sixteen hearths. By comparison, Arden Hall and Bramall Hall were both assessed at fifteen (the second largest figure for any house in the Borough at this time), Reddish Hall and Goyt Hall probably at seven and six respectively and Bridge Hall at five.[113]

One manorial hall, that of Cheadle Bulkeley, appears not to have been substantially altered in the late sixteenth century and early years of the seventeenth century, to judge from William Webb's reference in about 1620 to the Bulkeleys, the lords of the manor, having 'a fair house of the old timber building'.[114] This may reflect the particular circumstances of Sir Richard Bulkeley, the manorial lord from 1573 until his death in 1621. Towards the end of his life, at least, his principal residence appears to have been on Anglesey, where he was constable of Beaumaris Castle, an office held by his family since the fifteenth century. Curiously, the manorial hall is not mentioned in an account of Sir Richard's lands and properties in Cheadle Bulkeley compiled in 1622, and his immediate successor to the lordship seems to have lived not in Cheadle but at Peel Hall in the neighbouring township of Northen Etchells.[115] In 1664 by far the largest assessment in Cheadle Bulkeley was for the residence of the rector, Peter Harrison, with thirteen hearths, with the next highest number being the five hearths at Bridge Hall.[116] Two decades earlier the occupancy of the rectory had been the subject of a dispute between two successive rectors and Humphrey Bulkeley, the lord of the manor, who claimed the building for his own use.[117] This dispute in particular may lend weight to a local tradition that the rectory had once been the manor house of Cheadle Bulkeley, a change of use which may possibly have occurred during the absence of Sir Richard Bulkeley. The rectory stood on the south side of Cheadle village, on a site which is in keeping with Webb's description of the residence of the Bulkeleys as being near to the parish church.[118]

Another house which poses something of a puzzle with regards to its origin is Woodford New Hall, located about 750 metres to the east of the timber-framed Old Hall. From the datestone over the door, it would appear to have been built in 1630 by the eldest son of the local branch of the Davenport family.[119] Several years earlier, however, William Webb mentioned a place named 'Newhall' in this same locality.[120] Whatever its precise date, Woodford New Hall has the distinction of being the earliest known building in the Borough to be constructed of brick (Ill 4.8).

The second half of the seventeenth century saw a further major phase of building activity on the part of members of the local gentry. The dwellings involved were typically the homes of freeholders, a factor which may reflect the growing wealth and number of this class at this time. Among such buildings are Harrytown Hall in Bredbury (constructed in stone in 1671), and in the parish of Cheadle the houses known as Adswood Hall (built in 1659), Millington Hall (which like Adswood was built in brick) and Cheadle Moseley Hall (timber-framed and perhaps erected in 1666) (Ill 4.9).[121] Marple Hall was rebuilt in stone, probably in the 1650s by Henry Bradshaw after he inherited the family estates. The building was perhaps extended about fifty years later, but in 1664, when Henry Bradshaw was charged for thirteen hearths, it was already one of the largest dwellings in the Borough (Ill 4.10).[122] Mellor Hall, the centre of an extensive freeholding, was constructed in stone by James Chetham, shortly after his purchase of that estate in 1686. It replaced an earlier, and evidently substantial, building which was assessed at five hearths.[123]

Yeoman houses

Following the lead of the gentry, in the seventeenth century yeomen and husbandmen were constructing new farmhouses. Many of these buildings still survive in the Borough. Others are known from pictorial evidence and the accounts of local antiquarians. The most important room in these dwellings was the hall or 'house'. This was heated by a fireplace, usually in the form of an inglenook from which smoke was carried

Ill 4.8 Woodford New Hall.
This is the earliest known building in the Borough to have been constructed of brick. A datestone over the doorway was carved with the year 1630 and the initials of William Davenport and his wife Elizabeth. William was the eldest son of the lord of the manor, whose own residence was the timber-framed Woodford Old Hall.

Ill 4.9 Cheadle Moseley Hall.
Some of the largest houses built in the Borough in the late seventeenth century were constructed by freeholders, a class which may have been growing in terms of both wealth and numbers. This house was perhaps built in the 1660s by Robert Sidebottom and his wife Mary. Sidebottom was one of twenty-one freeholders listed in Cheadle parish in 1671.

out of the building via a timber-framed funnel. Such 'smoke hoods' rarely survive. Most were later replaced by a brick or stone chimney stack.[124] Cooking was carried out in the inglenook, which was often the only source of heating in the house.

The design of these new dwellings, known as 'yeoman houses', could vary. Some were long rectangular structures, such as the timber-framed farmhouse at Vale Close off Didsbury Road in Heaton Mersey.[125] Others could resemble more compact versions of the homes of the gentry, with a wing and even a porch. As with the halls of the gentry, stone and brick came to be used where these materials were locally available. Yeoman houses of stone were being built in the eastern townships of the Borough by the end of the 1650s, the same decade which saw the rebuilding of Marple Hall in this material. Brick was used in the latter part of the seventeenth century, but only rarely. A notable surviving example is Halliday Hill Farm in Offerton, which in the eighteenth century was home to a branch of the Dodge family. Here this

new material was used to rebuild the external walls of an earlier timber-framed building *(Ill 4.11)*.[126] The occupants' pride in their 'modern' yeoman house was often expressed by incorporating the date, usually with their initials, on the exterior, a practice adopted from the gentry. One farmer at Strines went one better. His datestone reads 'Peers Swindels purchest this land and built this house in the yeare 1694'.[127]

The building activity of the late sixteenth and seventeenth centuries did not only involve houses. Many new farm outbuildings were constructed, and several barns of this period still stand in the Borough. Shippons or cowsheds were also erected to shelter animals which in the days of the medieval longhouse would have shared the same roof as the farmer and his family.

LOCAL GOVERNMENT AND JURISDICTION

In the sixteenth and seventeenth centuries local government in the Borough took on a form which

Ill 4.10 Marple Hall, about 1906.
This substantial house was probably built in the 1650s by Henry Bradshaw and perhaps enlarged about fifty years later. The Bradshaws were wealthy freeholders in Marple and the most important family in the township in the seventeenth century. Marple Hall was demolished in 1959.

remained largely unchanged until the nineteenth century. It was a system divided between three main bodies: the manorial courts, known as court barons and court leets; the officers of the parishes and their subdivisions, the townships; and the justices of the peace, who were appointed for each county. The first and last of these also had a judicial role. All involved unpaid officials, who were required to balance these duties with their other daily activities.

The manors

Manorial courts and officers

Manorial courts were a continuation from the medieval period. They were presided over by the lord's steward, and for many tenants attendance was compulsory, with fines being imposed on absentees. It was from the ranks of these tenants that the juries of the courts were selected. As well as hearing minor civil actions (in particular for the recovery of debts under

£4) and dealing with petty criminal offences, the courts were empowered to make and enforce local byelaws.[128] The complexity of the business of these courts might vary from manor to manor. At Bramhall in the mid-seventeenth century much of the routine work of the court involved the obligations of tenants to keep in good repair their buildings and roadways, to maintain their boundaries and to clean out drainage ditches. At Stockport the duties of the court leet included regulating the market. The task of reporting to the local court, and ensuring that its instructions were carried out, fell to officers appointed from among the tenants. Their numbers and duties again varied from place to place. All manors would be expected to have a constable, entrusted with maintaining law and order and responsible both to the local court and to the county JPs. Bramhall's officers included two 'weirlookers', who were given charge of the weirs on the Lady Brook which provided the cornmill with its head of water, and four 'moorlookers', each responsible for one of the four peat mosses in the manor which

Ill 4.11 Halliday Hill Farm, Offerton.

In the seventeenth century yeomen followed the example of wealthy landowners by building or remodelling their homes in a more 'modern' style. The farmhouse at Halliday Hill was originally a timber-framed building. It was modernized by being encased in brick, with stone mullion windows. In the eighteenth century Halliday Hill was home to a branch of the Dodge family. This family is documented in the Stockport area from the medieval period.

served as a source of fuel. Among the officers appointed at Stockport were 'scavengers', who reported the dumping of refuse in the street, and 'marketlookers', 'alefounders' and 'officers for flesh' who between them presented cases of false weights and measures and other breaches of market regulations.[129]

Stockport's mayor and aldermen

By the mid-sixteenth century the office of mayor at Stockport had evidently become a bone of contention between the lord of the manor and his burgesses. Under the thirteenth-century borough charter, the burgesses had been allowed to choose the mayor, subject to

approval by their lord. Perhaps over time his had become the only voice in this matter. Whatever the cause of the quarrel, in 1565 it was agreed that in future the lord was to nominate four candidates from among the burgesses, one of whom was to be then selected as mayor by the jury of the court leet. Under the same agreement, former mayors were to sit on the same jury, if so required. Perhaps they had previously claimed exemption.[130]

By the early seventeenth century the former mayors of the borough were known as 'aldermen'. The title is more usually associated with corporations, that is towns with governing councils. How this title had arisen at Stockport, where local government remained under manorial control, is uncertain. A further change evident at this time is that the mayor had assumed some limited power as a local magistrate. In the medieval period it had been the duty of the mayor to ensure that cases of breaches of the peace were brought before the manorial court.[131] In the seventeenth century he heard such cases himself, with some evidence suggesting that he did so with the assistance of aldermen.[132]

Punishments and Stockport's dungeon

This delegation of a duty of the manorial court may have been a consequence of an increasing workload, but it may also have arisen from the question of profitability to the manorial coffers. The cases heard by the seventeenth-century court leet were punished by fines. Those heard by the mayor were punished by more physical measures, which included imprisonment in the town's dungeon, and the public indignity of the stocks and ducking stool.[133] It may be a reflection of the lack of interest by the manorial lord in such punishments that in 1664 the court leet itself ordered him to put the 'cage', stocks, 'rogue's post' (the whipping post) and 'cuckstool' in a state of good repair, or pay a fine of £5.[134] Other townships may be expected to have had at least stocks. There are surviving examples in the courtyard of Bramall Hall, at Memorial Park in Marple (in both cases they have been moved from their original position), and in the churchyard of St Thomas's at Mellor.[135]

Stockport's ducking, or cuck, stool in the early eighteenth century was situated by a watercourse to the west of the town. The whipping post and stocks were located in the Market Place, and it was here that, when required, the pillory was also set up. These last three punishments were still being administered in the town in the early nineteenth century. The list of local punishments also included the 'brank'. It was used to silence scolding women and was hung on public display on market days as a warning to would-be offenders (*Ill 4.12*).[136]

The dungeon, used for the short-term incarceration of offenders, was described in a deed dated 1692 as a 'little Roome, under the said Oulde Court House'. In 1790 the town's gaol, at that date comprising several cells, was situated at the top of Mealhouse Brow, on the south side of the Market Place. In that year it was replaced by a new gaol built on the present Warren Street. It is assumed that the site of the pre-1790 gaol was that of the seventeenth-century dungeon. If this is correct, the 1692 deed would also provide the earliest known evidence for the location of the town's manorial court house. Its description as the 'Oulde Court House' implies that at this date meetings were

Ill 4.12 The Stockport 'brank' or 'scold's bridle'.
This iron contraption was a manorial punishment for scolding women in the town's market. It was fitted over the head and has a spiked bar which held down the tongue. An attached leather strap, of which only a stub now remains, was used to lead the offender through the Market Place. The date of the brank is not recorded, but its actual use appears to have been obsolete by the mid-nineteenth century.

held elsewhere within the town.[137] We shall return to the matter of the changing location of the town's court house in a later chapter.[138]

Stockport's 'Town Books'

Crime and punishment were not the only concerns of Stockport's mayor in the seventeenth century. Along with certain 'ancient aldermen' and the rector of the parish church, he was given responsibility for managing bequests made to the town's grammar school and the poor. The funds were loaned out in various small sums and the interest given to the appropriate charities, with a record of these transactions being kept in the 'Town Books'. The system was plagued by defaulting borrowers but continued into the 1770s.[139]

The court of the Stockport rectors

At Stockport in the seventeenth century the rectors also held their own court. No records of this body are known to survive (some were confiscated during the Civil War) and its function is uncertain. One possible role was to manage the church's property in the township, which included houses on Churchgate as well as agricultural glebe land. In 1663 a survey recorded twenty-two tenants of the church, eighteen of whom each rented a house and garden, including eleven who rented other glebe land.[140]

The parishes and townships

Overseers of the poor and surveyors of the highways

In the second half of the sixteenth century two areas of local administration were made the responsibility of the parish: the maintenance of the main roads or 'highways', and the application of new legislation dealing with the 'poor', those unable to provide themselves with a living. New officials, the 'surveyors of the highways' and the 'overseers of the poor', were appointed from among the parishioners, who were themselves required to provide labour for the roads and to pay a rate levied for the upkeep of the poor. Responsibility for the highways might be devolved to the divisions of the parishes, the townships, and involve the existing manorial courts. (In much of the Borough the boundaries of the manors and townships were one and the same.) Surviving court records for Bramhall and Etchells show instructions being given to tenants to turn up at a fixed time and place to carry out road repairs. In both places the surveyors of the highways were probably themselves appointed by these courts.[141] The enforcement of the poor laws was usually carried out on a parish-wide basis, although in the extensive parish of Prestbury, of which Woodford was part, the separate townships levied their own rates.[142]

Charity

Charitable donations to the poor in the Borough had been made in the wills of wealthy individuals in the medieval period.[143] Such bequests continued to be made after the introduction of the compulsory poor rate, usually by the well off, and were sometimes fairly specific as to how the money was to be spent. In the townships of Cheadle Bulkeley and Cheadle Moseley in the 1660s and 1670s money was left to pay for children of poor tenants to learn a trade, to help support ten 'aged persons' and to buy bread to be given to the poor who attended church, a bequest which in 1688 was also made by Madam Christian Stafford of Bottoms Hall in Mellor.[144] In 1605 money to help poor craftsmen and tradesmen in Stockport was left by Alexander Torkington, himself a tanner.[145]

Edward Warren, the lord of Stockport manor, outdid them all. He built a row of almshouses at the south-east corner of the parish churchyard as dwellings for six 'poore old men'. In his will of 1684 Warren directed that each was to receive £1 a year 'for ever whilest this world lasteth'. Later members of the Warren family made further donations to this cause. By the early twentieth century the almshouses, which were approached from Millgate along the street known as The Folley, were in a state of disrepair and in 1927 were demolished.[146]

Managing the poor laws

Charity, whether in bequests or from the daily goodwill of others, could only provide limited assistance. In the late sixteenth and early seventeenth centuries poor laws were passed under whose provisions the able-bodied were to be provided with work by the parish, and the aged and sick with shelter, food and clothing, while unemployed migrants or 'strangers' might be returned to the parish of their birth. The possibility that strangers might fall destitute within their parish was a continual worry to local authorities. In Bramhall in the mid-seventeenth century tenants were repeatedly instructed by the manorial court to remove lodgers, while those wishing to sell or let property were ordered that it should be offered to other people in the township before any outsider.[147] It was in the town of Stockport that the numbers of poor were at their greatest, both among the native residents and by those drawn there in the hope of making a living. In 1640 there were reported to be

ninety-four lodgers in the town who were already, or likely to become, eligible for poor relief unless they were removed.[148] Legislation passed in 1662 required all individuals moving to a new parish to give security against becoming dependent on the local ratepayers. Those who failed to comply might be forced to leave, as in the case of a saddle-maker and his family in Stockport in 1666.[149] In 1674 the Stockport court leet ordered that from time to time the overseers of the poor were to submit reports on all outsiders who had come into the manor.[150]

If the lot of the poor was not a happy one, neither always was that of the overseers, who had to balance the needs of those legally entitled to poor relief with the demands of the ratepayers. In 1640 the problem which the ninety-four lodgers posed to the overseers was compounded by the fact that in some townships, in protest to the already high level of the rate, many were refusing to pay. Perhaps most difficult of all, the overseers were also accountable to the JPs.

The justices of the peace

The real power in local government in the Borough rested with the justices of the peace, an office introduced in Cheshire in the late 1530s, but already well established in other counties. Through the courts of the quarter sessions (the nearest of which to the Borough were held at Manchester and Knutsford), other regular meetings, attendance on committees and work conducted from their own homes, the JPs carried out a wide range of duties both judicial and administrative.[151] It was one of their tasks to ensure that the local officers in the parishes and townships were fulfilling their own responsibilities. In 1658 an Adswood man was called before the quarter sessions at Knutsford for negligence in his office as supervisor of the highways, while in 1642 the overseers of the poor in Stockport parish were summoned for refusal to give an account of the money which they had levied.[152] In 1577 one local JP is found questioning a vagrant arrested in Marple; in 1607 two ordered the apprehension of a man who had fathered a child by a Stockport woman but refused to provide maintenance (this otherwise would have had to be found from the poor rate).[153] Those wishing to build on waste land were required to obtain permission from the JPs as well as from their local manorial lord. JPs also had responsibility for bridges designated as being of particular importance in their county, from where money was raised for their repair. In the Borough by the early seventeenth century these included the bridge at Stockport over the Mersey, Beight Bridge over the Tame (on the road between

Stockport and Denton, the present A6017), and New Bridge, Otterspool Bridge and Marple Bridge over the Goyt. (At this date two of these bridges, Otterspool and Beight, were only wide enough for packhorses.)[154] The JPs might also be called upon to deal with local emergencies. During the terrible famine of 1623, the justices of the Macclesfield hundred arranged for corn supplies to be brought to Stockport market.[155]

In the sixteenth and early seventeenth centuries JPs were appointed from the higher ranking gentry and more occasionally the clergy. In the 1600s Alexander Reddish of Reddish Hall, John Arderne of Arden Hall, and William Davenport of Bramall Hall were among those serving in this office; in the 1630s and early 1640s the JPs for the Macclesfield hundred included William Nicholls, the rector of Cheadle.[156]

Somewhat exceptionally, in 1634 Edward Warren, the lord of Stockport, was given permission for his steward to be raised to this office, on the grounds that there was as yet no JP residing in this busy market town. Consequently, it was claimed, it served as a refuge for 'the worser sorte of people' from neighbouring counties, 'with divers great enormities and offences' going unpunished.[157] In the late 1640s and the 1650s the ranks of the JPs included new men, supporters of Parliament such as Robert Duckenfield and Henry Bradshaw of Marple, but this was after the upheaval of the Great Civil War.[158]

THE CIVIL WARS

In 1642 national politics intruded upon the lives of the people of the Borough as the quarrel between Charles I and Parliament escalated into the four-year long conflict of the Great Civil War. A number of local people would already have access to arms and have received some military training as members of the militia, the defence force of each county. Few are likely to have had actual experience of warfare. Although both sides drew support from the Borough, for most of the conflict it lay firmly under the control of the Parliamentarians. At the beginning of the war, north-east Cheshire and south-east Lancashire, particularly Manchester, were the main areas of Parliamentarian support within the region.[159] Elsewhere, the Royalists were the stronger. In the summer and autumn of 1642, as the two sides began to raise troops, the region proved a fertile recruiting ground for the king. He visited Chester in September to gather men, arms and ammunition for an intended march on London, a campaign which ended with the battle of Edgehill and the establishment of the king's headquarters at Oxford.[160]

Many within the North-West initially attempted to avoid conflict. In that same summer a group of Cheshire gentry organized a petition, urging against the taking of sides. Among those who signed this document, known as the Cheshire Remonstrance, were 159 men from Stockport, ninety-four from Marple and apparently thirty-eight from Bredbury. Neutrality proved to be a difficult position to maintain, and several of the men from these places who signed the Remonstrance are later found in the service of Parliament.[161]

The defence of Manchester

In September 1642 those local men who were prepared to fight for Parliament were put to the test. While the king was at Chester, Lord Strange, the leading Royalist commander in the region, laid siege to Manchester. (During the course of the siege, on the death of his father, Lord Strange became earl of Derby.) A number of the gentry from the neighbourhood came to the defence of the town, bringing with them troops raised from among their tenants and neighbours. Among them were Ralph Arderne of Arden Hall in Bredbury, Edward Hyde of Norbury, and Robert Duckenfield, lord of the manor of Dukinfield and also of Brinnington (*Ill 4.13*).[162] From the Lancashire part of the Borough came Edward Stanley of Wood Hall, in Reddish.[163] During the siege, the Parliamentarian defenders heard that a force of 400 men from Cheshire under Thomas Legh of Adlington Hall was on its way to help the earl of Derby. Ralph Arderne was sent out with troops to oppose them, but Legh's forces came no further than Stockport, refusing to move into Lancashire.[164]

Some of the lesser local men who came to the defence of Manchester and who were later to serve in Cheshire may have been prompted by an obligation to their manorial lord. However, one instance clearly demonstrates a considerable degree of independence. On the 17th of September William Davenport was taking supper at Bramall Hall when he received a written petition from twenty-four of his tenants. Davenport had evidently been pressing these men to enlist for the king. The petitioners asked him to lead them in their own proposed course of action (which as events would soon show was to support the Parliamentarian cause) or at least not to think badly of them for their decision. The next day, before receiving Davenport's reply, they and other tenants enlisted with Edward Hyde of Norbury. Presumably, a week later, these men were among the troops who accompanied Hyde to the defence of Manchester.[165]

Ill 4.13 Robert Duckenfield.
Lord of the manors of Dukinfield and Brinnington, Robert Duckenfield played a prominent part in the Civil War in the North-West. He was one of several members of the local gentry who rallied to the Parliamentarian cause by coming to the defence of Manchester in September 1642. His later active service, first as captain and then as colonel, included the ill-fated defence of Stockport in May 1644 when Parliamentarian troops were routed by the numerically superior army of Prince Rupert.

Local men on active service

The siege of Manchester ended, after several days' fighting, with a Royalist withdrawal. This, the first significant engagement in the Civil War, helped determine the future course of the conflict in the North-West. From their base at Manchester, the Parliamentarians were able to strike out into Lancashire. By June 1643 nearly all the county was under their control. The one main exception was Lathom House (near Ormskirk), the stronghold of the earl of Derby.

In Cheshire the Parliamentarians also enjoyed early success, operating from their base at Nantwich. This, the second largest town in the county after Chester, became the headquarters of the Parliamentarians in Cheshire in January 1643 under the leadership of William Brereton. Chester itself was a stronghold of the Royalists. Its surrender to the Parliamentarians in February 1646 effectively marked the end of the conflict in the region.

William Brereton, who for much of the war was commander-in-chief of the Parliamentarian forces in Cheshire, was the lord of Handforth, where his family residence was at Handforth Hall, and also of Bosden, now part of Hazel Grove.[166] Among the members of the gentry who joined him at Nantwich early in 1643, bringing with them their troops, were Robert Duckenfield and Edward Hyde, two of the former defenders of Manchester.[167] By spring, if indeed not earlier, Brereton's officers also included Ralph Arderne and Humphrey Bulkeley. The latter was lord of Cheadle Bulkeley, although at this time his residence appears to have been at Whatcroft near Northwich.[168] In May of the same year Henry Bradshaw of Marple enlisted as a captain in the regiment of Robert Duckenfield, who by this date had been promoted to the rank of colonel.[169]

Of these various officers, Robert Duckenfield saw active service in the region until the end of the conflict, when he was present at the surrender of Chester.[170] At that time Henry Bradshaw, who was wounded in the war, was still serving in Duckenfield's regiment.[171] Ralph Arderne and Edward Hyde, for unknown reasons, both appear to have given up their commissions while the war was still in progress, although they continued to serve the Parliamentarian cause in an administrative capacity.[172] Humphrey Bulkeley's active service came to an end when he was captured by the Royalists near Wrexham in the spring of 1645.[173] Towards the end of the war at least one other individual from the Borough was serving as an officer in the Parliamentarian army. William Siddall, a captain under Colonel Duckenfield, was a yeoman from Bramhall. In September 1642 his name had headed the list of petitioners to William Davenport. William Smith, also a captain in Duckenfield's regiment, may have been the individual of that name on the same petition.[174] We know less about the local men who served in the ranks under these officers, but a list of army pensioners in the Stockport area in 1653 includes men who were wounded, and widows whose husbands were killed, at several engagements in Cheshire.[175]

The early campaigning of the Parliamentarians in the region was not without setbacks. In April 1643 troops led by Ralph Arderne were repulsed from Warrington during an attempt to take the town, which was finally captured in the following month.[176] In June of that year Humphrey Bulkeley's men were among the troops ambushed during a raid into North Wales.[177] Nevertheless, only on two occasions was the Parliamentarian supremacy in the region relinquished. Both involved the intervention of Royalist forces from outside the area. The first was in the winter of 1643-4 when troops from Ireland and Oxford entered

Cheshire and laid siege to Nantwich. This crisis was ended when the Parliamentarians themselves brought in reinforcements from outside the county, in particular from Manchester, and defeated the besiegers of Nantwich outside the town. The second occasion was in the spring and early summer of 1644 when a Royalist army under Prince Rupert advanced through the region, inflicting especially heavy damage in Lancashire before turning eastwards to suffer defeat at Marston Moor near York. It was during this campaign that Stockport itself saw military action.

The war comes to Stockport

After the withdrawal of Thomas Legh's troops from Stockport in September 1642, no Royalist troops, as far as is known, marched on local soil for nearly two years. By December 1642 the town had been fortified. In that month a truce was arranged between Cheshire Royalists and Parliamentarians, the terms of which included the dismantling of the defences 'latelie made' by either side in Stockport and other towns in the county.[178] The precise nature of the fortifications at Stockport is not recorded. At the very least, barricades are likely to have been erected across the roads leading into the town.[179] The truce was short-lived, but with the subsequent Parliamentarian successes in Lancashire and Cheshire the need for defences at Stockport may have seemed less necessary. In the spring of 1643 captured Royalists were held prisoner in the town. So too was Edmund Jodrell, an east Cheshire landowner, whose main offence appears to have been his refusal to meet Parliamentarian demands for funds.[180]

Between the time of the siege of Manchester and the arrival of Prince Rupert's army, the closest fighting to the Borough involved Parliamentarian attempts to capture the halls of two members of the local gentry. Adlington Hall, the home of Thomas Legh, was surrendered in February 1644 after a fortnight's siege.[181] Nine days later the Parliamentarians took Wythenshawe Hall, the residence of Robert Tatton. The siege of the hall had been begun in November 1643 by a small contingent of Colonel Duckenfield's regiment under the command of a Captain Adams. He was killed during the siege and was buried at Stockport parish church.[182]

On the 19th of May 1644 Prince Rupert led his army north into Cheshire. The king's nephew, he had already proved himself the ablest Royalist leader in the war, with a fearsome reputation among his opponents. His main intention was to relieve the Royalist troops beleaguered behind the walls of York, but he also aimed to revive the king's fortunes in the North-West, and in particular to end the siege of Lathom House.

The Parliamentarians' hope was to check his advance by holding the bridges over the Mersey at Warrington and Stockport. In the event Rupert's chosen course took him to Stockport. On the 25th of May he advanced on the town from the west, passing through Cheadle. Defending Stockport was a force of about 3000, under the command of Colonel Duckenfield and Colonel Mainwaring. Captain Humphrey Bulkeley was also among the garrison. Rupert's force was estimated to be about 8000 or 10,000.[183]

Parliamentarian accounts of what happened on that day are short in detail but are in agreement as to the general outcome: the defending forces fled the town before the advance of Rupert, and sought safety in Lancashire.[184] William Davenport of Bramhall also refers to the Parliamentarians fleeing from Stockport and adds that earlier in the day a troop of Parliamentarian cavalry, stationed on guard at Cheadle, had also beat a hasty retreat at Rupert's approach.[185] Ironically, it is left to a jubilant Royalist 'newspaper' of the time to show that the Parliamentarians at Stockport had made some attempt at resistance. According to this account, they had advanced out of the town to meet the Royalist cavalry. For a while there was stand-off until the arrival of Rupert's infantry at about six o'clock in the evening. The main Parliamentarian force then withdrew, but men armed with muskets were stationed behind the hedgerows, to fire on the Royalist troops as they advanced. These musketeers were driven from their positions by Royalist dragoons and in the ensuing pursuit Rupert's men followed the fleeing Parliamentarians into the town. The same Royalist report claims, perhaps with some exaggeration, that all of the garrison's cannon and most of the arms and ammunition were captured, along with 800 prisoners.[186]

The victorious Royalists remained in and around Stockport on the following day. Some were billeted with William Davenport at Bramall Hall, where Parliamentarian troops had stayed on the night of the 23rd of May before proceeding to Cheadle.[187] There is a tradition that Battle Lane, leading to Arden Hall, was the scene of a skirmish at the time of Rupert's stay in the Borough. A cannon ball which is possibly of the Civil War period has been unearthed near this location, but the supposed attack on the hall remains unconfirmed. A further tradition states that a bell, which still survives, cast with the name of Jane Done and the date 1642, was hung at Arden Hall as an alarm. Jane and Mary Done were daughters of Sir John Done of Utkinton Hall in Cheshire and came to live at Arden after their sister Eleanor married Ralph Arderne (Ill 4.14).[188]

By the 27th of May Rupert's forces had crossed the Mersey into Lancashire and were at Barlow Moor. On

Ill 4.14 The Jane Done bell.
The bell carries the date '1642' as well as the name of Jane Done,
a sister-in-law of Ralph Arderne of Arden Hall. He took part
in the Parliamentarian defence of Manchester in September 1642
and in the following year was serving as a captain in Cheshire.
Jane Done lived at Arden Hall and is said to have had the bell
cast to be hung at the hall as an alarm.

the same day Colonel Duckenfield may have re-entered the town, since a letter of that date which he wrote urgently requesting money for his troops is addressed from Stockport. (This letter was sent to the same Edmund Jodrell who two years earlier had been held prisoner in the town by the Parliamentarians.) It was also on the 27th that the Stockport parish register recorded the burial of 'a souldier slayne at the takinge of Stockport'.[189]

On the following day a second Royalist force entered the Borough, from Derbyshire. Commanded by Lord Goring, these troops, mostly consisting of cavalry, are variously reported to have numbered between 3000 and 8000. For the next few days they were quartered in Stockport and the surrounding countryside, including Bramall Hall again, before proceeding into Lancashire where they met up with the army of Prince Rupert. Perhaps not surprisingly after Rupert's success in Stockport, Lord Goring's force appears to have met with no opposition in the Borough. Any Parliamentarian troops who had returned to the town after Rupert's

departure presumably now saw fit to make a speedy withdrawal.[190]

A year later, in May 1645, the threat of Royalist forces marching through the Borough resurfaced when an army led by the king and Prince Rupert advanced northwards towards Cheshire. Once again the order was given to defend the Mersey crossings. The Royalists, however, after approaching the southern boundary of Cheshire, moved on into the East Midlands, and to their defeat at the battle of Naseby.[191]

Sequestrators and delinquents

As well as serving in the army, local men assisted Parliament in an administrative capacity. A continuous problem was the raising of funds. A system of voluntary loans was begun in 1642, with Robert Duckenfield being given the responsibility for their collection in the Macclesfield hundred. From 1643 a series of compulsory measures was introduced, which included a first weekly, then monthly taxation. In Cheshire its collection was entrusted to a committee which also included Duckenfield, as well as Brereton and John Bradshaw. The last of these, the younger brother of Henry Bradshaw, was in fact too busy serving on parliamentary committees in London to attend meetings in his native county. The same body was also given the initial responsibility for what proved to be the main source of Parliamentarian revenue in Cheshire. This was the confiscation, or 'sequestration', of the personal property and estates of 'delinquents', that is known or suspected Royalists, the rents from whose lands now passed into Parliamentarian hands.[192]

From a slow beginning, the number of sequestrations in the county increased after this responsibility was transferred, in the summer of 1644, to committees appointed for each hundred. The chairman of the committee for the Macclesfield hundred was Henry Bradshaw. Of its five other members in August 1644, one was William Siddall of Bramhall, and two were Stockport aldermen. Acting on their behalf were a group of agents. They had the task of searching the homes of delinquents to compile a detailed inventory of their property, of selling off their confiscated goods and of collecting the rents from their lands. These agents too included men from the Borough.[193]

William Davenport of Bramhall was summoned before the sequestration committee in Stockport on the grounds that in the autumn of 1642 he had attended Royalist musters of troops at Knutsford and Macclesfield. He has left a vivid account of his visit by the sequestrators' agents, and of how they went into every room in the hall, searching every corner and ordering that all boxes and chests be opened, and threatening that they would otherwise break them open themselves. All the while, musketeers stood guard around the house.[194]

A number of sequestered estates in the Borough belonged to absentee manorial lords. Ludworth, as part of the manor of Glossop, had passed by marriage to the earls of Arundel earlier in the seventeenth century.[195] The manor of Cheadle Moseley (as it became known) had been acquired in a similar way by the marquis of Winchester, whose residence at Basing House in Hampshire was besieged and sacked during the war.[196] The Goyt Hall estate of the Davenports had recently passed into the guardianship of the Royalist Sir Thomas Millward, chief justice of Chester.[197] The manor of Heaton Norris belonged to Sir Edward Moseley, who was among the Royalists taken prisoner at the battle of Middlewich in March 1643.[198] The Moseley family, however, later managed to make some gain from the sequestration process. It was perhaps Sir Edward himself who bought the manor of Cheadle which had been confiscated from the marquis of Winchester.[199]

The manor of Etchells was sequestered as part of the estates of Robert Tatton, the defender of Wythenshawe Hall.[200] Edward Warren, the lord of Stockport, suffered sequestration for less. In about 1655 he wrote to Cromwell that he had never taken up arms or carried out any other action against Parliament, a point agreed upon by William Brereton. However, the charge laid against him by the sequestrators of his estates was that in February 1644 he, together with his two uncles, had visited the Royalist headquarters in Shropshire. Later his daughter married a local Parliamentarian officer, and he himself married the widow of another. His first wife had died in childbirth in April 1644. Tradition has it that her death was brought on after she was pulled from her horse by Parliamentarian troops searching for horses and arms at the family's Poynton estate.[201]

John Davenport, the lord of Woodford, while perhaps not taking any action against Parliament himself, had relatives who did. A brother had marched with the king's army from Cheshire in 1642 (and later died as a prisoner of the Parliamentarians). A son, Captain John Davenport, was serving with the Cheshire Royalist forces by March 1643 when he was captured at the battle of Middlewich. He escaped jail and was later recaptured, but was probably the John Davenport of Woodford who towards the end of the war was among the Royalist defenders of Exeter.[202]

Edmund Shallcross, the rector of Stockport, and William Nicholls, the rector of Cheadle, were among many Cheshire ministers who were expelled from their livings and suffered sequestration. Nicholls moved to Royalist Chester and, after the surrender of the city, to Denbigh Castle, itself a Royalist stronghold.[203] Edmund Shallcross allegedly fell foul of the sequestrators because of a dispute with the Bradshaws of Marple over the collection of tithes. As at Bramall Hall, the agents of the sequestration committee made a detailed search of his house. The inventory which they compiled included Shallcross's library of nearly 600 books and a chest containing curtains and other materials found hidden at the back of a chimney in his wife's chamber. Shallcross appealed against his sequestration to the parliamentary authorities in London and made several journeys to the capital in connection with his case. On one of these trips the party of Parliamentarian cavalry with whom he was travelling was attacked by Royalists from Dudley Castle, and Shallcross was killed.[204]

Manorial lords and rectors were not the only individuals in the Borough to suffer sequestration. Henry Stanley of Wood Hall in Reddish also fell foul of the sequestrators on the grounds that he had taken up arms for the king at the beginning of the war.[205] It will be remembered that another Stanley of Wood Hall had fought on the Parliamentarian side during the siege of Manchester. We know less about the charges of several other men who can be identified as living in the Borough, at Stockport, Woodford, Bredbury and High Greaves in Gatley. Three of these, all husbandmen, were described in a list of sequestered delinquents as men believed 'to have beene very active against the Parliament and to continue extreamelie malitious'.[206]

From 1645 sequestered delinquents were allowed to recover their estates by swearing allegiance to Parliament and paying a fine to the national treasury. This process, known as compounding, required the individual to present himself before a committee in London. Edward Warren was among the first compounders from Cheshire to make this journey to the capital, in November 1645. Others with sequestered estates in the Borough followed suit. Those with estates worth less than £200 were exempted from a fine.[207] William Davenport of Bramhall had the misfortune of being fined twice. Although this was not within its authority, the Macclesfield sequestration committee offered to return his estates if he paid £500 into its coffers. The national committee for compounding then proceeded to levy its own fine of £745. Whether he was reimbursed by the local sequestrators is not recorded.[208]

Accounts for the Macclesfield hundred for 1643-5 show that money raised by the sequestrators was put to a variety of local uses. Money was taken from this source for payment to officers and their troops. Payments were made to men supplying pikes and bullets. Widows in Stockport and Brinksway whose husbands had been killed in the service of Parliament each received £2 10s. Thomas Priestnall, the surgeon to Colonel Duckenfield's regiment, was paid 10 shillings for 'cureinge wounded souldiers'. When the rectorship of Stockport temporarily fell vacant after the removal of Edmund Shallcross, the sequestrators paid the wages of the ministers serving the outlying chapels in the parish and preaching at the parish church. In Stockport manor they also took over some of the administrative duties of the court leet, which during the sequestration of Edward Warren may have ceased to be held. Money was spent on repairing the mill weir and in sweeping the town's streets.[209]

Sequestrations and composition fines were not the only financial burden placed on local people as a result of the war. There were the weekly and monthly taxes, which in the case of William Davenport of Bramhall amounted to £60 a year. As Davenport also repeatedly experienced, arms and horses might be requisitioned, and troops billeted in people's homes. Promises were made for future reparations, but were probably only rarely fulfilled. Between March 1643 and August 1645 Parliamentarian troops were quartered at Bramall Hall on five separate occasions, in addition to the Royalists who were billeted there in May 1644. As well as the weapons which were removed from the hall, Davenport lost nearly fifty horses, most of these being taken by the Parliamentarians. On the 20th of May 1644 he suffered the indignity of having his own mount forcibly taken from him by Parliamentarian troops while he was visiting the Davenports of Woodford.[210]

The most widespread loss of property most likely occurred during the brief stay of Rupert's forces. The will of George Ridgeway, a linen weaver, was taken away by the prince's men, presumably along with other items.[211] William Davenport lost linens and other goods, to the value of over £100, from a house which he owned at Mile End, near Stockport Great Moor.[212] In 1755 'a large earthen pot' was uncovered in Stockport, containing silver spoons, a silver salt cellar, and coins including gold pieces dating from the reigns of Edward VI to Charles I. It has been suggested that this hoard had been buried for safekeeping during the Civil War. Possibly the owner hoped to prevent this falling into the hands of the occupying Royalist troops, or those of the sequestrators. What befell this hoard after its discovery in 1755 is unknown.[213]

Changing attitudes

In May 1645 Parliamentarian troops were themselves unwelcome visitors in the Borough. A Yorkshire regiment of cavalry, sent to help Brereton in Cheshire, stayed put in and around Stockport, refusing to leave until they received pay owing to them. As the Yorkshiremen began to eat them out of house and home, 'the oppressed inhabitants and soldiers' of the parishes of Stockport and Prestbury sent an ultimatum to Brereton. Either the Yorkshire regiment was to be removed, or they would cease to pay the taxes levied 'by the occasion of the trouble of these times'. Robert Duckenfield's regiment, then serving at the siege of Chester, even threatened to return home if action was not taken.[214]

There are other signs that towards the end of the war a weariness was setting in. In August 1645 the constable of Marple was serving on guard duty with instructions from Henry Bradshaw to allow no-one through without written permission or the password. When John Dand, a local man who had neither, was turned back by the guard, his nephew retaliated by attacking the constable when he next met him at Stockport market. Instructed by Bradshaw to requisition a horse from the township to carry ammunition to Chester, the constable met with refusals and threats from the two people he approached.[215]

The Second and Third Civil Wars

More serious local resistance arose during the Second Civil War of 1648, after the king had forged an alliance with the Scots. With the threat of a Scottish invasion of the North-West looming, the order was given for troops to be raised in Cheshire under the overall command of Robert Duckenfield. He nominated Henry Bradshaw as one of three officers with responsibility for recruitment in Macclesfield hundred. Local men who had fought in the previous war were still owed backpay, and Bradshaw's fears of a poor response proved well-founded. One muster was attended by fewer than forty men, most of whom turned up unarmed. Many of the people of Cheadle and Etchells openly refused to enlist.[216]

In the Third Civil War, of 1649-51, the old enthusiasm seems to have been rekindled. In 1651 Robert Duckenfield and Henry Bradshaw, who was himself now promoted to colonel, were called on again to raise troops, when the future Charles II marched southwards through the North-West in his attempt to win back the kingdom. On the 3rd of September Bradshaw's regiment took part in the defeat of Charles's army at Worcester. From a list of the names of the officers who fought under Bradshaw in the battle, the regiment was evidently raised in his native north-east Cheshire.[217] Later in that year Duckenfield and Bradshaw sat on the court martial at Chester which condemned to death the earl of Derby for his part in this attempted restoration.[218]

The Booth Rebellion

For the people of the Borough the Civil Wars were not quite yet at an end. In 1659, a year before the actual restoration of the monarchy, a rebellion took place in Cheshire under the leadership of Sir George Booth. Support seems to have been strongest in the north-east of the county, precisely that area which in earlier years had been most firmly behind Parliament. Humphrey Bulkeley, the lord of Cheadle and former Parliamentarian captain, busied himself raising local troops, as did John Davenport of Woodford. Edward Hyde of Norbury may also have been actively involved. Peter Harrison, the rector of Cheadle, appears to have preached rebellion from the pulpit, although he later claimed that his words had been misconstrued. At both Cheadle and Norbury the whole township met and agreed to send troops. Henry Bradshaw, though instructed by Parliament to recruit troops to help suppress the uprising, did not comply but wrote to Booth, warning him of the dispatch of a Parliamentarian army and advising him to desist.[219] The rising ended in defeat on the 19th of August, at Winnington Bridge, outside Northwich, the last battle to be fought in the north of England.[220]

John Bradshaw

Finally, mention must be made of the most famous individual from the Borough at the time of the Civil Wars. When Charles I was brought to trial in 1649, the Lord President of the court, who pronounced sentence and whose signature heads the list of names on the death warrant, was a Marple man, John Bradshaw (Ill 4.15). His elder brother Henry being heir to the family estate, John had chosen a career in law which took him away from his native township. By 1648 he had risen to the position of chief justice of Chester, the highest judicial office in the county. His election to the presidency of the court set up to try the king is attributed to the reluctance of others to take up that responsibility. However, it resulted in his appointment as President of the Council of State, so that from 1649 until 1651 he held the highest office in the country. He died in 1659, the year before the monarchy was restored under Charles II, and was buried in Westminster Abbey. In 1661, on the anniversary of the execution of Charles I, the bodies of Bradshaw, Cromwell and the Parliamentarian general Ireton were exhumed, drawn on sledges to Tyburn, hanged and their heads then cut off, a posthumous punishment for what was now considered to have been an act of treason. Bradshaw had been baptized at Stockport parish church on the 10th of December 1602. Next to the entry of the baptism in the parish resister, someone was later to write 'Traitor' (Ill 4.16).[221]

RELIGION

New chapels of ease

From the late sixteenth century onwards the number of places of public worship in the Borough increased, with the establishment of new chapels of ease in Stockport parish. Marple Chapel appears to have been the first of these, and was constructed by the mid-1570s. Like Chadkirk, which was built earlier in the century, it was a timber-framed building.[222] Norbury Chapel followed in the early seventeenth century. It was set on land belonging to the Hyde family, close to their residence at Norbury Hall.[223] In the 1640s the old chapel at Chadkirk was also reinstated as a place of worship. The years of neglect since the Reformation had evidently taken their toll on the building, for at some point in the seventeenth century two of its timber-framed walls were replaced with stone.[224] The construction or re-establishment of these chapels may reflect a growth in local population, but Norbury Chapel may also have been built for the benefit of the Hyde family.

Puritanism

After the establishment of Protestantism as the official, state religion in the mid-sixteenth century, few in south-east Lancashire and north-east Cheshire appear to have clung for long to the old Catholic faith. In the Borough, the Davenport families of Bramhall and Woodford may both have included Catholic members in the 1580s but they are notable exceptions.[225] Furthermore, the form of Protestantism which gained strength in the locality was that generally described as Puritan. It rejected those rituals and trappings of the Established Church considered to be too close to Catholicism.

Lancashire and Cheshire lay within the diocese of Chester, created in 1541. In the late sixteenth century the diocesan authorities had largely tolerated Puritanism, which they saw as an ally in their opposition to Catholicism.[226] In 1616-19, under Bishop Moreton, attitudes became more rigid. During these years Moreton also held the rectorship of Stockport, and on one occasion is recorded as castigating local Puritan ministers at a meeting in the town's rectory.[227] What has been described as a 'full-scale campaign'

Ill 4.15 John Bradshaw.

John Bradshaw was the most famous individual to hail from the Borough in the seventeenth century, and arguably in any era. A younger son of Marple's leading family, he pursued a highly successful career in law which took him away from the place of his birth. In 1648 he was appointed to the highest judicial office in Cheshire. In the following year he was propelled to national fame, and notoriety, when he was elected president of the court which condemned Charles I to death.

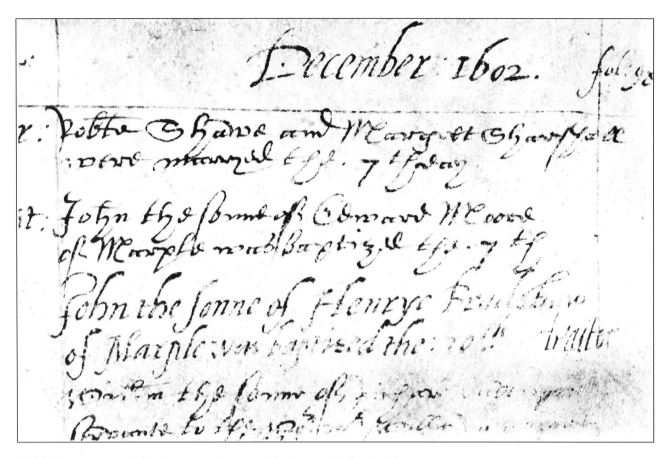

Ill 4.16 Stockport parish church register, the entry of the baptism of John Bradshaw.
The word 'traitor' was added in a later hand. John Bradshaw had the good fortune to die before the Restoration of the monarchy. He was buried in Westminster Abbey but in revenge for his part in the death of Charles I, his body, along with the bodies of Cromwell and Ireton, was exhumed, hanged and beheaded.

against Puritanism in the diocese began in 1633, as part of the national persecution conducted by the Established Church with the backing of the king. The response was a hardening of Puritan attitudes.[228] In Cheshire in 1641 William Brereton organized a petition, said to contain over 1000 signatures, directed against episcopacy, the rule of the Church by bishops.[229] It was perhaps religion which most determined the allegiance of other local men who fought against the king in the forthcoming conflict. Robert Duckenfield, Ralph Arderne and Edward Hyde were, like Brereton, men with Puritan views.[230]

The Parliamentarian successes in the region early in the Great Civil War meant that the bishop of Chester was now head of his diocese in name only. The rectors of both Stockport and Cheadle, as we have seen, were both removed from their livings by the sequestrators. Their successors were men appointed by the Parliamentarian Committee of Plundered Ministers, originally set up in 1642 to help ministers who had themselves been ejected from their livings by the Royalists.[231]

Presbyterians and Congregationalists

In the early 1640s most opponents of episcopacy hoped to replace it with a Presbyterian church, as had existed in Scotland since the mid-sixteenth century, organized at local levels through committees, or classes, of ministers and laymen and at national level through an assembly. In 1646, the same year in which it abolished episcopacy, Parliament authorized the creation of a Presbyterian state church. Classes were immediately established in Lancashire, but in Cheshire the new church was more loosely organized.[232]

During the Great Civil War a rival movement grew in influence, which wanted individual congregations to have a greater measure of independence. Henry Bradshaw was one of a number of hard-line Presbyterians who in 1646 petitioned, unsuccessfully, for such congregations to be suppressed.[233] Robert Duckenfield, on the other hand, by this date had become a firm supporter of the movement. He was the patron of Samuel Eaton, one of the most ardent Congregationalist preachers in the region. In the chapel of Dukinfield Old Hall, Eaton founded what was possibly the first Congregational church in England. In the early 1650s, following a split in this congregation, Eaton moved to Stockport where he preached in the grammar school. Although Eaton was at first supported by voluntary contributions from his congregation, in 1652 he was granted an annual income of £40 by the state; by 1657 subsequent grants had raised this figure to £100.[234] Congregationalism won particular favour with Cromwell and other hard-liners in the army and Parliament. In 1659 its continuing influence was one of the main factors behind the Cheshire uprising, whose participants believed themselves to be defending the Presbyterian church.

Quakers

Dukinfield Old Hall Chapel is also associated with another religious movement, for it was here in 1647 that George Fox, the founder of Quakerism, preached his first sermon.[235] There were Quakers in Stockport by 1653. The movement at this time was viewed as subversive by other religious groups. When, in that year, one Stockport Quaker, Richard Waller, married a woman of Samuel Eaton's congregation, the incident led to a fierce dispute between the sects. At first letters were exchanged between the newly weds and Eaton. Later, in response to a list of doctrinal questions delivered by the Quakers in the presence of his congregation, Eaton went into print, prompting the Quakers in turn to publish a reply in which they accused him of being a blasphemer and a liar.[236]

Nonconformity

In 1660, with the return of the monarchy, the Church of England was also re-established. The new king had promised freedom of worship, but in 1662 Parliament passed the Act of Uniformity, under which any minister who refused to conduct his services according to a new revised Prayer Book or who was not ordained by a bishop was to be removed from his living. At Cheadle the rector Peter Harrison conformed.[237] At Stockport, Thomas Paget, the last rector to be appointed before the Restoration, was not to be faced with the prospect of ejection, dying in 1660.[238] Samuel Eaton was removed from his living in the town. He died in 1665 at Bredbury, where the hearth tax returns suggest he lived at either Goyt Hall or Bredbury Hall.[239] At Mellor Chapel John Jones was ejected in 1660, even before the Act of Uniformity, as an alleged opponent of the Restoration. He had first come to the Borough as domestic chaplain at Arden Hall, and in the mid-

1640s had served as the minister at Marple.[240] At Chadkirk, Thomas Norman, who had been minister here since the early 1650s, appears to have remained in his office after the Act of 1662, although whether he in fact conformed is a matter of uncertainty.[241]

Francis Lowe, the curate at Marple Chapel since about 1648, also stayed on. In John Bradshaw's native township, feelings against the monarchy could still run high. In May of 1662 two local men nailed fast the door of the chapel to prevent the official announcement of a forthcoming service commemorating the Restoration. The curate and his congregation broke down the door, but before the commemorative service was held the protest was repeated. The protesters next changed the chapel lock and finally even replaced the chapel door. The offenders were brought before the diocesan court, but the case may have been abandoned in 1663 when Lowe, perhaps with some relief, moved to another appointment.[242]

The Act of Uniformity was followed in 1664 by the prohibition of nonconformist meetings at which more than four people, in addition to the members of the household, were present. In the following year nonconformist ministers were excluded from coming within 5 miles of a town, or of a parish from which they had been ejected. Despite such official attempts at suppression, religious dissenters continued to gather in worship. In 1669 it was reported that meetings were being held in the houses of two nonconformist ministers in Marple, one of whom was John Jones. They were even being held at Chadkirk Chapel, which was used by several ministers and was attended by worshippers from as far away as Disley. It seems that, after the death of Thomas Norman in 1667, the chapel was poorly served by curates attached to the mother church in Stockport, and that local nonconformists took full advantage of this lapse.[243]

When in 1672 freedom of worship was granted to all but Catholics, several licences were taken out allowing nonconformist meetings in Stockport parish. The places at which these meetings were to be held is not always specified, but one may have been a house in Marple. Another allowed John Jolly, a Presbyterian, to hold meetings at the Hydes' residence at Norbury Hall.[244] In January 1673 Jolly also preached in the neighbouring chapel. The incident led to him being arrested and brought before the king's council, where the charge against him was dismissed.[245] However, in 1673 all the licences for nonconformist meeting houses were cancelled.

Some, denied religious freedom at home, sought it abroad. In 1683 Francis Stanfield of Marple was among a group of Quakers who sailed for North America. He bought land in what is now Marple Township near Philadelphia, said to have been named by him after his Cheshire home.[246] In the same year as Stanfield's departure, the Quaker Jeremiah Owen, the town's baker at Stockport, was fined by the churchwardens for the failure of himself and his wife to attend the parish church. When he refused payment, the churchwardens took the equivalent amount in bread, which they attempted to sell at the market cross. In what appears to have been a local expression of sympathy, they found no buyers. When the churchwardens were reduced to giving the bread to the poor, they in turn handed it back to Owen.[247]

A lasting freedom of worship for Protestant nonconformists came with the Toleration Act in 1689. Among the places now licensed as meeting places was Chadkirk Chapel, its first minister being John Jones's son Gamaliel, whose house at Marple was also registered.[248] Chadkirk served a nonconformist congregation until 1705-6, when this moved to a new purpose-built chapel in neighbouring Bredbury. The departure from Chadkirk was forced, but by the order of the landlord not by an edict of the state. As Methodists learnt later in the eighteenth century, religious differences could still provoke individual acts of intoleration.

CHAPTER FIVE

STOCKPORT'S FIRST INDUSTRIAL REVOLUTION, 1700-80

'A large and handsome town...with the large silk mills belonging to the chief tradesmen of the place'

INTRODUCTION

The Industrial Revolution in the North-West is perhaps most commonly associated with the cotton industry. More particularly it is linked with the spinning mills powered first by water and then by steam. Their arrival in the closing decades of the eighteenth century not only led to massive growth in the region's textile trade but also brought about fundamental changes in local society. The Borough, as we shall see later, was itself to experience the far-reaching effects of this upsurge in the cotton industry. Here, as elsewhere in the region, the introduction of the cotton factory followed a rise in the importance of cotton in the earlier decades of the century. Cotton-spinning mills were not, however, the first factories in the Borough. For over forty years before the establishment of its first water-powered cotton mill, a factory system had been in operation in Stockport. The industry which lay at the centre of the town's first, and often overlooked, industrial revolution was silk.

This pre-1780 era saw other important local changes. There was expansion in other industries, in hatting and coal mining. The various branches of the textile finishing industry, dyeing, printing and bleaching, were either first introduced or grew in significance. There were improvements in transport, through the creation of the Borough's first turnpike roads. Schemes to establish a link with the emerging network of inland waterways and canals were also devised. Attitudes to religion changed, with a growing disenchantment with the Church of England giving rise to an evangelical crusade of religious revival. In Stockport people were willing to challenge manorial authority and to press for a system of local government to suit the changing needs of the time. In 1745 the Borough experienced an event of more momentary local significance, the Jacobite rebellion.

THE SILK INDUSTRY

The origins of the silk industry in Stockport can be traced back to the local manufacture of buttons and weaving of silk lace in the seventeenth century.[1] Button making was listed among the chief industries of Stockport in 1769, and was still documented in the town, although seemingly in a much reduced form, in the 1790s.[2] In the eighteenth century, as in the seventeenth, button making also appears to have been carried out in Gatley, with three 'button men' being mentioned here between 1735 and 1779.[3] The branch of the silk industry which came to dominate the economic life of the town in the eighteenth century was the manufacture of yarn. Some yarn was produced for the local button trade, but the principal market was London, the country's main centre of silk weaving.[4]

Silk throwing in early eighteenth-century Stockport

There were three main elements to the manufacture of silk yarn. The imported raw material consisted of skeins of silk unravelled from the cocoon of the silk worm. These were first wound onto bobbins, creating a manageable yarn. This was then twisted, a process known as 'throwing'. Thirdly, in the 'doubling' process, separate yarns were twisted together to create a stronger thread.[5] Yarn was being produced in Stockport in the early eighteenth century by the process known as hand-throwing. This involved attaching the ends of the threads on a number of bobbins to an upright wheel and then running with the bobbins to a fixed rail set between 25 and 35 yards (23 and 32 metres) away. Turning the wheel gave the yarn its twist.[6] A 'shade', the name of the long rectangular building in which hand-throwing was carried out, is mentioned as being under construction in the town in 1723. It stood in Petty Carr Green, the area now occupied by Mersey Square and the bus station. It was built of brick on a plot of land 35.5 yards long, and was to be used for the twisting of 'mohair', the term for a type of silk yarn used in the button-making industry.[7] 'Twisting alleys' are mentioned in the town in 1731, although it is possible that these were used for rope making.[8]

Sir Thomas Lombe's patent

The yarn used for the warp of the finest-quality silk cloths was known as 'organzine'; 'tram', a coarser yarn, was used for the weft. Until the early eighteenth century the English silk industry had the ability only to produce tram. Organzine needed to be imported from Italy, where it was produced on water-powered machinery whose design was a closely guarded secret. In about 1704 Thomas Cotchett attempted to produce his own organzine at Derby, in what is thought to have been the first water-powered textile mill in this country. The venture proved unsuccessful, but in 1716 John Lombe travelled to Italy and, in an early example of industrial espionage, smuggled the design of the Italians' winding and throwing machines out of the country. In 1718 Parliament granted his half-brother, Sir Thomas Lombe, patent rights over the machinery for fourteen years. Secure of a monopoly, the Lombes proceeded to build a large new silk mill adjacent to Cotchett's building at Derby. When in 1732 Sir Thomas Lombe sought a renewal of his patent, Parliament refused, granting him £14,000 as compensation and requiring him in return to place a model of his machinery on public display in the Tower of London.[9]

In March 1732 a petition against the renewal of Lombe's patent was sent to Parliament from the 'principal traders' of Stockport, among these being 'the manufacturers of mohair and yarn'. Similar petitions were received from Manchester, Macclesfield and Leek. These towns were also already involved in the manufacture of silk yarn.[10] However, it was Stockport which on the expiry of the patent was the first place in which a silk mill was established.

Stockport's first silk mill, 1732

The site of this new mill lay in the Park, close to the manorial cornmill (*Ill 5.1*). It was an area which was already being opened up to development. By 1731 next to the cornmill stood a logwood mill, built to grind dyestuffs for the local textile industry. In June 1732 Edward Warren, the lord of the manor, leased land here to a partnership of six individuals, for the purpose of erecting one or more buildings. They were to be suitable for housing silk manufacturing machinery, powered by water and constructed to 'a design imitable of Sir Thomas Lombe's'. The lease included permission to use the existing 'sluice' or millrace and to drive a tunnel from this to turn a waterwheel. Five of the six lessees were either members of the local gentry (one was Warren's younger brother) or local businessmen (two were Heaton Norris 'chapmen'). The sixth was a London merchant, who perhaps already had a connection with the silk industry. To build the new mill, the help was enlisted of the Italian John Guardivaglio, a former employee of Lombe. He brought to Stockport a number of other workers from the Derby factory. In 1740 the shareholders also acquired the lease of the logwood mill.[11] The water-supply to the mills in the Park was subsequently improved by the construction of a new millrace from a point on

the River Goyt above New Bridge. At Millgate this millrace was an open channel, but to the east and west of this point the water was carried through a tunnel (*Ill 6.5*). Part of the new millrace ran through glebe land (land belonging to the parish church), and here its construction and maintenance were sanctioned by an Act of Parliament passed in 1742.[12]

The Park silk mill was the earliest known water-powered factory not only in Stockport but also in the North-West, as well as being one of the first to be established in the country. Of the two other major centres of silk production in Cheshire, Macclesfield was not to have its first water-powered mill until 1743-4. It was built by Charles Roe, a button merchant, and contained machinery based on 'a perfect model' of that in use at Lombe's mill in Derby. Congleton's first water-powered silk mill is believed to have been Old Mill, built in 1753 by a partnership which included a Stockport silk throwster.[13]

After the construction of the Park mill, nearly thirty years passed before a second water-powered silk mill was built in Stockport. Possibly the financial outlay was prohibitive. The initial investment in the Park mill had been £12,000, of which a quarter seems to have been payment to the lord of the manor for a long-term lease.[14] There may also have been fears about the availability of Italian raw silk, suitable for producing organzine. In 1732 Thomas Lombe himself had claimed that there was such a shortage, in order to deter would-be competitors.[15] Stockport's later silk mills may have specialized in the production not of organzine but the coarser yarn, tram, for which supplies of raw silk were readily available from Persia.[16]

Later water-powered silk mills, 1759-73

The Stockport mills

The second area in Stockport to see the establishment of a water-powered silk mill was the Carrs (*Plate IV*). This was the name given to the valley of the Tin Brook (here known as Carr Brook) to the east of Middle Hillgate. In 1759 land in the Carrs was acquired by four Stockport men, including two silk throwsters, who were allowed to build one or more silk mills and to dam the stream.[17] In 1768 the partnership of Richard Blackburn and Thomas Tatlock, who then owned Carr Mill, bought the rival Park mill.[18] By this date a third water-powered silk mill had been built in the town. This lay in Adlington Square on the north side of Chestergate, close to the point at which the Tin Brook flowed into the Mersey (*Ills 5.1 & 5.2*). It was owned by Joseph Dale, who took up residence in the nearby Mansion House.[19]

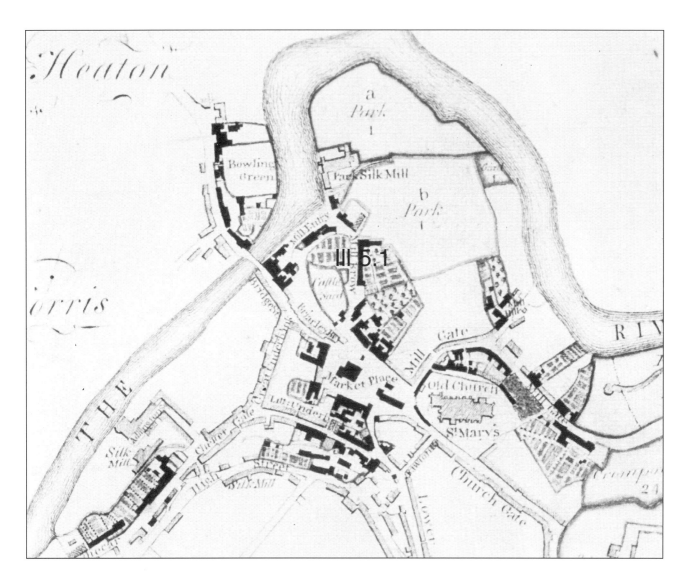

Ill 5.1 Detail of plan of Stockport township, 1770.
In the eighteenth century Stockport's first textile mills were erected for the production of silk yarn. The earliest of these was the Park silk mill, located within the bend of the Mersey and the Goyt. Built in 1732, this was one of the first water-powered textile mills in the country. Later silk mills included one in Adlington Square (lower left), which was powered by the Tin Brook, and one in High Street.

The Park, Carr and Adlington Square mills probably accounted for three of the four large mills which according to the findings of a parliamentary committee had been built in Stockport by 1773. The fourth may have been Crowther's Mill, across the Mersey in Heaton Norris (*Ill 5.2*). It is said to have been built after 1768, and is very likely one of two silk mills in Heaton Norris owned by the firm of Crowther and Venables and described in 1773 as 'new'. Its water-power was provided by a reservoir known as Crowther's Dam, which was fed by the Stitch Brook, a tributary stream of the Mersey. (In the late nineteenth century the site of the reservoir became the Heaton Norris Recreation Ground.)[20]

The Cheadle mill

By the early 1770s the silk mills of the Borough were not confined to the township of Stockport or the neighbouring area of Heaton Norris. In 1771 a water-powered silk mill was built in Cheadle, and was said to be capable of producing tram, organzine and sewing silks.[21] Its location is uncertain. It may have been on the Micker Brook to the north of Gatley Road, where a water-powered cotton and silk mill stood in the nineteenth century. Another possible location is on the site of one of two printworks, Demmings and Cheadle Grove, established near Cheadle village towards the end of the eighteenth century (*Ill 6.10*).[22]

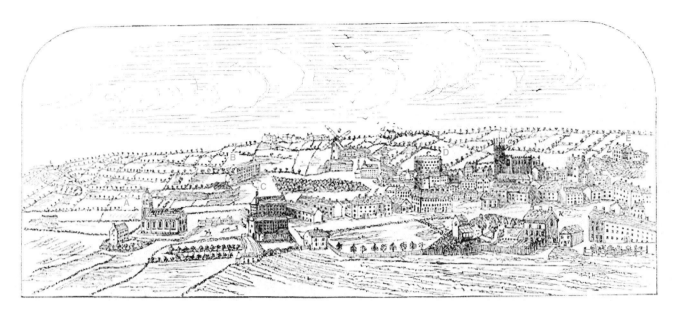

Ill 5.2 View of Stockport from the south.
This view of the town, probably dating from the late 1780s, shows two of the town's eighteenth-century silk mills, Crowther's Mill, in Heaton Norris, and the silk mill in Adlington Square, by this date converted to cotton spinning. The town's first cotton mill was the curiously designed Castle Mill, which came into operation in 1778.

Key:
A St Peter's Church   B Crowther's Mill   C Adlington Square Mill   D Castle Mill   E Rectory

The smaller mills

In 1773, as well as the four large mills, there were 'other smaller mills' in the town. Three mills listed in 1768 probably fell within this category: 'Tetlock's' in the Market Place, Guardivaglio's on Hillgate, and Ashbrook's on 'Top o' th' Hill', the present High Street (*Ill 5.1*).[23] None of these mills was in a location with an obvious water-supply to drive the machinery. The same may be said of two silk mills reported to have been established after 1768, Foster's or Bird Cage Mill on Old Road in Heaton Norris, and an unnamed mill on Lower Hillgate.[24] If the machinery in these mills was not simply hand-operated, it may have been literally horse-powered, with the animal harnessed to, and turning, a mechanism known as a 'gin'. (The name is a shortened form of 'engine'.) Such smaller mills could be set up in existing buildings. In 1776 silk throwster's machinery was advertised for sale in rooms in a building on Chestergate described as the Old Hall.[25]

The mill buildings

As far as is known, none of the eighteenth-century silk mills in the Borough has survived even in part, but something of the appearance of the larger mills can be gleaned from contemporary descriptions, pictorial and map evidence (*Ills 5.1 & 5.2*) and from other examples

of silk-mill buildings. By 1769 the larger mills had become a prominent feature of the townscape. According to an account of that date, Stockport was 'a large and handsome town occupying three hills and three valleys which are so serpentine as to form many pleasing prospects of churches, pieces of water, etc., with the large silk mills belonging to the chief tradesmen of the place'. The same source describes the mills in which the silk was thrown as 'of prodigious bulk'; at least one factory, the Park mill, was five storeys high.[26] Like known silk mills in other towns (including the Lombes' mill in Derby), they were rectangular in plan, and almost certainly had a regular arrangement of windows. In 1785 the Carr silk mill, by this date no longer used for that purpose, included two factories, both six storeys high, 28 yards (25.5 metres) long and 8 yards (7.3 metres) wide.[27] The Cheadle silk mill is reported to have been 14 yards (12.7 metres) long, 7 yards wide inside and four storeys high; two rooms contained the throwing machinery, another the winding machinery, while a fourth was used for doubling.[28]

The workforce

The silk mills gave rise to a new phenomenon in Stockport, the presence of a large body of factory workers. In 1769 there were said to be nearly 2000 people employed in the town's silk mills. The parliamentary committee in 1773 gave a roughly similar figure, noting that in recent years 1000 people had been employed in the four large silk mills in the town and about 600 in the 'other smaller mills'. A total of 1600 would have represented more than a third of the population of the township at this date, though presumably some of the workforce lived within the surrounding district. Such was the level of employment offered by the silk industry that it was said of Stockport in 1769 'At this place poverty is not much felt except by those who are idle, for all persons capable of tying knots may find work in the silk mills...where children of six years old earn a shilling a week and more as they grow capable of deserving it'.[29] Perhaps not surprisingly, those running the silk mills could be described as the town's 'chief tradesmen' and 'the principal people in the place'.[30]

The industry in depression, 1772-3

A society with this measure of dependency on a single industry ran the risk of being severely affected by a downturn in that industry's fortunes. By 1772 the country's silk industry was in depression, as a result, it was believed, of the government's inability to quell the illegal importation of foreign silk cloth.[31] In July 1772 the firm of Blackburn and Tatlock, by this date probably the single largest employer in the town, was declared bankrupt. In June 1773 the local press was advertising the forthcoming auction of their Carr and Hill mills. (The location of this last mill is uncertain.) At the same time the auction was announced of the two Heaton Norris silk mills of Crowther and Venables, also now bankrupt.[32] Earlier in the year the parliamentary committee reported that the workforce of the four large Stockport silk mills had been reduced from 1000 to less than 200; of the smaller mills, three-quarters were now standing idle.[33]

The changeover to cotton

By the end of 1773 the town's silk industry appears to have been in the process of recovery. Carr Mill found a new owner. With the assistance of Tatlock, his former partner, Blackburn bought the Park mill from his creditors, and over the next ten years was able to pay off half his debts.[34] In Heaton Norris, Crowther resumed business. In 1781 the Stockport poor rate book provides evidence for eight silk mills in the township alone, five shades, and 'silk rooms' on High Street.[35]

Nevertheless, in the 1780s the silk mills were being given over to a new rising industry, one in which local manufacturers may have hoped to avoid the uncertainties of silk manufacture. That new industry was cotton. It was a sign of the times that Carr Mill was bought in 1781 by a Stockport silk throwster who intended to convert it to cotton spinning. In 1783 Blackburn sold the Park mill to Henry Marsland for the same purpose.[36] At Adlington Square, Joseph Dale already had a 'cotton works' adjacent to his silk mill in 1780. By 1784 he had converted the silk mill itself to cotton.[37]

This process did not spell the sudden end of silk throwing in Stockport. Some twelve 'silk manufacturers' are listed in the town in the 1790s, and silk throwing was still being carried out here into the 1830s.[38] In Heaton Norris, Crowther's Mill appears to have undergone only a gradual change in use. William Crowther was manufacturing cottons by the 1800s, but he also continued silk throwing until perhaps the early 1820s.[39] However, while the silk-throwing industry continued after the 1780s, the changeover of other factories to cotton meant that it was now conducted on a much reduced scale.[40]

That changeover was not too difficult to make. The very design of the large water-powered silk mills, as rectangular multi-storey blocks, had probably helped shape the earliest cotton mills. The old machinery would have needed to be stripped out and the new machinery for the manufacture of cotton yarn installed, but fifty years of the silk industry in Stockport had given the town a body of trained mechanics. Most importantly of all, it had created a local workforce accustomed to the pace and routine of factory life.

THE COTTON INDUSTRY

The domestic industry, 1700-70

When cotton first became a part of the textile industry of the Borough is uncertain, but a date towards the very end of the seventeenth century or in the early eighteenth century seems likely.[41] Before the great expansion of the 1780s, the cotton industry had already witnessed two main phases of organization. The first, lasting until about 1770, was domestic in nature. The processes of production, as in the older linen and woollen industries, were carried out by individuals and families working in their own homes. However, unlike those older trades, the cotton industry is likely from the outset to have been operated through a putting-out system, in which manufacturers hired the labour of that domestic workforce. The second phase of organization, in the 1770s, saw the introduction of new machinery, resulting in manufacturers themselves beginning to undertake the processes of production.

The earliest use of locally spun yarn was in mixed cloths, known as 'checks', with a cotton weft and a linen warp. John Aikin in 1795 described how in Stockport the cotton industry had progressed from the spinning of weft to the weaving of checks. In 1732 the manufacturers of cotton yarn were among the 'principal traders' of Stockport who petitioned against the renewal of Thomas Lombe's patent.[42] Check manufacturers are mentioned in the town in the 1750s and 1760s.[43]

In the eighteenth century, as previously, many textile workers were also engaged in farming. William Radcliffe recalled how in 1770 in his native Mellor there were between fifty and sixty farmers, of whom only six or seven were not involved 'in some branch of trade, such as spinning and weaving woollen, linen or cotton'.[44] In Heaton Norris in 1776 several small farms of 4-6 acres were advertised as being suitable for weavers, each with cowsheds and 'large loom houses'.[45] In Mellor those without farms were even more dependent on the textile industry. According to Radcliffe, in 1770 the cottagers, whose land comprised no more than a garden, 'were employed entirely in this manner except for a few weeks in the harvest'. Some cottages, he adds, included a 'convenient loomshop'.[46]

The impact of new machinery, 1770-80

By the mid-eighteenth century the region's textile industry was facing a serious practical difficulty. The fly-shuttle, patented by John Kay of Bury in 1733, greatly increased the amount of cloth which a weaver might produce. The yarn which was used in that cloth continued to be produced on spinning wheels, each with only a limited output. William Radcliffe reported of this period that it required six other workers to prepare and spin enough yarn, whether wool, cotton or linen, to supply a single weaver.[47] There were several unfruitful attempts to solve this problem by inventing a new spinning machine. One such device was created in 1753 by Lawrence Earnshaw of Mottram-in-Longdendale. Earnshaw's spinning machine is said to have been destroyed by its inventor who feared that it would rob the poor of work.[48] The machine which was eventually to provide an answer to the industry's needs was the spinning jenny, invented in the mid-1760s by James Hargreaves, a weaver at Stanhill near Blackburn. Hargreaves patented the jenny in 1770, but by this date the machine was already in widespread use in and around Manchester and elsewhere in Lancashire.[49] Spurred on by the spread of the jenny, attempts were made to perfect a machine to carry out the initial process of carding, the combing of the fibres of the raw material. The most successful of these carding engines, as they

were known, was that patented by Richard Arkwright in 1775, but in the 1770s other types of carding machine were in use.[50]

Radcliffe describes how in Mellor, from 1770, the spinning wheels 'with the exception of one establishment were all thrown into lumber-rooms, the yarn was all spun on common jennies', while carding engines were used for all but the finest yarns. Not everyone in Mellor benefited from the changes; 'what was gained by some families who had the advantage of machinery, might, in a great measure, be said to be lost to the others, who had been compelled to throw their old cards and hand-wheels aside as lumber'.[51]

Early cotton factories

Arkwright's carding engines were powered by water, but early carding machinery was also driven by hand or by horse-gin. Hand-powered engines could be used in domestic workshops, but manufacturers quickly came to install carding machines in their own premises. Alongside these they might also add jennies. Works of this type had been established in Cheadle Hulme by 1773 and Heaton Norris in 1780. The machinery in the former included five spinning jennies in 1777, that in the latter, thirteen. At both sites textile manufacture did not end with the production of spun yarn. The Heaton Norris works also contained seven looms, while the Cheadle Hulme property included five houses 'with room to contain ten looms'.[52]

Such small cotton works might be the springboards to larger concerns. Henry Marsland appears to have begun his textile career in about 1770 by installing carding machinery in a building which he had erected next to his house in Bullock Smithy, the present Hazel Grove. In 1776 he patented a machine which he claimed could be used for 'doubling, throwing and winding cotton, silk, linen, mohair, or any other sort of yarn whatsoever' and which could be powered by water as well as by hand. In 1782 he expanded his Bullock Smithy factory by buying an adjacent plot of land. The site lacked water-power and Marsland was only able to drive his machinery here by a horse-gin. This difficulty was overcome in 1783 when he leased the former Park silk mill and turned this over to cotton spinning.[53] From this new beginning Marsland's firm grew into one of the largest textile businesses in the region.

Stockport's first water-powered cotton mill, 1778

The country's first purpose-built water-powered cotton mill was erected by Richard Arkwright in 1771 at Cromford, near Matlock in Derbyshire. It housed the spinning machines of Arkwright's own invention, which were known as 'water-frames' after their method of power and for which in 1769 he had taken out a patent for fourteen years.[54] From 1776 Arkwright was busy constructing new mills, creating a textile empire and earning for himself a very considerable fortune. As we shall see in the following chapter, Arkwright was also to play a significant part in the development of the cotton industry in Stockport, by providing financial backing to Samuel Oldknow.

Although former silk mills, such as the Park and Carr, were among Stockport's earliest water-powered cotton factories, they were not the first in the town. That distinction goes to Castle Mill, which was also one of the earliest water-powered cotton factories in the region. It was built by Sir George Warren, the lord of the manor, and was ready to begin operation in 1778. It stood on Castle Yard at the north-west corner of the Market Place. To bring water to its 40 feet (12 metres) diameter wheel, a branch was dug off the existing tunnel leading to the mills in the Park (Ill 5.3). The design of Castle Mill was possibly unique. Arkwright's mills were rectangular in plan. It was a form which was probably adopted from the silk industry and which remained the

norm for textile factories into the twentieth century. Castle Mill was circular or, perhaps more strictly, oval, with a central courtyard. In 1778 it was described as including 'a dwelling house', evidently on the side facing the Market Place. Illustrations show the building dominating this end of the town, its tower-like appearance emphasized by the battlements which crowned its walls (Ills 5.2 & 7.20). To John Byng, who visited Stockport in 1790, it looked 'like one of the grandest prisons in the world'.[55]

The design of the mill was no doubt influenced by the fact that the town's castle had stood on this same site. Sir George Warren, as we shall see, was a man for whom the idea of continuity with the medieval past was inseparable from his own self-interest. At Stockport his determination to exercise what he believed to be his traditional manorial rights brought him, in the late 1760s, into a bitter conflict with a number of the townspeople. At the time that Castle Mill was built, he was hoping to prove his entitlement to the ancient earldom of Surrey which had been held by his ancestors, the Warennes. Perhaps a desire of Sir George to make a personal statement to his contemporaries played a part in its design.

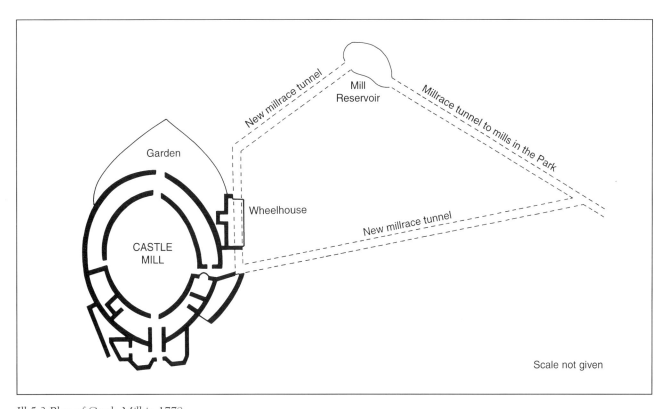

Ill 5.3 Plan of Castle Mill in 1778.
While cotton mills were typically rectangular in plan, Castle Mill was oval with a central courtyard. Water was supplied to its waterwheel along a new tunnel, leading from an existing tunnel which fed the mills in the Park. The front part of the building contained domestic accommodation which came to be used as an inn. The unusual plan of the mill may have presented difficulties in the transmission of power to its machinery, and in 1800 the building ceased to be used as a cotton factory. Castle Mill was demolished in 1841.

The first occupant of Castle Mill was John Milne, who is believed to have installed pirated versions of Arkwright's machinery in the building.[56] Milne's tenancy was short-lived but not uneventful. In 1779, during a depression in the textile trade, workers attacked several mills in Lancashire, destroying machinery which they believed to be a threat to the domestic-based industry. When the rioters threatened to march on Stockport, the rector asked for militiamen to be sent to the town and members of the local gentry began to organize its defence. Cannons were set on the battlements of Castle Mill, facing the approach from Lancashire, but the feared attack did not materialize.[57]

In the meantime the Milnes were involved in their own, secretive scheme. Within a few months of the opening of Castle Mill, they were in touch with an agent of the French government. Despite the fact that exportation of textile machinery was prohibited by law and that France was at war with Britain on the side of the rebellious American colonies, a son of John Milne agreed to go to France to build a carding engine of the Arkwright type. Other family members and relatives subsequently joined him, including in 1782 John Milne himself. Together, the 'Milne clan' were responsible for setting up Arkwright-type machinery across France and in at least one place in Spain.[58]

After John Milne's departure, Castle Mill continued in use as a cotton factory until 1800 when, under the terms of an agreement made nine years earlier between Sir George Warren and Henry Marsland of the Park mills, water-power ceased to be supplied to the site. The building was then used for the sale of muslins and, when this project failed, became storage space for stall holders in the market. Perhaps in or shortly after 1800, the 'dwelling house' part of the building became an inn.[59]

The reasons for its early closure as a cotton factory are uncertain, but the very design of the building may have played a part. Power in mills was transmitted from the waterwheel to the machines via a series of gears and horizontal and vertical shafts. It was a system to which the rectangular blocks of other mills were admirably suited, but which in a circular building may have introduced all manner of practical difficulties.

TEXTILE FINISHING

Silk throwing and spinning and weaving were not the only branches of the local textile industry between 1700 and 1780. In the early eighteenth century dyeing was also being carried out in Stockport. A dyehouse had been built at Petty Carr Green by 1720. Others stood between Little Underbank and High Street, in the valley of the Tin Brook which provided the necessary supply of water.[60] Dyestuffs, as has already been noted, were produced at the logwood mill, near to the manorial cornmill in the Park.

The bleaching of yarn and cloth at this period still involved the material being exposed to sunlight. A White Field, a name associated with such outdoor bleaching, is shown adjacent to Bridge Hall in Adswood on a map of about 1780. Possibly it was an existing tradition of bleaching in this area which in 1790 contributed to the establishment of one of the Borough's largest bleachworks on a nearby site in Edgeley. The same field-name is found in the Cheshire part of the Borough at Bramhall, Brinnington and Norbury. In the Lancashire part of the Borough a 'whitster' or bleacher is recorded in 1772 at Heaton Moor, and another at Reddish. The neighbouring township of Levenshulme at that date was an important centre of this local industry, with no fewer than six bleachers.[61]

Printing on cloth, or calico printing, was introduced into the region's textile industry in the mid-eighteenth century. The site of the first printworks in the North-West is uncertain, but one candidate is Chadkirk where such works were established by the River Goyt between 1755 and 1766.[62] In about 1777 printworks were set up on the Mersey at a site known as Sheep Wash, on what was then the western edge of Stockport.[63] The early calico-printing industry was littered with failed businesses and bankruptcies. The first printworks at Chadkirk went bust within a short time, but subsequently reopened. Aikin in 1795 described the works as 'a large printing ground, one of the oldest in these parts'.[64]

HATTING

Hat making had been established in Stockport by the 1650s. Between 1700 and 1780 probate records from Heaton Norris, Bredbury and Cheadle Bulkeley provide evidence that the industry was spreading to neighbouring townships.[65] The organization of the local industry was also beginning to change. The early hat makers in the region had bought their raw materials and sold the finished hats. In the eighteenth century a putting-out system was introduced, whereby felt makers still operated from their own premises but hired out their labour to a manufacturer. The felt makers produced the basic hat bodies, but manufacturers might carry out the finishing process as well as the marketing of the final product. This system seems to have been in operation by 1769 when hat manufacturers were listed, alongside the manufacturers of checks, mohair and buttons, among the 'warehousemen' in Stockport.[66] Some hats were sold locally, but of growing importance towards the end of the eighteenth century were commissions for the large hatting firms in London. Both aspects of the trade are illustrated by the Stockport firm of Worsleys. In 1752 a Mr Worsley was one of two hatters renting stalls in Stockport's Market House.[67] From 1797 Thomas and John Worsley were making hats on commission for the London firm of Christys, which in the nineteenth century would forge even closer links with Stockport.

THE GEORGIAN TOWN

Population

In 1664 Stockport appears to have been the fifth largest town in Cheshire, with the population of the township numbering about 1400 or 1500. In 1731 the figure was, at a very rough estimate, about 2250. In 1754, when a count was made of the number of individuals and families in Stockport parish, the total population given for the township stood at 3144. In 1765 it was 3713. By 1779, when some 995 houses are recorded in the township, the population has been estimated to have reached roughly 5000.[68] By this date the largest town in Cheshire was still Chester, whose population in 1782 was said to be 14,700. The only other town in the county which appears to have exceeded Stockport was Macclesfield, whose population by 1786 is reported to have stood at about 7000. Manchester, earlier in the century, had become the largest town in the region. By 1773-4 its population numbered over 24,000.[69]

The population of mid-eighteenth-century Stockport was a broad mixture. The owners of the silk mills may have been considered to be 'the principal people in the place' but in 1769 the town could still be described as 'inhabited by a great number of the gentry'.[70] There were also manufacturers engaged in other industries, domestic-based workers employed by them, and workers in the silk factories. There were artisans, or craftsmen, shopkeepers and other traders. Stockport's artisans now included a small number of clockmakers, a trade found in and around other Cheshire towns at this period.[71] There were other local clockmakers in the mid-eighteenth century at Gatley Green and at Bents Lane in Bredbury.[72]

There were also the poor. In 1722 an Act of Parliament enabled overseers of the poor to establish workhouses, in which the able-bodied were to work for their keep, and the old, very young and the sick could be looked after. Stockport had a workhouse by 1731, with sixty people being accommodated here in 1777.[73]

The market and shops

In the eighteenth century as the townspeople grew in number, more and more were dependent on the market and shops for food and other necessities. By the 1760s corn grown in the township itself was no longer sufficient to meet the needs of its inhabitants.[74] Much was imported, both from the neighbouring countryside and from further afield. Aikin in 1795 listed Stockport, Manchester and Macclesfield as the chief markets for the surplus grain grown in Cheshire. Of Stockport's market he wrote, 'A great quantity of corn and oat-meal are sold at it, and it is accounted the best market for cheese in the county'.[75] Oatmeal, made into bread, cakes and porridge, was an important part of the diet of the less well-off, that is the majority of the local population. In the eighteenth century both corn and cheese were increasingly sold by the producer to middlemen, or 'factors', with transactions between the two moving away from the open market to inns. Cheese, as well as being sold to local consumers, was also exported to more distant markets, and in particular London.[76]

The market at Stockport did not always meet local needs. In times of a poor harvest there could be not only a shortage of grain but also a sharp rise in prices. The years 1756-7 were especially bad. Grain prices at Manchester rocketed to twice the level of only a few years previously, and riots erupted in many parts of the country. At Stockport, to help quell the situation, a charitable fund was set up to buy oatmeal, wheat and cheese, which were then sold at or under cost price.[77]

At other times some produce available in the market seems to have been surplus to local needs, although as the population grew this may have been less the case. Aikin noted that in the past surplus oatmeal had been brought to Manchester from Stockport. In the mid-eighteenth century the Manchester court leet records show that traders in the town's Saturday market included a sizeable group of Stockport butchers, who were perhaps selling meat left over from Stockport market the day before. Their attendance at Manchester seems to have decreased from the 1770s, suggesting a growing demand in their home town.[78]

By 1786 there seem to have been over 100 shops in the town. Elsewhere in the Borough they were still few and far between, with Cheadle and Marple each having perhaps no more than one.[79] In the 1750s some of the town's shops evidently carried a similar mixture of goods to their seventeenth-century predecessors, with at least one Stockport linen draper at this time dealing in groceries as well as cloth. In the same decade there is also evidence of one Stockport shop which served as a general provisions store. Its stock included cheese,

Ill 5.4 Adlington Square, in 1935.

Most of the expansion of the town in the early and mid-eighteenth century took place along existing thoroughfares, but Adlington Square (in fact a right-angled street) was a new development. It was laid out in the 1720s on land belonging to the Leghs of Adlington Hall and situated between Chestergate and the Mersey. The early occupants of its houses included artisans or craftsmen. Later this degenerated into one of the slum areas of the town. The site of Adlington Square is now part of the Merseyway shopping precinct.

butter, bacon, wheat, flour, oatmeal, potatoes, eggs and sugar, as well as household necessities such as candles. Shops of this type, specializing in the day-to-day needs of the town's growing workforce, seem to have been on the increase by the end of the century.[80]

The layout and appearance of the town

The growth in population, commerce and industry meant that the 'large and handsome' town, as it was described in 1769, had expanded beyond its seventeenth-century limits. In 1770 a plan of the township was produced by the surveyor William Tunnicliff, to show the land and properties owned by the lord of the manor, Sir George Warren (*Plate IV & Ill 5.1*). In some parts of the town centre, properties in other ownership were omitted from the plan, but elsewhere these too were included. Much of the expansion which had taken place since about 1680

occurred along two existing streets at the town's edge, Chestergate and Hillgate, which at this time was still the main route into Stockport from the south. In 1770 the western side of the town extended along Chestergate to include Petty Carr Green, where since the early decades of the century a number of buildings had been erected on what was formerly common land. Along Hillgate, by 1770 buildings straggled southwards for a distance of about 800 metres. Here, as at Petty Carr Green, some had been built on former common land, in this case along the verge of the main thoroughfare.[81]

The 1770 plan also shows two new developments off existing streets: Watson Square off Hillgate; and Adlington Square, a right-angled street between Chestergate and the Mersey (*Ill 5.4*). This last development lay on land which had belonged to the Leghs of Adlington Hall. In 1577 this had been the site of a yarn croft, bounded by the Tin Brook and the river. It was later known as the 'Schole Croft', after the grammar school which from the early seventeenth century was housed in a building on the opposite side of the Tin Brook (*Ill 4.2*). The square seems to have originated in the 1720s when the Leghs were selling off plots of land in Schole Croft for building houses, alongside what was then described as the 'new street'. Its houses included artisans' dwellings (in 1731 the occupants of the square included a 'plummer' and a joiner), and also the large Mansion House. This is said to have been built by the Leghs as a dower house but was later occupied by Joseph Dale, the owner of the Adlington Square silk mill.[82]

By the 1770s the demands for land for new buildings, and the profits which might be made from this, were such that even some of the glebe land was opened up for development. Until that time, with the exception of the rectory and Churchgate, the glebe land was reserved for agricultural use, and it required an Act of Parliament to allow it to be used otherwise. Passed

in 1773, this permitted the rector, the Reverend John Watson, and his successors to lease out much of the glebe land for building for terms of up to ninety-nine years. Two semi-detached late eighteenth-century town houses which still stand at Nos 78 and 80 Churchgate were erected on land leased for building under the provisions of this Act.[83]

On the Market Place, Staircase House in the eighteenth century was divided into two separate premises, each containing a ground-floor shop (*Plate V*).[84] Other properties in the town were presumably also subdivided to meet a growing need for domestic accommodation and business premises. There is also evidence that people were extending their properties by exploiting the soft sandstone cliffs which lay to the rear of some of the town's streets. By cutting the cliffs into a vertical face, a building might be extended backwards. By hollowing out the rock, additional storage space could be created. An early recorded instance of

Ill 5.5 Samuel Oldknow's house, Higher Hillgate.
In the eighteenth century brick replaced timber as the common material for new buildings in the town. This Georgian house, with a door surround in a classical style, is believed to have been built in the early 1740s. In the 1780s it was the home of Samuel Oldknow, the country's leading manufacturer of muslins.

the first process concerns an area of land to the rear of a house on one of the Underbanks, described in 1727 as 'lately obtained by the hewing, felling or cutting of rock'. Two years previously William Stukeley had visited Stockport and noted that the people 'cut themselves houses in the rock here as at Nottingham', another town built on sandstone. Aikin recorded that on the Underbanks 'some of the houses have apartments hollowed out of the rock, and the appearance of the whole to one who surveys it is very singular'.[85]

New buildings of brick

Another visitor chose to pass comment on a different aspect of Stockport's appearance. 'All the houses of this town were formerly built of oaken timber; this, now, in general has given way to brick', wrote John Byng in 1790, adding that his own lodging place in the town,

the White Lion on Great Underbank, was 'striped and barr'd with as much black timber, as would build a man of war'.[86] Brick, which had been used only sparingly in the seventeenth century, in the early eighteenth century was adopted as the common material for new buildings in the town. Houses with symmetrical facades, sash windows and, where the owner could afford this, a door with a classical-style surround, were now the order of the day (Ill 5.5).

The core of the town became a mixture of the old and the new, as a number of earlier dwellings were rebuilt or remodelled in brick. At Millgate Hall, the town house of the Warrens, the original timber-framed building was dwarfed by two new brick wings, one built in 1732, the other at a somewhat later date.[87]

The present rectory was built in about 1743 by Samuel Stead, rector from 1742 to 1749. Its basement ceiling included beams reused from an earlier timber-

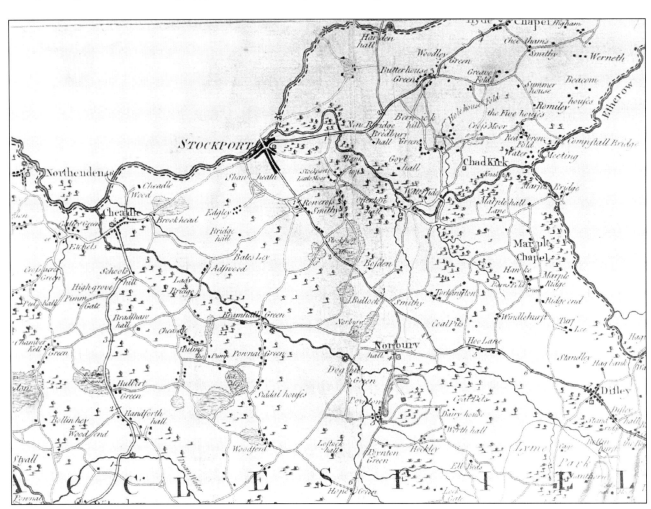

Ill 5.6 Detail of Burdett's map of Cheshire, 1777.

The map shows a pattern of settlement largely based on scattered farmhouses and hamlets. After the town of Stockport, the largest settlement at this date was probably Cheadle village. A sizeable village was also beginning to develop at Bullock Smithy, although its buildings are inexplicably omitted from Burdett's map. The large-scale enclosure of common uncultivated land was under way at this date, but dotted across the landscape there were still areas of mossland and heath.

framed building, probably the rectory shown on the map of the town of about 1680.[88] The size of the Georgian rectory reflects the wealth of the rectorship. We have already noted that by the late medieval period this was among the most profitable benefices in Cheshire. In 1768 the income received by the rector was £1621 5s 4d, of which by far the greatest part, approximately £1310, was derived from tithes.[89] It is also an indication of the wealth of the rectors that, probably in the early nineteenth century, an icehouse was built in the rectory grounds. Such subterranean structures were designed so that ice collected and stored in the winter months would be available throughout the year for use in the owner's kitchen. Icehouses, for all their usefulness in the days before refrigeration, were very much a rare luxury. Sir George Warren had one constructed on his Poynton estate in the late eighteenth century. Another was built in the nineteenth century at Highfield House in Bredbury, the home of a succession of wealthy industrialists.[90]

A cheaper option to rebuilding a house in brick was simply to change its external appearance. At Staircase House the seventeenth-century gabled facade was hidden behind a more fashionable brick frontage, which even seems to have included windows painted on the brickwork to suggest an upper storey.[91]

Leisure

Inns

Stockport's many inns remained a central part of its social life, and increasingly its business life. In the mid-1750s there were thirty-one inns in the township, one for every 100 residents. In 1731 there were at least four inns in the Market Place: the Black Swan, the Ship, the Sun and the Bull's Head. On Millgate was the Blew Stoops, described as an 'ancient' property in 1709 and said to have been replaced by the Arden Arms. Next to Lancashire Bridge, and extending across what later became Warren Street, was the Anchor, a timber-framed building. A passageway, arched over, led through this property to the mills in the Park.[92] The principal hostelry in the eighteenth-century town was the White Lion. This was Stockport's main coaching inn and was the venue for banquets held after meetings of the court leet.[93]

Races, bowling greens and the Assembly Room

Horse races were held on Stockport Great Moor. The earliest recorded meeting here may have been in 1711, the last in 1767. At the meetings in August 1763 and

July 1764 three races were held over as many days, the winner of each receiving £50. These may not have been the first meetings near the town, for in 1677 there is a reference to 'Shawe Heath Race'.[94]

For those in the town seeking leisurely exercise there was a bowling green off Hillgate and another just across Lancashire Bridge in Heaton Norris, next to an inn which was itself known as the Bowling Green (*Ill 5.1*). A third existed, prior to the early nineteenth century, alongside the Mersey at the rear of the White Lion.[95]

Genteel tastes were catered for by the town's Assembly Room, the venue for concerts and balls. It is said to have been a favourite spot for youths to loiter 'to see the ladies arrive in their Sedan chairs, carried by liveried footmen and a torch bearer walking or running in front'. If, as is reported to have been the case, the Assembly Room was in fact part of the grammar school building on Chestergate, attendance must have been very limited. That building, two storeys in height, is said to have been about 36 feet (11 metres) long, by about 16 feet (5 metres) wide, smaller than many a modern village hall.[96]

AGRICULTURE AND THE COUNTRYSIDE

Population and the rural economy

Outside the town of Stockport the population of the Borough was also growing. Between 1664 and 1754 the population of most of the townships which lay in Stockport parish seems to have increased in the order of 40% to 100%. The least populated township in 1754 was Brinnington with only 104 inhabitants, which was probably only a slight increase on the population nearly a century earlier.[97] In 1770 its little community was centred on a group of dwellings set around the fringe of Brinnington Moor, with the southern part of the township being occupied by the Portwood Hall estate. At this date Cheadle was probably still the second largest settlement in the Borough after Stockport. Its buildings lined the main east-west road through the village, with others extending southwards along Wilmslow Road (*Ill 5.6*).

In the eighteenth century the ways in which an individual outside the town might make a living were becoming more diverse. Industry in its various local forms was growing in importance in the countryside as in the town. By the mid-eighteenth century small rows of brick-built cottages were being erected, perhaps most notably at Bredbury Green, probably for the specific use of individuals or families engaged in handloom weaving or other domestic industries.[98] For many in the

Ill 5.7 The Spade Forge, Marple Bridge.
By 1780 many people in the countryside were involved in industry, in particular spinning and weaving, but farming still played an important part in the local economy. In this small water-powered mill, in existence by 1776, agricultural implements were manufactured using a tilt hammer. The forge continued in production until about 1920.

countryside, a trade or craft would not have been their only occupation. The majority are likely to have had some involvement in agriculture, either farming their own plot of land or hiring out their labour to others. It may be a measure of the continuing importance of farming that by 1776 a small water-powered mill was operating on the Mill Brook in Marple Bridge, making agricultural implements using a tilt hammer (*Ill 5.7*).[99]

Farm produce

In 1768 oats, perhaps not surprisingly in view of their importance in the local diet, were the most common arable crop grown in Stockport parish.[100] Not all oats would have been destined for the market, for some would have been consumed on the farm, including as animal feed. Wheat, on the other hand, seems to have

been grown primarily as a cash crop. In the 1770s Mr Burchall, a farmer in the Outwood area (between Heald Green and Handforth), was receiving about £30 a year from the sale of wheat, and a little less from oats. Both crops were sold in bulk, probably to corn factors or to millers who were also involved in the trade.[101] By the mid-eighteenth century potatoes were being grown in the Borough. It was feared that they took nutrients from the soil, and at Bramhall and Werneth landlords limited their tenants to growing only as much as could be consumed by their households. Their cultivation increased towards the end of the century to meet the growing demands of a rapidly increasing population.[102]

Those same requirements also began to bring about a change in pastoral farming. While some cheese sold at Stockport market is likely to have been brought from further afield, much was also produced in the

Borough. In the 1770s Mr Burchall was earning £50 to £100 a year from the sale of this produce.[103] Cheese making, however, tied up labour on a farm and required a necessary period of storage while the product matured. Milk provided a faster return of money but, while transport was restricted to roads, could not be carried any great distance. The farmland close to Stockport was ideally located to make capital out of this market and in the late eighteenth century was perhaps increasingly given over to milk production. In 1776 Edgeley, at this date an agricultural estate beyond the western edge of the town, was advertised for lease as a milk farm. Aikin in 1795 could report that 'The land in the neighbourhood of Stockport is chiefly pasture, and in general very good, supplying the town plentifully with milk and butter'.[104]

Enclosure

By the beginning of the eighteenth century the large-scale enclosure of common uncultivated land was under way in the Borough. The earliest recorded instance may be the enclosure of a large part of Bolshaw Outwood, near Heald Green, between 1699 and 1710, by William Tatton as lord of Etchells, a scheme which appears to have been undertaken solely for his private gain.[105] Enclosure might involve a wider, public benefit. In 1712 an agreement was made between Edward Warren and forty-two principal burgesses to enclose and sell a considerable part of the common land in Stockport township. The intention was that this sale would generate £60 each year in chief rents. Two-thirds of this was to be given to the overseers of the poor to be used as poor relief. A sixth was to be given to the mayor as a salary. The remaining sixth was to provide an additional income for the master of the grammar school. The greater part of the common land lay in the east of the township, and it was here that most of the enclosure under the agreement of 1712 took place, including part of Stockport Great Moor. On the western side of the township, the enclosure included land at Shaw Heath, and the small area of common land known as Heap Ridings, lying between the Mersey and Chestergate.[106]

Elsewhere in the Borough, Bosden Moor was enclosed in 1749, by agreement between Sir George Warren and seven others, who as freeholders in the township could claim a share of this common land.[107]

Ill 5.8 Hill End, Greave, about 1900.
Greave originated as a scattered group of dwellings, including these cottages, built in the mid-eighteenth century on former common land on the western slope of Werneth Low.

In the south-east of Mellor township the common land of Mellor Moor, which had been granted to the local freeholders shortly before the Civil War, was enclosed in 1779. This high ground is still crossed by drystone walls and unmade roads, giving it an appearance which has perhaps changed little since that time. The moorland in the north-east corner of the township was enclosed at an earlier date by the Chethams of Mellor Hall. Here two new farms were established, both of which in 1780 are reported to have had workshops for weaving or hat making.[108] In the township of Romiley in the mid-eighteenth century a farm and cottages were built in the area now known as Greave on newly enclosed land at the western end of Werneth Low. As at Mellor, domestic industries, and in particular weaving, played a part in the economy of this small community (Ill 5.8).[109]

Country houses

Compared with the feverish activity of the late sixteenth and seventeenth centuries, the eighteenth century appears to have seen little new building by the traditional landowning gentry. Offerton Hall, the home of the Wright family, was rebuilt or remodelled in brick at the beginning of that century.[110] Towards its close the Leghs of Booths near Knutsford re-established a residence in the Borough by building an 'occasional dwelling', known as Torkington Lodge, in their manor of Torkington. Their previous residence here, long abandoned, had been at the medieval Broadoak Moat.[111] A new mansion, Cheadle Hall, was built in Cheadle village. Its origin is uncertain, although according to one account it was constructed by the rector of the parish, after he had bought the manor of Cheadle Bulkeley in 1756.[112]

As a whole, the number of traditional wealthy landowners who resided on their estates in the Borough seems to have been in decline. In about the 1720s the local branch of the Davenport family left their Woodford home for the grander surroundings of Capesthorne Hall, thanks to a fortuitous marriage to the heiress of the Capesthorne estate.[113] In Mellor, the Chethams of Mellor Hall in the early eighteenth century purchased the one other large freeholding in the township, Bottoms Hall, whose previous owners now moved to Stockport.[114] Bridge Hall in Adswood had ceased to be a home of the gentry by 1712.[115]

When halls were no longer lived in by their owners, they were usually leased to tenants. In the eighteenth century these were often yeoman farmers, who had neither the money nor the inclination to modernize the building to suit the latest fashion. Nor might such tenants be able or willing to keep the building in good repair. Arden Hall in Bredbury was left in the hands of tenant farmers when the Ardernes moved to a newly acquired property in Yorkshire in about 1790. In the early nineteenth century one occupant had no qualms about tearing down the wooden panelling from the walls of the great hall to burn as fuel, while the paintings which still hung in this room became a target for a child's bow and arrows. More serious structural damage was caused in 1822, when a storm brought one of the chimneys crashing through the roof. By the second half of the nineteenth century the main part of the building was a shell.[116] Norbury Hall, once one of the largest halls in the Borough, was 'ruinous' by 1819.[117] Reddish Hall was demolished, albeit for unknown reasons, in about 1780.[118]

There were, however, some in the eighteenth century who had the resources and ambition to emulate the traditional gentry by building substantial dwellings. These were men who had made their money through manufacture or other professions. Their houses were typically built in a fashionable classical style. Brabyns Hall in Marple was constructed in 1750 for Henry Brabyn, a Stockport physician.[119] Gatley Hall and Gatley Hill House may both have been built in the mid-eighteenth century by local cotton manufacturers, while a third mansion erected in Gatley during this period, High Grove House, was built for a member of a wealthy hatting family of Yorkshire and Manchester.[120]

COAL MINING

Between 1700 and 1780 documentary evidence for mining in the Borough, although still sporadic, is more plentiful than for earlier periods. This was a period in which coal output in the Lancashire coalfield has been estimated to have risen more than tenfold, with the greater part of this growth occurring after 1750.[121] In the Borough itself more coal was required not only to heat the homes of a growing population but also to fuel the local brick-making industry. In 1745 Richard Arderne of Arden Hall bought coal from a local mine-owner for the brick kiln which he had recently erected on his Bredbury estate.[122]

At Norbury coal mining was already in the process of expansion in 1707-8, when one pit was in operation, producing about 700 tons a year, and a second pit was being dug.[123] At Woodley, in Bredbury township, in 1732 a local landowner who had exhausted the seams beneath his own estate leased the right to continue his workings under the neighbouring land of Richard Arderne. By 1762 the Ardernes were themselves involved in mining, operating two pits in Bredbury in

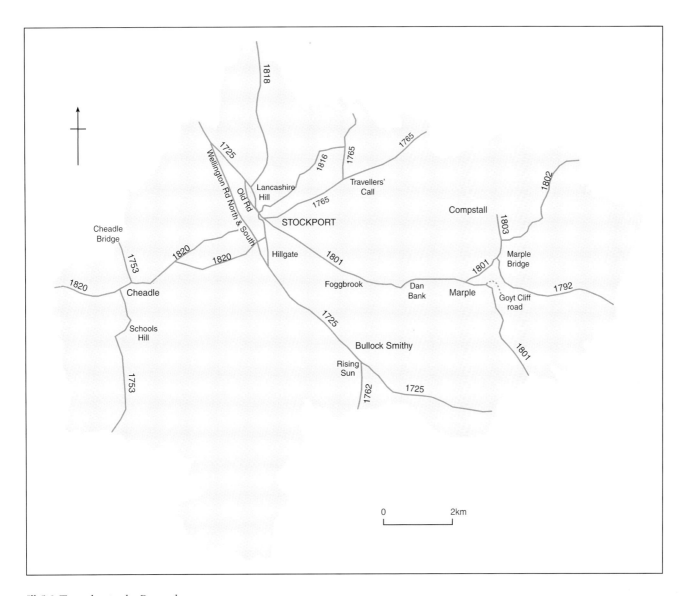

Ill 5.9 Turnpikes in the Borough.
The creation of turnpike roads, whose maintenance costs were paid by the user, greatly improved local transport. Each turnpike was authorized by its own Act of Parliament. The years marked on the map refer to the year in which that Act was passed.

which they employed seven full-time colliers. By the early 1780s only one of these pits was still being worked, with the same total number of men, but the maximum weekly output was nearly three times that twenty years previously.[124]

Rises in production in the eighteenth century were achieved by digging mines of greater size and depth, but this also increased the problems of ventilation and drainage. In the Arderne pits at Bredbury a pump system was used, either to circulate air or to remove water.[125] Drainage might be improved by digging a 'sough', a gently sloping tunnel which carried water out of the mine. In 1780, immediately to the south of the Borough, such a tunnel was dug from the mines below Sir George Warren's Poynton estate to discharge water into Norbury

Brook. Water was also lifted from mines by machinery. This was perhaps most commonly achieved using a horse-powered 'gin', but water-power was also employed. In 1707 it was planned to drain the coal workings at Norbury by a waterwheel sited on the brook.[126] By the mid-1770s a weir across the River Tame near Woodley provided the water for a wheel serving the Ardernes' coal workings.[127]

The first steam engines, known as atmospheric or Newcomen engines after their inventor, were themselves used to pump water from mines. An atmospheric engine was installed at Norbury at some date prior to 1764, when it was advertised for sale. It was reported to be drawing water from a depth of 240 feet (73 metres) and was to be replaced by a larger engine as a result of the

Ill 5.10 Milestone at Schools Hill, Cheadle.
Schools Hill formed part of a turnpike between Manchester and Wilmslow, created by Acts of Parliament passed in 1749 and 1753. This milestone is believed to date from the early nineteenth century.

mine being sunk to an even deeper seam, probably 100-150 feet (30-45 metres) lower. In 1766 the installation of this new engine was used as an argument in favour of a proposed canal which, it was claimed, would allow 10,000 tons of coal a year to be transported from Norbury to Macclesfield.[128] In the event, as we shall see below, rival interests helped to ensure that this canal scheme did not see fruition.

EARLY TURNPIKES AND CANAL SCHEMES

Turnpikes

At the beginning of the eighteenth century responsibility for the upkeep of the highways or main public roads passing through the Borough lay with the parishes and townships, under the supervision of the county JPs. The creation of turnpikes shifted the cost of maintenance onto the road user. A turnpike was a designated section

of road which by an individual Act of Parliament was placed under the management of a group of local trustees. The Acts themselves were usually promoted by wealthy landowners, industrialists and tradesmen. Road users paid a toll collected at gates across the road. (The spikes, or 'pikes', which were set on the gates, gave the turnpike roads their name.) Next to the gate, small cottages were built as accommodation for the toll gate, or 'toll bar', keeper. Money borrowed by the trust, using the tolls as security, paid for providing the road with an adequate surface and for any other improvements. The early turnpike Acts were concerned with existing routeways of national importance, but later Acts also authorized the construction of new, and often more localized, roads.

The first road passing through the Borough to be made a turnpike was that from Manchester to Buxton (*Ill 5.9*). Continuing through Derby, it provided the most direct route between Manchester and London. The Act creating the Manchester and Buxton turnpike trust was passed in March 1725.[129] The significance of this road is underlined by the fact that it was only the second to be turnpiked in Lancashire and Cheshire.[130] In 1739 the section between Manchester and Stockport was reported to be 'five yards in breadth paved throughout' and 'was thought to exceed any in the kingdom of that sort'.[131] In 1749 an Act was passed allowing a branch road from Ardwick Green, near Manchester, to Didsbury also to come under the care of the trust. Four years later a further Act extended this turnpike from Didsbury to Wilmslow, via Cheadle (*Ill 5.10*). This involved the construction of a stone bridge over the Mersey, the forerunner of the present Cheadle Bridge, at or near to the old Cheadle ford.[132]

Other local turnpikes were established in the 1760s. In 1762 a new turnpike was authorized linking Stockport with the south. Branching off the Stockport to Buxton turnpike at Hazel Grove, this turnpike continued as far as Sandon near Stafford. Its course through the Borough is now Macclesfield Road (the A523).[133] This routeway offered an easier, and consequently preferred, alternative for southward-bound traffic than the Manchester to Buxton turnpike, whose original course involved a steep climb and descent beyond Disley.[134] To the north of the Borough, an Act of 1732 allowed the creation of a turnpike from Manchester to Saltersbrook at the head of the Longdendale pass. In 1765 two turnpike roads were authorized between Stockport and this important trans-Pennine route. One was the road linking Stockport with the Saltersbrook turnpike at Mottram (the present A560). The other (the present A6017) branched off

114

this road at Bredbury, and joined with the Saltersbrook turnpike at Audenshaw, near Ashton-under-Lyne. Between 1834 and 1841 a public house, the Travellers' Call, was built at this Bredbury junction.[135]

The improvement of these last two roads was undertaken by the most famous road-builder of the time, John Metcalf or 'Blind Jack' of Knaresborough. He was closely connected with Stockport. While he was involved in road making in Cheshire, his wife took up residence in the town. She died here in 1778 and was buried in the parish churchyard. A daughter of the couple married a Stockport cotton manufacturer. In about 1780 John Metcalf himself took up this same business in the town, beginning with six spinning jennies and a carding engine and later adding looms. He failed to make a success of the venture and, passing his machinery to his son-in-law, returned to road making.[136]

The change in traffic

One consequence of the establishment of turnpikes was an increase in wheeled traffic, which allowed goods to be carried more economically than by packhorse. The Manchester to Buxton road, prior to the passing of the 1725 Act, was described as 'dangerous, narrow and at times impossible'. By as early as 1729, because of widening and other improvements, the shift from packhorses to wheeled carriages along this road had been so great that a second Act of Parliament allowed the tolls to be revised to take this change into account.[137] In 1754 a direct passenger coach service between Manchester and London was begun using this road.[138]

Pickfords, a local firm

One family which took advantage of the profits which might be made from transporting goods during this

Ill 5.11 The Grapes and The Three Tuns, Hazel Grove, in 1910.
Hazel Grove, or Bullock Smithy as it was originally known, owed much of its growth to the traffic along the main turnpike route linking Manchester and Stockport with the Midlands and London. By 1754 the village is believed to have contained about nine inns along this route. The place gained a reputation for lawlessness, and it was to improve its public image that a change of name from Bullock Smithy to Hazel Grove was first mooted in 1795. The problem of maintaining law and order cannot have been helped by the fact that the village straddled four local administrative boundaries. The Grapes (left) was in the township of Norbury, while next door The Three Tuns lay in Bramhall.

115

period were the Pickfords of Poynton, who established the firm which still bears their name. By 1756 James Pickford was operating a twice weekly wagon service between London and Manchester, via Macclesfield and Stockport. His son Matthew increased this service to three times a week in 1777, and in 1788 to six. In the 1780s one local manufacturer who used Pickfords was Samuel Oldknow of Mellor. The firm's wagons carried his muslins to London, and brought back to Mellor raw cotton, money and even a piano.[139]

Bullock Smithy – Hazel Grove

While improved road transportation helped the growth of industry in the Borough, in one locality it was probably the decisive factor behind the rise of a community. The place in question was Bullock Smithy, now known as Hazel Grove. From modest beginnings, by the end of the eighteenth century this had developed into 'a village of considerable length'.[140] Strung along the Manchester to Buxton turnpike, it included parts of the townships of Bramhall, Bosden, Norbury and Torkington.

The earliest known mention of Bullock Smithy dates from 1592. The name has sometimes been supposed to show that cattle drovers once had their animals shod here. However, there can be little doubt that the place was so called after a local person. In 1560 a Richard Bullock of Torkington, a blacksmith, renewed his lease of a property which included a house and smithy. These lay towards the eastern end of the present village, close to the junction of London Road (the A6) with Torkington Road. By the end of the seventeenth century travellers were able not only to have their horses shod here, for in 1674 there is mention of Bullock Smithy Inn.[141]

As traffic increased, other inns were established in this locality, providing places at which coach drivers could change and stable their horses, and passengers could buy refreshments *(Ill 5.11)*. These inns on the Buxton turnpike, of which there are said to have been about nine in 1754, stretched eastwards as far as the Rising Sun at the junction with the turnpike through Poynton.[142] The inns did not stand in isolation. Cottages and houses were built along this same stretch of the Buxton road. Passing trade may have provided one source of livelihood, but

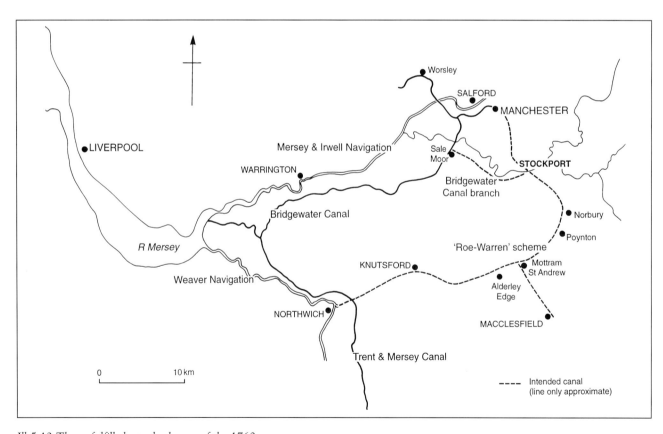

Ill 5.12 The unfulfilled canal schemes of the 1760s.
In the 1760s two rival schemes were proposed which would have provided Stockport with a canal link with Manchester and Liverpool. One scheme involved the creation of a branch from the canal system of the duke of Bridgewater. The other was promoted by Charles Roe, a leading Macclesfield industrialist, and Sir George Warren, the lord of Stockport manor and the owner of coal pits at Poynton. The 'Roe-Warren' scheme was successfully defeated by the duke of Bridgewater in Parliament, but he failed to complete his own canal link to Stockport.

the village also became a centre of domestic industry, and in particular weaving. Henry Marsland began his cotton manufacturing business at Bullock Smithy. Employment might also be found in the nearby coal mines at Norbury and Poynton.[143]

As the village grew, it gained a distinctive reputation. In 1788 John Wesley described Bullock Smithy as 'one of the most famous villages in the country for all manner of wickedness'. Another report said of the place in the early nineteenth century that 'Its inhabitants, colliers, handloom weavers, farm labourers, etc. drank more ale, fought more cock fights and had more rows with one another than the residents of any similar locality, barring Denton'.[144] (This last village, to the north of the Borough, across the Tame, had itself rapidly developed in the late eighteenth century, when it was 'principally occupied by hatters, cotton-spinners, and colliers'.)[145] In the eighteenth and early nineteenth centuries the day-to-day responsibility for maintaining law and order at Bullock Smithy fell to the local constables. Their task cannot have been made easier by the fact that the village was divided by four manorial boundaries.

By 1795 the place's reputation was having a detrimental effect on trade. The proposed solution was simple. If Bullock Smithy was a byword for anti-social behaviour, then why not change the name? At a meeting of the local business community it was decided, with the advice of a local lawyer, to 'Annihilate the name of Bullock Smithy, and revive the ancient and proper name of Hazelgrove'. Where this 'ancient and proper name' was found is uncertain. One possibility is that it was derived from 'Hessel Grave', a name which in the late seventeenth century was attached to the locality of the present Robin Hood Hotel, further to the east along the Buxton road. Whatever its origin, the new name was advertised to travellers on boards set up at either end of the village. Perhaps not surprisingly, the old name, and the reputation of the place, persisted. In September 1836 the name of Hazel Grove was 'revived' for a second time, with a great public celebration which included a procession through the village and the issuing of a souvenir medal. Commemorative celebrations of the 1836 renaming have been held at Hazel Grove every fifty years since.[146]

Early canal schemes

If the turnpike was one platform on which improvements in transport rested in the eighteenth century, the other was the inland waterway. These were of particular use for the transportation of coal and other minerals, goods which involved high costs if carried more than a short distance by road.

In the early 1720s a series of Acts of Parliament allowed a number of rivers in the North-West to be made navigable.[147] These included part of the Mersey and its tributary the Irwell, thus enabling boats to travel between Liverpool and Manchester. The 1750s brought a radical development in inland navigation, with schemes now being proposed for the digging of new waterways, or canals.[148] Among these was the duke of Bridgewater's canal, which was constructed to enable the cheaper transportation of coal from his mines at Worsley. The scheme was the subject of three Acts of Parliament between 1759 and 1762. The result was that the duke had permission to construct not only a canal from Worsley to Manchester but also a branch leading across north Cheshire to the Mersey near Runcorn. This Cheshire section of the Bridgewater Canal provided a rival waterway to the Mersey and Irwell Navigation. It also raised the possibility of a further branch, leading to Stockport.

This matter may have been considered by the duke even before the third Act was passed by Parliament. It is reported that in January 1762 James Brindley, the duke's consulting engineer, made a rapid survey of the course for such a branch, between Stockport and Sale Moor on the proposed line of the duke's Cheshire canal.[149] At this time the scheme does not appear to have been pursued any further. However, three years later, in February 1765, shareholders in the Mersey and Irwell Navigation noted with some alarm that the townspeople of Stockport intended to petition Parliament for the town to be linked to the duke's canal. Plans for this branch had been produced which showed that it would draw water from the Mersey.[150]

How this matter progressed in the following few months is uncertain, but by November 1765 an alternative and more ambitious scheme was being proposed, in which the duke's own canal was to play no part. A new canal was to be built running south from Manchester to Petty Carr Green in Stockport and on to Mottram St Andrew. From here a branch was to lead to Macclesfield, while the main canal was to continue westwards via Knutsford to Witton Bridge near Northwich. Here the new canal was to join with the Weaver Navigation, which had been created under an Act of Parliament of 1721 to link the salt-producing Cheshire 'wiches' with the Mersey (Ill 5.12).[151]

Among the main promoters of this scheme were Charles Roe of Macclesfield and Sir George Warren. Both men had good financial reasons for wanting the canal to be built. Roe, the man behind the first water-powered silk mill in Macclesfield, had co-founded a copper-smelting company in the town in the late 1750s. The proposed canal would have reduced the costs of transporting both ore and the coal required for smelting. By the 1760s Macclesfield's own coal pits were nearing exhaustion, but to the north lay the seams at Norbury and the Poynton estate of Sir George Warren, in close proximity to the proposed canal. As early as 1763 a request had come from Macclesfield for the duke of Bridgewater to build a branch from his own canal to the town, but he had turned this down.[152]

From the outset, what has been termed the 'Roe-Warren' scheme was viewed by the duke with hostility.[153] It has been suggested that personal feelings played a part in this, for in 1758 George Warren had eloped with Jane Revell, to whom the duke had himself been engaged.[154] The duke, however, had his own financial considerations. The prospect of Manchester being linked by canal to Norbury and Poynton threatened his coal trade in the town, while the joining up of the 'Roe-Warren' canal with the Weaver Navigation amounted to competition with his own canal between Manchester and the Mersey.[155]

Evidently in response to this rival scheme, the duke revived the plan to build a branch from his canal at Sale Moor to Stockport. His intention was no doubt to weaken support for the 'Roe-Warren' scheme in Stockport, where his own proposal did indeed find some backing. Dissatisfaction in the town with Sir George Warren's high-handed view of his manorial rights at this period may well have helped the duke's cause. In a further attempt to divide the opposition, he also raised the possibility of a branch from the Sale Moor to Stockport canal, running from Cheadle to Macclesfield.[156]

On the 15th of January 1766 Parliament received a petition from the 'Roe-Warren' camp requesting that their scheme be introduced as a bill. Either by coincidence or design, it was on this same day that petitions for a bill for the duke's own canal to Stockport came from the duke himself and from 'several gentlemen, tradesmen, and others, residing in and near the market town'.[157] The duke, by this date a seasoned campaigner in such matters, had the satisfaction of seeing his own bill passed by Parliament and the 'Roe-Warren' bill being killed off in the Lords, where James Brindley was called to give evidence against it.[158]

The duke had beaten the opposition but his own canal to Stockport, though evidently begun, was never completed. In 1772 it was reported that 'the Duke has already broke ground the length of about two miles, from Sale Moor towards Stockport'. In 1776, ten years after the passing of the Act, the duke was said to be intending to 'finish his Navigation to Stockport' in the following year, an intention which was not fulfilled.[159] His initial delay in constructing this canal may have resulted from the more pressing need to complete the line to Runcorn, which did not finally open in its entirety until 1776. His failure to construct the Stockport canal after that date is more difficult to account for, particularly given that the continuing growth of the town would have made such a link an increasingly lucrative venture. Whatever the reasons for the duke's inaction, the people of Stockport would not acquire a canal link until the 1790s.

LOCAL GOVERNMENT IN STOCKPORT

While the town of Stockport was undergoing an accelerating process of social and economic change, its local government remained largely unaltered. Here, as in other parts of the Borough, local administration was still controlled through the manor, the parish and, above these, the JPs. By the mid-eighteenth century to help regulate the day-to-day business of the town some forty officers were appointed each year by the court leet. Under the terms of the enclosure of 1712 the mayor had received a salary, but by the mid-eighteenth century his right to hear and punish cases of breach of the peace appears to have ceased. This duty now fell to the local JPs. They acted as individual magistrates, although at times they preferred to share responsibility for a final judgement with their colleagues, by deferring the case to the quarter sessions. By the 1760s the rector of Stockport was among those serving as a JP, a practice which continued into the nineteenth century.[160] Since the rectors were themselves chosen by the lord of the manor by a right dating back to the medieval period, their additional appointment as local magistrates may have been particularly welcome to Sir George Warren.

Sir George Warren

George Warren had inherited the lordship of Stockport from his father who died in 1737, when George was aged two. At this date the Warren family was in severe financial difficulty, a situation from which George was saved only by the astute actions of his guardians. This reversal of fortune was completed in 1758 by his marriage to the wealthy heiress Jane Revell. In the same year he entered Parliament as the member for Lancaster and in 1761, at the coronation of George III, was made a Knight of the Bath. Sir George then set his sights on a peerage. It was to this end that he appointed the Reverend John Watson as rector of Stockport. Sir George hoped, in vain as it transpired, that the researches of this antiquarian clergyman might prove him to be the heir to the title of the medieval Warennes, the ancient earls of Surrey.[161]

Despite the financial security brought by his marriage to Jane Revell, Sir George was determined to draw as much profit as possible from his position as lord of the manor of Stockport. As the town was growing, so too were the revenues which might be claimed for the manorial coffers. Unfortunately for Sir George, attitudes in the town towards manorial rule were also changing. Some not only resented what they believed to be unjust profiteering on Sir George's part but also had the confidence to defy him openly. The leaders of this opposition were, according to Sir George himself, 'people who live in new-erected burgages, and have not a perch of land to their burgage nor an acre in the fields according to the charter'. In other words, these were relative newcomers to the town, presumably manufacturers and tradesmen, people with no long-standing sense of loyalty to the manorial lord.[162]

The quarrel was at its bitterest in 1767 over the issue of common land. Sir George had enclosed a plot of the commons next to the Mersey at Petty Carr Green. In a scheme which was a forerunner of the erection of Castle Mill in the next decade, he planned to erect here a new industrial building, probably a silk mill. His opponents in the town argued that the burgesses should be compensated for this loss of common land. Believing that this would justify their claim, they demanded that Sir George should produce his copy of the borough's medieval charter (the original had been lost). When he refused, a public meeting of all burgesses was called, at which it was decided to present him formally with their grievances. Hard-liners among them, however, rejected negotiation and threatened to demolish any building which Sir George might build on any part of the commons.[163]

There were other causes of resentment. All freeholders in the town were required to be formally enrolled as burgesses at the court leet and to attend subsequent meetings of that body. Those who refused to be enrolled or failed to attend the court could be fined. For the 'privilege' of enrolment, Sir George charged 5s, but some freeholders would not pay this. They argued that they should pay no more than 4d, the figure stipulated in the medieval charter.[164] Even bricks became a subject of dispute. The principal source of clay for brick making in the township was the common land. In the 1760s, a time when the local demand for bricks was outstripping the supply, Sir George was selling clay from the common land to brick makers from outside Stockport, from whom the burgesses had to buy bricks which they felt were rightfully their own.[165]

These were not the only matters in which Sir George was eager to preserve and extend what he believed to be his manorial rights. There had been a manorial bakehouse at the foot of Mealhouse Brow since at least the seventeenth century. Sir George had invested in two new bakehouses here and objected to the presence of other bakers in the town. Burgesses were still required

to grind their corn at the manorial cornmills, and Sir George also attempted to impose a toll on corn which had been ground and bought outside Stockport.[166]

A close eye was kept on the Market Place. To avoid paying rent for a stall and a toll on the commodities which they sold, traders were hiring nearby rooms or shops from which to conduct their business. The practice was not peculiar to Stockport (it is also reported in Macclesfield in the 1750s), but the response may have been. The market, Sir George threatened, would be moved to one of his fields. Cheesemongers who chose to operate in the Market Place were required to have their produce weighed, at a charge, on the lord's scales. That the same charge should be made to burgesses and non-burgesses alike was a further cause of discontent.[167] Perhaps it was to avoid such difficulties that in 1776 and for some years afterwards Sir George leased the collection of market tolls. Surviving records until 1784 show that the lessee made an increasing loss.[168]

Improvement schemes

With Sir George Warren concerned with protecting his financial interests, it was left to others to try to address the problems posed by the growing town. Petty crime was one anxiety. In 1762 a voluntary subscription was begun to pay for the town to be lit at night with forty-five lights. In 1773 an association was established to catch and prosecute criminals. It may not be coincidental that the same year saw high unemployment in the town resulting from the slump in the silk industry. Other such associations followed in the 1780s.[169]

More far-reaching improvements could not be achieved without an Act of Parliament. In 1775 a petition 'of the inhabitants and owners of houses and lands' in the township was put before Parliament requesting permission to submit a bill. Under its provisions, powers would be given to light the town and relieve the problem of traffic by widening its streets. To pay for those measures there was to be a new local rate.[170] No more is heard of this particular proposal. Perhaps the idea of the rate created opposition within Stockport itself.[171] Ten years later a second, more ambitious, improvement scheme was put before Parliament, but again without success. Stockport's attainment of a local government which matched its requirements as an expanding and industrializing town would be a slow, piecemeal process.

THE 'FORTY-FIVE'

In the winter of 1745, just a century after the capture of Stockport by the Royalist forces of Prince Rupert, an army was again to pass unwelcome through the

Ill 5.13 Hatherlow Chapel, Bredbury, about 1905.
In the early eighteenth century local nonconformists began to erect purpose-built chapels. Hatherlow Chapel was opened in 1706 by a congregation which had previously met at Chadkirk Chapel in neighbouring Romiley. The local influence of Hatherlow Chapel was particularly strong. In 1754 there were three times as many nonconformist families in Bredbury, Romiley and Werneth as families adhering to the Church of England.

Borough. These were the Jacobite troops of Bonnie Prince Charlie, who had invaded England to overthrow the Hanoverian George II and place his father James Stuart on the throne. Their march south from Scotland took them through Cumbria and Lancashire, meeting only feeble resistance at Carlisle.[172] To impede the Jacobites' progress the order was given for the bridges over the Mersey to be destroyed. The task fell to troops of the Liverpool Blues, a recently raised regiment of volunteers. Lancashire Bridge at Stockport was breached early in the morning of the 27th of November.[173] The next day the prince arrived with his army in Manchester.

On the 30th the Jacobites sent out advance parties from Manchester to find a suitable crossing point over the Mersey. One group of some fifty-five men proceeded to Gatley ford, and passing through Cheadle crossed the river again by Cheadle ford. On that same day others entered Stockport by the ford above the demolished bridge. At both Stockport and Macclesfield they attempted to enlist men into the prince's army, but with little or no success. That same night and early the following morning the main army advanced into Cheshire, with Macclesfield as its next goal. The cavalry and artillery crossed at Cheadle ford, where a bridge was

hastily put together from tree trunks and planks. Contemporary sources differ as to the prince's own crossing point. According to one account, this too was at Cheadle ford, but another says that marching on foot with his infantry he forded 'the river above Stockport, which took him up to the middle', a reference which should be to the ford near Lancashire Bridge.[174]

From their temporary base at Manchester the rebels had requisitioned such horses as they could find.[175] It is said that a Stockport butcher, returning to the town from Gorton, heard that the rebels were seizing horses in Reddish and decided to make a detour of the place. He was himself mistaken for a rebel and was shot at and fatally wounded.[176] At Stockport the churchwardens took the precaution of hiding the church plate.[177] In the town, as at other places along their march, the Jacobites collected for their own use excise duties normally paid to the crown.[178]

The Jacobite march south, which was intended to end in triumph in London, finished in an acrimonious council of war at Derby. Having failed to raise the expected support in England, the prince's advisors pressed for a retreat. On the night of the 7th of December Jacobite troops were arriving back in

Macclesfield, while a few were already on the road between Stockport and Manchester. Advance parties found the Mersey crossing more difficult than on the outward journey. At Cheadle ford a force of 400 or 500 men under a Captain Hilton of Manchester stood guard. Four rebels who rode through the ford at Stockport were fired at by the night watch, and one of their horses hit. When the Jacobites arrived at Stockport in force, their mood was grim. In reprisal for the attack on their comrades, they threatened to burn down the town and hang the constable, who along with several others was led off to Manchester. Several people in the town were wounded by the rebels' swords.[179]

Jacobite troops are reported to have been billeted for the night in Stockport under the command of Lord Elcho.[180] On the 10th, however, their army was moving northwards from Manchester. By this time government forces were in close pursuit. When these passed through Stockport the churchwardens ordered the bells to be rung for two and a half days. The next year they would ring again when news reached the town of the Jacobites' defeat at Culloden.[181]

The excise duties which tradesmen had paid to the Jacobites were subsequently written off by the government, which also footed the bill for the rebuilding of the Mersey bridges.[182] Traumatic as the experience may have been for those who lived through it, 'the Forty-five' was, to borrow a phrase used of this event at Macclesfield, an 'irrelevant irruption' in the life of the Borough.[183]

RELIGION

Nonconformity

It is a measure of the strength of the local groups of nonconformists in the early eighteenth century that in place of the private houses and barns in which they had previously met they now began to erect meeting houses and chapels. To the south-west of the Borough such a chapel had already been built by the Presbyterians at Dean Row in the late seventeenth century. In 1702 the Congregationalists erected a chapel on Middle Hillgate in Stockport. Known as the Tabernacle, this is believed to have been the first purpose-built nonconformist meeting place in the Borough. In 1721 a split within the congregation resulted in the building of a Presbyterian chapel on High Street. This was the third purpose-built dissenters' meeting house in Stockport, for in 1705-6 the Quakers had erected a meeting house on Lower Hillgate.[184]

Two new nonconformist chapels were built during this same period outside the town. Chadkirk Chapel in Romiley had been registered as a dissenters' meeting place since 1689. In 1705, after the Chadkirk estate had changed hands, the minister, Gamaliel Jones, and his congregation were told that the building was no longer available for their use. Their response was to buy land at Hatherlow in Bredbury and build a new chapel there (Ill 5.13).[185] At Mill Brow in Ludworth a chapel was built in 1716 for a congregation which had previously met in an adjoining barn.[186] Some dissenters continued to meet where best they could. A meeting place in Etchells registered in 1722 may perhaps have been a house in Gatley.[187]

The largest of the nonconformist groups in the Borough in the early eighteenth century were the Presbyterians and the Congregationalists or Independents. In about 1715 the congregation of the Tabernacle was said to be 629, that of Hatherlow 300, and that of Dean Row as many as 1309, the largest nonconformist congregation at this time in Cheshire.[188] In 1730 at Mill Brow a visiting minister delivered a sermon to 'a very great congregation from all parts about', some crowding into the chapel, others standing outside, and many wet from the day's rain.[189] As also seems to have been the case in the seventeenth century, local Quakers were much fewer in number. Most appear to have lived in Stockport, where ten Quaker families were recorded in 1754. In the Cheshire part of the Borough, one or two Quaker families are also recorded from the early to mid-eighteenth century in Gatley, Cheadle and Offerton.[190]

After the 1720s the strength of nonconformity in Cheshire appears to have decreased, until it entered a revival towards the end of the eighteenth century.[191] The evidence from the Borough suggests that, while there were local variations, the long-established tradition of religious dissent continued to draw strong support. In one township in Stockport parish, Norbury, there does seem to have been a sharp decline in numbers. In 1722 Norbury and neighbouring Poynton are said together to have contained 145 families, half of whom were Presbyterian and Independent. By 1754 the number of nonconformist families in Norbury had been reduced to three, while in 1778 there was only one. The reason for this near-disappearance of nonconformity in a township which was once home to the hard-line Presbyterian Edward Hyde is uncertain, but the influence of the Leghs of Lyme may be suspected. They were both patrons of Norbury Chapel and lords of the manor.[192]

However, in 1754, across Stockport parish as a whole, dissenters accounted for more than a third of families.[193] The local influence of Hatherlow Chapel was particularly strong. In Bredbury, Romiley and Werneth in that year there were roughly three times as many dissenting families as families adhering to the Church of England. In 1778 it was said of Romiley and neighbouring townships that the people were 'almost all Presbyterian...they increase as the population increases', although the force of this statement is somewhat lessened by the fact that these so-called 'Presbyterians' were also said to include a number of Methodists. The register of baptisms carried out by the ministers of Hatherlow between 1732 and 1781 indicates that the congregation also included members scattered across much of the Cheshire part of the Borough, from Cheadle in the west to Marple in the east.[194] At Stockport in 1778 the best that the Reverend Watson could report about the strength of local nonconformists was that their number was not on the increase. The parish of Cheadle, according to its rector, contained 'great numbers' of dissenters.[195] That the rising tide of nonconformity in the Borough was stemmed in the mid-eighteenth century may be suggested by the apparent halt to the building of new chapels. It does not, however, appear to have been significantly turned back. By the late 1770s there is one local piece of evidence of a new expansion, with the building in 1779 of an Independent chapel at Gatley by a congregation which for at least two years previously had met in a private house.[196]

The Anglican Church

In the mid-eighteenth century the number of Anglican places of worship in the Borough was on the increase, with the building of a second church at Stockport, the construction of a new chapel in the township of Heaton Norris and the reinstatement of the old chapel at Chadkirk. After the departure of the nonconformist congregation from Chadkirk in 1705, the chapel remained unused as a place of worship for over thirty years. In the meantime the building was converted to a cowshed. In 1703 the owner of the Chadkirk estate, Reginald Bretland, had left the modest sum of £5 a year towards the salary of an Anglican curate at the chapel, with the hope that this figure would be matched by the rector of Stockport. It was not until 1747 that sufficient money was made available to fund both this post and what was by then a much needed restoration of the building (*Ill 3.19*). Money for this work is said to have been provided by members of the local gentry, among these being George Nicholson, the owner of the Chadkirk estate who in 1755 was buried beneath the chapel's communion table.[197]

A proposal to build a church in Heaton Norris in the parish of Manchester had been put forward as early as 1650. In the event, such a building was not erected until the construction between 1758 and 1765 of St Thomas's, paid for by voluntary contributions. Situated by the junction of Wellington Road (the present A6) and Manchester Road, it gave the north-eastern part of the township of Heaton Norris the name of Heaton Chapel.[198] In Stockport, St Peter's Church was built in 1768, amidst what were then fields and gardens at the western end of the town (*Plate IV & Ill 5.2*). The money was provided by William Wright, a wealthy landowner. He was the lord of Offerton and Mottram St Andrew, and owned land and property in Stockport, where he built as his town house the Mansion House on High Street. Wright also constructed a new road linking that street with the church. As St Petersgate, this routeway subsequently helped open up this part of the town for development.[199]

In addition to these new Anglican churches, the seating capacity of existing church buildings was increased by the installation of wooden galleries. At Stockport parish church a wooden gallery had been installed as early as 1697. Eventually there were four in the church, all of which are said to have been in place by about 1747.[200] At St Thomas's in Mellor the first gallery was built in the 1730s. Two others were added in 1783, increasing the seating capacity to 700 but with unfortunate results for the building itself. The galleries caused the church walls to bulge to such an extent that in the early nineteenth century most of the church had to be rebuilt, leaving only the tower from the medieval building.[201]

In some cases there appears to have been a direct and simple relationship between the local strength of the Anglican Church and nonconformity: the greater the one, the lesser the other. Chadkirk Chapel, prior to its reinstatement in 1747, had not been used as a place of Anglican worship for roughly sixty years. In the meantime a local nonconformist congregation had flourished first at Chadkirk itself and then at Hatherlow. The installation of a gallery at the west end of Chadkirk Chapel in 1761 has been interpreted as evidence of a growing attendance. However, in 1778 the congregation was described as 'small', consisting mostly of 'weavers or labouring people', and with only eight or ten members taking communion. The parish authorities seem to have done little to help the situation. There were no funds set aside for repairs to the building and in thirty years the churchwardens of Stockport parish had presented the chapel with only two worn surplices, and an old Common Prayer Book which was so tattered that the minister had to conduct services from memory.[202] At Norbury, by contrast, with its solitary dissenting family, absenteeism from services in the chapel by local Anglicans was said to be unknown. Given that the township included part of Bullock Smithy it might be wondered whether this was an entirely accurate picture. Certainly elsewhere in the Borough in 1778 ministers were reporting non-attendance among their parishioners.[203]

Non-attendance

Absenteeism from church, for reasons other than religious dissent, was already a problem for the local church authorities in the late seventeenth century, despite the fact that non-attendance was punishable by a fine.[204] In the eighteenth century in churches and chapels in the Borough, as indeed across the country, the number of absentees increased. Some kept away out of choice, preferring to spend their Sundays in other ways, and encouraged by the fact that church authorities were now abandoning the practice of fining non-attendance. At Marple there were some twenty miners and others who would 'not be prevailed upon to attend any place where public worship is performed'.[205] Others may have kept away reluctantly. Despite the establishment of new churches and the installation of galleries, seating capacity may not have kept pace with the rise of population. Most seating in churches was in any case privately owned or rented, a system which would have debarred many of the worse off. In Stockport parish church in 1810 there were 124 pews altogether, of which only twenty were free.[206]

It was in Stockport, of all the places in the Borough, that the church seems to have been faced with the greatest dislike or indifference. In 1778 the Reverend Watson reported that even Anglicans in the town often had their children baptized not in the parish church but by nonconformist or Methodist ministers. Given the quarrel between Sir George Warren and a number of the townspeople, attitudes may have been hardened by the fact that the rector was his own appointee, particularly in the case of the Reverend Watson. His antiquarian research, which included not only his investigation into the ancestry of the Warrens but also the completion of his history of Halifax, perhaps left him little time to devote to his duties as rector. Watson himself appears to have taken an unsympathetic view of his parishioners, blaming non-attendance on the failure of the churchwardens to fine absentees.[207]

A documented case of public dislike of a local minister concerns Chadkirk Chapel. In 1747, shortly after it had been rebuilt, the preacher John Bennet advised a number of his followers against attending the chapel. The minister, he had learnt, was not only overcharging for pew rents but also 'did frequently go a hunting, shooting &c and which was worse co'd sware and did actually do so'.[208] Bennet himself represented a new force attempting to revive religious beliefs, that of evangelicalism.

Evangelicalism and Methodism

The early evangelistic movement saw the formation of small societies of worshippers meeting in private houses and visited by itinerant preachers whose services were often held in the open air. Although the movement is most commonly associated with John Wesley, there were other pioneers. The first evangelical preacher in the region was David Taylor, who was active in north-east Cheshire and north-west Derbyshire in the early 1740s and whose converts included John Bennet of Chinley. In 1743 Bennet joined John Wesley's own Methodist movement and was by then serving as a full-time preacher, visiting in turn the societies of converts which had already been established in the locality and organizing new ones. In the Borough the first societies to be founded appear to have been at Woodley, Marple and Ludworth. Bennet added a new society at Bramhall in 1743, but in the following year this was one of several Cheshire groups which turned instead for preachers to the sect known as the Moravians. (A Moravian chapel and minister's residence were erected in the township in about 1771 on a site, at the west end of Bullock Smithy, which became known as Chapel Houses.)[209] Later in 1744 the remaining groups under Bennet's leadership were visited for the first time by Charles and John Wesley. On a visit to Mellor in the following year, John Wesley recorded in his diary how he rode to the farmhouse known as the Banks, 'a lone house on the side of a high, steep mountain wither abundance of people were got before us'.[210]

Although in such rural areas Methodist preachers might receive a warm reception, the situation was very different in the towns where their presence could result in mob violence. It was not until 1748 that Bennet preached to a society in Stockport. In the following year he was prevented from entering the society's meeting place by a crowd which had been incited by 'some young tradesmen in the town'. To the sound of the beating of a drum, the mob even marched off to Shaw Heath on the rumour that Bennet was to preach there instead.[211]

Within the ranks of the Stockport society, personal loyalty to Bennet was strong. When he and Wesley quarrelled and went their separate ways in 1752, all but two members of the society followed Bennet. The setback for mainstream Methodism was only temporary. John Bennet's circuit was now reorganized, with its centre at

Ill 5.14 Hillgate Methodist Chapel.
Methodism originated as an evangelical movement, intended to bring about a religious revival. In 1759 a purpose-built chapel was erected by local Methodists in Stockport, the first of its kind in Cheshire. This was replaced by a larger chapel, shown here, in 1781.

Manchester and its visiting preachers appointed by Wesley. In the 1750s popular hostility in the towns began to decrease. Wesley himself visited Stockport in 1759 and preached without disturbance 'on a green near the town's end'. In that same year local Methodists felt confident enough to build a chapel on Hillgate. Although the building was small, without pews and with only a second-hand pulpit, it was nevertheless the first purpose-built Methodist meeting place to be erected in Cheshire.[212]

At this date Methodists did not see themselves as a separate church. The movement had been begun in order to make up for what its founders considered to be shortcomings in the Church of England, but it was part of Methodist teaching that society members should still attend Anglican services, particularly for communion. When in 1747 John Bennet voiced criticism about Chadkirk Chapel, he did so to members of his own 'brethren' who were considering attending the chapel, and his words were directed against the minister, not their wish to attend an Anglican place of worship. It was only after the death of John Wesley in 1791 that Methodism developed into a distinctive church, creating in the process divisions within its ranks.[213]

John Wesley's own tireless journeys to visit local societies and to win new converts brought him repeatedly to the Borough. Between 1759 and 1790 he visited Stockport no fewer than seventeen times. In 1764, when he again preached on one of the township's areas of common land, 'a few wild men strove to make a disturbance, but none regarded them'. The number of converts did not always live up to Wesley's expectation.

Ten years later he preached at what he described as 'poor, dull, dead Stockport, not without hopes that God would raise the dead'.[214]

Evidence for the number of Methodists in the Borough before the very end of the eighteenth century is scarce.[215] In 1778 it was reported that there were seven Methodist families in the township of Marple and that this figure represented a considerable decrease in recent years. The curate of Chadkirk at this date, on the other hand, noted that 'That sect certainly increases'.[216] In Stockport Methodists were sufficiently numerous by 1781 to warrant the demolition of the Hillgate chapel and its replacement with a larger building *(Ill 5.14)*. Five years later Stockport became the head of a circuit.[217]

The second Methodist chapel to be opened in the Borough was in 1786 at Bullock Smithy. Wesley's own views on the place, expressed in 1788, have already been noted. The chapel is said to have been originally built in about 1774 for the Reverend David Simpson, who had been a curate at Macclesfield parish church. While most Anglican clergymen viewed the spread of Methodism with distrust, Simpson was a friend of Wesley. His sympathy for the evangelical movement resulted in the loss of his Macclesfield curacy, but later in the 1770s he was appointed minister at a new Anglican church in Macclesfield, built especially for him by the industrialist Charles Roe.[218] In the late eighteenth century evangelicalism was also spreading to the old nonconformist groups. It seems to have provided the impetus for the Congregational group at Gatley first to employ a full-time minister and in 1779 to build their chapel.[219]

CHAPTER SIX

THE DOMINATION OF COTTON, 1780-1842

'The chief dependence of the town at present is on the vast number of power looms at work herein'

INTRODUCTION

Between the 1780s and the 1830s industry within the Borough underwent a truly massive expansion. At the centre of this growth lay the spinning and weaving of cotton, activities which during this period transformed a considerable part of the region. The heart of this textile industry was Manchester. It was both a major producer of cotton yarn and cloth and the commercial centre for the region's wider cotton-manufacturing area. This encompassed not only south-east Lancashire but also neighbouring parts of Cheshire and Derbyshire. Cotton made this into one of the foremost manufacturing districts in the country, supplying an international as well as the home market.

That Stockport had once played a part in the cotton industry may be deduced from the mill buildings which still stand in and around the town. However, the number of such buildings, much reduced in the late twentieth century, belies the magnitude of Stockport's actual role. By the early nineteenth century cotton mills dominated the townscape. They lined the river banks and dotted the higher ground on both sides of the Mersey valley. 'Mills and factories rise out of the dense mass of houses', wrote a commentator in 1842, 'and around, a forest of chimneys shoot into the air' *(Ill 6.1)*.[1] One visitor in 1814 believed that 'the town promises to become a second Manchester'. Indeed, within the region at that time only Manchester surpassed Stockport as a cotton-spinning centre.[2]

Stockport may well have held that rank from the 1780s. The first cotton mills in the region had been established in the late 1770s. They included one at Stockport itself, the curiously designed Castle Mill. However, factories had been built in the town for over forty years before that time, to house the silk industry. In the 1780s the silk mills provided a ready-made stock of suitable buildings, some of which were quickly converted to cotton. No less important was the fact that, thanks to the silk industry, there also already existed a sizeable workforce used to factory work. Water-power had been the main motive force in the town's silk mills, as it was also to be in the region's first cotton mills. At Stockport new, purpose-built cotton mills were erected which were powered by the local rivers, and water-power continued to play an important part in the cotton industry long after the introduction of steam. Water also drove the machinery in a number of mills built outside the town. The township with the greatest number of such sites was Mellor, where steep, fast-flowing streams were most abundant. The earliest rural mills were generally smaller than their urban counterparts. One notable exception was the Mellor Mill of Samuel Oldknow, a figure of national significance in the cotton industry.

The rise of that industry played a major part in a considerable increase in the population of the Borough in the late eighteenth and early nineteenth centuries. It has been estimated that from the late 1780s onwards up to three-quarters of the population of Stockport and the surrounding area 'was supported by wages earned in this industry – either as workers or their dependents'.[3] The greatest rise in population was at Stockport itself.[4] To accommodate the swelling numbers the town expanded. At times its growth reached proportions which amazed contemporary commentators. In Stockport township much of this expansion occurred within the Hillgate area, but the urban spread also extended beyond the township boundary, to neighbouring parts of Heaton Norris, to Portwood and to Edgeley *(Ill 7.1)*.

The development of the local, and regional, cotton industry from the 1780s was not one of continual growth, but rather was subject to a series of economic booms and slumps. Particularly damaging was the depression which began to be felt in Stockport in 1837 and from which the town did not show signs of recovery until 1843.[5] Although other parts of the region's cotton district experienced hardship during this period, Stockport appears to have been hit especially hard. A government commission of enquiry, dispatched to the town in January 1842, was offered several explanations for the severity of its distress. Some blame was laid at the door of mill-owners who had borrowed heavily to upgrade their operations during a boom in the mid-1830s, but were now unable to meet repayments and were forced out of business. The age of some of Stockport's factories was also identified as a cause. The town's long involvement in the cotton industry meant that the buildings and machinery of some firms were too antiquated to allow them to remain competitive. Some blamed the wage levels of the town's factory workers, which were the highest in the cotton district with the possible exception

Ill 6.1 *Stockport, looking north-west from the Stockport Sunday School, about 1921.*
In the late eighteenth and early nineteenth centuries the cotton industry transformed Stockport. Cotton mills dominated the town, which greatly expanded as new houses were built for its swelling population.

of Manchester.[6] Whatever the reasons were for the particular difficulties of Stockport's cotton industry during these years, following the depression the town experienced a prolonged period of stagnation. While other cotton towns in the region continued to grow, for over three decades the population of Stockport either remained virtually unchanged or even fell. It would not resume its growth until the local cotton industry itself experienced a revival. By the early 1880s, when that revival was under way, Stockport had fallen to fifth in a league table of the region's cotton-spinning towns.[7]

Between the initial upsurge in the early 1780s and the slump more than fifty years later, the shape of the cotton industry in the Borough altered considerably. At the heart of this transformation lay the introduction of new machinery. The beginnings of that process can be traced to the 1770s. Prior to that decade local manufacturers had been dependent on a putting-out system, with spinning and weaving taking place in the workers' own homes. In the 1770s, with the advent of carding engines and jennies, manufacturers themselves began to undertake some of the processes of production on their own premises. In the closing decades of the eighteenth century, powered cotton mills and new spinning machinery would vastly increase the output of yarn, and cause the demise of the domestic spinning industry. That increase in output also produced a massive growth in weaving. Mechanization of this branch of the industry lagged behind that of spinning. However, in the early nineteenth century the development of a powered weaving machine or 'powerloom' shifted the process to the factory and effectively brought about the end of domestic cotton handloom weaving.

As well as tracing changes in the cotton industry, this chapter will examine four other industries: silk, hatting, coal mining and engineering. We will also look at the changing face of the Borough's transport system on which these various industries were dependent: the extension of the turnpike system, the arrival of the canals and, in the early 1840s, of the railways. Social and political developments which occurred in this period, themselves often of a momentous character, will be examined in the next chapter.

COTTON FACTORIES AND COTTON FIRMS IN STOCKPORT, 1780-1820

The growth of the town's factories

The early rise of the cotton mill in Stockport was dramatic. In 1780 Castle Mill was the only such building in the town. There were also a number of 'cotton works', probably workshops lacking the use of water-power. Fifteen years later, John Aikin reported that 'The cotton trade at Stockport is now so considerable, that besides a large number of cotton spinning shops, there are twenty-three large factories'.[8] Some of these were former silk mills, but others had been purpose-built for the cotton industry. As that industry expanded, a mill-owner might add one or more factories to his site, which could also include other buildings such as warehousing. Many of the larger mills in Stockport were built by this piecemeal process.[9]

The first great burst of factory building in the town's cotton industry appears to have occurred in the early 1790s. This activity was temporarily curtailed by a crisis in the national economy in 1792-3 as war between England and France first became a likelihood and then a reality. The crisis saw the bankruptcy of a number of Stockport businesses. It also helped bring about the closure of the town's first bank, founded in 1791, which had provided credit during the pre-war building boom.[10] A revival in the industry's fortunes in the mid-1790s gave way to a slump in 1797-8, but the following years until 1803 seem to have witnessed a new spurt of factory building in Stockport, as elsewhere in the region. The period from 1803 (when war with France resumed after a short-lived peace) to 1817 was characterized by a number of difficult years for the cotton industry and, overall, seems to have seen a more moderate growth in the number of factories in the town.[11] Nevertheless, in 1815, according to John Corry, 'Stockport and its vicinity contained forty large buildings occupied by cotton spinners'.[12]

Early water-powered mills

The Marslands and Park Mills

One of the town's largest concentrations of cotton factories was situated in the Park, in the bend of the Mersey and the Goyt. In 1780 there was already a group of water-powered buildings here, comprising the manorial cornmill, the town's first silk mill and the former logwood mill. Three years later the silk mill became one of the town's first cotton mills, when it was bought by Henry Marsland of Bullock Smithy.[13] It was an astute purchase. Marsland's business was now located on the prime water-power site in the town, and next to the existing mill buildings was vacant land, ripe for further expansion. From 1789 to 1791 Marsland was busy buying from Sir George Warren, the lord of the manor, neighbouring plots on which factory buildings were to be erected. Water for these factories was provided by the millrace which had been constructed in the 1740s from a point on the Goyt above New Bridge and which for much of its length was carried through tunnels (*Ill 6.5*). Until 1791 the cornmill in the Park and the millrace were the property of Sir George, but in that year these too were bought by Henry Marsland. With them came the right to build further tunnels. In the early 1790s others, John Collier and Abraham Illingworth, acquired land in the Park for their own factories.[14]

Henry Marsland retired from his business on the 1st of January 1792, passing the reins on to his two sons. The elder son, Samuel, left the firm about three years later for a new partnership with a Manchester spinning company. The younger, Peter, was now in sole charge of Stockport's most powerful cotton firm.[15] William Radcliffe later wrote that the name of Peter Marsland carried great weight 'in Glasgow, London etc; wherever the cotton trade was mentioned'.[16] Part of Marsland's wealth was spent on the purchase of his own country estate, Woodbank, to the east of the town. There he had a new residence built between 1812 and 1814 to a design by Thomas Harrison, one of the leading architects of the day (*Ill 7.6*).[17] Both the Park and Woodbank, as we shall see in the following chapter, figured in another of Peter Marsland's ventures, the provision of a public water-supply to the town.

A nineteenth-century local song described the Marslands' Park Mills, with an understandable exaggeration, as 'half-a-mile long'.[18] Their site is now occupied by Sainsbury's, but the importance of water-power to these mills is still evident from a row of great arched openings in a surviving wall on the riverside. Through these the water which had been brought along the tunnel system to turn the mills' waterwheels was discharged into the Mersey (*Ill 6.2*). In 1851 this same riverside site was the scene of one of the town's worst disasters. Twenty-two lives were lost when one of the factories of the Park Mills caught fire after a boiler exploded (*Ill 6.3*).[19]

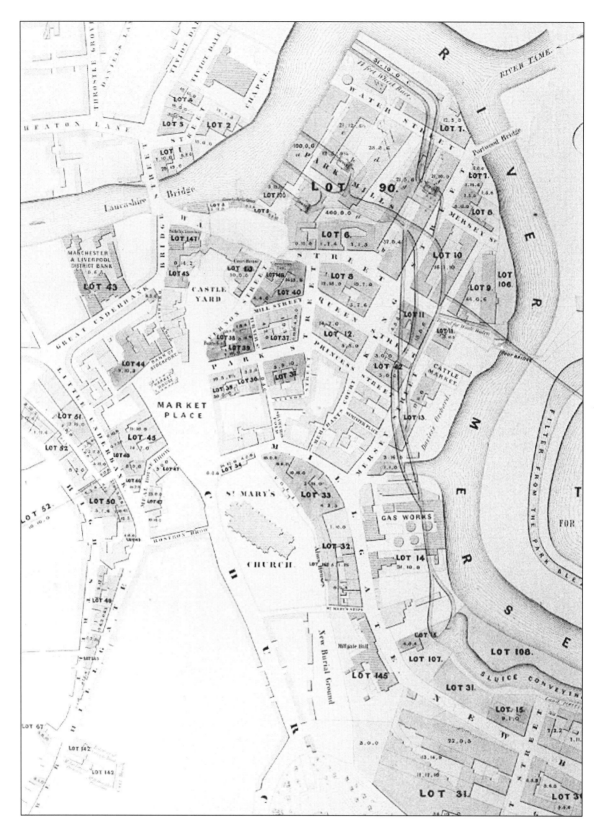

Ill 6.2 Detail of plan of Stockport showing millrace tunnels to the Park Mills, 1850.
Water-power played a key role in the early growth of Stockport's cotton industry. Despite the development of the steam engine, mill-owners continued to use water-power as a cheaper means of driving their factories. The Park Mills were fed by a network of tunnels. The mills themselves were demolished in the late 1970s, but the arched openings through which water was discharged into the Mersey can still be seen along its bank.

Ill 6.3 The Park Mills fire, 1851.
One of the earliest depictions of the Park Mills was drawn for the Illustrated London News *to show the disastrous fire which occurred there on the 17th of March 1851. A boiler exploded, hurling itself through the air and embedding itself in a factory in its path, setting the building on fire. Twenty-two lives were lost.*

Mills and weirs along the Mersey

To the west of the Park, by the mid-1790s there were five new water-powered cotton mills along the Mersey as far as Brinksway. Next to these factories their owners built weirs across the river, to build up a sufficient head of water to turn their waterwheels.[20] In 1794 the owner of a weir which crossed the river opposite Adlington Square was ordered to reduce its height, after the owners of mills downstream complained of their own lack of water.[21] One of these complainants was John Collier. As well as owning a mill in the Park and the former silk mill in Adlington Square, he had built two mills facing each other across the Mersey, with a weir strung between them. The waterwheels of both factories seem to have been located in small wings which projected into the river *(Ill 6.4)*. The lower part of one of these two wheelhouses, at the aptly named Weir (or Wear) Mill, still survives and is possibly Stockport's oldest remaining mill structure.[22]

New Bridge Lane

To the east of the town, in the early 1790s a large factory complex was rising along New Bridge Lane.

It was served by its own millrace tunnel bringing water from above a weir on the Goyt. This barrier became known as Stringer's Weir, after a manager at New Bridge Lane *(Ill 6.5)*. In 1795 Aikin reported that in the summer months, when the river level would have been at its lowest, the new tunnel drew 'every drop of water' from the Goyt. The water would have been returned to the river below the New Bridge Lane site but, between the weir and the outlet, travellers were puzzled by the fact that New Bridge seemed to have been built over a perfectly dry channel.[23] The Marslands' own tunnel inlet lay in this section of the river. How they dealt with the problem at that time does not appear to have been recorded, but in the nineteenth century the issue of water-rights was a hotly contested issue between themselves and the Howard family who were mill-owners at New Bridge Lane.

James Harrison and Portwood

Another area to see the building of early water-powered factories was Brinnington. In the 1770s, despite its proximity to Stockport, the township still had a rural character. Its southern part was occupied by the estate of Portwood Hall, once a residence of the Duckenfields

Ill 6.4 Stockport from the west, in 1819.
In the early 1790s purpose-built cotton mills were built along the Mersey. They were powered by waterwheels turned by the river, which was harnessed by the construction of weirs. One such barrier lay between the two mills shown on either side of the river in this illustration. The wheelhouse of one of these factories, the aptly named Weir Mill, can be seen projecting into the river and is identifiable by a great arched opening. The lower part of this original wheelhouse still survives and may be the oldest standing factory structure in Stockport.

but now leased to tenants.[24] Close to the Tame stood the manorial cornmill. In the early 1780s the manor of Brinnington was bought by James Harrison, who has been variously described as 'a Manchester cotton merchant' and 'a speculator and developer'. At about this time he also acquired the manor of Reddish on the Lancashire side of the Tame. These two purchases gave him not only land but also control of the water-rights along the section of the Tame immediately above the town of Stockport. Harrison lived at Cheadle Hall, on the eastern edge of Cheadle village, but it was at Portwood that he left an enduring mark. In 1786 he provided the place with a direct communication with Stockport by building Portwood Bridge across the Goyt. Prior to that time, access to the town had involved crossing a bridge over the Tame between Portwood and Heaton Norris, and then crossing Lancashire Bridge over the Mersey. By 1790 Harrison had three factories in Portwood and others were to follow. In 1796, to provide sufficient water-power to this growing industrial area, he constructed a substantial millrace. Known as the Portwood Cut, it carried water from above a weir which he built across the Tame between his Reddish and Brinnington estates. Harrison also planned the construction of factories at Wood Hall in Reddish, but the scheme was abandoned after his death in 1806.[25]

Wind-power

Water was not the only natural resource used by Stockport mill-owners as a source of power. In the 1780s two windmills stood on the skyline above the town. One was situated on Edward Street, off Hillgate, on a site opposite the later Town Hall. It appears to have been built in 1784-5 to provide power to a cotton factory. The other windmill stood on Lancashire Hill, in Heaton Norris (*Ills 5.2 & 6.25*). It was used as a cornmill but in the late eighteenth century may also have driven textile machinery.[26] A wind-powered cotton mill in Stockport was visited in 1791 by Peter Ewart who inquired what the workforce did when there was no wind. 'We play us', was the reply. Perhaps not surprisingly, no other wind-powered cotton mills are known within the region.[27] Presumably it was in recognition of the unreliability of wind-power that by 1795 the owners of the Edward Street windmill had invested in a steam engine.[28]

Steam-power

The earliest known use of a steam engine in a Lancashire cotton factory was at Richard Arkwright's mill on Shudehill in Manchester in 1783. This was a

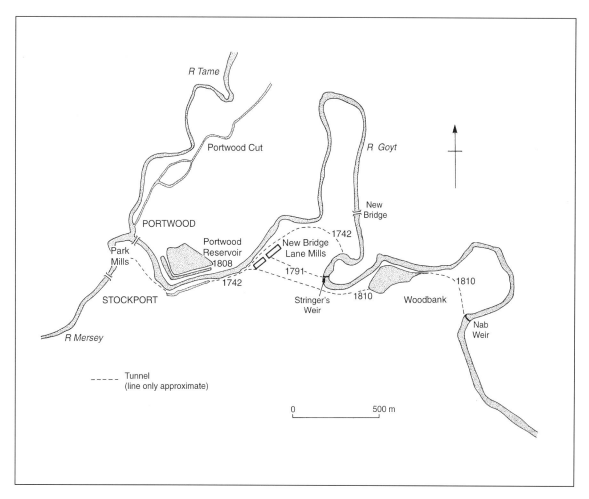

Ill 6.5 Millraces in Stockport and Portwood.
In the late eighteenth and early nineteenth centuries water-power was the subject of fierce competition between mill-owners at New Bridge Lane and the Marslands who owned the Park Mills. Both drew water from the Goyt, and successive schemes gave first one, and then the other, the upper hand.

pumping engine, used to raise water onto a waterwheel, which was the real driving force in the factory. In September 1785 work was under way on an engine for Stockport's Carr Mills. It too was probably used in conjunction with a waterwheel. By March 1791, however, Samuel Oldknow seems to have been using winding machinery at the Carrs powered directly by steam.[29]

The first successful engine with a 'rotative' action, and therefore capable of driving machinery, went on sale in 1785. Its manufacturers were Matthew Boulton and the inventor James Watt, operating from works at Soho, near Birmingham. Manchester received its first Boulton and Watt engine in 1789.[30] The first mill-owner in Stockport to place an order with the Birmingham firm was Samuel Oldknow in 1791, for a new factory on Higher Hillgate. The elevated position of the site made the use of water-power out of the question. Before the engine was installed, machinery in the factory was powered by a horse-gin. So great a novelty was this engine that the drivers of London stagecoaches travelling along Hillgate are said to have slowed down to inform their passengers.[31] By mid-1792 four other orders had been placed with Boulton and Watt by Stockport mill-owners. The subsequent slump in the cotton industry curtailed this demand but orders resumed in 1796. By 1809 seventeen Boulton and Watt engines had been installed in mills in Stockport, Heaton Norris and Portwood.[32] Boulton and Watt engines were sold under patent until 1800, but in the meantime other firms had produced their own, if somewhat inferior, designs of rotative engines. By 1795 the firm of Bateman and Sherratt, with works in Salford, was providing most of the engines installed in mills in and around Manchester.[33] At that same date, two Stockport factories had rotative engines acquired from a source other than Boulton and Watt, one being the factory on Edward Street.[34]

Steam engines were essential to the expansion of the cotton industry in Stockport. Water could only bring a limited amount of power to a limited number of factories. Steam-power still required water for boilers and condensers but placed less demand on that resource. Steam-powered mills could draw their supply from springs and wells or from the town's rivers. In the nineteenth century mills continued to be built along the Mersey even though they made no use of water-power. By the 1820s there were also factories next to the Ashton Canal on Lancashire Hill.[35] Canal-side locations not only offered another source of water but also had a particular convenience. Coal and raw cotton were both brought into the town by canal; yarn and finished cloth were transported out in the same way.

Steam also allowed the motive power of a mill to be upgraded. Engines could be replaced with larger versions; others could be added to power new buildings.[36] Eventually, in most mills in the town, steam replaced water-power.[37] It was, however, a slow process. The disadvantage of steam-power was one of higher running costs, which profit-motivated mill-owners were keen to keep to a minimum. In the late eighteenth and early nineteenth centuries some steam engines were installed in local mills only as a stand-by, taking over from waterwheels in periods of water-shortage. Initially this need may have been most acute in factories whose water was supplied not from the town's rivers but from the local tributary streams. Among these were the Carr Mills, which were supplied with water from the Carr Brook. When their new owner Thomas Hope ordered a Boulton and Watt engine in 1797, his intention was for it to be used 'in droughty weather'.[38]

The continuing use of water-power

Seven Stockport mill-owners are known to have still made some use of water-power in 1833, although by this date all of these were also using steam. It was reported at the same time that the supply of water was becoming increasingly irregular as a result of improved drainage of land upstream.[39] In 1842, however, there were still waterwheels in at least three Stockport mills: Brinksway Mill, the Marslands' Park Mills, and the New Bridge Lane factories owned by Jesse Howard.[40]

The Marslands and the Howards

In the early nineteenth century the Marslands and the Howards placed such a high value on water-power that they invested in costly new engineering works, and faced each other in litigation. In 1808 Peter Marsland bought

an area of meadowland in Portwood, and converted it to a reservoir which was linked, via a tunnel system, to his mills on the other side of the river. Two years later he turned his attention to improving his water-supply from the Goyt. By excavating a new section of tunnel, which passed under his Woodbank estate, Marsland was able to draw water from a point much higher upstream than previously. That point, Nab Weir, was also upstream of the inlet of the tunnel which fed the Howards' factories on New Bridge Lane (*Ill 6.5*).[41] The ensuing dispute which arose over water-rights between the two families was not finally settled until 1833, when Jesse Howard was awarded a share in the water-supply carried along the Marslands' tunnel. That decision is believed to have caused the abandonment of Howard's own ambitious engineering scheme. In 1825 he had bought a considerable portion of the Arderne estates in Bredbury, and on this land subsequently began the construction of a great millrace leading westwards from the Goyt at Otterspool Bridge. The millrace is said to have been intended to serve a new factory which Howard was planning to build. It may also have been intended to rejoin the river below Nab Weir, thereby diverting water from the Marslands' tunnel.[42]

Billies and mules

In the late eighteenth century the town's factories were used predominantly for the production of yarn. Weaving was still usually carried out in a workshop at the home of the weaver, who hired his labour to a manufacturer. In the 1770s output of yarn had been increased by the introduction of carding engines and hand-operated spinning jennies. The 1780s brought other improvements, in which Stockport played a part. Between carding and spinning came the process of producing a 'roving', a continuous rope of cotton. A roving machine had been invented by Richard Arkwright, but like the other machines of his invention it was protected by patent. After a prolonged dispute with other cotton spinners, Arkwright's patents were finally declared null and void in 1785. In the meantime, by 1782-3, no fewer than three Stockport men, John Swindells, John Milne at Castle Mill, and William Mycock, may have each come up with an alternative roving machine. The most important device of this type to appear in this decade was the 'billy'. The name of its inventor is not recorded, but he is said to have come from Stockport, and Swindells has been put forward as the most likely candidate.[43]

The annulment of Arkwright's patents meant that others were now free to use and copy his inventions without paying him a premium. The decision may have had ramifications for another relatively new invention, which would play a major part in the cotton industry in Stockport. This was the spinning machine known as the 'mule', invented by Samuel Crompton at his home at Hall i' th' Wood near Bolton. Crompton had made the invention public in 1780. Its design could have been considered to be an infringement of Arkwright's patents and it is believed that its use did not become widespread until these were finally annulled.[44] Mules soon developed into much larger machines than the prototype produced by their inventor. They were at first worked by hand, but from the early 1790s could also be partly driven by power.[45] With the annulment of Arkwright's patents, his powered spinning machine known as the water-frame was freely available for use. In the early nineteenth century an improved version of the water-frame was developed, the 'throstle', which could be powered by steam. However, it was the mule which became the most widely used spinning machine in the region. In 1811 Crompton recorded roughly 351,000 mule spindles in Stockport, compared with about 85,000 jenny spindles and 30,000 water-frame spindles.[46] A survey of 1832, by which date jenny spinning had virtually disappeared, recorded over 416,000 mule spindles in the town, compared with nearly 117,000 throstle spindles.[47] A major advantage of the mule was its ability to spin yarn fine enough for muslins. These were cotton fabrics which were much in demand in the late eighteenth century, but which previously had needed to be imported from India. In the 1780s, as we shall see, it was Stockport which was home to the country's leading muslin manufacturer.

Factories, workshops and 'room and power'

Factories, powered by whatever source, were not the only premises in which cotton spinning was carried out in Stockport. Some yarn in the late eighteenth century was still spun by workers, usually women, operating hand-powered machines in their own homes. A visitor to the town in 1794 described how there were 'large fires blazing in every house, by the light of which women were frequently spinning'. Such domestic spinners owned or perhaps rented their machines and hired their labour to manufacturers who provided them with the raw materials. Their small machines could not compete, however, with the town's increasingly larger jennies and mules, and by the turn of the century the domestic spinner was probably becoming a thing of the past.[48]

Between the house of the domestic spinner and the factory were Aikin's 'large number of cotton spinning shops'. These contained a number of spinning machines owned by an individual who employed others to work in his shop and, in small establishments, might work there himself. These spinning workshops may have been either purpose-built or converted from existing property. Some formed part of premises otherwise used for domestic purposes. In 1798 one local shoemaker owned four houses on Hillgate, with the attic being leased as a cotton-spinning shop.[49]

The success of the cotton shops was linked with the practice of local mill-owners to lease out floor space in their factories, and more particularly 'room and power'. This meant that the tenant could install machinery which was driven by the factory's power-system. In the late eighteenth century 'power' was usually the ability to drive carding engines. In the 1790s it was a common arrangement in the town for a firm to have hand-powered spinning machines in a cotton shop, and powered carding machines in rented space in a factory.[50] This combination could still be found in the 1820s.[51] Alternatively, both spinning and carding machines might be housed in rented factory rooms, perhaps the more common system as the early nineteenth century progressed.

Although the practice of renting out space is found among a number of mill-owners, it was of particular value to those who were not themselves cotton spinners. Thomas Hope, a hatter, acquired the Carr Mills in 1797 and reserved only a portion of the mills for his own use. Within six years the rents which he received from other occupants enabled him to give up his own business.[52] In 1819 the Lower Carr Mill alone was reported to accommodate twenty-seven 'masters', employing a total of 250 people.[53]

Workshops and the 'room and power' system enabled many small firms to set themselves up in business. Costs could be kept to a minimum. Workshops themselves appear to have been often leased, rather than owned, by the occupants. Jennies were the typical spinning machine used by Stockport's smaller firms until the 1820s, and these could be relatively cheap to buy. In 1795 spinning firms which did not own their own factories were very much in the majority in the town, outnumbering mill-owners by more than two to one. Within each group there were variations in the scale of a firm's operations. The smallest workshop operators owned only a few jennies. The largest in 1795 had machinery whose value equalled or surpassed that of some of the town's cotton spinners in possession of their own powered factories.[54]

In the late eighteenth century the typical cotton factory at Stockport, as elsewhere, took the form of a multi-storey rectangular block with a symmetrical arrangement of windows. Machinery was housed in open rooms, without dividing walls, and with wooden floors carried on wooden ceiling beams. In the early nineteenth century it became usual for those beams to be supported by cast-iron columns. Although both Aikin in 1795 and Corry in 1817 described Stockport's factories as 'large' buildings, that general phrase masks variations in their scale. Factories of the late eighteenth and early nineteenth centuries were generally narrow in width compared with some later counterparts, which were built to house longer spinning machinery. The greatest variations in size in Stockport's factories of this earlier period probably lay in their number of storeys, ranging perhaps from between three and six, and their length. The original factory at Weir Mill, built by John Collier in 1790, was four storeys high, 10 yards (9.1 metres) wide, and some 30 yards long. While some factories were of a similar length, others may have approached twice this figure.[55] One of the largest mills, on Higher Hillgate, was built as a rectangular arrangement of factory buildings set around a central courtyard. The mill was four storeys

Ill 6.6 Samuel Oldknow's Hillgate Mill, about 1880.
This mill was built by Samuel Oldknow in about 1790. Its scale and pioneering design, with a central courtyard, reflect Oldknow's position as one of the foremost figures in the cotton industry. It was also one of the earliest mills in Stockport to be powered solely by steam. Adjoining the mill, to the right, is the house built in about 1740 which Oldknow made his Stockport residence.

in height, above a basement. Its facade was crowned with a triangular pediment, a feature found in other large mills of the late eighteenth and early nineteenth centuries (*Ill 6.6*).[56] Its size, courtyard design and relatively early date, of about 1790, made this an exceptional building, but then its builder, Samuel Oldknow, was no ordinary mill-owner (*Ill 6.7*).

Samuel Oldknow and muslin manufacture

From Anderton to Stockport

Samuel Oldknow was born in 1756 at Anderton near Bolton, the son of a textile manufacturer. He served an apprenticeship with his uncle, a Nottingham draper, and became a partner in that business, before returning in 1782 to Anderton to set himself up as a manufacturer. There, in addition to other cloths, he began to produce muslins.[57] The muslin industry in this country was then in its infancy. The mule, the first machine capable of producing a yarn fine enough to be used in these fabrics, had been unveiled only two years previously by Samuel Crompton of Hall i' th' Wood, a few miles from Oldknow's home. Crompton himself is known to have provided Oldknow with some of his yarn.[58] Oldknow may not have been the first manufacturer in this field (a muslin business is said to have been established at Bolton as early as 1780), but he was the first to achieve prominence.[59]

In January 1783 Oldknow opened a salesroom in Manchester. Here his muslins attracted the attention of two London firms engaged in the wholesale distribution of textiles. For the next few years they would be the principal outlet for his products.[60] In order to expand his business, Oldknow needed to raise more capital. For this he looked to Richard Arkwright, whose firm already supplied him with yarn. In the winter of 1783-4 Oldknow made several visits to Arkwright who agreed to a loan of £3000.[61] With this financial backing, in 1784 Oldknow set up a new branch of the business at Stockport, which now became the main centre of his operations.

A considerable body of documentary evidence, including correspondence, survives for Oldknow's career, much of it discovered in the 1920s in a derelict building at his Mellor Mill.[62] This evidence does not, however, appear to offer an explicit explanation of his choice of Stockport. It has been suggested that his decision was influenced by the strong presence in the town of Unitarians, nonconformists of the same persuasion as Oldknow himself.[63] From a purely commercial point of view, Oldknow can hardly have been unaware of the recent upsurge in the cotton

Ill 6.7 Samuel Oldknow.

Born in Anderton in Lancashire in 1756, Oldknow moved in 1784 to Stockport where he established himself as the country's leading manufacturer of muslins. In this portrait, painted by Joseph Wright of Derby in about 1791, he is appropriately shown resting his arm on a length of muslin cloth. Oldknow built up a local textile empire which included finishing works in Heaton Mersey and spinning mills in Stockport and Mellor. At Marple and Mellor he also became the owner of an extensive estate. His ambitions exceeded his financial resources and in the mid-1790s his cotton business contracted to the operation of his Mellor Mill.

industry at Stockport, particularly since he must have recently passed through the town on his visits to Arkwright in Derbyshire. According to Aikin in 1795, muslin manufacture had been introduced into Stockport 'about ten years since'.[64] That Oldknow was responsible for its arrival is likely enough.

Operating from the Hillgate warehouses, 1784-9

The site which Oldknow chose for his Stockport business was on Higher Hillgate, then the main road south through the town. It included a town house, built

about forty years earlier and still standing to this day *(Ill 5.5)*. It was next to this building that several years later Oldknow built his great factory. At first, however, the focus of his business was his warehousing, with three buildings being constructed for this purpose between 1784 and 1789.[65] Until that last year, when Oldknow himself began spinning, his yarn was obtained from a variety of sources. Some was supplied, ready spun, by the Arkwrights. Other yarn was produced by small spinners in and around the town, using raw cotton which Oldknow provided.[66] Some weaving was carried out in a workshop at the Hillgate site, but most was undertaken by domestic workers. Evidence from 1784-5 shows that most of the weavers then in his employment lived within an arc to the east of the town, extending from Bullock Smithy to Ashton-under-Lyne. The weavers themselves appear to have collected the yarn from the Hillgate premises, and returned with the cloth.[67]

During the first year of his Stockport operation Oldknow was producing as much calico as muslin. The proportion of the two products subsequently shifted in favour of muslins, so that in 1790 these accounted for nine-tenths of his output.[68] By 1786 Oldknow had become the foremost muslin manufacturer in the country. At this date his Stockport branch employed over 300 weavers, compared with seventy when it began early in 1784. Another 159 were employed by the Anderton side of the business. His range of products now included 'flowered' muslins, whose decoration was said to be a good imitation of needlework. For these the weavers needed expensive specialized looms which they hired from Oldknow.[69]

The beginnings of the Heaton Mersey works

In 1784, the same year in which Oldknow set up business in Stockport, he also established a finishing works, to the west of the town, at Heaton Mersey *(Ill 6.10)*. For the next seven years it was under the charge of his brother Thomas, until his sudden death in 1791. The site was initially used for bleaching, but printing and dyeing were added later in the 1780s. It is believed likely that ready-to-wear items, such as dresses and petticoats, were also produced by the Oldknows at the Heaton Mersey site.[70]

From the introduction of spinning to the end of Oldknow's Stockport and Heaton Mersey businesses, 1789-94

It was at rented premises in the Carrs that Samuel Oldknow began spinning his own yarn in 1789.[71] Two years later he opened his mill on Higher Hillgate. It was equipped with mules, capable of producing fine muslin yarns.[72] However, from that very same year the balance of Oldknow's production was shifting away from muslins. In 1793-4 they represented roughly half his output, the same as ten years previously, and were now mostly plain goods. The demand for the finer home-produced muslins had fallen and Oldknow had been forced to reorganize his production accordingly.[73]

By the early 1790s Oldknow was also in deepening financial trouble. Between 1787 and 1791 he had acquired several neighbouring estates in Mellor and Marple. Some of this land he bought, some he exchanged for other property.[74] On the first of these acquisitions, the Bottoms Hall estate in Mellor, he began in 1790 to build his second great mill. In 1792 additional land was bought near his Heaton Mersey works.[75] His land purchases and the building of the two mills were a severe drain on his resources. He was already heavily in debt when the national economic crisis of 1792-3 occurred.[76] By the end of March 1793 Oldknow's trade had dried up. In order to pay the workforce even a third of their wages, desperate measures were required. A cart was loaded up with goods from his warehouses and made the rounds of retailers. Entrusted with this task was Peter Ewart. He had previously worked for Boulton and Watt, installing steam engines in the Manchester area. Among these assignments was the engine in Oldknow's Hillgate Mill. In 1792 he accepted an offer of a partnership with Oldknow. It was a decision which he must have soon come to regret. In 1793 Ewart's mission as a travelling salesmen proved successful for only three weeks. He was then sent to Liverpool, where he hoped to collect money owing to the firm, but found himself unable to raise 'a single guinea'. Ewart's partnership with Oldknow ended later in that year.[77]

Following the crisis of 1793, Oldknow began to contract his business empire. The Heaton Mersey works were the first to go. In November of that year they were taken over by Robert Parker. He was probably a partner in one of the two London firms to which Oldknow sold much of his output.[78] His Stockport spinning and weaving business continued for another year, before also coming to an end. In 1795 the Hillgate factory was probably rented out. By that time the Anderton branch also seems to have ceased to exist.[79] Oldknow's Mellor Mill continued to operate, but his career as a muslin manufacturer was over.

Other local muslin manufacturers

However, where Oldknow led the way, others followed. In the 1790s other men are named as local muslin manufacturers, not only in Stockport but also in Bredbury, Romiley, Bullock Smithy, Marple and Mellor.[80] One of these, Richard Heys of Bullock Smithy, had worked for Oldknow as a manager at Hillgate in the 1780s.[81] Another of Oldknow's managers who became a muslin manufacturer was John Bentley, who in 1819 bought Oldknow's Hillgate Mill.[82] The Oldknow connection could take other forms. In the 1780s William Sykes was a dealer in textiles, first at Halifax and then at Manchester. He traded, among other goods, in muslins bought from Oldknow. In the early 1790s Sykes belonged to a partnership which set up a muslin-manufacturing business in Stockport, sole control of which passed in 1795 to Sykes. The firm had its own bleachworks at Edgeley. It was also at Edgeley that Sykes's muslin-manufacturing business was based, with yarn being put out from here to handloom weavers.[83]

Another muslin manufacturer with links with Samuel Oldknow was William Radcliffe, who was born in Mellor in 1761, the son of a weaver (*Ill 6.14*). He took up the same trade, and by 1785 had saved enough money to set himself up as a manufacturer. Within four years he was, according to his own account, employing 'many hands both in spinning and weaving'. From 1789 to 1794 his main business was selling yarn to muslin manufacturers, chiefly to Oldknow, but he was also producing a few muslins himself. Following Oldknow's abandonment of muslin manufacture, Radcliffe appears to have greatly expanded this side of his own business. By 1801 he was putting out work to 'upwards of 1000 weavers, widely spread over the borders of three counties'. In 1799 he entered a partnership with Thomas Ross, the son of a wealthy Scottish merchant, whose arrival brought additional capital to the business.[84] In the following year they began to sell their products from Stockport's own newly opened muslin market. Known as the Muslin Hall, this was housed in Castle Mill, which had now ceased to be used as a factory.[85]

The decline of muslin manufacture

Although the production of muslins seems to have been widely taken up by local manufacturers by the end of the eighteenth century, other cotton fabrics were also made locally. These included checks and fustians, materials which combined a cotton weft with a linen warp, and calicoes.[86] In the second decade of the nineteenth century muslin manufacture in the town appears to have been in decline.[87] By 1825 the town's Muslin Hall was a thing of the past.[88] The decline of local muslin production was accelerated in the 1820s by the rapid spread of the powerloom, capable of producing only coarser fabrics. We shall return to this important development later.

WATER-POWERED MILLS AND COTTON FIRMS OUTSIDE THE TOWN

Samuel Oldknow's Mellor Mill

Like his Hillgate Mill, Oldknow's factory in Mellor was built on a grand scale. His contemporaries described it as 'a large, handsome, and very imposing cotton mill', and 'the largest cotton mill in this part of the country'.[89] It was situated in the valley of the River Goyt, whose water provided it with power. The main building was six storeys high, 14 yards (12.7 metres) wide and roughly 70 yards (64 metres) long (*Ills 6.8 & 6.9*). Like the Stockport mill, it was crowned with a central triangular pediment. Set within this was a piece of oval stonework (now in Memorial Park in Marple) carved with Oldknow's initials, a weaver's shuttle and the date 1790. At either end of the six-storey block was a three-storey wing. The date 1790 is believed to refer to the year in which the foundations were laid. The mill came into operation in 1792.[90]

The mill was initially powered by a waterwheel placed centrally within the main building, a not uncommon arrangement. Later Oldknow added the 'Waterloo Wheel', housed in a detached wheelhouse. The water left this building at a level lower than that of the nearest point of the river, into which it was to be discharged. To get round this difficulty, Oldknow had a tunnel dug which carried the water under the river bed and discharged it into the Goyt roughly 500 metres downstream. A third waterwheel powered a cornmill, built at one end of the cotton factory.[91]

To provide a sufficient supply of water, on the valley floor upstream of the mill Oldknow constructed two large reservoirs which were fed by the Goyt. One covered what had previously been the course of the river, which Oldknow diverted along a new cutting. Since the late nineteenth century this reservoir has been known as the Roman Lakes. A third, and smaller, reservoir was constructed in a neighbouring clough. Thanks to these engineering works the factory continued to be powered solely by water until as late as 1860, when steam-power was introduced.[92]

Ill 6.8 Samuel Oldknow's Mellor Mill.
This great spinning mill, shown here reflected in one of the reservoirs which provided it with water-power, came into operation in 1792. An oval stone, set within its central crowning pediment, was carved with the date 1790, probably the year in which the foundations were laid.

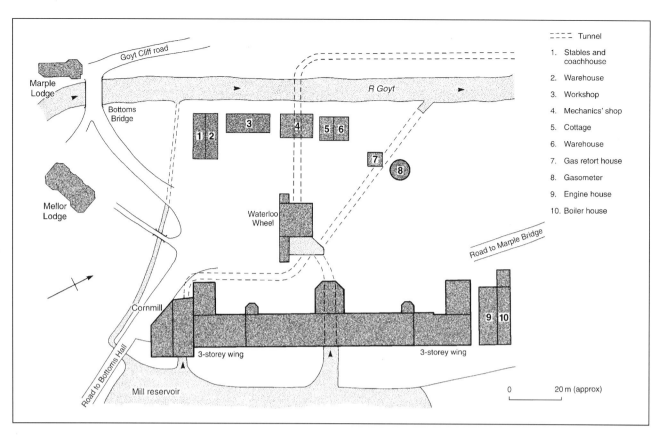

Ill 6.9 Plan of Mellor Mill, 1867 (after Ashmore 1989).

Machinery in the mill was originally powered by a centrally placed waterwheel. This was later supplemented by a second wheel, the 'Waterloo', located in a separate wheelhouse. A tunnel carried water from this wheelhouse under the Goyt to be discharged into the river further downstream. Attached to the cotton mill was a cornmill with its own waterwheel. Mellor Mill was powered solely by water until as late as 1860, when two steam engines were installed.

Oldknow's continuing financial difficulties

The construction of the mill was accompanied by other works on Oldknow's Mellor and Marple estate – roads, a new bridge over the Goyt, and housing – all of which contributed to his financial difficulties in the early 1790s. Having jettisoned his businesses at Heaton Mersey and Stockport, Oldknow poured money into the estate's further development. Lime kilns were built, and money was spent in experimenting with new farming techniques. He also invested heavily in the Peak Forest Canal. We shall examine these various projects in more detail later. The overall result was that his financial position remained precarious. By 1800 his debts exceeded the value of his property and he was only saved from bankruptcy by the intervention of Richard Arkwright junior. In 1786 there had been the possibility of the two men going into partnership. Although Oldknow had turned down such a move, Arkwright had advanced him money and provided him with yarn on credit. In the 1790s he helped to keep Oldknow afloat by making a succession of substantial loans, and

even taking over another of Oldknow's debts. The arrangement reached in 1800 amounted to a partnership which allowed Oldknow to manage Mellor Mill and the surrounding estate, but gave the real financial control to Arkwright. The partnership lasted five years. In the meantime the amount of money which Oldknow owed to Arkwright had increased, and was to continue to do so. When Oldknow died in 1828, the debt was over £200,000. In lieu of payment, his Mellor and Marple estate passed into the ownership of Arkwright, 'his chief creditor and former partner by whose capital it had been mainly acquired'.[93] To put Oldknow's debt in some perspective, the highest paid workers in Stockport's cotton factories in 1829 (the 'overlookers', or foremen, in charge of powerloom weaving) might earn about £100 a year.[94]

Mills on the streams of Mellor and Ludworth

Oldknow's mill was not the only early water-powered factory in this part of the Borough. The tributary streams flowing into the Goyt from the high ground on the east were used to power a number of small cotton mills (*Ills 1.5 & 6.10*). The earliest of these are believed to have been established in the late 1780s. By the mid-1800s there were at least eight such sites. The power of the Mill Brook, forming the boundary between Ludworth and Mellor, had been harnessed since perhaps the thirteenth century to drive the Ludworth cornmill. Four of the eight known early cotton mills were established on this stream. One of these, Primrose Mill, is believed to have previously been a fulling mill, used by the local woollen industry. On the stream which flows through Moor End in Mellor there were three mills belonging to William Radcliffe and his partner Thomas Ross. Two other mills may have been powered by the same stream during this early period. To the south-west,

on a third stream, was Damsteads Mill, probably built by 1794.[95]

Fast-flowing upland streams provided the power for many of the region's earliest cotton mills. To build up a sufficient head of water to turn a wheel, such streams were usually fed into one or more reservoirs. Even so, the power which they provided was often limited. William Radcliffe took some pride in the fact that he had been able to build up his extensive manufacturing business in Mellor despite the disadvantage of 'small streams of water for turning machinery'.[96] This limitation is reflected in the known scale of these early local mills. The largest of the three mills belonging to Radcliffe and Ross measured 18 by 10 yards (16.4 by 9.1 metres). Clough Mill, built on the Mill Brook

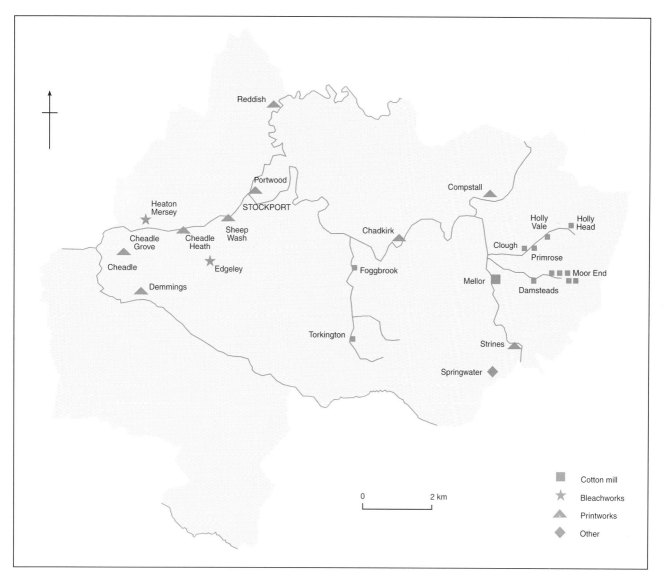

Ill 6.10 Rural water-powered cotton mills and bleaching and printing works, 1780-1803.
Outside the town of Stockport, most early water-powered cotton mills in the Borough were established on the fast-flowing streams of the upland townships of Mellor and Ludworth. Bleaching and printing works required a considerable supply of water and extensive sites. They were concentrated along the lowland river valleys and their tributaries.

between 1800 and 1805, was of the same dimensions, though of five storeys compared with the other's four (*Ill 6.11*).[97]

William Radcliffe appears to have been typical of the occupants of these mills in coming from a family already well-established in the locality. Some, again like Radcliffe, are known to have had an earlier involvement in the textile industry. Apart from Radcliffe, in the 1790s and early 1800s three were described as muslin manufacturers, and two others as mule spinners, suggesting that they were producing yarn for that same trade.[98]

Cheadle, Offerton and Torkington

Away from Mellor, cotton mills on the other rural streams in the Borough were relatively few. The tributary stream of the Mersey, variously known as the Norbury Brook, the Lady Brook and the Micker Brook, had some

four cornmills along its banks in 1780. A fifth was built at Adswood in about 1800.[99] In the mid-nineteenth century a small silk mill stood on this stream to the north-west of Cheadle village. It is said to have been converted, by 1832, from a water-powered cotton mill, but no details have been recovered of its earlier history.[100] Cheadle and Gatley, however, were noted by Aikin in 1795 as places to which handloom weaving of checks and fustians had spread from Stockport.[101]

To the east of Stockport at least three water-powered cotton factories existed in Offerton and Torkington along the Poise Brook and Ochreley Brook. One was Foggbrook Mill in Offerton, so-called after the local name for this northern section of the Poise Brook (*Ill 6.12*). It was built by William Lavender, a Stockport linen draper who moved into cotton manufacturing. The mill was certainly in existence by 1796, and very probably in 1791. By 1812, when the site was advertised for sale, Lavender had also built a second

Ill 6.11 Clough Mill, Ludworth.
The majority of early water-powered cotton mills built outside the town were on a fairly modest scale. Clough Mill, now demolished, was erected between 1800 and 1805 for the spinning of yarn from cotton waste.

Ill 6.12 Foggbrook Mill, Offerton.
This small cotton mill was probably built in the early 1790s. In the nineteenth century it seems to have become increasingly difficult for such rural mills to compete with their larger urban counterparts. Foggbrook Mill itself went through a succession of uses, eventually becoming a bleaching and dyeing works. The mill reservoir has been filled in, but the factory still stands.

factory, powered by this stream. This was a substantial building, 28 yards (25.5 metres) long and 12 yards (10.9 metres) wide and six storeys high. It is reported to have gone unsold and to have been allowed to go to ruin. The earlier mill went through a variety of uses, as a printworks in 1816, as a cotton mill again, as a cornmill, as a cotton mill for a third time, and by the 1840s as a bleaching and dyeing works.[102]

Further to the south, a little-known water-powered cotton-spinning factory at the Torkington end of Bullock Smithy was in operation by the beginning of January 1791. At that date part of the factory was used by Samuel Oldknow for carrying out 'some part of the muslin manufacture'.[103] Its precise site is not certain, but it is probably to be associated with a factory later mentioned in Torkington. This building was described in 1814 as 'a cotton shop' and from 1816 as a 'factory', although it was in use as a printworks by 1822 when

it was advertised to be let. The lease does not appear to have been taken up and by 1825 the building had been demolished. Its reservoir, fed by the Ochreley Brook, was incorporated into the grounds of the nearby house known as Torkington Lodge *(Ill 7.8)*. The factory itself presumably fronted that reservoir.[104]

No single explanation may lie behind the relatively rapid demise of the water-powered cotton factories in Offerton and Torkington. In the case of the second factory at Foggbrook, the timing of the sale suggests that Lavender undertook its construction at a time when trade was reasonably buoyant, only to be faced with a subsequent slump. The streams may also have proved to be an unreliable source of power. It may be significant that the older of the two Foggbrook factories was equipped with a steam engine in 1812, the earliest known example of the use of such an engine in a rural cotton mill in the Borough.

Ill 6.13 Seventeen Windows, Offerton.
The upper floor of these three-storey cottages, lit by a row of windows which gave the building its name, was used for handloom weaving.
The cottages were burnt down in 1944, but their name is still preserved in the neighbouring building, shown here on the extreme left.
In the late eighteenth and early nineteenth centuries handloom weaving of cotton was a major source of employment in the Borough.

COTTON WEAVING

The rise of handloom weaving

As cotton spinning increased, so too did handloom weaving. William Radcliffe described how at Mellor from about 1788 'The fabrics made from wool or linen vanished, while the old loom-shops being insufficient, every lumber-loom, even old barns, cart-houses, and outbuildings of any description were repaired, windows broke through the old blank walls, and all fitted up for loom-shops. This source of making room being at length exhausted, new weavers' cottages with loom-shops rose up in every direction; all immediately filled'.[105]

It is doubtful whether there was any township in the Borough during the late eighteenth and early nineteenth centuries without a share of this industry. In April 1800 cotton manufacturers from Stockport and the neighbourhood gathered at the town's Castle Inn. William Radcliffe later reported of this meeting that 'on comparing notes, we found that there was not a village within thirty miles of Manchester, on the Cheshire and Derbyshire side, in which some of us were not putting out cotton warps, and taking in goods, employing all the weavers of woollen and linen goods who were declining those fabrics as the cotton trade increased'.[106] In 1816 it was claimed that until recently there had been 15,000 people in Stockport and its neighbourhood who were engaged in this occupation.[107] The profession was fairly easy to take up. The weaving of plain cloths was not difficult to learn, and looms were inexpensive and could also be rented.[108]

Weavers' cottages

In the late eighteenth and early nineteenth centuries the classic form of weavers' dwelling was a three-storey cottage, two rooms deep and a single room wide, either free-standing or part of a short terrace. The lower two storeys provided domestic accommodation for the weaver and his family, while the upper storey served as his workshop. Three-storey cottages of this period survive at Moor End in Mellor. In Offerton a pair of three-storey cottages stood at the junction of Marple Road and Offerton Road. Their upper storey was lit by a row of small, close-set windows which gave the place its name of Seventeen Windows *(Ill 6.13)*.[109] In Mellor some three-storey cottages were built close to factories, probably by the mill-owners for weavers in their employment.[110]

Such specialized structures, however, appear to have accounted for only a small proportion of handloom workshops in the Borough. Most weavers probably worked within more conventional two-storey dwellings, in small purpose-built loomshops attached to the side or rear of their house or, as Radcliffe vividly describes at Mellor, in converted outbuildings.

William Radcliffe at Stockport

In the late 1790s cotton spinners in the region were exporting an increasing amount of their yarn to the continent, which had its own weaving industry. This apparent encouragement of foreign competition prompted some local manufacturers to call for the export of yarn to be restricted.[111] It was to discuss these demands that the meeting was held at the Castle Inn in Stockport in April 1800, whose proceedings were later recorded by William Radcliffe. There was perhaps no stronger advocate of such export control than Radcliffe himself, who had built up his own manufacturing business, employing 'upwards of 1,000 weavers', by selling cloth to the continental markets (Ill 6.14).[112] The meeting at the Castle Inn, however, revealed a major obstacle to the success of the campaign – there were not enough weavers within the district to cope with the present supply of yarn. Radcliffe, undeterred, suggested that what was needed was new machinery which would increase productivity, and volunteered to take on the role of its inventor. His condition was that the other manufacturers present would swear to support the prohibition of the export of yarn if his efforts proved successful.[113]

To put this plan into effect, in the next year Radcliffe and his partner Thomas Ross leased Oldknow's Hillgate Mill in Stockport. The intention was to fill these premises 'with looms, &c on some new plan, and just so much spinning machinery as would supply the yarns with weft'.[114] Thomas Johnson, the son of one of Radcliffe's weavers and a talented mechanic, was enrolled as an assistant, and at the start of 1802 work began at the Hillgate factory on not one, but two inventions, designed to speed up the weaver's job. One, which became known as the 'dandyloom', was a handloom fitted with a mechanism for taking up the finished cloth without interrupting the weaving process. The new machine is believed to have speeded output by as much as a half, although unlike earlier handlooms it could only weave plain cloth, using coarse yarns. The other innovation was a machine for

Ill 6.14 William Radcliffe.
Born in Mellor in 1761, Radcliffe rose from being a handloom weaver to the owner of a cotton-manufacturing firm which employed over 1000 handloom weavers in 1801. In that year he took over Samuel Oldknow's Hillgate Mill, where he developed a new form of handloom and a machine for 'dressing' warps. Radcliffe was a fierce opponent of the sale of yarn to foreign manufacturers. His inventions were intended to increase the productivity of handloom weavers working in their own homes, thereby reducing the need for such exports. This grand plan was unfulfilled, but Radcliffe's machines directly influenced the development of the powerloom.

'dressing' the warps, that is pasting them with flour and water to prevent them breaking on the loom. Normally the weaver himself carried out this task, once the warps were on the loom, but it was a process estimated to occupy a third of his working time.[115]

Although Radcliffe's inventions were developed and used at his Hillgate factory, his plans centred on the domestic industry. The aim was to distribute his new loom among the cottages of families whose children had been trained at the factory. Warps would also be delivered to these cottages, already dressed on Radcliffe's other new machine. Some looms were indeed distributed in this way, but Radcliffe's grand scheme was not to see fulfilment.[116] In 1806 Radcliffe and Ross were also running a factory in Adlington

Square, 'well filled with weaving machinery'. When their partnership ended in that year, this factory was kept by Ross, while Radcliffe retained the Hillgate factory and the rights to the patents on his loom and dressing machine. Radcliffe's enterprise, however, required heavy investment and he now found himself without the financial support of his partner at a time when the cotton industry was going through a major slump. Despite the profits which he made from weaving and from the patents, he was forced to borrow heavily, and in 1807 was declared bankrupt.[117]

Radcliffe resumed his business, paying back his debts by 1817. In the meantime his patents had passed to his creditors who allowed the collection of premiums to lapse. In his old age a number of attempts were made to gain some financial reward from the government in recognition of his contribution to the textile industry. Finally, in May 1841, he was awarded £150. His shock at learning that he was to receive such a meagre sum is said to have led to his death, three days later.[118] It was indeed a poor recognition of his contribution to the textile trade. Although Radcliffe made his inventions for the handloom-weaving industry, they influenced another development, which revolutionized manufacturing. This was the powerloom.

The rise of the powerloom

The importance of Stockport's role in the development of powerloom weaving is difficult to exaggerate. It has been seen as the single most important aspect of the town's cotton industry. 'Above all, Stockport pioneered from 1803 the development of the steam loom, accomplished for power weaving what Arkwright had done for machine spinning and became the first great centre of powerloom weaving, as Cromford had been for machine spinning'.[119]

The application of power to the weaving of wide cloths had been first achieved in the 1780s by an unlikely inventor, the Reverend Edmund Cartwright. The efficiency of his machine left much to be desired, and manufacturers were reluctant to take it up. Samuel Oldknow's curiosity seems to have been sufficiently whetted for him to visit Cartwright's Doncaster factory in 1787, but if Cartwright was hoping to make a sale he was disappointed.[120] He did supply looms to a new mill in Manchester in the early 1790s, but this had been operating for barely a month when it was burnt down by angry handloom weavers. The action is said to have deterred other mill-owners from repeating the experiment, and no further Cartwright looms are known to have been licensed before the end of the eighteenth century.[121]

William Horrocks's and Peter Marsland's powerlooms

In the 1800s two Stockport mill-owners were each engaged in an attempt to devise a more efficient powerloom. One was William Horrocks, the owner of a mill in the Park. He is reported to have been weaving with fifty powerlooms, presumably models of the Cartwright machine, when he decided to try to improve their performance. His new powerloom was patented in 1803, with a patent being taken out on a further improvement two years later. It is said that William Horrocks's father, Thomas, had woven cloth using both handlooms and powerlooms at Castle Mill in Stockport as early as 1795-6, and had sworn his workforce to secrecy.[122] Thomas Horrocks was certainly leasing Castle Mill at that time, while he was awaiting completion of his mill in the Park, but the story of his role in the introduction of powerloom weaving into Stockport is yet to be confirmed.[123]

The other Stockport mill-owner experimenting with a new powerloom in the 1800s was no less a figure than Peter Marsland, who patented his own machine in 1806. Marsland had a reputation as a skilled mechanic, but his powerloom was judged to be too complex and was not adopted by other manufacturers.[124] William Horrocks, on the other hand, became a victim of his own success. His attempts to enforce his patents were opposed by manufacturers. In order to fight them in the courts, Horrocks was forced to mortgage and later sell his mill.[125]

William Horrocks's role in the development of the powerloom was due in no small measure to the work of William Radcliffe. Horrocks's machine of 1803 borrowed the taking-up mechanism of the dandyloom. (Radcliffe himself claimed that this was its only new feature.) Furthermore, his powerloom was used in conjunction with the dressing machine, to which with Radcliffe's permission he made his own improvements.[126] Cartwright had attempted, unsuccessfully, to include a mechanism for dressing the warps on the loom. Radcliffe's method of using a separate machine for this process, adopted by Horrocks, became the norm within the powerloom-weaving industry.[127]

Horrocks's powerloom is said to have played a considerable part in manufacture only after he patented further improvements in 1813. By that date, however, it had already been adopted by other Stockport mill-owners. Among the first of these were some of Horrocks's own relatives. In about 1806 they installed spinning machines and 100 powerlooms in a factory on Millgate. In 1808 the firm went bankrupt, and was taken over by a London merchant, John

Goodair. He added to the business by building a new spinning mill at Edgeley and, next to this, a weaving factory housing 200 powerlooms.[128]

The Luddites

At least six Stockport firms were using powerlooms by 1812.[129] In that year rioters attacked powerloom factories in Stockport, Manchester and some of the handful of other places in the region where these machines were now in use. The name Luddite, which was attached to these rioters, has passed into the language as a byword for opposition to technological innovation. The attacks on factories, however, took place against a background of particular circumstances, of rising food prices and a slump in the textile industry. Handloom weavers in particular were badly hit, as manufacturers reduced their piece-rate and the amount of available work diminished. In the case of Stockport, the attacks on factories occurred after manufacturers went back on an agreement to raise the handloom weavers' wages.[130] The first attack was on the 20th of March when as many as 500 men tried unsuccessfully to set fire to William Radcliffe's factory. Radcliffe was still weaving at this date using his dandyloom, but in the previous year he had founded a monthly club for powerloom manufacturers, enabling them to share 'such practical improvements as daily experience brought out, either in the system itself, or in the teaching and management of the hands'. His aim was the same as in 1800, to ensure that cotton spinners had no need to export yarn abroad, but in the climate of 1812 his championship of the powerloom made him an obvious target.[131] On the 14th of April a mob marched through the town, breaking the windows of several factories, including Radcliffe's and Peter Marsland's. The rioters then wrecked the powerlooms at John Goodair's mill at Edgeley, and set fire to both the mill and Goodair's house. Two days later an anonymous letter sent to a Stockport mill-owner threatened the destruction of all powerlooms and dressing machines. However, after the violence of the 14th, no further attacks occurred on Stockport factories in that year.[132] In 1818 powerloom weavers in the town protested against a reduction in their own wages by going on strike, the earliest known industrial action by this class of workers in the country.[133]

The expansion of the 1820s

The adoption of the powerloom in the town's mills quickened in the first half of the 1820s. This was a prosperous time for the textile industry, ended by a sharp

economic downturn in 1826. It was also during this period, in 1822, that Sharp and Roberts of Manchester patented a new powerloom. Their machine has been described as 'a much improved form of the Horrocks loom'. Further improvement came with William Dickinson's 'Blackburn Loom' of 1828. Both of these machines were widely used in the industry.[134]

According to a survey carried out in 1832, since 1822 the number of firms in Stockport weaving by power had increased from ten to thirty-two, and the number of powerlooms had risen from 1970 to 11,003. In 1825 Edward Baines listed twenty-seven firms in the town using powerlooms, with some 5730 machines.[135] The number of firms weaving by power, it would thus appear, had nearly trebled between 1822 and 1825, with the number of machines rising by roughly the same proportion. By 1832 the number of powerloom firms had undergone only a modest increase, but the average number of machines worked by these firms had risen from 212 to more than 340. By 1825 Stockport had been overtaken as the region's foremost centre of powerloom weaving by Manchester, but it nevertheless contained more than a quarter of the total number of powerlooms in the United Kingdom. In 1833 there were estimated to be up to 12,000 powerlooms in the town, out of a national total of 100,000.[136] Where Stockport manufacturers had played a leading role in the widespread adoption of the powerloom, others were now following suit.

In 1825 all of the powerlooms in the town were worked by combined firms, that is firms which also carried out spinning. Only two spinning and weaving firms at that time did not have these machines. Well might it seem to James Butterworth, two years later, that 'The chief dependence of the town at present is on the vast number of power looms at work herein'.[137]

Powerlooms transformed the nature of the cotton industry in Stockport. In 1825 there were some forty-five firms in the town which carried out only cotton spinning. The majority of these, however, appear to have been relatively small concerns. Most of the larger spinning firms were by this date also weaving by power. Furthermore, to all intents and purposes, the town's combined firms seem to have been weaving solely by power.[138] In the 1820s while the number of powerlooms increased, that of handloom weavers fell drastically.

The decline of cotton handloom weaving

Perhaps particularly after the improvements in the powerloom in the 1820s, handloom weavers could not compete in terms of productivity. It was said in 1827 that a child of twelve or fourteen could be placed in charge of two powerlooms and produce up to three times as much cloth as a handloom weaver.[139] Until the 1830s powerlooms were capable of producing only coarser types of cloth, such as calicoes and heavy shirtings. Here, handloom weavers might have had an advantage, in that their machines could produce much finer materials. However, even before the 1820s the local production of such fabrics seems to have been diminishing. The spread of the powerloom in that decade meant that coarser fabrics were now decisively the main product of the town. In 1836 Stockport was noted for its 'stout printing calicoes', made entirely by power, and cotton shirtings, made mainly in the same fashion.[140] To cater for the production of such materials, the town also became a centre for the spinning of coarse yarns.[141]

The decline in the number of handloom weavers of cotton in Stockport was said by one weaver in 1834 to have been greater than in any other place. In 1816 over 5000 handloom weavers were counted in Stockport township, Heaton Norris and Edgeley. In 1822 a figure of 2800 was given for the town. By 1832 the number had fallen to 800, and in 1834 to 300 or 400. In Union Street alone, off Higher Hillgate, there were more than 160 weavers in 1813; in 1838 there were only fourteen.[142]

During the slump in the textile industry in 1826, there was a fresh outbreak in the region of powerloom wrecking by distressed handloom weavers. On this occasion Stockport was spared, although its working population was suffering considerable hardship. Attacks on the town's mills were feared, but the danger was seen as coming from outsiders. The contrast with 1812 suggests that Stockport's own cotton handloom weavers were now so few that they no longer posed any serious threat.[143]

Outside the town, figures for the decline of cotton handloom weaving are less readily available, but the case of Mellor may serve as a general guide. In the late eighteenth and early nineteenth centuries handloom weaving shops could not be opened in the township quickly enough. In 1851, out of a total population of 1777, only five people were cotton handloom weavers.[144] It may be a reflection of the demise of the industry in the township that from as early as the 1820s its population was in decline.[145]

Some former handloom weavers took up work in the factories. There were those, however, particularly among older weavers, who shied away from the move, reluctant to lose the greater independence enjoyed in the domestic industry.[146] Some handloom weavers found new employment in a reviving silk industry, on which more will be said below.

The demise of the handloom weavers of cotton also seems to have meant the end for a number of the firms which had employed them. In 1825 some thirteen firms were named in the town as carrying out only weaving by handloom. By 1834 most of these names had disappeared from a list of cotton manufacturers. One exception was Francis Smith Clayton, who still carried out only weaving, but by power. His workforce of about 150 operated some 300 powerlooms, accommodated in a shared factory. Clayton was evidently a survivor but, as the owner of a specialist power-weaving firm in the town, he was also something of a rarity at this time. Only one other such firm is listed in 1832, and that was operating on a smaller scale, with 150 powerlooms.[147] The vast majority of powerlooms in Stockport were always owned by combined firms. In the 1820s it could be said of the mills of such firms that each 'forms a complete manufacturing colony, in which every process, from the picking of the raw cotton to its conversion into cloth is performed, and on a scale so large, that there is now accomplished in one single building as much as would in the last age have employed a large district'.[148]

COTTON FACTORIES AND COTTON FIRMS, 1820-42

New machines and new factories

The 1820s and 1830s saw not only investment in powerlooms but also considerable expenditure in new factory buildings and steam engines. There were also changes in spinning machinery. In the 1820s manufacturers began to install much longer mules. In 1811 mules in Stockport held up to about 200 spindles. This was still reported to be the usual maximum number in 1822, but ten years later the figure was often 300 or 400.[149] In 1830 Richard Roberts of Manchester successfully produced a fully-powered or 'self-acting' mule. Over the next decade these new machines were installed in mills in Stockport and its neighbourhood.[150]

In 1822 there were fifty-one steam engines in Stockport, providing a total of 1298 horse-power. Three years later the number had risen to seventy, with a total of 1960 horse-power. By this period steam engines were being used in other industries in the town, in calico printing, cornmilling and engineering. Nevertheless, sixty-two of these seventy engines were employed in the town's cotton mills.[151]

After the opening years of the nineteenth century, the construction of new factory buildings in Stockport had lost much of its initial momentum. The early 1820s, however, saw a boom in factory building. In August 1822

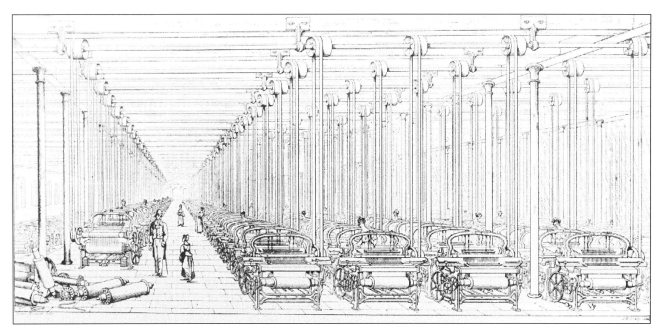

Ill 6.15 Powerlooms at Spring Bank Mill, 1835.
Stockport was the cotton industry's first great centre of powerloom weaving. William Horrocks, a Stockport manufacturer, patented a powerloom in 1803, which after further improvements became the first powerloom to be widely used in the cotton industry. The weight and vibration of powerlooms meant that they were housed either on the lower floors of a cotton-spinning factory or, as shown here at Spring Bank Mill, in a single-storey weaving shed.

eight factories were under construction.[152] The severe economic downturn in 1826 seems to have brought an end to this fever-pitch activity. A short-lived revival in the industry was followed by a fall in profits, and in 1829 by a protracted strike by factory workers in response to a cut in wages. Towards the end of 1831, however, the industry was showing the signs of a revival.[153] It brought a fresh mill-building boom until the effects of renewed depression began to be felt in the later 1830s.[154]

Housing powerlooms

Much of this building activity in the 1820s and 1830s was a result of the need of combined firms to find additional and suitable accommodation for their powerlooms. The weight and vibration of these machines meant that they were housed on a ground floor, and perhaps also on the floor above it. This might be within a multi-storey spinning mill, whose upper floors were used for the preparatory processes and spinning. Alternatively, powerlooms were housed within single-storey weaving sheds, which were characterized by their 'saw-tooth' roofs. These contained banks of windows which usually faced north, an arrangement designed to provide an even light. Weaving sheds could be very large structures indeed. The sheds of the firms of Joseph Lane at New Bridge

Lane and of Thomas Robinson at Spring Bank Mill were roughly 1830 and 1650 square metres in area respectively. Lane's weaving shed was advertised in 1842 as capable of accommodating 547 looms (*Ill 6.15*).[155] Some local mills contained even higher numbers of powerlooms. The Mersey Mills, on the Heaton Norris side of the river, had 900 in 1842.[156]

Fireproof factories

By the 1820s some mill-owners in Stockport were building multi-storey factories with a 'fireproof' construction. In these mills the floors were made not of wood, but of non-flammable materials which included cast-iron ceiling beams and stone flagging. Fireproofing raised the cost of construction, and at first was mainly confined to large factories built by the most successful firms. The first fireproof factory in Greater Manchester was erected in Salford in 1802.[157] Stockport's earliest example was perhaps the aptly named Cast Metal Factory, built on Warren Street before 1823. Between 1824 and 1833 at least four others may have been built in the town, among these being Wellington Mill which today rises above the bus station at Daw Bank.[158]

At seven storeys, Wellington Mill was one of the tallest factories ever to be built in Stockport. It was constructed in 1828 by Thomas Marsland, who was already one of the wealthiest industrialists in the town thanks to a highly successful printing and dyeing business. For the construction of his factory Marsland used what appears to have been the most common form of fireproofing. In this method, cast-iron ceiling beams supported brick vaulting. This was covered with a layer of sand or ash, onto which a floor surface was laid. More unusually, Wellington Mill also had cast-iron roof trusses. At the time this would have been a rare feature even in fireproof mills, with timber being the normal method of construction. Wellington Mill was used for both spinning and weaving, with the latter probably being carried out in the lower part of the building.[159] In 1833 Marsland's combined firm employed a workforce of 947, the largest in the town at this date.[160]

Orrell's Mill

This total was soon surpassed by the combined mill of Ralph Orrell, built on the western outskirts of the town at Travis Brow in Heaton Norris. In 1842 Orrell's Mill was reported to be 'by far the largest in Stockport', with a workforce of 1264. It was built in about 1834, and was designed by one of the leading experts in mill construction, the engineer William Fairbairn. One contemporary described the building as 'a model of factory architecture'. The main mill building was of six storeys, with a projecting wing at either end (*Ill 6.16*). Its spinning machinery included self-acting mules. The mill was designed to accommodate 1100 powerlooms, but in 1842 contained 1300. They were housed on the ground floor and in a large single-storey shed at the rear. In place of ground-floor windows on this side of the mill were doorways leading into the shed, effectively creating one large weaving area. Careful attention was also given to the position of the mill's chimney. Set a little distance away, on a natural knoll, it is said to have enabled the factory to be entirely free of smoke. Orrell's business had begun in a modest way. His father was the landlord of a public house on Lancashire Hill, where he started to manufacture sewing thread. Success in this enterprise led to the family spinning and weaving, as well as producing thread, in factories in Heaton Norris and Portwood, before Ralph Orrell established his great mill at Travis Brow.[161]

The size of firms

Thomas Marsland and Ralph Orrell belonged to a very small body of Stockport mill-owners operating on a

Ill 6.16 Orrell's Mill, 1835.
This great factory, used for cotton spinning and powerloom weaving, was built in about 1834. It was designed by William Fairbairn, a leading exponent of factory design, and was considered to be a model of its type. The chimney was built some distance away, allowing the factory to be free from smoke.

massive scale. This number also included Joseph Lane, who owned factories at New Bridge Lane and Higher Hillgate, and William Smith who owned the Mersey Mills. In 1833 their workforces numbered 873 and 761 respectively. Both firms collapsed in 1841 during the depression, throwing 'about 3,000' people out of work.[162]

In the early 1830s at the other end of the scale of the town's combined firms were a small number of employers with workforces of between 100 and 150. The majority of combined firms lay between these two extremes, and typically had a workforce of between 250 and 450. By this period, firms which carried out only spinning rarely seem to have employed more than 150 people (the known maximum in 1833-4 appears to have been 211 at a Brinksway mill). Some had workforces of between twenty-five and fifty.[163]

The decline of jenny spinning

The nature of small firms changed in the 1820s. Beginning in the late eighteenth century, the jenny had allowed many individuals to set themselves up as small cotton spinners. As the use of longer mules became more widespread, jenny spinning no longer proved competitive. In 1818 there were between 900 and 1100 jenny spinners in Stockport. Their numbers fell to about 500 in 1825 and to 120 in the early 1830s.[164] Some owners of jenny shops converted to mules, but it was a process which might require a change of premises. In the 1820s jenny firms occupied a number of the older, smaller mills and the cellars of other buildings.[165] Some jenny shops of this time still operated on a tiny scale. The machinery of one such business in 1823 consisted of two carding engines, two billies, a 'willow' (used to open and clean the raw cotton) and seven jennies, each with 120 spindles.[166] Among those who successfully made the transition to mule spinning was Thomas Fernley junior, whose father owned one of the town's larger jenny-spinning firms, based in Portwood. In 1824 Fernley took over Weir Mill where, in keeping with the times, he also carried out powerloom weaving.[167]

Cotton waste spinning

In the late 1820s and the 1830s the number of spinning firms in Stockport seems to have been rising. Many of these, however, were producing coarse yarn using the waste cotton produced by other spinners. In 1828 there were already thirty such firms listed in the town. The industry gave rise to its own manufacturing branch, producing candlewicks, heavy fabrics which were used for bed covers. Firms involved in both branches of the industry were generally small, some with perhaps no more than a handful of employees. The Carr Mills, which continued to be rented out as 'room and power', were the town's chief centre of this trade. In 1828 three-quarters of Stockport's cotton waste-spinning firms were based here, as in 1836 were five of its ten candlewick manufacturers.[168]

Peter Marsland and wool weaving

In one factory in Stockport powerlooms were used for a purpose which at the time was certainly unique locally and perhaps also nationally. In 1822 Peter Marsland bought an additional plot of land in the Park on which he built a 'large new factory of immense strength, secured by cast-iron beams and pillars'. Here woollen yarn was produced on great spinning machines, and woven into cloth on powerlooms which Marsland had modified for this purpose. The cloth was also dyed on the premises. The quality of the product was said to equal and even surpass French woollen cloth, at that time considered to be the finest of its kind. George IV had a suit made of Marsland's material. Production seems to have ceased as a result of the onset of the depression in the late 1830s. The machinery was sold and is said to have been taken to a town in the woollen-manufacturing county of Yorkshire.[169]

Cotton mills outside the town

Mellor and Ludworth

The 1820s and 1830s brought new challenges and opportunities to mill-owners outside the town, as within. In Mellor and Ludworth the small water-powered factories built in the late eighteenth century and the opening years of the nineteenth saw a variety of changes, as their owners erected new buildings and added new machinery. The most ambitious development in these townships was the construction of Mellor New Mill, later known as Dove Bank Mills. It was built at Moor End between 1817 and 1825, and probably stood on the site of one of the three mills which had belonged to Radcliffe and Ross. By 1836 Dove Bank Mills were of a considerable size, with a valuation two-thirds that of Samuel Oldknow's Mellor Mill.[170] Primrose Mill, on the Mill Brook, was more than doubled in size in 1823 by the addition of a new factory building. Ten years later it was being used as a combined mill.[171] At Damsteads Mill powerloom weaving was added to spinning by as early as 1822.[172]

These attempts at upgrading were not an unqualified success. Perhaps increasingly the location of these mills, along upland roads, became a disadvantage. Dove Bank suffered its own particular difficulties, with legal wrangling over the ownership of the firm contributing to its bankruptcy in 1840.[173] Furthermore, there was a problem of economy of scale, for the size of some local firms remained small in comparison with many in the town. Primrose Mill, even after expansion, had only seventy-six employees in 1833.[174] At Damsteads Mill the total number of powerlooms was only twenty. Perhaps it was the meagre scale of the business which led to the bankruptcy of the occupant of the mill during the slump of 1826. There does not appear to have been a rush of new applicants for the lease. When a new tenant did take over the mill, he converted it to cotton waste spinning, employing a mere nineteen people in 1833.[175] Cotton waste spinning had a long history in the district. Clough Mill, on the Mill Brook, had been built in the early 1800s specifically for this purpose.[176] It may be a sign of growing difficulties among the local spinning mills that by the early 1840s two, including Dove Bank, were involved in candlewick making, while a third had become a bleachworks.[177]

Heaton Mersey

Elsewhere within the Borough in the 1820s other industrialists were also attracted by the profits which might be won from the rapidly changing industry. At the Heaton Mersey bleachworks Samuel Oldknow's successor, Robert Parker, had added spinning and weaving by 1815. Some of the yarn was woven by powerlooms but much was still put out to handloom weavers. When Samuel Stocks assumed control of the works in 1824, he reshaped the firm by discontinuing printing and expanding the powerloom side of the business. By the late 1840s the site included a five-storey mill and a large weaving shed.[178]

The Andrews and Compstall

There was one other place in the Borough at which manufacturing by power was added to an established finishing industry. This was Compstall. Printing was begun here in the early 1800s by the firm of Thomas Andrew and Sons, who already owned a printworks at Harpurhey near Manchester.[179] A bridge had crossed the Etherow at Compstall since at least the seventeenth century, but when the Andrews set up business here the place was agricultural land, 'with only one small farmhouse'.[180] Under the Andrews' ownership this sparsely populated corner of Werneth township would develop into Compstall village, built to house their workforce (Ill 6.17).

The establishment of the village seems to have been directly connected with a reorganization and expansion of the Andrews' business in the early 1820s. As part of these changes, a new printworks was built in 1822. This side of the business, however, now became secondary to spinning and powerloom weaving, for which two new mills were constructed in 1823-4.[181]

The Etherow provided the main source of power to these factories, but to harness the river required considerable engineering work. Upstream of Compstall the Etherow flows through a deep and narrow gorge. At the end of this, where the river valley begins to broaden out, a great weir was now created to build up a head of water. From here a millrace was constructed, ending at an extensive reservoir by the Compstall mills. By the 1840s the mills were driven by two giant waterwheels. The larger of these, 50 feet (15 metres) in diameter and 17.5 feet (5.3 metres) wide, was constructed by the engineers Fairbairn and Lillie and was known as the 'Lily Wheel'. When it was installed in 1838 it was said to be the largest in the country (Ill 6.18).[182]

The broad millrace also served a second purpose, as a private canal. In 1828 George Andrew began mining at a colliery on the edge of Ernocroft Wood, high on the valley side upstream of his mills. From this mine, coal was transported by a tramroad which descended the hillslope. It appears to have had two tracks, and probably used the weight of a descending coal wagon to pull up an empty one. The tramroad was carried on a trestle bridge over the Etherow, to end at the millrace-canal where the coal was loaded onto barges for the short journey to Compstall. There, among other uses, it fuelled the steam engines which powered the cotton mills at times of water-shortage.[183]

Perhaps few mill-owning families in the region had the level of self-sufficiency achieved by the Andrews. The building of the new factories meant that they had control of the complete process of manufacture, from opening the bales of cotton to printing the finished cloth. Their engineering works provided water-power on a large scale and, if this failed, their mine in Ernocroft Wood could supply the mill boilers with coal brought along their private canal. Many of their workforce also lived immediately at hand in the village, and paid the Andrews rent for the privilege. 'The earth is the Lord's and the fullness thereof', one member of the family is credited with saying, 'But Compstall and all within is Juddy Andrew's'.[184]

Steam-power and canal-side mills

By the late 1820s new mills were being constructed outside the town which were powered only by steam.

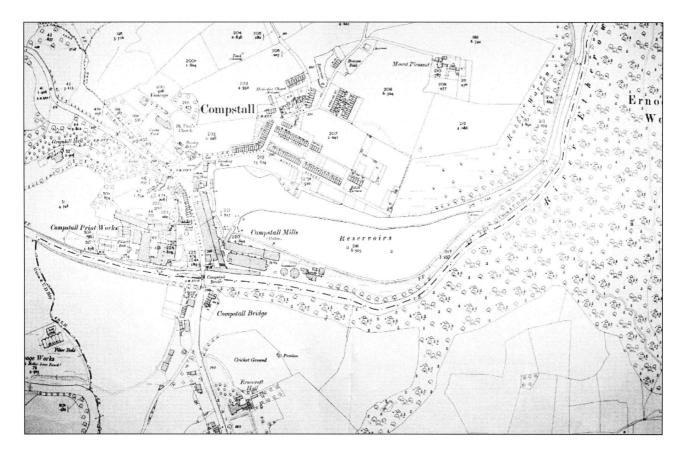

Ill 6.17 Compstall, detail of an Ordnance Survey map of 1910.
Compstall village owed its creation to the Andrew family, who established a printworks here in the 1800s. In the 1820s mills were built for cotton spinning and weaving, and houses were erected to accommodate the growing workforce. This period of expansion saw the construction of a great mill reservoir, fed by a broad millrace carrying water from the River Goyt. The millrace also served as a canal, along which coal mined in Ernocroft Wood was carried by barge to Compstall.

Such mills might still be built by local streams, to provide the necessary water-supply. In 1837 a site by the Poise Brook in the north-east of Hazel Grove was used for a large new cotton factory known as Wellington Mill (*Ill 7.8*). It was built by Thomas Moseley, whose family firm had earlier in the century taken over the Bullock Smithy premises of Henry Marsland.[185]

The preferred location for new steam-powered mills built outside the town was by a canal. Among the first of the canal-side factories in the Borough was Woodley Mill. This large fireproof factory was sited close to the Peak Forest Canal to which it was linked by a short canal branch. It was built in about 1828 by Samuel Ashton, a member of an important mill-owning family whose textile empire was centred on neighbouring Hyde.[186] Hollins Mill, constructed on Market Street in Marple in 1830, was served by its own short branch leading from the Peak Forest Canal. Oakwood Mill in Romiley was built next to the same canal in the mid-1830s.[187] By 1841 Rhode House Mill stood by the Macclesfield Canal at Hawk Green.[188] As we shall see in a later

chapter, from the mid-1840s canal-side mills would transform Reddish from a rural township into a centre of cotton spinning second only in the Borough to Stockport itself.

SILK

Silk throwing and spinning

The fortunes of the silk industry during this period were mixed. In the 1780s silk throwing, the production of yarn from raw silk, had rapidly been ousted from its role as the town's most important industry by cotton. Although the early years of that decade saw the owners of silk mills converting these buildings to cotton, the silk industry was not entirely replaced. Silk throwing continued at Crowther's Mill in Heaton Norris into the early nineteenth century. For a while other silk-throwing firms continued in business, although most of these were probably operating from small-scale premises.[189] By the mid-1820s the industry was very much reduced

Ill 6.18 The Lily Wheel, Compstall Mills.
Built by the Manchester engineering firm of Fairbairn and Lillie, this great wheel was installed at Compstall Mills in 1838. At that time it was said to be the largest waterwheel in the country.

indeed. Crowther's Mill, which in the 1800s had been producing cotton as well as silk, was given over entirely to cotton by 1823. Two years later only one silk throwster was listed in the town.[190] At that same period, however, two other branches of the silk industry were enjoying local success. One was silk spinning, the other silk weaving.

Silk spinning used the waste material produced by the throwing industry. In view of the local decline of that industry much of this material must have been imported into the town. This new branch of the trade appears to have been established in Stockport by 1815, when perhaps two firms were engaged in spinning silk as well as cotton. By 1825 the number of silk spinners had risen to five, of whom all but one seem to have specialized in that trade. Edward Baines's remark in this year, that 'there is not one silk mill in the parish', suggests that these specialist firms were leasing 'room and power'.[191] However, two years later the continuing steady rise of the silk-spinning industry enabled the firm

of Michael Newton to occupy a new factory in Heaton Norris. This mill was in a prime position, close to the terminus of the Ashton Canal on Lancashire Hill.[192] At about the same time a newly built factory in the centre of the town was also described as a 'silk mill'. Situated between High Street and Royal Oak Yard, this building still survives, although its High Street facade was altered during the early twentieth century.[193]

The rise of the town's silk-spinning industry was short-lived. In 1826 legislation came into effect which reduced the duties paid on the import of raw and woven silk. Stockport's spinners were not opposed to the changes, but competition from imported fabrics was to have a drastic effect on the home market. By the 1830s the town's silk spinners were one by one ceasing business.[194] Among these was a firm which for some years had also been involved in silk throwing, and whose closure may have marked the end of this industry in the town.[195] At his factory in Heaton Norris, Michael Newton continued in production, although at one stage

152

he is said to have had £30,000 of unsold yarn in his warehouse.[196]

Silk throwing survived longer outside the town. Reference has already been made to a water-powered factory at Cheadle and its conversion from cotton to silk by 1832. An advertisement for its sale in 1839 shows that it contained both silk-spinning and throwing machines. In 1851 its occupant was described as a silk throwster, with a workforce of thirty-six.[197]

Silk weaving

Much of the impetus for the growth in silk weaving in the Borough may have come from Macclesfield. Unlike at Stockport, the silk industry in that town continued to flourish in the late eighteenth century, despite the fact that cotton mills were being built there from the mid-1780s. Indeed, in the first quarter of the nineteenth century while the silk industry continued to expand, cotton seems to have made little progress. At that time Macclesfield silk throwsters were increasingly taking up the manufacture of cloth. Although some weaving was carried out within the town's mills, Macclesfield manufacturers also employed handloom weavers operating from their own workshops.[198] By the 1820s these domestic silk weavers included a considerable proportion of the population of Bullock Smithy.

Silk weaving played an important part in the economic life of this village into the second half of the nineteenth century. It was usually carried out in purpose-built workshops at the rear of the weavers' homes, although the cellars and upper floors of houses were also used.[199] Yarn was brought from Macclesfield by carriers, who were paid by the handloom weavers for this service. The woven cloth made the return journey in the same way. When times were hard, to save money Bullock Smithy weavers walked to Macclesfield and back themselves.[200]

Until the mid-1820s this local industry prospered, but it was hit hard by the economic downturn in 1826. It was reported in April of that year that of 582 weavers in Bullock Smithy as many as 459 had no work.[201] The depression of the late 1830s and early 1840s also affected the village badly. In 1839 Bullock Smithy was 'in considerable distress through the depression of the silk trade', while in 1842 it was reported that 'work has never been so slack and wages so low'.[202]

As well as the large number at Bullock Smithy, silk weavers were said in 1826 to comprise a significant proportion of the population of the townships of Cheadle Bulkeley and Cheadle Moseley. A 'silk manufacturer' listed at Rose Hill in Marple in the mid-

1820s suggests the presence of a further body of weavers. Others may well have been found at Gatley Green.[203]

The majority of known silk manufacturers in the Borough were to be found in Stockport. Here they seem to have specialized in goods such as scarves and handkerchiefs, woven with yarn produced by the local silk spinners. When the silk-spinning industry declined in the 1830s, so too did the number of silk manufacturers in the town. The number of weavers in their employment is difficult to assess, but it has been suggested that the meagre 250 handloom weavers said to be left in Stockport township in 1838 included the silk industry as well as the cotton.[204]

'WHERE BLEACHERS AND PRINTERS ARE BOTH MUCH WANTED'

The finishing branches of the textile industry, bleaching, printing and dyeing, were already established in the Borough before the upsurge in cotton manufacture in the late eighteenth century. Although some firms specialized in one or other of the finishing branches, there was considerable overlap. Calico printers needed first to bleach the cloth, and they might also carry out some bleaching as an end in itself. Bleaching firms might diversify their interests by taking up printing.[205] Dyeing could also be carried out as an additional, rather than specialized, business.

Stockport seems to have been the main centre within the Borough for specialized dyeing. Two firms describing themselves as dyers were listed in the town in 1798. By 1834 the number stood at six, with one other in Reddish.[206] Bleaching and printing firms were more widely spread. They required an ample supply of water and a fairly extensive site, particularly while the bleaching process still involved exposure to sunlight. The majority, therefore, were to be found outside the town, located along the rivers or their tributary streams (*Ill 6.10*).

Heaton Mersey and Edgeley bleachworks

The most important bleachworks in the Borough were at Heaton Mersey and Edgeley. The Heaton Mersey works, as we have already seen, were begun by Samuel Oldknow and his brother Thomas in 1784, the same year in which Oldknow set up his manufacturing business in Stockport. Edgeley, or Sykes's, bleachworks were founded by William Sykes and his partners in 1792. Three years later, on the dissolution of the partnership, he became the sole owner of what would become one of the Borough's longest-established family firms. The site, formerly part of an agricultural estate, had been advertised in the local press in November 1792 as 'an eligible situation for bleach ground, or print field...very contiguous to the populous manufacturing town of Stockport, where bleachers and printers are both much wanted'.[207] An earlier mention of a White Field next to Bridge Hall, a short distance to the south of this site, suggests that bleaching was already under way in the locality.[208] Water for Sykes's works was initially provided by a local stream, the Edgeley Brook, but in the early nineteenth century a more abundant source was achieved by the digging of wells. By the mid-1840s an extensive series of reservoirs, which still survives to this day, had been built along the course of the brook.[209]

In the late eighteenth century two developments began to transform the bleaching industry. One was the introduction of chemical bleaching, which moved the bleaching process indoors. At the Heaton Mersey works Thomas Oldknow was experimenting with his own chemical agent by 1790. The Edgeley works were converted to chemical bleaching after William Sykes passed them on to his son in 1804.[210] The other development was mechanization. Power was first applied to dash wheels, wooden drums used for washing the cloth, but also came to be used for other stages of the bleaching process. Water-power was in use at Edgeley in the 1790s. In 1803 this was supplemented by steam, one of the earliest instances of its application to the finishing industry.[211] A waterwheel was installed at the Oldknows' works in 1786. As in the cotton-spinning industry, it was only with some reluctance that the finishing trades entirely dispensed with water-power. A new waterwheel was fitted at the Heaton Mersey works in 1824, although by this date steam was also in use on the site. Defects in the construction of this wheel are reported to have made it more a hindrance than a use.[212]

Both the Edgeley and the Heaton Mersey works underwent considerable expansion in the nineteenth century. At Heaton Mersey, as we have already seen, spinning and weaving were added to finishing. An upper bleachworks was also added to the site in the early 1830s, towards the top of Vale Road. The Heaton Mersey works, however, were particularly badly hit by the depression in 1842, when the workforce of 500 was laid off.[213]

Early printworks

Two calico printworks are known to have been established in the Borough before 1780. One, at Chadkirk on the River Goyt, was among the very first (possibly the first) printworks in the region. The other, founded somewhat later, was at Sheep Wash on the

Mersey to the west of Stockport town. By 1800 there were about five times that number. The earliest of these new sites may have been the Reddish Mills printworks, in existence in 1784. By 1805 water was brought to these works from the Tame along a millrace over 900 metres long.[214] The Oldknows may have been printing at their Heaton Mersey works in 1787.[215] Two printworks were established in the vicinity of Cheadle village: Cheadle Grove to the north, and Cheadle Vale (also known as Demmings works) to the south. Closer to Stockport were works at Cheadle Heath, part of which was housed in a converted barn.[216] James Heald carried out printing in the growing industrial suburb of Portwood until 1806, when he moved this business to a site in Disley.[217] At the south-east extremity of the Borough were the Strines printworks.[218] The date at which a small printworks at Brinksway Bank was established is uncertain, but a time in the 1780s or 1790s seems likely. They were located on a site cut out of the natural rock, probably a short distance downstream on the Mersey from the Sheep Wash works.[219] In the early 1800s the Compstall printworks opened.

This early expansion of the printing trade closely mirrored that of the cotton-spinning industry. As the building of new factories decreased after about 1803, so the printing branch entered a period in which any new investment seems to have been confined to existing sites. After Compstall no printworks are known to have been established in the Borough for well over a decade. At some works printing now ceased. In about 1809 both the Cheadle Heath and Sheep Wash sites closed. The Brinksway Bank works also appear to have been relatively short-lived. Foggbrook Mill in Offerton was converted to a printworks in 1816, but two firms failed in turn to make a success of the business and the building was converted back to cotton.[220] The end of printing at the former cotton mill in Torkington, as we have seen, seems to have resulted in the demolition of the building. The printworks at Chadkirk are reported to have closed in 1817, although they were reopened by 1824. From about this time the owner of the printworks was involved in a dispute with Samuel Oldknow at Mellor over the right to draw water from the Goyt.[221] The resumption of printing at Chadkirk was probably a consequence of the more buoyant state of local cotton manufacture in the early 1820s. This new economic climate was a situation from which one local printer took particular advantage.

Thomas Marsland's Daw Bank printworks

Among the dyers in Stockport in the 1790s was John Marsland, who passed on what was evidently a fairly successful business to his son Thomas. Shortly after 1816 Thomas Marsland took a crucial step and expanded this business into calico printing. At this date there appears to have been no other calico printer in the town itself. When cotton manufacture boomed in the first half of the 1820s, Marsland's trade soared. The firm had two neighbouring works. One was at Daw Bank (*Ill 6.19*), the other on Chestergate. Edward Baines in 1825 described Marsland's premises as 'an immense calico-printing establishment, connected with blue-dye works, said to be the most extensive in Europe'. It was estimated that at this time Marsland was printing 1,270,000 yards of cloth every six weeks.[222]

It was Marsland who a few years later built the seven-storey Wellington Mill, on a site immediately next to his Daw Bank works. He ran the cotton-spinning and weaving factory and the printing and dyeing works as two separate concerns. The first was in partnership with his sons, the second with his sons-in-law, presumably as a way of ensuring a good living for his daughters. Marsland also had a political career, serving as an MP for Stockport from 1832 to 1841. After losing his parliamentary seat, he settled in retirement at Henbury near Macclesfield, on his own newly purchased manorial estate.[223]

Later printworks

By the mid-1830s a few other works were also carrying out printing in the town. Among these were the Spring Vale printworks, on a riverside site behind Tiviot Dale. A firm occupying these works in the 1840s had the distinction of being owned by a woman, Elizabeth Hulme, whose policy was to employ only female printers.[224] The 1830s also saw expansion outside the town. In 1833 Springwater Mill, near Turf Lee in Marple township, was converted to printing. It had previously been used to grind dyestuffs, probably for use in the nearby Strines printworks.[225] Woodford, a township in which industry had been hitherto confined to domestic workshops, also became the site of a new printworks. Located near Deanwater Bridge, it was built in 1837 by a member of the Andrew family of Compstall. Even as the Woodford works were being built, the depression was perhaps already beginning to be felt within the printing industry. Springwater Mill may have been one

Ill 6.19 Daw Bank printworks and Wellington Mill.
In 1825 the Daw Bank printworks were reported to be the largest in Europe. They were owned by Thomas Marsland, who at this date was the only calico printer operating in Stockport. The seven-storey Wellington Mill was built by Marsland in 1828 for cotton spinning and powerloom weaving. In 1832 Marsland became one of Stockport's first two MPs. The printworks have been demolished, but Wellington Mill is still a prominent feature of the town.

casualty of that downturn, with the site becoming a bleachworks at some point between 1836 and 1849. Cheadle Grove works closed in the 1840s and an industrialist's mansion, Abney Hall, was built on the site. The Woodford works survived that decade, but were destroyed by a fire in 1850 and apparently not rebuilt.[226] The opening of these printworks probably accounts for the rise in Woodford's population from 403 in 1831 to 564 ten years later. In 1851, following the fire, the figure had fallen to 430, presumably as former employees left the area to find work elsewhere.

Machinery and buildings in the printing industry

Calico printing was originally carried out by hand, using wooden blocks engraved with the pattern. In the mid-1780s machine printing, using engraved rollers, was introduced into the region. By the 1800s most, if not all, of the printworks in the Borough were carrying out some printing by machine. At this period power was still mostly provided by water, although a steam engine was installed at Cheadle Grove in about 1805. Cheadle Heath and Brinksway Bank printworks each had one machine, turned by a horse-gin.[227] The local printing industry experienced its own troubles during the Luddite period. Towards the end of April 1812 printworkers in Cheadle were demanding the removal of machinery. Whether by coincidence or design, later in that year a Cheadle printworks, probably Cheadle Grove, was burned down. In the previous December the Andrews' printworks at Compstall had been ransacked and set on fire.[228]

Block printing was only slowly phased out. In the 1840s the printworks in the Borough appear to have been typical of the region, in using both methods of production. The change-over to machine printing occurred later in the nineteenth century.[229] Because the finishing trades involved the use of heavy equipment and the movement of cloth, often wet, from one process to the next, the works themselves usually consisted of an arrangement of one- or two-storey buildings. A notable exception was the Daw Bank printworks of Thomas Marsland, parts of which were four storeys high.[230]

HATTING

In the late eighteenth century and early decades of the nineteenth, while the textile industry was being radically changed by the introduction of new machinery, hatting was still carried out by hand. It was an industry divided between the workshops of small hatters and the premises of manufacturers who put out raw materials,

and may also have undertaken the finishing processes. An example of this last group is David Higham of Stockport, who in the 1790s had rooms for storing fur and wool (the raw materials of felt hat making), for dyeing and for finishing, and a warehouse for the finished hats.[231] Aikin in 1795 described hatting in the town as 'a considerable branch of employment'.[232] However, compared with the cotton industry, the numbers involved were small. Stockport was said to contain eighteen large hat manufactories in 1815, but one of the largest hatters in the town at this time provided work for only between 100 and 130 people.[233] Small hatters were to be found within both the town and the surrounding townships, perhaps particularly in those lying to the north and east. Some hatters living in the more rural areas obtained part of their income from farming. One hatter at Marple Bridge in the 1830s also ran a public house.[234] Most of the Borough's larger hatters were probably based within the town, or in fairly close proximity. The family firm of Carringtons had premises at Cale Green, while the firm of Barlow and Shawcross was based near Priory Lane in Reddish.[235]

Worsleys and Christys

By the late eighteenth century some local manufacturers were making hats on commission for London firms. Among these were Thomas and John Worsley, who from 1797 were producing hats for the firm of Miller Christy.[236] The Worsleys' business was based in Canal Street, located behind Hillgate and in the early nineteenth century home to several other hatting firms.[237] In 1826, in a move which marked a watershed in the development of Stockport's hatting industry, Christys bought out the Worsleys' firm and junior partners came to live in the town.[238] Christys are said to have acquired the firm out of admiration of its high standards and efficiency. While some hats produced by provincial manufacturers were finished in London, the Worsleys undertook the finishing processes themselves.[239] The town's reputation for a high-quality product was not entirely new. In 1814 it was said that 'The best English hats are made in London and Stockport'.[240]

Christys expanded their Canal Street site by acquiring the premises of neighbouring firms. In about 1840 they also erected a five-storey warehouse, almost certainly the largest building to be constructed for the hatting industry in the town at the time, and itself a sign of the firm's expansion.[241] By 1834 Christys were employing seventy-six workers to carry out the finishing processes.[242] In the following year the firm built a large hatting factory in Droylsden, to the north of the Borough. The building was not, however, put to its intended use but in 1837 opened as a combined cotton mill.[243] Precisely which hatting processes Christys had intended to undertake at the Droylsden factory is uncertain, but by this date another firm was carrying out the planking, or felt-making, process at its own Canal Street premises.[244]

The felt hat industry in depression

The depression which hit the textile industry in the late 1830s also affected hatting. In the case of the traditional form of this industry, the making of felt hats, this slump continued through the 1840s. Fashions were changing, and what was now in demand was the silk hat. At Reddish, Barlow and Shawcross were making silk hats by the late 1820s. Christys, perhaps because of the size of their operation, seem not to have suffered a serious decline in trade until about 1845-6, when the firm also took up the manufacture of this new product.[245]

The later revival of the felt hatting industry involved a decisive shift away from the old workshops to new factories in which the processes of manufacture were carried out by machinery. With that change, the local hatting industry greatly increased both in terms of output and the size of the workforce. As we shall see in a later chapter, it was a process in which Christys played a key role.

ENGINEERING

A second industry which assumed a much greater local importance in the later nineteenth century was engineering. The early development of this trade in the region owed much to the requirements of the cotton industry. Ironwork was needed for steam engines and boilers, for gearing and shafting, for machines and machine parts, and for use in the construction of factories.[246] Stockport had at least one iron foundry in the 1790s and 1800s.[247] In 1825 eight iron founders were listed in the town. They included a specialist boiler maker and two firms whose names also appear in a list of eleven local machine makers. One of these was also described as a millwright; another, John Garside at Portwood, operated a combined cotton mill as well as his iron foundry and machine-making business.[248] There were other local demands for the products of these firms. One foundry on Great Underbank produced gas brackets and lamp pillars installed to light the town's streets in the 1820s and 1830s.[249]

The importance of the engineering trade in the town during the early nineteenth century should not be exaggerated. One local machine maker was able to turn out 200 pirated copies of the Sharp and Roberts powerloom for a neighbouring cotton mill. (In the event these proved to be defective and were quickly replaced with the genuine article.)[250] However, compared with some other machine-making firms in the region, Stockport's are said to have been on a small scale, and most mill-owners seem to have preferred to order their machinery from Manchester, Bolton or, even further afield, from Preston.[251]

COAL MINING

The Borough's growing local population and expanding industry, based increasingly on steam, were both dependent on coal. From the 1790s this could be brought into Stockport by barge, along the Ashton Canal, from the coal-producing areas to the north of the Tame. In the Lancashire coalfield as a whole, output is believed to have quadrupled between 1800 and 1840.[252] That coal production within the Borough itself was rising in this period is also evident, although for the most part this increase may be impossible to quantify accurately.

Norbury

At Norbury, even while the Ashton Canal was under construction, a concerted effort was being made to improve output. The seams here continued beyond the township boundary along the Norbury Brook into the northern part of Sir George Warren's Poynton estate. In a move towards greater efficiency, in 1795 Warren leased the right to mine his share of these seams to Thomas Peter Legh, the manorial lord of Norbury. He in turn leased his rights to Nathaniel Wright, a Poynton man who at this date was already operating a coal pit in the southern part of that township. Wright invested considerably in his newly acquired seams. Even before his lease with Legh was finalized, he had begun to sink two new pits. Flooding had long been a problem in the Norbury mines. To raise water, an atmospheric engine had been installed before 1764, when it was replaced by a larger version. Wright himself installed two new pumping engines. One of these, on the Poynton side of the Norbury Brook, was a pirated version of the designs of Boulton and Watt. Unfortunately for Wright, the Birmingham firm had an agent operating in the region, James Lawson, whose job was to track down such infringements. Arriving at Poynton on Good Friday 1796, he made the pretence of being interested in the workings of another engine which had been erected two years earlier by Sir George Warren and was used for winding up coal. While a local engineer was busy starting this up, Lawson wandered off to examine the nearby pumping engine and confirmed that there had indeed been a breach of patent. Nathaniel Wright, rather than pay a premium to Boulton and Watt, had the engine modified.[253] The site of Wright's new engine in Norbury, and of the two earlier engines serving the Norbury pits, lay between the brook and Buxton Road (the A6), close to the Robin Hood Hotel. A later pumping engine house, built in about 1840, still stands in this location (Ill 6.20).[254]

The joint working of seams on either side of the Norbury Brook ceased in the early nineteenth century, after which Norbury and Poynton coals were mined independently.[255] It left an unfortunate legacy. In the 1860s water was reported to be entering workings in Poynton via a communication with the Norbury pits made during that earlier period. After mining stopped

at Norbury in 1892, water levels within the abandoned workings began to rise. At Poynton fears were expressed that this water would find its way 'through communications which were made in the upper Seams when the two Collieries were worked together some years ago'. Pumping equipment was installed to deal with the problem, and tunnels were dug to drain water from the Norbury workings.[256]

Norbury may well have been the first mining area in the Borough to witness significant expansion in response to the growing demand for coal. By 1842 the colliery employed 122 people, a medium-sized workforce for the Lancashire coalfield at this date. The Poynton collieries, owned by Lord Vernon, employed 418.[257] In 1825 Norbury was the only place in the Borough which Baines named as contributing to the 'abundance of coal' brought to Stockport.[258]

Ill 6.20 Norbury Colliery engine house.
Norbury was the site of one of the Borough's largest collieries in the late eighteenth and early nineteenth centuries. Drainage was a continual problem and from at least the 1760s steam-power was used to raise water from the workings. This engine house, now converted to a dwelling, dates from about 1840.

Bredbury

In 1817 there were at least two collieries in Bredbury township. One of these, in Woodley, was leased by the owners of the Heaton Mersey bleachworks. Some of the coal was sold to their workforce, some was used in the works themselves. The supply from Woodley proved inadequate, and more had to be brought from the mines at Poynton and Haughton Green.[259] Mining in Bredbury may have expanded by 1841 when, as well as a pit at Woodley, there appears to have been a concentration of small collieries in the Bents Lane area. However, it was perhaps not until some years later, with the opening of new, deeper pits, that mining in Bredbury was really to move up a gear.[260] The sinking of a shaft on Brinnington Moor by 1836, reaching seams down to a depth of 720 feet (218 metres), may have been an early attempt to widen the traditional areas of coal working in this locality.[261]

Marple, Ludworth and Mellor

In Marple coal was mined on Samuel Oldknow's estate. Here pits were conveniently located alongside the Peak Forest Canal and close to the lime kilns which they provided with fuel.[262] In 1811 there were also at least three mines in operation in Ludworth and Mellor: Ludworth Colliery, to the south of Compstall Bridge; and collieries at Ernocroft on the side of the Etherow valley, and at Longhurst Lane, near to the present Mellor War Memorial Park. The Longhurst Lane colliery appears to have closed by the late 1830s, although by that time other, possibly new, pits were being worked in Marple and Mellor.[263]

Ludworth Colliery was being worked by 1822 by the mining company of the Jowett family and was leased from the duke of Norfolk, as part of his manor of Glossop. The accounts of the manor show that over the next two decades the Jowetts greatly increased output. They paid the duke a percentage of the value of the coal which they extracted. These payments steadily rose from £74 in 1822, to £293 in 1830, and £603 in 1839.[264] From the 1840s the Jowetts also operated Mellor Colliery, on the eastern boundary of that township. During its early working life, coal was carried from this pit by packhorse to a wharf on the Peak Forest Canal at Newtown near New Mills.[265]

By comparison with the Jowetts' activities at the Ludworth and Mellor collieries, mining at Ernocroft was on a fairly small scale. At some time after 1811 mining in this area seems to have ceased, until 1828 when George Andrew leased from the duke of Norfolk the right to mine in Ernocroft Wood. This was not Andrew's first mining venture. In about 1825 he began mining operations at Ludworth Colliery, which he worked alongside the Jowetts until he moved his operation to Ernocroft. Between 1828 and 1838 he paid the duke the relatively low royalties of £33 to £42 a year, making it likely that most of the coal dug at Ernocroft Wood was intended for use at the Compstall mills. It may not be coincidental that in 1839, the year after the installation of the Lily Wheel at the mills, the royalties had fallen to a mere £13.[266]

TURNPIKES

The roads to Marple, Mellor and Compstall, 1792-1803

The earliest turnpikes to be established in the Borough had largely been to the benefit of Stockport. They had improved links between the town and Manchester, Yorkshire and the south.[267] From the late eighteenth century, as other places in the Borough grew in importance they too were provided with better communications by road. The first area to benefit in this way was Samuel Oldknow's estate at Marple and Mellor.

Oldknow's Mellor Mill lay close to an old road leading eastwards from Marple Bridge to Hayfield. This routeway was included in a turnpike Act of 1792 designed to improve communications in this north-west corner of Derbyshire (Ill 5.9).[268] By this date Oldknow had begun, and perhaps completed, his own road scheme on his estate. In March 1789 he was already planning to build a new bridge over the Goyt close to the proposed site of his mill. It was suggested to him that this should be of cast iron, to a design patented the year before. (The first iron bridge in the world had been built only ten years previously, at Ironbridge in Shropshire.) Oldknow, however, was impatient to proceed with his original plan. The result was the stone-built and elegant Bottoms Bridge. Beyond this a new road was cut into the rock face of the valley side, known as Goyt Cliff, to provide access from Marple (Ill 6.9). The road and bridge together cost at least £3000.[269]

In 1790 Oldknow turned his attention to improving the road between Marple and Stockport. He began by building or repairing the bridges along its line at Foggbrook and Dan Bank, on the boundary between Offerton and Marple. In 1792 he had the road between them repaired and gravelled.[270] This private enterprise was perhaps intended as only a temporary measure. By 1796 Oldknow and other local landowners were planning to establish a turnpike from Stockport, through

Marple, to New Mills and Hayfield. Oldknow developed his own views about this turnpike, which were patently motivated by self-interest. He soon decided that it should run only between Stockport and Marple Bridge. In the face of opposition from one of the joint promoters of the road, he conceded that it should continue from Marple to Hayfield. He then argued that this section should include his Goyt Cliff road and Bottoms Bridge, with the intention that some of the cost of their construction would be recovered from tolls collected from the turnpike. The scheme which was finally chosen and was approved by Parliament in 1801 ignored Oldknow's private road. Instead a new road was built, southwards from Marple, through Strines. For the section between Stockport and Marple, and for a branch from Marple to Marple Bridge, the turnpike made use of the roads already in existence.[271]

In 1802 Parliament sanctioned the creation of a turnpike from Marple Bridge to Glossop. This too involved the construction of a new line (the present A626), which followed the side of the Etherow valley.[272] In the following year a further Act allowed the establishment of a branch from this road to Compstall. Among the trustees named in this Act were George and Thomas Andrew, co-founders of the Compstall printworks.[273]

Stockport and turnpike Acts of 1816-20

Later turnpike Acts served Stockport and its vicinity. The main road leading westwards from the town, through Cheadle, Gatley, Altrincham and Northwich, was placed under a turnpike trust in 1820. By July 1822 a fast coach service was operating along this road between Stockport and the port of Liverpool, via Warrington, making it possible to spend six hours in Liverpool and return the same day.[274]

The 1820 Act included a branch road from Cheadle Heath to the Manchester to Buxton turnpike, passing through Edgeley, an acknowledgement of the growing importance of this area. Greek Street and most of Edgeley Road appear to have been built as parts of this branch.[275] In 1816 parliamentary consent had been given for the road between Bredbury and Portwood Bridge to be improved, as a branch of the Stockport to Ashton turnpike. Brinnington Moor had been enclosed in the previous year, and the new turnpike was intended to enable development in the northern part of the township.[276] The road from Lancashire Hill, through Reddish to Gorton was turnpiked under an Act of 1818. At Gorton this turnpike joined with a new road (the present Hyde Road) linking Manchester to Denton.[277]

Wellington Road – Stockport's first bypass

Arguably the most controversial turnpike Act to affect the Borough was passed in 1824. It involved the creation of a new road which redrew the map of Stockport. The ancient route for traffic passing from north to south through the town, turnpiked under an Act of 1725, involved the steep slopes of Old Road and Hillgate. Between these, traffic had to turn from Bridge Street into Little Underbank, and then negotiate a right-angled bend between that thoroughfare and Great Underbank. The narrowness of the town's old streets added to the difficulties. Originally laid out in the medieval period, in the eighteenth century they were proving inadequate for the rising volume of traffic, and in particular the growing number of horse-drawn vehicles. Attempts were made in 1775 and 1785 to obtain an Act of Parliament which, among other improvements, would have allowed the widening of streets in the town. Both ended in failure. In 1794 the route on the north side of the Mersey was partly improved by the construction of a new road, known as 'Lancashire Hill' after the name of this side of the Mersey valley. However, within a few years a canal link to Stockport was opened with a terminus on Lancashire Hill. The presence of this canal wharf created further congestion. Through traffic using Lancashire Hill now had to compete with local wagons collecting coal, cotton and other commodities from the canal wharf or delivering finished goods to be loaded onto barges.[278]

In the early 1820s, a period of boom in the town, the trustees of the Manchester to Buxton turnpike decided on a radical solution to the town's traffic problems. They would build a bypass. In a move which foreshadowed late twentieth-century road-building schemes, various routes were proposed, each known by a particular colour. The 'Orange Line', the most westerly of these, was eventually chosen. The idea of a bypass caused alarm among shopkeepers and manufacturers whose premises lay on the existing route and who anticipated a loss of trade. They argued that an adequate and cheaper solution could be found by improving the existing line. The trustees appeared to give in to this opposition, but within a short time an investigating committee, which they themselves had appointed, was reporting that a bypass was essential. When the trustees submitted their proposal to Parliament, the opposition petitioned in favour of their own improvement scheme. They omitted, however, to send a witness to back up their case, and in March 1824 the trustees' bill became law.[279]

Work on the project began the following month. The new road was 3.5 kilometres (2 miles) long, joining with the old turnpike route at Bramhall Lane and Heaton Chapel. It was carried across the Mersey valley on a new stone bridge of eleven arches, the widest of which spanned the river. With memories of the Napoleonic wars still fresh, both the road and the bridge were named after Wellington. A grand opening ceremony was planned for Monday the 19th of June 1826, eleven years and a day after the battle of Waterloo. The discovery that the county's parliamentary elections were to be held on that same day prompted a postponement to the 3rd of July. The opening procession, which was nearly as long as the road itself, included workmen who had built the road and bridge, carrying the tools of their trade, and stagecoaches representing the companies who would use this new route, as well as local civic dignitaries.[280]

Today, as part of the A6, Wellington Road is still part of a major north-south route but its original role as a bypass is scarcely recognizable (Ill 6.21). When first built, the new road cut across mostly open land (Ill 7.1). The report on the grand opening of the road in the *Stockport Advertiser* predicted that this would not remain the case; 'though many years may elapse before that event takes place, there can be no doubt that at some period or other, the new line will become the centre of a new town at once healthy and convenient'.[281] Among the first people to take advantage of the new opportunity for development were local industrialists. By its side, even as the road was under construction, a new six-storey cotton mill, Spring Bank, was being built by one of the members of the very investigating committee which had so strongly recommended the bypass.[282] On a neighbouring plot of land, between Wellington Road and his Daw Bank printworks, Thomas Marsland was soon to construct his seven-storey Wellington Mill.[283] In 1833 'neat and respectable dwellings' were being built along the new road.[284] Its junction with Edward Street and Greek Street became the site of several of the town's grandest buildings, beginning with a National School in 1825-6 and Stockport Infirmary in 1832-3, and ending in the early twentieth century with the Town Hall, and the War Memorial and Art Gallery.

CANALS

The Ashton Canal

Rival plans for a canal link to Stockport had been put forward in the 1760s but, as we have seen in the previous chapter, one scheme was successfully opposed by the duke of Bridgewater, while his own was begun but abandoned. In the early 1790s conditions were more favourable for the construction of a canal to the town.

This was the period of 'canal mania', when numerous proposals were made for the building of new waterways. Then, as previously, they were principally intended to carry heavy freight, and in particular coal. At Stockport the main market for this fuel must initially have been with the domestic needs of its rapidly expanding population, but from 1791 there was also a growing demand from factory-owners using steam as a source of power.

The revival of the idea of a canal link to Stockport can be traced to November 1790. In that month a proposal was announced for the building of a canal between Stockport and Sale Moor, where it would have joined with the duke of Bridgewater's own canal. This was the very same scheme which the duke himself had previously failed to complete. Although this plan quickly found financial backers, it does not appear to have been pursued any further.[285] However, a new proposal for a canal link to the town was soon to come from another quarter.

In 1792 Parliament authorized the construction of a canal linking Manchester with the coal-producing areas of Ashton and Oldham. The proprietors of this new canal were quick to seize the opportunity for further profits, offered by the growing market for coal at Stockport. In March 1793 an Act allowed a branch of this Ashton Canal to be built, which was to be Stockport's first and, in the event, only canal link. This branch left the main Ashton Canal at Clayton, to the east of Manchester. Passing southwards through Gorton and Reddish, it terminated on the north side of the Mersey at a canal basin on the top of Lancashire Hill (Ill 6.22). The branch opened in early 1797, although work was not finally completed until the following year.[286]

From the Stockport branch in Reddish the 1793 Act also allowed the construction of a branch eastwards to Beat Bank. It was intended to serve the collieries at Haughton Green. Work on the Beat Bank branch was begun, but financial difficulties forced the canal company to first suspend and in 1798 to abandon the scheme.[287]

The Peak Forest Canal

The 'canal mania' of the early 1790s resulted in not one, but two canals being built through the Borough. The Peak Forest Canal ran from a junction with the Ashton Canal at Dukinfield to Buxworth near Whaley Bridge in Derbyshire. Unlike the Ashton Canal, it was primarily designed to carry not coal but lime and limestone. From Buxworth its line continued as a tramroad to the limestone quarries at Dove Holes near

Ill 6.21 Wellington Road South, in 1939.

Wellington Road (the modern A6) was Stockport's first bypass. It was built in 1824-6 to relieve traffic congestion within the town and almost immediately was a focus for new development. Wellington Road South, seen here looking south, became the location for a succession of public buildings. These include the Central Library (lower left), opened in 1913; the Town Hall (centre left), opened in 1908 and built on the site of a National School erected in 1825-6; and, facing this, Stockport Infirmary, built in 1832-3.

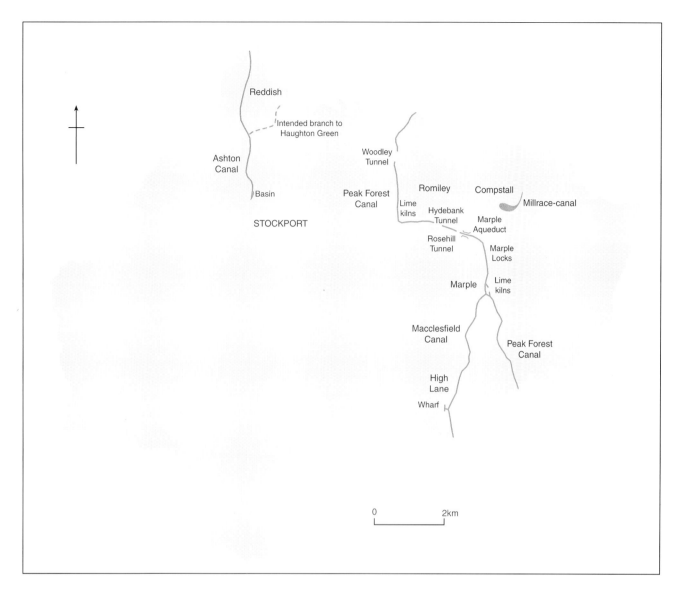

Ill 6.22 Canals in the Borough.
The 'canal mania' of the early 1790s resulted in two canals being built within the Borough. One was a branch of the Ashton Canal which terminated on Lancashire Hill and served the town of Stockport. The other was the Peak Forest Canal, built to carry limestone quarried at Dove Holes near Buxton. The Macclesfield Canal, which joined the Peak Forest Canal at Marple, was opened in 1831. A fourth canal in the Borough was the private waterway used to carry coal to Compstall Mills.

Buxton. Lime, produced by burning limestone, was an important commodity. Spread on fields, it served as a fertilizer. It was also used in the building industry and in the textile finishing trade. By the late eighteenth century limestone burning was a long-established industry around Dove Holes. Prior to the construction of the canal the lime was transported by packhorse.[288]

The Peak Forest Canal was initially planned as a branch of the Ashton Canal. In May 1793, only two months after the passing of the Act for their Stockport branch, the Ashton Canal Company decided to submit the new proposal to Parliament. Existing commitments seem to have soon led to a change of mind and in July a new company was formed to pursue

the Peak Forest scheme. The Act authorizing the construction of the canal was passed in March 1794. Links with the Ashton Canal Company remained close, for a third of the shareholders named in the Act had also invested in the Ashton Canal. The largest shareholder was Samuel Oldknow, despite the fact that he was still embroiled in financial difficulties.[289] He had a close personal interest in the new canal. It would pass through his estate at Marple and, as we shall see, would enable him to diversify his business interests.

The Peak Forest Canal presented considerable problems of engineering. Between its more low-lying northern terminus at Dukinfield and its southern terminus at Buxworth there was a difference in height

Ill 6.23 Marple Aqueduct.
This great aqueduct still carries the Peak Forest Canal across the River Goyt. It was designed by Benjamin Outram and opened to
traffic in 1800, having taken seven years to build. Circular openings lessen the weight of the arches while retaining their strength.

of over 60 metres. By following, as far as possible, the natural contours and enhancing these with engineering works, the greater part of the canal was built as two level sections. Linking these lower and upper levels is a flight of sixteen locks extending for a distance of about 1.5 kilometres (nearly 1 mile) at Marple. With an average depth of about 4 metres, these locks are said to be the second deepest in the country.[290]

The locks were part of the original scheme, but when the whole length of the canal opened in 1800, they had not yet been built. The upper level from Buxworth to Marple had been completed in 1796, but in the following year the canal company found that it was running out of money. To cut costs, in place of the locks a tramroad was built linking the upper and lower levels. Along this track, wagons were pulled by horses. Once the canal had opened the shortcomings of this alternative soon became apparent. The loading of limestone at Marple from barges onto tram wagons and back onto barges created such a bottleneck that first a night shift was introduced and then the tramroad was

increased from one track to two. Raising the money for the construction of the locks itself proved to be an uphill task, but the cost was finally met with the help of Richard Arkwright. The locks opened in 1804, and the tramroad itself remained in use until 1807. Part of its line can still be traced as a low curving bank on the recreation ground between Strines Road and Arkwright Road.[291]

The lower level included three tunnels, at Woodley, Hyde Bank and Rosehill in Romiley. The canal towpath was not continued into the Hyde Bank tunnel, and boatmen had to propel the barges through by lying on their back and 'walking' along the tunnel walls or roof. In the late nineteenth century, after a partial collapse, the roof of the Rosehill tunnel was removed.[292]

Marple Aqueduct

It is also on the lower level, a short distance from the first of the locks at Marple, that the most impressive of the engineering works on the canal is to be found.

Here the steep-sided valley of the Goyt was spanned with a great aqueduct which carried the canal at a height of 30 metres above the river (*Ill 6.23*). It was designed by the principal engineer of the canal, Benjamin Outram, and took seven years to build. George Borrow described the aqueduct as 'the grand work of England', and considered it to be surpassed only by the great canal of China. Circular openings were built into the shoulders of the aqueduct's three great arches. These reduced the weight of the arches, while still retaining their strength. The design of the piers from which these arches spring and the use of different coloured stone make the aqueduct a striking piece of architecture as well as a masterpiece of engineering.[293]

At one point in 1795 the canal company had approved a proposal by the American engineer Robert Fulton that the arches should be built of cast iron. Fulton had originally been employed as a contract engineer to excavate part of the canal but seems to have preferred to provide the company with his own ideas as to how the canal should be built and operated. Towards the end of 1795, however, Fulton disappeared from the scene. Outram may not have been sorry to see him go.[294]

Lime kilns

The establishment of the Peak Forest Canal not only made the transportation of limestone easier but also resulted in kilns for limestone burning being built along its banks. By the early 1820s there were several such kilns at Hole House Fold in Romiley.[295] Much better known are the kilns built in the 1790s by Samuel Oldknow at Marple. They were placed behind an elaborate stone facade, with buttresses and Gothic windows. Resembling a medieval castle, the building is said to have been designed as an eyecatcher from the opposite side of the Goyt valley (*Ill 6.24*). Limestone was unloaded at a canal basin behind these kilns. Together with coal which Oldknow mined nearby, it was tipped into the top of these kilns, and the burnt lime was collected from the bottom. This was carried away by cart or by canal barge, along a short branch leading to the main canal. The process of limestone burning was carried out here on a massive scale. It has been estimated that in 1800 the kilns produced 8300 tons of lime. The cost of production, however, was high and within a few years the business was running at a loss. In 1811 Oldknow leased the kilns out. Later operators of the kilns appear to have fared somewhat better, and production may not have finally ceased until the 1900s.[296]

The Macclesfield Canal and earlier schemes

After the completion of the Peak Forest Canal, no new waterways were built in the Borough until the 1820s, when two were constructed. One was the short length of private canal constructed through the Etherow valley below Ernocroft Wood to carry coal to Compstall. The other was the Macclesfield Canal. At its northern end this joined with the Peak Forest Canal immediately above the locks at Marple. Heading south, the new canal passed through Poynton and Macclesfield, and close by Congleton, to join with the Trent and Mersey Canal near Kidsgrove.

The idea for such a canal link had been put forward as early as the mid-1790s. Then the proposal included a branch canal or tramway along which coal from Norbury and Poynton would have been carried to Stockport. On that occasion the scheme for a Macclesfield Canal failed to win sufficient support, and a string of subsequent attempts in the early nineteenth century to revive the project were no more successful. Even a far less ambitious plan by the Peak Forest Canal Company in 1799 to build a branch from Marple to the Norbury and Poynton pits was dropped.[297]

It was against the background of a rapid expansion in the silk industry in Macclesfield in 1824-5 that the scheme for a canal link to the town was promoted for the final time. Ironically the Act allowing the construction of the canal was passed in 1826, the very year which saw that boom turn to bust. The line of the canal was surveyed by Thomas Telford, one of the leading transport engineers of the nineteenth century. Responsibility for its construction fell to William Crossley, formerly the engineer on the Lancaster Canal. Like the Peak Forest, the Macclesfield Canal was built on two levels. These were joined by a flight of locks at Bosley, between Macclesfield and Congleton. The canal opened in 1831.[298]

At High Lane a short branch from the canal led to a wharf next to Buxton Road (the A6). This provided a link between the canal and the main road to Stockport. Among the local businesses using this wharf was the firm of Pickfords, which had expanded its transport business in the late eighteenth century by acquiring a fleet of barges. Goods from Stockport, including hats made by Christys, were loaded by Pickfords onto their boats at High Lane and transported along the canal network to the Midlands and London. The High Lane branch of the Macclesfield Canal also provided access to a second wharf, where barges were loaded with coal mined at Norbury and Middlewood. To the south, another wharf served the Poynton collieries.[299] A canal link to the Norbury and Poynton pits, first proposed in the 1760s as part of the 'Roe-Warren' scheme which was defeated by the duke of Bridgewater, had finally been achieved.

'Our canal'

There was one other canal scheme relating to the Borough which was proposed in the 1820s but which did not come to fruition. It was put forward in 1822, a time when the cotton trade in Stockport was enjoying a boom and building in the town was going on at fever pitch. From the Bridgewater Canal at Stretford it was intended to build a canal eastwards as far as Heaton Norris. No aqueduct seems to have been planned across the Mersey. Instead, the canal would have resumed on Higher Hillgate. This southern section would have passed through Norbury and Poynton and finished at a tramroad leading to the stone quarries at Kerridge to the north-east of Macclesfield. Stockport was clearly

intended to be the main beneficiary. The northern section of canal would have enabled raw cotton, imported through Liverpool, to be brought to Stockport along a shorter route than that provided by the Ashton Canal. The southern section would have brought cheaper coal and building materials to the town. Most of the promises of financial backing for the scheme are said to have come from Stockport tradesmen. The *Stockport Advertiser* described it as 'our canal'. In February 1823 a petition was sent to Parliament asking leave to present a bill. The scheme was not, however, to the liking of Wilbraham Egerton of Tatton, the largest landowner in Heaton Norris and also an MP for Cheshire. He was sitting on the parliamentary committee to which the petition was referred for consideration and the scheme progressed no further.[300] Stockport's next major transport link was to take a very different form.

Ill 6.24 Marple lime kilns.
These lime kilns were built next to the Peak Forest Canal by Samuel Oldknow in the 1790s. Their facade, resembling a medieval castle, is said to have been designed as an eyecatcher from across the Goyt valley. Lime, produced by burning limestone, was spread on fields as a fertilizer, as well as being used in the building and textile-finishing trades.

Ill 6.25 Stockport Viaduct, in 1842.
The monumental viaduct across the Mersey valley was built in 1839-40 as part of the railway between Manchester and Crewe. That line first reached Stockport in 1840, when trains from Manchester terminated at a station at Heaton Norris. The viaduct itself was opened to traffic in 1842. It was widened in 1888-9. This early view of the viaduct, from the west, shows in the distance the windmill and other buildings next to the terminus of the Ashton Canal on Lancashire Hill.

THE ARRIVAL OF THE RAILWAY

Railways originated with the tramroads used to haul wagons in the mining and quarrying industries. The first steam locomotive was the invention of the Cornishman Richard Trevithick in the 1800s. The early locomotives were heavy and slow, and for many years the use of locomotion was mainly confined to private railways operated by mine-owners. Interest in railways widened in the 1820s, when many schemes were put forward for commercial lines which would carry more general freight. Even during this period it was generally the intention that wagons should be horse-drawn, with fixed steam engines being used for haulage up steep gradients. Some schemes proposed in the 1820s involved lines which, had they been built, would have crossed the Borough. When the Macclesfield Canal was

being planned in 1824, a railway was briefly considered as a possible alternative.[301] About this same time a proposal was put forward for a railway from Manchester to north-west Derbyshire. The idea was revived in 1828, this time with the intention of meeting the Cromford and High Peak Railway. That railway, authorized by Parliament in 1825, had been planned as a link between the Peak Forest Canal and the waterways network of the East Midlands. The 1824 and 1828 railway schemes each involved a route passing through Heaton Norris, Cheadle, Bramhall and Norbury. The first of these schemes, however, was quickly abandoned. The second was quashed by a parliamentary committee.[302]

In 1830 a railway was proposed between Manchester and Sheffield, along a route which from Stockport would have followed the Goyt valley, through Marple to

Whaley Bridge. An alternative route, put forward in the following year, would have seen the line turning north at Marple, following the Etherow valley past Compstall and then passing through Longdendale to a tunnel at Woodhead. This tunnel was eventually built, but the adopted approach followed a more direct route from Manchester, passing to the north of the Borough.[303]

The first commercial railway in the region to use locomotion opened between Bolton and Leigh in Lancashire in 1828. The widespread acceptance of locomotives, however, was largely a result of their use on the Liverpool and Manchester Railway. Opened in 1830 and carrying both passengers and freight, this line was a catalyst for the growth of a national railway network. In 1833 Parliament authorized the construction of the Grand Junction Railway between Birmingham and Warrington on the Liverpool and Manchester line. This provided Manchester with a somewhat circuitous railway link with the Midlands. It was to create a more direct route that the first railway line was built through the Borough, eventually joining with the Grand Junction Railway at Crewe.

The Manchester and Birmingham Railway

Such a link was originally promoted by the Manchester and Cheshire Junction Railway Company. It proposed a route which would have crossed the Mersey between Cheadle and Stockport. On the north side of the river a branch line would have served Stockport. In the town backing was given to a rival scheme, proposed by the Manchester South Union Railway Company. It intended to bring a main line from Manchester as close to Stockport as possible. Beyond the town this line would have taken a more easterly route to the Midlands, connecting Stockport with places of more commercial value than those linked by the Manchester and Cheshire Junction line. In 1837 a compromise was reached

between the two companies, which joined together as the Manchester and Birmingham Railway Company. The end result was not entirely satisfactory for Stockport. A change of plan meant that the railway did, after all, take a westerly route, to Crewe. Nonetheless, the line passed through Stockport itself.[304]

Stockport Viaduct

To achieve that link, a great viaduct was built across the Mersey valley on the western side of the town (*Ill 6.25*). More than 500 metres long, with twenty-six arches, it carried trains at a height of about 33 metres above the river. Some 11,000,000 bricks are reported to have been used in its construction. Work began in 1839, and in December 1840 the last stone was ceremoniously laid in place. The viaduct was widened on its western side in the late 1880s to cope with an increase in traffic.[305]

The line opens

The first section of the railway opened in June 1840, between Manchester and a station on the edge of the Mersey valley at Heaton Norris (*Ill 8.10*). Services did not cross the viaduct until May 1842, when the line was opened as far as Sandbach. The final section to Crewe opened in August of that year. Complaints were made that the Heaton Norris station, beyond the northern edge of the town, was too inconvenient. In response, in February 1843 the company opened a new station at Edgeley. This was originally intended only as an experiment, but in the following year it became the town's principal station. There were also stations on this line at Cheadle Hulme and, from 1852, at Heaton Chapel.[306]

CHAPTER SEVEN

REVOLUTIONS IN SOCIETY, 1780-1842

'Let ages yet unborn hear, when and how,
The sons of freedom fought on Sandy Brow'

INTRODUCTION

The cotton industry made Stockport one of the most important manufacturing towns in the country in the late eighteenth and early nineteenth centuries. It also brought wide-reaching social changes. The most fundamental of these was the massive growth in the population. To accommodate those growing numbers the town greatly expanded. Its very appearance also altered, with the most common form of building being the terraced workers' dwelling. Trade, which had long been a part of the town's economy, developed to cater for the needs of its largely working-class population. New forms of entertainment appeared in the town.

Outside Stockport new industrial communities were created, as mills and finishing works were established in rural locations. Agriculture was beginning to change, with local farmers, albeit in varying degrees, adopting more scientific methods of production. Cornmilling underwent significant developments in response to the requirements of the growing local population.

The scale of the growth of the town led to changes in its local government, but this was a slow, piecemeal process. The impetus for improvements in its administration came largely from within the ranks of its inhabitants, who at times were themselves divided on this issue. The town was also affected by national changes introduced in the 1830s by a reforming Whig government. The Reform Act of 1832 made Stockport a parliamentary borough, with its own representation in the House of Commons. Under the provisions of the Poor Law Amendment Act of 1834, the town became the centre of a new poor law union. The Municipal Corporations Act of 1835 created an elected town council. Although this initially co-existed with other administrative bodies, a 'police commission' and the ancient manorial court leet, it would in turn assume their authority.

There were also important developments in the provision of local services as a result of private initiatives. These resulted in improvements to the town's water-supply, in the introduction of gaslighting, and in greater provision of health care. Education also became more widely available to the lower classes, as religious groups established Sunday and day schools. This was a field in which Stockport enjoyed particular prominence, as the home of what was said to be the largest Sunday school in the world.

Stockport also had a reputation of a very different kind in the early nineteenth century, as one of the cotton district's main hotbeds of industrial unrest and political radicalism. The town was the scene of sporadic but at times violent confrontations between the forces of authority and sections of the lower classes striving to improve their economic condition.

THE GROWTH OF STOCKPORT

Population

It has been estimated that in 1779 the population of Stockport township was about 5000. At that date Stockport was surpassed among Cheshire towns only by Chester and perhaps Macclesfield.[1] In 1801, when the first ten-yearly census was taken, the population of Stockport township was 14,830.[2] In two decades the number of people had roughly trebled. The population continued to grow over the next four decades, though at a lesser rate. In 1841 it was nearly double that in 1801, at 28,431. To adhere simply to the population rise within the boundaries of Stockport township is, however, to present only a partial picture of the growth of the town. Beyond those boundaries were the rapidly growing communities in Portwood, Heaton Norris and Edgeley *(Ill 7.1)*. When these are taken into account, by the close of the eighteenth century the population of the town was already the largest in Cheshire.[3] In 1832, in recognition of the spread of the town beyond the township boundaries, the new parliamentary borough of Stockport included neighbouring parts of Heaton Norris, Brinnington, Cheadle Bulkeley and Cheadle Moseley *(Ill 7.2)*. In 1841 there were 50,154 people in the parliamentary borough.[4] Sixty years earlier the town had scarcely begun to spread outside the township boundaries. Now nearly half of its population lay beyond those bounds.

Portwood, Heaton Norris and Edgeley

The growth of Portwood was particularly striking. In the 1770s this corner of Brinnington township was still

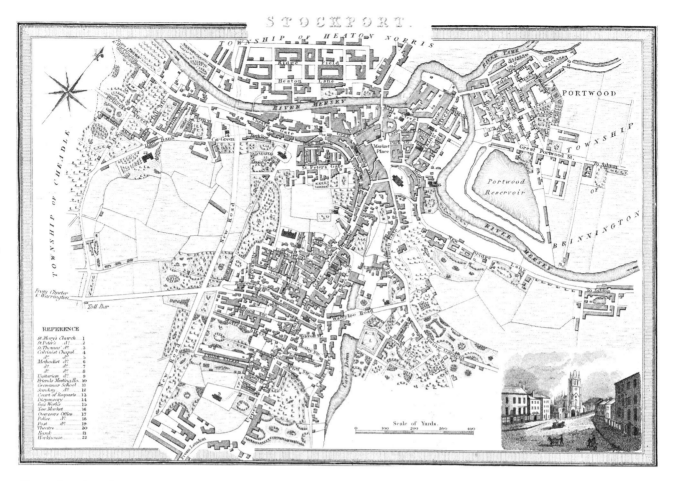

REFERENCE
St.Mary's Church.......1
St.Peter's   d°.......2
St.Thomas' d°.......3
Cohurst Chapel.......4
   d°   d°.......5
Methodist d°.......6
   d°   d°.......7
   d°   d°.......8
Unitarian d°.......9
Friends Meeting Ho. 10
Grammar School.....11
Sunday   d°.......12
Court of Requests...13
Dispensary.........14
Gas Works..........15
New Market.........16
Overseers Office.....17
Police.   d°.......18
Post.   d°.......19
Theatre............20
Bank...............21
Workhouse..........22

Ill 7.1 Plan of Stockport, 1824.
In the late eighteenth and early nineteenth centuries the size of the town greatly increased. In Stockport township the Hillgate area saw massive growth. The built-up area also spread beyond the township boundary into Heaton Norris and Portwood. Much of this expansion can be directly attributed to the rise of the town's cotton industry.

rural in character. Following the acquisition of Brinnington by James Harrison in the early 1780s, the situation changed dramatically.[5] On what had been farmland belonging to Portwood Hall, houses as well as new factories and workshops mushroomed. In 1754 the population of the whole of Brinnington township had been a mere 104. In 1801, mainly as a result of the growth of Portwood, it stood at more than eight times that level, at 890. John Aikin in 1795 described Portwood as 'a new and thriving village' and reckoned that it contained about 100 houses.[6] The population of the place may already have been 600-700.[7] In 1827 James Butterworth could note that 'Though a village, for population and extent, Portwood equals most of our market towns'.[8] In 1841, due largely to the continuing expansion of Portwood, the population of Brinnington stood at six times the level in 1801.

On the north side of the Mersey, the population of the township of Heaton Norris in 1774 was 769. By 1801 it had risen by nearly five times, to 3768. Forty years later the population was nearly quadruple the 1801

figure. The population of Heaton Norris was more scattered than that of Brinnington, but there were two concentrations of housing close to the boundary with Stockport. One was on the low ground between the Mersey and the steep side of the river valley. There had been a cluster of houses here at the north end of Lancashire Bridge since at least the seventeenth century (*Ill 4.2*). They lay along the main road to Manchester, but leading westwards towards Didsbury from this point was another roadway, Heaton Lane. The easternmost section of this road is now known as Prince's Street. In the 1820s it formed the main thoroughfare through an area which, like Brinnington, contained a mixture of mills and housing. The development of this area is believed to have been encouraged by the opening in 1826 of the new turnpike, Wellington Road, which joined with Heaton Lane.[9] The other concentration of population lay on the high ground above the Mersey, along Old Road and Lancashire Hill. Butterworth in 1827 described this area as 'a very large and populous village'.[10] It lay on the northern approach by road into

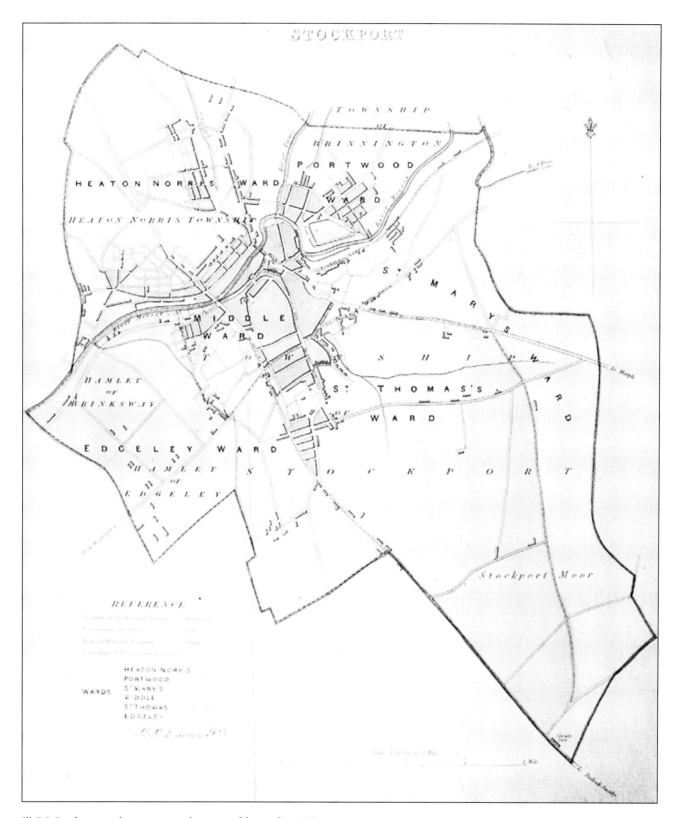

Ill 7.2 Stockport parliamentary and municipal borough, 1835.
Stockport was first given its own parliamentary representation by the Reform Act of 1832. In recognition of the growth of the town the new parliamentary borough included not only the township of Stockport but also neighbouring parts of the townships of Heaton Norris, Brinnington, Cheadle Bulkeley and Cheadle Moseley. The creation of the municipal borough in 1835 provided Stockport for the first time with an elected town council.

the town and was also the location of the terminus of the branch of the Ashton Canal.

Edgeley, like Brinnington, was used for agricultural purposes in the 1770s, when there was a dairy farm here. By the 1800s this area was undergoing a transformation, with the construction of factory buildings and streets of workers' houses.[11] Edgeley lay within the township of Cheadle Bulkeley, and accounted for much of the growth of the population of that township, which more than trebled between 1801 and 1841.

Immigrants and emigrants

A large proportion of the population rises of the late eighteenth and early nineteenth centuries was due to people moving into the town from elsewhere. Migration into Stockport had been going on since the medieval period, but for a long time the rate was probably slow. The building of the town's silk factories in the eighteenth century is likely to have quickened the

process. An unknown number of workers from the Lombes' silk mill in Derby came to work in Stockport's first silk mill, established in the Park in 1732.[12] Other workers can be presumed to have been drawn to the town to find work in the growing number of silk mills. With the rapid expansion of the cotton industry in the late eighteenth century, migration now became a flood. People arrived from other places in the North-West, from the West Riding of Yorkshire, Derbyshire, Staffordshire, Shropshire, North Wales, Scotland and Ireland.[13] More than half of the population of Stockport, Heaton Norris and Brinnington in 1841 were born outside Cheshire.[14]

Irish immigrants appear to have first arrived in the Stockport area in the 1790s. Some are said to have found low-paid work building the new canals and turnpikes, but others made a living from handloom weaving and the relatively well-paid occupation of calico printing. The vast majority of the 300 Roman Catholics who are reported to have been living in the town in

Ill 7.3 Rock Row, about 1895.
The most common form of workers' housing in the industrial towns of the late eighteenth and early nineteenth centuries was the two-storey terraced 'cottage', but Stockport also included some taller dwellings. The now demolished Rock Row was built against the sandstone cliffs on the south side of the Mersey valley, and was four storeys high. The dome in the background crowns the tower of St Peter's Church. The open space in the foreground is part of the present Mersey Square.

1798 were Irish. Many of these early immigrants appear to have settled in Edgeley, where a Roman Catholic church was built in 1802-3.[15]

At the close of the eighteenth century less than one in fifty of the population of the town may have been Irish. In 1841 roughly one in fourteen had been born in Ireland.[16] The number of Irish arriving in Stockport is believed to have greatly increased in the 1820s. With the sharp decline in handloom weaving in that decade, the range of their traditional occupations was diminished. Although many Irish women and children found employment in the cotton factories, the men now mostly worked in the various branches of the construction industry. In 1835 four out of every five bricklayers' assistants in Stockport were said to be Irish. Poorly paid, the Irish were now to be found living in the more run-down parts of the town, such as Edward Street off Middle Hillgate, and Adlington Square (Ill 5.4).[17]

Migration could also work the other way, particularly in times of economic depression.[18] In the early 1840s many of the town's unemployed who applied for poor relief and had no legal right of settlement were returned to their place of origin. During that same depression others left Stockport voluntarily. Some even quit the country, emigrating to Australia, the United States or Canada. In November 1841 there were 1901 empty properties in Stockport township. The vast majority of these were houses whose occupants had either left the town or moved into shared accommodation to save money. On the doors of vacated houses were the words 'Stockport to let'.[19]

The changing layout of the town

In 1790 John Byng had witnessed a very different picture: 'I walk'd over the stones of Stockport, which increases hourly'.[20] At this date the town was not only expanding at an astonishing rate but was also undergoing a fundamental change with regard to its layout. Growth earlier in the century had largely taken place as ribbon development along existing thoroughfares.[21] In the late eighteenth and early nineteenth centuries expansion primarily involved the creation of new networks of streets, spreading out over what had previously been gardens or farmland.[22] This often took the form of a 'grid-iron' pattern, with streets crossing each other at right-angles. It was a common arrangement during this period and created rectangular building plots well-suited for factories and terraced housing. In Stockport township streets were laid out in this fashion in the Park, along St Petersgate and on the western edge of the town in a new development

centred on King Street at Daw Bank (Ill 7.1). Beyond the township boundary the same principle was employed in the Heaton Lane area, at Portwood and at Edgeley.

The most extensive area of new development was along Hillgate. Here a succession of streets was laid out at right-angles to the main thoroughfare. Some were constructed on existing long, rectangular plots of land, which were the result of enclosure of the strip divisions within the town's medieval open-field system.[23] At the northern end of the Hillgate development was Crowther Street, so steep that the road surface was built as a series of low steps. A similar arrangement existed at Lavender Brow, descending from Churchgate towards the Carr Brook.

As more land was sought for building, even the valley of the Tin Brook behind Little Underbank was given over to development. Here in about 1790 a new street, Royal Oak Yard, was laid out between the brook and the steep cliffs which rose up to High Street. In the early nineteenth century the cliffs themselves were cut back into a vertical face to create space for workshops and even a silk mill.[24]

Workers' housing

In 1779 there are said to have been 995 houses in Stockport township. By 1801 this figure had risen to 2698 and by 1841 to 6785. At this last date there were roughly as many houses again in the rest of the town.[25] By far the majority of the new dwellings were built to house the growing number of factory, and other, workers. The rate at which houses were built did not always keep up with the increase in population. Aikin in 1795 noted that 'The population has of late years been amazingly on the increase, so that before the war, houses could not be built fast enough for the demand'.[26] The war was that with France, whose outbreak in 1793 marked a slump in the textile industry.

Between 1811 and 1821 the rate of population increase in Stockport township was the highest for any decade in the nineteenth century, but the number of houses within its boundary rose by a mere 153. The decade saw a succession of trade slumps, and people were evidently as unwilling to invest in new houses as industrialists were in new factory buildings. The early 1820s, on the other hand, saw a building boom. In August 1822, as well as eight factory buildings, 150 houses were under construction in the town. The housing shortage of the previous decade, and a continually rising population, meant that even in this new boom the demand outstripped the supply. In July 1823 it was said that no sooner were the foundations

Ill 7.4 *Stringer's Yard, New Bridge Lane, in 1909.*
The standard of workers' housing in Stockport, as in other industrial towns, varied considerably. Some of the town's worst conditions were found in its 'courts', confined areas lined with 'back-to-back' and 'blind back' dwellings. Shared privies and poor drainage made the courts breeding grounds for disease.

laid than there were a dozen applicants for every house. In 1834, also a time of expansion in the cotton industry, 1000 new houses were reported to have been built over the past year. By contrast, during the depression of the late 1830s and early 1840s house building in the town seems to have all but ceased. Although construction resumed in the mid-1840s, this was at a more modest rate.[27]

The developers

Workers' houses were built by several types of developer. Some were constructed by mill-owners to accommodate members of their workforce. The practice appears to have been less common in the town than in more rural areas, where other forms of housing were more scarce. Known examples in Stockport suggest that workers' houses tended to be associated with factories built on the periphery of the town, such as at Portwood, New Bridge Lane, Brinksway and Hope Hill in Heaton Norris.[28]

Other houses were constructed by their occupants, through a system of building clubs. Club members, who often included people in the building profession, paid a monthly subscription towards the construction of the required number of dwellings. Some of the houses built in the Higher Hillgate area in the 1780s and 1790s were paid for in this way, while in 1822 it was estimated that 1000 Stockport workers belonged to such clubs. At Edgeley and in the King Street area at Daw Bank there were terraces with the name of Club Row, which had evidently been built in this manner.[29]

The third and most common type of builder was a speculative developer, ready to cash in on the demand for housing. Such men could themselves be relatively low down in the social scale. In the last two decades of the eighteenth century they included a stonemason who built houses on Chestergate, and a weaver and carpenter who pooled resources to erect houses on Edward Street off Middle Hillgate.[30] Speculative builders were probably responsible for some of the worst excesses in housing conditions in the town in the nineteenth century.

The types of workers' housing

To save on costs, workers' housing was invariably built in terraces. These usually consisted of two-storey 'cottages', but Stockport also contained three- and even four-storey rows, most probably dating from the late eighteenth century (*Ill 7.3*). Such larger properties are likely to have contained multiple tenancies, although some may have degenerated into common lodging houses. These provided a cheap bed for the night, but were notorious for their overcrowded and squalid conditions.[31]

Engels in the 1840s was particularly scathing about the standard of workers' housing in Stockport. Describing the town as 'one of the darkest and smokiest holes in the whole industrial area', he added that 'the cottages and cellar dwellings of the workers are even more unpleasant to look at. They stretch in long rows through all parts of the town from the bottom of the valley to the crest of the hills'.[32] In reality, as in other towns in the region, the quality of workers' housing varied considerably. It should also be borne in mind that for some migrants the standard of their new accommodation must have been an improvement on their previous situation. Until the mid-nineteenth century the dwellings of agricultural workers in the north of England seem to have been often no more than a flimsy, single-storey cottage.[33]

At the higher end of the scale of workers' houses were two-up two-downs, so called after the number of rooms on each floor. Such houses might have a small rear yard containing an outside privy.[34] Other households shared a common privy with their neighbours. In both cases the human waste usually fell into a 'midden', or pit, into which household ash and rubbish might also be thrown through a separate access point. The cleaning out of these middens was often infrequent.[35]

Inferior to two-up two-downs were back-to-backs, blind backs and cellar dwellings. Back-to-backs superficially resembled two-up two-downs, but each side of the terrace comprised a row of dwellings one room deep and usually only one room wide. Blind backs also had one room on each floor, but were without a matching dwelling at the rear. In both types of housing the only doorway and windows were situated at the front, restricting ventilation.[36] These inferior forms of dwelling were built in increasing numbers from the 1820s. Often they were squeezed into the available space between existing houses or other properties,

where they were arranged around a narrow space, known as a 'court', into which a covered passageway typically provided the only entrance (*Ill 7.4*). Courts were especially numerous in the Hillgate area, where hidden behind the streets were dozens of cramped dwellings (*Ill 7.5*). Perhaps the most unsavoury of the town's back-to-backs were the two terraces known as Shepherd's Buildings. They were situated below Wellington Road North, in a deep hollow which they shared with the Heaton Norris gasworks. The privies here were built within the centre of each row, so that directly above them was sleeping accommodation. These houses also included a number of cellar dwellings.[37]

The renting of cellars as domestic accommodation was in Engels's belief particularly common in Stockport: 'I do not remember seeing elsewhere in the Manchester industrial district so many inhabited cellars in proportion to the total number of houses'.[38] Cellar dwellings were entered by their own door, approached by steps leading from the street. The presence of such an outside entrance, however, did not necessarily mean that a cellar was used for this purpose. Some served as small industrial workshops. Their use as dwellings may have been most common in times of a housing shortage or economic depression.[39] Although damp was commonplace, conditions in cellar dwellings must have varied from case to case. An example in Heaton Norris in the 1850s shows them at their most primitive. Here a family of five lived in a cellar in which 'the sleeping place was excavated from a rock, their beds were made of shavings on the ground environed by bestial filth and moisture'.[40]

Overcrowding could add to already poor conditions. In Stockport township the average number of people living in a house in 1821 was 6.4. In 1831, even after the building boom of the 1820s, the figure was 5.1, and was to remain at about that level for the rest of the nineteenth century.[41] One extreme case was reported in 1825. Eighteen Irishmen were living in a house with sufficient room for only a family of four; they slept on the floor. Three blind back houses off Higher Hillgate, built in 1835, were each home to a family of three or four; the two rooms in these houses were 12 feet (3.6 metres) square.[42]

In 1842 the commissioners, sent by Parliament to investigate the economic distress in the town, listed the housing in Stockport township according to its rateable value in 1841 and its typical occupants. Their evidence provides the best indication of the relative numbers of the various types of workers' housing and other properties in the town. Of a total of 7300 dwellings and shops in the township, 975 (or 13%) were cellar dwellings, while 2307 (or 32%) were described as 'back-houses' (presumably blind backs and back-to-backs). These types of dwelling were said to be the homes of lower-paid factory workers and labourers, 'including Irish'. A total of 2898 houses (or 40%) were occupied chiefly by better-paid factory workers. Most of these dwellings were probably two-up two-downs. Next up the scale, but harder to identify as a particular building type, were 476 houses (7%) occupied by 'overlookers, book-keepers, and other persons holding places of trust'. A total of 303 properties (4%) were occupied by 'small shopkeepers, and persons of small independent means', while the remaining 341 were associated with 'larger shopkeepers, publicans and the higher classes of private residences'.[43] The various categories of dwellings and occupants presented in this list is not comprehensive. It does not appear to take into account, for example, the lodging houses which are known to have existed in the town. Nevertheless, it does suggest that at this date workers' dwellings, in all their various forms, accounted for over four-fifths of Stockport's housing stock.

Industrialists' mansions

In 1769 Stockport had been 'inhabited by a great number of gentry'. By 1842 the time when the town was 'a favourite place of residence' for traditional landowning families was a fading memory.[44] The departure of the gentry from their Stockport town houses may in part have resulted from a decline in the number of local landowners with a main residence in the neighbourhood. The decisive factor, however, must have been the increasingly industrial character of the town. Some of their former residences came to be used for non-domestic purposes. One town house on Millgate was converted to a cotton-spinning factory.[45] In 1823 Underbank Hall was bought by public subscription with the aim of using the building as a town hall, but a year later it opened as a bank, a purpose for which the building is still used to this day (Ill 4.5).[46]

In the late eighteenth and early nineteenth centuries the town's mill-owners were busy building their own large residences. In the 1790s John Collier chose a site next to his Weir Mill for his new house.[47] A later

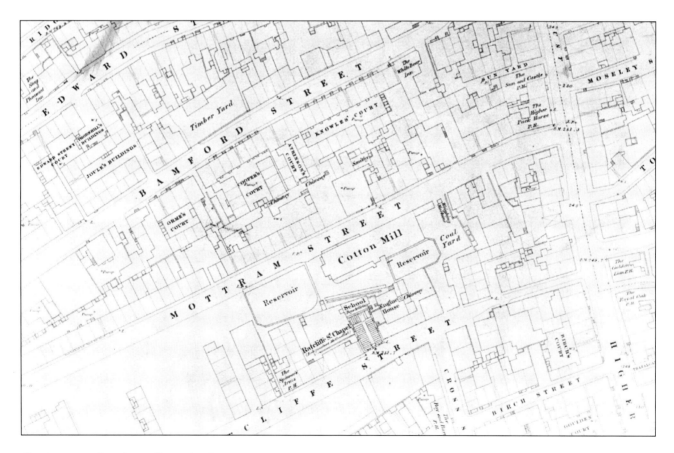

Ill 7.5 Courts off Higher Hillgate, detail of an Ordnance Survey map of 1851.
Courts enabled housing to be squeezed into the spaces between existing streets, a practice particularly common in the Hillgate area.
They were typically built by speculative developers, cashing in on housing shortages in the town.

Ill 7.6 Woodbank.

In the early nineteenth century Stockport's wealthiest mill-owners were building new residences for themselves, away from the smoke and overcrowding in the town. Woodbank was built in 1812-14 by Stockport's leading industrialist, Peter Marsland, and was designed by Thomas Harrison, a prominent architect of the day. The classical style of the building was typical of industrialists' mansions of this time.

preference seems to have been to live on the periphery of the town, away from its factory smoke. Peter Marsland was living in a house on Heaton Lane in 1812. Two years later his new residence was completed at Woodbank, set within its own estate *(Ill 7.6)*.[48] In the 1820s, at the opposite end of the town, Holly Vale near Brinksway was the home of Thomas Marsland, the owner of the Daw Bank printworks. This 'very elegant mansion', surrounded by a high wall, had a garden 'ornamented with pleasing walks, shades of perennials, fruit trees, and various exotics'. Other local industrialists lived in 'elegant mansions', beyond the northern edge of the town, in Reddish.[49] By the 1820s and 1830s Heaton Mersey was also considered a 'select' area. In the 1840s there was a string of substantial houses here, extending westwards along Didsbury Road from Norris Bank, with views over the Mersey and the Cheshire plain.[50] William Crowther, a Stockport silk throwster,

at some time prior to 1819 built his residence of Highfield House in an isolated spot overlooking the Goyt valley in Bredbury.[51]

The owners of rural mills typically lived close to their factories. Among the grandest of such residences was Oakwood Hall, built on a site high above the Goyt in Romiley. It was constructed in a 'Tudor revival' style in about 1845 for Ormerod Heyworth, whose Oakwood Mill lay nearby.[52] Other instances of rural industrialists' mansions will be noted below.

TRADE IN THE INDUSTRIAL TOWN

The worker as consumer

The presence of a large working-class population appears to have had a significant influence on both the character and organization of trade in the town.

Between the 1790s and 1830s the numbers of suppliers of foodstuffs, including butchers and bakers, greatly increased. By contrast, the numbers of wine and spirit dealers, glass and china dealers, and watchmakers and clockmakers seem to have shown at best only a modest growth, and one lagging far behind the rise in the local population. These shops sold non-essential items, for which demand is likely to have been more limited among the working class than those higher up the social scale.[53]

The importance of the working-class consumer is also suggested by a change in the town's weekly market. By 1825 this was held not only on Friday, its traditional day, but also on Saturday. The Friday market was used by farmers for the sale of cheese and other produce to dealers. The market on the following day was a more local affair. Here the townspeople bought meat and other provisions, with trading continuing until eleven

thirty at night. The arrangement was of obvious benefit to factory operatives, whose working week did not finish until Saturday afternoon, when they were also paid.[54]

Foodstuffs were also bought by the working class from numerous, small local shops. They were easy to set up, with little more than the front room of a house being required. Their success owed much to the fact that they sold food on credit. They also had a reputation for overcharging.[55] By the 1810s there were ready-made and second-hand clothes shops in the town. In 1833, however, it was estimated that half of the population of Stockport bought clothing from travelling salesmen. They called on their customers once every three weeks and were often the agents of firms based in Manchester. Payment was made in instalments, but the final cost could be as high as twice the normal price.[56]

For many people a visit to the pawnshop was also a regular occurrence. The number of pawnbrokers in the

Ill 7.7 The Court House.
This civic building was erected in 1824 and served a dual purpose. The ground floor housed the town's meal and cheese market. The upper floor was the meeting place of the town's manorial court and, after the creation of the municipal borough in 1835, of the town council.

town quadrupled in the twenty-five years before 1833, when a quarter of the population was estimated to pawn their best clothes at the start of each working week and to reclaim them the following Saturday.[57] 'Furniture brokers', who are documented in Stockport from the early nineteenth century, were dealers in second-hand furniture and were a further class of trader catering for working-class needs.[58]

Some workers had little choice as to how they spent their wages. Instead of being paid solely in money, they received part of their pay as foodstuffs and other goods, for which they might be charged well above the normal price. The truck system, as this method of payment was known, was illegal but was used by a number of Stockport mill-owners during the late 1810s. This was a time when there was a shortage of cash in circulation. It was also a period of unrest among workers, when mill-owners were eager to tighten their authority. The final demise of the truck system in Stockport seems to have been brought about by the prosecution in 1830 of one of its main local practitioners, Samuel Stocks, the owner of the Heaton Mersey bleachworks.[59]

By that date some workers in the town had begun to organize their own retail outlets by founding co-operative stores. The earliest of these was established at Shaw Heath in about 1828 and may have been one of the first in the country. It later moved to premises on Higher Hillgate. Another early co-operative existed in Portwood, founded by workers from a local cotton mill perhaps during the strike by the town's factory workers in 1829. It is believed unlikely that these stores survived the depression of the late 1830s and early 1840s. In 1839 local Chartists began their own, possibly short-lived, co-operative venture. The co-operative movement was revived in the town in 1860 with the establishment of the Stockport Industrial and Equitable Society and the opening of its first shop, on Chestergate.[60]

Improving the market

'Spacious and convenient' was John Aikin's description of the Market Place in 1795.[61] Some local people would not have agreed. Ten years earlier, when a scheme was drawn up to improve the state of the town, the Market Place was one of the priorities. Trade had so increased that the site was becoming overcrowded. The situation was not helped by the uneven surface of the natural promontory on which the Market Place was sited. The narrowness of the streets leading to the market added to the congestion.[62] The 1785 improvement scheme was aborted before it received parliamentary approval, and over thirty years would pass before the problem began to be addressed.

The first step was the widening in 1818 of Churchgate, the eastern approach to the Market Place. To achieve this, the bishop of Chester gave permission for the removal of part of the adjacent churchyard of St Mary's. Access was not much improved, since stalls quickly extended along the newly widened street, which became the site of a potato market. Two years later the Market Place was levelled and repaved, under the supervision of the township's surveyors of the highways.[63]

The new Cheese and Meal House and Court House

The next problem concerned the old Meal and Cheese Houses, which were situated at the east end of the Market Place (Plate V). Their dirty condition had for some years been deterring dealers from coming into the town to buy cheese. In 1824 the inhabitants of the Market Place clubbed together to buy these buildings from Lady Warren Bulkeley, the lady of the manor, and had them demolished. In their place a new Cheese and Meal House was built to the west of the Market Place, on the corner of Castle Brow and Mill Street, the present Vernon Street and Warren Street (Ill 7.7).[64]

The upper floor of this building was used to house meetings of Stockport's manorial court leet. These had previously been held in the upper room of the old, decrepit Meal House or in a 'dark and gloomy' room above the town's old prison at the top of Mealhouse Brow (Ill 7.13). It is said to have been the lack of suitable premises for conducting the official business of the town which prompted the purchase in 1823 of Underbank Hall. Within a year, however, that role had evidently passed to the new building on Castle Brow. Butterworth in 1827 described it as the place in which 'the chief affairs belonging to the town are settled. The justice meetings held and all public discussions on subjects connected with parochial affairs transacted.'[65]

The 'New Market' on Hillgate

In addition to the improvements to the existing Market Place, there was also an attempt to set up a second market place in the town. On a plot of land behind a public house on the corner of Middle Hillgate and Ridgeway Lane, a 'New Market' was built, containing small, one-room shops set around a central courtyard. In 1835 the court leet proposed that the potato market should be moved to this site. However, the lord and lady of the manor seem to have been unwilling to endorse a rival market place. The Hillgate site was instead used for a variety of other purposes, as stores, stables, a smithy and a butcher's slaughterhouse.[66]

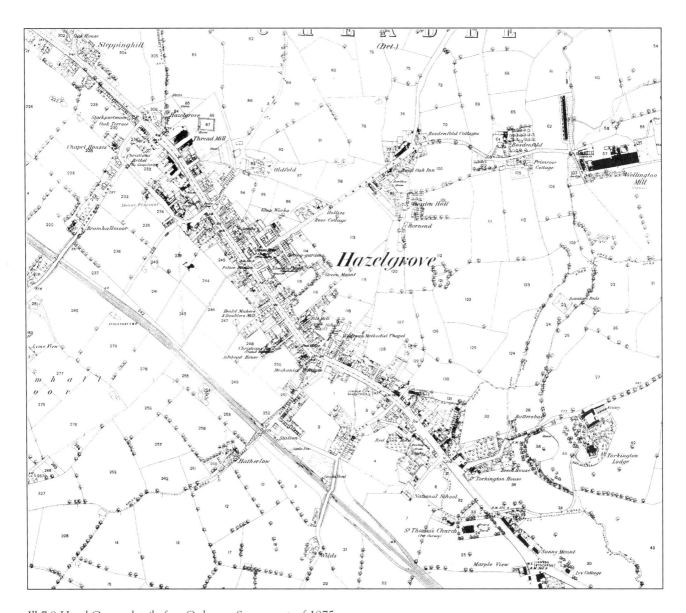

Ill 7.8 *Hazel Grove, detail of an Ordnance Survey map of 1875.*
The village of Hazel Grove, or Bullock Smithy until its change of name in 1836, developed along the main road from Stockport to London. It still retained a linear form in the late nineteenth century, with most properties lying on or close to that road. Torkington Lodge (lower right) was built in the late eighteenth century for the Leghs of Booths, the lords of Torkington manor. The neighbouring round pond (numbered '38' on the map) was once the reservoir of a cotton factory, demolished in the 1820s. The large Wellington Mill (upper right) was built as a cotton factory in 1836. The silk mill (centre) was one of several in operation in the village in the middle of the nineteenth century.

THE GROWING VILLAGES

Cheadle

After the town of Stockport, the largest settlement in the Borough had long been the village of Cheadle. In the late eighteenth and early nineteenth centuries the village was not immune to the growth of industry, but it was affected in a far more muted manner than the town. The village was a centre of handloom weaving and had, close to its outskirts, two printworks and a small mill, said to have been converted from cotton to silk.[67] However, no large factories were built here and the village seems to have retained much of its rural character. In the 1790s Cheadle was referred to as 'a pretty, little town', and 'a neat and pleasant village'. In 1825 it could still be described in similar language: 'This village is remarkable for the beauty of its situation, and for its very clean and neat appearance'.[68] In 1823 a fair for the sale of cattle and horses was established here, held on the

23rd and 24th of March. Cheadle, it was announced at that time, 'is situated in a respectable farming district, has a spacious green in the centre of the village, with three good inns for the accommodation of dealers'.[69] The village was also located on the Manchester to Wilmslow turnpike, and from 1820 on the turnpike route from Stockport to Liverpool.

Bullock Smithy – Hazel Grove

By that last date, Cheadle, one of the oldest places of settlement in the Borough, had very probably been overtaken in size by Bullock Smithy or, as it was renamed in 1836, Hazel Grove. An increase in traffic in the eighteenth century along the main turnpike road between Manchester and the south had provided the initial impetus for the development of this village. By the 1820s its buildings included 'a great number of shops', as well as ten public houses.[70] Its working-class population included agricultural labourers, handloom weavers, and some miners working in the Norbury and Poynton pits. A cotton factory, Wellington Mill, was built close to the village in 1837, and a less well-known mill was in operation at an earlier period.[71] Some of the villagers worked in the mills in Stockport.[72]

As in Stockport, terraced housing was built to accommodate a growing population but, in contrast to the sprawl of Hillgate, Hazel Grove remained a linear village. Even in the later nineteenth century, development was mostly confined to a narrow corridor along Buxton Road (Ill 7.8). The place was not without instances of inferior housing. One miner's house in 1842 was described as 'being in a court, a narrow and confined place without ventilation, with an open gutter in front of the door full of dirty water and refuse'.[73]

NEW INDUSTRIAL COMMUNITIES

A number of the cotton mills and printworks in the Borough were built in areas which had little or no housing in their close vicinity. In such cases, the industrialist himself often erected dwellings adjacent to his works to accommodate at least some of his

Ill 7.9 Stone Row, Marple, about 1900.
The establishment of large cotton mills or other industrial works in rural areas led industrialists to build dwellings to accommodate members of their workforce. The workers' houses shown here, dating from the early 1790s, were among several scattered rows of dwellings built by Samuel Oldknow on his estate in Marple and Mellor. The building in the background was intended by Oldknow to serve as a market hall, but itself came to be used as housing.

employees. Small-scale examples, in terms of the number of dwellings involved, include the houses erected near the Reddish Mill printworks, and three rows built next to Hollins Mill at Marple. Close to Rhode House Mill at Hawk Green an arrangement of terraces was built around a square, with yards and privies at the back.[74] Workers' housing might also be built for industries other than the textile trade. A 'few ranges of cottages' mentioned near coal workings at Redhouse Lane in Bredbury in the 1820s are a possible instance.[75] In three places within the Borough, the construction of houses by local industrialists and the provision of other facilities created what were in effect sizeable and self-contained communities. The places in question were the Marple and Mellor estate of Samuel Oldknow, Heaton Mersey and Compstall.

Marple and Mellor

The labour force of Samuel Oldknow at Marple and Mellor included men who worked at his lime kilns, in his coal pits and on his agricultural estate, as well as the mainly women and children employed in his great cotton mill. It was on the Marple side of his estate that

most of the workers' housing was erected. Butterworth noted that 'This place is built in no regular order', with houses being built in scattered terraces. Some of these were completed by 1794, others were built in the 1800s. Among the buildings at this 'New Marple' was a three-storey structure intended by Oldknow to be used as a market hall (*Ill 7.9*). It is reported that he tried to gain an Act of Parliament which would have allowed him to operate a market, and that permission was refused on the grounds of the proximity of the market at Stockport.[76]

Oldknow's building projects also included three grander dwellings. Bottoms Hall was rebuilt as an impressive house with substantial outbuildings (*Plate VI*). This site was the centre for the management of his agricultural estate, and also used for another purpose. Oldknow is one of only a few mill-owners in the Borough known to have employed child apprentices, a practice also carried out at another large rural mill, that of Samuel Greg at Styal in Cheshire.[77] Oldknow's apprentices were sent by two London orphanages (the Foundling Hospital and the Royal Military Asylum, established for the children of servicemen) and by parish workhouses in London and

Ill 7.10 Mellor Lodge (right) and Marple Lodge (left), about 1904.
Mellor Lodge, built by Samuel Oldknow as his own residence, lay adjacent to his great Mellor Mill. The smaller Marple Lodge, on the opposite bank of the River Goyt which is crossed here by Oldknow's Bottoms Bridge, was the home of the mill's manager.

Ill 7.11 Workers' housing, Vale Road, Heaton Mersey.
These houses formed part of an industrial community associated with the Heaton Mersey bleachworks, originally established by Samuel Oldknow and his brother Thomas in the 1780s. Houses were built for the workforce in a piecemeal process which continued well into the nineteenth century.[79]

its neighbourhood. At Mellor they were accommodated either in the new Bottoms Hall or in an adjoining dormitory block.[78] Adjacent to the mill was Oldknow's own residence, Mellor Lodge, 'a neat but not large mansion, embowered in trees'. On the opposite side of the river was Marple Lodge, the home of the mill-manager *(Ills 6.9 & 7.10)*.[79]

Heaton Mersey

At Heaton Mersey dwellings were built for workers employed in the local bleachworks and associated cotton mill. They were centred on the junction of Didsbury Road (the main road to Stockport) and Vale Road, leading down the side of the Mersey valley to the riverside site where Samuel Oldknow and his brother Thomas had first established the bleachworks in the 1780s (Ill 7.11). The growth of this community was a piecemeal process which seems to have been under way in the 1800s and continued into the late nineteenth century. Its housing included two-up two-downs and back-to-backs. The large purchase in 1820 of fire grates, hobs and ovens for the workforce may have been connected with the building of new dwellings. Some thirty-two others are known to have been built later in the 1820s.[80] The community's buildings included a Sunday school, which was built in 1805 by Robert Parker, Oldknow's successor as owner of these works. This was a branch of the much larger Stockport Sunday School, on which more will be said later.

Compstall

The development of Compstall village can be traced to the early 1820s, when the Andrews' printworks here were rebuilt and new factories were erected for cotton spinning and powerloom weaving. By 1827 Butterworth could describe the place as 'a populous village'. Twenty years later George and Thomas Andrew owned 250 dwellings here, the main area of housing being a series of two-up two-down terraces on the north side of the mill reservoir (Ill 6.17). In the 1850s other houses were built by the Andrews on the Ludworth side of the River Etherow, on land leased from the manor of Glossop.[81] The first known home of the Andrews themselves in the locality was Werneth Hall, on the summit of Werneth Low, a property which they bought in 1815. George Andrew subsequently built for himself the substantial residence known originally as Green Hill and later as Compstall Hall, on the western side of the village, and constructed or leased other houses for his sons and their families.[82]

In 1826 Compstall was provided with its first place of worship, a Wesleyan chapel. The Andrews added further facilities to the village, building a school in the mid-1830s, the Anglican church of St Paul in 1839-41, and the grandly named Athenaeum in the early 1860s, for the education of the village's adults. They were also involved in the establishment of the village's co-operative society in 1851. This developed into a highly successful venture, with stores in Marple, Romiley, Hawk Green, Marple Bridge, High Lane and Mellor.[83]

AGRICULTURAL IMPROVEMENTS

Nationally the late eighteenth and early nineteenth centuries saw two related developments in agriculture, each intended to increase food production. One was an increasingly scientific attitude to farming, the other was the virtual disappearance of common land as a result of large-scale enclosure. In Cheshire both movements had a limited impact. The process of enclosure had been under way in the county long before this period, so that only a relatively small proportion of common land still remained. On the question of farming techniques, commentators were in general agreement that the county lagged behind many other parts of the country, although by the mid-nineteenth century it was acknowledged that some improvements were in evidence.[84]

Enclosure

In 1780 most surviving common land within the Borough was probably heathland or moss (Ill 5.6). By the early 1840s virtually all local common land, including such waste land, had been enclosed. The process was partly achieved by a series of Acts of Parliament, beginning with that for Stockport in 1805, on which more will be said below. The enclosure of common land in the parish of Cheadle was authorized in 1810 and that of Norbury Moor, on the south side of Bullock Smithy, in 1811.[85] Other enclosures were carried out privately, without recourse to Parliament. Brinnington Moor in 1815 and, in Bramhall township, Woods Moor, Bramhall Moor and Kitt's Moss were all reclaimed and enclosed in this fashion.[86]

Improvements in farming

The extent to which agricultural practices changed within the Borough in the late eighteenth and early nineteenth centuries is difficult to assess. Certainly, it was not entirely lacking in exponents of scientific farming. Samuel Oldknow, though better known as a muslin manufacturer and cotton spinner, also had a deep interest in improvements in agriculture, which he put into practice on his Mellor estate. Oldknow introduced new breeds of livestock to the district and experimented with cross-breeding. As well as growing cereals, he created a garden for the production of fruit and vegetables. In 1813 Oldknow was reported to be the only person in Derbyshire using machinery to raise water for irrigation. The construction of Mellor Mill and other building and engineering works had involved the felling of a large number of trees on this estate. In their place, new plantations were established containing more than a dozen varieties of trees, and records were kept as to the effect of thinning and pruning on their growth. The management of Oldknow's estate was carried out on a commercial basis. The produce which was not consumed by his own household was sold, some to his own workforce. Even the islands in the mill's reservoirs were utilized; they were planted with osiers which were sold for basket making. Oldknow's experiments in agriculture won him praise from his contemporaries and, on two occasions, awards from the Manchester Agricultural Society, a body set up to encourage improvements in farming. In 1828, the final year of his life, he was made president of Derbyshire's own agricultural society.[87]

Other local farmers receptive to new ideas in the late eighteenth century were the Pownalls, freeholders who lived at Pownall Hall in Bramhall. Their farming routine between the years 1782 and 1789 is recorded in the diary of Peter Pownall. Among their crops were turnips, used as winter feed for cattle. Samuel Oldknow also grew turnips (one of his two awards from the Manchester society was for the best 'Swedish turnips', or swedes), but the crop is said to have been not widely grown in this area until the 1840s.[88]

The Pownalls also made use of lime as a fertilizer. In the 1780s this was an expensive commodity, but its cost was greatly reduced with the opening of the Peak Forest Canal in the following decade. After the opening of his kilns by the canal at Marple, Oldknow himself made extensive use of lime on his estate.[89] In the nineteenth century bones ground to a fine dust came to be commonly used as a fertilizer on pasture land. Its widespread use in Cheshire is reported to have begun in the 1830s, but the practice is recorded on some local farms (in Cheadle Bulkeley, Cheadle Hulme and Marple) in the early 1820s. Bone was being ground at Springwater Mill near Strines before 1833.[90] Manure had long been spread on fields. The human waste produced by the region's growing urban populations provided farmers with a new source of supply, which was politely known as 'nightsoil'. Samuel Oldknow obtained large quantities from the Manchester police commissioners, and had these conveyed to Marple by canal. In 1790 an advertisement for the lease of Portwood Hall and its remaining fields noted the suitability of this land for meadow, since it was close to Stockport 'where manure is plenty'.[91]

By the early 1830s improved land drainage upstream was reported to be affecting the water-supply of cotton mills in Stockport.[92] Samuel Oldknow and the Pownalls both employed a method of drainage which involved digging long, regularly spaced furrows, known as 'reins'. These carried off surface water from intermediate strips or 'butts'. (The resulting earthworks can be confused with 'ridge and furrow' found in medieval open-field systems.)[93] The major nineteenth-century innovation

in drainage, however, was the tile pipe, whose use was encouraged by three Acts of Parliament between 1840 and 1850.[94] By the early 1850s drainage tiles are recorded among the products of brickworks within the Borough.[95]

Market gardens and allotments

By the late eighteenth century the expansion of Stockport was influencing the local farming economy, as dairy farmers shifted from the production of cheese to that of milk.[96] Its growing population prompted another development, the creation of small plots of land on the outskirts of the town, which were used for the growing of fruit and vegetables. An early example is provided by 3 or 4 acres in Edgeley, which were advertised in 1793 as suitable for this purpose.[97] By the 1820s workers were renting their own small 'gardens', or allotments. In Heaton Norris the open hillslope to the east of Wellington Road was covered with such plots, the main crop here being potatoes. Allotments were particularly numerous on the south and east sides of the town. During times of economic boom, the plots risked becoming building sites. In the 1830s it was remarked that 'the rapid increase of building has made great havoc with these gardens'. On the glebe land, land belonging to the parish church, some allotments were to survive, however, into the twentieth century.[98]

CORNMILLS

In the 1760s the corn produced within Stockport township was already said to be insufficient to meet the local demand. Within the wider area known as the Stockport Division, most agricultural land in 1795 was reported to be pasture or meadow, 'with very little corn of any kind, particularly wheat, and never in any degree adequate to the consumption of the inhabitants'.[99] However, even when imported, corn was still ground locally. In 1770 there appear to have been ten water-powered cornmills in the Borough.[100] After 1780, and particularly in the early nineteenth century, new cornmills were built and existing mills upgraded, with water, steam and wind all being used to provide power. Additional milling capacity was needed not only for the production of foodstuffs but also for the cotton industry which used flour for 'dressing' yarns.[101] In 1842 it was reckoned that Stockport's powerloom factories, when in full work, required nearly as much flour as the population of the town.[102] In line with these two developments, the greatest increase in milling capacity was in Stockport and its vicinity.

Two water-powered cornmills were erected on new sites. That at Adswood is said to have been built in 1800 by the miller at Bramhall, where milling now ceased.[103] In Mellor a water-powered cornmill was attached to Samuel Oldknow's great cotton-spinning mill (Ill 6.9).[104] In the 1820s Foggbrook Mill in Offerton, itself originally built as a cotton factory, was briefly converted to cornmilling.[105]

Steam-power

As in the cotton industry, steam-power came to be used in local mills as a standby in times of water-shortage. An engine was installed at Norbury Mill by 1842.[106] That at Foggbrook cornmill was probably a legacy from the earlier use of the building as a cotton factory. In some cornmills steam was the sole source of power. A steam-powered mill was built by Oldknow next to the Peak Forest Canal in Marple.[107] Another, of uncertain date, stood alongside the same canal at Woodley.[108] In such cases the canal presumably served as a source of water for the engines' boilers and condensers, and as a means of transporting the grain and flour.

It was next to the terminus of the Ashton Canal that Stockport's earliest known steam-powered cornmill, Albion Mill, was built in about 1820. This was a substantial building, which in 1834 was described as being four storeys high, powered by two steam engines and containing fourteen pairs of millstones.[109] By comparison Foggbrook Mill contained three pairs of millstones, and the mills at Marple Bridge, Adswood and Portwood, five.[110] An Albion flour mill still stands on the Lancashire Hill site, but this is a later building, constructed in 1893 after the original mill was destroyed by fire (Ill 7.12).

Albion Mill was not the only large steam-powered mill in Stockport. On the south side of Warren Street stood the Park Corn Mill, towering six storeys high. It was built on the site of a Methodist chapel, which was sold in 1825 to help pay for a new chapel at Tiviot Dale. The mill was burnt down in 1868.[111] It should not be confused with the much older, water-powered cornmill in the Park, which lay further to the north. This had been bought from Sir George Warren, the lord of the manor, by Henry Marsland in 1791 and had gone out of existence by 1825.[112] A third early steam-powered cornmill in Stockport was built by 1830 on Hempshaw Lane. This mill, which contained five pairs of stones, does not appear to have been a success. In the 1830s the building was repeatedly advertised as being available for use as either a cornmill or a cotton factory.[113]

Wind-power

The extent to which wind-power was used for cornmilling in the Borough is uncertain. A 'Windmill Field' in Norbury suggests a possible early wind-powered site.[114] From the 1780s to the 1850s two windmills stood on the high ground above Stockport, one being on Edward Street, the other on Lancashire Hill. Only the last seems to have been functioning as a cornmill in 1825. Its continued existence may have owed much to the fact that, like the Albion Mill, it lay next to the canal.[115] In the late eighteenth century both of the town's windmills may have been used to power textile machinery.[116] A map of 1819 shows a windmill to the north-west of Hawk Green in Marple. Its origin and precise use appear to be unknown.[117]

LOCAL GOVERNMENT

In 1780 local government in the various parts of the Borough was of a form which had changed little since the seventeenth century. The highest local authority were the justices of the peace. They had administrative as well as judicial powers, which they exercised in the county quarter sessions and as resident magistrates in their own locality. In the parishes and townships, overseers were responsible for providing assistance to the poor, paid for by local ratepayers; surveyors supervised the repair of highways, where responsibility for their maintenance had not yet passed into the hands of a turnpike trust. In a number of townships, manorial courts were still held.[118] The powers of the lord of the manor were widest in Stockport, where the market and fairs were under his authority. Responsibility for enforcing the byelaws in the manors fell to local officers who brought offenders before the manorial courts. All of these positions were unsalaried, and the officials were required to balance their duties with their normal daily routine.

The 1785 Stockport improvement scheme

As the population expanded, the existing system of administration proved increasingly inadequate, in terms of both its manpower and its legal powers, at meeting local needs. In Stockport its shortcomings were already evident before 1780. Five years earlier an abortive attempt had been made to obtain an Act of Parliament to improve the town's streets.[119] In 1785 a second attempt was made, involving a much more ambitious package of proposals. They included not only the widening, lighting and cleaning of the streets but also the appointment of night watchmen, the levelling

Ill 7.12 Albion Mills, Lancashire Hill, in 1895.
In the early nineteenth century steam-powered cornmills were built in Stockport. These not only provided its growing population with foodstuffs but also supplied its cotton mills with flour used for the 'dressing' of looms. Albion Mill was built in about 1820, adjacent to the Ashton Canal. The original mill was destroyed by fire in 1893 and was rebuilt on a larger scale. This later mill still stands, but the canal itself is now infilled.

of the Market Place, the creation of a court to deal with cases of small debts, and the building of a new workhouse for the poor, and a new prison. The power to put these proposals into effect was to be given to a body of 'police commissioners', comprising the lord of the manor, the rector of the parish church, the minister of St Peter's, and other wealthy local individuals. To pay for the proposed improvements, the remaining common land in the township was to be enclosed and sold. A rate would be introduced only to make up any deficit.[120]

The promoters of the scheme were given permission by Parliament to present a bill or bills. Two were in fact drawn up, one dealing with the small debts court, one with the other improvements. For some reason the scheme was then aborted. Local opposition by ratepayers may have played a part. So too may have

the attitude of Sir George Warren, the lord of the manor. Whatever his views on the creation of police commissioners may have been, the plan for the remaining common land would seem to run contrary to his interests. Warren himself had sold plots of such land for his own profit. If the commons were enclosed this source of revenue would have been no longer available. It may not be coincidental that the improvement scheme was launched during the one short break, from 1784 to 1786, in his long career as an MP.[121]

1787-90, the new gaol and the night watch

Lacking parliamentary sanction for wider improvements, the town's inhabitants now looked to the highest local authority, the justices of the peace, for help in tackling at least some of their problems. In 1787 the JPs in the Knutsford quarter sessions agreed to contribute from county funds towards the building of a new gaol at Stockport. Sir George Warren provided the site, a plot of land by the entry to the manorial cornmill in the Park, and construction began in 1790. From 1795 the JPs also provided a salary for a gaoler, and made contributions towards the repair of the building. In return for this financial assistance, the gaol was to serve not merely Stockport township but also the whole of the Stockport Division of the Macclesfield hundred, comprising twenty-nine townships in five north-east Cheshire parishes. The gaol, which became known as the 'House of Correction' or 'New Bayley', was only a place of temporary confinement. The inmates included vagrants sent here as a punishment, and people who had been arrested for more serious crimes and who were waiting to be brought before a magistrate. Lengthy sentences of imprisonment were served at the gaols in Middlewich, Knutsford or Chester.[122]

Stockport's older prison had stood on the corner of the Market Place and Mealhouse Brow, also known as Dungeon Brow. The entrance to one cell is still visible on that street (Ill 7.13). Four other cells, cut into the rock below the Market Place, led off the main basement. In 1790 it was described as 'a very unhealthy and incommodious place for the confinement of any prisoners'.[123]

In 1790, the same year that work began on the new prison, the quarter sessions authorized the creation of a body of night watchmen in the town. They seem to have been funded entirely by voluntary contributions.[124] Despite their introduction, policing in the town must have been woefully inadequate. Until the 1820s the only official daytime police in the town were the manorial constables (Ill 7.14). They were not only part-time and unpaid – receiving only their expenses, which might admittedly involve some creative accounting – but also were ridiculously few in number. Stockport township had only two constables for a population which by 1821

Ill 7.13 The site of Stockport's gaol, the Market Place.
The town's gaol occupied this site until 1790 when a new prison was built by the Mersey close to Lancashire Bridge. The low door visible on Mealhouse Brow (centre right) is the entrance to one of the cells.

Ill 7.14 A Stockport police helmet of about 1820 and the truncheon of a special constable.
Despite the massive growth in the town's population, in the early nineteenth century its day-to-day policing fell to only a handful of constables. At times of civil unrest, however, the authorities swore in large numbers of special constables and mustered the yeomanry, a volunteer militia.

had risen to roughly 22,000. The problem was repeated in the areas of the town which lay within other townships. Arrests were also made by the paid gaoler of the New Bayley, who served unofficially as a 'deputy constable'.[125] In many instances the apprehension of offenders must have been left to the townspeople themselves. In contrast to their weakness in day-to-day policing, the authorities mounted a conspicuous show of force at times of industrial action or political demonstrations. On these occasions the magistrates enlisted 'special constables', and called out the local yeomanry; more on these forces will be said below.

The true level of crime in Stockport in the late eighteenth and early nineteenth centuries is difficult to assess, since the evidence relates mainly to charges which reached the courts rather than actual incidents.

Between 1791 and 1806 the Cheshire quarter sessions heard 656 cases arising from Stockport township, more than twice as many as in the period from 1760 to 1790. More than half of all these cases involved breaches of the peace; among the other charges were petty larceny, embezzlement and, more rarely, assault.[126] One local magistrate in the early nineteenth century described Stockport and its vicinity as 'the worst part of Cheshire' for crime; 'half the prisoners at the sessions come from that neighbourhood'.[127]

The 1805 Stockport Enclosure Act and the workhouse

In 1801 the body of Sir George Warren was carried with considerable state from his home at Poynton to be buried with his ancestors in the chancel of Stockport parish church. His daughter and heir was Lady Elizabeth Warren Bulkeley, whose principal residence was not at Poynton but in Surrey and who took a less rigid attitude than her father in the matter of the manor of Stockport.[128]

In 1805, for the third time, a petition was sent to Parliament requesting permission to introduce a Stockport improvement bill. Once more the intention was to enclose and sell the remaining common land. The proceeds were to be used to fulfil a number of the aims included in the scheme of 1785; the improvement of the streets, the funding of watchmen and the building of a workhouse. The poor of Stockport, Parliament was informed, had 'become very numerous, and are supported at a very great expense to the inhabitants'. A new workhouse would not only be of financial benefit to those paying the poor rate but also 'would tend to the better support, relief and comfort of the poor themselves'.[129] A workhouse had existed in Stockport as early as the 1730s.[130] Evidently as the population of the town grew, and with it the number of poor, the existing accommodation proved insufficient.

Unlike the schemes of 1775 and 1785, this new attempt did result in an Act being passed. However, during the progress of the bill through Parliament the clauses relating to the improvement of the streets and the appointment of watchmen were removed, so that the Act itself was concerned only with the disposal of common land to help tackle the problem of the poor. The revenue from the sale was to be placed in the care of a body of trustees, who included the lord and lady of the manor and the rector of the parish church. The Act stipulated that, after the costs of the enclosure and sale had been deducted, the proceeds were to be first spent on the construction of a new workhouse. The remainder was to be invested, with the annual profits being put towards the cost of poor relief.[131] The process of dividing up the common land began almost immediately and the first sale took place in the following year. A plot of common land at Daw Bank was earmarked for the new workhouse. The building, said to be capable of housing 170 people, was finished in 1812.[132]

Although Stockport had its new workhouse, it does not appear to have been paid for in the way laid down in the Act. The sale of common land raised more than £7000, but it was later declared that only £1000 of this had been spent on 'the skeleton of the workhouse' and that local ratepayers had footed the bill for the rest. Nor is there any evidence that the enclosure trustees ever delivered any money to the overseers of the poor. Stockport's common lands had passed into private hands, but the community as a whole gained precious little from the exercise. Precisely what happened to the proceeds remains a mystery. In 1836 the new Stockport borough council made a lukewarm attempt at investigation, but the matter appears to have been quickly dropped.[133]

The small debts court, 1806

In the year after the Enclosure Act, Parliament agreed to another of the proposals originally put forward in 1785, the creation of a local court 'for the more easy and speedy recovery of small debts'. Known as a 'Court of Requests', it was authorized to deal with cases involving sums of up to £5. In acknowledgement of the growth of the town, its jurisdiction not only included the township of Stockport but also extended into Brinnington, Edgeley and Brinksway. Cases were heard, without a jury, by commissioners appointed from among the town's more substantial property owners. The court was intended for the collection of private debts, and as such was of particular value to local industrialists and tradesmen. Those on the receiving end of its justice took a very different view. The commissioners imposed heavy court costs on the debtor. As an added grievance, people who failed to pay their local taxes, the poor rate and the highway rate, found themselves being summoned before the court. In 1813 a petition was sent to Parliament requesting the court's abolition, but without success, and the conduct of the court was still a matter of controversy in the late 1830s.[134]

Select vestries

In the first two decades of the nineteenth century a succession of trade slumps resulted in dramatic increases in the cost of the poor relief, as people were thrown out of work or saw their wages greatly reduced. In Stockport township the money spent on the poor more than trebled, while in some neighbouring townships the rise was even higher.[135] Escalating poor rates were a national problem in this period and resulted in legislation by Parliament designed to check expenditure. The long-established method of appointing overseers of the poor was by the vestry, a public meeting of ratepayers. Under an Act of 1819 each vestry was allowed to appoint a committee of up to twenty people who would meet regularly with the overseers to scrutinize all applications for poor relief. Mellor appears to have been among the first of the townships in the Borough to adopt this new system, with the first meeting of its select vestry being held on the 1st of July

1819. Stockport and Marple both appointed select vestries in the following year, and Heaton Norris followed suit soon after. The members of the select vestries were drawn from the more prosperous members of local society, from industrialists, landowners and well-to-do tradesmen.[136] Under the previous system, overseers had been accused of showing too much generosity to the poor.[137] It was difficult to level the same criticism against the select vestries. At Stockport applicants might be denied assistance if they were known to have taken part in strikes or to hold radical political views. Drunkenness, impertinence and even ownership of a dog were among other grounds for refusal. A policy of providing housing benefit was now scrapped, and though help was given with rents, this was in the form of loans. In the early 1820s Stockport's poor rates were considerably reduced, partly through the tactics of the select vestry but partly also through a new boom in the cotton industry.[138]

Although the select vestries were limited in law to the 'care and management of the concerns of the poor', they took on wider responsibilities. In Stockport township these included the scrutiny of the expenses of the manorial constables, which were paid out of the poor rate. The minutes of the select vestry also provide the earliest evidence for the existence of the Stockport fire brigade, itself financed by the poor rate. In 1820 the brigade consisted of a 'conductor' and eight firemen. All but one of these were dismissed by the select vestry after an examination of their accounts. The service was then organized on a new footing with the select vestry carrying out an inspection of the fire engines every three months. The firemen's assembly point was the parish church, to where they were summoned by the ringing of the bells as an alarm. Heaton Norris had a separate fire brigade which was established in 1821 and was equipped with an engine paid for mainly by the township's cotton manufacturers.[139]

The 1826 Stockport Police Act

By the early 1820s, through a piecemeal process, the inhabitants of Stockport township had achieved several of the aims of the grand scheme of 1785. They had a new prison and workhouse and, though many regretted this, a small debts court. The move to improve the streets had seen some progress, through the widening of Churchgate. The requested levelling of the Market Place had also been achieved. In 1821 it was proposed that the township should apply to Parliament for a power which had not yet been fulfilled, the levying of a new rate to pay for the lighting, policing and cleaning of the streets. To many the idea of such additional expense was

an anathema. 'Let those who are not content with the lights from the druggists' shop windows, carry lanterns', declared one critic, 'and those who want watchmen, or have anything to watch, pay for them'.[140]

In 1823 the township did take over, from the county JPs, responsibility for paying the salary of the gaoler-cum-deputy constable, and also appointed two paid assistants. The money, however, came from an existing and hard-pressed source of funds, the poor rate.[141] Responsibility for ensuring that streets were kept clean by their occupants lay with the manorial officers known as 'scavengers', who were required to bring offenders before the court leet. In 1823 several of these officials were themselves fined by that court for failing in this duty. One report of the time claimed that one of the scavengers' greatest faults was their respectability; they were 'above their business'. The town was in the middle of an economic boom, and yet it could be said that 'Stockport is what Stockport was, an irregular, ill built, badly lighted, dirty place, which no traveller ever passed through and wished to see again'.[142]

By 1825 there was an acceptance in the township that the dreaded introduction of a new rate could not be delayed indefinitely. A petition was drawn up asking Parliament leave to present a bill. Much political infighting followed concerning the criterion for membership of a new body of police commissioners who would manage this rate, and the scope of their powers. The eventual result was the Stockport Police Act, passed by Parliament on the 26th of May 1826.[143] Under its terms the commissioners were to be appointed according to a property qualification which meant that those eligible seldom numbered more than 150 people. (Under a higher property qualification which had originally been proposed, this figure would have been only about fifty.) The commissioners were to hold monthly meetings, and could appoint salaried officials to put the Act into operation. In keeping with local worries about expenditure, the new rate which they were allowed to levy on households was only half of the amount charged in neighbouring Manchester. Furthermore, houses in streets not lit by the commissioners were exempt from payment, as were those with low rateable values.[144]

After a slow start, the commissioners did succeed in bringing about some improvements. Through co-operation with the township's own gas company, to which we will return below, street lighting became more widespread. Refuse collectors were hired. Some streets were paved and provided with sewers, under the supervision of a new, salaried assistant surveyor. Another paid officer, the 'comptroller', was responsible for bringing prosecutions for obstructing the streets and numerous other public nuisances prohibited by the Act. In 1827 the police commissioners took over the cost of the deputy constable and his two assistants, and appointed a third. In the following year they also assumed full control of the fire brigade, which now operated from an engine house on Edward Street. As the commissioners took over such administrative powers from the select vestry, that body was reduced to its originally intended role of administering assistance to the poor. In 1831 the select vestry system was abandoned in Stockport township.[145]

The commissioners' own ability to tackle the problems of the township was limited, however, by the low level of the new rate and its many exemptions. In the 1830s the number of refuse collectors employed was normally only five or six for the whole township. Between 1830 and 1833 the cost of paying the deputy constable and his assistants was even shifted back onto the poor rate, on the grounds that the police rate was insufficient. From 1833 between four and eight 'Sunday constables' were employed, as a cheaper alternative to increasing the permanent staff.[146]

The JPs and petty sessions

While the Stockport police commissioners endeavoured to enforce the 1826 Act, the local JPs retained their powers of jurisdiction. In contrast with the membership of the select vestries and police commission which included industrialists and tradesmen, the JPs of the late eighteenth and early nineteenth centuries were mostly appointed from a narrow social elite. They included successive rectors of Stockport parish, John Watson who died in 1783 and Charles Prescot who held the rectorship until his death in 1820. Other magistrates were drawn from among the diminishing class of local gentry. The first, and for many years only, Stockport industrialist to be made a JP was Peter Marsland, the town's leading mill-owner.[147]

By 1825 local JPs held a fortnightly court or 'petty sessions' in Stockport, with a jurisdiction which covered all the Stockport Division of the Macclesfield hundred. Magistrates were also on hand in the town between these sittings, with one JP in attendance three days in the week, and generally two once a week. The slight increase in the number of local police in the 1820s seems to have had little effect. In 1833 it was noted that a 'prodigious number of prisoners' annually passed through the town's gaol (there had been about 1400 in the past year, none staying longer than three days). However, the conclusion drawn was 'that the magistracy of the district are more successful in the detection than in the prevention of crime'.[148]

The municipal corporation

In 1835 the Municipal Corporations Act created a new administrative body in Stockport, an elected town council, with power to levy a rate to carry out local improvements. Forty-two councillors were to be directly elected and were in turn to appoint twelve aldermen. The town's mayor, who had previously been appointed at meetings of the manorial court leet, was to be chosen by members of the town council, and was to preside over council meetings. The 'municipal borough', the area designated for this new system of corporate government, was the same as the parliamentary borough created three years earlier (Ill 7.2). For the purposes of council elections, this was divided into wards, each of which was allocated a number of seats. Under the provisions of the Act the municipal borough also received its own JPs.[149]

Stockport's was one of 178 municipal corporations in England and Wales authorized by the 1835 Act. However, the very inclusion of the town in the Act seems to have been the result of a parliamentary misunderstanding about its actual status. The places named in the Act were all believed to have existing but antiquated corporations, which Parliament was determined to reform. Stockport was not a corporate borough, but it did have a mayor, a title normally reserved for the chief officer of a corporation. On this basis alone, the government seems to have assumed that Stockport had corporate status and included the town within the 1835 Act.[150]

The qualifications for eligibility to vote for the new council were such that the electorate comprised no more than 2300 adult males out of a total population in the municipal borough of about 41,000.[151] At the first election for the new council in December 1835 this was sufficient number, however, to change the political complexion of local government in the town. Prior to that time, both the select vestry and the police commission were dominated by a small group of upper-middle-class inhabitants. Its members have been described as drawn from the town's mill-owners, large shop-keepers, lawyers and Anglican clergy. This group appears to have worked in harmony with the manorial court leet, and may well have provided the officials of that court. By the mid-1820s the rule of this clique was being opposed by the lower-middle class of small shop-keepers and traders, who were radical in their politics and nonconformist in their religion. By the early 1830s divisions seem to have developed within the ruling group itself on religious and political grounds, between Anglican Tories and nonconformist Whigs. At the first municipal election in 1835 not a single Tory was elected.

Instead, the new council was controlled by nonconformists and radicals.[152]

The Municipal Corporations Act allowed the new councils to levy an unlimited rate, and also gave them general powers of policing and lighting. It did not, however, abolish existing bodies of police commissioners but allowed them to transfer voluntarily their power to the town councils. The more reactionary members of the Stockport police commission had opposed the incorporation of the town, and were unlikely to agree to this new proposal. Other, more radical police commissioners, however, were now themselves councillors. In early March 1837 they outmanoeuvred their opponents by calling a special meeting of the commissioners at short notice. At this it was voted that the commission should be abolished and its powers given over to the council.[153] The authority of the police commission, however, had only extended over Stockport township. On the 16th of March the council decided to seek Parliament's consent to widen those powers across the municipal borough. This was obtained in an Improvement Act passed in 1837. The Act reduced by a third the already low rate which the council was permitted to levy, but it also empowered the council to buy the town's highly profitable gas company. That power, as we shall see, was soon put into effect.[154]

Poor law unions

The Poor Law Amendment Act of 1834 reorganized the way in which poor relief was managed across the country. Parishes and townships, while continuing to bear the cost of their own poor, were amalgamated in larger 'poor law unions'. Within each union, assistance was administered by a central body, a 'board of guardians'. Under the Act, the able-bodied were to receive only 'in-door' assistance, that is if they and their families entered a workhouse. Within their walls men, women and children, and the aged and infirm were housed separately. It was a system specifically designed to save costs by deterring all but the very desperate from seeking relief.

In January 1837 Stockport became the centre of a poor law union comprising sixteen townships, to which Handforth and Bosden were added shortly afterwards. While most of the union's component townships were in Cheshire, it also included Heaton Norris and Reddish in Lancashire. Woodford was part of the Macclesfield union, established in 1836. In Derbyshire, Ludworth was part of the Glossop union, while Mellor formed a union with New Mills and Hayfield, its workhouse being at Ollerset.[155] At Stockport the workhouse at Daw Bank, built to house the poor of the township, was found to be inadequate for the needs of the new union. It was replaced by a new workhouse at Shaw Heath, which could accommodate 600 people and which opened on Christmas Day 1841 (Ill 7.15).[156]

Despite the directive of the Act, the Stockport board of guardians at this time still provided 'outdoor relief'. In 1837 the district first began to feel the economic depression which would continue into the early 1840s. The guardians' priority was to house the most vulnerable, the old, the infirm and the young. In January 1842, of more than 500 inmates only a very small proportion came from the ranks of the able-bodied unemployed. More usually people in that category received assistance in the form of cash or as chits which could be exchanged at the workhouse for basic foodstuffs.[157]

The end of manorial government

The creation of the new corporation in 1835 did not mean the end of the manorial court leet, and for a number of years to come the two bodies were to function in the town side by side. As if to underline the continuing authority of the court leet, in 1840 the steward of the manor had the oaths and duties of the officers of the court published.[158] The lord of the manor was keen to ensure that he maintained his rights which brought in revenue. These included the requirement for all freeholders to be enrolled, at their own cost, as burgesses at the court leet, and for all burgesses to attend its sessions, with fines being imposed on those who failed to comply on either account.[159] These practices were a long-standing grievance among the townspeople. By 1840 their legitimacy was evidently being challenged by Henry Coppock, the Whig town clerk, prompting the lord of the manor to seek legal advice.[160] Equally contentious was manorial policy towards the market. The right to collect market tolls had been leased to a Mr Moore at some date prior to 1840, but in that year the lease expired and their collection now passed back into the hands of the manorial authorities.[161] By 1843 complaints were being made about the inadequacy of the market facilities and the severity with which tolls were being collected. In the spring of that year the borough magistrates even summoned the collectors of the tolls to the Court House on charges of extortion and referred the case to the county assizes.[162]

In 1845 the council began negotiations for the purchase of the manorial rights from Lord Vernon. Two years later Parliament gave its consent to this transaction in the Stockport Manorial Tolls and Bridge Act. Under its provisions, for an agreed sum of £22,500 the council would assume the manorial rights and

Ill 7.15 Stockport Workhouse, Shaw Heath.
A new workhouse was opened at Daw Bank in 1812 to accommodate the poor of Stockport township. In 1837, as part of a national reorganization of the system of poor relief, Stockport became the centre of a sizeable poor law union. The change necessitated the construction of a much larger workhouse, at Shaw Heath, which opened on Christmas Day 1841. In August 1842 striking cotton workers broke into the building to help themselves to bread. The workhouse building is now St Thomas's Hospital.

acquire property in the Market Place. It was also to take over from Lord Vernon an area of farmland known as Stringer's Fields for use as a public park, on which more will be said in the following chapter. The bill met with local opposition which questioned whether the sale was justifiable by the profits which might be acquired from the manorial tolls.[163] This controversy is said to have been the major cause of the Tories' success in the local election of November 1848, when they gained a majority of seats on the town council, and promptly removed Henry Coppock from the office of town clerk.[164] In August of the following year, however, a special committee reported to the council that it was honour bound to fulfil the agreement with Lord Vernon. In 1850 the purchase was completed.[165] New, lower market tolls were introduced, which became the responsibility of a new council committee.[166] Almost immediately work began on improving the Market Place facilities, as we shall see in the following chapter. With the purchase of the manorial rights, the council also

assumed control of the court leet. The town clerk now acted as the court's steward. Meetings of the court leet continued to be held until 1858. With the holding of the last meeting on the 21st of October of that year, this 'ancient ceremonial', as it was described in the press at that time, became extinct.[167]

LOCAL SERVICES

Gaslighting

In the early nineteenth century gas, produced by burning coal, transformed the night-time appearance of Stockport. The early development of the gas industry owed much to the adoption of gaslighting by mill-owners in the region. The long hours worked in the cotton industry required artificial lighting which was initially provided by candles or oil lamps. In 1805 a Salford mill was the first in the region to install gas-making plant.[168] It was designed by William Murdoch, the pioneer of gaslighting and an employee of the Birmingham firm of Boulton and Watt, better known for the manufacture of steam engines. In the following year Peter Marsland, Stockport's leading mill-owner, commissioned Murdoch to provide him with designs for gas-making plant, which was later installed in Marsland's Park Mills.[169] Other mill-owners in the town also installed gas-making plant, so that by 1825 Baines could describe how Stockport's factories 'rising in tiers above each other, when lighted with the brilliant gaseous vapour of modern discovery, present in the evenings of the winter months a towering illumination of the imposing grandeur of which it is difficult to convey an adequate idea'.[170] At this date it was common for mill-owners who were manufacturing gas also to use it to light the immediate surroundings of their factories.[171]

In 1820 a private commercial gas company was established in the town. Among its founders was Thomas Claye, a printer and bookseller, who for several years previously had lit his shop window with gas produced on the premises. In 1822 the new company leased premises on Millgate as the site of its gasworks. A supply was initially provided to the Market Place but by 1824 mains extended to Higher Hillgate. Customers paid for the lighting of their property by subscription.[172] After the 1826 Police Act gave the police commissioners power to light the town, this new local authority set up its own street lights, to which the company provided the gas.[173] By 1832 the company had extended its operations to supply Heaton Norris. Here for a short while a rival company was also in operation until its Heaton Lane works were bought by the Stockport company. Portwood also had a gas supply by the 1830s, provided by a local cotton firm.[174]

From the outset the Stockport Gas Light Company proved highly profitable, a position which its shareholders were determined to preserve. In March 1825, in anticipation of a Stockport police bill, the company strengthened its position by being incorporated by an Act of Parliament. The Police Act of the following year permitted the police commissioners to manufacture gas, but a clause allowing them to sell it was removed from the bill in the face of opposition from the gas company. By the early 1830s radicals in the town were complaining about the level of prices charged by the company. They were also looking enviously at the situation in Manchester, where the gas company was owned by the town's police commissioners and where profits were used for public improvements. In 1834 the Stockport Gas Light Company responded to criticism by reducing its charges, but with the election of the municipal council in 1835 the writing was on the wall. When the Stockport Improvement Act was passed in

1837, it included a provision empowering the council to buy the gas company. At the start of 1839, for the sum of £21,493, this passed into council ownership.[175]

Water

The origins of a public water-supply at Stockport are obscure. Aikin in 1795 reported that the 'old part of the town' was chiefly supplied with water from springs in the Barn Fields. These were on the high ground to the south of St Peter's church, near which was a reservoir where this spring-water was collected. From here the water was carried 'by pipes to different parts of the town, as well as into the houses on the rocks in the market-place'. A 'conduit', or fountain, had been built on the north side of the Market Place by the late seventeenth century and is said to have been supplied from this same source. At the southern end of the town, water was obtained from springs at the head of Hempshaw Brook. From here, as late as the 1840s, water was distributed for sale by carriers with yokes and cans, or carts. By the early nineteenth century a much-used public pump stood opposite the grammar school on Chestergate, and drew water from a well cut into the natural sandstone. A second pump stood on this street, with another in Spring Gardens near the rectory.[176]

By the early 1820s the pollution of existing sources by sewage and the requirements of a growing population were resulting in a water-shortage. The solution was provided by an artesian well, over 45 metres deep, sunk by Peter Marsland at his Park Mills. So plentiful was the supply of water which this produced, that Marsland applied to Parliament for permission to lay mains for its distribution. An Act, passed in 1825, gave him the right to supply water not only to Stockport but also to several of the surrounding townships, including, to the north of the river, Heaton Norris and Reddish. The Park Mills' waterwheels and a steam engine were used to raise the water to a reservoir at Marsland's Woodbank estate, giving it sufficient pressure to supply all but the highest parts of the district. Marsland's Stockport Water Works came into operation in 1827. Customers who wanted to bring water into their homes or business premises were expected to lay their own pipes from Marsland's mains. Many householders appear to have been reluctant to pay this additional expense. Instead, two or three households shared a standpipe to which each had a key. The water supplied from the Park Mills' well was hard, but on one day each week the supply was replaced with soft water drawn from the River Goyt above Woodbank.[177]

HEALTH CARE

The Stockport Dispensary

Until the late eighteenth century the local provision of medical care seems to have been confined to the private practices of physicians, to apothecaries, or to whatever treatment may have been available to the sick under the local system of poor relief. At Stockport the first significant extension of the provision of health care is attributed to James Briscall. He arrived in the town in about 1774 to practise as a doctor, and subsequently opened a dispensary where he offered treatment to the poor at his own expense. In the 1790s the financing and management of the Dispensary were taken over by a committee of local mill-owners and other prominent townspeople, and new premises were erected in Petty Carr Green. (Its site is now part of Stockport's bus station.) Peter Marsland, a member of that committee, also provided most of the money for the erection close by of what was later euphemistically known as the 'House of Recovery'. It comprised nine wards and dealt with cases of highly infectious diseases. This facility was much needed. In the unsanitary conditions of the expanding town, outbreaks of typhus seem to have been an almost annual occurrence. There were also epidemics of smallpox and scarlet fever.[178]

The cholera epidemic of 1832

In the early 1830s cholera was added to this list. The disease first reached England in October 1831, and almost immediately Parliament advised towns to set up special committees to improve local sanitary conditions. Such a committee, or local board of health, was established in Stockport in November 1831. It brought together officers from the various existing branches of local government, the mayor, overseers, surveyors, police commissioners and constables, as well as including local doctors. Resolutions were passed to enforce street cleansing and for inspections to be made of lodging houses, where conditions were often at their most squalid, but there was little that could be effectively done to prevent the epidemic reaching the town. It was brought, in June 1832, by a poor man and his wife, who travelling between Manchester and Birmingham spent the night in a lodging house in Adlington Square. The woman was taken ill and was brought to the House of Recovery, where she died. With the House of Recovery already full of other patients, a 'Cholera House' was quickly erected at Daw Bank. By October there had been thirty more deaths from the disease, out of seventy reported cases,

although compared with some other places Stockport was considered to have got off lightly.[179]

The Stockport Infirmary

In the same week that cholera reached Stockport, the foundation stone was laid for a new infirmary. It was intended to replace the premises at Petty Carr Green, which had become increasingly inadequate over the years. In 1815 the Dispensary and House of Recovery had dealt with just under 1000 patients. By 1831 the number had doubled. The existing buildings also lacked adequate facilities for surgical operations. Work on surgical wards had started at the Dispensary in the early 1820s but was suspended as a result of the construction of Wellington Bridge immediately adjacent to the Dispensary site. The new Infirmary, completed in 1833, stood on what was then the edge of the town, next to the new turnpike, Wellington Road. Its facade included a central portico in the classical style which was then much in fashion for large public buildings (*Ill 7.16*). The Infirmary was later enlarged by the addition of wings at the south and north ends of the original block in 1870 and 1898 respectively. Other additions were made in the twentieth century.[180] After serving Stockport for over 160 years, the Infirmary closed in 1996 and its services were transferred to Stepping Hill Hospital. That hospital was itself founded in 1905 to accommodate the sick of the Stockport poor law union.[181]

RIOTERS, STRIKERS AND RADICALS

The massive industrial and urban growth which led to developments in local government and the provision of services also fostered popular unrest. The cotton industry was subject to cycles of booms and slumps, and during downturns in trade mill-owners reduced the wages of their workforce. Handloom weaving saw a more long-term trend. In the 1780s, with the first upsurge in the cotton industry, local handloom weavers were able to command high wages. In the 1790s wage levels began a general decline which was accentuated in the early nineteenth century.[182] Sharp rises in the price of corn and bread, part of the staple diet of the working class, added to the problems. The Corn Laws of 1815 and 1828, which restricted the import of grain, gave parliamentary sanction to the continuation of high food prices.

The responses of the lower classes to their economic difficulties took a variety of forms. At the turn of the nineteenth century anger at food shortages or high prices erupted into rioting in Stockport. In 1812, as we have seen in the previous chapter, Luddites attacked

Ill 7.16 Stockport Infirmary.

Improvements in the provision of health care in the industrial town owed much to the charity of private individuals. A free dispensary was established in Stockport in the late eighteenth century by Doctor James Briscall. In the 1790s this developed into a new charitable institution housed in purpose-built premises. The need for larger accommodation led to the construction in 1832-3 of the Stockport Infirmary, an imposing structure designed in a classical style and built alongside the Wellington Road turnpike.

factories and other property in the town.[183] In a change of tactics this initial phase of violence in that year was replaced by 'rural levies'. At first these involved gangs of workers visiting the homes of landowners and farmers to exact money; later they became night-time robberies of isolated homes by armed men. For their part in robberies committed in the Stockport area in 1812 two men were hanged at Chester.[184]

'Turnouts' or strikes were the most common of direct industrial action, perhaps the earliest recorded in Stockport being a strike by hatters in 1775.[185] In the course of the late eighteenth and early nineteenth centuries most sizeable local industries witnessed sporadic strike action.[186] Dissatisfaction among the lower classes was directed not merely against employers. By the 1790s some local men were espousing the view that improvements could only be achieved by changes in national government, and in particular by the widening of the right to vote. Prior to the Reform Act of 1832 the franchise within the area of the Borough was limited to freeholders who were entitled to vote for county MPs. The Reform Act gave Stockport its own parliamentary representation, but, as we shall see, the Act's own property qualification meant that the vast majority of the working class were still without a vote. The degree of support enjoyed by political radicals was not constant. Parliamentary reform was for many of its advocates a last resort when other attempts at improving their economic condition had failed.

The reaction of the authorities

Although the police force within the town was barely able to meet the day-to-day problems of crime, the authorities were able to call on other assistance to deal with popular unrest. Beginning in 1794 sizeable local forces of volunteers were enrolled not only to guard against a possible French invasion but also to quell any civil disturbances.[187] The volunteers were disbanded in 1808. Some were reformed as a permanent militia, but after this date the authorities relied mainly on loyalists who were sworn in as special constables at times of emergency. Acting alongside these were the Stockport Yeomanry, a volunteer troop of cavalry founded in the mid-1810s when it numbered thirty-seven men. Only a minority of these lived in the town; most were said to be farmers.[188] From 1818 regular troops were also stationed in Stockport. They were first housed in temporary barracks, probably in Adlington Square, but in 1819 the government approved the construction of purpose-built quarters on Hall Street on the east side of the town.[189]

John Lloyd

The task of mustering these various forces was normally the responsibility of the local magistrates. For a number of years in the early nineteenth century, however, the main opponent of radicals and strikers was the magistrates' clerk, the lawyer John Lloyd. Fervently loyal to king and country, Lloyd took it upon himself to act as an agent of the government. He hired his own spies, and sent reports of local activities to the Home Office. In return he was sent his expenses by the Treasury.[190] Lloyd was himself a member of the local permanent militia and the Stockport Yeomanry. In 1816, in response to unrest among local handloom weavers, he secretly organized a force of special constables; they were instructed to provide themselves with a pistol, powder and shot and, at the first sign of trouble, to assemble at the old Castle Mill 'in order to act in a body with the magistrates if required'.[191] The courts were another weapon in Lloyd's armoury. In 1815 he obtained evidence which resulted in the conviction and imprisonment of twelve members of a hatters' 'combination', or trade union, on a charge of conspiracy. Three years later he successfully brought the same charge against workers who had staged a walk-out at the Mersey Mills.[192] His activities at Stockport, on which more will be said below, came to an end in 1822 when he was promoted to the position of chief clerk of the court at Chester.[193]

Food riots, 1795-1812

In 1795 Stockport was one of several Cheshire towns to suffer disturbances as a result of escalating corn prices. The focus of the crowd's anger was Bradford Norbury whose house, one of the largest in the Market Place, was pelted with stones (Plate V). Norbury was a prominent figure among Stockport's corn factors, middlemen who bought corn from farmers and who were seen as profiteering at the cost of the poor.[194] There was rioting again in the Market Place in 1799, when a crowd seized carts bringing meal and flour for sale, and shops were attacked.[195] In January of the following year the local JP Charles Prescot, fearing more trouble, asked farmers to bring corn, meal and flour to the market, and to sell it not to middlemen, but 'there retail it to the poor at a reasonable profit'.[196]

High food prices also fuelled the civil unrest of 1812. At Stockport in that year a voluntary subscription was raised to buy food which was then sold to the poor at a reduced price.[197] The action seems to have deterred a repetition of earlier food riots in the town. In Bredbury, however, Arden Mill was attacked by a crowd which marched across the bridge over the Tame, having already seized food in Hyde and Gee Cross. The ransacking of the mill was stopped by the arrival of cavalry led by John Lloyd. Seven men were subsequently tried at Chester for their part in the

incident; four were found guilty and were transported to Australia for seven years.[198]

Early radicals and revolutionaries

Radicalism can be traced in Stockport to 1792 when the Stockport Friends of Universal Peace and the Rights of Man was founded in the town. This was one of a number of radical societies which were formed in the country in the early 1790s, and which quickly inspired a loyalist backlash. When in December 1792 a royal proclamation outlawed 'seditious' literature, the local JPs swore in a force of seventy special constables at Stockport to put this ban into effect. In the Market Place, immediately following that meeting, a crowd burnt an effigy of Thomas Paine, the author of the recently published *Rights of Man*. As the decade progressed, repression of radicalism became harsher and radical views more extreme. In 1797 meetings were being held in Stockport and Heaton Norris by members of the United Englishmen, an underground organization which advocated revolution. The movement was suppressed in 1798 but in the early 1800s a further revolutionary organization, the Union Society, was in existence in the town. Despite the fears of the authorities, the membership of these early radical organizations remained limited to only a tiny minority of the local population. It was not until the 1810s that radicalism both in Stockport and elsewhere in the Manchester region won mass support. That change came about as one particular body of workers increasingly gave up hope of improving their condition by means other than parliamentary reform. These were the handloom weavers.[199]

The road to Peterloo, 1816-19

Stockport Union Society and the Blanketeers, 1816-17

In 1816 the cotton handloom weaving industry was at one of its lowest ebbs. In June of that year more than half of the handloom weavers in Stockport township, Heaton Norris and Edgeley lacked work. For those who had employment, piece-rates had fallen. Local weavers petitioned Parliament and the Prince Regent for a minimum wage and the prohibition of the export of cotton yarn. When their voice was ignored they looked for a solution in the reform of Parliament itself. In the autumn of 1816 the Stockport Union Society was established, one of a number of so-called 'Hampden clubs' founded in the country during this period to organize a campaign for parliamentary reform. Its membership brought together weavers, hatters and lower-middle-class radicals. At Stockport and elsewhere within the Manchester area mass meetings were held to promote the radicals' demands. By early 1817 the strategy was being advocated that weavers should march to London to deliver a petition. On the 10th of March a mass meeting in Manchester witnessed the start of that march of the 'Blanketeers', so-called after the blankets which some carried for use on the journey. The authorities had no intention of letting the event proceed. The meeting at Manchester was broken up by magistrates and military, and arrests were made. Many of the marchers themselves got no further than Stockport. There they were met by John Lloyd and Holland Watson (a Congleton JP, formerly of Stockport), leading a force of yeomanry and special constables. Some marchers were stopped at Lancashire Bridge. Others waded across the river, only to be arrested within the town. The prisoners were held in the yard of the old Castle Mill, before being marched back to Manchester. Although the marchers had committed no offence, Lloyd suggested that they should be charged with vagrancy. The government eventually recommended their discharge. The events of the 10th of March caused one fatality at Stockport. A cabinet-maker living on Old Road, hearing the commotion outside his house, went to shut his yard gate and was struck on the head by one of the yeomanry. An inquest returned a verdict of wilful murder, but the assailant was never identified.[200]

A summer of strikes, 1818

The slump in the cotton industry in 1816-17 had brought reductions in wages across the cotton industry. In 1818, with an improvement in trade, a succession of workers in Stockport took industrial action in support of their demands for a return to earlier wage levels. The jenny spinners were the first to strike, in May. Their dispute ended after six weeks when they agreed to a rise of half the amount originally demanded.[201] Dressers and powerloom workers went on strike in July. Their action escalated into violence when one manufacturer, Thomas Garside, brought in replacement workers. On the night of the 15th of July a crowd of angry protesters battled with special constables and yeomanry outside Garside's factory. The violence was resumed on the following evening when the authorities' forces were reinforced by cavalry dispatched from Manchester. Further rioting was prevented by the threats and persuasions of John Lloyd. One protester later died from his injuries, but an inquest delivered the verdict that he had 'Died by the Visitation of God'. Charges were brought against one of the yeomanry and

a special constable for firing shots through the door of the house of Dr Thomas Cheetham during the disturbances, but John Lloyd ensured their acquittal. (Cheetham was one of the town's radicals, who gave their support to the strike.) The strikers received a very different treatment from the courts. Legislation passed in 1799-1800 against 'combinations' or trade unions was used by Lloyd to convict four strikers found in possession of strike funds. The dispute ended with strikers returning to work without achieving their goal.[202]

At the start of September handloom weavers in Stockport and across the Manchester district began their own strike.[203] The dispute saw handloom weavers parading with banners through the streets of Stockport but passed without violence in the town, and the weavers returned to work when their employers agreed to the demanded rise. They soon reneged on this agreement and wages again began to fall.[204]

Stockport Union for the Promotion of Human Happiness

In 1817 support for the radicals' cause was weakened first by repression by the government and local loyalists and then by an improvement in economic conditions. During their strike in 1818 handloom weavers in the Stockport district distanced themselves from radicals who were resuming the call for parliamentary reform. When that strike failed to achieve a lasting wage settlement, handloom weavers once again gave their support. For a while some weavers continued to press for parliamentary legislation for a minimum wage, but by June 1819 these moderates had abandoned such hopes and were also backing the campaign for reform.[205]

In October 1818 a new radical organization was established in Stockport, the Union for the Promotion of Human Happiness, which in the first months of its existence may have enjoyed the active support of as many as one in ten local people. Members met in weekly classes, each with up to twelve persons. The town was divided into twelve districts, and members in each district appointed two people to sit on the Union's committee. Its permanent treasurer and leading light was the Reverend Joseph Harrison, a nonconformist who called himself 'chaplain to the poor and needy'. The 'Windmill Rooms' on Edward Street served as the society's headquarters. They also housed the Union's own Sunday school, the first to be organized by a radical group in England. The Union's political aspiration was a Parliament elected annually in a secret ballot in which all male adults were entitled to vote, an aim earlier espoused by the Hampden clubs and later taken up by

Ill 7.17 The breastbone of Constable Birch and the Memoir of Jacob McGhinness.
In 1819 a series of mass meetings were held at Sandy Brow in Stockport by radicals pressing for parliamentary reform. The authorities, who had failed to break up these gatherings by force, ordered the arrest of two of the speakers on a charge of sedition. After Constable William Birch enforced one of these arrests, he was shot in the chest by an unemployed weaver, Jacob McGhinness. Birch survived the attack and after his death in 1834 the bullet was found lodged in his breastbone. McGhinness was sentenced to death for his crime. His Memoir, written while he was awaiting execution, gave his own account of the crime, and of his religious conversion in prison.

the Chartists. In support of their menfolk, women founded their own Stockport Female Union in 1819, which held its own classes and had its own committee.[206]

The Sandy Brow meetings and the shooting of Constable Birch

During the early months of 1819 local radicals grew in confidence. In January of that year Henry Hunt, a leading national figure in the campaign for reform, visited Stockport and addressed a crowd in the Market Place from a window of the Bull's Head.[207] On the 15th of February radicals held a mass meeting on Sandy Brow, not far from the Windmill Rooms. When a 'cap of liberty', a symbol of revolution, was raised, the Stockport Yeomanry and special constables moved in to break up the meeting, but were forced back by the crowd. The episode became a cause of celebration among radicals in the region, and was even commemorated in verse.[208] Over the coming months Sandy Brow was the venue for further radical demonstrations. On the 19th of April a mass meeting was held here to protest against the sentences of two years' imprisonment imposed on three locally prominent radicals, John Bagguley, Samuel Drummond and John Johnston. They had been found guilty at Chester assizes of making seditious speeches in Stockport in September of the previous year. On the day of the Sandy Brow meeting a total of 4550 people signed a petition for a retrial. When constables confronted the crowd, they were met with a hail of stones.[209]

On the 28th of June Sandy Brow was the scene of perhaps the greatest of all the radical meetings held in the Manchester area in the heady year of 1819, with the exception of Peterloo. The crowd was variously estimated at between 4000 and 20,000 and included contingents from Bullock Smithy, Ashton, Oldham and Manchester. The aim of the meeting was to consider measures for delivering petitions for reform to the Prince Regent and to make 'a solemn appeal to the people of Great Britain, praying them to join us in forming a National Union, for the purpose of achieving Radical Reform'. With the exception of the removal of a Manchester constable from the scene, the meeting passed without violence. Some of the crowd, however, were armed and a cap of liberty was again on display.[210]

At the next quarter sessions two of the speakers at the meeting were indicted on a charge of sedition. One was Sir Charles Wolseley, who had been invited to chair the meeting. The other was the Reverend Harrison. Two constables, one being William Birch, were sent from Stockport by John Lloyd to arrest Harrison, who had left the town to address a radical meeting in London. When the three arrived back in Stockport on the evening of the 23rd of July, Harrison was taken to Birch's house, where he was questioned by Lloyd. As Birch himself stood outside, three men approached. One pulled out a pistol and shot the constable in the chest. The culprit, a silk-weaver from Edgeley named Jacob McGhinness, escaped immediate arrest but was later captured in Ireland. He was tried at Chester, along with James Bruce, one of his two accomplices. Both men were sentenced to death, although Bruce's sentence was commuted to transportation for life. Birch recovered from the attack and was awarded a government pension. Radicals suggested that the assailant had fired only wadding from his pistol, or that the constable had not been shot at all, but after Birch's death in 1834 the bullet was found lodged in his breastbone (*Ill 7.17*).[211]

The assizes of April 1820 which tried McGhinness and Bruce also heard the case against Harrison and Wolseley. Both were sentenced to eighteenth months' imprisonment. In a separate trial in that same month, Harrison was found guilty of preaching two seditious sermons subsequent to the Sandy Brow meeting. For these offences two years were added to his sentence. The occasion of one of those sermons had been the 15th of August 1819, the eve of the great radical meeting which ended in the 'Peterloo Massacre'.[212]

Stockport and Peterloo

That meeting, held at St Peter's Fields in Manchester, had originally been called for the 9th of August. When magistrates were informed that the meeting would include the election of a 'representative' to Parliament they declared it to be illegal. With the offending topic removed from the agenda, the meeting was postponed to the 16th. The principal speaker, Henry Hunt, had been invited by the Stockport Union to stay overnight in the town on the 8th of August, an appointment which he still kept. The following morning a crowd escorted him to Manchester. With Hunt were the Reverend Harrison and James Moorhouse, a long-standing Stockport radical, in whose house Hunt had lodged for the night.[213]

A week later people in tens of thousands – the true figure may never be known – converged on St Peter's Fields. A large proportion was from Manchester itself; others came from the surrounding towns and countryside. Estimates for the number attending from Stockport range from 1000 to 5000. A figure of 1400 or 1500, including about forty women, is believed to be the most accurate. One eyewitness described how they marched along the turnpike road to Manchester in a well-ordered file. Casualty lists suggest that the largest single occupational group among this contingent were weavers, the same being also true for the demonstration as a whole.[214]

A total of 1500 cavalry were stationed at the ready in Manchester that day. The violence began when the Manchester Yeomanry were ordered through the crowd to assist in the arrest of Hunt and the others on the hustings. The 15th Hussars were then sent in to disperse the crowd. Four years earlier they had fought at Waterloo, and it was their action at St Peter's Fields which provided the tragic episode with its name of Peterloo.[215] In all twelve people were killed, and more than 600 injured. The vast majority of the casualties were demonstrators. Some of these were sabred, others were trampled or crushed in the panic. Of the wounded, forty-six, including eight women, are reported to have come from Stockport township or its neighbourhood.[216] One Stockport man survived despite having part of his skull cut away. He kept it as a grim souvenir, and it was later exhibited by Hunt to the House of Commons as evidence of the military's brutality.[217] James Moorhouse was one of nine people who along with Hunt were charged with conspiracy in connection with Peterloo. Five of these, including Moorhouse, were acquitted.[218]

The contingent of demonstrators were not the only people from Stockport at St Peter's Fields that day. Helping the hussars disperse the crowd were John Lloyd and the Stockport Yeomanry, who viewed the occasion as a chance to revenge their humiliation at Sandy Brow. A witness described how the Stockport Yeomanry 'cut their way through in form'. One member of the yeomanry seized banners from the crowd. These were later burnt in Stockport's Market Place. Lloyd himself spoke of 'the glorious day at Manchester. We have come back with honour'.[219]

In the aftermath of Peterloo, radicals in the Stockport area were reported to be preparing for revolution. There were rumours of men arming and drilling in Torkington, Offerton and Marple, and the authorities took the precautionary measure of removing cannons from Lyme Park to Chester Castle to prevent them falling into the radicals' hands. At Stockport, special constables made nightly patrols through the town.[220] Fears of an uprising were soon to evaporate. Repressive legislation by Parliament, the so-called 'Six Acts', undermined support for the radical cause. In the early 1820s Stockport enjoyed a period of economic boom during which the call for parliamentary reform lost its previous urgency. Those same years also saw the sharp decline in the numbers of workers who had given their support to that cause, as the handloom weaving of cotton gave way to the unstoppable advance of the powerloom.

The strike of 1829

The bitterest and most prolonged of strikes in Stockport in the early nineteenth century occurred in 1829. In late December of the previous year, faced with falling profits, some twenty local cotton-spinning and manufacturing firms announced a reduction in wages. The response was a strike by mule-spinners, powerloom weavers and dressers, which by the 23rd of January involved 10,000 workers. The dispute was initially peaceful, but by April 1829, to the anger of the strikers, the mill-owners were bringing in blackleg labour. As these replacement workers arrived in the town, strikers offered them money to return home or hurled stones.

Violence reached its height on the evening of the 6th of May when a crowd assembled on Wellington Bridge. Two magistrates, Peter Marsland and Captain Humphreys of Bramall Hall, arrived with a force of special constables and infantry. When they tried to steer the front of the crowd off the bridge down steps leading to Chestergate, they themselves were forced back under a hail of bricks and stones. The demonstrators reached Spring Bank Mill on Wellington Road, one of the factories employing blackleg labour, and gave way only when, on Humphreys' orders, shots were fired over their heads. The strike saw no further large-scale disturbances, but attacks on individuals continued. There were incidents of acid throwing, one of the victims being the son of William Smith, owner of the Mersey Mills. For attacking a blackleg, three men were sentenced to transportation and another to death. The powerloom weavers had returned to work by mid-August, and by late September the other striking workers had also given up the fight. In that same month Peter Marsland died at the age of fifty-nine, possibly as a result of injuries sustained in the May riot.[221]

The Reform Act and the parliamentary borough's early elections, 1832-7

The cause of radicalism saw a brief revival in the early 1830s. In the aftermath of the failed strike of 1829, and labouring under a severe economic depression, workers in Stockport looked to the reform of Parliament as a means of achieving their own aims. On this occasion the radical cause was also encouraged by the coming to power of a Whig government itself pledged to some measure of parliamentary reform. By the beginning of 1831 a Political Union had been established in Stockport, by workers and lower-middle-class radicals. The latter group, which included campaigners from the Peterloo era, comprised the individuals who supported reform in the local administration of the town. One of a number of radical pressure groups established at this time, the Stockport Political Union petitioned the government for annual Parliaments, the right of all adult males to vote, and election by secret ballot. The government's own proposals were supported by both local Whigs and Tory mill-owners who saw the possibility of parliamentary representation for Stockport as being to their own commercial advantage. Those proposals fell far short of the aspirations of the radicals, and were denounced by Henry Hunt during two visits to Stockport. The Reform Bill roused some support among the town's working class, but the disillusioned radical faction had abandoned its own agitation long before the bill became law in June 1832.[222]

The Reform Act made Stockport one of the country's new parliamentary boroughs, and gave it two seats in the Commons. The right to vote, however, was still based upon a property qualification, as a consequence of which the local electorate in 1834 numbered only 936. These included mill-owners and shop-keepers, but only a few, better-off, factory workers.[223] Four candidates stood in the town's first electoral contest, one Tory, one Whig and two radicals. On the 12th of December 1832 they were formally nominated at a meeting in the Market Place which was attended by an estimated 12,000 people, said to have been the largest gathering which the town had ever seen. Of the two men who were elected, one was Thomas Marsland, the Tory owner of the Daw Bank printworks and Wellington Mill. The other, perhaps to the surprise of local radicals, was one of their own candidates, John Horatio Lloyd. The son of John Lloyd, the arch-enemy of Stockport radicalism in the 1810s, he appealed to Tory voters for their support in order to defeat the Whig candidate, Henry Marsland, the owner of the Park Mills. Lloyd claimed to endorse radical views in reaction to his father's own politics, but once elected he did little to further the radicals' cause. At the next election, in 1835, he was not invited to stand. In a straight three-sided contest, the radical candidate was defeated, Henry Marsland was now elected, and Thomas Marsland retained his seat. While radicals could tolerate Henry Marsland's victory, the re-election of Thomas Marsland provoked rioting in the town. The two Marslands were re-elected in 1837, despite the fact that the Whigs brought in a candidate whom they believed could defeat Thomas Marsland.[224] Richard Cobden, a Manchester calico-printer, had already begun his rise to national prominence as an advocate of 'free trade', the removal of the government's tariffs on the importation of goods. He attributed his defeat in the 1837 election to bribery of the electorate by Thomas Marsland.[225] Cobden was to reverse that defeat four years later. In the meantime local radicals found a new wave of popular support, as Stockport became one of the region's main centres of Chartism.

Chartism, 1838-9

In the late 1830s as the national economy worsened the agitation for parliamentary reform was revived. It now found a focus in the People's Charter published in May 1838 by the London Working Men's Association. Its 'six points' called for the vote for all adult males, secret ballots, constituencies of roughly equal size, annual Parliaments, the abolition of a property qualification for MPs and for MPs to be paid. At a meeting in Birmingham in early August the campaign was launched for the collection of a national petition to be presented to Parliament. By the end of that same month a Radical Association in support of the Charter had been established in Stockport.[226]

In September the Association held public meetings in the town which voted in favour of the Charter and the National Petition. The intended venue of each meeting was a room in the Bull's Head in the Market Place, but so great was the attendance that the audience adjourned outside and was addressed by speakers from a first-floor window of the inn. Chartists were busy rallying support elsewhere in the Manchester area at this time. On the 24th of September supporters of the Charter converged on Kersal Moor, to the north of Manchester, for a great rally. Members of the Stockport Radical Association, or as it had now become known, the Stockport Working Men's Association, were among those present.[227]

At the beginning of October two of the movement's leading figures, Fergus O'Connor and Joseph Rayner Stephens, addressed a crowd from the window of the Bull's Head. They had been escorted into the town in a torchlight procession, a hallmark of the early Chartist movement and to the authorities a cause of serious concern. In early December torchlight processions and assemblies were banned by royal proclamation. By this time Stockport's town clerk, Henry Coppock, was writing to the Home Office for advice about dealing with the Chartists, while the mayor refused to allow the Chartists to meet in the Court House for the purpose of choosing delegates to their National Convention. That meeting was instead held a week later on the 12th of December at the Bull's Head and elected Joseph Rayner Stephens as one of the town's two delegates. His appointment was short-lived. On the 27th of December Stephens became the first notable Chartist to suffer arrest, the charge being one of making seditious speeches. A month later local Chartists held a dinner in his support at the Stanley Arms on New Bridge Lane. Over the next few months this was to be the venue for further Chartist gatherings. It was here on the 11th of February that Bronterre O'Brien, another prominent figure in the movement, was elected to replace Stephens as a delegate. At the end of that same month O'Brien presented the National Convention with £9 10s collected in Stockport for 'the National Rent', the Chartists' central fund. The town also provided 13,000 names towards the National Petition.[228]

In the early months of 1839 some Chartists within the Manchester area were busy arming themselves. This shift from 'moral force' to 'physical force' Chartism may

PUBLIC NOTICE.

The Magistrates of the Borough of Stockport having received a Communication from different Trades in this Borough, that many of the work-people are desirous and willing

To Return to their Work,

GIVE THIS

PUBLIC NOTICE,

THAT MEASURES ARE TAKEN TO SUPPRESS

ANY ATTEMPTED RESISTANCE

TO THEIR GOING TO WORK;

AND

That any Persons desirous of following their usual

EMPLOYMENTS,

WILL BE PROTECTED.

WILLIAM NELSTROP,

MAYOR OF STOCKPORT.

Court House, Stockport, August 16. 1842.

T. M. KING, PRINTER, BRIDGE-STREET, STOCKPORT.

Ill 7.18 A magistrates' poster issued during the 'Plug Plot' strike of 1842.
In August 1842, during a severe economic depression, workers in Stockport became involved in what was effectively a general strike in the factories of the Manchester area. The dispute originated in response to a reduction in wages, but local Chartists attempted to use the strike as a means of achieving their own goal of parliamentary reform.

have taken place more slowly in Stockport than in some neighbouring towns, but by late March local Chartist leaders were advocating the arming of the working class and in mid-April weapons were being sold in the Market Place. By early May the government was promising to provide arms to local authorities to help quell Chartist activity. Evidently encouraged by this government sanction, when the Chartists organized a meeting at the Stanley Arms on the 9th of May, Henry Coppock declared it to be illegal and swore in a force of special constables. The meeting itself was postponed for two days, when between 6000 and 7000 people assembled at New Bridge Lane in defiance of Coppock's ban. One speaker urged the crowd to arm themselves against the authorities, and several pikes were on display. The message appeared to have an effect; on the following Monday numerous applications are reported to have been made at ironmongers' shops for firearms. Henry Coppock responded to the meeting by writing to the Chartists, listing the various penalties which they faced if they did not give up their arms in favour of peaceful protest. The Chartists themselves launched a recruitment drive in advance of another great meeting on Kersal Moor, held on Whit Saturday. That meeting reiterated the right of the working class to be armed and called for a general strike known as the 'National Holiday' or 'Sacred Month'. It was followed by a feverish week of Chartist gatherings in Stockport, culminating in a meeting on the 1st of June at the Stanley Arms addressed by Bronterre O'Brien. Local magistrates expected trouble, particularly when on the 8th of June the Chartist Peter Murray M'Douall was arrested and brought to Stockport's gaol. It was the Chartists themselves, however, who were now subject to violence. When M'Douall was released on bail and was making his way with a body of Chartist supporters towards the Stanley Arms, a missile was hurled from a mill on New Bridge Lane, injuring a boy.[229]

On the 12th of June Parliament rejected the National Petition. In response the Chartists' National Convention voted to begin a general strike in August. At Stockport meetings were organized to put the plan into effect. One assembly, on the 20th of July, drew between 10,000 and 12,000 people from the town and the surrounding area. On the following day, a Sunday, Chartists even took over the parish church, forcing the congregation to give up their pews. The next day, the 22nd, the JPs issued instructions to the special constables. At the first sign of further trouble the bells of the parish church were to be rung as an alarm, and the special constables were to present themselves at once at the Court House to assist the magistrates; if necessary use would also be made of the military. Over the following days additional

Ill 7.19 Richard Cobden's statue, St Peter's Square.
Cobden, a political figure of national importance, was an MP for Stockport from 1841 to 1847. He was a prominent advocate of free trade and a leader of the Anti-Corn Law League, whose campaign received widespread support among local mill-owners. The bronze statue of Cobden in St Peter's Square was erected in 1886, twenty-one years after his death.

special constables were sworn in; at the request of the magistrates and mayor, 500 firearms and 800 cutlasses were sent from the government's stores at Chester.[230]

On the night of the 30th of July, when the authorities learnt that a consignment of arms had been delivered to a leading local Chartist, James Mitchell, they took immediate action. The superintendent of police with a group of constables searched Mitchell's house, and finding arms, took him into custody. With the support of troops from the barracks, the police then searched other homes, and discovering more arms carried out further arrests. The following day the

Ill 7.20 Tiviot Dale Methodist Chapel, in 1831.
By the mid-nineteenth century Wesleyan Methodists had become the largest nonconformist denomination in Stockport. Of all the denominations they were also the most prolific local builders of chapels. Among the largest of these was Tiviot Dale Chapel, designed with a fashionable classical facade and built in 1825-6. The battlemented building shown here to the right of the chapel was the old Castle Mill.

Chartists attempted to hold mass meetings in the town but these were broken up by the authorities. On this and subsequent days, when the prisoners appeared before the magistrates, Stockport was in a state of alert. The Court House itself was under guard and, as after Peterloo, special constables patrolled the streets. In August Mitchell and three others were tried at Chester on a charge of conspiracy, and sentenced to eighteen months' imprisonment. The general strike did not materialize and the 'Sacred Month' passed without incident in Stockport. Ralph Pendlebury, the mayor, was later knighted for his part in the arrests in the town.[231]

The 'Plug Plot' strike, 1842

Local Chartists enjoyed their last wave of mass support in 1842 when, with the economy even deeper in depression, they collected 14,000 signatures towards the second National Petition for the Charter. In August of that year Chartists also took advantage of what was effectively a general strike in the factories of the Manchester district (*Ill 7.18*). The dispute became

known as the 'Plug Plot', after the strikers' ploy of pulling the plugs from factory boilers to immobilize the machinery, and from the belief that the strike had been organized from the outset for wider political ends. The dispute began in Stalybridge and Ashton-under-Lyne, following a reduction in wages, and rapidly widened as strikers marched on neighbouring towns and districts and brought out other workers. In Stockport people joined the strike only with a measure of reluctance. Two years earlier the town's powerloom weavers had fought a bitter strike for nearly three months before being forced to return to work, and local workers appear to have been unwilling to repeat the experience. The turnout in Stockport took place on the 11th of August when other strikers arrived en masse from Hyde and Compstall. That same day also saw strikers breaking into the workhouse at Shaw Heath where they seized bread and about £7 in cash. They were interrupted by the arrival of the magistrates with troops and special constables who carried out about forty arrests. Others who arrived to rescue their companions withdrew when they found cavalry formed up with drawn swords ready to charge, and infantry and the special constables in the workhouse yard. Although the strike was initiated for economic reasons, local Chartists saw it as an opportunity to press for their own demands and succeeded in carrying a number of the strikers with them. As the strike began to collapse in late August and early September, they paid the price for associating themselves with the dispute. Once again the Chartist leaders suffered arrest, among them being James Mitchell and Richard Pilling, a weaver who had helped to initiate the strike.[232]

The Anti-Corn Law League and Richard Cobden

In the late 1830s, while the town's lower classes were lending their support to the Charter, manufacturers were involved in a separate reform campaign for the abolition of the Corn Law. The repeal of the legislation of 1815 restricting the importation of cheap foreign corn had formed part of the agenda of local radicals in the Peterloo era. The call for repeal was resumed during a brief but sharp economic slump in 1826, and figured in the petitions of the Stockport Political Union to Parliament in the early 1830s. In Stockport's first parliamentary election in 1832 repeal had formed part of the electoral platform of Henry Marsland. Until the 1830s, however, the issue was of little interest outside the lower classes.[233]

While hungry workers sought repeal out of desperation, the manufacturers who adopted the cause in the late 1830s and 1840s were guided by thought of profit. By removing restrictions on the importation of corn, they hoped to promote the market at home and abroad for their own goods. Manchester lay at the centre of this campaign. An Anti-Corn Law Association was established in the town in September 1838, and in March 1839 was transformed into a national body. Stockport members were among those who in January 1840 attended the banquet which marked the opening of the Anti-Corn Law League's new meeting place, Manchester's first Free Trade Hall.[234]

Local Chartists shared the aim of repealing the Corn Law but viewed the League itself with distrust. Their view was that only once the reform of Parliament had been achieved could the question of the Corn Law be properly resolved. They argued that, by lowering the price of corn, manufacturers hoped to reduce wages. Personal animosity also played a part. The local membership of the League included the very members of the town's administration who opposed the Chartists in 1838-9 and caused the arrest of the movement's leadership. Repeatedly, Anti-Corn Law meetings held in the town were interrupted by Chartists who tried to bring the discussion around to parliamentary reform.[235]

It is probably a measure of the growing support for the repeal campaign among Stockport's upper-middle class that at the parliamentary elections of 1841 it was a League candidate who finally ousted the Tory Thomas Marsland from his seat. The town's new MP was Richard Cobden, by this date the acknowledged leader of the League. Cobden accepted the request to stand in Stockport on condition that he was to be free from normal constituency duties and be allowed to devote necessary time to the League. He himself wrote of his election victory that he had received the active support of even mill-owners who 'were against me at the former contest'.[236]

When the Corn Law was eventually repealed in 1846, mill-owners in Stockport celebrated by declaring a general holiday. Some 2500 people were entertained with a tea-party held in the giant weaving shed of the newly-opened India Mill.[237] In the following year Cobden's association with Stockport came to an end. Without his knowledge, he was nominated as a candidate for the West Riding of Yorkshire in the parliamentary election of that year. He was also once again a candidate in Stockport, and found himself in the awkward position of winning in both seats. Forced to make a decision as to which he should represent, Cobden opted for the Yorkshire constituency, the largest in the country.[238] His resignation resulted in a by-election at Stockport, contended by Thomas Marsland, who hoped to regain his seat, and James Kershaw, a co-owner of India Mill and Mersey Mills, who emerged the victor. The contest was marked by violence by the supporters of both sides, which left two people dead and others injured.[239]

Marsland had fought his last election in the town, but success in future contests meant that James Kershaw served as an MP for Stockport for seventeen years.[240] His enduring legacy to the town was the building of Vernon Park Museum, for which he and his fellow MP provided the funding and on which more will be said in the following chapter. Richard Cobden was given his own monument in the town, a bronze statue, paid for by subscription. In 1886, twenty-one years after his death, a crowd filled St Peter's Square to witness its unveiling by his daughter (*Ill 7.19*).[241]

RELIGION

From the late eighteenth century the face of religion in the Borough became more diverse. The number of local Roman Catholics was negligible in the 1780s, but from the following decade was greatly multiplied as Irish

Ill 7.21 St Thomas's Church, Higher Hillgate, about 1903.
In 1818 a shortage of Anglican places of worship within the country's growing towns prompted Parliament to set aside a million pounds for the construction of new churches. St Thomas's, built on the edge of Stockport's densely populated Hillgate area, was the only church in Cheshire erected with money from that fund. This great classical building, designed by George Basavi and erected between 1822 and 1825, could accommodate nearly 2000 worshippers.

immigrants began to arrive in the Borough.[242] Methodists during the lifetime of John Wesley had considered themselves members of the Anglican Church, but after his death in 1791 the movement was established as a church in its own right.[243] In 1797 seventy-six of the 450 members of Stockport's Hillgate Chapel joined the breakaway and more democratic Methodist New Connexion.[244] Primitive Methodism, a second breakaway movement, originated in the late 1800s with large open-air meetings held at Mow Cop near Congleton, and attended by Methodists from Stockport. In 1820 a Primitive Methodist society was organized in the town, from where preachers carried out missionary work among other local communities.[245] Between the late eighteenth and the mid-nineteenth century, despite fluctuations in the number of its local members, Wesleyan, or mainstream, Methodism grew

in influence. In 1834 Wesleyan Methodists were said to comprise the largest nonconformist denomination in Stockport.[246]

Nonconformist chapels

Between 1780 and 1842 the number of churches and chapels within the Borough more than doubled. The majority of new places of worship were chapels built by nonconformists, including the various Methodist sects, with the Wesleyans being the most prolific of local chapel builders. Nonconformists were the first to establish purpose-built places of worship in some of the rising industrial communities of the Borough: at Compstall, where a Wesleyan chapel was built in 1826; at Portwood, where a Methodist New Connexion chapel was built in 1834-5;[247] and at Heaton Mersey where

Congregationalists erected a chapel in 1839-40.[248] The Wesleyans also appear to have been the first to build a Protestant chapel at Edgeley, in 1818.[249] A Roman Catholic chapel had been consecrated here in 1803 to serve the local Irish community.

The grandest of these new chapels stood in close proximity to each other in Heaton Norris. One was the Hanover Chapel on Lancashire Hill, which was built in the style known as Strawberry Hill Gothic and opened in 1821.[250] The other, on nearby Tiviot Dale, close to Lancashire Bridge, was erected in 1825-6. This chapel, which was said to be able to accommodate 1600 people, was constructed of brick but with a stone facade built in an elegant classical design (Ill 7.20).[251] A third great nonconformist chapel, the Methodist New Connexion Mount Tabor Chapel, was built in the town later in the nineteenth century. It was constructed in 1865-9, at the junction of Wellington Road South and Edward Street, after the congregation had outgrown the town's first Mount Tabor Chapel built off Middle Hillgate in 1798. None of these chapels still stands, although the stone capitals of the classical portico which once adorned the nineteenth-century Mount Tabor Chapel still mark its site.[252]

Anglican churches

After the building of St Peter's in Stockport in 1768, no new Anglican churches were established within the Borough for over fifty years. In the meantime three of the existing churches saw complete or major rebuilding. By the beginning of the nineteenth century the old timber-framed chapel at Marple was in a poor state of repair, as well as being too small for the needs of the growing local population. Funds for its replacement were provided by voluntary donations, principally from the Isherwoods of Marple Hall and Samuel Oldknow. It was Oldknow who was entrusted with the rebuilding work and who also diverted the road from the east side of the chapel to the west to provide easier access. The new chapel was completed by 1812. Later in the nineteenth century a new, larger church was built on an adjacent site. In 1959 Oldknow's chapel was demolished leaving only its tower still standing.[253]

At Mellor Chapel the insertion of galleries in the eighteenth century caused so much structural damage that in 1815 a subscription was begun for the rebuilding of all but the tower. Although the estimated cost was less than £700, the money came in only slowly, and the work does not appear to have been finally completed until 1829.[254]

The most costly, and controversial, rebuilding project involved Stockport's parish church of St Mary.

By the late eighteenth century its ancient fabric, built of soft local sandstone, was in an advanced state of decay. The tower, already in a dangerous condition, is said to have been further damaged in 1805 when the church bells were rung for three days in celebration of the victory at Trafalgar.[255] By 1810 for safety reasons the nave could no longer be used by worshippers. In that year demolition began, leaving only the medieval chancel still standing. On the 5th of July 1813 the foundation stone of the new church was laid, with work being completed four years later (Ill 1.1).[256]

To pay for the rebuilding, an Act of Parliament was sought in 1810, allowing the levying of a rate on all occupiers and tenants of property in the parish. The move was opposed by nonconformists in the town, acting under the leadership of Peter Marsland. They failed to prevent the bill from becoming law and in 1815, since existing funding was proving insufficient, a second Act allowed the raising of an additional rate. The funding of the rebuilding was still a contentious issue in 1833, when ratepayers, having already provided £32,000, were asked to pay off an outstanding debt of over £7000. In the following year the matter ended in a compromise under which half of this money was provided by private donations.[257]

Despite the rebuilding of St Mary's, church accommodation in Stockport lagged far behind the rising population. In 1818 the number of church seats in the town was said to be only 2500. The shortage of church accommodation was a problem common to many of the country's towns. As a result, in 1818 an Act of Parliament set aside a million pounds to be spent on the construction of new churches. Responsibility for putting this Act into effect was entrusted to a new national body, the Church Building Commissioners, after whom the resulting buildings came to be known as 'Commissioners' churches'. In Cheshire the only place to receive a grant from the million-pound fund was Stockport, where a new church was erected off Higher Hillgate. Dedicated to St Thomas, this was designed by the architect George Basavi and built between 1822 and 1825 at a cost of £15,611, which was met wholly out of the Commissioners' grant. It has been described as 'the grandest classical church in the Manchester region' (Ill 7.21). Nearly 2000 worshippers could be accommodated within its walls.[258]

The Commissioners received a second allocation of government funds in 1824. A grant from this provided the greater part of the money for the next Anglican church to be built in the Borough. This was St Thomas's, which was constructed in 1833-4 in the Norbury part of Bullock Smithy and replaced the then ruinous Norbury Chapel as the local Anglican place of worship.[259] At the close of that decade, with the construction of St Paul's in Compstall, the Borough entered a concerted period of Anglican church building. By 1851 new churches had been erected in Woodford,[260] Heaton Norris,[261] Heaton Mersey,[262] Portwood[263] and Woodley.[264] However, in that same year, only one seventh of the population of the parish of Stockport could have been seated within its Anglican churches.[265]

EDUCATION

The evidence for the local provision of education before the late eighteenth century may be far from complete, but it is very probable that schooling was limited to a minority of children. There had been a free grammar school in Stockport since the late fifteenth century, established under the bequest of Edmund Shaa.[266] In the seventeenth century, thanks to other local benefactors, free grammar schools had also been founded at Marple and Mellor, where the school building stood within the churchyard.[267] Nationally the cause of education was helped by the establishment in 1699 of the Society for Promoting Christian Knowledge, or SPCK. Its aim was to encourage the creation of charity schools providing elementary education and religious instruction to the children of the poor. A letter sent to the society's London headquarters in 1714 by the rector of Stockport reveals that he had established two schools in the town and a third in another, unspecified, part of the parish. These had some fourteen pupils, who were taught to read and to say the catechism.[268] The respective lords of the manor funded the building of schools at Bramhall Green in 1741 and at Norbury in 1761. The Bramhall school may not be well documented but that at Norbury is known to have served the poor.[269] Marple's grammar school, which had ceased to exist by the early eighteenth century, was re-endowed in 1739. This new donation was to be used for the teaching of reading, writing and religious instruction to eight poor children.[270] At Cheadle Heath a school established in 1785 was supported by local subscriptions, a method of funding advocated by the SPCK.[271] By this date, however, another form of educational institution was winning local support, and one which first made education widely available to the children of the working class.

Sunday schools

Although Sunday schools existed at an earlier date, the movement first gathered real momentum when a school founded by Robert Raikes in Gloucester in 1782 was widely publicized in the press.[272] Both Raikes and his imitators viewed the elementary and religious education provided by Sunday schools as a means of moral improvement among the young. The movement found particular appeal among Methodists, but it was also widely supported by other denominations. The conservative ethos of the Sunday schools, which taught respect for the status quo, meant that they were guaranteed the patronage of Stockport's mill-owners and other members of the town's upper-middle class. That same ethos also meant that the schools received the condemnation of local radicals and prompted the Reverend Harrison, as we have seen, to establish his own Sunday school.[273]

The first Sunday schools in Stockport were established in 1784 in a joint venture by Anglicans, Methodists and nonconformists. The town was divided into six districts, each of which was to be provided with at least one school. It was agreed that pupils should attend from 9am to noon and from 1pm to 6pm, with the afternoon session including attendance at a service in a church or chapel. Funding was provided by collections made among the town's various congregations. In 1793 there were eight schools in operation under this system, with a total of 1148 pupils.[274]

The most successful of these schools was associated with the Methodist chapel on Hillgate. In 1794 it separated from the control of the committee which jointly administered the town's Sunday schools. Henceforward it was run independently, and remained interdenominational. In 1783 it had 534 pupils. By 1803 the figure had risen to 2865, with over 200 teachers. To provide the necessary accommodation the school first expanded into neighbouring vacant rooms and houses, but in 1805 work began on a new building into which the school moved in the following year. It was known from the outset as 'The Stockport Sunday School'. The building occupied a commanding position on the hillslope off Lower Hillgate, and in size was probably surpassed in the town only by the largest cotton factories. Four storeys high, it contained fifty-eight classrooms and, on the top floor, a great assembly room (Ill 7.22). In 1825 it was said to be the largest Sunday school building in the world. It was extended in 1835-6 by the addition of a wing which itself could accommodate 2000 pupils.[275]

The success of the Hillgate school was such that its governing committee also established auxiliary schools. Two of these were opened in 1801, at Brinksway and Heaton Mersey where a new building was erected for this purpose by Robert Parker, the owner of the local bleachworks. Other auxiliary schools were established in the early 1820s at Lancashire Hill and Heaviley.[276]

Ill 7.22 Stockport Sunday School, about 1905.
From the 1780s the establishment of Sunday schools made an elementary education more widely available to the lower classes. The Stockport Sunday School was the largest of many such institutions in the Borough. Its building, set in a prominent position off Hillgate, was erected in 1805-6. In the early nineteenth century this Sunday school was said to be the biggest in the world.

After the schism within the town's Sunday schools in 1794 local Anglicans ran their own schools. In the late 1820s these were combined in a single large, new building, the National School, on which more will be said below.[277] From the late 1830s Sunday schools were also established in connection with individual Anglican churches in the town, the first being at St Thomas's.[278] Other denominations opened their own Sunday schools in Stockport. The Methodists were at the forefront of this movement, but from the 1830s other religious groups were following suit.[279]

Communities outside the town were also served by their own local Sunday schools. At Bullock Smithy a school was established in the 1780s by its most prominent industrialist, Henry Marsland.[280] In Marple a Methodist Sunday school was begun in 1795 and within two years was attended by 130 pupils.[281]

The success of Stockport's Sunday schools seems particularly astonishing. In 1817 they were estimated to provide teaching to about 7000 children. In 1825 the total number of pupils stood at 9380. The Stockport Sunday School, and its auxiliary schools, accounted for 3965 of these pupils, the remainder of whom were fairly evenly divided between the Anglican schools and the Methodist. In 1833 two-thirds of the town's children were reckoned to be Sunday school pupils.[282] Attendance was not compulsory, and for many of these pupils Sunday was the one day of the week when they were not required to work.

Day schools

The provision of day schools for working-class children lagged behind that of Sunday schools. Across the country in the early nineteenth century two main types of day school were established for children of that class: National Schools, which were associated with the Church of England; and British Schools, founded by nonconformists. It was probably a reflection of the success of the local Sunday schools that such day schools were not established until a relatively late date in Stockport. A National School was built in the town in

THEATRE, STOCKPORT.

MR HOWARD

Most respectfully announces the opening of the Theatre, and hopes to meet that encouragement he is anxious to deserve. The house has been decorated in a manner which he has reason to flatter himself will be universally approved, and every possible care has been taken in the selection of a respectable Company.

On SATURDAY Evening, October 22, 1825,

Will be performed (not acted here for many years) the celebrated Comedy of THE

HYPOCRITE;

Or, TREACHERY UNMASKED!

As performed in London by command of His Majesty!

Sir John Lambert,............Mr SHIELD	Tipstaff,...............Mr FARQUHAR
Dr Cantwell,..............Mr GRIERSON	Servant,... ....Mr HAIGH
Colonel Lambert,.............Mr SMITH	Old Lady Lambert,.........Mrs GREEN
Darnley,................Mr STODDART	Young Lady Lambert,.....Mrs STODDART
Seyward,...... .. ..Mr EGERTON	Charlotte,...... ....Mrs HOWARD
Maworm,................Mr PHILLIPS	Betty,......................Miss MOODY

A Comic Song, by Mr Phillips.

To conclude with a Romantic Melo Drama, (never acted here,) entitled THE

TWO GALLEY SLAVES;

Or, The Unknown, and the Convicted Felon!

Henry,....................Mr SMITH	Claude,................Mr FARQUHAR
Major de Lisle,..........Mr STODDART	The Unknown,............Mr GRIERSON
Bonhomme,..................Mr SHIELD	Lenoir,................Mr HAIGH
La Ronte, (the Postmaster,)...Mr EGERTON	Louise,.....,............Mrs HOWARD
Basil, (a simple honest fellow,) Mr PHILLIPS	Marian,... ....Mrs GREEN
Felix,................Mrs STODDART	Claudine,................Miss MOODY

Act 1st.—Appearance of the Unknown—Mysterious meeting between Henry and the Unknown—A Dance by the Characters.—Act 2nd.—Sudden re-appearance of the Unknown—Henry is wounded—The Unknown escapes—The fatal mark is discovered on Henry's arm, H. L!!!—The Mystery developed—Henry innocent—The villainy of the Unknown exposed, and virtue triumphant.

Doors to be opened at Six, and the performance to commence at Seven.
BOXES, 8s.—PIT, 2s.—GALLERY, 1s.
Tickets to be had of Mr HOWARD; and of Mr LOMAX, *Advertiser-Office,* where places for the Boxes may be taken.
** *Tickets for the Season will be issued, and may be had on the usual terms by applying to Mr HOWARD.*

ON MONDAY,
GUY FAWKES; OR, THE DUMB GIRL OF GENOA.
On Tuesday, Der Frieschutz, the Black Huntsman of Bohemia; or, the Demon of the Wolf's Glen, and the Seven Charmed Bullets.

☞ APARTMENTS WANTED,—Apply to Mr Howard at the Theatre.

Ill 7.23 A Stockport Theatre playbill, 1825.

As Stockport grew with the rise of the cotton industry, new forms of entertainment appeared in the town. The Stockport Theatre was established by the 1790s and by 1805 was located in a venue on Park Street. Much of the fare consisted of variety acts and melodramas. The theatre closed in about 1834.

1825-6, on a site adjacent to the new turnpike road, Wellington Road South. This is now the site of the Town Hall, built in the 1900s. Stockport's first British School was established nearby on this same road as late as 1843.[283]

There was a third school in this area of the town, for in 1832 the grammar school moved from its cramped premises on Chestergate to a new building on Wellington Road, virtually opposite the National School. (In the early twentieth century the grammar school moved to new premises near Heaviley and the War Memorial and Art Gallery was built on its site.) Admittance to the grammar school by this time was only on the recommendation of its 'visitors'. Since these comprised a select group of figures belonging to the local establishment (the rector of the parish church, the manorial steward, the mayor and a magistrate), it is believed likely that its pupils were themselves drawn from among the high-ranking local families.[284]

Perhaps midway between the exclusiveness of the grammar school and the basic education of the Sunday schools and denominational day schools were private schools catering for the children of manufacturers and tradesmen. Their numbers mushroomed in the early nineteenth century; in 1833 it was reported that since 1818 forty-two day schools had been established in the town.[285]

Further education

Sunday and day schools provided an elementary education for the young, but in the early nineteenth century there were several attempts in the town to establish educational institutions for adults. The first of these were the pioneering classes of the Stockport Union for the Promotion of Human Happiness. In the 1820s, in common with many other factory towns, a mechanics' institute was set up in Stockport. It was established in 1825 with the backing of local mill-owners, but membership appears to have been badly affected by the economic slump of the following year and it closed in 1827. A new institute, the grandly titled Stockport Institution for the Diffusion of Useful Knowledge, was launched in 1834, occupying what had previously been a theatre on Park Street. In 1850 the institute moved to Lower Hillgate, and in 1862 to new purpose-built premises on the corner of Wellington Road South and St Petersgate. These institutes were attended mostly by professionals and the highest paid workers. In 1841, in an attempt to make education more accessible to the working class, supporters of the Socialist Robert Owen erected their own educational institution in the town. Known

originally as the Hall of Science, and later as the Lyceum, it was opened by Owen himself. Its upper room became a venue for political meetings, but the institute itself failed to attract sufficient support and the building was sold in 1855.[286]

LEISURE

Public houses

For many workers in the industrial town of the early nineteenth century the main social outlet was the public house. Not every part, however, was well served by 'locals'. Portwood, despite its large working-class population, had only one licensed premises, the Millstone, until the mid-1820s when two others were added. The number of drinking establishments in the town greatly increased after 1830. In an attempt to reduce the level of spirit drinking, Parliament passed legislation encouraging the establishment of premises which sold only beer. In 1833 there were no fewer than 160 beer-shops in Stockport, in addition to 103 other public houses.[287]

Public houses served a wide number of social uses. They were used for meetings by local societies and political groups. Here business transactions were often carried out, and workers were often given their wages. Inns provided overnight accommodation and were the termini or stopping points for stagecoach services. In the early nineteenth century it was a cannon fired outside one of these inns, the White Lion on Great Underbank, which alerted the townspeople to the arrival by coach of any important news. In the eighteenth century the White Lion had been the town's most fashionable inn, and the venue for the banquets held for members of Stockport's court leet. By the 1820s, however, that position had passed to the Warren Bulkeley Arms, situated on Warren Street and conveniently close to the town's new Court House.[288] During that same decade, billiard rooms in the town were a haunt of the 'young and affluent'.[289]

The theatre and music

A 'Stockport Theatre' was in existence in the 1790s. At one time this was housed in a room behind the Angel inn in the Market Place, but by 1805 was established in a building on Park Street. Billings in the 1820s included the occasional Shakespearean tragedy, but the staple fare seems to have been a mixture of melodramas and variety acts (Ill 7.23). Despite being 'neatly embellished' the theatre does not appear to have been well frequented by the town's middle class. It finally closed in the mid-1830s and the building was acquired by the town's new mechanics' institute. The demise of the theatre seems to have been brought about by competition from travelling companies which charged only a few pennies for admission. The landlords of public houses in the town were also beginning to open 'singing rooms' in their premises, in which local people performed popular songs. They were the forerunners of Stockport's late nineteenth-century music halls.[290]

For lovers of more serious music, from the 1790s there were annual oratorio performances at Stockport Sunday School, and by the early nineteenth century choral and instrumental societies existed in the town. In the 1830s a group of musicians gave occasional concerts in the mechanics' institute.[291]

Circuses, menageries, balloonists and pleasure gardens

By the early 1820s it was usual for a circus company to come to the town at the time of the May fair.[292] Another regular visitor by this time was Mr Wombwell, with his travelling menagerie of wild animals. An elephant, claimed to be the largest in Europe, even figured in the billing at the Stockport Theatre in February 1832, when it was found necessary to pull down a large portion of one gable end of the building to allow the animal access. In the 1840s, following the demolition of the old Castle Mill, Mr Wombwell's own collection of animals was displayed on the vacant space of Castle Yard.[293] In the late 1820s the courtyard of the Castle Mill had been the scene of another visiting attraction, when balloonists set off from here on display flights.[294]

Some local attractions were of a more permanent nature. Despite the considerable growth of the town, even in the 1840s there were few points within the built-up area which were more than a few minutes' walk from the surrounding fields and other open spaces. Sunday walks in the countryside provided workers with a brief respite from the smoke and overcrowding of the town.[295] At Adswood they might call at the pleasure gardens owned by John Jennison. These began as his own private plot in which Jennison, a jobbing gardener, grew strawberries. He first admitted the public to the Strawberry Gardens, as they became known, in 1826. Two or three years later he added a display of caged British birds, pheasants and macaws, and began to charge for admission. As a further attraction a public house, 'The Adam and Eve', was opened on the site. At some stage the animal collection was expanded by the addition of monkeys, earning the place the nickname of the Monkey House. In 1836 Jennison opened a new zoological garden on a larger site, Belle Vue, off Hyde Road on the east side of Manchester. By the 1850s the Adswood property had become a private house, but Belle Vue developed into a major regional attraction and its zoo finally closed only in 1977.[296] Jennison was buried at Cheadle parish church, in a family vault crowned with one of the tallest monuments in the churchyard.

Before opening the Strawberry Gardens, Jennison is said to have worked for a while at John Lawton's Pleasure Gardens. They were situated in Portwood, next to the great reservoir built by Peter Marsland in 1808 and later a part of his waterworks. The pleasure gardens housed a small collection of animals but the main attraction was the reservoir itself on which Lawton, an employee of the waterworks company, had a number of pleasure boats for hire.[297]

Animal baiting and races

An entertainment of a very different kind, bear baiting, was forbidden in Stockport township by the Police Act of 1826. (So too, though this was no doubt rather more difficult to enforce, was 'playing at foot-ball to the annoyance of the inhabitants'.)[298] Animal baitings survived longer outside the town where they formed part of the annual holiday or 'wakes'. A bear bait was held at Hatherlow as late as 1837, and bull baits are reported to have been held at Hazel Grove and in Marple township even later still. Cock fighting, which was once a common sport, was made illegal in 1849 but is said to have continued in Hazel Grove until at least the 1920s.[299]

Horse races had been held on Stockport Great Moor until at least the 1760s. No evidence has been found for a similar event within Stockport township after that date, but a race meeting at Woodford was noted in his diary by Peter Pownall of Bramhall in 1784.[300] Norbury wakes, as the holiday at Bullock Smithy was known, in 1810 included four days of jackass races, while in 1830 horse races were held in the village, run over what was described as 'the old race ground'.[301]

Plate I The 'Portwood Urn'.
This was one of three Bronze Age vessels which were accidentally discovered in Portwood in 1896 and which belonged to a prehistoric burial. At least seven Bronze Age funerary vessels have been unearthed within the Borough, but with the exception of the 'Portwood Urn' all of these were irreparably damaged at the time of their discovery.

Plate II Medieval tomb effigies in the parish church of St Mary, Cheadle. These alabaster figures, wearing armour of the fifteenth century, lie in the church's Brereton Chapel. Both may represent lords of the manor of Handforth, whose private chapel this once was. Another possibility is that one of these figures marked the resting place of Richard Bulkeley, lord of the manor of Cheadle Bulkeley, who died in 1454.

Plate III The Withdrawing Room, Bramall Hall.

This spacious room, with decorative plasterwork on the ceiling and around the fireplace, was created by William and Dorothy Davenport as part of a 'modernization' of their residence in the late sixteenth century. Above the hearth the royal arms with the inscription 'Vive la Royne' (Long live the Queen) declare the Davenports' loyalty to Elizabeth I.

Plate IV 1770 map of Stockport township.

This map, one of the earliest known of Stockport, was surveyed to show the lands and properties belonging to the lord of the manor, Sir George Warren. By this date the town was expanding from its historic core around the Market Place, with buildings extending for some considerable distance along Hillgate, the main approach to the town from the south. Most of the township, however, still comprised agricultural land.

Plate V The Market Place, Stockport.

This painting by William Shuttleworth (1785-1829), a native of the town, shows the parish church of St Mary prior to the commencement in 1810 of the demolition of the tower and the nave and their subsequent rebuilding. The central property on the north side of the Market Place (left) is Staircase House, whose brick facade hides its much older timber-framed origins. The three-storey house on the far left was the home of Bradford Norbury, a wealthy corn merchant. At this date meal and cheese were sold in the buildings immediately in front of the church.

Plate VI Bottoms Hall, Mellor.

Bottoms Hall, the centre of an ancient freeholding in Mellor, was rebuilt by Samuel Oldknow, whose great cotton mill stood close by. Oldknow's elegant new building, which is believed to have been erected in the 1790s, served as the centre of his own agricultural estate and also provided accommodation for child apprentices working in the mill.

Plate VII Pear Mill, Lower Bredbury.

The construction of this great cotton-spinning mill was begun in 1908, on the site of Pear Tree Farm. The mill's own name is represented by the giant copper fruit which crowns its tower, and by smaller pears set at the corners of the building.

Plate VIII King's Valley, Stockport.
Completed in the early 1990s, this pyramid-shaped office building by the M63 is the most striking of the late twentieth-century additions to the townscape. It also symbolizes the importance of commerce in the modern town.

CHAPTER EIGHT

FROM POWERLOOMS TO PLANES, 1842-1939

'Structures whose vastness and capacity of production is at once a marvel and a gratification to see'

INTRODUCTION

Between the 1780s and 1830s Stockport had played a leading role in the region's cotton industry and as a consequence witnessed a massive growth in its population. The severe depression of 1837-43 marked the beginning of a period of stagnation. Over the next four decades the population of the town showed little overall increase.[1] An influx of new immigrants from Ireland helped heighten racial tensions which erupted in an anti-Irish riot in 1852. Immigration, however, was counterbalanced by a flow of workers leaving in search of a better life elsewhere.[2]

The town's cotton industry, on which so many of its inhabitants remained dependent, continued to be badly hit by depressions. After a brief revival in the industry, the late 1840s saw a further downturn. Wages were greatly reduced as mill-owners, to avoid closure, cut the working week, in many cases by a half. High food prices at this time compounded the misery.[3] The years 1861-5 brought the severe depression known as the 'Cotton Famine', at the time of the American Civil War. The name arose from the belief that the crisis was caused by the naval blockade of the southern states from where the Lancashire cotton industry derived much of its raw material. Current thinking sees the basis of the depression as over-production in the industry in the years immediately before the war. Whatever the cause, the result was devastating for the Borough, with some mills closing and others going on short time. The existing system of providing relief to the poor through the Guardians of the Stockport Poor Law Union was overstretched. Voluntary committees were set up to provide additional assistance, while mill-owners and other industrialists organized soup kitchens and other forms of relief.[4]

When a further depression hit the cotton industry in the late 1870s, Stockport was more badly affected than any other town in the Manchester area.[5] In the 1880s, however, the fortunes of the town entered a new era. Its ailing cotton industry was revived by the construction of massive new mills. Other local industries began to expand. Hatting had already embarked upon a long-awaited process of mechanization. Of particular importance for the long-term future of the town was the growth of engineering.

Previously of only minor significance in the local economy, it now developed into a major employer. As a result of its broader industrial base, Stockport was better placed than many other towns in the region to weather the terminal decline which began to affect the cotton industry in the 1920s.

This chapter, as well as considering the changing face of local industry between the mid-nineteenth and early twentieth century, will also examine some of the other important local developments during this period. Local government took on wider powers and became increasingly involved in the provision of services and the improvement of housing. The administrative map was changed as new local authorities were created. Stockport became a county borough in 1889 and greatly expanded in size in the early twentieth century with the addition of areas previously under the control of other local authorities.

Transport also underwent a revolution. The spread of the railway network, from the 1840s, encouraged the expansion of local industry and laid the foundations for the growth of the suburbs. Concurrent with the growth of the railways was the evolution of other forms of public transport, from the horse-drawn vehicles of the nineteenth century to the electric tramways and motor buses of the twentieth. Shorter working hours, coupled with improvements in both public and private transport, provided new opportunities for leisure.[6]

THE STOCKPORT RIOT OF 1852

By 1851 there had been an Irish population in Stockport for about sixty years. The earliest Irish immigrants had been relatively few in number, but in the 1820s the scale of immigration to the town began to increase.[7] The potato famine which devastated the population of Ireland in 1845-7 further accelerated the process. In the census of 1851 the number of people recorded in both Lancashire and Cheshire who had been born in Ireland was roughly twice as great as ten years previously. The increase in Stockport was somewhat less than this regional average, but nevertheless the proportion of Irish-born in the town increased from roughly one in fourteen to one in ten of the population. These figures do not represent all of the town's Irish community, which also included persons born outside Ireland.[8]

Hostility towards the Irish was not a new phenomenon in Stockport in the 1850s. As their numbers began to grow from the 1820s, they appear to have been increasingly viewed with disdain by other members of local society, who considered them ill-educated and uncivilized. In that same period opportunities for employment among Irish males became mainly limited to poorly-paid jobs in the construction industry.[9] Nor was violence between English and Irish in Stockport new in the 1850s. As early as 1823 a brawl between two men in a public house in Adlington Square escalated into a free-for-all between Irish and English, which left a number of people injured and caused damage to local property.[10] What set apart the rioting of 1852 was the scale and ferocity of the violence, and the heightened mood of tension against which that rioting took place. Increasing animosity towards the Irish in the early 1850s was not unique to Stockport, nor in 1852 was this the only town in the region in which such unrest led to violence. It was Stockport, however, which was the scene of the most serious disturbance of that year.[11]

As the events of the riot were to demonstrate, one focus of hostility towards the Irish was their Roman Catholic religion. The restoration of a Catholic hierarchy in England in 1850 provided fuel for such sectarianism.[12] Anti-Catholic feelings may have been further roused by the opening in 1851 of the town's second Roman Catholic church, St Michael's (housed in the former Stockport Theatre and mechanics' institute).[13] The main grievance against the Irish, however, would appear to have been an economic one. A modern study of the census returns has shown that between 1841 and 1851 a new trend in employment among the Irish had emerged. The number of Irish females employed in Stockport's cotton factories had markedly increased, and a growing number of Irish males were also now working in those factories.[14] Shortly after the riot an editorial in the *Stockport Advertiser*, a paper not averse to expressing anti-Irish sentiments within its columns, explained that 'It is well known to every one that, for some years, large numbers of Irish have come into the town until their numbers amount to about 14,000 or one fourth of the whole population of the borough'. These immigrants, the paper continued, 'have found employment in our cotton mills to so great an extent as in some establishments to equal or even outnumber the English employed, and that they are generally regarded by the latter, and not unnaturally, as taking the bread out of their mouths and reducing their wages'.[15] The belief that poorly-paid Irish workers reduced the general levels of wages in any industry in which they were employed was a widely held one,

although was not necessarily substantiated by the facts.[16] Whether or not the true number of Irish in Stockport at this time amounted to a quarter of the population is itself uncertain. In 1852, however, popular perceptions must have proved a stronger motivating force than reality. The Irish had long been viewed as socially inferior. Now that same group, swollen by the recent influx of immigrants, seemed to be gaining the upper hand by squeezing the English out of their main traditional source of employment in the town.

The catalyst which turned resentment to rioting was a procession of Catholic schoolchildren through the town. This event, on the 27th of June 1852, had taken place annually, and apparently without incident, since the early 1830s. On the 15th of June, however, a royal proclamation had forbidden the carrying of Catholic symbols in procession and the wearing of robes by Catholic priests in public places other than their place of worship. Canon Frith, the priest of Ss Philip and James in Edgeley, and Robert Foster, the priest of St Michael's, adhered to the letter of this proclamation by walking with the procession in ordinary clothes. A large body of Irishmen marched at the head of the procession, evidently with the intention of deterring any attempt to break up the march. Their presence may have served to strengthen the view of some in the town that in the light of the royal proclamation the very holding of the procession was an act of defiance. Animosity against the Irish was further inflamed on the following evening, when an Englishman came off the worse in a brawl with Irish customers in the Bishop Blaize public house (now the Gladstone Arms) on Middle Hillgate. Later that night there was trouble in the Edward Street area, with stones being thrown. This was only a prelude to the more serious violence which erupted on the next evening, the 29th of June. The events of that evening began with marauding English youths giving chase after Irishmen, and quickly deteriorated into a pitched battle in St Peter's Square where gangs from both sides hurled stones at each other. Irish homes in the neighbouring Rock Row were attacked and ransacked (*Ill 8.1*). This violence was quelled by the arrival of magistrates with a force of regular troops and hastily sworn-in special constables. In the meantime a body of the rioters had headed for Edgeley. There they set about ransacking Ss Philip and James Church and the neighbouring presbytery, burning fittings and books on a bonfire in the street, and forcing Canon Frith and a companion to take refuge first in the church belfry and then on the presbytery roof. The destruction ended when the magistrates and their forces arrived from Rock Row, but news quickly arrived that the chapel of St Michael's on Park Street

Ill 8.1 The Stockport Riot, 1852.
In June 1852 Stockport was the scene of an anti-Irish riot which resulted in one fatality and the ransacking of the town's two Catholic churches. This drawing, one of several of the event which appeared in the Illustrated London News, *shows rioters attacking Irish homes in Rock Row.*

was being attacked. The interior of this building was also wrecked before the situation was brought under control. Although the worst of the violence was over, there was further trouble the following night when Irish homes on John Street, off Hillgate, were attacked.[17]

The rioting left about 100 people wounded and one Irishman dead. He had been mistakenly struck by one of his fellow countrymen, who was subsequently found guilty of manslaughter and transported for fifteen years. At the same assizes, for their part in the disturbances, seven other Irishmen were given sentences of between two and twelve months' imprisonment with hard labour. Two Englishmen were sentenced to eighteen months and a third to two years, again with hard labour; seven others were acquitted of the charges brought against them. The cost of repairing the

damage to Stockport's two Catholic churches was eventually met by the ratepayers of the Macclesfield hundred.[18] (In 1861 Stockport's Irish community built a third Catholic church, St Joseph's, on St Petersgate.)[19] Divisions between the English and the Irish in the town were harder to repair. Although the scale of the violence of 1852 was not repeated in the town, minor disturbances between members of the two communities continued. At the end of the nineteenth century some public houses in Stockport still contained wooden partitions to keep their English and Irish customers apart.[20] When there was a renewed outbreak of anti-Irish rioting in the region in 1868, Stockport may only have been spared by the omission of the chief instigator of that violence, William Murphy, to visit the town.[21]

THE TEXTILE INDUSTRY

In 1851 the textile industry employed more than half of Stockport's working population. By 1921 the proportion had been reduced to about a quarter, but the industry was still the largest single local employer.[22] In the interim period it had undergone a number of fundamental changes. Some traditional branches had declined almost to the point of extinction, while others had been introduced or had experienced a revival. The geography of the industry had also altered. Mellor's long-established involvement in textiles had virtually come to an end, while Reddish had risen from economic obscurity to become a major local centre of the industry. In and around Stockport new mills were built on a monumental scale. These represented only a minority of the Borough's working factories in the late nineteenth and early twentieth centuries, but their massive spinning capacity played a key role in reviving the local cotton industry.

The years immediately after the First World War were a boom time in the region's cotton industry. The mills of Stockport and its neighbourhood reached the peak of their spinning capacity in 1920. In 1926, however, the industry was severely affected by a trade depression which marked the beginning of its demise. In 1939, although there were about sixty textile sites in operation in the Borough, others, including some of the larger mills, had already suffered closure.[23]

Ill 8.2 Mills along the Ashton Canal (centre) and Greg Street (right), South Reddish, about 1931.
From the mid-nineteenth century the construction of cotton mills and other works alongside the Ashton Canal transformed Reddish into a major local centre of manufacturing. This aerial photograph shows from bottom to top: the large complex of the Albert Mills, including a factory built by R H and J Greg in 1845, one of the first in Reddish; Hanover Mill, built in 1865; Spur Doubling Mill, opened in 1907, a rare example of a single-storey cotton mill; Victoria Mill, also built by the Gregs in 1845, and located immediately beyond Broadstone Hall Road with its bridge over the canal; and the 'Guardian' (later the CWS) printing works, built in 1899.

Cotton mills and firms, 1843-80

Reddish

Before the 1840s, despite its proximity to Stockport and the presence of the Ashton Canal, the township of Reddish had few outward signs of industry. There were the calico printworks, established by the mid-1780s near the old cornmill at Reddish Vale, and the hat manufactory of Barlow and Shawcross. By the 1840s handloom weaving, once carried out in the township, had probably all but ceased.[24]

From the mid-nineteenth century this situation changed dramatically. First cotton mills, and later works housing a range of other industries, were established alongside the canal. Today, although the canal itself has been filled in, its course can still be traced at Greg Street, Broadstone Road and Houldsworth Street by the line of surviving industrial buildings. The industrial development of Reddish in turn led to the growth of housing within the area and a rise in population at a rate not witnessed in the Borough since the early years of the cotton factory. In 1901 the number of people living in Reddish stood at 8688, more than six times the figure forty years earlier.[25]

This process of industrial growth began with the construction in 1845 of the Victoria Mill and Albert Mill (Ill 8.2). They were built by Robert Hyde Greg and his brother John, sons of Samuel Greg. The founder of a mill-owning dynasty, he is perhaps best remembered as the builder of Quarry Bank Mill and its associated housing at Styal in Cheshire. In the 1800s Samuel began to buy land in Reddish and by the time of his death in 1834 was the largest estate holder in the township. A portion of the family's land, close to the Ashton Canal, had been earmarked for the construction of mills by the end of the 1830s, but building work was evidently postponed as a result of the economic depression at that time. The two mills built in 1845 were originally leased separately to other firms, but the business at Albert Mill soon failed. The Gregs themselves then took over its operation, first in partnership with the firm at the Victoria Mill and from 1853 as sole proprietors.[26]

The growth of the cotton industry in Reddish continued in the 1860s when two other mills were erected next to the Ashton Canal. One was Hanover Mill, built in 1865 close to Albert Mill (Ill 8.2).[27] The other, situated further to the north at Reddish Green, was Houldsworth Mill (Ill 8.3). This was one of the largest, if not the largest, mills to be built in the Borough up to that time. Unusually for the period, it was named after its founder, William Henry Houldsworth. The mill was built on farmland which he had bought in 1863

or 1864, with the aim of relocating his cotton-spinning business from Manchester. The building carries the date of 1865, but is said to have been completed and opened two years later.[28] In 1870 another great mill was built on a neighbouring site by four members of the Houldsworth family, including William Henry, and other business partners, under the name of the Reddish Spinning Company.[29]

Adjacent to his Reddish mill, Houldsworth established a new industrial community. Terraced houses were built to accommodate his workforce, and other buildings were provided. A working men's club was opened in 1874, designed by A H Stott, the architect of the mill. Alfred Waterhouse, the architect of Manchester Town Hall, was employed by Houldsworth to design the community's school, its church of St Elisabeth and the rectory.[30]

Other new mills

The mid-1840s, which saw the building of the Gregs' Reddish mills, also witnessed a mini mill-building boom in Stockport. Two new mills were built on opposite banks of the Mersey during this period, the larger being India Mill, constructed by the firm of Kershaw & Leese. In 1847 it was reported to have a workforce of about 1200 people, making it one of the most substantial local textile concerns at this time. One later visitor described it as the finest mill he had ever seen in operation.[31] No comparable period of building activity has been identified in Stockport until the early 1880s, although new factories are known to have been erected in the interim.[32]

By the 1870s four new mills had been established by the canals to the east of Stockport, continuing a process which had begun in the 1820s. Three were sited on the Peak Forest Canal, at Woodley, Romiley and by Marple Aqueduct.[33] The fourth was at Windlehurst on the Macclesfield Canal.[34]

The demise of the cotton mills in Mellor

In Mellor the last quarter of the century saw the textile industry all but disappear. Unlike many of their competitors, the upland factories on the Mill Brook and the stream at Moor End had no ready access to a canal or railway (Ills 1.5 & 6.10). Coal for the boilers of these mills could be obtained from nearby pits, but by the late 1870s the local mining industry was itself in a process of terminal decline. Economies of scale may have added to these problems, for even the largest of these upland mills were relatively modest in size in comparison with their urban counterparts. Closures

Ill 8.3 Houldsworth Mill (left) and Broadstone Mills (right), Reddish, about 1931.
Houldsworth Mill was built in the mid-1860s by William Henry Houldsworth. Broadstone Mills were constructed in 1903-7 and briefly
held the record as the largest cotton-spinning mill in the world. Both Houldsworth Mill and Broadstone Mills were 'double mills', comprising
twin factories powered from a central engine house.

began in the 1870s, when Primrose Mill and Dove Bank Mills ceased operation. In the case of Dove Bank Mills, the end was brought about by a fire in 1876, the second in three years to damage the site. Damsteads Mill seems to have closed in the early 1880s. It is probably a reflection of the increasing difficulties of another local mill, Holly Vale, that in the late 1870s it expanded its activities into bleaching. By 1891 bleaching and dyeing had also been introduced at the small Clough Mill (*Ill 6.11*). Of all the branches of the cotton industry, the finishing trades, which required a plentiful supply of clean water, could provide upland mills with their best chance of survival. Despite these efforts, by 1900 Holly Vale and Clough mills had closed. Perhaps significantly, the one upland textile site which remained open was involved solely in finishing, Holly Head bleachworks.[35]

Mellor's largest mill was the great factory built by Samuel Oldknow (*Ill 6.8*). Situated on the Etherow in relatively close proximity to both the Peak Forest Canal and the railway station at Marple, it would seem to have had a greater chance of remaining a viable concern. New equipment had only recently been installed in the mill, when in November 1892 the main building was destroyed by fire. The mill had been the largest single employer in Mellor. Although the workforce had declined since the mid-nineteenth century, at the time of the fire it still numbered about 200.[36] Collectively the mill closures of the late nineteenth century had a devastating effect on the local population. While other parts of the Borough were experiencing a population rise in this period, Mellor continued to suffer a decline which had begun as early as the 1820s. Although the trend was reversed in the 1890s, this is believed to have been due primarily to the growth of suburban housing in the area.[37]

In about 1890, against the background of the closure of long-established local factories, a new mill opened at Cataract Bridge on Longhurst Lane in Mellor, not far from Marple Bridge. Its purpose-built single-storey main building was used for the production not of cotton yarn but of cotton wool and wadding.[38]

The changing face of the textile industry

The decline of weaving

At the beginning of the nineteenth century Stockport had become the cotton industry's first great centre of powerloom weaving. By the early 1830s most of the large and medium-sized firms in the town carried out both spinning and weaving by power. The second half of the nineteenth century saw a shift in the region's cotton industry away from such 'combined firms' to specialization in one of the two branches. In south-east Lancashire and the adjoining parts of Cheshire and Derbyshire, spinning became the dominant branch. The mills of eastern Lancashire came to specialize in weaving.

Stockport, despite its long association with the powerloom, was not immune to this change. Twenty-two combined firms were listed in the town in 1860. In 1884 the number had fallen to six, with nearly a third of their looms being at India Mill. Thirty years later the number had fallen to three. By 1939 the town's combined firms were only a memory. In the late nineteenth and early twentieth centuries there was also a handful of small weaving firms in the town, specializing in the manufacture of towels. Their numbers also decreased, and by 1939 only two remained.[39]

Elsewhere in the Borough powerloom weaving fared rather better. In 1884 combined firms still operated at Compstall Mills, Woodley Mill, and Oakwood Mill in Romiley. A fourth ran both Hollins Mill in Marple, where weaving had actually been added to spinning since 1859, and Wellington Mill in Hazel Grove. By 1939 weaving was still being carried out at two of these sites. One was Compstall Mills, which since 1926 had been used solely for weaving (from 1936 this was of the new synthetic fibres). The other was Hollins Mill, the last bastion of the Borough's combined firms.[40]

The demise of cotton waste spinning

In the second quarter of the nineteenth century the spinning of coarse yarns from cotton waste had provided the livelihood of a large number of small firms in the town. By the 1850s as a centre of cotton waste spinning Stockport is said to have been second only to Manchester. The late nineteenth and early twentieth centuries saw this industry virtually disappear. In 1872 there were still some twenty-nine cotton waste spinners listed in Stockport. Nearly half were occupying premises in the Carrs, the traditional focus of the industry. By the early 1900s the number of such firms had fallen to about seven, while by 1939 only one seems to have remained.[41]

The rise of cotton doubling

While the late nineteenth century saw the decline of weaving and waste spinning, cotton doubling was growing in importance. (Doubling is the twisting together of two or more yarns to produce a stronger thread.) In 1872 eighteen firms were listed in the town as either doubling or doubling and spinning. Their number had seen only a moderate rise, to about twenty-three, by 1914. In the meantime, however, firms had increased their doubling capacity, while in the late 1900s Spur Doubling Mill in Reddish had been built specifically for this branch of the trade.[42]

Some manufacturers specialized in producing particular types of doubled yarn. A number made thread for sewing and crochet work. In the 1890s the Gregs at the Albert Mill in Reddish began to specialize in fancy yarns for use in the upholstery trade. By the 1910s this was a rapidly expanding market, and for a while the firm enjoyed a near monopoly. Its range of fancy yarns expanded from 350 in 1897 to over 3000 by 1930.[43]

The return of woollens

The production of woollens had once been one of Stockport's staple industries. It had been briefly revived in the town in the 1820s by Peter Marsland, but production at his factory in the Park is believed to have ended in the depression of 1837-43.[44] In the late nineteenth century the industry saw a new revival. Meadow Mill, in Portwood, was built in about 1880 for both wool and cotton spinning. By 1892 production of woollen yarn had also begun at Shaw Heath Mill. Both of these mills were still being used for wool spinning in 1939.[45]

Ring frames

In the late nineteenth century the region's cotton industry began to adopt a faster spinning machine, the ring frame. In Stockport a dozen mills are known to

Ill 8.4 Houldsworth Mill.
Houldsworth Mill was designed by A H Stott, a leading figure in this field. The imposing central block contained offices and warehousing, flanked by taller staircase towers. The symmetry of the design extended to the placing of the mill's great chimney on an alignment behind its central clock.

have installed ring frames before 1914. In some cases these replaced existing mules, but new mills were also built to house ring frames from the outset. Ark Mill in Bredbury, later known as Welkin Mill, was built for this purpose in the 1900s. The largest concentration of ring spindles in the town was to be found in the three Stockport Ring Mills, on the north bank of the Mersey opposite Brinksway. They were built between 1892 and

1911. When first completed, Ring Mill No 1 and No 2 each held the record as the largest ring-spinning mill in the world.[46]

The mills of the Stockport Limiteds, 1880-1913

By the mid-1880s a number of the town's older and less economic mills had been closed and the buildings pulled down. Even the Mersey Mills, at one time one of the largest factory complexes in Stockport, was in 1886 'slowly undergoing a process of demolition'.[47] By this date, however, the first in a succession of giant new mills had been built in the town, described by one contemporary as 'structures whose vastness and capacity of production is at once a marvel and a gratification to all concerned'.[48]

In the early days of the cotton factory, firms had been owned by an individual, by members of the same family, or by other select business partners. In Stockport and its neighbourhood this was still usually the case at the end of the nineteenth century, although from the 1880s these cotton masters were providing themselves with greater financial security by registering their firms as private limited companies. One of the first of the town's large new mills, Meadow Mill, was built by the private firm of T & J Leigh.[49]

Other large mills were built by firms with a different organization, that of the joint stock limited liability company. In these capital was raised by the sale of low denomination shares, and by loans from investors who were paid a fixed rate of interest. The joint stock companies were most predominant in and around Oldham, which in the 1860s had become the single most important centre of spinning in the cotton industry. The 'Oldham Limiteds' were set up either to build new mills or to inject fresh capital into existing concerns. Seventy were established in a boom in 1873-5 alone.[50]

The first of Stockport's own limiteds, floated in 1881, constructed Vernon Mill in Portwood, later rebuilt after a fire in 1902. A second limited followed in 1884, formed to rebuild and refit the neighbouring Palmer Mill. The third, established in 1891, was responsible for the construction of the first of the Stockport Ring Mills. By 1894 these three companies accounted for nearly a fifth of the total of spindles in the town. Stockport, the fifth largest spinning town in the region in 1884, had now become the fourth.[51]

The town's next limited was not established until 1900, and was formed to take over the existing Kingston Mill on Chestergate. The 1900s saw the formation of limiteds in the Borough at its height, with a flood of new mill-building companies. This was a period of prosperity in the cotton industry in general, and the occasion of the region's last great mill-building boom. In Reddish the two Broadstone Mills were built by a limited founded in 1903.[52] The completion of Broadstone Mill No 2 in 1907 meant that together the two factories briefly held the record as the industry's largest spinning mill with 262,500 spindles, until this figure was surpassed in the following year by Times Mill in Middleton.[53] Between 1905 and 1907 no fewer than seven limiteds were set up to erect new mills in the Borough. These included Stockport Ring Mill No 2 and No 3, Ark Mill and Pear Mill in Bredbury and, in Reddish, Spur Doubling Mill and a ring mill which was planned but never built. The seventh company was responsible for the building of Goyt Mill, erected next to the Macclesfield Canal at Hawk Green in Marple.[54]

Mill design

In the mid-nineteenth century factories were built to greater widths to accommodate longer mules. The main block of Orrell's Mill, built in the 1830s and considered at the time to be a model of factory design, was about 17 yards (15.5 metres) wide (Ill 6.16). The width of Heaviley Mill, built by Ephraim Hallam in 1859, was 28 yards (25.5 metres).[55] While mills were still typically built as rectangular blocks, there were exceptions. Houldsworth Mill was an early example of a 'double mill' (Ill 8.3). This type comprises two factory blocks sharing a central engine house, a design also still found at Meadow Mill in Portwood.[56] The impressive facade of Houldsworth Mill was made up of twin factories and a taller central block which contained offices and warehousing. Flanked by staircase towers and crowned by a clock, this central block hid the engine house and boiler houses to the rear. The symmetry of the arrangement extended to the positioning of the great chimney, which was centrally placed at the rear of the complex (Ill 8.4). Its decorative architectural style also set this building apart from the more restrained exteriors of most contemporary mills. A H Stott, the architect of Houldsworth Mill, was the founder of a family firm of architects which in the late nineteenth and early twentieth centuries was at the forefront of mill design. Pear Mill, Goyt Mill in Marple, and the Broadstone Mills were all designed by A H Stott & Sons.[57]

By the 1900s improvements in methods of construction meant that mills were being built to even greater widths and with walls dominated by window glass. Staircase towers, which rose above these buildings and housed a water tank in their upper storey, offered a particular opportunity for architectural embellishment. One of the most flamboyant instances

Ill 8.5 Mechanized hat making at Christys, Hillgate, in 1933.
Christys played a leading role in the mechanization of the hatting industry in the late nineteenth century. The machinery shown here
was used for the preparatory process known as 'fur forming', the creation of basic conical hat bodies.

was Pear Mill, named after Pear Tree Farm which previously occupied this site. Its tower was capped with a giant copper version of the fruit, with smaller pears being set at the corners of the building (*Plate VII*). Pear Mill was originally planned as a double mill and if completed would have been the largest of this type. Following a not uncommon practice, the intention was to build the second half of the mill once the first half had become operational. The blank wall on one side of the building still indicates where the missing structure would have been added, while the distinctive staircase tower, which would have been centrally placed in the facade of the completed building, has remained a feature of one corner.[58] The two Broadstone Mills were also built at separate times to create a double mill, of which only one half now remains (*Ill 8.3*).

Ring frames took up less space and were heavier machines than mules. Consequently mills built specifically for ring spinning were usually narrower and

lower in height. Stockport Ring Mill No 1, No 2 and No 3 were three, five and two storeys respectively.[59] A further variation in mill design is represented by the Spur Doubling Mill in Reddish (*Ill 8.2*). It was built as a single-storey shed, a form more commonly associated with the weaving industry. This design was advocated for new spinning mills by some architectural writers in the early twentieth century, but appears to have been rarely adopted in practice.[60]

SILK

The handloom weaving of silk was the last great domestic industry in the Borough, its principal centre being Hazel Grove. In 1901 it was reported of the village that 'Fifty years ago a large business was done in silk weaving for...almost every house having accommodation for two or three looms'.[61] The 1851 census bears this out, with 404 and sixty-nine silk handloom weavers being recorded respectively in Bosden and Norbury townships, which included parts of the village.[62] At this time smaller groups of silk weavers were to be found scattered across the Cheshire part of the Borough, from Gatley to Marple. A few are also recorded in Mellor.[63]

The silk weavers of Hazel Grove wove cloth for the manufacturers of Macclesfield, the main centre of the silk industry in Cheshire. In the 1850s some yarn was produced locally. At Stockport the firm of Michael Newton may have still spun yarn from waste silk.[64] A silk mill at Cheadle was still operating in 1851.[65] The census for Bosden in that same year provides evidence for a small mill in Hazel Grove. This may have been one of four mills in the village which were said to have been purpose-built for the silk industry, but by the 1870s the process had begun of converting these factories to other purposes (Ill 7.8). One was made into a thread mill, two others became hatting works, while the fourth was used for the manufacture of silk braids for the hatting industry.[66]

The conversion of these mills appears to reflect a more general decline in the local silk industry. In the 1860s the industry nationally entered a period of depression. Although trade had recovered by the mid-1870s, Macclesfield manufacturers were now increasingly carrying out silk weaving by power.[67] In the 1880s it was said of the silk weavers in Bramhall that the 'rickety-rick of the loom...is now rapidly becoming a memory of the past'.[68] In 1901 there were estimated to be about 200 handloom weavers in Hazel Grove, less than half of the number suggested by the census fifty years earlier.[69] It is believed unlikely that by 1935 any remained.[70] The industry in Hazel Grove was to experience one final revival. In 1939 Wellington Mill, built a century earlier for cotton spinning, housed a company producing, possibly artificial, silk yarn.[71]

HATTING

In the second half of the nineteenth century the hatting industry in Stockport grew dramatically. In 1860 the number of people living in the town who worked in this industry is said to have been 473. Thirty years later there were estimated to be ten times that number.[72] The growth was a consequence of a revival in the popularity of felt hats, after a slump in the 1840s when silk hats became the fashion, and of changing methods of production which allowed hat manufacturers to meet this demand. New machinery now carried out the processes previously undertaken by hand, and moved these from the domestic workshop to the factory (Ill 8.5).

The Stockport firm of Christys played a leading role in this development. In the early 1850s, having previously switched their own production to silk hats, the firm shifted back to the manufacture of felt hats in response to the changing market. The workforce was increased and in 1858 a five-storey warehouse on the firm's Canal Street site, erected nearly twenty years earlier, was extended. The key turning point for both Christys and the hatting industry occurred in 1859 when two representatives of the firm visited the United States. There the hat-making industry had already reached an advanced stage of mechanization. Early in the following year the firm installed machinery bought on that trip in Hillgate Mill, the former cotton factory built by Samuel Oldknow (Ill 6.6). Other machinery was acquired from the continent in the 1860s, a decade which also saw the firm taking out patents on its own device for shaping hats. The works underwent further expansion. In 1864 the large Canal Street building was again extended. Four years later the whole building was said to be 'the largest hat-factory in England, probably in Europe'.[73]

By the 1880s further substantial buildings had been added to the works. In 1842, when most of the processes were still undertaken in domestic workshops, Christys' Canal Street premises had comprised a somewhat ramshackle group of buildings with the new warehouse rising in their midst. Now the firm occupied one of the most extensive factory complexes in the town.[74]

Christys' lead in the field of mechanization was followed by other hatting firms, which likewise either built or acquired suitable factory premises. The firm of Battersbys was founded in 1865, at which date its workforce of forty carried out the hat-making processes by hand. By 1886, however, the firm required a large new purpose-built factory, on Hempshaw Lane in Offerton.[75] Another hatting firm which was in the ascendant was Wards. In 1856 this family firm started a hat manufactory on Redhouse Lane in Bredbury, presumably taking advantage of the renewed demand for felt hats at this time. Twelve years later Wards opened the substantial Victoria hatting factory nearby on Bents Lane (Ill 8.9), and in the 1890s moved to the seven-storey Wellington Mill in Stockport. The firm also retailed its hats locally, through shops in the Market Place and on Lower Hillgate.[76]

There are reported to have been ten or twelve sizeable hatting firms in Stockport in the late nineteenth century.[77] In 1931 roughly 3200 people in the county borough worked in the hatting industry, putting it in third place behind textiles and engineering. The 1920s and 1930s, however, saw a decline in the industry. Changing fashions reduced the number of hats bought in this country, while foreign competition was beginning to eat away at both the home market and exports.[78]

COAL MINING

In the mid-nineteenth century coal mining in the Borough was in a state of change. Most notably in Bredbury, a number of pits ceased working.[79] Output across the Borough, however, is likely to have been rising as other pits were opened and existing mines, such as Norbury Colliery and Ludworth Colliery, continued in operation. The organization of the local coal industry was also altering, with mining now being dominated by a small number of colliery owners.

In 1852 a survey of mines in the region listed only two colliery owners in the Cheshire part of the Borough: the firm of Clayton and Brooke at Norbury Colliery, and J & J Jowett in Bredbury. In the 1850s this last firm operated two pits in that township, both of which appear to have been opened only in recent years. One was on the north side of Stockport Road, facing the junction with Bents Lane; the other, the Demesne Pit, lay to the north-east, close to the River Tame.[80] Other members of the Jowett family mined Ludworth Colliery, between Compstall Bridge and Marple Bridge, and Mellor Colliery on the eastern edge of Mellor township.[81] In Marple mining was carried out by the firm of J & M Tymm, which in 1851 had taken out a lease on Samuel Oldknow's lime kilns and the adjacent coal workings. Nine years later the firm opened a new shaft, the Peacock Pit, between the kilns and the Peak Forest Canal. In the 1870s it extended its mining operations to a new colliery. This was located on the southern edge of the village of Marple Bridge, but was somewhat confusingly named Bottoms Hall Colliery after the house a kilometre away to the south.[82]

Although mining in this period never reached the same importance as textiles as a local employer, the numbers involved were not insignificant. In the case of Bredbury the census report of 1861 attributed a recent rise in the township's population in part to an increase in local mining operations.[83] The returns of 1851 list 157 people in Marple township working in the mining industry and sixty-six in Mellor, representing roughly 8% and 7% of the working populations of those townships.[84] In the Bosden part of Hazel Grove in that same year at least 124 people were employed in the industry, presumably at the collieries at Norbury or Poynton.[85]

The days of the industry were, however, numbered. The last quarter of the nineteenth century saw a succession of closures as workings became exhausted or no longer profitable. Mellor Colliery ceased to operate in 1879. Jonathan Jowett, writing of his decision to close the mine, described it as 'unproductive both to master and man'. Mining at Ludworth Colliery ceased in about 1882. The Peacock Pit in Marple was abandoned as exhausted in 1896, a few years before the lime kilns were closed down. Bottoms Hall Colliery had been abandoned by 1899.[86] Norbury Colliery closed in 1892. Some of its workforce, living in Hazel Grove, are reported to have found new work on the railways.[87]

Bredbury also experienced closures during this period. Demesne Pit closed in 1875. (Later the colliery manager's house and weighing machine collapsed into the pit.) Bents Lane Pit ceased working at about this same time. It was reopened in 1881, but finally closed twelve years later. After this date the only mine operating in Bredbury was Lingard Lane Colliery, which had been begun in 1889. It was finally abandoned in 1936 as a result of flooding.[88]

ENGINEERING

The rise of engineering was one of the great success stories of the Borough in the late nineteenth and early twentieth centuries. In 1851 the number of people employed in machine making and metal working in Stockport municipal borough was roughly 400. In 1931 the total for the county borough was over 5000, making this the second largest industrial employer after textiles.[89] The growth of engineering in the interim saw an increasingly diverse number of products. It was also a process which owed much to the relocation or expansion of existing firms into the area.

Machine making and metal working

It had been the need for metalwork in the local textile industry which in the early nineteenth century had first encouraged the growth of engineering in the town. A century later Stockport manufacturers were still supplying machinery and other goods to the textile trade. As that industry changed, so too did the range of their products. In the 1860s these included powerlooms and boilers (*Ill 8.6*). By 1911 the town's largest firm making textile machinery, based at the Sovereign Works in Brinksway, was manufacturing ring-doubling frames.[90] The mechanization of the hatting industry offered further opportunities for local engineers. Two Stockport firms were advertised in the early 1880s as manufacturers of hat-making machinery.[91]

In the late nineteenth and early twentieth centuries new engineering works were established in the

Ill 8.6 A product of Wellington Boiler Works, Lancashire Hill, 1887.
The mechanization of first the cotton industry and later the hatting industry encouraged the growth of engineering firms in Stockport,
supplying machinery and power systems. This illustration shows one of the 'Lancashire' boilers constructed at the Wellington Boiler
Works, founded in 1863 by Thomas Oldham (right). In the late nineteenth and early twentieth centuries local engineering industry
diversified, with firms specializing in such products as cranes, gas engines and printing presses.

Borough by firms with other specialized products. Following the lead of the textile industry, several such works were set up on green-field sites in Reddish. The Reddish Iron Works, off Gorton Road, were opened in 1880 by the Manchester firm of Furnivals for the manufacture of printing presses. The Atlas Steel Rope Wire Works were built in 1880 by a firm making cables for the mining industry, and previously based in Longsight. In 1900 Craven Brothers moved from Manchester to new premises, the Vauxhall Works, on Greg Street. The firm was one of the country's leading manufacturers of cranes as well as producers of machine tools for the railway industry. In the early 1920s it employed between 1300 and 1400 people. Other firms, established in North Reddish in the early twentieth century, specialized in making electrically powered lifting and moving equipment, such as overhead travelling cranes, pulley blocks and hoists.[92]

Bredbury and Cheadle Heath also saw the development of heavy industry. Bredbury steelworks developed from a small beginning. In 1850 James Mills had begun to manufacture engineers' keys in a factory outbuilding in Stockport. The business was continued by his son and in 1874, the firm, then comprising thirty employees, moved to new premises in Bredbury.[93] The firm of Henry Simon Ltd opened works in Cheadle Heath in 1926 for the manufacture of flour-milling machinery. Simon, a Silesian engineer, had emigrated to Manchester where in 1878 he introduced the continental system of roller milling into this country. Steel roller mills produced a finer flour than millstones, and their adoption by large urban mills was a significant factor in the demise of the old rural cornmills. Among the cornmills in which this new system was installed was the Albion Mills in Stockport *(Ill 7.12)*. Simon-Carves Ltd, an associated firm founded in 1880, also established works at Cheadle Heath, making coke ovens, coal-washing equipment, and boilers for power stations and collieries.[94]

Engine makers

Stockport's involvement in the manufacture of new forms of machinery also extended to the field of engines. J E H Andrew of Stockport originally made machinery for the tobacco industry. After seeing the 'Bisschop' gas engine at a Paris exhibition, he bought the sole right to manufacture the machine in this country and went into production in 1878. The engine was a small-scale device, with limited power; its uses included the driving of printing machinery, and potato-washing machinery in chip shops. Andrew's firm subsequently developed the much larger 'Stockport' gas engines. In 1887 the business moved to new works in Reddish, where its products included a gas engine of 400 horse power, at that time the largest ever made.[95]

Another pioneer of the gas engine was Henry Neild Bickerton, with works in Ashton-under-Lyne. He was also a partner in Mirlees, Bickerton & Day Ltd. In 1908 this company opened a factory at Bramhall Moor Lane in Hazel Grove to manufacture diesel engines for which it held the British patent.[96]

Cars and planes

Heaton Chapel

In the early twentieth century the manufacturing industry of the Borough also came to include the construction of motor vehicles and aeroplanes. Both industries were carried out at Crossley Road on the northern edge of Heaton Chapel, where their history was closely interlinked. In October 1917, during the First World War, work began here on the building of National Aircraft Factory No 2, one of three such factories commissioned by the government. Its construction, management and operation were entrusted to Crossley Motors Ltd. This company, a subsidiary of the firm of Crossley Bros Ltd based at Gorton in Manchester, had been founded in about 1910 primarily to manufacture passenger vehicles but also produced aero engines. The completed National Aircraft Factory No 2 was 15 acres in extent and employed a workforce of 2500. The first aircraft left the factory in March 1918. A total of 400 de Haviland DH9 fighter bombers, and at least seven large DH10 bombers, came off its production lines *(Ill 8.7)*.[97]

After the war the aircraft factory was taken over by another Crossley company, Willys Overland Crossley, set up to produce saloon cars designed by the American Willys Overland Corporation. Sales were disappointing and in 1934 the company went into liquidation.[98] The Heaton Chapel factory was bought by Fairey Aviation of Hayes in Middlesex. The Fairey company was already a major supplier of aircraft to the RAF, and the purchase was made with the encouragement of the government

Ill 8.7 National Aircraft Factory No 2, Heaton Chapel.
In 1917, during the First World War, Heaton Chapel was chosen by the government as the site of one of three national aircraft factories. The Heaton Chapel factory, operated by the Manchester-based firm of Crossley Motors, produced 400 de Haviland fighter bombers. After the war it was used for the manufacture of motor cars by the Willys Overland Crossley company, until production ceased in 1934.

Ill 8.8 The first Woodford aerodrome.
Woodford's association with aviation began in 1924 when New Hall Farm was bought by the Avro company for use as an aerodrome.
The hangar shown here was transferred from an earlier airfield in south Manchester. Woodford was used by Avro for the assembly and
flying of aircraft manufactured at works at Newton Heath and, from 1938, at Chadderton. The assembly plant at Woodford saw massive
expansion in the 1930s and 1940s. During the Second World War the site produced over 4000 of Avro's perhaps most famous aircraft,
the Lancaster bomber.

as part of its rearmament programme. Faireys' staff began to move into the Heaton Chapel factory in September 1935. The first aircraft to be built here by Faireys were fourteen of the company's Hendon bombers. While the main aircraft components were built at Heaton Chapel, these needed to be transported elsewhere for final assembly before test flying or delivery. Initially use was made of Barton aerodrome, but by June 1937 aircraft produced at Heaton Chapel were flying from the aerodrome at Ringway, now the site of Manchester International Airport.[99]

Avro and Woodford

It was the need for an aerodrome which brought another great aircraft company to Woodford. Avro, the world's first aeroplane-manufacturing company, was established by Alliott Verdon-Roe and his brother in 1910 in Manchester and greatly expanded during the First World War. Until 1924 the company flew its aircraft from the Alexandra Park airfield in south Manchester, which was leased by the Air Ministry from Lord Egerton of Tatton. With the lease about to expire, Avro was forced to look for an alternative site. Eventually an available location was found at New Hall Farm in Woodford, the land

was bought and a hangar was transferred here from Alexandra Park (*Ill 8.8*). The airfield also provided a new home for the Lancashire Aero Club. In September 1925 a crowd of 25,000 people watched an air display in which the RAF, Avro, the aero club and a few private owners took part. Air shows are still held at Woodford to this day. In the mid-1930s the airfield's facilities were expanded with the building of three new hangars. It was during this period, in 1935, that the prototype of Avro's Anson reconnaissance bomber first flew from Woodford. The Anson was to become one of the world's most widely used aircraft, with more than 11,000 being built, of which nearly 5000 were assembled at Woodford. In 1938 work began on the construction of a new assembly plant at the aerodrome. In that same year, with government funding, the company built a massive new factory at Chadderton, near Oldham.[100] The finest hour of both Woodford and Heaton Chapel was soon to come.

OTHER INDUSTRIES

As well as engineering firms, in the late nineteenth and early twentieth centuries the industry of the

Ill 8.9 Ramie gas mantle advertisement, 1906.

In the late nineteenth and early twentieth centuries the range of manufacturing industries in the Borough widened. The Ramie Company, founded in 1897, manufactured mantles for gaslights using the fibres of the plant 'Ramie Rhea'. (Its brand name 'Zeimar' is 'Ramie' in reverse, with the addition of a 'z'.) The Victoria Mills, shown in this advertisement, were originally built as a hatting factory.

Borough included a number of other specialist manufacturers. Some were established in new works, most notably, but perhaps not unexpectedly, in Reddish. Among the earliest large manufactories to be built here was a chemical works, established in 1867. Later arrivals were the Guardian Printing Works which opened on Greg Street in Reddish in 1899, and the 'Chairman' tobacco factory, built off Broadstone Hall Road South in the early 1920s.[101]

Other manufacturing firms were housed in buildings originally erected for other industrial uses. At Woodley, the Trianon (or Unity) Mill had been converted by the 1890s from a cotton factory to a rubber works.[102] The Victoria hat works in Bredbury and the Primrose cotton mill in Mellor were taken over by the Ramie Company. Established in 1897, it manufactured mantles for gaslights, which were made using fibres from a plant of the nettle family, 'Ramie Rhea', and sold under the brand name of Zeimar. According to the company's advertising, this was the only gas mantle to be 'all British made' (Ill 8.9).[103] Arden Mill in Bredbury ceased to be used for cornmilling in 1850 and was subsequently acquired by a firm manufacturing wallpaper. Under its ownership the mill was rebuilt and cottages were erected nearby for the workforce.[104] In the early twentieth century Oakwood Mill in Romiley, a former cotton mill, was also given over to the manufacture of paper.[105]

A local industry which underwent considerable expansion in the late nineteenth century was the making of ropes. Perhaps the largest of several rope works in Stockport was that on Turncroft Lane. From a small beginning in 1844, thirty years later it employed a workforce of between 300 and 400. Its products then included rope drives, which in the cotton industry were coming to replace upright shafts as the means of transmitting power from engine houses. The works closed in about 1930.[106]

Food and drink

Commercial brewing was a long-established local industry. Public houses across the Borough initially brewed their own beer, but by the early nineteenth century wholesale breweries had begun to appear in, or close to, the town. These often developed from existing 'pub' brewhouses, but some were set up as new businesses. One of the first was the Portwood Brewery. It was established in about 1796 by a Manchester brewer and in 1827 was said to be capable of producing 270 barrels a week. The industry was greatly expanded in the late nineteenth century, when six sizeable breweries emerged. Two, Bell's and the Brookfield breweries, were situated on Hempshaw Lane, and a third, Clarke's, in

South Reddish. Robinson's Unicorn Brewery and the Windsor Castle Brewery in Edgeley were each situated behind the public house from which they had developed. The sixth large brewing concern was Royal Oak Brewery on Higher Hillgate, itself an offshoot from a nearby inn. In the 1880s this last business expanded into the production of mineral water.[107] Today Robinson's is the only brewing company still operating in the Borough.

In the late nineteenth and early twentieth centuries large food works were also established in the Borough. In 1885 a Burnley firm making jam and marmalade moved its operation to Heaton Norris, and five years later to Reddish. By the mid-1890s the Silver Pan Fruit Preserving Works had been established off Didsbury Road in Heaton Norris, in premises which subsequently became the Squirrel Chocolate Works. McVitie & Price's biscuit works in Heaton Chapel is said to have been established in 1917, the same year as the neighbouring aircraft factory.[108]

THE RAILWAYS

The impact of the railways

Between the 1840s and 1900s the Borough came to be crossed by an extensive network of railways, which by 1910 included more than twenty stations, as well as goods yards and warehouses. This system provided a major source of employment, and in 1931 accounted for 2400 jobs in the county borough alone.[109] The railways also helped shape the map of the Borough. Their extension to Reddish Green in the late 1840s, to Bredbury and North Reddish in 1875, and to Cheadle Heath in 1902 encouraged the settlement and development of industry in those areas. Rail transport was facilitated by private sidings. These served a range of industrial sites, including the collieries at Norbury and Lingard Lane, the Edgeley bleachworks and the factories at Heaton Chapel. In other places the arrival of the railways led to the growth of residential developments, notably at Marple, Cheadle Hulme and Bramhall.

Existing systems of transport were affected by the railways. Stagecoach and long-distance haulage wagons could not compete with the speed of the new system and quickly disappeared. The end of those services reduced the revenues of the turnpike trusts and contributed to their own demise. By the 1880s the turnpike trusts which had once operated within the Borough had all ceased to exist.[110] The revenues generated by the local canals also decreased as freight shifted to the railways.[111] (As we shall see below, from the 1840s those canals, the Ashton, Peak Forest and

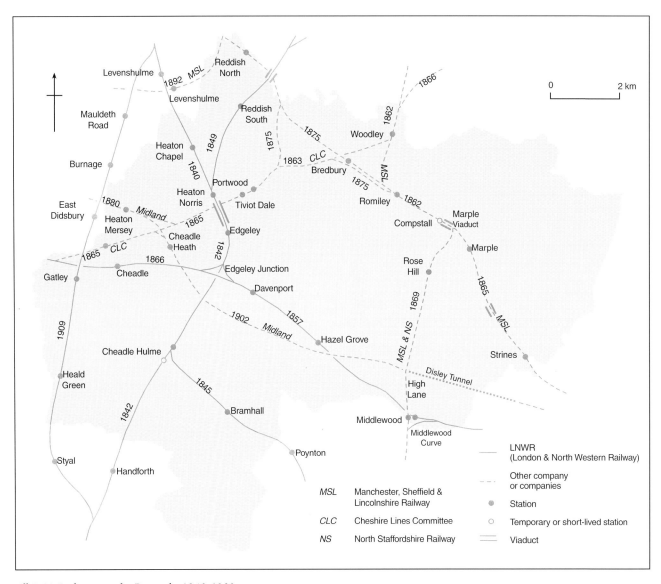

Ill 8.10 Railways in the Borough, 1840-1909.
The development of the local rail network owed much to the competition between rival railway companies, eager to profit from the carrying of passengers and freight between Manchester and London. The railways had a profound impact on the Borough. Their growth encouraged the spread of industry and the building of suburban housing, and opened new opportunities for leisure.

Macclesfield, were themselves owned by a railway company.)

The spread of the railways brought about a change in agricultural practice. Farmers in the vicinity of Stockport were already providing the town with milk.[112] Rail transport meant that milk could now be carried greater distances to supply the region's towns, and dairy farmers in more outlying parts shifted their production away from cheese to cash in on these newly opened markets. Milk produced in the Stockport and Marple areas was sent by train to Manchester, Oldham and Bury, as well as being sold more locally. By 1860 some milk produced in the Stockport district was even being sent to London.[113]

The railways also helped change patterns of leisure. Local scenic spots became more accessible to excursionists. More distant resorts such as Blackpool became the destination of holidays for local workers. Greater freedom of movement could also have adverse effects on the local economy. In the 1840s Stockport's shops and the market lost trade as customers began to travel by train to Manchester.[114]

The development of the railway network

The growth of the railway network in the Borough was a piecemeal process involving a number of railway companies and has a history which often seems daunting in its complexity (*Ill 8.10*). However, behind much of this development lay one obsession, the establishment of new routes to Manchester from London and the Midlands. The Borough, in short, owed a significant proportion of its rail system to its proximity to one of the railway companies' main prizes. Those companies were not oblivious to the profits which might be made from local traffic along the main lines or subsidiary routes. Although this was often a secondary motive in the creation of the network, it provided the Borough with the stations and other rail facilities which from the mid-nineteenth century played a key role in its economic and social development.

The M&B and LNWR 1845-9: Cheadle Hulme, Bramhall and Reddish South

The first railway to be opened in the Borough, in 1840-2, had been the line between Manchester and Crewe. Built by the Manchester and Birmingham Railway Company (the M&B), it included stations at Heaton Norris, Cheadle Hulme and, from 1843, at Edgeley. The company had also been granted the power to construct a branch line from Stockport to Macclesfield, but its construction was delayed by the depression in the early 1840s. When economic conditions improved, the M&B opted for a less expensive branch to Macclesfield from a junction at Cheadle Hulme. The first section of this line to be opened, in June 1845, extended as far as Poynton, and provided Stockport with a rail link with the local collieries. A station was opened at the Cheadle Hulme Junction, replacing the station established three years earlier a short distance to the south. The branch line included a station at Bramhall.[115]

It was also in 1845 that the M&B obtained Parliament's consent for a branch line between Heaton Norris and Guide Bridge on the line between Manchester and Sheffield. This important trans-Pennine route was built by the Sheffield, Ashton-under-Lyne and Manchester Railway Company, which in 1847 joined with two other companies to form the Manchester, Sheffield and Lincolnshire Railway (MS&L). The Heaton Norris to Guide Bridge line was opened in 1849, by which date the M&B had become part of the London and North Western Railway (LNWR). The line included a station at 'Reddish', later called 'Reddish South'.[116] Along with the Ashton Canal, this station became a focal point for industrial development in the area. The LNWR and MS&L were both to play a major role in the further development of the Borough's rail network.

The Stockport, Disley and Whaley Bridge Railway: Davenport and Hazel Grove

The Stockport, Disley and Whaley Bridge Railway was an LNWR scheme. It ran from Edgeley Junction (on the Stockport to Crewe line) to Whaley Bridge. The last place was of importance as the northern terminus of the Cromford and High Peak Railway, which provided a link, across Derbyshire, between the East Midlands and the North-West. It had been built in the 1820s between the Cromford Canal and, at Whaley Bridge, a branch of the Peak Forest Canal. The SD&WB opened in 1857, with an extension to Buxton being completed six years later. In the Borough it included stations at Hazel Grove and at Davenport, on the northern edge of Bramhall township. This last station opened in 1858 at the request of Colonel William Davenport of Bramall Hall.[117]

The MS&L and the Marple, New Mills and Hayfield Junction Railway: Woodley, Romiley, 'Compstall', Marple and Strines

The opening of the SD&WB was not welcome news to another railway company. In 1846 the Sheffield, Ashton-under-Lyne and Manchester Railway had received Parliament's consent for the building of a branch from Hyde Junction on its trans-Pennine line. Passing through Marple, this branch would itself have reached Whaley Bridge, to provide the SA&M with a link with the Cromford and High Peak Railway. To remove any competition between its new line and the local canal network, the SA&M took the precaution of buying the Peak Forest, Ashton and Macclesfield canals. Responsibility for the Whaley Bridge line passed in 1847 to the MS&L. In the following year, as an economic depression set in once again, work on the line stopped. It was the failure of the MS&L to complete the line in the allotted time which left the way open for the SD&WB.[118]

In 1858 the MS&L received Parliament's approval for work to begin again on its own branch line. The terminus was now to be a station known as 'Compstall'. The line opened in 1862 and also served stations at Woodley and Romiley. 'Compstall' station was also known as 'Marple', but was in fact a good walk from either place. It was situated on the west side of the Goyt valley, close to the Peak Forest Canal aqueduct. This was only a temporary arrangement. In 1860, while work on the line was still under way, Parliament agreed to its continuation into Derbyshire. This extension was to be built by a new company, the Marple, New Mills and Hayfield Junction Railway. The section of the line as far as New Mills was opened in 1865. Four days later the MNM&HJ was amalgamated with the MS&L.[119]

The line included two great viaducts over the River Goyt. The more northerly of these, at a height of 38 metres above the river, dwarfed the nearby canal

Ill 8.11 Tiviot Dale railway station, about 1901.

This elegant station, shown here with a line of waiting horse-drawn cabs, opened in 1865. It lay on an east-west railway through Stockport operated by the Cheshire Lines Committee. From 1880 this station was used by Midland Railway services between Manchester and London. Its importance diminished with the opening in 1902 of a new route, which bypassed the town and included a sizeable station at Cheadle Heath. Stockport's other main line station, at Edgeley, was operated by the rival LNWR. Tiviot Dale station was demolished in 1968, but Edgeley station still serves the town.

aqueduct. The second viaduct, 27 metres high, crossed the river to the south of the reservoirs of Mellor Mill. With the opening of the new line, the temporary station at 'Compstall' was replaced by a new 'Marple' station, built where the railway was crossed by the Stockport road, a short distance from Marple Bridge. A station at Strines opened in 1866.[120]

The Macclesfield, Bollington and Marple Railway: Rose Hill, High Lane and Middlewood

The line from Hyde Junction to New Mills was the springboard for several other railways built within the Borough in the 1860s. These were financed by the MS&L jointly with other railway companies. In the case of the Macclesfield, Bollington and Marple Railway, the partnership was with the North Staffordshire Railway. The line opened in 1869, when it included stations at Rose Hill (to the west of Marple village) and High Lane.[121] The MB&M crossed over the LNWR's line between Stockport and Whaley Bridge at Middlewood. In 1879 a station was built on each of the two lines at this point, allowing passengers to change trains. Six years later the two lines were

physically joined with the opening of the linkage known as the Middlewood Curve.[122]

The Cheshire Lines Committee and the LNWR: Portwood, Tiviot Dale and Cheadle

In 1860 an Act of Parliament allowed the building of a railway from the MS&L's line at Woodley to a terminus at Portwood. This Stockport and Woodley Junction Railway opened in 1863 and ended the LNWR's sole control over rail services to Stockport. It would soon also become part of a new through-route, for in 1861 Parliament had authorized a railway to be built to Altrincham as a continuation of the Portwood line. Known as the Stockport, Timperley and Altrincham Junction Railway, it opened in 1865. To avoid the built-up area of the town, beyond Portwood the line was carried over the Tame and passed through tunnels and a cutting excavated from the sandstone at the foot of Lancashire Hill. At Heaton Mersey a viaduct carried the line over to the south side of the Mersey. In Stockport itself a new station, notable for its elegant facade, opened at Tiviot Dale, on a site previously occupied by the Spring Vale printworks *(Ill*

8.11). It was more centrally placed than the station at Portwood, which closed for passenger services in 1875 but remained in use as a goods yard. There was also a station on this line to the north of Cheadle village, which opened in early 1866.[123]

Later in that same year another line opened through Cheadle. This was built by the LNWR, between Edgeley Junction and Northenden on the Stockport, Timperley and Altrincham Junction Railway. The LNWR had its own station at Cheadle, conveniently located within the village. From here passengers were able to travel via Edgeley station to Manchester. The station closed, however, as early as 1917, as a result of competition from the electric tram service between Stockport and Gatley.[124]

The Stockport and Woodley Junction and the ST&AJ were each jointly financed by the MS&L and the Great Northern Railway. The two lines formed part of a grander scheme which enabled those companies to extend their services westwards from the Manchester area to Chester and Liverpool. The partnership worked through the joint board of directors known as the Cheshire Lines Committee (CLC). In 1866 this body was joined by a third company, the Midland.[125]

The Sheffield and Midland Rail Committee: Bredbury, Reddish and the promotion of Marple

In 1861 the Midland, eager to extend its services northwards from Derbyshire to Manchester, entered into an agreement for a link-up with the Marple, New Mills and Hayfield Junction Railway. Six years later Midland trains were running between London and Manchester along this route, in competition with the LNWR's line through Edgeley.[126]

In 1869 the line between New Mills and Hyde Junction was formally transferred to a joint committee of MS&L and Midland directors. This Sheffield and Midland Rail Committee also took on the task of finishing the Manchester and Stockport Railway. Its construction had originally been authorized in 1866 to enable trains to travel between Tiviot Dale and Manchester, and between Romiley and Manchester, without the need for a detour via Woodley and Hyde Junction. When the Sheffield and Midland Rail Committee took over the scheme, they also added a more direct link between Tiviot Dale and Romiley. The significance of Romiley in the grander scheme of things was its position on the Midland's route into Manchester.[127]

The Manchester and Stockport Railway opened in 1875 and included stations at Bredbury and Reddish. A fourteen-arch viaduct carried the line over the Tame

valley at Reddish Vale. With the opening of these various new links the station at Marple took on a new importance. Trains on the Midland's London and Manchester route now stopped here, to allow Liverpool coaches to be attached and detached and to enable passengers to connect with other local services. To meet this new role, Marple station was considerably enlarged.[128]

The Midland: Heaton Mersey and the promotion of Tiviot Dale

The Midland's trains to Manchester originally terminated at London Road station, later renamed Piccadilly. In 1875, with more and more trains using this station, the Midland was given notice to quit. Ironically this was the very year in which the company had achieved a more direct route to Manchester, via the new line from Romiley. However, it was also in 1875 that the Cheshire Lines Committee began the construction of Manchester's Central station (now GMEX). The Midland saw in this the answer to its own need for a Manchester terminus. To establish a link with the new station, the company took over an existing project, the building of the Manchester South District Railway. This line opened in 1880 and joined with the CLC's line at Heaton Mersey, which was also now served by a station.[129] The opening of the new line meant the beginning of a new era for Tiviot Dale. This was now a main line station, with services to many parts of the country.[130]

The Midland: Cheadle Heath, Hazel Grove and the demotion of Tiviot Dale and Marple

The heyday of Tiviot Dale was to last for just over two decades. Its demotion was sealed in 1898 when the Midland was empowered to build a new route to Heaton Mersey. Designed to speed up services between London and the North-West, it bypassed New Mills, Tiviot Dale, and all the stations and junctions in between. These included Marple, whose own heyday now came to an end with the completion of the 'new line', as this route was known. Its role as an interchange was taken over by a station at Chinley, to the south of New Mills.[131]

The building of the 'new line' involved the last great piece of railway engineering undertaken in the Borough. To maintain as direct a route as possible, a tunnel 2 miles and 346 yards (roughly 3.5 kilometres) long was excavated below the high ground to the west of Disley. Digging was carried out from both ends of the tunnel, and in each direction from the bottom of

Ill 8.12 Horse-drawn trams in St Peter's Square, about 1902.
In the late nineteenth century horse-drawn trams operated between St Peter's Square and Manchester and Hazel Grove. In the 1900s these services were each in turn replaced by electric trams, powered from overhead cables. The imposing building in the background of this photograph is the Theatre Royal and Opera House. This was one of two music halls in the town at this date.

eleven shafts sunk along its length, creating twenty-four working faces. Ten of these shafts were later capped with brick towers and were used for ventilation.[132]

The 'new line' was completed in 1902. It included a large station at Cheadle Heath, where a junction with the CLC's line was also provided. A station was also opened at Hazel Grove. This was the second to be built here, the other being on the LNWR's line to Whaley Bridge and Buxton. Few trains, however, stopped at the Midland's station and it was closed in 1917.[133]

The LNWR: Heald Green and Gatley

The opening of the Midland's new approach to Manchester prompted the LNWR to follow suit. In 1909, in an attempt to reduce travelling time between Crewe and Manchester, the company opened the 'Styal Line', running between Wilmslow and Slade Lane Junction and bypassing Stockport. In the Borough it included stations at Gatley and Heald Green and would play a part in the growth of suburbia in these areas. Its use as an alternative to the route through Edgeley ended in 1939, but the line remained open for local services.[134]

TRAMWAYS AND BUSES

Horse-drawn buses and trams

A horse-drawn omnibus service was operating in the Borough as early as 1830 when a service began between Manchester and Stockport, with a terminus at the Warren Bulkeley Arms. The first railway station to serve Stockport, opened in Heaton Norris in 1840, was itself linked to the town by bus. Rival bus services were operating in the 1870s between Stockport and Hazel Grove. At about this same date a service was begun between Stockport and Bredbury.[135]

Buses were running between Cheadle and Manchester, via Didsbury, by 1851. In 1875 the Cheadle Omnibus Company which operated on this route was bought out by the much larger Manchester Carriage Company, which continued to provide a local service. Fletcher Moss organized his own form of transport from Cheadle to Manchester. In 1876 he acquired an old stagecoach which he ran in the summer months for the benefit of a group of wealthy Cheadle residents. A cold wet summer in 1879 put an end to the service.[136]

In 1880 the Manchester Carriage Company, which

operated omnibus services between Manchester and Stockport and Cheadle, became part of a new business concern, formed to build and operate horse-drawn tramways in and around Manchester. In May of that year this Manchester Carriage and Tramways Company opened a tramway service between Manchester and Stockport, bringing the days of the omnibuses along that route to an end. Among the company's many other tramway routes was one from Manchester to Withington, which now became the terminus for the omnibus from Cheadle. At Stockport, the original terminus for the tramway was the George Hotel in Mersey Square, but by the beginning of 1881 the service had been extended to St Peter's Square (Ill 8.12). It was also from there that in 1890 a separate company began to operate a tramway service to the Bull's Head in Hazel Grove, with a branch line to Edgeley.[137]

Gatley does not appear to have had any public transport until 1896, when the postmaster started a cab service. Two years later a Mr Potts began to operate a service to Stockport with a single omnibus which he seems to have acquired from the Manchester Carriage and Tramways Company. This service continued until May 1904, by which date the route between Gatley and Cheadle was being served by a new form of public transport, the electric tram.[138]

Electric trams and trolley buses

Electric trams, powered from an overhead wire, began to run between Manchester and Stockport in June 1902, and replaced the horse-drawn tramways on that route. They were operated by Manchester Corporation, under an agreement with Stockport Corporation which owned the track within the county borough. The first electric trams in the Borough, however, had begun operation in August of the previous year. Run by Stockport Corporation, they provided a service between the town, Sandy Lane in Reddish, and Woodley railway station. The Woodley line was rapidly extended to Pole Bank on the Hyde boundary, enabling a service to begin between Stockport and Hyde Town Hall. The Reddish service was also extended, to reach the Bull's Head on the Gorton boundary. A new line was built westwards from the town, so that by March 1904 trams were running through Cheadle to a terminus at the Horse and Farrier in Gatley (Ill 8.13). The corporation also bought out the private horse-drawn tram company operating between Stockport, Hazel Grove and Edgeley, and began to run electric trams on these routes in July 1905.[139]

In 1913 a service was begun from Stockport to Offerton, using trackless electric trams, or trolley buses.

These were a recent innovation, the country's first trolley bus services having come into operation only two years previously in Leeds and Bradford. Stockport's trolley buses, however, proved unreliable. On several occasions the cable which carried power to the vehicles was detached from the overhead wires. More serious was the frequent failure of the tram's back axle. In 1919 the trolley buses on the Offerton route were replaced by the corporation's first motor buses.[140]

Motor buses

Stockport's first known motor bus service had begun in about 1908. It was privately run by Frank Clayton of Foggbrook in Offerton and operated between the Thatched House, on Churchgate in Stockport, and the Jolly Sailor in Marple. Financial difficulties brought the service to a sudden end in July 1912.[141] In the 1920s and 1930s an explosion in the number of corporation and privately run services made the bus a familiar sight across the Borough. One private operator, the North Western Road Car Company, in 1923 relocated its headquarters to Stockport from Macclesfield.[142] In 1931 buses replaced the trams between Cheadle Heath and Gatley, but other tram services continued into the post-war period.[143]

LOCAL GOVERNMENT

Public health and local boards

By the end of the 1830s Stockport had acquired a corporate form of local government, with councillors appointed by a local electorate and empowered to collect rates to carry out improvements. The electorate as yet comprised only a relatively small proportion of the population and the specific powers of the council were limited. Nevertheless, the system contained the basic elements of local government which continues to this day.

Outside the municipal borough, local government developed more slowly. A key issue which led to change was the need to improve public health. In 1849 Stockport was struck by cholera and typhus. In the 1850s outbreaks of disease remained a regular occurrence in the town.[144] That same decade saw a series of measures being introduced to help ameliorate the town's more unsanitary conditions. A local board of health was established in 1852.[145] In the following year the Stockport Amendment Act was passed by Parliament which included a provision compelling mill-owners to reduce smoke emissions.[146] In 1854 sewers were laid in Higher Hillgate, Edgeley and Heaton

Ill 8.13 The electric tram terminus at the Horse and Farrier, Gatley, about 1905.
Between 1901 and 1905 Stockport came to be served by a network of electric tram services which linked the town with Manchester, North Reddish, Hyde, Hazel Grove and Gatley. As electric trams had replaced horse-drawn trams and omnibuses, so they in turn were eventually replaced by motor buses. Trams ceased to operate between Gatley and Cheadle Heath in 1931. The remaining services in the Borough were withdrawn between 1947 and 1951.

Norris, and in 1855 ten 'scavengers' were appointed to deal with the disposal of waste.[147] The town's first public baths, built by the corporation on St Petersgate, opened in 1858. (In 1886 this facility, which provided a place to wash as well as to swim, was improved by the opening of a much larger baths on an adjacent site.)[148] A further programme of laying sewers was begun in the 1860s.[149] Despite such efforts, however, it was reported in 1869 that the death rates in Stockport and Manchester, at roughly thirty-one or thirty-two people per 1000, were higher than in any other town in the country.[150]

Other communities in the Borough had their own share of unsanitary conditions. A public inquiry into Marple's water-supply, held after the establishment of its own local board in 1875, found examples of poor housing (including a family of seven living in a cellar) and of four to six houses sharing a single privy. Marple also suffered from factory smoke and other industrial emissions. Its water was mainly provided by wells and pumps, but these supplies were often polluted.[151]

Although an Act of Parliament was passed in 1848 to allow the setting up of local boards of health, the initial response was not enthusiastic. In Cheshire few were established before the 1860s. Among those created in that decade was a local board for Bredbury, founded in 1865.[152] Legislation in the 1870s introduced a more uniform system for maintaining public health, and a new measure of compulsion. An Act of 1872 divided the country into urban and rural sanitary districts. The first were areas under the control of a municipal corporation, police commissioners or a local board of health; the second comprised those parts of the poor law unions which lacked such an existing local authority. Under the Public Health Act of 1875 both types of sanitary district were required to have an adequate water-supply and sewerage system, and to appoint medical officers of health and sanitary inspectors.[153]

Perhaps as a direct consequence of this new legislation, other parts of the Borough set up local boards of health. A board was established for Heaton Norris in 1872, Marple in 1875 and Reddish in 1881. Cheadle and Gatley formed a joint local board in 1886. In that same year, and again in 1892, an unsuccessful attempt was made to establish a local board for Hazel Grove.[154]

Urban and rural districts

Under the Local Government Act of 1894 those areas controlled by local boards of health were designated 'urban districts', while rural sanitary districts became 'rural districts'. In line with recent developments in county government, both types of district were to be administered by elected councils. Within rural districts the Act also allowed for the creation of councils for the civil parishes, the successors to the townships.[155] Stockport Rural District Council was relatively short-lived. Within a decade of the 1894 Act all of its component civil parishes had been included within urban districts.[156] Hazel Grove and Bramhall Urban District was created in 1900, and comprised Bosden, Norbury, Offerton, Torkington and Bramhall.[157] Compstall Civil Parish, created in 1897 from part of the old Werneth township, was promoted to an urban district in 1902. In terms of both its area and its population (a mere 875 in 1901) it was said to be the smallest urban district in the country.[158]

The growth of Stockport County Borough

The Local Government Act of 1888 gave counties their own elected councils, and transferred the administrative work formerly carried out by the JPs to these new bodies. Under the provisions of the Act, on the 1st of April 1889 Stockport became a 'county borough', largely independent from the control of the new Cheshire County Council.[159] The Act also involved a local boundary change, with the area of the county borough previously in Lancashire now becoming part of Cheshire.[160] The county boundary, which from before Domesday had run along the River Mersey, now lay in Heaton Norris.

In 1901 the area of the county borough was more than doubled by the first Stockport Extension Act. The new acquisitions included neighbouring parts of Cheadle and Gatley, Hazel Grove and Bramhall, and Brinnington (the remaining part of which passed in the following year to Bredbury and Romiley). The greatest prize in 1901, however, was the whole of the urban district of Reddish. The arrangement was to the benefit of both parties. Stockport Corporation received Reddish's valuable rates, and fulfilled a promise to provide Reddish with a fire station, public baths and library.[161] There was a further substantial addition to the county borough in 1913, when both Stockport and

Manchester corporations applied to take over the urban district of Heaton Norris. It was Stockport which won the day, receiving the lion's share of the district, with only a small portion, on the western boundary, going to Manchester.[162]

In 1933-4 Manchester and Stockport were in competition again, as each proposed the annexation of Cheadle and Gatley Urban District. Stockport's ambitions at that time went even further, for they also included taking over the whole of the Hazel Grove and Bramhall Urban District and part of Poynton. The proposals met with fierce local opposition. In Cheadle and Gatley an opinion poll of nearly 10,000 residents recorded almost unanimous support for the council's fight to retain the district's independence. Manchester abandoned its own plans to extend its boundaries in this direction. The outcome for Stockport was the Extension Act of 1934, which came into effect the following year. It fell short of the corporation's original aspirations but transferred Offerton to the county borough from Hazel Grove and Bramhall.[163]

Changes in local government, 1936-9

The year 1936 brought widespread changes in local government in Cheshire, involving the reshaping of some authorities and the abolition of others. Marple Urban District was greatly expanded by the addition of Ludworth and Mellor. This change was much resented in the two civil parishes, since it also involved these being transferred from Derbyshire to Cheshire.[164] It was also in 1936 that Compstall Urban District was abolished. Part went to the municipal borough of Hyde, but the largest portion, including Compstall village, was added to Bredbury and Romiley Urban District.[165] The boundaries of Cheadle and Gatley saw minor adjustments, resulting from the abolition of Handforth Urban District.[166] A further local change came in 1939, when Woodford was transferred from Macclesfield Rural District to Hazel Grove and Bramhall.[167] There was to be one further significant addition to the county borough of Stockport in 1952, when Brinnington was annexed from Bredbury and Romiley, but otherwise by the end of 1939 a pattern of local authorities had been established which in 1974 was to become the Metropolitan Borough of Stockport.

HOUSING

Workers' housing

Between the late eighteenth and the mid-nineteenth century dwellings of varying quality were built to house the working class. At the upper end of the scale were two-up two-downs; inferior to these were the back-to-backs, blind backs and cellar dwellings.[168] This housing was built with only the minimum of regulation by local government. In the case of Stockport the Improvement Act of 1836 legislated against such public hazards as doors opening outwards and unguarded cellar openings, but ignored the standard of accommodation behind the street facade.[169] Even in the 1850s, when the council was endeavouring to reduce the unsanitary conditions in the town, it rejected a proposal to restrict the use of cellars as dwellings.[170] In 1868, however, an Act of Parliament laid down national standards for new housing, requiring streets to be wider and dwellings to be higher to improve ventilation.[171] The terrace continued to be the norm for workers' housing into the early twentieth century, but the individual dwellings within those rows now commonly comprised two-up

two-downs with a two-storey extension to the rear and their own privy in an enclosed yard.[172]

The older, inferior types of dwelling still remained and many people continued to live in overcrowded conditions. The 1891 census for Stockport shows that there were 132 cases of a family living within a single room. Two of these were families of seven. One family of twelve lived in a two-roomed dwelling. Overcrowding continued into the twentieth century. In 1921 in the county borough the average number of occupants of a house was lower than nineteenth-century levels but was still 4.2 persons.[173]

Although the Act of 1868 allowed local authorities to demolish or improve property, it was perhaps not until the early twentieth century that such powers were utilized on any significant scale within the Borough. Between 1910 and 1914, when the outbreak of the First World War curtailed this process, over 300 houses in

Ill 8.14 The drawing room, Abney Hall, Cheadle.
Abney Hall is an important example of a mansion of a Victorian businessman. It was the home of James Watts, a wealthy Manchester merchant, who in the 1850s commissioned J G Grace to create its lavish interiors. Grace's work at Abney incorporated designs by A W Pugin, a leading figure of the nineteenth-century Gothic Revival. In 1857 Watts played host to Prince Albert at Abney. The house also has a literary connection, for Agatha Christie spent childhood holidays here.

the county borough were demolished and more than 100 back-to-backs were made into through-houses. In the early 1930s, however, there were still 295 blind backs, 889 back-to-backs and seventy-five cellar dwellings in Stockport which were inhabited. Even in the 1960s there were many dwellings in the town which were considered to be a danger to health.[174]

Local authorities were empowered by Parliament in 1879 to build new houses with government loans to replace demolished property, but it was not until the Addison Act of 1919 that they were made responsible for meeting the housing needs in their area.[175] Within the Borough, Cheadle and Gatley Urban District Council was at the vanguard of the construction of council housing, having completed its first new dwellings by 1920. Stockport Corporation began building council houses in the following year.[176]

Victorian mansions

Terraced housing was built for the working class in the town and close to other local centres of industry and employment. The preference among the middle class was to live outside the town in more secluded, semi-rural areas. The process was already under way in the first half of the nineteenth century as wealthy manufacturers moved into residences away from the overcrowding and grime of Stockport. Some local mansions also became home to people from Manchester. Mauldeth Hall in Heaton Norris, built in about 1830, was bought in 1854 by the Ecclesiastical Commissioners as a residence for Manchester's first bishop.[177]

Perhaps the grandest of all the nineteenth-century mansions in the Borough was the home of James Watts, a partner in a family firm which owned the largest wholesale drapery business in Manchester. The house, situated off Manchester Road to the north of Cheadle village, had been begun in 1847 by Alfred Orrell, a Stockport cotton spinner. It was built on the site of the Cheadle Grove printworks and was originally called The Grove. Orrell died fourteen months later, before the building was completed, and the property was bought by James Watts who renamed the house Abney Hall. Under his ownership the building was remodelled on a larger scale and its rooms lavishly decorated in the Gothic Revival style in fashion at this time (*Ill 8.14*). The interiors were designed for Watts by the London firm of J G Grace. He was an associate of Augustus Pugin, one of the leading exponents of the Gothic Revival, who shortly before his death in 1852 provided Grace with sketch designs for Abney. In the splendour of Abney, Watts played host to some of the leading figures of the day. Guests included Disraeli and Gladstone, but for Watts the high point came in 1857 when Prince Albert stayed here during a visit to Manchester. Agatha Christie, whose sister married into the Watts family, spent Christmas holidays here as a child. In 1959 the house was bought by Cheadle and Gatley Urban District Council and became the district's town hall.[178] For the previous fifteen years the town hall had been another Gothic mansion, Bruntwood, built to the south of Cheadle village in 1861.[179]

New homes for the middle class

From the mid-nineteenth century the demand for dwellings outside the town was growing. Where mill-owners and wealthy professionals led the way, other members of the middle class, including tradesmen and shopkeepers, followed. In the late nineteenth and early twentieth centuries sizeable detached and semi-detached houses, complete with gardens and known as 'villas', were built in increasing numbers for such individuals and their families. Typically they were constructed by speculative developers. At Bramhall in 1877, the whole of the ancestral estate of the Davenports was bought by one such business, the Manchester-based Freeholders Company. It planned to resell some plots of the estate for building, and on others to erect houses for lease. Bramall Hall itself was bought from the company in 1882 by the owner of the Strines printworks and became the residence of his son, Charles Nevill.[180]

It was the railways which enabled the growth of 'villadom', by providing the middle class with a convenient means of commuting between their homes and their place of work. Following the opening of the Heaton Chapel station on the LNWR's Manchester to Stockport line in 1852, villas were built along the neighbouring Heaton Moor Road.[181] Cheadle Hulme, which had been served by a railway station as early as 1845, was also one of the first places in the Borough to see an influx of new middle-class residents. In 1864 it was described as 'rapidly improving, containing some handsome, suburban residences'.[182] Marple, after the arrival of the railway in 1865, saw a similar development, with large new houses being built in convenient proximity to the station. This area had the additional attraction of the scenery of the Goyt valley.[183] Improvement in sanitation also encouraged the spread of middle-class housing. In Mellor new residences were rapidly built along the lower stretch of Longhurst Lane after the laying of a sewer along that road in 1902 to serve the existing community at Moor End.[184] For much of the nineteenth century the population of Mellor had been declining in numbers. Between 1901 and 1911 it increased by over 40%.[185]

The inter-war growth of suburbia

In the 1900s the development of the local electric tram system further facilitated the growth of suburbia in the Borough. It was in the 1920s and 1930s, however, that the building of suburban housing really gathered pace. Buyers now had the benefit of mortgages from either the local authority or building societies.[186] The growth of motor transport was also a major factor, allowing greater flexibility in the location of new homes. Much of the suburban housing built within the Borough during the inter-war years was situated in the western and southern districts. New residences were erected in Bramhall and in neighbouring Woodford, where the population nearly doubled between 1921 and 1931, from a mere 413 to 801.[187] (In 1936, as we have seen, Woodford was incorporated within Hazel Grove and Bramhall Urban District.)

The spread of suburbia was at its most feverish in Cheadle and Gatley Urban District. In 1921 its population was a little over 11,000. By 1931 it had reached nearly 18,500 and by 1939 was over 27,000. The rate of increase was among the highest in the region during this period. New housing not only spread out around the established local centres, Cheadle, Cheadle Hulme and Gatley, but also mushroomed in the previously mainly rural area of Heald Green.[188]

Much of the increase in population of Cheadle and Gatley during the inter-war years was a result of people moving into the area from Manchester.[189] The county borough of Stockport also evidently saw a significant number of its residents moving to homes further afield. Between 1921 and 1931 its population rose by less than 2%.[190]

Rural hospitals

By the mid-nineteenth century it was not only middle-class commuters who were moving into new accommodation in the more rural areas in the Borough. Hospital trustees looked to such locations to provide a healthier environment for patients. Cheadle Royal Hospital and Barnes Hospital in Gatley, which opened in 1850 and 1875 respectively, were both associated with the Manchester Royal Infirmary. Cheadle Royal was built for the care of the mentally ill, and replaced an earlier hospital in Manchester's Piccadilly. Barnes Hospital, built with the aid of money left by Robert Barnes, a cotton spinner, was for convalescents.[191] Existing buildings were also converted for hospital use. Mauldeth Hall in Heaton Norris was converted in 1882 to a hospital for incurables by the Northern Counties Supplementary Hospital.[192] At Nab Top in Marple a nursing home, established in 1912, was re-opened by Salford Corporation in 1920 as a sanatorium.[193]

PUBLIC AND PRIVATE UTILITIES

Water

In 1825 the enterprising Peter Marsland had received Parliament's consent to supply piped water to the town. The Stockport Waterworks remained under the sole control of the Marslands until 1850, when this private business was reformed as a joint stock company. It immediately set about improving the supply. Previously water had only been available for two hours a day, and even then the supply was liable to be intermittent. In 1850 the new company became one of the first in the country to provide a constant supply. Shortly afterwards indoor taps replaced the shared standpipes from which half of the Marslands' customers had drawn their water. The number of people supplied by the waterworks also increased. In the 1840s many still depended on public pumps and water carriers. By the end of 1852 as many as 40,000 of the town's 56,000 inhabitants were receiving the company's supply.[194]

Within a few years the Goyt, from which the Stockport Waterworks Company took its water, was becoming visibly polluted. In 1859 an agreement was reached for the company to be provided with water by Manchester Corporation, which owned extensive reservoirs in the Longdendale valley. By the beginning of 1863 a main linking Stockport with Manchester's service reservoir at Denton had been completed and pumping from the Goyt now ceased. In the meanwhile, however, a rival water company had been set up. This Stockport District Waterworks Company planned to supply water to both Stockport and a much wider area from reservoirs at Lyme Park. In late 1863 competition was avoided when the two companies amalgamated. Lyme Park now became the chief source of supply to the town.[195]

Stockport Corporation had originally given its support to the Lyme Park scheme but in 1867, dissatisfied with the quality, quantity and high price of the new company's supply, it applied to Parliament for powers to establish its own waterworks. The attempt failed, but the corporation was empowered to buy the existing company by agreement. The asking price, and the council's reluctance to commit itself to high expenditure, ensured that this power was not exercised for over thirty years.[196]

In 1899 the company finally passed into the corporation's hands. Four years later work commenced on a new reservoir. It was constructed in the Kinder valley in Derbyshire and officially opened in 1912. Later the requirements of the increasing local population resulted in the construction of the Fernilee reservoir in the Goyt valley to the south of Whaley Bridge. The project began in 1932, with the reservoir opening seven years later. In the 1960s a second reservoir was built in this valley by the newly created Stockport and District Water Board.[197]

Gas

From the mid-nineteenth century the local provision of gas for lighting underwent a massive expansion. In 1849 Stockport Corporation's gasworks had only 1530 customers. In 1889 there were ten times as many. To meet the growing market, the corporation first expanded the production and storage plant at its Heaton Lane works, and in the late 1870s erected a new works on the former site of the Marslands' Portwood reservoir. The town's Millgate gasworks shut in the 1890s. The Heaton Lane site closed in 1930. Its storage capacity was no longer required as a result of the construction at the Portwood works of a towering new gasholder, 77 metres high. This remained a local landmark until it was dismantled in 1988.[198]

Marple Urban District Council ran its own gasworks, situated on Lower Fold on the north side of Marple Bridge. It had originated as a privately owned gas plant, which in 1865 was taken over by a joint stock company. In 1887 this Marple Gas Company was in turn acquired by the Marple local board. Compstall and part of Ludworth were supplied by privately owned gasworks at Compstall Mills until as late as the 1920s, when the supply to these areas passed to Marple UDC.[199]

Electricity

Stockport Corporation was among a number of local authorities which in the 1890s invested in the nascent electricity industry. The corporation's Electricity Supply Undertaking was established in 1898, and a generating station was constructed at the former gasworks on Millgate. In 1900 it supplied power to the corporation's new electric tramway system. The application of the supply to other uses was slow at first. By 1904 only 217 consumers were connected, and though the town had its first electric street lamps, these numbered only forty-five. By the time of the First World War, electric cranes were being used in the town's growing engineering industry, but more than half of the Millgate station's output was still accounted for by the tramways. The use of electricity became more

widespread in the 1920s and 1930s. During this period industry increasingly made use of electricity, and a range of domestic appliances came onto the market. In 1933 an electricity showroom was opened at Tiviot Dale, where cookers, washing machines, refrigerators and other appliances were on display. (A gas showroom had opened on St Petersgate three years earlier.) The Millgate power station had itself been greatly enlarged by 1931. Its generating capacity increased from a mere 156 kilowatts in 1900, to 11,000 in 1918. By 1922 the figure had risen to 22,000 and by 1935 to 55,000. Early in 1933 the Millgate power station was connected to the newly created national grid. The corporation also supplied electricity in bulk to Bredbury and Romiley and Hazel Grove and Bramhall urban district councils which undertook its distribution within their areas. Cheadle and Gatley Urban District was similarly supplied by an arrangement with Manchester Corporation, while under an agreement made in 1930 the Trent Valley and High Peak Electrical Company supplied Marple Urban District. The first electric lamp in the Marple area was powered by electricity generated by a considerably more modest source, the waterwheel at the Spade Forge.[200]

IMPROVEMENTS TO THE TOWN

The Market Place

The year 1850 marked a turning point in the long history of Stockport's Market Place. Since the medieval period the right to collect market tolls had belonged to the lord of the manor, and the market had been regulated by officers of his manorial court. In 1850 the corporation completed the purchase of the manorial rights from Lord Vernon. Their acquisition, at a cost of £22,500, had aroused considerable controversy. Doubts were expressed about the profitability of the market tolls at a time when the convenience of rail transport meant that customers were forsaking Stockport for Manchester. The council, however, was honour bound to carry through the purchase.[201] Once the manorial rights had exchanged hands, it quickly set about improving the market facilities. A timber-framed building on the west side of the Market Place, which had been used as a post office and which was included within the purchase, was demolished. In its place, in 1851, was built a new Market Hall, later known as the Farm Produce Hall or Hen Market. Its imposing frontage, designed in a classical style, included a first-floor balcony from which election speeches and public announcements were made (*Ill 8.15*).[202] In 1853 Castle Yard was lowered to make it suitable for use as a cattle

Ill 8.15 *The west side of the Market Place, in 1896.*
In 1850 the ancient manorial rights over the town's market were bought by the corporation, which promptly began to improve the facilities.
In 1851 a new Market Hall, with a colonnaded facade, was erected at the west end of the Market Place (right). In 1860 the centre
of the Market Place was covered over by a structure of glass and cast iron, designed as protection from the weather. The easternmost
bay of the covered market, visible on the left in this photograph, was taken down in 1912 to allow trolley buses to pass en route between
St Peter's Square and Offerton.

market, which was now moved here from a site in the Park.[203] (Castle Mill, which once stood on this site, had been demolished by the lord of the manor in 1841.)[204] The sale of cattle in the heart of an industrial town may now seem incongruous, but livestock had long been sold in Stockport and the continuation of this practice was essential if the town was to be supplied with fresh meat.

Other changes were to follow. In 1860 the council authorized the construction of a covered market in the Market Place (*Ills 1.6 & 8.15*). It was built of cast iron and glass, with the lower half of the sides being originally open. The intention was to provide traders and shoppers with protection from the weather, and the design earned the building the nickname of the 'glass umbrella'.[205] The council turned next to the problem of access. In 1864 it was decided to build a bridge linking the Market Place with St Petersgate, to provide an easier approach from

the west of the town and the Edgeley railway station. St Petersgate Bridge comprised five arches of brick (mostly hidden from view by the adjoining buildings) and a cast-iron section spanning Little Underbank (*Ills 1.6 & 8.16*). It was opened in 1868, much to the consternation of shopkeepers in the Underbanks who feared that the new access route to the Market Place would reduce their own passing trade.[206]

The Town Hall

In the nineteenth century it was common for the larger local authorities in the region to build a grand town hall. These buildings were a symbol of civic pride. They not only provided the setting for council meetings, and housed the various departments of an expanding local administration, but also served as a venue for public

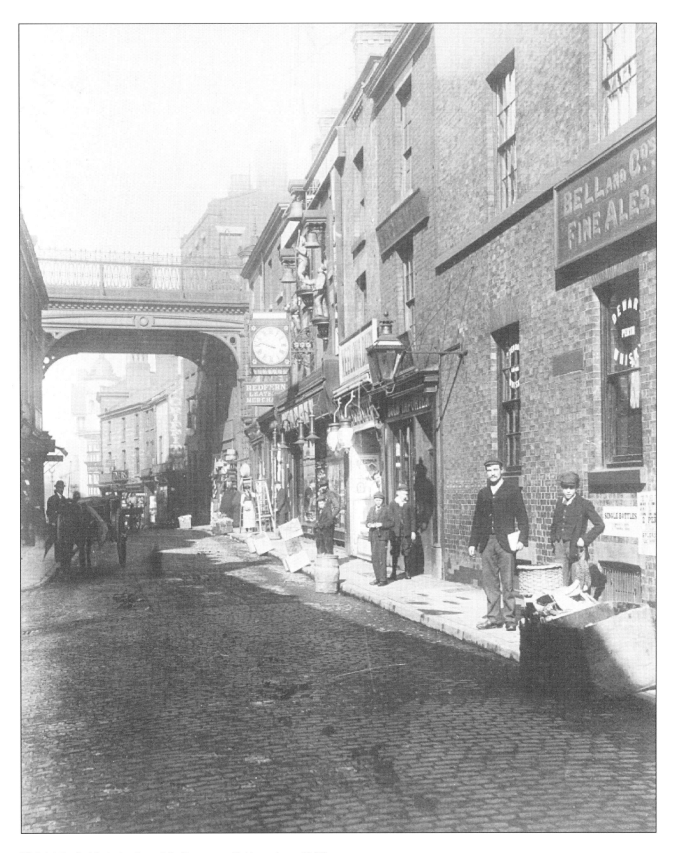

Ill 8.16 Little Underbank and St Petersgate Bridge, about 1905.
Little Underbank lies within the natural ravine of the Tin Brook, below the south side of the Market Place. St Petersgate Bridge opened
in 1868 and linked the Market Place with St Petersgate, providing easier access to the market from Edgeley railway station. A feature
of note in Little Underbank is the late nineteenth-century clock (right), flanked by mechanized figures of a sailor, a soldier and Father
Time, which chimed bells above their heads on the quarter-hour.

Ill 8.17 Stockport Town Hall, in 1908.
While other municipal councils in the region were busy building imposing town halls in the nineteenth century, Stockport Corporation was reluctant to commit itself to such an expense. It was not until 1904 that the foundation stone of the Town Hall was laid. The building was designed by the architect of Belfast Town Hall, which it is said to resemble. The street decorations in this photograph were set up for the official opening of the building by the Prince and Princess of Wales on the 7th of July 1908.

functions. Stockport Corporation did not have such a central facility. The right to erect a town hall had been among the powers granted to the corporation by the Stockport Improvement Act of 1837, but successive councils considered such a project an unnecessary expenditure. Council and other public meetings were held at the Court House on Warren Street, which in 1845 the corporation bought from Lord Vernon.[207] Later in the nineteenth century the spacious drill hall of the Stockport Armoury on Greek Street, built in 1861-2 for a local force of rifle volunteers, doubled as the venue for large civic, social and political functions.[208]

By 1892, with Stockport's status promoted to that of a county borough, the council's attitude towards the prospect of a new town hall had softened. A committee was appointed to investigate a suitable location. It would be five years before a decision was finally made in favour

of a prominent position on Wellington Road South, at that date occupied by the National School (*Ill 6.21*). A competition was launched for a design, the successful applicant being Sir Alfred Brumwell Thomas, who had previously designed Belfast City Hall. The limestone facade and colonnaded clock-tower of the completed building gave it the nickname of the 'wedding cake'. The official opening was carried out by the Prince and Princess of Wales, later George V and Queen Mary, in July 1908 (*Ill 8.17*). This, the town's first royal visit, was also the occasion of the renaming of part of Heaton Lane as Prince's Street.[209]

Mersey Square and Merseyway

In the early 1930s the Mersey still flowed uncovered through the centre of the town. By the 1900s,

Ill 8.18 Mersey Square, about 1931.
In the 1900s Mersey Square, located on either side of the river below Wellington Bridge, became the site of new municipal developments.
An imposing new fire station, with a lofty tower, was opened in 1902 (centre left). Adjoining it was a depot for the corporation's electric
trams.

alongside Wellington Bridge, an open public space known as Mersey Square had been created on either side of the river, its two halves being linked by a new bridge. It was at the north-east corner of Mersey Square that an impressive new station was built for the county borough's fire service, which opened in 1902 (*Ill 8.18*). To its rear was the corporation's first tramway depot. Both of these buildings occupied the site of the demolished Mersey Mills.[210] As the tramway service expanded new premises were required. In 1924 a new depot was built on the corner of Wellington Road North and Heaton Lane, on the site of the old Heaton Lane gasworks. The gasworks' coal stores were retained and converted to a bus depot, but in 1932 a new depot was added to the site, capable of holding over 100 buses.[211]

In 1935, as part of an improvement of Mersey Square and Wellington Bridge, the river was covered over between the two neighbouring bridges. It was the

precursor to a much grander scheme on which work began in 1936. This was the covering over of the river between Mersey Square and Lancashire Bridge (*Ill 8.19*). Above the river now ran a new road, Merseyway, which was opened in 1940 and was designed to relieve traffic along the existing through-routes of Prince's Street and Chestergate. In the 1960s the corporation would find a new role for Merseyway.[212]

EDUCATION

Local school boards and Local Education Authorities

In the late eighteenth and early nineteenth centuries elementary education had been made more widely available for working-class children in the Borough by the establishment of Sunday schools, the largest of these being the Stockport Sunday School, off Hillgate. The popularity of the Sunday schools, both among their middle-class patrons and the working class itself, probably accounts for the relative slowness with which public day schools were established in Stockport in the early nineteenth century.[213] In 1870 the government attempted to address a national shortage of day schools through Forster's Education Act. It allowed locally elected school boards to be set up where the existing provision of education was considered to be inadequate. The activities of these boards were to be funded by the ratepayers. In Stockport by this date the provision of elementary day schooling, with some 7000 places, had considerably improved. Anglicans, Methodists and Roman Catholics all maintained several schools in the town. There were some local black spots. Heaton Norris, despite its large population, possessed no public day school; neither, outside the town, did Bramhall.[214]

Within the region opposition from the supporters of the existing system of voluntarily maintained schools helped ensure that relatively few local school boards were created. A board was established in Bramhall in 1875 and opened a school two years later. In Cheadle

the creation of an elected board was rejected, and although a new rate was introduced this was used to support voluntary schooling.[215] At Stockport the council voted in 1870 in favour of a school board, but its elected membership came to be dominated by supporters of the voluntary system. They seized upon a provision within the Forster Act, empowering local boards to make schooling compulsory for children aged between five and thirteen, and used this to more than double school attendance in the town. They did not, however, build a single school and charged a rate so low that they claimed the board to be the cheapest in the country for a town of that size. The Stockport local board was also short-lived, being dissolved in 1879.[216]

The long reliance on voluntary schools in the town placed the council at a disadvantage in 1902, when an Education Act made both elementary and secondary education the responsibility of new Local Education Authorities. This meant that Stockport council now had responsibility for education in its area, while elsewhere within the Borough that duty fell to the county councils. In Stockport the building stock of the

Ill 8.19 Merseyway under construction, in 1939.
In the 1930s, in an ambitious programme of engineering, the corporation covered over the River Mersey between Lancashire Bridge and Mersey Square to create a new road. Known as Merseyway, it was intended to relieve traffic congestion on the older routes through the town.

voluntary schools was found to be inadequate for the town's needs. New sites were bought by the council, and by 1912 six new council schools had been erected, with others being added in the late 1920s and 1930s.[217]

Stockport Technical School and Stockport College

Between 1879 and 1902 there was one educational institution which was under the council's control. This was the Technical School, located on Greek Street, which opened in 1889. It was built in response to a growing awareness, at both local and national levels, that improvement in technical skills was needed if industry was to match the advances made by foreign competitors. The teaching facilities in the new Technical School included art rooms, joinery and engineering workshops, a metallurgical room and a dyehouse. Shortly afterwards a weaving shed was added. Money was initially provided by private benefactors, and included substantial donations from Joseph Leigh, mayor of Stockport and owner of Meadow Mill in Portwood, and from the estate of Sir Joseph Whitworth who died in 1887. Whitworth, a pioneer of precision engineering and the inventor of the standard screw thread, is most closely associated with Manchester, but previous members of his family had resided in Stockport for at least 200 years. The Technical School was donated to the corporation by its governing committee in 1892.[218]

In 1927 the Technical School was reorganized as Stockport College for Further Education. In 1935 it had 1700 students, and the number greatly increased in the post-war period. Today as Stockport College of Further and Higher Education, it is one of the country's largest centres of further education. By the early 1990s 15,000 students were enrolled on full-time and other courses.[219]

LEISURE

Public parks and recreation grounds

Vernon Park

The public park was largely an innovation of the 1830s and 1840s. At that date it was viewed as a means of 'improving' the working class, particularly if it could divert their attention away from the public house. Stockport's first public park was Vernon Park, established on what had previously been farmland, known as Stringer's Fields (Ill 8.20). Most of this land was offered to the corporation in 1844 by Lord Vernon. He proposed

to retain the areas immediately fronting New Bridge Lane and New Zealand Road, as building plots, but in 1851 these were bought by a local benefactor, and presented to the corporation. At the time of Lord Vernon's offer, Stringer's Fields were already unofficially used for public recreation – the view across the Goyt valley made this something of a local beauty spot, and it was also a popular place for swimming in the river. Stringer's Fields finally passed into corporation ownership in 1850 along with the manorial rights, but the council showed a reluctance to spend money on improving the site. In 1857 its own market committee forced the issue by buying 47,000 trees and shrubs for just under £50 at auction. The council, after some opposition, ratified the purchase, plans were drawn up for the landscaping of the park and £300 was set aside for their implementation. The park was officially opened in September 1858 before an estimated crowd of over 30,000. The ceremony included the firing of two Russian guns, which had been set up in the park as trophies of the Crimean War.[220] In 1860 a voluntary subscription was raised to build a tower and observatory in the park. The celebrations organized in town to mark the laying of its foundations ended in tragedy. Seven people were trampled to death and others were injured when a crowd rushed down Mealhouse Brow to watch a firework display. Work on the observatory was subsequently abandoned through lack of funds.[221]

Later parks and recreation grounds

Despite the popularity of Vernon Park and the need for other public open spaces, it was only by the casting vote of the mayor that the council in 1868 decided to buy Crowther's Dam and Fields. Situated on the edge of the high ground above the Mersey and the location of an early mill reservoir, this site was opened in 1876 as the Heaton Norris Recreation Ground.[222] The number of corporation parks and recreation grounds gradually increased from about 1890, thanks to donations of land by public benefactors and a greater willingness on the part of the council to commit public funds. The Woodbank estate, adjoining Vernon Park, was presented to the corporation in 1921 as a memorial to the dead of the First World War.[223] In Marple Urban District, Memorial Park, which opened in the following year, originated with a similar gift.[224]

Museums, libraries and stately homes

Vernon Park Museum

Amid the euphoria of the opening of Vernon Park, the town's two MPs, James Kershaw and John Benjamin

Ill 8.20 Vernon Park, about 1905.
Stockport's first municipal park, straddling the slope of the Goyt valley to the east of the town, was opened with great celebration in 1858. It was named after Lord Vernon who had donated the land to the corporation.

Smith, offered to donate money for the building of a public museum, sited in the park. Under the Public Libraries and Museums Act of 1855 the council was allowed to maintain such a building from the rates, but its members were in no eagerness to do so. It was suggested to Kershaw and Smith that their donation should be used instead for 'a lounge, Park-Keeper's house adjoining thereto, and a store-room for bedding-out plants'. The MPs stuck to their original plan and in October 1860 the town's museum was officially opened. The following February the council agreed to adopt the 1855 Act. Later in that year, Smith loaned to the museum a collection of over forty paintings which he had bought in Rome. These works were later discovered to be not the old masters which Smith believed, but they did have the effect of saving the museum from an embarrassing lack of exhibits. They also encouraged a stream of other donations, which necessitated, in 1866, the enlargement of the building by the addition of a new wing. From 1901 Vernon Park was served by the corporation's tram service, and the following years, until the First World War, saw the museum at the peak of its popularity, with between 50,000 and 60,000 visitors a year.[225]

Libraries

Vernon Park Museum also housed the corporation's first public library until the mid-1870s, when this moved to above the Farm Produce Hall in the town's Market Place. The new premises were more centrally placed, but the smell rising from the market below was at times overpowering until the building's ventilation was sufficiently improved. In 1913 the library moved again, to a new building erected on the corner of Wellington Road South and St Petersgate (*Ill 6.21*). It was erected on the site of the Mechanics' Institute and was the gift of the millionaire benefactor Andrew Carnegie. He is said to have been convinced of the town's need for a new library after being shown photographs of the existing facilities.[226]

The War Memorial and Art Gallery

The establishment of a public art gallery in Stockport was already under consideration in 1919, when it was proposed that this building should incorporate a memorial to the 2200 men from the town killed in the First World War. Voluntary donations funded the construction of the War Memorial and Art Gallery, which was built on the corner of Wellington Road South and Greek Street on a site previously occupied by the grammar school. The building was officially opened in 1925.[227]

Bramall Hall and Marple Hall

In that same year Stockport Corporation attempted to purchase Bramall Hall and its grounds. At the time the property was coming up for auction by its owner Captain Thomas Nevill who proposed to dismantle the building and sell off its fittings if no single buyer could be found. The corporation's offer was rejected and the auction failed to reach the reserve price, but the hall was saved from an unexpected quarter. In a private sale the property was bought by John Davies, a highly successful Manchester businessman and the president of Manchester United FC. In 1935 Bramall Hall was bought from Davies's widow by Hazel Grove and Bramhall UDC. The grounds became a public park and the hall itself was opened to the public, with the first visitors being shown round the building in April 1936.[228]

In the 1930s Marple Hall, once the home of the Bradshaws, was also open to visitors. In the 1950s it was offered to Marple UDC by its owner Richard Isherwood who lived at Wybersley Hall. (Richard was the brother of the novelist Christopher Isherwood who was himself born at Wybersley.) The extent of the repairs needed to the building led the council to decline the offer, and in 1959 it was demolished.[229]

Music halls, theatres and cinemas

In the late nineteenth century the music hall was perhaps second only to the public house as a place of working-class entertainment. Stockport at this time had two music halls and theatres on St Petersgate. One, with a main entrance on High Street, was the New Theatre Royal which opened in 1869 and was later renamed the Grand. The building was pulled down in 1904, and replaced by a new theatre, the Empire. (In 1915 this was renamed the Hippodrome.) The other, in St Peter's Square, was the Theatre Royal and Opera House, built by Frank Matcham, the foremost designer of theatres and music halls of his day *(Ill 8.12)*. It replaced an older building, which was converted from a temperance hall to a music hall in 1869 and was destroyed by a fire in 1887.[230]

It was at the Theatre Royal and Opera House that Stockport's first cinema show was presented in June 1896. The earliest shows were provided by travelling companies. It was not until 1908, when one such company settled in the town, that the cinema became a permanent feature. The venue for those first regular shows was the Mechanics' Institute, later the site of Stockport Central Library. The town's earliest purpose-built cinema, the Electric Theatre, opened in 1912, and stood almost opposite the Mechanics' Institute on a site now occupied by Stockport's main post office. Between 1908 and 1939 twenty-seven cinemas were established in the county borough and thirteen others elsewhere in the Borough, in most cases either in the years before the First World War or during a boom in cinema building in the 1930s. In that later period cinemas were being built on a massive scale and to lavish designs. The first of such 'super cinemas' in Stockport was the Plaza, which opened in 1932 and whose tiled facade still dominates the south side of Mersey Square. The Carlton on Wellington Road South followed in 1937 and the Ritz, situated on Duke Street and with 2343 seats the largest cinema in the town, in 1938.[231]

The great outdoors

The coming of the railways opened up a new field of leisure in the Borough, that of the excursion. Marple quickly became an especially popular destination for Sunday school picnics and day trippers. By 1865 pleasure gardens had been established at Compstall to cater for such visitors. Their attractions included an arcade covered by gooseberry and redcurrant bushes, providing room for 200 diners. After the destruction of Mellor Mill in 1892, the higher of its two main reservoirs was converted to a boating lake, which drew thousands of visitors each year. A nearby packhorse bridge over the River Goyt proved an additional attraction. This had been built in the eighteenth century when it was known as Windy Bottom Bridge. With the advent of visitors a new origin was invented for the structure which now became known as the Roman Bridge *(Ill 8.21)*. The reservoir itself was named the Roman Lakes.[232]

The tramways also brought the countryside closer to the town. Local advertisements encouraged people to travel 'To the Heart of Cheshire by Electric Car'. One account of a tram ride to Gatley described how 'through the pretty village of Cheadle, the passenger can see a vast difference from Brinksway, – creepers clinging to the sides of dwellings in lovely luxuriance'.[233] Some preferred more energetic ways of viewing the countryside, and from the 1880s the beauty spots of the Borough became part of the itineraries of rambling and cycling clubs.[234]

To cater for the influx of visitors, numerous farms and cottages sold refreshments. In the 1930s some also found customers in the owners of chalets. These wooden

Ill 8.21 A family outing at the 'Roman Bridge', about 1910.
The spread of the railways in the nineteenth century made local beauty spots accessible to excursionists. The Goyt valley at Marple and Mellor was a popular resort. Visitors could hire boats on the 'Roman Lakes' and admire the nearby 'Roman Bridge'. The boating lake had in fact been constructed in about 1790 as one of the reservoirs serving Samuel Oldknow's Mellor Mill, destroyed by fire in 1892, while the bridge had been built in the eighteenth century as a crossing for packhorses.

shacks, built on land leased by farmers, were used for weekend country breaks and longer holidays. Examples were to be found alongside the Norbury Brook. There was also a sizeable number on Ludworth Moor; they and their occupants, mainly young people from Manchester, were a cause of complaint among local residents and the shacks were eventually removed by Marple UDC in the 1950s.[235]

Stockport County FC

In the late nineteenth century sports came to be established on a more organized basis. Stockport County Football Club, the best known and most successful of the local clubs founded during this period, originated with the formation in 1883 of a team associated with Wycliffe Congregational Church. From being known as Heaton Norris Rovers, the team changed its named to Stockport County in 1890, a year after the town had been made a county borough. The club began to play league football in the 1891-2 season as part of the Football Combination, at which time the team was drawing crowds of 2000-4000. After six seasons in the Lancashire League, the team won promotion to the Football League in 1900. At the beginning of the 1902-3 season County moved from Green Lane to its present home at Edgeley Park, previously used by Stockport rugby club. On the 1st of May 1937 the club's record crowd, variously estimated at 26,135 or 27,304, watched County win the League's Division 3 by defeating promotion contenders Lincoln City.[236]

CHAPTER NINE

FROM 1939 TO THE PRESENT

'Those were the nights Stockport saved itself'

INTRODUCTION

The post-war years brought far-reaching local changes. The textile industry, once the driving force of the local economy, contracted in size so as all but to disappear. Hat making also declined, although Stockport was to be one of the country's last centres of the industry. Balancing these losses, other occupations grew in importance. Engineering at first continued on the ascendance begun in the late nineteenth century, but as the late twentieth century progressed this industry was itself to see contraction and the closure of several large firms. The expansion of Stockport's shopping facilities, from the 1960s, ensured the continuing success of the retail trade in the town. The growth of office blocks in the late twentieth century is testimony to the increasing importance of service industries within the local economy. By the 1990s a large proportion of industry within the Borough was based on high technology.[1]

Demolition and redevelopment in this post-war era altered the appearance of some parts of Stockport beyond recognition. Outlying districts also experienced considerable change, as a result not merely of the replacement of the old with the new but also of the continuing spread of suburbia. In the 1950s and 1960s, while the population of the county borough remained fairly static, the number of people living in the urban districts of Cheadle and Gatley, and Hazel Grove and Bramhall roughly doubled. Marple, and Bredbury and Romiley also saw considerable rises.[2] By the 1990s a substantial proportion of the Borough, however, retained a rural or semi-rural character, with a quarter of its area being Green Belt.[3] A growing ecological awareness in the late twentieth century also resulted in a more general 'greening', as trees were planted either as part of council policy or by private initiative.

There were sweeping changes in local government. In 1972 an Act of Parliament redrew the map of local administration across the country. Among the provisions of this legislation, which came into effect on the 1st of April 1974, was the creation of Stockport Metropolitan Borough, formed by the amalgamation of the county borough and Bredbury and Romiley, Cheadle and Gatley, Hazel Grove and Bramhall, and Marple urban districts. The Borough was one of ten districts which now made up the new Greater Manchester County. This two-tier system of local government included the amalgamation of the county borough's police force and fire service with those of other member districts. (The corporation's transport department had merged in 1969 with those of ten other local authorities in the Manchester area.) The Greater Manchester Council was abolished, along with other metropolitan councils, by the Conservative government in 1986. That Act, it should be added, did not abolish the county of Greater Manchester.

Other changes occurred in the field of transport. The last half of the twentieth century saw the disappearance of local trams, the reduction of the local railway network, the arrival of the motorways and the growth of Manchester International Airport which lies immediately beyond the Borough's south-western boundary. The pattern of local leisure facilities also altered. The multitude of cinemas which were once scattered across the town disappeared in the face of competition from television. At the same time the local-authority provision of leisure facilities widened, embracing rural as well as urban parks, and creating new museums and other attractions.

New international links were forged. In 1972 the county borough 'twinned' with the French town of Béziers. The relationship was maintained by the Metropolitan Borough, which in 1982 celebrated the tenth anniversary of this link by twinning with Bézier's twin German town, Heilbronn.

The town found a new prominence in the fields of popular music and sport. Strawberry Studio, which was established in 1967 in premises next to Underbank Hall and in the following year moved to a building on Waterloo Road, was the first fully professional recording studio outside London. Its association with the local band 10cc helped it to achieve an international reputation.[4] In 1996-7 Stockport County FC enjoyed its most successful season, winning promotion to the First Division and reaching the semi-final of the Coca-Cola Cup.

The town was also to make news headlines in other, unhappy circumstances. In 1967-8 it was the scene of a bitter and at times violent industrial dispute, after the American-owned textile engineering firm of Roberts-Arundel sacked the workforce for taking strike action.[5]

Ill 9.1 Air raid damage at the LNWR goods depot, Wellington Road North.
Stockport was hit by bombs in a succession of air raids from October 1940 to April 1941. The heaviest attacks occurred on the 22nd and 23rd of December 1941, during a blitz on Manchester – the crater shown above was caused on the second of those nights. The last attack on Stockport occurred in the early hours of Christmas Eve 1944, when a V1 flying bomb, one of a number launched at Manchester, fell on Adswood.

On the 4th of June 1967 Stockport also experienced one of the most tragic events in its history, the crash of an airliner within the town.

The following chapter considers some of the more prominent changes to the face of the Borough in the last half century. It also describes some of the main aspects of the local Home Front during the Second World War, and touches upon the fatal crash of 1967.

THE HOME FRONT, 1939-45

Bombing

The air raids, 1940-1

Although it was feared that the outbreak of war would be followed by the bombing of British towns and cities, there was nearly a year's respite before this nightmare became a reality. Liverpool was the first to suffer a major attack, on four consecutive nights in late August 1940.[6]

Stockport was hit on the night of the 2nd of October 1940, the first of a dozen occasions ending in April 1941 when bombs fell within the county borough. These attacks reached their height during an all-out attack on Manchester on the nights of the 22nd and 23rd of December. They were later described as 'the nights Stockport saved itself', when the emergency services prevented incendiary bombs showered on the town from taking hold. The number of fatalities during these October to April raids was thankfully low. Eleven people are reported to have been killed within the county borough and two others in Cheadle. The highest single number of deaths occurred during the very first raid, when bombs missed the town's gasworks by only a few hundred metres but killed four people in Portwood. The raids demolished private houses, and a remand home on Didsbury Road in Heaton Mersey. The railway goods depot on Wellington Road North was hit, probably by a parachute mine, which left a huge crater and caused considerable damage to railway wagons and delivery vehicles *(Ill 9.1)*. The town, however, escaped lightly compared with the wholesale destruction in Manchester.[7]

On the night of the 7-8th of May 1941 a Heinkel bomber crashed into a field on the edge of Torkington golf course. The plane, returning from the raid, had been shot down by a patrolling Defiant nightfighter. The crew of four bailed out in a line from Cheadle to Hazel Grove and were taken prisoner. This was the only German bomber shot down over Greater Manchester during the war.[8]

The V1 attack

There was an isolated bombing in Stockport in December 1944 when, in the early hours of Christmas Eve, V1 flying bombs were launched towards Manchester from Heinkel bombers off the Yorkshire-Lincolnshire coast. Apart from one bomb which fell in Didsbury, Manchester itself was not hit, but seven bombs landed elsewhere in Lancashire, two in north Derbyshire and six in Cheshire. One of these fell at Garner's Lane

in Adswood. Two houses were totally destroyed, forty-two were seriously damaged and over 700 were affected by the blast. There was one fatality. At Oldham thirty-two people died in this same attack.[9]

Evacuees

The relative safety of the Stockport area, its large population and its ready access via the railway network resulted in the area becoming home to a sizeable number of evacuees. The first to arrive came from Manchester on the 1st of September 1939, two days before war was declared. In anticipation of bombing raids, children, expectant mothers, the blind and some of the disabled were being moved out of the city to less vulnerable areas. Those arriving in Stockport were found accommodation in the rural and suburban districts. Cheadle and Gatley alone eventually housed 12,000 evacuees. Many of those evacuated from Manchester returned home during the first year, before the bombing began.[10] There were, however, to be other evacuees who were found accommodation in the

Ill 9.2 Chestergate air raid shelters.
In 1938 Stockport Corporation began the construction of a system of public air raid shelters without parallel in the region. Below the sandstone cliffs which flank Chestergate, engineers excavated a network of tunnels which could shelter several thousand people. Tunnel shelters were also constructed in Heaton Norris, Portwood and Brinksway.

Ill 9.3 *Halifax bombers at the Errwood Park 'shadow factory', Heaton Chapel.*
In the Second World War, as in the First, Heaton Chapel was an important centre of aircraft production. National Aircraft Factory No 2 had been taken over by Fairey Aviation in the mid-1930s and was used for the manufacture of planes of their own design. Other aircraft, including 600 Halifax heavy bombers, were produced by Faireys at the neighbouring Errwood Park shadow factory.

Borough. June 1940 saw the arrival of 400 refugees from the German occupation of the Channel Islands.[11] A final wave of evacuees began to arrive in Stockport in July 1944, escaping from the flying bomb raids in London and the South.[12]

Stockport's underground air raid shelters

Of all the towns in the region, it was Stockport which offered perhaps the greatest security in the event of an air raid. Refuge could be found not only in conventional shelters but also within rock-cut tunnels specifically excavated by the corporation for this purpose (*Ill 9.2*). The idea originated in 1938 when, as part of a road-widening scheme, property on the south side of Chestergate was demolished, revealing cellars cut into the sandstone cliff. It was initially suggested that these should be extended to form an underground parking area. After the Munich crisis, when war seemed increasingly likely, the possibility was

considered of creating underground air raid shelters. Trial digging into the cliff at Chestergate showed that a tunnel 7 feet (2.1 metres) in width and height could be excavated without the need for shoring and at a fairly low cost. The government initially refused to provide a grant for the work, fearing that a direct hit on a large public shelter might result in massive loss of life. The corporation, however, pressed on with the work and the Chestergate shelters were officially opened on the 28th of October 1939. At this date the complex consisted of two main parallel tunnels, linked by nineteen shorter cross-tunnels, and could accommodate nearly 4000 people. Four other rock-cut shelters were excavated in the town. Two lay on the north side of the Mersey, at Stewart Street and Hatton Street. (Blocked tunnels belonging to these shelters can be seen in the face of the sandstone cutting of the M63.) The others were at Portwood and at Brinksway, the latter serving the population of Edgeley. The shelters were first put to use in September 1940, following the beginning of the Blitz on British cities. They drew people from not only Stockport itself but also Manchester and its suburbs – so many in fact that in 1941 the council introduced a system whereby Manchester residents were required to apply to the town clerk for a place in the shelters. Many people also came to the shelters night after night, whether the air raid sirens had sounded or not. By late October 1940 the Chestergate shelters had 200 such 'permanent residents'. Facilities were primitive. Although there were toilets, most were of the chemical type, made from scrap-iron drums set into the floor, with canvas screens separating the cubicles. Wooden benches were provided along the sides of the tunnels, but not enough for the anticipated number of people. On the 29th of October 1940 it was announced at a council meeting that Stockport was to receive 1000 bunks for use in the town's underground shelters, and that the Chestergate tunnels were to be extended. Eventually those shelters stretched from Lower Hillgate to Mersey Square.[13]

There were still between fifty and seventy people staying each night in the 'Chestergate Hotel' in December 1942. As the threat of bombing receded, the number fell to eight by October 1943. In that month the council decided that there was no longer a need to keep the shelters open and staffed each night. Instead, the keys were kept by on-duty ARP wardens who were to open the doors in case of an emergency. After the war, the shelters were closed and the interior fittings were left largely intact. As we shall see below, this was not to be the end of their story.[14]

The plane makers

Local firms and factories geared their production towards the war effort. Palmer Mill in Portwood, for example, provided anti-gas clothing for the Admiralty.[15] Kay's of Reddish, a firm whose peacetime products included fly papers, were commissioned to produce 'sticky bombs', adhesive covered grenades used as anti-tank weapons.[16] However, it was in the field of aircraft production that local industry made its most outstanding contribution.

Faireys and Heaton Chapel

Wartime manufacture at Faireys in Heaton Chapel reached over thirty planes a week, with final assembly taking place at six hangars at Ringway. At the outbreak of the war, the former National Aircraft Factory No 2 was producing Fairey Battle light bombers, a plane which had been first tested at Barton aerodrome in

April 1937. A Battle manufactured at Heaton Chapel was the first RAF plane to shoot down an enemy aircraft during the war, a Messerschmitt Me 109 over northern France. A total of 1360 Battles were built at Heaton Chapel before their production ceased in 1942. By that date Fairey Fulmar fighters were on the factory's assembly lines. In all, 600 Fulmars were manufactured here. While their production was building up, Faireys received and reconditioned 100 Swordfish biplanes. Like other major aircraft manufacturers during the war, Faireys also undertook the production of planes designed by other firms. In 1938 the government had established a 'shadow factory' at Errwood Park next to the former National Aircraft Factory No 2. This plant was placed under the management of Faireys, which received a contract for 500 Bristol Beaufighters, followed by one for 600 Handley Page Halifax heavy bombers (Ill 9.3). In the later years of the war Heaton Chapel produced over 1000 Barracuda torpedo bombers for the Fleet Air Arm. The Heaton Chapel production lines were supported by parts factories, one being at Reddish. The scale of wartime production required a massive increase in the size of the workforce. In October 1935, shortly after Faireys had begun to move into the Heaton Chapel factory, there were 140 staff. By 1943 the number of employees had risen to 15,000. Six years later it had fallen to 2700.[17]

Avro and Woodford

At Woodford, at the peak of wartime production, Avro's assembly section employed 2529 people and the flight section 480. As in the case of Faireys, wartime production was not limited to Avro's own designs. In 1938 the firm was contracted to build Bristol Blenheim medium bombers. By November 1941, when this work was complete, 1000 had been constructed. In July 1939 the prototype of Avro's own heavy bomber, the Manchester, was tested at Ringway. An order for 200 was placed by the Air Ministry, but the Manchester's Rolls Royce Vulture engines proved to be unreliable. When Rolls Royce stopped production of the Vulture engine, Avro's chief designer, Roy Chadwick, looked to the Rolls Royce Merlin engine, which had proved its power and reliability in the Spitfire and Hurricane fighters. The result was the modified version of the Manchester, equipped with four Merlin engines, which became known as the Lancaster. The first test flight was on the 9th of January 1941 at Woodford. It was also here, on the 31st of October in that same year, that the first Lancaster to be delivered took to the air. By the end of the war the Woodford plant had assembled 4101 Lancasters produced at Avro's factory at

Chadderton or at the Metropolitan-Vickers works in Trafford Park. (In all 7377 were produced, the remainder at other plants.) In August 1943 seven Lancasters were leaving Woodford's production lines every day. Local firms in the Manchester area were involved in the production of parts for the Lancaster, among them Stockport Manufacturing, a metal-working company. The wartime service record of the Lancaster became legendary. Of the total tonnage of bombs delivered by the RAF from mid-1942, two-thirds was dropped from Lancasters. The reputation of the plane also owed much to its part in such individual actions as the Dambusters raid and the sinking of the battleship *Tirpitz*.[18]

INDUSTRY

Textiles

The region's cotton industry had entered a decline in the 1920s. Although the immediate post-war years saw

a brief revival, in the 1950s the downward trend continued.[19] Hollins Mill, in Marple, the last bastion of the combined firm in the Borough, closed in 1956 and was subsequently demolished.[20] To reduce surplus capacity, in 1959 Parliament authorized the paying of subsidies to firms leaving the industry. Three of the Borough's largest remaining spinning mills, the Broadstone Mills at Reddish, the Stockport Ring Mills and Goyt Mill in Marple, closed in the same year, taking advantage of that legislation.[21] By 1962 the spinning capacity of the Stockport district had fallen to less than an eighth of the total less than ten years earlier.[22] In 1970 fewer than 1500 people in the county borough were employed in the cotton industry. 'Stockport', it was said in 1975, 'has ceased to be a cotton town'.[23]

Hatting

Hat making, like the cotton industry, had seen its markets beginning to slip away in the 1920s. In 1942 government pressure led to local hatting firms sharing

Ill 9.4 Merseyway shopping precinct.
Shoppers in Merseyway may be oblivious to the fact that beneath their feet flows the River Mersey. The section of river between Mersey Square and Lancashire Bridge was covered over in the 1930s to provide a new road through the town. In the 1960s this road gave way to a new pedestrianized shopping precinct, extending from the existing shops on Prince's Street to Chestergate and Great Underbank.

factories, production and profits. At the end of the war they resumed their old independence and competition, but in the 1950s and 1960s, to cut costs, Stockport firms were once again working in shared premises. In 1966 the two leading Stockport hatting firms, Christys and Battersbys, and the two largest Denton firms, Moores and Wilsons, were formally amalgamated, and adopted the name of Associated British Hat Manufacturers Ltd. As the industry continued to shrink, the company concentrated its operations at Stockport and the name of Christys was revived. By the early 1970s this was the last substantial hatting firm left in Stockport and one of only four remaining in the region. It outlived those competitors, but in 1997 the announcement was made of the factory's closure.[24]

Engineering

In 1972 engineering was described as the staple industry of Stockport. Three years earlier, two of the Borough's largest engineering firms, Simon Engineering based at Cheadle Heath and Mirlees International at Hazel Grove, had workforces of 3500 and 2500 respectively, far outnumbering the total workforce of the dwindling textile industry.[25]

The face of the local engineering industry itself saw continual change. The motor vehicle industry in the Borough was revived in 1946 when the firm of Crossley Motors transferred its operations from Gorton to the wartime shadow factory at Errwood Park in Heaton Chapel. The works were used for the manufacture of buses. (Crossley Motors had by this date ceased to make cars.) Like the earlier manufacture of cars by Willys Overland Crossley at the neighbouring former National Aircraft Factory No 2, production of buses at Errwood Park was relatively short-lived, coming to an end in 1957.[26] Faireys, Crossley Motors' neighbour at Heaton Chapel, had moved by the early 1960s into the field of nuclear engineering, producing reactor components. By the late 1980s the company had shed its nuclear engineering division, and now supplied portable military bridges.[27] In the changing economy of the late twentieth century, some long-established local firms disappeared altogether. Craven Bros in Reddish closed in 1970. Bredbury steelworks shut in 1983.[28]

Woodford remained an important centre of the aeronautical industry. In 1977 the aerodrome became part of the new British Aerospace. By 1989 a staff of 3000 were employed here, on marketing, design, research, final assembly of aircraft and flight testing. In the 1990s the name of Avro was revived at Woodford with the establishment of Avro International Aerospace,

for the production of updated versions of British Aerospace's 146 airliner.[29]

THE CHANGING TOWN

The 1945 plan

In March 1945 Stockport's borough surveyor published plans for the possible future development of the town. They included the confinement of industry to six main zones, the building of a new market hall to the north of Prince's Street, and the construction of a sports stadium at the brickworks in Heaton Mersey. The implementation of the scheme was impractical in the years of post-war austerity, but some elements of this plan foreshadowed subsequent developments in the town. One proposal in 1945 was the creation of a civic centre on a site bounded by Wellington Road South and Edward Street, incorporating the Town Hall, a new health centre, civic hall and law courts. Today offices housing administrative divisions of the Metropolitan Borough, the magistrates' court and the police station all lie within this general area. The building of a new bus depot on the east side of the viaduct in the late 1960s and of a new bus station between the viaduct and Wellington Road in the 1970s fulfilled a proposal in the 1945 plan to establish a new terminus here at Daw Bank.[30]

From Merseyway to King's Valley

In 1940 work was completed on the culverting of the River Mersey between Mersey Square and Lancashire Bridge to create a new relief road, Merseyway. In the 1960s this road and adjoining property between Prince's Street and Chestergate were redeveloped as an extensive new pedestrianized shopping precinct (Ill 9.4).[31] Its Mersey Square facade in part lies over the site of the county borough's fire station, demolished in 1967 after sixty-five years' use.[32]

At the eastern end of Merseyway, further redevelopment occurred in the 1980s on Warren Street, Vernon Street and Bridge Street. The largest projects here were the construction of Sainsbury's (on the site of Park Mills, demolished in 1979) and Asda, on land between Warren Street and Millgate.

The Warren Street development involved taking down the Warren Bulkeley public house, the facade of which was rebuilt on neighbouring Bridge Street. On the north side of Warren Street, Lancashire Bridge disappeared as the result of further culverting of the river, although a plaque, recording the widening of the bridge in 1891, was recovered and set within a new wall.

Ill 9.5 The M63, west of Stockport Viaduct.
In the 1970s and 1980s the staged construction of a motorway link through the Borough, from Gatley to Bredbury, radically changed the local landscape. At Stockport the M63, following the natural communications corridor of the Mersey valley, passed under the arches of the great railway viaduct and skirted the very edge of the town centre.

This same development saw the demolition of the Buck and Dog, which once stood on the north side of the bridge. Its ornate carved entrance, also dating from the time of the widening of the bridge, was saved and built into the rear of the new property on its site. Alongside it is set an earlier relic from the town's past, an inscription recording a great flood of the Mersey on the 31st of August 1799 and bearing the name of the landlord of the public house at that time, James Brown.[33]

The most striking new development in the town was built in the late 1980s. At Brinksway, on a site close to the M63, offices were built in the form of a massive glass-sided pyramid named King's Valley. The building is now occupied by the Co-operative Bank (*Plate VIII*).

The Market Place

In 1960 Stockport celebrated the 700th anniversary of its market charter. Somewhat ironically, in 1962 and again in the early 1970s plans were put forward for the modernization of the Market Place which involved the demolition of some of its most historic buildings.[34] Although these plans did not come to fruition, by the 1980s a number of these buildings were in a state of neglect. Proposals were made in the late 1980s to demolish Staircase House but were successfully opposed by a local conservation group, Stockport Heritage Trust. This and neighbouring buildings on the north side of the Market Place, together with property on Millgate, are currently being restored by the council. This

redevelopment project also involves the construction of new property, in keeping with the character of the old. The process of revitalizing the Market Place area has been greatly furthered by the council's bid in 1996 to the Single Regeneration Budget, from which £5.18 million has been awarded to the town.

HOUSING

The clearance of slum dwellings halted during the war had resumed by the mid-1950s. The problem of unfit housing was at its greatest in Stockport, where between 1955 and 1967 nearly 6000 houses were demolished by the corporation.[35] The process continued into the 1970s, and on Hillgate and in Portwood swept away the terraced streets which had characterized those communities. New council house estates were built in the 1950s at Bridge Hall in Adswood and at Brinnington, which in 1952 the corporation took over for this purpose from Bredbury and Romiley Urban District. In the 1960s new council housing projects included the building of multi-storey blocks of flats at Lancashire Hill and on Mottram Street off Hillgate, developments which changed the skyline of the town.

In the suburban areas the trend changed from demolition to restoration. What had once been the cheaply rented homes of the working class were to become desirable commuters' dwellings.[36] Compstall, in particular, underwent a remarkable change of fortune. When Compstall lost its urban district council in 1936 and was amalgamated with Bredbury and Romiley, the village built by the Andrews still lacked a sewerage system. It was to remain that way for a number of years, as a result of a reluctance on the part of Bredbury and Romiley to foot the bill. By 1952 it was the view of government officials that the village had only a limited time before it finally died. Local pressure, however, forced a change of heart. The urban district council acquired a long leasehold on most of the property in the village in 1958 and undertook the long-awaited improvements to its sanitation and housing.[37]

THE INFRASTRUCTURE

Gas and electricity

In the late 1940s nationalization of the gas and electricity industries ended Stockport Corporation's control of two local services. It also ended Marple Urban District Council's own provision of gas from the works at Marple Bridge. The Marple gasworks were closed in 1952.[38] In Stockport, coal gas continued to be manufactured at the Portwood gasworks until 1968. The works continued to operate until 1976, producing gas derived from oil and serving a diminishing market as the conversion to natural gas neared its completion.[39] The Millgate electricity power station also remained in operation until 1976, when production ceased as part of a national closure of uneconomic plant. Since 1943 the dominant feature of the site had been a cooling tower, 80 metres high. This was demolished in 1981.[40]

Transport

The end of the trams

From 1947 Stockport's tramway routes were one by one given up in favour of bus services. The services to Hyde and Bredbury were the first to end, followed by those to Manchester. The last corporation tram service, between Stockport and Reddish, ceased to run on the 25th of August 1951, the eve of the fiftieth anniversary of the inauguration of the town's tramway system. This was also the last tram service to operate in Greater Manchester before the establishment of the Metrolink, four decades later.[41]

Railways

In the 1960s, as passengers and freight shifted increasingly to road transport, the Borough's rail network did not escape the closure of stations and lines undertaken by British Railways to reduce its mounting financial losses.

Lack of use by passengers led to the closure of the Middlewood station on the Marple to Macclesfield line in 1960 and of Heaton Mersey station in the following year.[42] Cheadle North, on Manchester Road, closed in 1964.[43] The main losses, however, occurred on the 2nd of January 1967, with the closure of both Cheadle Heath and Tiviot Dale, where the elegant station building was demolished in the following year. The line through Heaton Mersey was taken up in 1969. That through Tiviot Dale disappeared in the 1980s (at Brinnington, a section of this line, including the Brinnington tunnel, became a public footpath).[44] High Lane lost its station in 1970, when the Marple to Macclesfield line was abandoned to the south of Rose Hill. In the 1980s this abandoned railway was converted to a new use as a footpath and bridleway, known as the Middlewood Way.[45]

By the mid-1970s official attitudes towards the railways were more favourable. In 1977 a completely new station was opened in the Borough, to serve the Brinnington estate.[46] Following this, a station was also built at Woodsmoor, on the line between Stockport and Hazel Grove. The late 1980s saw the Borough's best known railway landmark receiving a much needed face-lift, when Stockport Viaduct was cleaned of nearly 150 years' of grime. Floodlighting was installed to illuminate the viaduct, providing a dramatic night-time backdrop to the town.

Motorways

Since the 1970s no fewer than three motorways have been built within the Borough. The first to be opened, in 1974, were the M56 and M63. They bypassed Gatley and joined with each other and with Kingsway at the Borough's own spaghetti junction, encircling Barnes Hospital. (Kingsway, a main south-bound road in Manchester, had been extended across the Mersey in 1959.)[47] The M63 initially ended on the east side of Cheadle, but in the early 1980s it was continued eastwards along the Mersey valley, cutting a swathe through Stockport as far as Portwood (Ill 9.5).[48] Later in the 1980s the motorway was further extended, passing Brinnington and in the process changing from the M63 to the M66, to end, for the time being, at Denton. (In the 1990s work began on the northern continuation of the M66, to complete a circle of motorways around Manchester.)

The junction of the M63 and M66 was planned to take into account a fourth motorway. This proposed A6(M) Stockport North-South Bypass, a continuation of the M66, would pass through the Goyt valley at Bredbury and Offerton and skirt Hazel Grove to link with the A6.

If built, this motorway, would also join with the new Manchester Airport Eastern Link Road, part of which, between Handforth and Woodford, has already been constructed. That road in turn joins with the new Handforth Bypass, which forms a continuation of Kingsway. This junction is the site of a further new development, an out-of-town shopping area.

Manchester International Airport

Ringway Airport, owned by Manchester Corporation, came into operation in 1938. The timing of its establishment enabled it to be used for wartime purposes (which included the training of parachute forces) and to share in the post-war growth in civil air transport. In 1947 about 34,000 passengers used the airport. In 1962, when Ringway was renamed Manchester Airport, the number was over a million. Twenty-one years later it stood at five million. The 1970s brought a further change of name, to Manchester International Airport, and a new joint management by Manchester City Council and Greater Manchester Council. The growth of the airport involved a progressive expansion of its facilities, leading in the 1990s to the commencement of work on a second runway. It has been said that the airport 'arguably does for the region what the Manchester Ship Canal did almost a hundred years ago: it links directly with commerce and industry of the world'. Its location means that the Borough is well-placed to benefit from those links. The reverse of this coin has been the noise pollution, about which the residents of neighbouring Heald Green were already voicing their complaints in the early 1960s.[49]

The Stockport air crash

On the morning of Sunday the 4th of June 1967 Stockport suffered the worst disaster in its recorded history, when an Argonaut airliner carrying holiday makers to Manchester Airport from Majorca crashed at Hopes Carr, off Hillgate. The official enquiry revealed that two of the plane's four engines had ceased to deliver power, one as a result of a design fault which had cut off the fuel supply, the other for reasons which remained undetermined. It was also concluded that the pilot, as the plane rapidly lost height over the town, had deliberately forced a landing at Hopes Carr as the one available open space within the heavily built-up area. Police and other rescuers were on the scene in minutes and managed to extract ten passengers from the plane, but sixty-nine others were killed either by the impact or in a fire which broke out in the fuselage and forced back the rescuers. Three of the five crew members also died.[50]

LEISURE

Cinema and theatre

The Second World War saw cinema-going increase in popularity. It also saw a long-running row over whether the county borough's cinemas should be allowed, for the first time, to open on Sundays. A request for Sunday opening was made to the council by local cinema owners in 1941. Despite their offer to donate £1000 a year to charity, the strength of feeling in favour of keeping Sunday a day of religious observance was such that the plea was rejected. The demand among cinema-goers was shown by the full houses in May 1944, when cinemas were permitted to open their doors on Red Cross Sunday to raise money for prisoners of war. The following year a ballot conducted in the town showed a majority of two to one in favour of Sunday opening, which was finally permitted in 1946.[51]

With the growing popularity of television in the 1950s, particularly after ITV began broadcasting in the area in 1956, local cinema attendances began to decline sharply. There were twenty-nine cinemas in the Borough in the late 1940s. By the end of 1961 the number stood at fourteen.[52] The following year the town's Theatre Royal, in St Peter's Square, was demolished after closing in 1957. It had been one of two theatres in the town during the war. The other, the Hippodrome on St Petersgate, had been converted to a cinema in 1931, but between 1940 and 1951 was once again used as a theatre.[53]

The opening of the Forum in Romiley in 1971 by Bredbury and Romiley Urban District Council provided a new venue for a variety of live shows and other events, but the number of cinemas continued to fall. By late 1997, of the pre-war cinemas in the Borough only three remained open, at Gatley, Heaton Moor and Marple. The last to have closed was the Davenport on Buxton Road, which was also the venue for pantomimes and other live performances. However, following a recent trend, the 1990s also saw the opening of Stockport's first new cinema since 1939, a multi-screen complex in the new Stockport Grand Central. This development on the site of the former coal and goods yard at Edgeley station contains a number of leisure facilities, which include a swimming pool, replacing the public baths on St Petersgate.[54]

Lyme Park, Etherow Country Park and Sykes's Reservoirs

It was a reflection of the optimism in local government in the post-war period that Stockport Corporation took on the responsibility of managing Lyme Park and Hall. The house and over 1000 acres of land had been offered to the National Trust by Lord Newton. Acceptance of that donation was made possible by the corporation's willingness to lease the property from the Trust and shoulder the cost of its maintenance. The hall and park were officially opened to the public in June 1947 and became a major local attraction.[55] In April 1994 their management passed from the Borough council to the National Trust.

Etherow Country Park at Compstall originated in 1965 when Bredbury and Romiley UDC bought land alongside the Etherow between Compstall village and George Andrew's great weir. It was extended with the purchase of land around Keg Pool, above the weir, and the acquisition by the Borough council in the late 1980s of Ernocroft Wood. The park includes the millrace-canal and the remains of the tramroad along which coal from George Andrew's mine in Ernocroft Wood was once carried to the Compstall mills. The park also contains a Site of Special Scientific Interest, while the mill reservoir is used by anglers.[56]

The same use is also made of the extensive reservoirs constructed in the nineteenth century at the Sykes's bleachworks in Edgeley. The works closed in 1986 and houses were built on their site. The reservoirs, however, were bought by the Borough council and the banks landscaped. This new public amenity lies adjacent to Alexandra Park. It is the site of the Sykes's house and private gardens which in the 1900s was acquired from the family by the corporation and opened as a public park.[57]

Canals

Pleasure cruising has a long history on the canals which pass through the Borough. By the 1900s this activity was being encouraged by the Grand Central Railway Company which then owned the Ashton, Peak Forest and Macclesfield canals. The North Cheshire Cruising Club, based at the High Lane wharf on the Macclesfield Canal and founded in 1943, was one of the first to be established in the country. In the years following the war commercial traffic on the local canal network came to an end. Following nationalization in 1948, little maintenance was carried out. While the Macclesfield

Canal and upper level of the Peak Forest Canal (above Marple locks) remained open for pleasure cruising, it seemed that the writing was on the wall for the lower level and for the Ashton Canal. The Stockport branch of the Ashton Canal was officially declared closed in 1962 and was subsequently filled in. The 1960s, however, saw sustained local efforts to maintain the lower level of the Peak Forest Canal. Marple Aqueduct, threatened with demolition because of frost damage, was restored by Bredbury and Romiley UDC, and a voluntary body, the Peak Forest Canal Society, was founded with the aim of achieving the canal's complete restoration. That work, along with the restoration of the main Ashton Canal, was finally authorized by the British Waterways Board and was carried out with the financial support of local authorities and the muscle-power of an army of volunteers. The Macclesfield and Peak Forest canals form part of the 'Cheshire Ring', a chain of inland waterways which also includes the Trent and Mersey Canal and the Bridgewater.[58]

Heritage projects

In the 1990s the Borough council has undertaken a series of ambitious projects for the preservation and presentation of the heritage of the Borough. These have been helped by a variety of sources of funding, including the European Union and the National Lottery. Chadkirk Chapel, now owned by the council, has been restored and opened to the public. The adjoining farm is used for educational visits. The Chestergate air raid shelters, to which visitors had been admitted on the occasional guided tour in the 1980s, have been opened on a regular basis and the facilities enhanced by a new reception area and an audio-visual show. A museum of Stockport's hatting industry has been established in the former Battersby hat factory in Offerton. This is only a temporary arrangement. Work is in hand for a new hatting museum in Wellington Mill, itself once used as a hat factory by the firm of Ward Bros. Staircase House is currently undergoing a restoration, along with neighbouring property in the Market Place. One of these renovated buildings, a large Georgian house on the corner of Park Street, is intended to house a new museum presenting the history of the town. It is planned to develop Staircase House itself as a heritage attraction, fulfilling the ambition of those local people who campaigned to save this important building in the 1980s. Even as this volume was nearing completion, the announcement was made of a successful bid to secure National Lottery funding which will enable Vernon Park to be restored to its Victorian splendour.

Appendix: Population Tables

Township	1664[a]	1754[c]	1774[d]	1801	1811	1821	1831	1841	1851	1861	1871
Bosden	NA			NA	NA	NA	1389	1713	2021	1779	1795
Bramhall	347	534		1033	1134	1359	1401	1396	1508	1615	1960
Bredbury	299	597		1358	1706	2010	2374	3301	2991	3408	3596
Brinnington	90	104		890	1705	2124	3987	5331	5203	5346	5042
Cheadle Bulkeley	337			1577	2509	3229	4228	5463	5489	6115	6927
Cheadle Moseley	390			971	1296	1534	1946	2288	2319	2329	2612
Heaton Norris	290		769	3768	5232	6958	11,238	14,629	15,697	16,333	16,481
Ludworth	238[b]			NA	NA	NA	NA	1476	1578	1640	1735
Marple	304	548		2031	2254	2646	2678	3462	3558	3338	4100
Mellor	280[b]			1670	1760	2099	2049	2015	1777	1733	1447
Norbury	171	313		592	451	680	671	808	848	1305	1291
Offerton	119	169		351	493	401	431	354	352	297	316
Reddish	195		302	456	532	574	860	1188	1218	1363	2329
Romiley	190	376		825	1015	1181	1290	1465	1364	1468	1804
Stockport	1463	3144		14,830	17,545	21,726	25,469	28,431	30,589	30,746	29,931
Stockport Etchells	238	380		623	627	749	701	749	805	860	977
Torkington	76	161		218	254	293	284	345	358	218	261
Werneth[e]	252	358		1152	1304	1804	3462	3904	3635	3464	3402
Woodford	NA			NA	376	383	403	564	430	392	351
Stockport Municipal Borough[f]								50,154	53,835	54,681	53,014

Key
a – Estimate based on Hearth Tax Returns
b – Figure for 1670
c – Enumeration of Stockport parish
d – Enumeration of Manchester parish
e – Note that much of the growth in Werneth township in the nineteenth century is accounted for by the area of Gee Cross, now part of the Metropolitan Borough of Tameside.
f – The municipal borough included Stockport township, and parts of the townships of Brinnington, Cheadle Bulkeley, Cheadle Moseley and Heaton Norris.
NA – Not available (the figure is included within the return for a wider area).

Sources
1664: CRO Mf 13; LRO Hearth Tax Returns; Edwards 1982
1754 & 1774: Watson Mss, vol 1, 129, SLHL; Heginbotham 1892
1801-71: Harris 1979; Abstracts of census returns

District	1881	1891	1901	1911	1921	1931	1951	1961	1971
Bosden CP	1962	2342							
Bramhall CP	2682	3365							
Bredbury & Romiley UD	5553	5821	7107	8683	9168	10,876	17,818	21,621	28,529
Brinnington CP (part not in Stockport MB)	452	485	502						
Cheadle CP (part not in Stockport MB)	5969								
Cheadle & Gatley UD		8252	10,820	9913	11,036	18,473	31,511	45,621	60,799
Compstall UD			875	908	944	865			
Hazel Grove & Bramhall UD			9791	9631	10,127	13,300	19,674	29,917	39,619
Heaton Norris UD	5797	7164	9474	11,240					
Ludworth CP	NA	1804	1775	1726	1684	1926			
Marple UD	4421	4844	5595	6483	6608	7389	13,073	16,300	23,665
Mellor CP	1242	1096	1218	1711	1876	1712			
Norbury CP	1499	1495							
Offerton CP	358	372							
Reddish UD	5557	6854	8688						
Stockport MB & CB	59,553	70,263	78,897	108,682	123,309	125,490	141,650	142,543	139,644
Stockport Etchells CP	1369								
Torkington CP	244	294							
Werneth CP (part not in Hyde MB)	1107								
Woodford CP	362	332	304	338	413	801			

	1981	1991
Stockport Metropolitan Borough	288,980	284,420

For the various changes in local administrative districts after 1871 see pp 238-9 of this volume.

Key
CB – County Borough
CP – Civil Parish
MB – Municipal Borough
UD – Urban District

Sources
1881-1971: Harris 1979; Abstracts of census returns
1981-91: Abstracts of census returns

Notes

1. Introduction

1. Engels 1971, 52
2. Heginbotham 1882, 54 citing *The Lady Shackerley, a Cheshire Story, by one of the House of Egerton* (1871), 279. The basis of the saying is uncertain. It may have arisen among Royalists in reaction to the support given in Stockport to Parliament during the Civil War or refer to the religious radicalism in the seventeenth-century town.
3. Heginbotham 1882, 313
4. Williams with Farnie 1992, 26 citing W H Barker *Journal of the Manchester Geographical Society* 43 (1927), 35
5. Corry 1817, 245-6 wrote of the industrial town, 'Instead of the obscure and miserable place which formerly appeared on the Cheshire side of the river Mersey, a new town was erected as if by inchantment...the scene became equally gratifying, interesting, and important, to the merchant, the philosopher, and the statesman'.
6. Williams with Farnie 1992, 24 citing R H Tawney (ed) *Studies in Economic History: The Collected Essays of George Unwin* (1968), xii
7. Wardle & Bentham 1814
8. For the drift geology of the Borough see Geological Survey of Great Britain (England and Wales) Drift sheet 98 (Stockport) & sheet 99 (Chapel en le Frith) with Taylor *et al* 1963 & Stevenson & Gaunt 1971.
9. For the solid geology of the Borough see Geological Survey of Great Britain (England and Wales) Solid sheet 98 (Stockport) & sheet 99 (Chapel en le Frith) with Taylor *et al* 1963 & Stevenson & Gaunt 1971.
10. On the mosses of the Borough see Hall *et al* 1995.
11. Smith 1910, 24
12. Webb's description of the town and its locality is published in Ormerod 1882, vol 3, 545-6; for the description in Defoe's *Tour* see Unwin 1968, 26.
13. Moss 1894; Wainwright 1899; Fletcher 1901
14. Professor Unwin, of the University of Manchester, was himself born in Stockport in 1870. His *Samuel Oldknow and the Arkwrights: The Industrial Revolution at Stockport and Marple* was first published in 1924.
15. Giles 1985 & 1950
16. Glen 1984; Reid 1974
17. Phillips & Smith 1985 & 1992

2. Origins

1. N Redhead, Greater Manchester Archaeological Unit, personal communication
2. Jackson 1934-5, 74; Harris 1987, 53 'Cheadle (b)'; GMSMR 802
3. Shone 1911, 38, 94; Harris 1987, 53 'Cheadle (a)'; GMSMR 2822
4. *Cheshire Archaeological Bulletin* 4 (1976), 36; Harris 1987, 55; GMSMR 1255
5. Shone 1911, 40, 98, fig 13.2; Harris 1987, 88; GMSMR 801
6. Jackson 1936, 114, pl 7.6; Harris 1987, 87 'Cheadle (b)'; GMSMR 841. A prehistoric origin has also been ascribed to an object found at Gatley and described as a round stone hammer, about 60mm in diameter, 'with perforations on each face' (Shone 1911, 40, 98; GMSMR 3662).
7. Earwaker 1877, 185; Harris 1987, 82; GMSMR 800
8. Jackson 1936, 114; Harris 1987, 87 'Cheadle (a)'; GMSMR 799
9. *CN&Q*, new and enlarged edition, 1 (1896), 144
10. *TLCAS* 30 (1912), 214; Jackson 1936, 113; GMSMR 789
11. *Cheshire Archaeological Bulletin* 4 (1976), 38, fig19; GMSMR 794
12. Phelps 1909, 15; GMSMR 848
13. Tindall 1985, 69
14. *TLCAS* 14 (1896), 150-3; GMSMR 918
15. Shone 1911, 41, 93, fig 14; GMSMR 3665
16. Stockport Heritage Services STOPM L.60.75
17. Correspondence between Charles Roeder and Edward Sykes, engineer and surveyor to Cheadle and Gatley UDC (information provided by Stockport Heritage Services). The subsequent whereabouts of this palstave appear to be unknown and no illustrations have been found, but from the correspondence it was evidently of the unlooped type.
18. Shone 1911, 80, 99, fig 13.5; Davey & Forster 1975, no 34; Harris 1987, 101 'Cheadle (b)'; GMSMR 793
19. Jackson 1936, 115-16, fig 2; Davey & Forster 1975, no 42; Harris 1987, 101 'Cheadle (a)'; GMSMR 798
20. *Cheshire Archaeological Bulletin* 8 (1982), 70, figs 11 & 12; P Wroe, personal communication
21. Burton, *History of Bramhall*, vol 1, 63
22. Shone 1911, 43, 93, fig 16; GMSMR 795; Manchester Museum 28915
23. Burton, *History of Bramhall*, vol 1, 63
24. Hall *et al* 1995, 148
25. *Cheshire Archaeological Bulletin* 8 (1982), 70, fig 13
26. *JCAS*, new series, 46 (1959), 79, pl XII.a; Harris 1987, 88; GMSMR 791
27. Marriott 1810, 378-9; Lowe *et al* 1975-6; Harris 1987, 85 'Marple (a)'
28. Marriott 1810, 376-8, 381-4; Harris 1987, 85 'Marple (b)'
29. Lowe *et al* 1975-6
30. Marriott 1810, 253
31. Nevell 1992a, 38, fig 5.5
32. Harris 1987, 78, 90; GMSMR 792
33. Nevell 1992a, 49-50
34. Nevell 1992b
35. Harris 1987, 216 citing M V Taylor *Archaeologia Cambrensis*, 6th series, 10 (1910), 439
36. Heginbotham 1892, 107
37. Watkin 1883, 55-6; Rylands 1887, 4-5, 66-9
38. Gelling 1978, 153
39. P Wroe, personal communication. I am grateful to Mr Wroe for sharing the results of his own research into the Roman roads of the Borough. The extent to which the account of those roads given in the present work is indebted to his work will be obvious from the following notes.
40. *TLCAS* 4 (1886), 243; Heginbotham 1882, 13; Marriott 1810, 254-5
41. P Wroe, personal communication; Harris 1987, 235
42. Taylor 1950, 274
43. P Wroe, personal communication
44. Richardson 1987, 22 and personal communication. In 1997 a silver coin of Sapor I (AD 241-72), Sassanid king of Persia, was discovered at a depth of about 1 metre during the digging of a garden pond at Whalley Road, Offerton. The find is reported to have been made within a soil also containing fairly modern material. Although it is tempting to relate this coin to the line of the Roman road, its provenance must be considered uncertain (GMSMR 228; N Redhead, Greater Manchester Archaeological Unit, personal communication).
45. Margary 1973, 365
46. Heginbotham 1892, 295
47. Clemesha 1921, 23; Dodgson 1970, 260
48. Ormerod 1882, vol 3, 530; Dodgson 1970, 45
49. Burton, *History of Bramhall*, vol 1, 69
50. Ormerod 1882, vol 3, 530
51. Bredbury Particular and Sales 1825, SLHL

52. *JCAS*, new series, 44 (1957), 54; Harris 1987, 235; GMSMR 786
53. Information provided by Stockport Heritage Services
54. Moss 1894, 5
55. Dodgson 1970, 238, 243
56. Watkin 1886, 78
57. Burton, *History of Bramhall*, vol 1, 69
58. *Britannia* 26 (1995), 348; P Wroe, personal communication; Ormerod 1882, vol 3, 688 n 'b'; Dodgson 1970, 45
59. *Britannia* 26 (1995), 348; P Wroe, personal communication
60. Bruton 1909, ii, 125; Shotter 1990, 225
61. Moss 1894, 2
62. Shotter 1990, 222, 225
63. GMSMR 790; SLHL S/16 26277 & 26279; D & P Seddon, personal communication. For the coin hoard from Alderley Edge see Nevell 1996.
64. Richardson 1987, 18-31; Nevell 1992a, 58-62, 65
65. Earwaker 1880, 5; Ormerod 1882, 539 n 'f'; *Cheshire Sheaf*, 3rd series, 18 (1921), 19 no 4260; Dodgson 1970, 9-10
66. Harris 1987, 235; Richardson 1987, 22; GMSMR 787
67. Dodgson 1970, 293
68. Crump 1939, 130-4; Dodgson 1970, 49-50
69. Richardson 1987, 23-5, 32-4; Nevell 1992a, 61-2
70. Heginbotham 1882, 7-9
71. Heginbotham 1882, 15 & 1892, 88; Watkin 1886, 293
72. Watkin 1886, 294
73. Heginbotham 1882, 12; Watkin 1886, 294
74. Heginbotham 1892, 88
75. *CN&Q*, new and enlarged edition, 1 (1896), 83, 143 & 7 (1902), 153
76. Cf Tindall 1985, 69
77. Marriott 1810, 261; Earwaker 1877, 330 n 'b'; Heginbotham 1882, 15
78. *CN&Q*, new and enlarged edition, 1 (1896), 142-3
79. Bruton 1909, ii, 129; Shotter 1990, 226
80. McLean 1993-4, 19
81. Moss 1894, 3-5; Shotter 1995, 56 & personal communication to T D W Reid, SLHL
82. GMSMR 790; SLHL Frank Mitchell, newspaper cutting 'The mystery of an old Roman track'
83. Clarke 1972, 1; SLHL S/16 26279; GMSMR 790
84. D & P Seddon, personal communication
85. M Nevell, University of Manchester Archaeological Unit, personal communication
86. GMSMR 842; Harris 1987, 231
87. SLHL, Frank Mitchell, newspaper cutting 'The mystery of an old Roman track'
88. Owen Mss, vol 26, 21-2; Heginbotham 1892, 136; Hall *et al* 1995, 148
89. *Cheshire Archaeological Bulletin* 4 (1976), 39, figs 20 & 21; GMSMR 846, 847
90. Marriott 1810, 369
91. The only evidence recovered for earthworks in this locality relates to a field, adjacent to the moated Arden Hall. Known as Battle Field, it contained 'two mounds about a bowshot from each other' around which arrow-heads are said to have been found (Earwaker 1877, 479). This last tradition does not appear to have been recorded by antiquarians before the late nineteenth century. Nor does the name Battle Field appear in the catalogue of the sale of the Arden Hall estate in 1825 (Bredbury Particular and Sales 1825, SLHL).
92. Cf Harris 1987, 242-3; Kenyon 1991, 86-7; Higham 1993, 94
93. Dodgson 1970, 31-2, 36; Kenyon 1991, 78; Higham 1993, 77
94. Dodgson 1970, 302
95. Cameron 1959, 144; Gelling 1993, 128-9
96. Dodgson 1970, 247; Higham 1993, 94
97. Dodgson 1970, 256; Gelling 1993, 141-2, 155
98. Cameron 1959, 144-5
99. Cox 1975-6, 62-3, 66
100. Dodgson 1970, 262
101. Dodgson 1970, 287-8
102. Cox 1975-6, 60, 63, 65-6
103. Ormerod 1882, vol 3, 788, 806; Dodgson 1970, 268
104. Ekwall 1922, 30; Mills 1976, 94
105. Dodgson 1970, 290 & 1981, xxii
106. Dodgson 1970, 299
107. Dodgson 1970, 282; Harris 1987, 348 no 66
108. Dodgson 1970, 263, 282, 292
109. Dodgson 1970, 244, 248, 296
110. Dodgson 1970, 258; Gelling 1993, 106, 110
111. Cameron 1959, 143; Cox 1975-6, 66; Kenyon 1988-9, 46-7. See also Nevell 1992a, 88-9.
112. Ekwall 1922, 30; Mills 1976, 125
113. Morris 1983, 13
114. Dodgson 1970, 281-2; Gelling 1993, 27-8
115. Dodgson 1970, 217
116. Dodgson 1970, 239-40; Gelling 1993, 231
117. Earwaker 1877, 266, 322 & 1880, 110; Ormerod 1882, vol 3, 604, 619-20; Heginbotham 1892, 172-3
118. Dodgson 1970, 294-5
119. Kenyon 1988-9, 23-5
120. Higham 1993, 114-16
121. Dodgson 1970, 247, 292
122. Kenyon 1986
123. Heginbotham 1882, 22
124. *TLCAS* 3 (1885), 190
125. Morgan 1978a, R5
126. Harris 1987, 359 no 230
127. Harris 1987, 353 no 129
128. Harris 1987, 359 no 237
129. Harris 1987, 348 no 66
130. Harris 1987, 364 no 308
131. Earwaker 1877, 79; Ormerod 1882, vol 3, 849; Heginbotham 1892, 206-7; Moss 1894, 9-12; Axon 1909, 71-2; Dodgson 1970, 246-7, 292-3; Harris 1987, 364 no 308
132. Morgan 1978b, 1.30
133. Ormerod 1882, vol 3, 834-5, 838
134. Gibbons 1994, 40
135. Dodgson 1970, 268
136. Dodgson 1970, 292; Griffith 1952-3, 159
137. Arrowsmith 1996, 62-6
138. Earwaker 1877, 457-9 & 1880, 78-81; Ormerod 1882, vol 3, 821, 848-9
139. See pp 32-3.
140. Heginbotham 1892, 207; Higham 1993, 207; Arrowsmith 1996, 66-7
141. Dodgson 1970, 263
142. Phelps 1919; Harris 1987, 86
143. Harris 1987, 281
144. Harris 1987, 275-81. It is possible that at least one of the three crosses reported to have been found in the 1870s stood in or next to the Cross Fields, two neighbouring fields documented by that name in the early nineteenth century. These lay on the north side of Gatley Road to the west of Cheadle village, and their site is now bisected by Kingsway (Mitchell 1976-7, 27, 31; Mitchell & Mitchell 1980, 6-7).
145. Dodgson 1970, 212; Higham 1993, 172-5
146. Higham 1993, 175
147. The evidence for Nico Ditch is recently summarized by Nevell 1992a, 78-83.
148. Connor *et al* 1991; Arrowsmith 1996, 54-5
149. Arrowsmith & Fletcher 1993; Hall *et al* 1995, 154
150. Farrer 1902, 328-9
151. Farrer 1907, 65
152. Crofton 1905, 154-61; Richardson 1983 & 1986
153. Hart 1977, 53; Kenyon 1991, 71; Nevell 1992a, 83
154. J Walker, University of Manchester Archaeological Unit, personal communication

3. The Medieval Town and Countryside, 1069-1540

1. Harris 1987, 359 nos 230, 237

2. Higham 1982, 18-19; Harris 1987, 336-7
3. Harris 1987, 348 no 66
4. Morgan 1978b, 1.30M
5. Morgan 1978a, R5
6. Harris 1987, 364 no 308, 352 no 129
7. Higham 1993, 172-4, 200-1
8. Harris 1987, 331-2
9. Cf Higham 1982, 19.
10. Stubbs 1867, 47-8 & 1872, 216-17
11. Heginbotham 1882, 11; Ormerod 1882, vol 3, 788 n 'e'; Farrer 1902, 370-1; Barraclough 1962, 35 & 1988, 192; Pipe Roll Society 1909, 117; 1910, 34 & 1911, 90-7
12. For the confiscation and demolition of castles following the revolt see Allen Brown 1959, 252-4.
13. Earwaker 1877, 349
14. Dent 1977, 3-4; Arrowsmith 1996, 28-31
15. Farrer 1902, 69, 208
16. Earwaker 1977, 337-8, 485
17. Calendar of Inquisitions Post Mortem, vol 1, 30-1; Calendarium Inquisitionum post mortem sive Escaetarum, vol 1, 7
18. Dodgson 1970, 241-2
19. Ormerod 1882, vol 3, 848-50
20. Heginbotham 1882, 112-30; Ormerod 1882, vol 3, 788
21. As well as Stockport itself, the de Stokeports held Mottram St Andrew of the de Spensers. Bredbury and Brinnington were held of the de Masseys of Dunham, as was Stockport Etchells as a separate fee. Poynton and Woodford were held of the Poutrells; Hattersley of the lordship of Longdendale; and Bosden of the de Buctons. Norbury, Torkington, Offerton, Old Withington and a half of Marton were held of the de Ardernes of Aldford, as were the estates in Sharston and Ragel (Calendar of Inquisitions Post Mortem, vol 1, 30-1; see also Ormerod 1882, vol 3, 789).
22. For the medieval castles of Cheshire see Cathcart King 1983, 66-9, giving further bibliographical details. To the list given there may be added Buckton Castle (Nevell 1991, 115-17).
23. Earwaker 1877, 456-7; Ormerod 1882, vol 3, 61 n 'c', 724, 789; Heginbotham 1892, 293-4
24. See p 25.
25. Barraclough 1988, 169-70 no 164
26. Earwaker 1877, 423; Ormerod 1882, vol 3, 823; Heginbotham 1892, 296
27. Earwaker 1877, 264; Ormerod 1882, vol 3, 636
28. Earwaker 1880, 49; Ormerod 1882, vol 3, 839-40; Heginbotham 1892, 295; Barraclough 1988, 403-5 no 408
29. Ormerod 1882, vol 3, 806, 820, 834-5, 838
30. Earwaker 1880, 40, 102; Ormerod 1882, vol 3, 807, 810, 834
31. Farrer & Brownbill 1911, 324; Farrer 1903, 157
32. Farrer & Brownbill 1911, 326
33. Kerry 1893, 67-8, 73-7; Hanmer & Winterbottom 1991, 27-30. The last authors suggest that the grant of 1157 was a confirmation of an earlier grant by one of the Peverels.
34. Hanmer & Winterbottom 1991, 41
35. Earwaker 1877, 338-43 & 1880, 274-81, 286-7; Ormerod 1882, vol 3, 681-7, 792-6
36. Ormerod 1882, vol 3, 682-3, 838
37. Ormerod 1882, vol 3, 806, 812
38. Heginbotham 1892, 153-4
39. Ormerod 1882, vol 3, 813; Stewart-Brown 1916, 107
40. Earwaker 1877, 461-80; Ormerod 1882, vol 3, 820-2, 848; Reeves & Turner 1991, 20-4
41. Earwaker 1877, 457-8 & 1880, 109, 269-70; Ormerod 1882, vol 3, 689, 821, 848, 850
42. Ormerod 1882, vol 3, 823-8
43. Earwaker 1877, 170; Ormerod 1882, vol 3, 622-6, 634; Dodgson 1970, 247
44. Earwaker 1877, 196-7; Ormerod 1882, vol 3, 636
45. Ormerod 1882, vol 3, 619-20
46. Coates 1965, 93-6; Morris 1983, 25
47. Heginbotham 1892, 297, 410
48. See p 23.
49. Coates 1965, 105
50. Stewart-Brown 1925, 230, 239
51. Tait 1904, 44; Morris 1983, 27
52. Coates 1965, 108-9
53. Davies 1961, 7; Bayliss 1992, 22
54. Stewart-Brown 1925, 232, 237-8
55. Stewart-Brown 1925, 229-30, 237, 239
56. Tait 1904, 92-4; Davies 1961, 8-9
57. Stewart-Brown 1925, 215, 230, 239
58. Stewart-Brown 1925, 209
59. Highet 1960, 54, 73
60. Tait 1904, 98, 100; Stewart-Brown 1916, 47
61. Tait 1904, 111-14, 199, 202; Barraclough 1988, 433-6 no 435
62. Earwaker 1877, 334-6; Ormerod 1882, vol 3, 790-1 n 'f'; Heginbotham 1892, 291-3; Tait 1904, 60-108
63. Earwaker 1877, 345-6; Ormerod 1882, vol 3, 790 n 'e'
64. A similar amalgamation of the portmoot and baronial court, between the late fifteenth and mid-sixteenth century, is evident at Manchester (Tait 1904, 57-8).
65. Taylor 1974, 4, Appendix 1. Records of the portmoot and court leet, the earliest dating from 1464 and 1479, are held by SLHL.
66. Heginbotham 1892, 257-8, 266-7
67. Earwaker 1877, 345; Ormerod 1882, vol 3, 790 n 'e'
68. Heginbotham 1882, vol 3, 162-3
69. Stockport Moss Room Rolls, SLHL
70. Heginbotham 1882, 125
71. Stewart-Brown 1925, 243; Davies 1961, 9; Morris 1983, 38
72. Ormerod 1882, vol 3, 829
73. Earwaker 1877, 349
74. Stockport Moss Room Rolls, SLHL. See also Earwaker 1877, 349; DKR 39 (1878), 171.
75. See also Earwaker 1877, 349; Heginbotham 1882, 291; DKR 39 (1878), 6-7.
76. See also DKR 39 (1878), 103-4.
77. See also Earwaker 1877, 188-9; DKR 39 (1878), 233.
78. Stewart-Brown 1925, 214, 219
79. Ormerod 1882, vol 3, 797
80. Stewart-Brown 1925, 130; Phillips 1988a, 21
81. Earwaker 1877, 349; Highet 1960, 49
82. Stewart-Brown 1910, 273
83. Earwaker 1877, 346-7 & 1880, 108-9; Heginbotham 1892, 204-5, 266-7
84. Morris 1894, 402. Oliver Dodge was accused of exporting this cloth fraudulently, under another merchant's mark.
85. Morris 1983, 35
86. Heginbotham 1892, 204-5, 266-7
87. Cunliffe Shaw 1958, 15-22; Varley 1957, 23, 25, 44-6; Nevell 1991, 61
88. Varley 1957, 23-4, 36-8, 49, 55, 307-8
89. Harris 1980, 196, 213
90. Dent 1977, 2-12; Arrowsmith 1996, 17-18, 28-31
91. Dent 1977, 4; Kay 1896; Powlesland 1974, 3-4
92. Arrowsmith 1996, 28, 31
93. Earwaker 1877, 347; Dodgson 1970, 296; Stockport Moss Room Rolls, SLHL; Cheshire Sheaf, 3rd series, 18 (1921), 111 no 4484
94. Smith 1977, 14-15; Hartwell & Bryant 1985, 76-8; Arrowsmith 1996, 16-17; Phillips 1988b
95. Heginbotham 1882, 290; Arrowsmith 1996, 34-5
96. Smith 1910, 24
97. Morris 1983, 36-7, 39
98. Heginbotham 1892, 90, however, believed the 'maner place' to be a building later known as Old Farm on New Bridge Lane.
99. Earwaker 1877, 334; Ormerod 1882, vol 3, 790; Heginbotham 1892, 296
100. Ormerod 1882, vol 3, 793 n 'e'
101. Earwaker 1877, 349; Ormerod 1882, vol 3, 629, 797; Heginbotham 1892, 95-6; Stewart-Brown 1916, 47-8; Dodgson 1970, 297

102. Earwaker 1877, 420; Heginbotham 1882, 290-1; *Cheshire Sheaf*, 3rd series, 55 (1962), 49 no 10,617, 58 no 10,630; Morris 1983, 38

103. See pp 15-16.

104. Harrison 1894, 10-11, 14

105. Heginbotham 1892, 96

106. Ormerod 1882, vol 3, 545

107. Coutie 1992, 32-3

108. Earwaker 1877, 349; Dodgson 1970, 296; Heginbotham 1892, 91

109. Barraclough 1957, 30-1

110. Groves, nd, 14 & 1990-1, 36, 40

111. Dodgson 1970, 218-19 (Woodford), 245-6 (Stockport Etchells), 251-3 (Cheadle), 257 (Bosden), 261-2 (Bramhall), 265-7 (Bredbury), 269 (Brinnington), 286-7 (Marple), 289-90 (Norbury), 291-2 (Offerton), 294 (Romiley), 300-2 (Torkington), 304-5 (Werneth); Cameron 1959, 144 (Ludworth), 146-7 (Mellor). See also Coutie 1989a, 38 on Bramhall.

112. Sylvester 1956, 5-6; Youd 1961, 3, 12; Coutie 1989a, 35

113. Youd 1961, 1

114. Two examples in Bredbury, at Crookilley Farm and Highfield Cemetery, are illustrated in Reeves & Turner 1991, 6, 27.

115. Harris 1987, 353 no 129, 359 nos 230 & 237, 364 no 308

116. Stewart-Brown 1925, 245

117. Farrer 1907, 52, 74-5

118. Ormerod 1882, vol 3, 688

119. Barraclough 1957, 30-2; *Cheshire Sheaf*, 3rd series, 53 (1958), 35 no 10, 377; Dodgson 1970, 253

120. Farrer & Brownbill 1911, 328-9; Ormerod 1882, vol 3, 629; Arrowsmith 1996, 56-9

121. Farrer 1903, 244-9 & 1907, 48-75

122. Tait 1904, 28, 30 n 1

123. Barraclough 1957, 31 (Cheadle) & 1988, 403-5 no 408 (Marple and Wybersley); Ormerod 1882, vol 3, 688 (Woodford); Kerry 1893, 80, 84-5 (Mellor)

124. Barraclough 1988, 169-70 no 164

125. Husain 1973, 25, 34

126. Yeatman 1892, 172; *Calendar of the Charter Rolls*, vol 4, 100; Ashworth & Oldham 1985, 14

127. Piccope 1860, 26; Heginbotham 1892, 154

128. Stewart-Brown 1916, 62

129. Ashworth & Oldham 1985, 15-16, 22

130. Piccope 1857, 79; Driver 1971, 94

131. Dodgson 1970, 253

132. Cf Sylvester 1956, 15.

133. Giles 1950-1, 87-8, 90-1; Hall *et al* 1995, 145, 151; Stockport Moss Room Rolls, SLHL; Heginbotham 1882, 137 n 6

134. Ormerod 1882, vol 3, 688; Dodgson 1970, 219

135. Farrer 1907, 65-6; Crofton 1905, 160

136. Harris 1987, 353 no 129, 359 nos 230 & 237, 364 no 308; Moorhouse 1909, 81; Husain 1973, 28

137. Dore 1972, 20-3, 145-7; Heginbotham 1892, 293-4

138. Husain 1973, 54

139. Kerry 1893, 67-8

140. Harris 1979, 178

141. Earwaker 1880, 5; Ormerod 1882, 539 n 'f'; *Cheshire Sheaf*, 3rd series, 18 (1921), 19 no 4260; Dodgson 1970, 9-10

142. Yeatman 1895a, 209, 211; Kerry 1893, 84-5; Ashworth & Oldham 1985, 15

143. Earwaker 1880, 49; Ormerod 1882, vol 3, 839-40; Heginbotham 1892, 295; Barraclough 1988, 342-3 no 341

144. Barraclough 1988, 342-3 no 341; Dodgson 1970, 16

145. Yeatman 1895b, 241, 301, 302, 305

146. Stewart-Brown 1925, 245-6

147. Yeatman 1895b, 237-9, 301

148. Stewart-Brown 1925, 212, 224

149. Barraclough 1988, 403-5 no 408

150. *Calendar of Inquisitions Miscellaneous*, vol 1, 39; Yeatman 1895a, 211; Kerry 1893, 73-7; *Calendar of the Charter Rolls*, vol 2, 373; Hanmer & Winterbottom 1991, 34-5

151. Earwaker 1877, 334; Ormerod 1882, vol 3, 790; Heginbotham 1892, 296; *Cheshire Sheaf*, 3rd series, 18 (1921), 111 no 4484; Dodgson 1970, 298

152. Dodgson 1970, 253. Note also the place-name Edgeley in Cheadle, 'clearing in an enclosed park' (Dodgson 1970, 248).

153. Dodgson 1970, 210

154. Piccope 1860, 27; Ormerod 1882, vol 3, 806

155. Moorhouse 1909

156. Singleton 1952, 89; Driver 1971, 82; Pevsner & Hubbard 1971, 278

157. Arrowsmith 1996, 56-9

158. Pevsner & Hubbard 1971, 112; Figueiredo & Treuherz 1988, 39-43; Stockport MBC 1992a; Piccope 1857, 76-81; *Cheshire Sheaf*, 3rd series, 19 (1922), 62 no 4614

159. Walker & Tindall 1985, 59-72

160. Ormerod 1882, vol 3, 835-7; Taylor 1950, 272 no 277, 274 no 287; Dodgson 1970, 299; Walker & Tindall 1985, 34-5; Harrop 1983, 8-15

161. Farrer & Brownbill 1911, 326

162. Dodgson 1970, 241

163. *TLCAS* 3 (1885), 192-3; Crofton 1905, 161-4, 167-71

164. Farrer 1903, 246

165. Ormerod 1882, vol 1, 131

166. Burke & Nevell 1996, 32-3

167. Dodgson 1970, 294

168. Tait 1904, 98-102

169. Farrer 1903, 246 & 1907, 61, 64

170. Harris 1987, 347 no 60

171. Barraclough 1957, 31

172. Dodgson 1970, 250; Ormerod 1882, vol 3, 623; Moss 1894, 21-2, 139-40

173. Tait 1904, 100; Watson 1782, vol 2, 202, 211; Heginbotham 1892, 103-4, 300; Earwaker 1877, 349

174. Hart 1886, 17

175. *Calendar of the Charter Rolls*, vol 4, 100; Ashworth & Oldham 1985, 14; Ashmore 1989, 67-9; Marple Local History Society 1993, 13

176. Dodgson 1970, 285; Stewart-Brown 1925, 244; Marple Local History Society 1993, 13, 33; Ashmore 1989, 65-6

177. Ashmore 1989, 69

178. Heginbotham 1892, 244; Farrer 1907, 61; Farrer & Brownbill 1911, 324

179. Ormerod 1882, vol 3, 688

180. Booker 1857, 198-9; Astle 1922, 142; Owen Mss, vol 44, 261-2

181. Ormerod 1882, vol 3, 820

182. *Cheshire Sheaf*, 3rd series, 33 (1938), 104-5 no 7485; Dodgson 1970, 264; Ormerod 1882, vol 3, 821; Stewart-Brown 1934, 8-11; Reeves & Turner 1991, 22, 42

183. Bulkeley 1889, 62; Stewart-Brown 1934, 161-6; Hunter 1974; Marple Local History Society 1993, 33

184. Heginbotham 1892, 154; Earwaker 1880, 10; Ormerod 1882, vol 3, 806; Stewart-Brown 1934, 193-6; Burton 1877, vol 5, 298

185. Arrowsmith 1996, 77

186. William Hope of Bramhall, miller, was buried at Stockport parish church on the 30th of December 1622 (Bulkeley 1889); see also Clemesha 1921, 13, 14, 17.

187. Ormerod 1882, vol 3, 798, 835

188. Ormerod 1882, vol 3, 823

189. Nevell 1991, 119

190. Heginbotham 1882, 274 & 1892, 229-30; Bennett 1972, 7, 23

191. Earwaker 1877, 380-1; Heginbotham 1882, 186-8, 285-6

192. Ormerod 1882, vol 3, 630-1, 685, 798-9; Driver 1971, 130; Bennett 1972, 7, 10

193. Earwaker 1877, 362; Heginbotham 1882, 186-93; *Cheshire Sheaf*, 3rd series, 19 (1922), 63 no 4618

194. Earwaker 1877, 198-211; Chivers 1995

195. Earwaker 1877, 212-13, 239-44; Ormerod 1882, vol 3, 632,

638-9; Moss 1894, 76-7; Chivers 1995, 11, 30 n 17

196. Earwaker 1877, 356-65; Ormerod 1882, vol 3, 804; Heginbotham 1882, 197-203; *Cheshire Sheaf*, 3rd series, 19 (1922), 62, no 4614; Varley 1957, 41-3

197. Cox 1877, 218, 221-2; Richards 1947, 232; Ashworth & Oldham 1985, 12; Hanmer & Winterbottom 1991, 37; Marple Local History Society 1993, 18-19

198. Earwaker 1877, 459-60 & 1880, 80-81; Ormerod 1882, vol 3, 707-8, 849; Heginbotham 1892, 207-8; Axon 1909; *Cheshire Sheaf*, 3rd series, 25 (1928), 86; Griffith 1952-3; Arrowsmith 1996, 62-4

4. Building a New World, 1540-1700

1. The early cartographic evidence for the Borough also includes maps of land within the Peak Forest, one drawn in 1589, another in 1640, which include sketches of the church, houses and boundary crosses in Mellor (Cox 1907, 280-306; Ashworth & Oldham 1985, 6, 24); and a plan of the Portwood estate of Sir Robert Dukinfield, dated 1692 (a later copy of which is to be found in Burton 1877, vol 5, 298).

2. Earwaker 1877, 430-3; Gibson 1862-3; Groves 1990-1

3. Phillips & Smith 1985 & 1992; Groves nd & 1994; Lee 1979, 430-3; Oldham 1995. Transcripts of some wills and inventories from Cheadle parish, 1660-1760, are to be found in Trunkfield nd. Members of the Stockport Historical Society are currently transcribing the probate records from Stockport township in the period 1670-1800 for publication (S McKenna, personal communication).

4. The early textile industry in Lancashire has been the subject of detailed studies; see Wadsworth & Mann 1931; Lowe 1972. The early industry in Cheshire has received less attention.

5. Lee 1979, 51-2; Phillips & Smith 1985 & 1992; Groves nd, 53-4 & 1994, 27-8; Wadsworth & Mann 1931, 24, 79; Lowe 1972, 97-8

6. Wadsworth & Mann 1931, 14, 30; Phillips & Smith 1994, 42

7. Phillips & Smith 1985, 6-7, 36-7

8. Phillips & Smith 1985, 1-2; Irvine 1901, 12

9. Phillips & Smith 1985, 85-6, 100-1 & 1992, 323-5

10. Adlington Survey, SLHL

11. Groves nd, 19

12. Groves nd, 53 notes that inventories from Etchells and the neighbouring township of Northenden in the seventeenth century show that almost every household with wives or daughters had at least one spinning wheel.

13. Piccope 1857, 81

14. An early example of this practice may be provided by the inventory of John Browne of Gatley in 1642, who seems to have been a yarn dealer and shearman and also had woollen cloth out 'at weaving', but Groves nd, 53 believes it likely that this cloth was for his own use.

15. Lowe 1972, 53-4

16. Wadsworth & Mann 1931, 30

17. Stockport Moss Room Rolls, SLHL; Earwaker 1877, 347, 349, 350; Heginbotham 1892, 267; *Cheshire Sheaf*, 3rd series, 19 (1922), 63-4 no 4618; Ormerod 1882, vol 3, 352-3

18. Ormerod 1882, vol 3, 353

19. Wadsworth & Mann 1931, 9; Axon 1902, 7; Farrer & Brownbill 1911, 324-5

20. Axon 1902, 4-5

21. Phillips 1987

22. Adlington Survey, SLHL; Phillips 1987

23. Earwaker 1884, 28

24. Phillips & Smith 1985, 7-14, 130-8

25. Phillips & Smith 1985, 103-8; Phillips 1987

26. Adlington Survey, SLHL; Phillips 1987; Phillips & Smith 1992, 156. For the Burdsells' renting of glebe land see the Adlington Survey, SLHL; Phillips & Smith 1985, 34-5.

27. Phillips & Smith 1985, 48-50

28. Phillips & Smith 1992, 215-17

29. Phillips & Smith 1985, 38-9; Oldham 1995, 5

30. Phillips & Smith 1985, 54

31. Lowe 1972, 36-8; Nevell 1991, 87-8

32. Marple Local History Society 1993, 17; Ashmore 1989, 3, 15, 70

33. Earwaker 1884, 29-30; Rylands 1880, 253

34. Phillips & Smith 1994, 36-7; Lee 1979, 51; Groves nd, 53-4 & 1994, 28-9; Mitchell & Mitchell 1980, 36

35. Davies 1961, 42-3, 122-4; Calladine & Fricker 1993, 16

36. Heginbotham 1892, 317; Mitchell & Mitchell 1980, 36, 43

37. Kerridge 1985, 79; Calladine & Fricker 1993, 17-18; Wadsworth & Mann 1931, 106-7

38. McKenna & Nunn 1992, 33, 50-1

39. Phillips & Smith 1994, 53-4, 98

40. Phillips & Smith 1985

41. Oliver 1984, 2-3; Phillips & Smith 1985, 55

42. Lee 1979, 48; Shercliff *et al* 1990, 14

43. Oliver 1984, 4

44. Shercliff *et al* 1990, 14

45. Hurst-Vose 1987-8

46. Taylor 1974, Appendix II(c)

47. Willan 1980, 69, 132-4; Mitchell 1975, 125

48. Ormerod 1882, vol 3, 546

49. Gibson 1862-3, 83-93

50. Heginbotham 1892, 410

51. Bloome's *Britannia*, cited by Heginbotham 1892, 96

52. Groves 1990-1, 36-8 & 1994, 20

53. Taylor 1974, 20, Appendix II(a); McKenna & Nunn 1992, 27

54. Thorp 1940, 160-1. For Preston market see Tupling 1945-6, 19.

55. McKenna & Nunn 1992, 47

56. Heginbotham 1892, 99, 300

57. Phillips & Smith 1985, 44-6 & 1992, 248-61; Earwaker 1877, 31

58. Phillips & Smith 1992, 159-71; McKenna & Nunn 1992, 33

59. Phillips & Smith 1985, 63-5

60. Phillips & Smith 1992, 220-3

61. Phillips & Smith 1992, 180-1; McKenna & Nunn 1992, 35

62. Taylor 1974, 20; Earwaker 1877, 31, 353; Heginbotham 1892, 264. For inns in the seventeenth-century town see also Phillips & Smith 1992, 217-19; McKenna & Nunn 1992, 23, 29, 49-51.

63. Heginbotham 1892, 261; Greenhalgh 1887, 49-50; Varley 1957, 108; Groves 1990-1, 38; Giles 1950-1, 89

64. Bennett & Dewhurst 1940, 166

65. Taylor 1974, Appendix V

66. McKenna & Nunn 1992, 3

67. Hodson 1978, 93

68. Blackwood 1978, 8

69. Phillips & Smith 1985, x; Willan 1980, 38-9

70. Earwaker 1877, 406; Bulkeley 1889

71. Willan 1982, 29-33

72. McKenna & Nunn 1992, 4

73. Earwaker 1877, 406; McKenna & Nunn 1992, 35, 49

74. Taylor 1974, 19, 21, 22, Appendix II

75. Heginbotham 1882, 258-9; Willan 1982, 29; Phillips & Smith 1994, 10-11; Rogers 1975; McKenna & Nunn 1992, 4, 63

76. Phillips & Smith 1992, 204

77. Phillips & Smith 1985, 138. The location of this burgage has not been identified.

78. Heginbotham 1892, 299-300

79. Phillips & Smith 1985, 85, 88 & 1992, 153-6, 315

80. Phillips & Smith 1985, 12, 34, 131 & 1992, 177, 206, 237, 254; McKenna & Nunn 1992, 61-2

81. Arrowsmith 1996, 32-3; Stockport Moss Room Rolls, SLHL

82. Heginbotham 1892, 112

83. Phillips & Smith 1992, 191-3

84. Phillips & Smith 1985, 123-9; Arrowsmith 1996, 32. A

banking hall built in 1915 now adjoins the rear of the timber-framed building.

85. Smith 1977; Hartwell & Bryant 1985; Arrowsmith 1996, 19-25
86. McKenna & Nunn 1992, 21, 61-2; Phillips & Smith 1985, 11-13 & 1992, 130-4, 245-6
87. Heginbotham 1892, 105-7
88. CRO Mf 13; McKenna & Nunn 1992, 24
89. McKenna & Nunn 1992, 52-7
90. Phillips & Smith 1994, 8
91. See Appendix.
92. One hamlet known at this time formed the nucleus of the later Bramhall village. A group of timber-framed houses still stood here in the late nineteenth century when the hamlet was known as Siddall Houses. The place took its name from a family resident here until about 1700 (Earwaker 1877, 455; Dean 1990, 34-7).
93. Earwaker 1880, 42, 102; Nevell 1994, 80
94. Earwaker 1877, 460
95. Earwaker 1880, 52-3, 61-2; Ormerod 1882, vol 3, 841-2; Marple Local History Society 1993, 22-3
96. Groves nd, 7 & 1994, 14
97. Earwaker 1877, 460; Ormerod 1882, vol 3, 822
98. Earwaker 1877, 184, 193
99. Gibson 1862-3, 83
100. Morrill 1975, 115
101. Earwaker 1884, 35-6; Lee 1979, 39-44; Groves nd; 1990-1 & 1994, 16-20, 22-6; Phillips & Smith 1985 & 1992, passim. Marl was being used in Torkington by 1465 (Taylor 1950, 274 no 287).
102. Adlington Survey, SLHL; Phillips & Smith 1985, 6 & 1992, 175, 194, 199, 235; Stockport Poor Rate Books 1731 & 1781, SLHL; Davies 1960, 54; Coutie 1992, 32
103. Groves 1990-1, 36-7 & 1994, 16
104. Taylor 1950, 276 no 302, 277 no 305
105. Bennett & Dewhurst 1940, 111; Heginbotham 1892, 92
106. Groves nd, 17-18 & 1990-1, 37. The waste in Reddish is said to have been reclaimed in 1597 (*SH* 5 (1988), 25).
107. Somerville 1977; Ashworth & Oldham 1985, 24
108. Earwaker 1877, 459
109. Earwaker 1877, 477-9; Figueiredo & Treuherz 1988, 237. Burton 1877, vol 5, 137-41 includes a plan of the hall.
110. Booker 1857, 211
111. Arrowsmith 1996, 59; Earwaker 1880, 268
112. Figueiredo & Treuherz 1988, 42
113. CRO Mf 13; Tait 1924, 102
114. Ormerod 1882, vol 3, 545
115. Earwaker 1877, 174-8; Ormerod 1882, vol 3, 624-5. In 1618 Sir Richard Bulkeley built the mansion of Baron Hill outside Beaumaris (Earwaker 1877, 182).
116. CRO Mf 13
117. In 1644, when the incumbent William Nicholls was removed from the living, Humphrey Bulkeley forcibly gained entrance to the rectory and refused to surrender the house to the new rector, Thomas Gilbert. A judgement made in favour of Gilbert noted that two verdicts had already been given against Bulkeley's claim by judges in Chester (Earwaker 1877, 221-2).
118. A late eighteenth-century illustration shows the rectory as a substantial structure, and suggests that at least part of the building was timber-framed. This building was demolished in 1939 and a post office now occupies part of its grounds (Hudson 1996, 24). Moss 1894, 121-2 records two other traditions concerning the location of the manorial hall of Cheadle Bulkeley, one associating it with a building on Massie Street, the other with a moderately-sized timber-framed house, which still stands towards the east end of the village and is said to date from 1664 (DOE *List of Buildings of Special Architectural or Historic Interest: Borough of Stockport*, 5/39). By the early nineteenth century the latter building was known as the 'Manor House', but this is a name which frequently came to be applied to buildings which were not in fact of manorial origin.
119. Earwaker 1880, 268, 273; Ormerod 1882, vol 3, 690-1
120. Ormerod 1882, vol 3, 546
121. Reeves & Turner 1991, 28; Moss 1894, 120-1, 129-32, 138; Seddon 1989
122. Earwaker 1880, 77-8; CRO Mf 13
123. Ashworth & Oldham 1985, 17-18; Lee 1979, 27, 29; Edwards 1982, 54
124. A rare survival is reported in a cottage on Chester Road in Bramhall (DOE *List of Buildings of Special Architectural or Historic Interest: Borough of Stockport*, 6/8).
125. Arrowsmith 1996, 71-3
126. Hartwell & Hunt 1987-8
127. DOE *List of Buildings of Special Architectural or Historic Interest: Borough of Stockport*, 7/158
128. Harris 1984, 21
129. Clemesha 1921; Taylor 1974
130. Heginbotham 1892, 258-60
131. Earwaker 1877, 345
132. Heginbotham 1892, 261-2, 264-5
133. Heginbotham 1882, 171; Taylor 1974, 29, Appendix V(a)
134. Taylor 1974, 28. The Warrens were quick, however, to safeguard the profitable, judicial rights of their own court. In 1613-14 they challenged the hearing of cases of small debt by the earl of Derby's court of the Macclesfield hundred, when these fell within the jurisdiction of their court in Stockport (Coward 1983, 115).
135. Bramhall's stocks were previously at Bramhall Green, near the gates to the hall (Dean 1990, 19), and Marple's at Church Lane (Wainwright 1899, 71). At Mellor, when the old school in the churchyard was rebuilt in 1806, the stocks were used within its foundations. They were rediscovered when that building was demolished in the 1880s (Ashworth & Oldham 1985, 28).
136. Heginbotham 1882, 171-5; Giles 1950-1, 89
137. Heginbotham 1882, 175. On the pre-1790 gaol see p 188.
138. See p 179.
139. Phillips & Smith 1985, 41, 59-60 & 1992, 235; Varley 1957, 63-5
140. Phillips & Smith 1985, 89 & 1992, 175, 201, 231-2; Heginbotham 1882, 275, 277, 302; *Cheshire Sheaf*, 3rd series, 59 (1965), 69-72 nos 11,266, -68, -71; Map of Stockport Glebe Land, 1750, SLHL
141. Clemesha 1921, 17; Shercliff 1974, 41
142. Bennett & Dewhurst 1940, 97-9
143. Varley 1957, 25 (Edmund Shaa 1488); *Cheshire Sheaf*, 3rd series, 19 (1922), 63 no 4618 (Nicholas Elcock, 1536); Piccope 1860, 139 (Robert Arderne, 1540)
144. Earwaker 1877, 217; Ashworth & Oldham 1985, 20; Oldham 1995, 9
145. Phillips & Smith 1985, 40-1
146. Earwaker 1877, 378; Ormerod 1882, vol 3, 880-1. The almsmen had moved in 1884 to new almshouses on Turncroft Lane. By 1952, however, they too were empty and were later pulled down (*SH* 2 (1988), 18 & 10 (1990), 24).
147. Clemesha 1921, 19-20
148. Bennett & Dewhurst 1940, 100-1
149. Taylor 1974, 20-1, Appendix II(d); see also Shercliff 1974, 101.
150. Heginbotham 1882, 167
151. Harris 1984, 11-21
152. Bennett & Dewhurst 1940, 117, 166
153. Bennett & Dewhurst 1940, 42-3, 59-60
154. *Cheshire Sheaf*, 3rd series, 22 (1925), 59-60 no 5253; see also Bennett & Dewhurst 1940, 137-8, 160.
155. *Calendar of State Papers Domestic 1619-23*, 542
156. Wilkinson 1982, 65; Bennett & Dewhurst 1940, 59, 104; Morrill 1974, 166 & 1975, 115-16
157. *Calendar of State Papers Domestic 1634-5*, 434; Taylor 1974, 33-5

158. Morrill 1974, 224
159. Dore nd & 1991, 49-50. The events in the Civil Wars in Lancashire and Cheshire are discussed by Broxap 1973 and Dore 1966.
160. Dore nd & 1991, 41-2
161. Dore 1991, 51-5; Heginbotham 1892, 8-12
162. Ormerod 1844, 45, 52
163. Booker 1857, 227-9
164. Ormerod 1844, 46, 333
165. Earwaker 1877, 429-30; Morrill 1975, 128-9
166. On the career of William Brereton see Dore 1990, 31-59.
167. Hall 1889, 36
168. Hall 1889, 62; Atkinson 1909, 151
169. Earwaker 1880, 62
170. Nevell 1991, 73-4
171. Earwaker 1880, 62; Ormerod 1882, vol 3, 845
172. Dore 1966, 60; Morrill 1974, 80
173. Dore 1990, 27
174. Dore 1984, 330-1. On the Siddalls of Bramhall see n 92 above.
175. Earwaker 1880, 68-9
176. Hall 1889, 44
177. Hall 1889, 62
178. Hall 1889, 32
179. Heginbotham 1882, 12 supposed the reference in the case of Stockport to be to a refurbishment of the walls on Castle Hill. Cf, however, Dent 1977, 2.
180. Hall 1889, 50, 245, 247
181. Hall 1889, 121-2
182. Earwaker 1877, 314-15; Groves 1992, 14-16
183. Broxap 1973, 117; Ormerod 1884, 182
184. Calendar of State Papers Domestic 1644, 193, 206; Hall 1889, 130
185. Earwaker 1877, 430
186. Earwaker 1877, 351
187. Earwaker 1877, 430
188. SH 10 (1990), 15 & 11 (1990), 6; Ormerod 1882, vol 2, 247, 249; Heginbotham 1892, 193
189. Hall 1889, 252; Earwaker 1877, 408
190. Calendar of State Papers Domestic 1644, 188, 194; Earwaker 1877, 430-1
191. Dore 1966, 47-9
192. Morrill 1974, 85-6, 99-106
193. Morrill 1974, 86-7; Earwaker 1877, 432; Dore 1984, 181-2; Heginbotham 1892, 9
194. Earwaker 1877, 432
195. Hanmer & Winterbottom 1991, 51
196. Earwaker 1877, 25, 192
197. Earwaker 1877, 26; Ormerod 1882, vol 3, 708
198. Axon 1902, 10-11
199. Ormerod 1882, vol 3, 634 n 'b'. In 1650 it was reported that profits from the lease of the marquis's manor of Cheadle had been used 'for Irish affairs for some years'. In June 1652 a house within that manor was sold by the Committee for Compounding to Robert Bancroft; and in August of that year the manor itself was bought by Walter Strickland and others. See, for these and other references to the manor under the Commonwealth, Calendar of the Committee for Compounding, vol 1 (1889), 194-5, 242; vol 3 (1891), 2374; vol 4 (1892), 2533.
200. Earwaker 1877, 25
201. Earwaker 1880, 26, 279-80; Calendar of the Committee for Compounding, vol 2 (1890), 1038
202. Ormerod 1882, vol 3, 691; Dore 1984, 122 n 3; Calendar of the Committee for Compounding, vol 2 (1890), 1409
203. Groves 1992, 21, 23
204. Earwaker 1877, 386-7; Heginbotham 1882, 302-3
205. Brownbill 1941, 14
206. The three were Francis and Richard Barton of Woodford, and Robert Renshaw (or Wrenshawe) of Stockport. Other sequestered men who can be placed in the Borough were William Hulme of Woodford, Ralph Grantham of Bredbury, Reginald Ryle of High Greaves and William Skelhorne senior of Stockport. See Catalogue of the Harleian Manuscripts, vol 2, 381 no 1999; Earwaker 1877, 24-5, 27; Calendar of the Committee for Compounding, vol 4 (1892), 2399.
207. Morrill 1974, 203-6; Earwaker 1880, 280; Calendar of the Committee for Compounding, vol 2 (1890), 1038
208. Morrill 1975, 126-7
209. Earwaker 1877, 28-9, 31, 402-3; Heginbotham 1892, 300-1
210. Earwaker 1877, 430-1; Morrill 1974, 107-8
211. Phillips & Smith 1992, 323
212. Earwaker 1877, 432
213. Earwaker 1877, 353
214. Dore 1984, 356, 376-8, 407, 424, 517-20
215. Bennett & Dewhurst 1940, 120
216. Dore 1966, 71; Ormerod 1882, vol 3, 845 n 'a'
217. Dore 1966, 75-6; Earwaker 1880, 64, 68
218. Broxap 1973, 197-9
219. Dore 1966, 86-93; Morrill 1974, 300-25, especially 310, 312-14, 317; Earwaker 1877, 226-30
220. Four members of the gentry, escaping from the battle, were attacked in Stockport parish by 'countrymen' brandishing pitchforks, and were only saved by the arrival of the constable (Parkinson 1845, 141-2).
221. Earwaker 1880, 69-72; Marple Local History Society 1993, 23-7
222. Marple Local History Society 1993, 18; Heginbotham 1892, 190
223. Heginbotham 1892, 200; Ormerod 1882, vol 3, 546
224. Axon 1909, 73; Arrowsmith 1996, 63-4
225. Wark 1971, 49-50, 146, 179
226. Morrill 1974, 18-19
227. Heginbotham 1882, 299-300, 306
228. Morrill 1974, 19-20
229. Dore 1966, 11-12
230. Morrill 1974, 52; Nevell 1991, 73-4 & 1994, 21-2; Dore 1991, 49
231. Earwaker 1877, 221, 388
232. Urwick 1864, xxiv-vi, xxxii-iii; Harris 1980, 102-3
233. Morrill 1974, 264
234. Nevell 1994, 25, 28-31; Heginbotham 1892, 17
235. Nevell 1991, 125
236. Heginbotham 1892, 16, 19-20
237. Earwaker 1877, 222
238. Earwaker 1877, 390-1
239. Earwaker 1877, 33; CRO Mf 13
240. Urwick 1864, 317-19; Earwaker 1877, 403
241. Axon 1909, 73; Griffith 1952-3, 155-6
242. Thacker 1980, 160-70
243. Axon 1909, 73-4; Griffith 1952-3, 166-7
244. Heginbotham 1892, 22; Axon 1909, 76
245. Jolly had been resident in the neighbourhood as early as 1664, but the tradition that he was minister at Norbury in 1662, and was ejected under the Act of Uniformity, seems to be mistaken. John Jolly was probably one of the ministers preaching at Chadkirk Chapel in 1669. See Earwaker 1880, 103; Fishwick 1895, vii-viii; Axon 1909, 74.
246. Swindells 1974a; Marple Local History Society 1993, 35
247. Heginbotham 1892, 58-9
248. Axon 1909, 75, 78

5. Stockport's First Industrial Revolution, 1700-80

1. See p 70.
2. Unwin 1968, 26. Tunnicliff 1787, 67-8 lists four button manufacturers in the town. In the 1790s the Universal British Directory (vol 4, part 1, 477-82) lists only one.
3. Mitchell & Mitchell 1980, 36-43
4. Unwin 1968, 26; Heginbotham 1892, 318
5. Calladine & Fricker 1993, 8
6. Calladine & Fricker 1993, 19-20

7. CRO DVE 10/5, 88
8. Stockport Poor Rate Book 1731, SLHL
9. Calladine & Fricker 1993, 8-9; Calladine 1993-4, 83-7
10. JHC vol 21, 840
11. Stockport Poor Rate Book 1731, SLHL; Unwin 1968, 23-5; Heginbotham 1892, 318; Notes by P M Giles on Abstract of Title of Park Mills 1886, SLHL
12. JHC vol 24, 167, 178, 184; 15 Geo.2 Ch. 14
13. Chaloner 1950-1, 134-7; Calladine & Fricker 1993, 9-10
14. Unwin 1968, 24; Giles 1990, 50
15. Calladine 1993-4, 87-8, 99
16. Calladine 1993-4, 96-7
17. Hadfield 1934, 124-5; Giles 1950, 9
18. Unwin 1968, 27; Hadfield 1934, 125-6
19. Heginbotham 1892, 113, 318
20. JHC vol 34, 240; MM 29 June 1773; Heginbotham 1892, 318, 356; Greenhalgh 1886, 97; Unwin 1968, 22
21. MM 12 May 1773
22. See p 154.
23. Heginbotham 1892, 318
24. Heginbotham 1892, 318
25. MM 16 July 1776
26. Unwin 1968, 26; Wadsworth & Mann 1931, 305 n 6
27. MM 20 September 1785
28. MM 12 May 1776
29. Unwin 1968, 26; JHC vol 34, 240
30. Unwin 1968, 26; Aikin 1795, 445
31. JHC vol 34, 96
32. Hadfield 1934, 136; MM 29 June & 6 July 1773
33. JHC vol 34, 240
34. Hadfield 1934, 126; Unwin 1968, 27; Tunnicliff 1787; Heginbotham 1892, 113
35. Stockport Poor Rate Book 1781, SLHL. The mills were those in the Park and Adlington Square, and others on 'Top of Hill' (High Street), Higher Hillgate, Watson's Square, Chestergate, Churchgate and one seemingly outside the town, at Heaviley or Shaw Heath. Of the shades, three were on Higher Hillgate, the others being on Chestergate and High Street.
36. Hadfield 1934, 126-7; Glen 1984, 32; Unwin 1968, 27, 120
37. Stockport Land Tax Returns 1780, 1784, SLHL; Stockport Poor Rate Book 1781, SLHL
38. *Universal British Directory* (vol 4, part 1), 477-82; Ashmore 1975, 10
39. Holden 1805, 273; Giles 1950, 295-6; Greenhalgh 1886, 97. In the 1790s the *Universal British Directory* (vol 4, part 1), 478 named William Crowther's father, Robert, as a silk manufacturer.
40. In the 1820s the silk industry in the town underwent a modest revival, but this involved the spinning, rather than the throwing, of silk. See pp 151-3.
41. Wadsworth & Mann 1931, 116
42. Aikin 1795, 445; JHC vol 21, 840
43. Wadsworth & Mann 1931, 156; Unwin 1968, 26
44. Radcliffe 1828, 59
45. Wadsworth & Mann 1931, 319
46. Radcliffe 1828, 59
47. Radcliffe 1828, 61
48. Wadsworth & Mann 1931, 472-3; Nevell 1994, 26
49. Wadsworth & Mann 1931, 477, 481
50. Wadsworth & Mann 1931, 487
51. Radcliffe 1828, 61-2
52. Wadsworth & Mann 1931, 305-6, 493-4; Ashmore 1975, 10
53. MM 16 July 1776; Heginbotham 1892, 343-4; Wadsworth & Mann 1931, 495; Coutie 1982, 15; Glen 1984, 31-2
54. Fitton 1989, 28-30
55. Watson 1782, vol 2, 190; Giles 1950, 55; Hurst nd, vol 1, 117-21; SH 12 (1990), 9; Andrews 1935, 179
56. Glen 1979, 15-16 & 1984, 31
57. Wadsworth & Mann 1931, 496-500; Glen 1984, 67-8
58. Glen 1979

59. Giles 1950, 55-6; Baines 1825, 720; Greenhalgh 1888, 64
60. CRO DVE 10/5, 71, 86, 95; Stockport Poor Rate Book 1731, SLHL; CRO DVE 13282
61. SLHL Map Collection 844; Dodgson 1970, 261, 269, 289; Higgins 1924, 28-9
62. Wadsworth & Mann 1931, 307-8 n 5; Phillips & Smith 1994, 97; Glen 1984, 31
63. Graham 1846, 424
64. Aikin 1795, 449
65. Phillips & Smith 1994, 179
66. Phillips & Smith 1994, 98; Unwin 1968, 26
67. Thorp 1940, 161
68. Watson Mss, vol 1, 129, 164; Thorp 1940, 294; Mitchell 1982, 43
69. Phillips & Smith 1994, 68
70. Aikin 1795, 445; Unwin 1968, 26
71. The trade may have been established at Stockport by 1717, when a clockmaker, John Bancroft, is mentioned as owning property in the town (CRO DVE 10/5, 65). In *Cheshire Sheaf*, 3rd series, 55 (1960), 38 no 10,596, Josiah Stringer is named as a clockmaker in Stockport in 1742-50, and James Heaph, James Hopper and H Clarkson in 1770. The inventory of John Shepley, a Stockport clockmaker, survives from 1750 (Mitchell 1975, 325, 373). Lawrence Earnshaw of Mottram-in-Longdendale (1707-67), perhaps the most skilled of all local clockmakers, spent a brief period working for 'Mr Shepley' of Stockport, before setting himself up in the trade. The culmination of Earnshaw's career was the making of an astronomical clock or 'orrery'. Of four which he is reported to have made, one was ordered by William Wright of Stockport and Offerton, another perhaps by Sir George Warren (Nevell 1994, 26-8).
72. These were David Collier and Samuel Kellett (Mitchell & Mitchell 1980, 37; Reeves & Turner 1991, 43-4).
73. Thorp 1940, 30, 250; Stockport Poor Rate Book 1731, SLHL
74. Giles 1950, 61
75. Aikin 1795, 45, 446
76. Mitchell 1975, 89-90, 97-8 & 1982, 43-9
77. Wadsworth & Mann 1931, 358-9; Mitchell 1982, 55-6. A similar fund was set up in Manchester.
78. Aikin 1795, 203; Mitchell 1975, 133
79. Mitchell 1975, 230-2
80. Mitchell 1975, 343-4, 350 & 1980, 50. According to Mitchell the twenty-eight 'hucksters' listed in Stockport in the *Universal British Directory* of the 1790s were almost certainly general provisions dealers.
81. CRO DVE 10/5
82. Varley 1957, 22; Heginbotham 1882, 167 & 1892, 113; Adlington Survey, SLHL; Stockport Poor Rate Book 1731, SLHL
83. Heginbotham 1882, 277-9; Giles 1950, 51-2; Galvin 1986, nos 31, 32. Similar Acts had been passed in 1754 to allow the leasing of glebe land in the expanding towns of Manchester, Bury and Rochdale (Wadsworth & Mann 1931, 312 n 3).
84. Arrowsmith 1996, 26
85. CRO DVE 10/5, 93; Heginbotham 1892, 96; Aikin 1795, 443
86. Andrews 1935, 179
87. Heginbotham 1892, 105-6; Giles 1990, 48, 50-1
88. Heginbotham 1892, 101; Arrowsmith 1996, 35. William Nicols, the rector from 1694 to 1716-17, claimed in a poem to have himself built the rectory, at his own expense (Heginbotham 1882, 313). Possibly this refers to some renovation of that timber-framed building.
89. Heginbotham 1882, 275-6
90. Arrowsmith 1996, 35-6; Reeves & Turner 1991, 25
91. Arrowsmith 1996, 26
92. MacGregor 1992, 66; Stockport Poor Rate Book 1731, SLHL; Ogden 1987, 28; Greenhalgh 1887, 86
93. Greenhalgh 1887, 278-9. The White Lion was also used for administrative business by the JPs; see Heginbotham 1892, 420.

94. Earwaker 1877, 353; Giles 1950-1, 88; Butterworth 1827, 288-9; *CN&Q*, new series, 8 (1888), 24-6, 40-1; *Cheshire Sheaf*, 3rd series, 55 (1960), 117
95. Heginbotham 1882, 327 n 8; Thorp 1940, 112; CRO DVE 13282; Greenhalgh 1887, 85-6, 279
96. Astle 1922, 124; Coutie 1989a, 19, 90; Greenhalgh 1887, 85-6, 254; cf Varley 1957, 121
97. See Appendix.
98. Reeves & Turner 1991, 59-61. In the eighteenth century domestic weavers in the Barrack Hill area of Bredbury specialized in the production of artists' canvas (Reeves & Turner 1991, 55).
99. Ashmore 1989, 70
100. Mitchell 1975, 65-6
101. Norbury 1888 & 1889; Mitchell 1975, 66-7
102. Davies 1960, 50; Coutie 1989a, 77 & 1993, 16
103. Norbury 1888 & 1889; Mitchell 1975, 66-7. See also Coutie 1989a, 37.
104. MM 9 July 1776; Aikin 1795, 448
105. Groves nd, 17-18 & 1990-1, 37
106. Giles 1950-1, 74-9
107. Fletcher 1901, 13-14
108. Davies 1960, 69-70; Ashworth & Oldham 1985, 24
109. Frost & Simpson 1988, 35-8
110. Earwaker 1880, 108
111. Coutie 1982, 18; Walker & Tindall 1985, 34
112. Moss 1894, 150; Ormerod 1882, vol 3, 629
113. Earwaker 1880, 272-3; Ormerod 1882, vol 3, 690
114. Ashworth & Oldham 1985, 18-19
115. Arrowsmith 1996, 59
116. Reeves & Turner 1991, 22; Earwaker 1877, 477-8
117. Ormerod 1882, 835
118. Booker 1857, 211
119. Marple Local History Society 1993, 39
120. Mitchell & Mitchell 1980, 9, 15, 16
121. Phillips & Smith 1994, 102
122. Oliver 1984, 7
123. Shercliff *et al* 1990, 14
124. Oliver 1984, 8-10
125. Oliver 1984, 8
126. Shercliff *et al* 1990, 14-15
127. Yates's map of Lancashire, 1786; Aikin 1795, 451
128. Shercliff *et al* 1990, 15
129. JHC vol 20, 425, 464, 469
130. Harrison 1886, 83-4. A section of the Chester to Whitchurch road, part of the route linking Chester with London, had been turnpiked under an Act of 1705.
131. Wadsworth & Mann 1931, 220 n 2
132. Harrison 1916, 138-41
133. Shercliff *et al* 1990, 35-6
134. Harrison 1886, 88; Phillips & Smith 1994, 85
135. Harrison 1892, 240; Reeves & Turner 1991, 40
136. Heginbotham 1892, 250-1; Smiles 1904, 112, 117
137. Speake 1964, 64
138. Tupling 1952-3, 55-6
139. Turnbull 1979, 15-23, 70; Shercliff *et al* 1990, 40-1
140. Aikin 1795, 442
141. Earwaker 1877, 405 & 1880, 5; Fletcher 1901, 10-12, 16-21; Dodgson 1970, 256 & 1981, xx-xxi; *Cheshire Sheaf*, 5th series, 1977-8, 65 no 128; Trowsdale 1985, 23-4, 35-7; Coutie 1982, 4-5, 18-19
142. Trowsdale 1985, 24. Three of Bullock Smithy's inns can be identified by name in the 1750s, this number increasing to eight by the early 1780s, and ten by 1811 (MacGregor 1992, with which compare Baines 1825, 726-7).
143. Trowsdale 1985, 25-8; Turner 1991
144. Trowsdale 1985, 33, 54. Turner 1991 attributes Bullock Smithy's notoriety to outsiders preying on unwary travellers.
145. Aikin 1795, 449
146. Turner 1991; Fletcher 1901, 32-4; Trowsdale 1985, 33-40; Coutie 1989b
147. Phillips & Smith 1994, 85-6
148. Wadsworth & Mann 1931, 221-2
149. Chaloner 1950-1, 148 n 48
150. Malet 1977, 109
151. Chaloner 1950-1, 145-7; *Kenyon Mss* (1894), 500. The prospectus for the scheme is published in *CN&Q*, new & enlarged edition, 6 (1901), 6-8.
152. Chaloner 1950-1, 140-2, 145, 150-1
153. Chaloner 1950-1, 148; *Kenyon Mss* (1894), 500
154. McLean 1988, 10. On the engagement and elopement see Giles 1990, 51-4.
155. Chaloner 1950-1, 155-6 n 75. The linking of the 'Roe-Warren' canal with the Weaver Navigation may have been prompted by a grander scheme. Since the 1750s a plan had been under way to create a 'Grand Trunk', a canal which by linking the River Trent with the Mersey provided a navigable waterway between the west coast and the east. Until late 1765 it seemed that the northern end of the Grand Trunk might join with the Weaver Navigation. In the event the duke of Bridgewater secured an agreement for the Grand Trunk to join with his own canal. The bill for the Trent and Mersey Canal, passed by Parliament on the 14th of May 1766, included a clause that it should be carried on an aqueduct over the proposed 'Roe-Warren' canal. See Willan 1951, 89-93; Chaloner 1950-1, 146, 150 n 52.
156. Chaloner 1950-1, 150
157. JHC vol 30, 452-3
158. JHC vol 30, 452-3; Chaloner 1950-1, 150-5
159. Hadfield & Biddle 1970, vol 1, 31
160. Thorp 1940, 183-7, 196-7
161. Giles 1990
162. Giles 1950-1, 81-2
163. Giles 1950, 56-7 & 1950-1, 80-82
164. Giles 1950, 89-92
165. Giles 1950-1, 88
166. Giles 1950, 91; Mitchell 1975, 95
167. Giles 1950, 91; Mitchell 1975, 162, 175; Taylor 1974, 35-6
168. Giles 1950, 93; Thorp 1940, 159
169. Newton 1925, 320; Glen 1984, 49
170. JHC vol 35, 153, 190
171. See Giles 1950-1, 85 on the 1785 improvement proposal.
172. On the events of the '45 in the North-West see Smith 1993.
173. Heginbotham 1882, 65; Jarvis 1958, 76-8
174. Heginbotham 1882, 66-7; Earwaker 1877, 33-4; Moss 1894, 57-8; Million 1969, 55-8; Smith 1993, 31-2
175. Heginbotham 1882, 66; Earwaker 1877, 34; Smith 1993, 22
176. Burton 1877, vol 5, 367
177. Heginbotham 1882, 270
178. Jarvis 1947
179. *Kenyon Mss* (1894), 486; Heginbotham 1882, 68; Earwaker 1877, 37-8
180. Heginbotham 1882, 69
181. Heginbotham 1882, 270
182. Jarvis 1947 & 1958, 83-4
183. Davies 1961, 105
184. Heginbotham 1892, 24-5, 28, 50-1, 59-60
185. Urwick 1864, 322; Griffith 1952-3, 168
186. Urwick 1864, 332-3; Marple Local History Society 1993, 35
187. Mitchell & Mitchell 1980, 8, 52
188. Urwick 1864, lxi
189. Ashworth & Oldham 1985, 28
190. Raines 1845, 270; Heginbotham 1882, 87; Mitchell & Mitchell 1980, 52
191. Harris 1980, 108
192. Raines 1845, 295; Heginbotham 1882, 87; CRO Mf 44/2; *Cheshire Sheaf*, 3rd series, 53 (1958), 32 no 10,368
193. Heginbotham 1892, 87
194. Hodson 1978, 41; CRO Mf 44/2; *Cheshire Sheaf*, 3rd series, 53 (1958), 38 no 10,384
195. CRO Mf 44/2; *Cheshire Sheaf*, 3rd series, 53 (1958), 21 no 10,338

196. Shercliff 1976; Mitchell & Mitchell 1980, 52-3
197. Raines 1845, 302; Urwick 1864, 322; Earwaker 1880, 81-2; Griffith 1952-3, 169-70; *Cheshire Sheaf*, 3rd series, 53 (1958), 38 no 10,384; Arrowsmith 1996, 64
198. Booker 1857, 189; Farrer & Brownbill 1911, 325
199. Heginbotham 1882, 115, 236-7; Giles 1950, 52-3; Thorp 1940, 187-8; CRO DVE 13282
200. Heginbotham 1882, 196-7, 212; Varley 1957, 115-16
201. Ashworth & Oldham 1985, 26, 60
202. Richards 1947, 90; Griffith 1952-3, 172; *Cheshire Sheaf*, 3rd series, 53 (1958), 38 no 10,384; Hodson 1978, 48; Addy 1977, 187
203. CRO Mf 44/2
204. McKenna & Nunn 1992, 5
205. Harris 1980, 52-3; CRO Mf 44/2; Hodson 1978, 48
206. Heginbotham 1882, 212
207. CRO Mf 44/2; *Cheshire Sheaf*, 3rd series, 53 (1958), 37 no 10,382; Harris 1980, 53; Giles 1990, 66-7. Watson also visited and recorded archaeological sites in the Stockport area and was an early contributor to the journal *Archaeologia*.
208. Rose 1975, 29-30
209. Rose 1975, 22-3; Marple Local History Society 1993, 61; Heginbotham 1892, 140
210. Rose 1975, 23; Ashworth & Oldham 1985, 28
211. Rose 1975, 25
212. Rose 1975, 26-8; Heginbotham 1892, 64-5
213. Rose 1975, 29-30 & 1982, 84-5
214. Marple Local History Society 1993, 61; Ashworth & Oldham 1985, 28; Rose 1975, 29 with map 4; Hodson 1978, 41; Heginbotham 1892, 64-9
215. Rose 1975, 33-5
216. CRO Mf 44/2; *Cheshire Sheaf*, 3rd series, 53 (1958), 40 no 10,391; Hodson 1978, 41
217. Glen 1996, 3; Rose 1975, 33
218. Fletcher 1901, 26-8; Rose 1975, 30-1
219. Shercliff 1976, 12, 17

6. The Domination of Cotton, 1780-1842

1. Ashmore 1975, 65
2. Henderson 1968, 136; Williams with Farnie 1992, 24-5
3. Glen 1984, 66
4. See Appendix.
5. Giles 1950, 673; Reid 1974, 76-100
6. PP 1842 XXXV; Giles 1950, 673-4
7. Farnie 1979, 223
8. Stockport Land Tax Returns 1780, SLHL; Stockport Poor Rate Book 1781, SLHL; Aikin 1795, 446
9. Giles 1950, 254
10. Giles 1992
11. These trends are based on the dates of their buildings given in returns submitted by thirty-six cotton firms in Stockport, Heaton Norris, Portwood and Edgeley (PP 1834 XX, D1, 2-5, 29-35, 64-85, 165-79). For the economic changes in this period see Edwards 1967, 10-28; Glen 1984, 34-6, 38.
12. Corry 1817, 246
13. See pp 98, 102.
14. Unwin 1968, 119-23; Notes by P M Giles on Abstract of Title of Park Mills 1886, SLHL; Giles 1992, 63-4
15. Heginbotham 1892, 344-5
16. Radcliffe 1828, 35
17. Figueiredo & Treuherz 1988, 284; *Cheshire Sheaf*, 4th series, 3 (1968), 35 no 145. As well as designing houses for wealthy private clients, Harrison's work included substantial new buildings at Chester Castle, the Grosvenor Bridge at Chester, the Shire Hall at Lancaster Castle, and the original Exchange building and the Portico Library at Manchester.
18. Greenhalgh 1886, 260
19. Smith 1994, 16
20. Unwin 1968, 121
21. Notes by P M Giles on Abstract of Title of Park Mills 1886, SLHL

22. Williams with Farnie 1992, 179-80
23. Unwin 1968, 121-2; Nisbet 1991; Aikin 1795, 444
24. Heginbotham 1892, 66
25. Horrocks 1994; Ormerod 1882, vol 3, 629, 807; Farrer & Brownbill 1911, 327; Heginbotham 1892, 152; Chapman 1970, 246
26. Stockport Land Tax Returns 1785, SLHL; R Glen, personal communication. In the 1790s William Hardy, the occupant of the windmill on Lancashire Hill, was listed as a 'miller and cotton-manufacturer' (*Universal British Directory* (vol 4, part 1), 479).
27. Hills 1987-8, 32; Williams with Farnie 1992, 24
28. GMSMR, notes on Guildhall Ms 11937/7 No 636607. On the later history of the Edward Street windmill see Simpson 1990.
29. Hills 1970, 136-7; Unwin 1968, 119 n 1; Giles 1985, 22-3
30. Hills 1970, 162
31. Chaloner 1949, 127, 132; Giles 1985, 26; Hills 1987-8, 32; Heginbotham 1892, 323
32. Chaloner 1949, 132-5
33. Aikin 1795, 176-7; Hills 1970, 149-51. These designs were based on the old, atmospheric type of engine.
34. Chapman 1970, 260. The other factory, belonging to the firm of Matthew Priestnall, Samuel Lee and John Oldham, was at Bullock Croft, in the Thomas Street area off Higher Hillgate (GMSMR, notes on Guildhall Ms 7253/32A No 164320).
35. Greenhalgh 1886, 132, 192
36. The power of steam engines could also be increased by adding a second cylinder, the most common form of this addition being that patented by William McNaught of Bury in 1845 (Williams with Farnie 1992, 88).
37. At the Park Mills, however, in a part used for bleaching, a waterwheel was later replaced with a turbine (Ashmore 1989, 31).
38. Chaloner 1949, 129, 133; Giles 1950, 22-3
39. Giles 1950, 21-2
40. Plans of all the Mills, &c in the Township of Stockport, 1842, SLHL
41. Giles 1950, 16
42. Giles 1950, 17-19; Reeves & Turner 1991, 31 (who place the building of Howard's millrace after the 1833 arbitration). The Marslands themselves owned part of the New Bridge Lane mills, immediately adjoining the property of Jesse Howard (Plans of all the Mills, &c in the Township of Stockport, 1842, SLHL).
43. Unwin 1968, 30-2; Wadsworth & Mann 1931, 496; Hills 1970, 122
44. Unwin 1968, 71-2
45. Hills 1970, 126-8
46. Giles 1950, 29-30
47. PP 1831-2 XV, 432-3
48. Glen 1984, 35; Unwin 1968, 70; Giles 1950, 30
49. GMSMR, notes on Guildhall Ms 7253/32A No 162333
50. There are numerous references in contemporary insurance records. See also Hills 1970, 190-1; Glen 1984, 41.
51. SA 30 May 1823
52. Heginbotham 1892, 369; Giles 1950, 323
53. Fitton & Wadsworth 1958, 193
54. Chapman 1970, 260-1
55. Plans of all the Mills, &c in the Township of Stockport, 1842, SLHL; Chapman 1970, 239, 245, 260
56. Unwin 1968, 199-200; Ashmore 1975, 38-9; Plans of all the Mills, &c in the Township of Stockport, 1842, SLHL. On this mill see also Giles 1985, 25-7.
57. Unwin 1968, 1-2, 4-6
58. Unwin 1968, 69; Giles 1985, 16
59. Unwin 1968, 3-4
60. Unwin 1968, 6-7, 103-4
61. Unwin 1968, 11, 16-17
62. Unwin 1968, v-vi

63. Giles 1985, 49
64. Aikin 1795, 445
65. Giles 1985, 7
66. Unwin 1968, 70-2, 78, 84-5; Giles 1985, 15-20
67. Unwin 1968, 42, 46, 110; Giles 1985, 7-8, 12-14
68. Unwin 1968, 43-5, 105, 244
69. Unwin 1968, 45-7; Aikin 1795, 446
70. Giles 1985, 35-40
71. Giles 1985, 21-2
72. Giles 1985, 28
73. Unwin 1968, 75, 244; Giles 1985, 29-32
74. Unwin 1968, 135-42
75. Giles 1985, 41-2
76. Unwin 1968, 149-51; Giles 1985, 56-8
77. Hills 1987-8, 29-35; Unwin 1968, xi-xv; Giles 1985, 60-1
78. Giles 1985, 42-3
79. Unwin 1928, 156; Giles 1985, 32, 64
80. Scholes 1794 & 1797
81. Unwin 1968, 51, 116
82. Giles 1985, 68, xi n 23, xiv n 66
83. Mason 1981, 59-62
84. Radcliffe, 1828, 9-10, 14-16
85. Radcliffe 1828, 14; Giles 1950, 55-6
86. Scholes 1797; Giles 1950, 29
87. Giles 1950, 37-8, 247; Mason 1981, 61-2
88. Baines 1825, 720
89. Unwin 1968, 124; Aikin 1795, 482
90. Ashmore 1989, 33-4; Unwin 1968, 162-4
91. Ashmore 1989, 32-6
92. Ashmore 1989, 32, 36-7
93. Unwin 1968, 72-83, 85, 149, 156, 194, 200-2; Giles 1985, 52, 57-8, 64, 65, 67-8; Fitton 1989, 235-9. The quotation is from Unwin (1968, 202).
94. Giles 1950, 277-8
95. Ashmore 1989, 3-5, 7, 9, 15, 18-19, 26
96. Radcliffe 1828, 17
97. Ashmore 1989, 4-5, 19, 21-2
98. Ashmore 1989, 6, 7, 9, 15, 19-20, 26; see also Oldham 1995, 14-15.
99. Reid 1979, 22. The other cornmills were Cheadle Higher and Lower mills, Bramhall and Norbury.
100. Reid 1979, 33; Moss 1894, 139. Bowden 1974, 17 mentions a silk mill in Cheadle in 1813, which in 1832 was being used for printing and bleaching, and in 1840 as a cornmill. This site has not been identified.
101. Aikin 1795, 446
102. Offerton Land Tax Returns 1791 & 1796, SLHL; Heginbotham 1892, 205; Preston 1992; Graham 1846. In 1797 the mill was described as comprising a cotton factory, a workshop and an adjoining warehouse (GMSMR, notes on Guildhall Ms 7253/32A No 156307). According to Heginbotham, 'the remains of the foundation' of the second mill could be seen 'in Gnat Hole, below Fogg Brook Bridge'. Greenwood's map of Cheshire, 1819, shows a water-powered site some distance upstream of the bridge, and closer to the confluence with the Mersey.
103. Giles 1985, 55; MM 4 January 1791. The owner was a Thomas Blackburn. The Torkington Land Tax Returns suggest that he acquired the site in 1790 from Peter Legh, lord of the manor and owner of Torkington Lodge.
104. Torkington Land Tax Returns 1814-25, SLHL; SA 14 June & 8 November 1822; Butterworth 1827, 343-4
105. Radcliffe 1828, 65
106. Radcliffe 1828, 11-12
107. Glen 1984, 255
108. Glen 1984, 141
109. Butterworth 1827, 333 described this locality as occupied 'chiefly by operative weavers'. The term 'operative' is normally used of factory workers. Since by 1827 the handloom weaving of cotton had largely been replaced by powerlooms, it is possible that these 'operatives' were former handloom weavers who had made the switch. According to Hearle 1997, 10 in the nineteenth century silk handloom weavers worked in the upper storey of Seventeen Windows.
110. Ashmore 1989, 13 (Holly Vale Mills), 18 (Primrose Mill). At Primrose Mill a terrace of three cottages included a third storey which was open the full length of the row and to which access was provided by an outside staircase. Similar buildings of this type are known along the Pennine fringe; a good example survives to the north-east of the Borough at Broadbottom (Burke & Nevell 1996, 56-8). A pair of weavers' cottages (now modernized and extended) with an external staircase giving access to the third floor also stood close to Damsteads Mill in Mellor (Hearle 1997, 56).
111. Glen 1984, 144, 147, 150-1; Bythell 1969, 68-9
112. Radcliffe 1828, 16
113. Radcliffe 1828, 12-14
114. Radcliffe 1828, 15; Giles 1985, 68
115. Radcliffe 1828, 19-23; Bythell 1969, 67, 71, 83-4
116. Radcliffe 1828, 13, 30, 42
117. Radcliffe 1828, 41-4
118. Radcliffe 1828, 45; Heginbotham 1892, 325-6
119. Williams with Farnie 1992, 25
120. Hills 1970, 216-17
121. Bythell 1969, 74; Hills 1970, 219
122. Heginbotham 1892, 326-7
123. In December 1796 a fire insurance record only mentions Thomas Horrocks having hand-powered spinning machinery at Castle Mill. While the same record shows that he had some powered machinery, this was in a carding room in one of Peter Marsland's mills in the Park (GMSMR, notes on Guildhall Ms 7253/32A No 154849).
124. Radcliffe 1828, 35, 37; Baines 1835, 234; Giles 1950, 35-6, 301
125. Heginbotham 1892, 327-8
126. Radcliffe 1828, 26-7, 36-8
127. Hills 1970, 215-16; Bythell 1969, 77
128. Ure 1836, vol 2, 234; Glen 1834, 37
129. Glen 1834, 37
130. The background to the Luddite attacks on Stockport factories is discussed in detail by Glen 1984, 167-75.
131. Glen 1984, 175; Radcliffe 1828, 4-5, 184
132. Glen 1984, 164, 176-8. In August 1816, during a further slump, a fire destroyed Peter Marsland's powerloom factory at the Park Mills. It occurred three days after an attack on the house of a powerloom weaver at Preston, but was believed to be unconnected and to have started accidentally (Glen 1984, 199-200).
133. Giles 1950, 191-4; Glen 1984, 73-4
134. Bythell 1969, 79. Ure 1835, 38-9, 351 mentions two unnamed Stockport mills using powerlooms made by Sharp and Roberts, 'the principal constructors of power-looms', and a third (that of Thomas Robinson at Spring Bank) using looms 'of a slightly different pattern'.
135. PP 1831-2 XV, 432-3; Baines 1825, 720, 725. These figures include the firm of Samuel Stocks at the Heaton Mersey bleachworks.
136. Giles 1950, 246
137. Butterworth 1827, 282
138. That a manufacturer with powerlooms might also have made use of handloom weavers is illustrated by the case of William Sykes of Edgeley. In 1804 he opened a factory in the former Millgate Hall, where some weaving was carried out using handlooms. By 1813 the factory had been converted to powerlooms, but as late as 1819 Sykes was also putting out work to handloom weavers in Stockport and surrounding villages (Mason 1981, 61-3).
139. Butterworth 1827, 285
140. Giles 1950, 247
141. Giles 1950, 245
142. Glen 1984, 255; Giles 1950, 249
143. Giles 1950, 354-7; Bythell 1969, 200-2

144. Ashmore 1989, 6
145. See Appendix.
146. Giles 1950, 250-1
147. Baines 1825, 725; Pigot 1834; PP 1834 XX, 175; Ure 1836, vol 1, 340; PP 1831-2 XV, 432-3
148. Butterworth 1827, 285
149. Glen 1984, 40; PP 1831-2 XV, 433
150. PP 1842 XXXV, 107. In 1835 an 'excellent mill' in Stockport was spinning using only self-acting mules (Ure 1835, 363).
151. Giles 1950, 24; Baines 1825, 720
152. Glen 1984, 39; Giles 1950, 352-3
153. Giles 1950, 359-71, 408, 411
154. PP 1834 XX, D1; Giles 1950, 412
155. Plans of all the Mills, &c in the Township of Stockport, 1842, SLHL
156. Ashmore 1975, 19
157. Williams with Farnie 1992, 59
158. Greenhalgh 1886, 50-1; PP 1833 XX, D2, 12; PP 1834 XX, D1, 71
159. PP 1834 XX, D1, 78; Arrowsmith 1996, 44-9; Williams with Farnie 1992, 59; Giles 1950, 263-4
160. Ure 1836, vol 1, 335. This figure may include the employees at two smaller factories owned by Marsland in Brinnington; see PP 1834 XX, D1, 78.
161. PP 1842 XXXV, 107; Ure 1836, vol 1, 297-304, 311-12; Williams with Farnie 1992, 76-7; Giles 1950, 292-3
162. Ure 1836, vol 1, 335; Plans of all the Mills, &c in the Township of Stockport, 1842, SLHL; PP 1842 XXXV, 69; Greenhalgh 1886, 87
163. Ure 1836, vol 1, 334-42; PP 1834 XIX, D2, 189
164. Giles 1950, 136; Glen 1984, 71. By 1824 the town's jenny spinners were said to be mostly either 'old pensioners' or 'disbanded soldiers' (Aspin with Chapman 1965, 52-3).
165. Greenhalgh 1887, 145-7, 161, 163-4, 183, 197
166. Ashmore 1975, 10
167. Greenhalgh 1886, 32; SA 14 June 1822; PP 1831-2 XV, 432; Williams with Farnie 1992, 179
168. Giles 1950, 258, 294-5
169. Giles 1950, 300-6
170. Ashmore 1989, 21-2
171. Ashmore 1989, 16-17; Ure 1836, vol 1, 341
172. SA 14 June 1822; Ashmore 1989, 26
173. Ashmore 1989, 24-5
174. Ure 1836, vol 1, 341
175. Ashmore 1989, 27; Ure 1836, vol 1, 342
176. Ashmore 1989, 19-20
177. Ashmore 1989, 7-8, 11, 25
178. Giles 1950, 317-18; Reid 1985, 7
179. Graham 1846, 368 states that the Andrews began printing at Compstall in 1804. According to PP 1834 XX, D1, 90 the earliest part of Compstall Mills was built in 1802. It is likely that this was originally part of the printworks.
180. Earwaker 1877, 406; Graham 1846, 368
181. PP 1834 XX, D1, 89-90; PP 1833 XX, D1, 28-30
182. Brumhead 1989; Thelwall 1972, 27; Wainwright 1899, 35
183. Brumhead 1989; Arrowsmith 1996, 86-7. See also Owen 1977, 102-5.
184. Thelwall 1972, 5
185. Fletcher 1901, 49-50; Heginbotham 1892, 344
186. Nevell 1994, 12-15; DOE List of Buildings of Special Architectural or Historic Interest: Borough of Stockport, 1/227
187. Figueiredo & Treuherz 1988, 260
188. Ashmore 1989, 39, 41
189. See p 101.
190. Baines 1825, 729
191. Baines 1825, 720, 729
192. Giles 1950, 295-7
193. GMAU 1994; Arrowsmith 1996, 40-1
194. Giles 1950, 296-7, 299
195. The firm was that of John Priestnall. See SA 21 November 1834 & 6 March 1835; Pigot 1834; Ashmore 1975, 10.
196. Greenhalgh 1886, 170
197. Ashmore 1975, 10; Reid 1979, 33
198. Calladine & Fricker 1993, 36, 39, 54
199. Coutie 1982, 6, 10
200. Giles 1950, 297
201. SA 14 April 1826
202. PP 1842 XXXV, 9, 13
203. Giles 1950, 297-8; Ashmore 1989, 50; Mitchell & Mitchell 1980, 36
204. Giles 1950, 298-9
205. Higgins 1924, 56-7
206. Universal British Directory (vol 4, part 1), 479-80; Pigot 1834. See also Ashmore 1975, 32.
207. Mason 1981, 60-1, 65-6
208. See p 104.
209. Mason 1981, 68
210. Fitton & Wadsworth 1958, 295 n 2; Giles 1985, 37; Mason 1981, 67; Ordnance Survey 6in to 1 mile First Edition Lancashire sheet 110
211. Mason 1981, 66-7; Glen 1984, 36
212. Giles 1985, 35-6 & 1950, 21-2, 318; SA 9 May 1823
213. Giles 1950, 318, 321
214. Glen 1984, 37-8; MM 16 March 1784
215. Giles 1985, 37-9
216. Graham 1846
217. Glen 1984, 83-4; Graham 1846
218. Marple Local History Society 1993, 49
219. Graham 1846
220. Graham 1846
221. Graham 1846; Giles 1985, 75-7. The Chadkirk estate, of which the printworks were part, was advertised for sale in 1822 (SA 21 June 1822).
222. Baines 1825, 720
223. Arrowsmith 1996, 44; Ormerod 1882, vol 3, 706
224. Pigot 1834; Graham 1846
225. Ashmore 1989, 47
226. Graham 1846; Woodford Women's Institute nd, 16
227. Graham 1846
228. Glen 1984, 189-90
229. Ashmore 1969, 66 & 1975, 34-5
230. Plans of all the Mills, &c in the Township of Stockport, 1842, SLHL
231. Giles 1950, 42; Phillips & Smith 1994, 98
232. Aikin 1795, 446
233. Giles 1950, 42-3
234. Butterworth 1827, 239; Giles 1950, 43, 328 & 1959, 115; Ashmore 1989, 73
235. Heginbotham 1892, 320; Astle 1922, 106, 142-3; Condon 1983, 3
236. Astle 1922, 106-7; Heginbotham 1892, 320
237. Barber 1965, 3-5. The street was named after the long canal-like reservoir, the Upper Carr Dam, which provided water to the Carr Mills.
238. Giles 1959, 117
239. Giles 1950, 325
240. Henderson 1968, 146
241. Barber 1965, 4, 7; Plans of all the Mills, &c in the Township of Stockport, 1842, SLHL
242. Giles 1959, 119
243. Giles 1959, 117-18; Nevell 1993, 40, 73
244. Giles 1950, 327; see also Ashmore 1975, 37.
245. Astle 1922, 143
246. Ashmore 1975, 43
247. Universal British Directory (vol 4, part 1), 478; Holden 1805, 274
248. Baines 1825, 725, 727-8; Greenhalgh 1886, 32
249. Giles 1950, 307. This foundry, belonging to the firm of Johnson and Scott, lay to the rear of houses on Great Underbank, between Underbank Hall and the White Lion inn (Plans of all the Mills, &c in the Township of Stockport, 1842, SLHL).

250. Ure 1835, 38-9
251. Giles 1950, 307
252. Nevell 1993, 99
253. Shercliff *et al* 1990, 15, 25; Chaloner 1949, 129-31
254. Shercliff *et al* 1990, 16, 17, 19
255. Shercliff *et al* 1990, 16
256. Shercliff *et al* 1990, 21, 23-4
257. Winstanley 1995, 146
258. Baines 1825, 721
259. Oliver 1984, 13; Giles 1950, 315-16. Greenwood's map of Cheshire of 1819 shows 'coal' at two sites in Woodley, and also in the bend of the River Tame above Arden Mill.
260. Oliver 1984, 13
261. Oliver 1984, 19
262. Unwin 1968, 216, 220; Marple Local History Society, nd. A list of collieries in and around Derbyshire in 1811 includes three which can be located in Marple township: Chapel-house, Brabins, and abandoned workings at Hoo-lane (High Lane). The first of these is the known colliery site by Oldknow's lime kilns. The same list places an Old-hall-wood colliery two-thirds of a mile west-south-west of Mellor Chapel. This would appear to be the mine at Bottoms Hall noted by Ashmore (1989, 60); in 1811 it was said to be abandoned. See Farey 1811, 192, 193, 201, 206.
263. Farey 1811, 194, 196, 203, 209; Ashmore 1989, 59, 61
264. GMAU 1990; see also Ashmore 1989, 59-60.
265. Ashmore 1989, 59
266. GMAU 1990
267. See pp 114-15.
268. Ashmore 1989, 76
269. Unwin 1968, 222
270. Unwin 1968, 223
271. Unwin 1968, 229-30; Ashmore 1989, 77; Marple Local History Society, nd
272. Ashmore 1989, 77; Marple Local History Society 1993, 52
273. Brumhead 1989, 28
274. Giles 1950, 432-3
275. Mitchell & Mitchell 1980, 44. Cf Greenwood's map of Cheshire 1819.
276. Ormerod 1882, vol 3, 807; Heginbotham 1892, 153
277. Ashmore 1975, 58; Burdett's map of Cheshire, 1777; Nevell 1993, 121
278. Giles 1950, 435-6
279. Giles 1950, 436-41
280. SA 7 July 1826. The change of schedule came too late to alter a commemorative stone set in the bridge, which gave the day of opening as the anniversary of the battle.
281. SA 7 July 1826
282. Giles 1950, 439, 441
283. Arrowsmith 1996, 45-7. The lower part of this mill incorporates an abutment of Wellington Bridge.
284. Giles 1950, 413. Early houses still stand on Wellington Road South; see Galvin 1986, no 134.
285. MM 16 & 23 November 1790
286. Keaveney & Brown 1974, 4-6, 26
287. Hadfield & Biddle 1970, vol 2, 294-6; Keaveney & Brown 1974, 506. Nevell 1993, 103, 122 suggests that two of the shareholders in the Ashton Canal Company, who also had a stake in collieries near Oldham, were unwilling to continue with the scheme which would have benefited the Denton pits.
288. Hodgkins 1987, 73
289. Hodgkins 1987, 73-5. Oldknow's involvement with the canal is discussed in detail by Hodgkins 1977.
290. Hodgkins 1987, 74; Bowyer nd, 42
291. Hodgkins 1987, 77, 80, 81-3; Ashmore 1989, 84; Burton 1981, 1
292. Hadfield & Biddle 1970, vol 2, 306; Bowyer nd, 28, 36-8
293. Hadfield & Biddle 1970, vol 2, 306; Pratt nd, 13
294. Hadfield & Biddle 1970, vol 2, 307-8
295. SA 25 April 1823
296. Unwin 1968 215-21; Hodgkins 1977, 31-2; Ashmore 1989, 51-8
297. Hadfield 1966, 210; Keaveney & Brown 1974, 11, 13; Shercliff *et al* 1990, 16; Shercliff 1985, 87
298. Hadfield 1966, 211-12; Shercliff 1985, 88-9
299. Shercliff 1985, 114
300. Giles 1950, 430-1
301. Hadfield & Biddle 1966, 211
302. Giles 1985, 445-8
303. Burton 1981, 1
304. Giles 1950, 449-52; Holt 1978, 109-10
305. Ashmore 1975, 65; Chapman 1992
306. Holt 1978, 117-20

7. Revolutions in Society, 1780-1842

1. See p 105.
2. Population figures for Stockport and other townships in the Borough are given in the Appendix.
3. The population of Chester in 1801 was 15,052 (Harris 1979, 210). Aikin (1795, 442) reckoned that Stockport was 'probably superior to Chester itself in population'.
4. Giles 1950, 461
5. On James Harrison see pp 129-30.
6. Aikin 1795, 445, 447
7. The estimate is based on the average number of 6.7 people per house given in the 1801 census for Brinnington (Heginbotham 1892, 155).
8. Butterworth 1827, 249
9. Butterworth 1827, 251; Giles 1950, 443
10. Butterworth 1827, 249-50
11. MM 9 July 1776; Giles 1950-1, 89
12. See p 98.
13. Glen 1984, 19-21
14. Giles 1950, 461
15. Glen 1984, 21, 198; Heginbotham 1882, 353-4
16. Kirk 1985, 325
17. Glen 1984, 21-2; Giles 1950, 65, 495
18. Giles 1950, 65-6
19. PP 1842 XXXV, 21, 39-40, 42-3, 105; Engels 1971, 101. Engels's claim that the population of the town decreased by 20,000 at this time is clearly an exaggeration.
20. Andrews 1935, 180
21. See pp 106-7.
22. Byng himself noted how 'in every field adjoining, is land to be let for building' (Andrews 1935, 180).
23. Coutie 1992, 32
24. GMAU 1994, 4; Arrowsmith 1996, 40-1
25. Heginbotham 1892, 87; Abstract of census returns for 1801, 33; Giles 1950, 462. Byng in 1790 reckoned that the number of houses in Stockport was then more than 2000, and about ten years previously the figure had stood at about 700 (Andrews 1935, 180).
26. Aikin 1795, 446
27. Giles 1950, 46-7, 352-3, 413; Glen 1984, 25-6; Steele 1968, 49; PP 1842 XXXV, 20; PP 1847 XIX, 16. Coutie (1992, 37) identifies two main periods of house building in the Hillgate area between 1780 and 1840, the first from 1784 to 1808, the second from 1825 to 1835.
28. Glen 1984, 28-9; Giles 1950, 47
29. Coutie 1992, 35; Giles 1950, 47
30. Glen 1984, 25
31. Giles 1950, 467; Nevell 1993, 138
32. Engels 1971, 52
33. Burke & Nevell 1996, 44
34. Houses of this type on Hillgate are described by Coutie 1992, 38-42 and Hooley 1981, 1-6.
35. Coutie 1992, 51-3
36. Smith 1938, 150; Coutie 1992, 42-7
37. Glen 1984, 27; Coutie 1992, 51-2; Hooley 1981, 7; Giles 1950, 467-8

38. Engels 1971, 52
39. Coutie 1992, 47
40. Swindells 1972, 2
41. Glen 1984, 26
42. Steele 1968, 49; Coutie 1992, 47
43. PP 1842 XXXV, 6
44. Unwin 1968, 16; PP 1842 XXXV, 96
45. Heginbotham 1892, 107; PP 1834 XX, 64 no 45; Mason 1981, 62
46. Giles 1950, 330 n 1
47. Giles 1950, 290. By 1842 this building had been converted to store rooms (Plans of all the Mills, &c in the Township of Stockport, 1842, SLHL).
48. In 1812 the windows of Marsland's Heaton Lane house were broken by Luddite rioters. The action is said to have prompted the family to move to Brabyns Hall in Marple until the completion of Woodbank (Heginbotham 1882, 72 & 1892, 345).
49. Butterworth 1827, 248, 250
50. Giles 1950, 313; Ordnance Survey 6in to 1 mile First Edition Lancashire sheet 110. See also Reid 1985, 1-2.
51. Reeves & Turner 1991, 25
52. Figueiredo & Treuherz 1988, 260
53. Mitchell 1980, 41-4
54. Baines 1825, 721; Butterworth 1827, 246; Giles 1950, 459. The change appears to have been fairly recent. Corry (1817, 249) refers only to the Friday market.
55. Giles 1950, 502-3; PP 1842 XXXV, 99
56. Mitchell 1980, 45; Giles 1950, 504
57. Giles 1950, 501-2; see also PP 1842 XXXV, 27-8, 100-2.
58. Mitchell 1980, 45; PP 1842 XXXV, 1-3
59. Giles 1950, 314-15, 377-83
60. Giles 1950, 409-11; Reid 1974, 262-5; Smith 1938, 465
61. Aikin 1795, 443
62. Giles 1950, 454
63. Giles 1950, 454-5
64. Giles 1950, 455-7. The origin of these buildings is obscure. The 1680 town map shows only butchers' shops at this end of the Market Place. According to Greenhalgh (1887, 243-4) the Meal House was a square, brick building, with a gabled facade, and was in existence by 1745. Heginbotham (1892, 99) states that it was also in 1824 that the old Market House, which stood at the west end of the Market Place, was demolished, but this building appears on later maps of the town.
65. Greenhalgh 1886, 20 & 1887, 243, 253-5; Butterworth 1827, 274
66. Giles 1950, 457-8; Stockport History Trail nd, no 9
67. See pp 140, 154.
68. Andrews 1935, 178; Aikin 1795, 449; Baines 1825, 733
69. SA 14 February 1823
70. Butterworth 1827, 343; Baines 1825, 726-7
71. See pp 116-17, 141, 150-1.
72. PP 1842 XXXV, 124
73. Winstanley 1995, 137
74. SH 2 (1988), 19; Ashmore 1989, 41-2
75. Oliver 1984, 912
76. Butterworth 1827, 331; Unwin 1968, 209-10, 225 n 2; Wainwright 1899, 18. See also Hearle 1997, 37-9.
77. Giles 1950, 282-4. The London Foundling hospital had apprenticed girls to a silk mill in Stockport in 1769 (Glen 1984, 78).
78. Giles 1985, 79-84, xvii n 44; Unwin 1968, 137, 204; DOE List of Buildings of Special Architectural or Historic Interest: Borough of Stockport, 7/124 & 125
79. Marple Local History Society nd
80. Reid 1985, 2, 7, 17; Giles 1950, 314, 317
81. Butterworth 1827, 203; Brumhead 1989, 28; Thelwall 1972, 2-4
82. Ormerod 1882, vol 3, 850; Thelwall 1972, 9; Figueiredo & Treuherz 1988, 226

83. Thelwall 1972; Gent 1997; Marple Local History Society 1993, 67; Hearle 1997, 96-9
84. Scard 1981, 81-2
85. Moss 1894, 61-3; Tate 1978, 79
86. Heginbotham 1892, 136, 153; Hall et al 1995, 141, 148, 155
87. Unwin 1968, 204-14; Giles 1985, 78-9. In 1797 announcement (reproduced in the programme of the Dedication of Marple War Memorial Park & Historical Pageant 1922, SLHL) was made of a winter fair to be held in Marple on the first Thursday in November and a spring fair on the second Thursday in April. These fairs were intended 'for the shew of horned cattle, horses, sheep & pigs'. They appear to have been arranged by Oldknow, and probably stemmed from his own interests in animal breeding.
88. Coutie 1989a, 16, 18, 20, 21, 24, 95; Giles 1985, 79
89. Coutie 1989a, 6, 9, 13, 20, 61-2; Unwin 1968, 206-8
90. Scard 1981, 85-6; SA 5 April, 14 June, 25 October 1822; Ashmore 1989, 47
91. Unwin 1968, 209; MM 20 January 1790
92. Giles 1950, 21
93. Unwin 1968, 207; Coutie 1989a, 35
94. Scard 1981, 83
95. Reid 1979, 29 & 1985, 6. In Poynton output of a kiln which supplied tiles to tenants on the Vernons' estate more than quadrupled between 1845 and 1847 (Shercliff et al 1990, 31).
96. See pp 110-11.
97. Mitchell 1975, 20 citing MM 12 February 1793
98. Giles 1950, 61, 505; Ordnance Survey 6in to 1 mile First Edition, Lancashire sheets 110 & 111
99. Giles 1950, 61; Mitchell 1982, 45; Aikin 1795, 45
100. These were the mill in the Park at Stockport, the mills at Portwood, Reddish, Bramhall, Norbury, Marple Bridge and Ludworth, Arden Mill in Bredbury, and the Higher and Lower mills in Cheadle. See Burdett's maps of Cheshire, 1777, and Derbyshire, 1767, and Yates's map of Lancashire, 1786.
101. See p 143.
102. PP 1842 XXXV, 99
103. Speake 1964, 46. According to Dean 1990, 17 the mill at Bramhall was pulled down by the lord of the manor following a dispute with the miller.
104. Ashmore 1989, 33-6
105. Ashmore 1975, 46-7; Preston 1992, 24
106. Arrowsmith 1996, 83
107. The building, which lay close to the Marple lime kilns, was converted in the 1850s to a mineral mill. See Ashmore 1989, 57-8, 69; Hearle 1997, 113.
108. Wadsworth 1982, 50-1
109. Greenhalgh 1886, 191; Nelstrop & Co 1970, 2; Ashmore 1975, 47-9
110. Ashmore 1975, 46-7 & 1989, 66; SA 25 March 1831
111. Plans of all the Mills, &c in the Township of Stockport, 1842, SLHL; Heginbotham 1892, 69
112. Baines 1825, 725. The other early cornmill in the Borough, on Millgate, appears to have gone out of use by 1770; according to Astle (1922, 25) the mill building was demolished in 1822.
113. SA 14 May 1830; Ashmore 1975, 48-9. By 1842 the building appears to have been in use as a cotton factory (Plans of all the Mills, &c in the Township of Stockport, 1842, SLHL). In the late nineteenth century Throstle Grove Mill at the foot of Lancashire Hill, originally erected in about 1820 as a cotton mill, was converted to cornmilling (Ashmore 1975, 47).
114. Bott 1985, 32
115. Ashmore 1975, 46; Astle 1922, 36; Simpson 1990
116. See p 130.
117. Greenwood's map of Cheshire, 1819. The existence of a mill in this locality is also suggested by field-name evidence (Bott 1986, 32).

118. In 1819, in the Cheshire part of the Borough, manorial courts were held in Cheadle Bulkeley, Woodford, Brinnington, Bredbury, Bramhall and Norbury, as well as Stockport (Ormerod 1882, vol 3, 626, 690, 807, 822, 826, 835).
119. On the 1775 improvement scheme see p 119.
120. Giles 1950-1, 84-5; Stockport Corporation 1935, 14-15
121. Giles 1950-1, 85
122. Thorp 1940, 148-53; Giles 1950, 109-10
123. Thorp 1940, 145-6. Cells belonging to the New Bayley were rediscovered in 1973 (SH 2 (1988), 17).
124. Glen 1984, 50-1; Giles 1950, 594
125. Giles 1950, 104, 594-5
126. Thorp 1940, 196-7. It should be added that more than a quarter of the cases dealt with the maintenance of illegitimate children.
127. Glen 1984, 55
128. Giles 1990, 71-2 & 1950-1, 86, 93-4
129. Giles 1950-1, 92-3
130. See p 105.
131. Giles 1950-1, 94-6
132. Giles 1950-1, 97-8, 100
133. Giles 1950-1, 99, 100-4
134. Heginbotham 1892, 159-60; Giles 1950, 97-100; Glen 1984, 52, 55. In 1808 the township of Heaton Norris was included within the jurisdiction of a small debts court for the parish of Manchester.
135. Glen 1984, 56
136. Ashworth & Oldham 1985, 50; Giles 1950, 548; Glen 1984, 60-1; Swindells 1972; Mitchell 1978
137. Giles 1950, 112-13
138. The provision of relief to the poor by the select vestry is discussed in detail by Giles 1950, 552-69.
139. Giles 1950, 569-81; Smith 1994, 4-5; Greenhalgh 1887, 49. In 1828 a motion was passed by the select vestry of Cheadle Bulkeley to consider contributing towards the Stockport fire engines, so that 'this township might have the benefit of the same in case of fire' (Mitchell 1990, 19). The Heaton Mersey bleachworks had its own engine. So too did the Andrews of Compstall, who in 1834 dispatched it to fight a blaze at Dove Bank Mills in Mellor (Giles 1950, 264; Ashmore 1989, 24).
140. Giles 1950, 591-3
141. Giles 1950, 595-6
142. Taylor 1974, 41; Giles 1950, 104; Reid 1974, 13
143. Giles 1950, 597-603
144. Giles 1950, 603-4, 608-9; Stockport Corporation 1935, 14
145. Giles 1950, 581-4
146. The achievements and problems of the police commissioners are discussed in detail by Giles 1950, 610-33.
147. Glen 1984, 45, 46, 55; Giles 1950, 150-1
148. Baines 1825, 718; PP 1838 XXXV, 30-1
149. Heginbotham 1892, 272-3 gives details of the ward boundaries.
150. Stockport's inclusion within the Act occurred despite the fact that both the opponents and the supporters of the town's incorporation had pointed out its true status to the government. Moreover, an official inquiry into the local administration of Stockport had been carried out by T J Hogg in 1833. He could find no evidence which would classify Stockport as a corporate borough, but concluded that 'It would not be easy to select a town that is better suited for the experiment, should it ever be deemed expedient to grant to any borough a well-devised scheme of local government'. His report was not, however, presented to Parliament until 1838. See Giles 1950, 655-65; PP 1838 XXXV.
151. Reid 1974, 63
152. Giles 1950, 543-6, 666-8
153. Giles 1950, 669-70
154. Heginbotham 1892, 275; Giles 1950, 671
155. Heginbotham 1892, 216; Harris 1979, 76; Davies 1961, 265;

Marple Local History Society 1993, 57
156. Heginbotham 1892, 216; PP 1842 XXXV, 72. In 1827 there was also a workhouse on Lancashire Hill, serving Heaton Norris township; prior to 1841 this was converted to a poor law school (Butterworth 1827, 250; Smith 1938, 145).
157. PP 1842 XXXV, 35, 37, 70-2; see also Reid 1974, 64-7.
158. Taylor 1974, Appendix VI
159. Giles 1950, 94; Taylor 1974, 24, Appendix III(a)
160. Burton 1877, vol 9, 22-4; Taylor 1974, 39
161. PP 1847 XIX, 12; Taylor 1974, 43
162. SA 26 May & 2, 9 June 1843. Taylor 1974, 39 reports that the court leet book under the year 1842 includes copies of letters between the steward of the manor and a James Newton about rights in the market, followed by twelve pages of legal opinion on the right of the lord of the manor to erect permanent buildings on the Market Place.
163. Heginbotham 1892, 275; PP 1847 XIX
164. Smith 1938, 407; Taylor 1974, 42; Heginbotham 1892, 283-4
165. Taylor 1974, 42-4; Heginbotham 1892, 275
166. Taylor 1974, 44
167. Taylor 1974, 45, Appendix IV
168. Wilson 1991, 3-4
169. Giles 1950, 36, 260-1
170. Baines 1825, 721
171. Giles 1950, 469
172. Heginbotham 1892, 411; Giles 1950, 470-1; Loverseed 1997, 4-5
173. Giles 1950, 473-4
174. Giles 1950, 474-5
175. Giles 1950, 470-1, 597-8, 602-5, 620-2; Wilson 1991, 199-200; Loverseed 1997, 10-13
176. Aikin 1795, 445; Heginbotham 1892, 98-9, 417-18; Giles 1950, 475-6; Greenhalgh 1887, 49; PP 1847 XIX
177. Heginbotham 1892, 418; Giles 1950, 475-9
178. Heginbotham 1892, 380-1; Giles 1950, 486-7
179. Giles 1950, 488-92; SA 22 June 1832
180. Giles 1950, 487, 492-4; Heginbotham 1892, 382-3; Stockport History Trail nd, no 46
181. Stockport Corporation 1935, 35
182. Glen 1984, 142-3
183. See p 145.
184. Glen 1984, 179-80, 183-4
185. Glen 1984, 97
186. On strikes during this period see Glen 1984; Giles 1950 & 1959; Reid 1974.
187. Glen 1984, 51
188. Glen 1984, 57; Giles 1950, 148-50
189. Giles 1950, 211
190. Giles 1950, 153-6; see also Glen 1984, 57-9.
191. Glen 1984, 58; Giles 1950, 48-9, 170-1
192. Giles 1950, 157-9, 188-91
193. Giles 1950, 234-5
194. Mitchell 1982, 63; GMAU 1993, Appendix. In 1788 Norbury had been fined £50, after being found guilty of mixing good wheat with putrid pastry and wheat infected with grubs, grinding this up and selling it as flour. His dealings in corn made him a wealthy man and the owner of property in both Stockport and Marple. When he died in 1813 his personal estate was valued at £17,500 (Mitchell 1975, 326, 335-6).
195. Mitchell 1975, 188
196. Mitchell 1975, 183, 185 & 1982, 57
197. Mitchell 1982, 63. A similar subscription had been raised at the time of high prices in 1757; see p 105.
198. Mitchell 1975, 189 & 1982, 65; Glen 1984, 182; Reeves & Turner 1991, 41-2
199. Glen 1984, 117-39 provides a detailed account and discussion of radicalism in Stockport in the 1790s and 1800s.
200. Giles 1950, 162-78; Glen 1984, 194-207; Heginbotham 1882, 79-81
201. Giles 1950, 135-7, 187-8; Glen 1984, 68, 70-1

202. Giles 1950, 191-9; Glen 1984, 73-4
203. The weavers had previously struck in 1808; for the events of that strike in the Stockport area see Glen 1984, 154-9.
204. Giles 1950, 199-200, 205-6; Glen 1984, 221-4
205. Giles 1950, 202-4, 207, 213-16
206. Giles 1950, 143-4; Glen 1984, 225-32
207. Giles 1950, 217
208. Heginbotham 1882, 84-5; Glen 1984, 236-7
209. Heginbotham 1882, 85-6; Glen 1984, 238
210. Giles 1950, 207-9, 220-2; Glen 1984, 220-1, 240-1
211. Giles 1950, 223-4; Glen 1984, 242-3, 250, 323 n 66; Heginbotham 1882, 86-9
212. Glen 1984, 250-1; Giles 1950, 225
213. Glen 1984, 244; Reid 1974, 34-5. On Moorhouse's early career as a radical see Glen 1984, 133-7.
214. Glen 1984, 244-6; Bee & Bee 1989, 46-7
215. Kidd 1993, 92-4
216. Glen 1984, 246; Bee & Bee 1989, 44-6
217. Glen 1984, 246
218. Glen 1984, 251
219. Glen 1984, 245-6
220. Glen 1984, 247; Giles 1950, 149-50
221. Giles 1950, 359-73
222. Reid 1974, 47-52. Cf Giles 1950, 642-8.
223. Giles 1950, 648-9; Reid 1974, 52-3
224. Giles 1950, 649-55; Reid 1974, 53-5, 72-4
225. Edsall 1986, 45-8
226. Reid 1974, 74
227. Reid 1974, 108-11
228. Reid 1974, 111-17
229. Reid 1974, 117-31
230. Reid 1974, 132-7
231. Reid 1974, 138-47
232. Reid & Reid 1979
233. Giles 1950, 160, 243; Glen 1984, 236, 245; Reid 1974, 33, 41, 48, 53
234. Smith 1938, 332-4
235. Reid 1974, 301-4. In April 1844 the League tried unsuccessfully to turn the tables by arriving in force at a Chartist meeting attended by Fergus O'Connor (Reid 1974, 308).
236. Edsall 1986, 98
237. Smith 1938, 341
238. Edsall 1986, 189-90
239. Smith 1938, 344-5
240. Heginbotham 1892, 310-11
241. Heginbotham 1892, 309
242. Glen 1984, 21
243. Rose 1982, 84
244. Rose 1975, 34
245. Heginbotham 1892, 79-81
246. Glen 1996; Giles 1950, 78; PP 1838 XXXV, 132. See also Walker 1966, 93.
247. Heginbotham 1892, 78
248. Heginbotham 1892, 247-8
249. Heginbotham 1892, 69
250. Heginbotham 1892, 41-4
251. Heginbotham 1892, 70-2
252. Heginbotham 1892, 77-8
253. Wainwright 1899, 13-14; Marple Local History Society 1993, 60. Oldknow himself attended Marple Chapel despite evidently retaining Unitarian beliefs; see Giles 1985, 49-52.
254. Cox 1877, 219-20
255. Andrews 1935; Aikin 1795, 443; Heginbotham 1882, 188
256. Heginbotham 1882, 211, 215-16
257. Heginbotham 1882, 70-4, 210-15, 223; Giles 1950, 529-33
258. Port 1961, 5, 132-3; DOE List of Buildings of Special Architectural or Historic Interest: Borough of Stockport
259. Heginbotham 1892, 201; Port 1961, 140-1
260. Woodford Women's Institute nd
261. Heginbotham 1882, 342
262. Heginbotham 1892, 247
263. Heginbotham 1882, 340
264. Heginbotham 1892, 148-9
265. Walker 1966, 89
266. See pp 41-2.
267. Swindells 1974b, 5, 7
268. Cheshire Sheaf, 3rd series, 56 (1961), 27 no 10,777; Robson 1966, 28-9
269. Heginbotham 1892, 137; Cheshire Sheaf, 3rd series, 53 (1958), 41 no 10,394
270. Swindells 1974b, 5
271. Robson 1966, 22
272. Steele 1968, 15-16, 22
273. Dick 1981; Giles 1950, 183
274. Heginbotham 1882, 349 & 1892, 385
275. Heginbotham 1892, 385, 388-9; Steele 1968, 23-5; Baines 1825, 720; Elsdon 1997. In 1905 construction began on a further sizeable addition to the Sunday School, the Centenary Hall.
276. Heginbotham 1892, 389
277. The first Wesleyan Methodist Sunday school in Stockport was opened in 1810. Sunday schools connected with the Congregationalist Tabernacle and Orchard Street Chapel were opened in 1834. A school was established in connection with the Roman Catholic church in Edgeley in about 1840. See Heginbotham 1882, 355 & 1892, 35, 39, 74.
278. Heginbotham 1882, 351-3
279. Heginbotham 1892, 74-6, 81
280. Heginbotham 1892, 139
281. Marple Local History Society 1993, 61-3; Heginbotham 1892, 197
282. Corry 1817, 249; Baines 1825, 720; Giles 1950, 533
283. Giles 1950, 517-18; Steele 1968, 60-3, 139-43
284. Giles 1950, 521-2
285. Giles 1950, 517-18
286. Steele 1968; Heginbotham 1892, 398-9
287. MacGregor 1992, 68; Giles 1950, 499
288. Stockport History Trail nd, no 37; Greenhalgh 1887, 279
289. Butterworth 1827, 279
290. Glen nd, 15; Butterworth 1827, 279; Greenhalgh 1886, 20, 91, 101, 108-9, 130-1, 213 & 1888, 149-52, 177-180, 211-13, 241-3, 264-5, 275-7; Astle 1922, 130-1; Giles 1950, 506-7
291. Astle 1922, 124-5; Greenhalgh 1888, 265-6; Steele 1968, 82
292. Giles 1950, 508
293. Greenhalgh 1888, 241-2
294. Robinson 1977, 9; SH 12 (1990), 9; Loverseed 1997, 6. The first balloon ascent in Stockport was on the 18th of June 1827 by ballooning exhibitionists George and Charles Green, using locally produced coal gas.
295. Giles 1950, 505-6
296. Nicholls 1992, 1-8
297. Nicholls 1992, 1; SH 3.9 (1996), 8
298. Giles 1950, 608
299. Wainwright 1899, 71; Trowsdale 1986, 56, 59-60, 62; Coutie 1989a, 29, 34, 38, 96
300. Coutie 1989a, 10
301. Glen nd, 20, 39

8. From Powerlooms to Planes, 1842-1939

1. See Appendix.
2. On emigration from Stockport see Smith 1838, 368-9. Emigration was not restricted to the town; see Thelwall 1972, 10 on emigrants leaving Compstall for the USA.
3. Steele 1968, 120-1; Reid 1974, 102-6
4. On the provision of relief in Stockport during the Cotton Famine see Coutie 1979 & 1989c.
5. Farnie 1979, 232
6. Towards the end of the nineteenth century cotton towns within the region adopted the practice of an annual holiday

or 'wakes week' for factory workers. Stockport's 'wakes week', from 1899, was in August. See Walton 1987, 295; Astle 1922, 47; Worrall 1939.

7. See pp 172-3.
8. Kirk 1985, 325
9. Glen 1984, 22-3
10. Greenhalgh 1886, 19
11. Kirk 1985, 312-18
12. Harris 1980, 95
13. Heginbotham 1882, 356
14. Kirk 1985, 325-9
15. SA 9 July 1852, quoted in Reid 1974, 373
16. Kirk 1985, 329-30
17. Holland 1971
18. Holland 1971, 33-6; Harris 1980, 95
19. Heginbotham 1882, 357
20. Kirk 1985, 318-19; Glen 1984, 280. Continuing racial tensions may also be reflected in the distribution of Irish dwellings in the town in the 1860s and 1870s, which suggests a measure of segregation; see Hayton 1992.
21. Kirk 1985, 320
22. Kirk 1985, 48; Phillips & Smith 1994, 257
23. Worrall 1939
24. See pp 154, 156 & Booker 1857, 201.
25. See Appendix.
26. Condon 1983, 4; O'Connell 1988, 8-9; Rose 1986, 68
27. Astle 1922, 145
28. Astle 1922, 145; Condon 1983, 5
29. Astle 1922, 145
30. Ashmore 1975, 28-9; Holden 1992
31. PP 1847 XIX, 2; Heginbotham 1892, 310; Coutie 1979, 53. The other mill built on the Mersey in the 1840s was Kingston Mill, constructed by Ralph Pendlebury (PP 1847 XIX, 3; Heginbotham 1892, 349).
32. Cobbing nd, 3
33. These mills were Trianon (later Unity) Mill in Woodley, built in the 1860s (Frost & Simpson 1988, 6), Hatherlow Mill in Romiley and Aqueduct Mill in Marple, built by 1864 (Ashmore 1989, 48).
34. Ashmore 1989, 45-6. Windlehurst Mill was demolished after being severely damaged in a storm in 1908.
35. Ashmore 1989, 7-28
36. Ashmore 1989, 37
37. Ashworth 1979
38. Ashmore 1989, 29-31
39. White 1860; Cobbing nd, 10-16; Worrall 1939. One firm, Marriott's on New Bridge Lane, had carried out weaving, bleaching and dyeing in 1884 but by 1914 only the finishing side of this business remained.
40. Worrall 1884 & 1939; Thelwall 1972, 10-11
41. Giles 1950, 295; Cobbing nd, 32-4; Worrall 1939
42. Cobbing nd, 25-7
43. Cobbing nd, 28-30; Rose 1986, 98-9; O'Connell 1988, 24
44. See p 149.
45. Cobbing nd, 29; Worrall 1939
46. Ashmore 1975, 22-3, 81; Cobbing nd, 23-4; Williams with Farnie 1992, 200 n 57
47. Greenhalgh 1886, 87-8
48. Cobbing nd, 18 citing E B Wood Directory of Stockport (1887)
49. Cobbing nd, 42; Farnie 1979, 233; Ashmore 1975, 76
50. Farnie 1979, 224-76; Williams with Farnie 1992, 36
51. Cobbing nd, 43; Holden 1986, 96; Farnie 1979, 232-3
52. Holden 1986, 96
53. Williams with Farnie 1992, 25
54. Holden 1986, 96-7
55. Cobbing nd, 48
56. Ashmore 1975, 76
57. Holden 1986, 98-102 & 1987-8, 163-7
58. On the design of Pear Mill see Holden 1986, 68-74 & 1987-8.
59. Holden 1986, 78-9; Ashmore 1975, 81
60. Williams with Farnie 1992, 131

61. Fletcher 1901, 49
62. Shercliff et al 1990, 9; Reid 1979, 32
63. Mitchell & Mitchell 1980, 36; Reid 1979, 32; Ashmore 1975, 8 & 1989, 6; Swindells & Western 1980, 14
64. Bagshaw 1850
65. See p 153.
66. Reid 1979, 33; Fletcher 1901, 49; Heginbotham 1892, 140. See also Coutie 1982, 15.
67. Calladine & Fricker 1993, 14, 80, 102
68. Dean 1990, 24. Handloom weaving of silk in Woodford is said to have ended in the early twentieth century. See Woodford Women's Institute nd, 16; also Shercliff et al 1990, 10.
69. Fletcher 1901, 49
70. Trowsdale 1985, 69
71. Worrall 1939
72. Heginbotham 1892, 321
73. Barber 1965
74. Plans of all the Mills, &c in the Township of Stockport, 1842, SLHL; Ashmore 1975, 38. The buildings of Christys' hat works are discussed by McKnight 1996.
75. Battersby & Co Ltd 1925; Ashmore 1975, 91
76. Reeves & Turner 1991, 44, 47; Arrowsmith 1996, 51
77. Ashmore 1975, 38
78. Phillips & Smith 1994, 330
79. Oliver 1984, 13
80. Dickinson 1855, 101-2; Oliver 1984, 13, 18-19, 20-1
81. Ashmore 1989, 59-60
82. Ashmore 1989, 60-1
83. Harris 1979, 245
84. Swindells & Western 1980, 11-13; Ashworth 1979, 67
85. Reid 1979, 29
86. Ashworth & Oldham 1985, 48; Ashmore 1989, 59-61
87. Fletcher 1901, 49
88. Oliver 1984, 13-14, 18-19, 20-1
89. Kirk 1985, 48; Census of England and Wales 1931: Industry Tables (1934) HMSO
90. Cobbing nd, 39-41
91. Ashmore 1975, 38
92. Astle 1922, 145-9; Ashmore 1975, 45, 86
93. Hunter 1974; Reeves & Turner 1991, 45; Bredbury & Romiley UDC 1974, 35
94. Creighton 1989, 51-2; Kerr et al 1935, 86-8. On roller milling at Albion Mills see Nelstrop & Co 1970, 4.
95. Astle 1922, 146
96. Ashmore 1969, 95; Christie-Miller 1972, 22
97. Robinson 1977, 39-40; George 1987-8b, 120; SH 9 (1989), 9
98. George 1981 & 1987-8b, 120
99. Robinson 1977, 71; George 1987-8b, 118
100. Holmes 1990; 1993, 4-12 & 1994, 85-6, 186
101. Astle 1922, 145, 148-9; Ashmore 1975, 55, 86
102. Frost & Simpson 1988, 6. A second factory in Woodley, Botany Mill, became a rubber works in 1914.
103. Ashmore 1989, 17; Reeves & Turner 1991, 44, 48
104. Reeves & Turner 1981, 42, 45
105. Hunter 1974
106. Heginbotham 1892, 316; Ashmore 1975, 55, 91
107. Ogden 1987; Ashmore 1975, 52-4
108. Ashmore 1975, 54
109. Census of England and Wales 1931: Industry Tables (1934) HMSO
110. Harrison 1892
111. Hadfield 1966, 220; Hadfield & Biddle 1970, vol 2, 441-5
112. See pp 110-11.
113. Porter 1977, 143-5; Scard 1981, 75
114. Giles 1950, 453; PP 1847 XIX, 17
115. Holt 1978, 123; Jeuda 1983, 4; Squire 1976, 5
116. Holt 1978, 149; Ashmore 1975, 64
117. Holt 1978, 124-5; Jeuda 1983, 4; Creighton 1989, 57
118. Burton 1981, 2
119. Burton 1981, 3, 5

120. Burton 1981, 3-6
121. Jeuda 1983, 12
122. Jeuda 1983, 17; Burton 1981, 15
123. Holt 1978, 127-8; Burton 1981, 9
124. Holt 1978, 128
125. Burton 1981, 9-10
126. Burton 1981, 7-8
127. Burton 1981, 8, 10
128. Burton 1981, 10-11; Ashmore 1975, 86
129. Burton 1981, 13; Holt 1978, 132-3. In 1891-2 the MS&L began to operate its own approach line to Central Station. From a junction with the company's trans-Pennine line at Fairfield, this new railway swung in an arc to the south of Manchester to meet with the Midland's South District line at Chorlton Junction. The new line crossed the north-west corner of Reddish, where some sixty years later a maintenance depot was set up for serving newly introduced electric locomotives (Holt 1978, 133; Condon 1983, 9).
130. Chapman 1993, 4 & 1993-4, 8
131. Burton 1981, 25-6
132. Burton 1981, 26-7
133. Burton 1981, 27; Chapman 1993-4, 9
134. Holt 1978, 135
135. Marshall 1975, 12; Holt 1978, 117
136. Gray 1977, 15, 30; Moss 1894, 68-9; Seddon 1990, 22
137. Marshall 1975, 12-15; Gray 1977, 48, 65
138. Mitchell & Mitchell 1980, 45
139. Marshall 1975, 17-52
140. Marshall 1975, 59-64
141. Marshall 1975, 57
142. Marshall 1975, 68-9, 71
143. Marshall 1975, 93-4
144. Smith 1938, 408-10, 413, 424-5, 427-8
145. Coutie 1992, 53
146. Smith 1938, 417-19
147. Smith 1938, 422, 427
148. Smith 1938, 444-5; Heginbotham 1892, 417
149. Smith 1938, 502, 505; Coutie 1992
150. Smith 1938, 503-4
151. Marple Local History Society 1993, 72
152. Bredbury and Romiley UDC 1974, 39. The rise in the number of local boards of health in the 1860s may have been prompted by another piece of legislation, the Highways Act of 1862. Under its provisions, JPs could set up local highway boards with powers to maintain the roads in their district. In 1863 Cheshire was divided between twelve such boards, based on the existing divisions of the petty sessions – most of the Borough, therefore, came under the board for the Stockport Division. Areas under a local board of health were exempt from paying rates to the highway boards (Harris 1979, 77-9).
153. Harris 1979, 79, 188-9 & 1984, 27-8. Marple local board opened works at Dooley Lane by the Goyt in 1885. A short distance upstream were sewerage works for Bredbury and Romiley. Joint works for Mellor and Ludworth opened in 1903 (Marple Local History Society 1993, 73). By far the largest of the Borough's sewerage works were those of Stockport Corporation at Cheadle Heath, which opened in 1899 (Astle 1922, 77; Stockport Corporation 1935, 62-3).
154. Farrer & Brownbill 1911, 326, 334; Marple Local History Society 1993, 69; Bowden 1974, 25; Fletcher 1901, 55, 57
155. Harris 1984, 28
156. Harris 1979, 198
157. Fletcher 1901, 57-9
158. Thelwall 1972, 24
159. Harris 1984, 28; Heginbotham 1892, 287
160. Harris 1979, 188
161. Harris 1979, 209 n 'r', 233 n 'g'; Bowden 1974, 25; Astle 1922, 73-4; Rands 1989
162. Astle 1922, 74
163. Bowden 1974, 66-75; Stockport Corporation 1935, 17

164. Swindells 1974a; Marple Local History Society 1993, 71. Ludworth was previously a part of Glossop Dale District Council, and Mellor a part of Hayfield Rural District until 1934, when it briefly became part of Chinley RD. Marple UD also acquired part of Hazel Grove and Bramhall UD (Harris 1979, 223 n 'f').
165. Thelwall 1972, 24; Harris 1979, 213 n 'j'. Bredbury and Romiley UD also gained part of Hyde MB (Harris 1979, 219 n 't').
166. Harris 1979, 211 n 'o'. Cheadle & Gatley acquired an area of Handforth UD and lost part of its own territory to Wilmslow UD.
167. Harris 1989, 195-6, 217 n 'a'
168. See p 175.
169. Coutie 1992, 52
170. Smith 1938, 418
171. Coutie 1992, 52
172. On these later terraced houses with a rear extension (known as 'tunnel backs') see Burke & Nevell 1996, 64. Compstall provides a good illustration of the superior nature of such housing. In 1860, while most workers' houses in the village were merely two-up two-down with shared privies, there was one row, Edith Terrace, of tunnel backs with their own privies; they were occupied by foremen and office staff (Thelwall 1972, 4).
173. Coutie 1992, 51
174. Bowden 1974, 150; Astle 1922, 81; Coutie 1992, 54-5
175. Bowden 1974, 150
176. Bowden 1974, 46, 48; Stockport Corporation 1935, 41. Bredbury and Romiley UDC began building council houses in 1922. Marple UDC embarked on its first council house scheme in 1924 (Bredbury & Romiley UDC 1974, 41; Marple Local History Society 1993, 75-6).
177. Booker 183-4; Reid 1985, 19. The house, originally known as Leegate, was built by Joseph Chessborough Dyer, an inventor and financier.
178. Figueiredo & Treuherz 1988, 11-14; SH 10 (1988), 4-5 & 2.4 (1991), 24-5
179. Figueiredo & Treuherz 1988, 220; Bowden 1974, 51
180. Dean 1977, 54, 62 & 1990, i. Charles Nevill carried out extensive restoration and alterations at the hall; see Dean 1977, 64-8.
181. T D W Reid, Stockport Local Heritage Library, personal communication
182. Squire 1976, 6, 10. An increase in the population of Cheadle townships between 1861 and 1871 was attributed in the census report to these becoming a place of residence for people 'engaged in business at Manchester' (Harris 1979, 245).
183. Burton 1981, 6; Marple Local History Society 1993, 75
184. Ashworth & Oldham 1985, 65
185. See Appendix.
186. Marple Local History Society 1993, 76
187. See Appendix.
188. Bowden 1974, 30, 53; Phillips & Smith 1994, 303-5
189. Bowden 1979, 27
190. See Appendix.
191. Mitchell & Mitchell 1980, 61, 68
192. Farrer & Brownbill 1911, 323; Reid 1985, 19
193. Marple Local History Society 1993, 81
194. Stockport Corporation 1935, 102; Forsyth 1961, 15-16
195. Heginbotham 1892, 418; Forsyth 1961, 16-24
196. Forsyth 1961
197. Forsyth 1961; Christie-Miller 1972, 45
198. Heginbotham 1892, 412-13; Stockport Corporation 1935, 44, 99, 100; SH 4 (1988), 4-5; Loverseed 1997
199. Loverseed 1993a & 1993b
200. Astle 1922, 76; Stockport Corporation 1935, 105-6; Frost 1990 & 1993, 47-8; Marple Local History Society 1993, 77
201. See pp 193-4.
202. Heginbotham 1892, 275-6; Galvin 1986, no 72

203. Heginbotham 1892, 276; Astle 1922, 36
204. Heginbotham 1882, 13
205. Heginbotham 1892, 276; Galvin 1986, nos 49-52
206. Heginbotham 1892, 277; Galvin 1986, no 105; Astle 1922, 123
207. Heginbotham 1892, 275; *Stockport History Trail* nd, no 47
208. Christie-Miller 1969, 3-4, 7-8
209. *Stockport History Trail* nd, 47; Galvin 1986, nos 137-40
210. Smith 1994, 49-53; Stockport Corporation 1935, 109
211. Stockport Corporation 1935, 42, 45-7; Ashmore 1975, 60-1, 74
212. Stockport Corporation 1935, 49; *Express Annual for 1941*, 33-9
213. See pp 210-11, 213.
214. Harris 1980, 210; Steele 1968, 200-1
215. Phillips & Smith 1994, 296-7; Heginbotham 1892, 137; Harris 1980, 211
216. Steele 1968, 193-217; Harris 1980, 212
217. Astle 1922, 89-92; Stockport Corporation 1935, 73-4; Steele 1968, 260-6
218. Heginbotham 1892 400-2; Steele 1968, 229-40. On Sir Joseph Whitworth and his family connection with Stockport see Heginbotham 1892, 366-7.
219. Creighton 1989, 41; Stockport MBC 1992b, 24
220. PP 1847 XIX; Heginbotham 1892, 413-15
221. Heginbotham 1892, 415
222. Astle 1922, 41-2
223. Astle 1922; Stockport Corporation 1935
224. Marple Local History Society 1993, 78-80
225. Galvin 1991, 40-2
226. Galvin 1991, 41; *Stockport History Trail* nd, no 30; Heginbotham 1892, 416-17; Astle 1922, 93-4
227. *Stockport History Trail* nd, no 1
228. Dean 1977, 79-87
229. *SH5* (1988), 16-18; Marple Local History Society 1993, 68, 89
230. Graham 1992 & 1992-3
231. Shenton 1988
232. Shercliff 1987, 27; Swindells 1974a
233. Marshall 1975, 54-5
234. Shercliff 1987, 30-2, 48-52
235. Shercliff 1987, 85, 87-8
236. Freeman with Harnwell 1994, 8-11, 14, 37

9. From 1939 to the Present

1. Stockport MBC 1992b, 11, 39-41
2. See Appendix.
3. Stockport MBC 1992b, 11
4. Wadsworth 1990-1
5. Christie-Miller 1972, 29; Cliffe 1993-4
6. Phillips & Smith 1994, 354-5
7. *Express Annual for 1946*, 68-9; Reid 1995, 40-1
8. *Express Annual for 1946*, 69; Seddon 1995
9. *Express Annual for 1946*, 69-70; Phillips & Smith 1994, 355; Smith 1988
10. Reid 1995, 42; Bowden 1974, 55-6; Phillips & Smith 1994, 354
11. *Express Annual for 1946*, 73
12. *Express Annual for 1946*, 71; Reid 1995, 49
13. Nicholson 1990; Reid 1995, 38-9
14. Nicholson 1990, 21, 23
15. Christie-Miller 1972, 20
16. Reid 1995, 9-11
17. Robinson 1977, 85-6; George 1987-8a; *SH 9* (1989), 9
18. Jackson 1965, 339-41; Holmes 1993, 12-17 & 1994, 133, 185
19. Phillips & Smith 1994, 322-4
20. Ashmore 1989, 40
21. Phillips & Smith 1994, 324; Holden 1986, 65, 96-7
22. Williams with Farnie 1992, 46-7. The 'Stockport district' referred to here covers a somewhat wider area than the Borough.
23. Ashmore 1975, 27
24. Phillips & Smith 1994, 331-2; Christie-Miller 1972, 27
25. Christie-Miller 1972, 21; Phillips & Smith 1994, 317
26. Crossley Motors Ltd nd; George 1981 & 1987-8b, 121
27. Christie-Miller 1972, 24-5; *SH 9* (1989), 9
28. Bailey 1995, 18; Reeves & Turner 1991, 45
29. Creighton 1989, 50; Holmes 1993, 26; Jackson 1995, 8
30. *Cheshire Year Book for 1946*, 6, 68, 74; *Express Annual for 1946*, 5-11, 73
31. Christie-Miller 1972, 103
32. Smith 1994, 103
33. *SH 2* (1988), 3
34. Christie-Miller 1972, 109; Powlesland 1974
35. Christie-Miller 1972, 49
36. Ashworth & Oldham 1985, 78; Marple Local History Society 1993, 87
37. Thelwall 1972, 24-5; Bredbury & Romiley UDC 1974, 54
38. Loverseed 1993a, 77-8
39. SLHL Stockport Gas Works S P22; Loverseed 1997, 90
40. SLHL Stockport Power Station S P21
41. Marshall 1975, 108-15
42. Jeuda 1983, 51; Fox 1986 no 55
43. Holt 1978, 128
44. Burton 1981, 38; Chapman 1993, 5 & 1993-4, 9; *SH 12* (1990), 2
45. Jeuda 1983, 51-3, 55
46. Burton 1981, 50
47. Mitchell & Mitchell 1980, 70, 72; Bowden 1974, 125
48. Ball 1983
49. Frangopulo 1977, 180; Kidd 1993, 196; Bowden 1974, 132-4. The quotation is from Kidd.
50. Board of Trade 1968
51. Shenton 1988, 12
52. Shenton 1988
53. Graham 1992, 19 & 1992-3, 23
54. Chapman 1992, 22; *SH 3.7* (1995), 10
55. Christie-Miller 1972, 107-11
56. *SH 2* (1988), 21
57. *SH 2.10* (1993), 22; Astle 1922, 48-79
58. Owen 1977, 75-81, 87; Shercliff 1987, 61-3 & 1985, 107-9; Keaveney & Brown 1974, 27

Sources

Parliamentary Papers and Acts

PP 1831-2 XV Report of the Select Committee on Children's Labour.

PP 1833 XX First Report of the Factories Inquiry Commission.

PP 1834 XIX Factories Inquiry Commission, Supplementary Report, Part I.

PP 1834 XX Factories Inquiry Commission, Supplementary Report, Part II.

PP 1838 XXXV Report upon Certain Boroughs by T J Hogg.

PP 1842 XXXV Report into the State of the Population of Stockport (copy in SLHL).

PP 1847 XIX Minutes of Evidence upon a Preliminary Inquiry Respecting the Stockport Manorial Tolls and Bridges Bill.

15 Geo.2 Ch. 14 (1742) An Act to enable George Warren, Esquire, his Heirs and Assigns, to make a Sluice or Tunnel through Part of the Glebe belonging to the Rectory of Stockport (copy in SLHL).

Cheshire Record Office (CRO)

DVE 10/5 Stockport, Bosden and Offerton Estates Chief Rents.

DVE 13282 A Survey with maps of the Manor of Poynton and Town of Stockport and Sundry Farms and Tenements in the County of Chester belonging to the Hon Sir George Warren K.B. 1770.

Mf 13 Hearth Tax Returns for Macclesfield Hundred 1664.

Mf 44/2 Diocese of Chester, articles preparatory to visitation of Bishop Porteus, 1778.

Lancashire Record Office (LRO)

Hearth Tax Returns for Salford Hundred 1664 (mf).

Stockport Local Heritage Library (SLHL)

Adlington Survey, 1577 (transcripts of original ms in Chetham's Library, Manchester).

Bredbury Particular and Sales 1825.

Map collection No 844, land in Edgeley, c. 1780 (copy of original map in the Fairbank Collection in Sheffield Public Library).

Map of Stockport Glebe Land, 1750.

Offerton Land Tax Returns (mf).

Plans of all the Mills, &c in the Township of Stockport, 1842.

Plans of Chief Rents, Lands and Building Plots in the Borough of Stockport, and the Townships of Marple, Handforth-cum-Bosden and Offerton, 1850.

Stockport Land Tax Returns (mf).

Stockport Moss Room Rolls (photocopy of original mss in MCL).

Stockport Poor Rate Book 1731.

Stockport Poor Rate Book 1781.

Torkington Land Tax Returns (mf).

Published Primary Sources and Secondary Sources

Addy J 1977 'Bishop Porteus' Visitation of the Diocese of Chester, 1778' Northern History 13, 175-98.

Aikin J 1795 A Description of the Country from Thirty to Forty Miles Round Manchester, London (reprinted 1969, New York, Augustus M Kelley).

Allen Brown R 1959 'A List of Castles, 1154-1216' English Historical Review 74, 249-80.

Andrews C B 1935 The Torrington Diaries, vol 2, London, Eyre & Spottiswoode.

Arrowsmith P 1996 Recording Stockport's Past: Recent Investigations of Historic Sites in the Borough of Stockport, Stockport Metropolitan Borough Council with the University of Manchester Archaeological Unit.

Arrowsmith P & Fletcher M 1993 "Nico Ditch' and 'Carr Ditch': A case of mistaken identity?' Archaeology North-West 5, 26-32.

Ashmore O 1969 The Industrial Archaeology of Lancashire, Newton Abbot, David & Charles.

Ashmore O 1975 The Industrial Archaeology of Stockport, University of Manchester Dept of Extra-Mural Studies.

Ashmore O (ed) 1989 Historic Industries of Marple and Mellor, revised and updated by A Ashworth & T Oldham, Metropolitan Borough of Stockport Leisure Services Division.

Ashworth A M 1979 The Decline of Mellor in the 19th Century, unpublished Local History Certificate dissertation, University of Manchester Dept of Extra-Mural Studies.

Ashworth A M & Oldham T F 1985 Mellor Heritage, Parochial Church Council of St Thomas's, Mellor.

Aspin C with Chapman S D 1964 James Hargreaves and the Spinning Jenny, Helmshore Local History Society.

Astle W (ed) 1922 "Stockport Advertiser" Centenary History of Stockport, Stockport, Swain & Co Ltd.

Atkinson Revd J 1909 Tracts relating to the Civil War in Cheshire 1641-1659, Chetham Society, new series, 65.

Axon E (ed) 1902 'Moseley Family Memoranda', in Chetham Miscellanies, Chetham Society, new series, 1.

Axon E 1909 'A Note on Chadkirk' TLCAS 27, 71-8.

Axon G R 1927 'Hatherlow Chapel Baptismal Register 1732-1781' TLCAS 44, 56-99.

Bagshaw S 1850 History, Gazetteer and Directory of the County of Chester, Sheffield.

Bailey S 1995 'Where have all the factories gone?' SH 3.7, 18.

Baines E 1825 History, Directory, and Gazetteer of the County of Lancaster, vol 2, Liverpool (reprinted by David & Charles, Newton Abbot).

Baines E 1835 History of the Cotton Manufacture in Great Britain, London.

Ball W B 1983 M63: Motorway through a Town, Congleton, Old Vicarage Publications.

Barber W 1965 The Chronicles of Canal Street from B.C. (Before Christys) to 1868, with introduction and notes by J Christie-Miller, privately published.

Barraclough G (ed) 1957 Facsimiles of Early Cheshire Charters, Oxford, Blackwell.

Barraclough G (ed) 1962 'Some Charters of the Earls of Chester', in P M Barnes & L F Slade (eds) A Medieval Miscellany for D M Stenton, Pipe Roll Society (new series) 36, 25-43.

Barraclough G (ed) 1988 The Charters of the Anglo-Norman Earls of Chester, c. 1071-1237, RSLC 126.

Battersby & Co Ltd 1925 1865 to 1925: Sixty Years of Progress, Battersby & Co Ltd.

Bayliss D (ed) 1992 Altrincham: A History, Timperley, Willow Publishing.

Bee M & Bee W 1989 'The Casualties of Peterloo' Manchester Region History Review 3.1, 43-50.

Bennett J H E & Dewhurst J C (eds) 1940 Quarter Sessions Records with other Records of the Justices of the Peace for the County Palatine of Chester 1559-1760, RSLC 94.

Bennett M J 1972 'The Lancashire and Cheshire Clergy 1379' THSLC 124, 1-30.

Blackwood B G 1978 The Lancashire Gentry and the Great Rebellion 1640-60, Chetham Society, 3rd series, 25.

Board of Trade 1968 Civil Aircraft Accident: Report of the Public Inquiry into the causes and circumstances of the accident to Canadair C.4 G-ALHG which occurred at Stockport, Cheshire on 4th June 1967, London, HMSO.

Booker Revd J 1857 A History of the Ancient Chapels of Didsbury and Chorlton in Manchester Parish, Chetham Society 42.

Bott O 1985 'Cornmill Sites in Cheshire 1066-1850: Part 5. Evidence from Field Names' Cheshire History 16, 26-33.

Bott O 1986 'Cornmill Sites in Cheshire 1066-1850: Part 6. Mills Recorded 1701-1850' Cheshire History 17, 27-33.

Bowden T 1974 *Community and Change: A History of Local Government in Cheadle and Gatley*, Cheadle and Gatley Urban District Council.

Bowyer O nd *The Peak Forest Canal: Lower Level: Towpath Guide*, New Mills History Notes No 23, New Mills Local History Society.

Bredbury & Romiley UDC 1974 *The Official Guide Commemorative Edition*, Bredbury and Romiley Urban District Council.

Brownbill J (ed) 1941 *The Royalist Composition Papers, Vol VI. Part I, S-We*, RSLC 95.

Broxap E 1973 *The Great Civil War in Lancashire (1642-1651)*, 2nd edition with an introduction by R N Dore, Manchester University Press/Augustus M Kelley.

Brumhead D 1989 'The Geology and Industrial Archaeology of the Compstall Area of Cheshire' *Amateur Geologist* 13, 28-35.

Bruton F A (ed) 1909 *The Roman Fort at Manchester*, Manchester University Press.

Bulkeley E W 1889 *The Parish Register of Saint Mary Stockport containing the Baptisms Marriages and Burials from 1584-1620*, Stockport, Swain & Co Ltd.

Burke T & Nevell M 1996 *Buildings of Tameside*, Tameside Metropolitan Borough Council with the University of Manchester Archaeological Unit.

Burton A nd *A History of Bramhall*, vol 1, unpublished ms, SLHL.

Burton A 1877 *A Chronological History of the Town and Neighbourhood of Stockport*, Burton Mss, vols 5 & 9, MCL.

Burton W R 1981 *Railways of Marple and District from 1794*, Marple, M T & W R Burton.

Butterworth J 1827 *A History and Description of the Towns and Parishes of Stockport, Ashton-under-Lyne, Mottram-Long-den-dale and Glossop*, Manchester.

Bythell D 1969 *The Handloom Weavers: A Study in the English Cotton Industry during the Industrial Revolution*, Cambridge University Press.

Calendar of the Charter Rolls preserved in the Public Record Office. Vol II. Henry III - Edward I. A.D. 1257-1330, 1906, HMSO.

Calendar of the Charter Rolls preserved in the Public Record Office. Vol IV. 1-14 Edward III. A.D. 1327-1341, 1912, HMSO.

Calendar of Inquisitions Miscellaneous (Chancery) Preserved in the Public Record Office, vol 1, 1916, HMSO.

Calendar of Inquisitions Post Mortem and other analogous documents in the Public Record Office, vol 1, 1904, HMSO.

Calendar of the Proceedings of the Committee for Compounding &c, 1643-1660, 5 vols, 1889-93, ed M A E Green, HMSO.

Calendar of State Papers, Domestic Series, of the Reign of James I. 1619-23, 1858, ed M A E Green, London.

Calendar of State Papers, Domestic Series, of the Reign of Charles I. 1634-5, 1864, ed J Bruce, London.

Calendar of State Papers, Domestic Series, of the Reign of Charles I. 1644, 1888, ed W D Hamilton, HMSO.

Calendarium Inquisitionum post mortem sive Escaetarum, vol 1, 1806, London.

Calladine A 1993-4 'Lombe's Mill: An Exercise in Reconstruction' *Industrial Archaeology Review* 16, 82-98.

Calladine A & Fricker J 1993 *East Cheshire Textile Mills*, Royal Commission on the Historical Monuments of England.

Cameron K 1959 *The Place-Names of Derbyshire. Part I*, English Place-Name Society 27 (for 1949-50).

Catalogue of the Harleian Manuscripts in the British Museum, vol 2, 1808.

Cathcart King D J 1983 *Castellarium Anglicanum: An Index and Bibliography of the Castles in England, Wales and the Islands*, vol 1, Kraus International Publications.

Chaloner W H 1949 'The Cheshire Activities of Matthew Boulton and James Watt, of Soho, near Birmingham, 1776-1817' *TLCAS* 61, 121-36.

Chaloner W H 1950-1 'Charles Roe of Macclesfield (1715-81): an eighteenth-century industrialist, Part I' *TLCAS* 62, 133-56.

Chapman R 1992 'Ages of the train' *SH* 2.8, 22-3.

Chapman R 1993 'Railway Frenzy' *SH* 2.10, 4-5.

Chapman R 1993-4 'Continuing the story of Stockport's railways' *SH* 2.12, 8-9.

Chapman S D 1970 'Fixed Formation Capital in the British Cotton Industry, 1770-1815' *Economic History Review*, 2nd series, 23, 234-66.

Cheshire Year Book for 1946, Stockport Advertiser.

Chivers G V 1995 *The Parish Church of St Mary, Cheadle, Stockport: History and Guidebook*, The Rector and Parochial Church Council of St Mary's Parish Church, Cheadle.

Christie-Miller J 1969 *Stockport Volunteers*, Stockport, Swain & Co Ltd.

Christie-Miller J 1972 *Stockport and the Stockport Advertiser: A History*, Stockport Advertiser.

Clarke H 1972 *Cheadle Through the Ages*, Didsbury, E J Morten.

Clemesha 1921 'The New Court Book of the Manor of Bramhall (1632-1657)', in *Chetham Miscellanies*, Chetham Society, new series, 4.

Cliffe S 1993-4 'Storm in a pint mug' *SH* 2.12, 6-7.

Coates B E 1965 'The Origin and Distribution of Markets and Fairs in Medieval Derbyshire' *DAJ* 85, 93-111.

Cobbing S M nd *The Cotton Trade in Stockport 1865-1914: A Review*, unpublished Local History Certificate dissertation, University of Manchester Dept of Extra-Mural Studies.

Condon J A 1983 *Reddish Remembered*, Metropolitan Borough of Stockport Recreation and Culture Division.

Connor A, Fagan L & Fletcher M 1991 'Nico Ditch: Excavations at Kenwood Road, Reddish, Stockport' *Archaeology North-West* 1, 3-7.

Corry J 1817 *The History of Macclesfield*, London.

Coutie H 1979 *Stockport in the Cotton Famine: An Examination of the Methods of Relief Provided for the Unemployed 1861-1863*, unpublished Local History Certificate dissertation, University of Manchester Dept of Extra-Mural Studies.

Coutie H (ed) 1982 *Hazel Grove or Bullock Smithy: A Village History Trail*, Stockport Historical Society in association with Stockport Metropolitan Borough Recreation and Culture Division.

Coutie H 1989a *The Diary of Peter Pownall: a Bramhall Farmer 1765-1858*, Congleton, Old Vicarage Publications.

Coutie H 1989b 'Hazel Grove – a rose by any other name?' *SH* 7, 15.

Coutie H 1989c 'The Cotton Famine in Stockport' *Cheshire History* 24, 18-28.

Coutie H 1992 'How they lived on Hillgate: a survey of industrial housing in the Hillgate area of Stockport' *TLCAS* 88, 31-56.

Coutie H 1993 'Life on an 18th century farm' *SH* 2.10, 16-17.

Coward B 1983 *The Stanleys, Lord Stanley and Earls of Derby 1385-1672*, Chetham Society, 3rd series, 30.

Cox B 1975-6 'The Place-Names of the Earliest English Records' *Journal of the English Place-Name Society* 8, 12-66.

Cox J C 1877 *Notes on the Churches of Derbyshire. Vol II. The hundreds of High Peak and Wirksworth*, Chesterfield.

Cox Revd J C (ed) 1907 *Memorials of Old Derbyshire*, London.

Creighton J 1989 *Portrait of Stockport*, Wilmslow, Sigma Leisure.

Crofton H T 1905 'Agrimensorial Remains round Manchester' *TLCAS* 23, 112-71.

Crossley Motors Ltd nd *A Short History of Crossley Motors Ltd*, Crossley Motors Ltd.

Crump W B 1939 'Saltways from the Cheshire Wiches' *TLCAS* 54, 84-142.

Cunliffe Shaw R 1958 'Two Fifteenth-Century Kinsmen: John Shaw of Dukinfield, Mercer, and William Shaw of Heath Charnock, Surgeon' *THSLC* 110, 15-30.

Davey P J & Forster E 1975 *Bronze Age Metalwork from Lancashire and Cheshire*, University of Liverpool Dept of Prehistoric Archaeology.

Davies C S (ed) 1961 *A History of Macclesfield*, Manchester University Press.

Davies S 1960 *The Agricultural History of Cheshire 1750-1850*, Chetham Society, 3rd series, 10.

Dean E B 1977 *Bramall Hall: the story of an Elizabethan Manor House*, Metropolitan Borough of Stockport Recreation and Culture Division.

Dean E B 1990 *Bygone Bramhall: aspects of change in a rural community*, 2nd edition, Wilmslow, Sigma Press.

Dent J S 1977 'Recent Excavations on the Site of Stockport Castle' *TLCAS* 79, 1-13.

Dick M 1981 'Urban growth and the social role of the Stockport Sunday School c.1784-1833,' in J Ferguson (ed) *Christianity, Society and Education: Robert Raikes, past, present and future,* SPCK, 53-67.

Dickinson J 1855 'Statistics of the Collieries of Lancashire, Cheshire, and North Wales' *Memoirs of the Literary and Philosophical Society of Manchester,* 2nd series, 12, 71-107.

Dodgson J McN 1970 *The Place-Names of Cheshire. Part I,* English Place-Name Society 44 (for 1966-7).

Dodgson J McN 1981 *The Place-Names of Cheshire. Part V (1.i),* English Place-Name Society 48 (for 1970-1).

DOE *List of Buildings of Special Architectural or Historic Interest: Borough of Stockport,* Dept of the Environment.

Dore R N nd *The Great Civil War (1642-46) in the Manchester Area,* BBC.

Dore R N 1966 *The Civil Wars in Cheshire,* A History of Cheshire vol 8, Cheshire Community Council.

Dore R N 1972 *A History of Hale, Cheshire: From Domesday to Dormitory,* Hale Civic Society.

Dore R N (ed) 1984 *The Letter Books of Sir William Brereton, volume one, January 1st - May 29th 1645,* RSLC 123.

Dore R N (ed) 1990 *The Letter Books of Sir William Brereton, volume two, June 18th 1645 - February 1st 1645/6,* RSLC 128.

Dore R N 1991 '1642: the coming of the Civil War to Cheshire: conflicting actions and impressions' *TLCAS* 87, 39-63.

Driver J T 1971 *Cheshire in the Later Middle Ages,* A History of Cheshire vol 6, Cheshire Community Council.

Earwaker J P 1877/80 *East Cheshire Past and Present: A History of the Hundred of Macclesfield, in the County Palatine of Chester, from Original Records,* 2 vols, London.

Earwaker J P (ed) 1884 *Lancashire and Cheshire Wills and Inventories,* Chetham Society, new series, 3.

Edsall N C 1986 *Richard Cobden: Independent Radical,* Harvard University Press.

Edwards D G (ed) 1982 *Derbyshire Hearth Tax Assessments 1662-70,* Derbyshire Record Society 7.

Edwards M M 1967 *The Growth of the British Cotton Trade 1780-1815,* Manchester University Press.

Ekwall E 1922 *The Place-Names of Lancashire,* Manchester University Press.

Elsdon Revd B R 1997 'End of Sunday School?' *SH* 4.1, 13-15.

Engels F 1971 *The Condition of the Working Class in England,* translated and edited by W O Henderson & W H Chaloner, 2nd edition, Oxford, Blackwell.

Express Annual for 1941, Stockport Express.

Express Annual for 1946, Stockport Express.

Farey J 1811 *General View of the Agriculture and Minerals of Derbyshire,* vol 1, London, Board of Agriculture.

Farnie D 1979 *The English Cotton Industry and the World Market 1815-1896,* Oxford University Press.

Farrer W (ed) 1902 *Lancashire Pipe Rolls and Early Charters,* Liverpool, Young & Sons.

Farrer W (ed) 1903 *Lancashire Inquests, Extents and Feudal Aids A.D. 1205 - A.D. 1307,* RSLC 48.

Farrer W (ed) 1907 *Lancashire Inquests, Extents and Feudal Aids Part II. A.D. 1310 - A.D. 1333,* RSLC 54.

Farrer W & Brownbill J 1911 *The Victoria History of the County of Lancaster,* vol 4, London, Constable & Co.

Figueiredo P de & Treuherz J 1988 *Cheshire Country Houses,* Chichester, Phillimore & Co Ltd.

Fishwick H (ed) 1895 *The Note Book of the Rev. Thomas Jolly A.D.1671-1693,* Chetham Society, new series, 33.

Fitton R S 1989 *The Arkwrights: Spinners of Fortune,* Manchester University Press.

Fitton R S & Wadsworth A P 1958 *The Strutts and the Arkwrights 1758-1830: A Study of the Early Factory System,* Manchester University Press.

Fletcher R J 1901 *A Short History of Hazel Grove from Olden Times,* Stockport.

Forsyth D R 1961 *The Development of the Stockport Water Undertaking,* unpublished MA thesis, University of Manchester.

Fox G K 1986 *Scenes from the Past: 1. The Railways Around Stockport,* Romiley, Foxline Publishing.

Frangopulo N J 1977 *Tradition in Action: The Historical Evolution of the Greater Manchester County,* Wakefield, E P Publishing.

Freeman P with Harnwell R 1994 *Stockport County: A Complete Record,* Derby, Breedon Books.

Frost R 1990 'Power to the People' *SH* 10, 11-13.

Frost R 1993 *Electricity in Manchester. Commemorating a century of electricity supply in the city 1893-1993,* Radcliffe, Neil Richardson.

Frost R & Simpson I 1988 *Woodley and Greave: All About Two Villages,* Stockport Metropolitan Borough.

Galvin F 1986 *Stockport Town Trail,* Stockport Metropolitan Borough Leisure Services Division.

Galvin F 1991 '130 Years of Stockport Museum' *Manchester Region History Review* 5.1, 40-5.

Gelling M 1978 *Signposts to the Past: Place-Names and the History of England,* London, J M Dent.

Gelling M 1993 *Place-Names in the Landscape: the geographical roots of Britain's place-names,* London, J M Dent.

Gent J 1997 'Hall of Learning' *SH* 3.12, 14-15.

George A D 1981 *The Manchester Motor Industry 1900-1938,* Manchester Polytechnic Occasional Paper No 3.

George A D 1987-8a 'Fairey Aviation in the North-West' *Memoirs and Proceedings of the Manchester Literary and Philosophical Society* 127, 117-19.

George A D 1987-8b 'A note on the acquisition and disposal of capital and fixed assets by Crossley Motors Ltd. of Manchester during the shadow factory period 1934-47' *Memoirs and Proceedings of the Manchester Literary and Philosophical Society* 127, 120-1.

Gibbons P 1994 *A Multi-Disciplinary Study of the Origins of the Late Medieval Borough of Stockport,* unpublished BA dissertation, University of Birmingham.

Gibson A C 1862-3 'Everyday Life of a Country Gentleman of Cheshire in the 17th Century: as shewn in the private expenditure journal of Colonel Henry Bradshawe, of Marple and Wybersleigh' *THSLC* 2, 67-92.

Giles P M 1950 *The Economic and Social Development of Stockport 1815-36,* unpublished MA thesis, University of Manchester.

Giles P M 1950-1 'The Enclosure of Common Lands in Stockport' *TLCAS* 62, 73-110.

Giles P M 1959 'The Felt-hatting Industry, c.1500-1850, with special reference to Lancashire and Cheshire' *TLCAS* 69, 104-32.

Giles P M 1985 *Samuel Oldknow: A Postscript,* unpublished typescript, SLHL.

Giles P M 1990 'The Last of the Warrens: Sir George Warren, K.B. (1735-1801)' *THSLC* 140, 47-78.

Giles P M 1992 'The perplexed and ill-managed affairs of the Stockport Bank' *TLCAS* 88, 57-85.

Glen R nd *Stopfordiana: Bibliography of works printed or published in Stockport 1785-1840,* unpublished, SLHL.

Glen R 1979 'The Milnes of Stockport and the Export of English Technology during the Early Industrial Revolution' *Cheshire History* 3, 15-21.

Glen R 1984 *Urban Workers in the Early Industrial Revolution,* Croom Helm.

Glen R 1996 'Anatomy of a Religious Revival: Stockport Methodists in the 1790s' *Manchester Region History Review* 10, 3-13.

GMAU 1990 *Ernocroft Wood: Historical Background,* unpublished report.

GMAU 1994 *High Street – Royal Oak Yard, Stockport: An Archaeological Survey,* unpublished report.

Graham E 1992 'The Theatre Royal' *SH* 2.6, 18-19.

Graham E 1992-3 'Stockport Hippodrome' *SH* 2.9, 22-3.

Graham J 1846 *History of Printworks in the Manchester District from 1760 to 1846,* unpublished ms, MCL.

Gray E 1977 *The Manchester Carriage and Tramways Company,* Manchester Transport Museum Society.

Greenhalgh J 1886-9 'Recollections of Stockport', in *CN&Q*, new series, 6-9.

Griffith T M 1952-3 'Chadkirk Chapel' *TLCAS* 63, 156-74.

Groves J nd *The Communities of the Manors of Northenden and Etchells 1641-1820*, unpublished Local History Certificate dissertation, University of Manchester Dept of Extra-Mural Studies.

Groves J 1990-1 "Such a Day as is Seldome Seene': The Memorandum Book of a Cheshire Yeoman, John Ryle of High Greaves, Etchells, 1649-1721' *Manchester Region History Review* 4.2, 36-41.

Groves J 1992 *The Impact of Civil War on A Community: Northenden and Etchells in Cheshire 1642-1660*, Sale, Northern Writers Advisory Services.

Groves J 1994 *Piggins, Husslements and Desperate Debts: a social history of North-east Cheshire through wills and probate inventories, 1600-1760*, Sale, Northern Writers Advisory Services.

Hadfield B 1934 'The Carrs Silk Mills, Stockport' *The Manchester School* 5, 124-9.

Hadfield C 1966 *The Canals of the West Midlands*, Newton Abbot, David & Charles.

Hadfield C & Biddle B 1970 *The Canals of North West England*, 2 vols, Newton Abbot, David & Charles.

Hall D, Wells C E & Huckerby E 1995 *The Wetlands of Greater Manchester: North West Wetlands Survey 2*, Lancaster University Archaeological Unit.

Hall J (ed) 1889 *Memorials of the Civil War in Cheshire*, RSLC 19.

Hanmer J & Winterbottom D 1991 *The Book of Glossop*, Buckingham, Barracuda Books.

Harris B 1979 (ed) *The Victoria History of the County of Chester*, vol 2, University of London Institute of Historical Research.

Harris B 1980 (ed) *The Victoria History of the County of Chester*, vol 3, University of London Institute of Historical Research.

Harris B 1984 *Cheshire and its Rulers*, Cheshire Libraries and Museums.

Harris B 1987 (ed) *The Victoria History of the County of Chester*, vol 1, University of London Institute of Historical Research.

Harrison W 1886 'The Development of the Turnpike System in Lancashire and Cheshire' *TLCAS* 4, 80-92.

Harrison W 1892 'The Turnpike Roads of Lancashire and Cheshire' *TLCAS* 10, 237-48.

Harrison W 1894 'Ancient Fords, Ferries and Bridges in Lancashire' *TLCAS* 12, 1-29.

Harrison W 1916 'The History of a Turnpike Trust (Manchester and Wilmslow)' *TLCAS* 36, 136-65.

Harrop S A 1983 'Moated Sites in North-East Cheshire and their Links with the Legh Family in the Fourteenth Century' *Cheshire History* 11, 8-15.

Hart C 1977 'The kingdom of Mercia', in A Dornier (ed) *Mercian Studies*, 43-61, Leicester University Press.

Hart W H 1886 'A Calendar of Fines for the County of Derby from their Commencement in the Reign of Richard I' *DAJ* 8, 15-64.

Hartwell C & Bryant S 1985 'A Measured Survey of the Buildings at Numbers 30A and 31 Market Place, Stockport' *GMAJ* 1, 75-88.

Hartwell C & Hunt C 1987-8 'Halliday Hill Farm' *GMAJ* 3, 103-9.

Hayton S 1992 *The Irish Cellar Dwellers – Salford, Stockport and Rochdale 1861-71*, University of Salford Occasional Papers in Politics and Contemporary History No 28.

Hearle A 1997 *Marple and Mellor*, Stroud, Chalford Publishing.

Heginbotham H 1882/1892 *Stockport Ancient and Modern*, 2 vols, London, Sampson Low, Marston & Co.

Henderson W O 1968 *Industrial Britain under the Regency: The Diaries of Escher, Bodmer, May and de Gallois 1814-18*, London, Frank Cass.

Higgins S H 1924 *A History of Bleaching*, London, Longmans, Green & Co.

Higham N J 1982 'Bucklow Hundred: the Domesday Survey and the Rural Community' *Cheshire Archaeological Bulletin* 8, 15-21.

Higham N J 1993 *The origins of Cheshire*, Manchester University Press.

Highet T P 1960 *The Early History of the Davenports of Davenport*, Chetham Society, 3rd series, 9.

Hills R L 1970 *Power in the Industrial Revolution*, Manchester University Press.

Hills R L 1987-8 'Peter Ewart, 1767-1842' *Memoirs and Proceedings of the Manchester Literary and Philosophical Society* 127, 29-43.

Hodgkins D J 1977 'Samuel Oldknow and the Peak Forest Canal' *DAJ* 97, 27-35.

Hodgkins D J 1987 'The Peak Forest Canal – Lime and Limestone, 1794-1846' *DAJ* 107, 73-91.

Hodson J H 1978 *Cheshire, 1660-1780: Restoration to Industrial Revolution*, A History of Cheshire vol 9, Cheshire Community Council.

Holden R N 1986 *Pear Mill, Stockport, 1907-1978*, unpublished Local History Certificate dissertation, University of Manchester Dept of Extra-Mural Studies.

Holden R N 1987 'Pear Mill, 1907-1929: A Stockport Spinning Company' *Manchester Region History Review* 1.2, 23-9.

Holden R N 1987-8 'Pear Mill, Stockport: An Edwardian Cotton Spinning Mill' *Industrial Archaeology Review* 10, 162-74.

Holden R N 1992 'Reddish Clubhouse' *SH* 2.6, 12.

Holden W 1805 *Triennial Directory, 1805, 1806, 1807*.

Holland V 1971 *Anti-Catholic Riot in Stockport 1852*, unpublished typescript, SLHL.

Holmes H 1990 'History of Woodford Airfield' *SH* 12, 16-17.

Holmes H 1993 *Avro: The Story of Manchester's Aircraft Company*, Radcliffe, Neil Richardson.

Holmes H 1994 *Avro: The History of an Aircraft Company*, Shrewsbury, Airlife Publishing Ltd.

Holt G O 1978 *A Regional History of the Railways of Great Britain. Volume 10: The North West*, Newton Abbot, David & Charles.

Hooley J 1981 *A Hillgate Childhood – Myself when Young*, Age Concern Stockport.

Horrocks P 1994 'Portwood's Founder' *SH* 3.3, 17.

Hudson J 1996 *Cheadle*, Stroud, Sutton Publishing Ltd.

Hunter R 1974 *A Short History of Bredbury and Romiley*, Bredbury and Romiley Antiquarian Society.

Hurst J nd *Scrapbook*, vol 1, unpublished ms, SLHL.

Hurst-Vose R 1987-8 'Haughton Green, Denton: A Seventeenth-Century Coal-Fired Glass Furnace' *GMAJ* 3, 115-16.

Husain B M C 1973 *Cheshire Under the Norman Earls 1066-1237*, A History of Cheshire vol 4, Cheshire Community Council.

Irvine W F (ed) 1901 'A List of the Freeholders in Cheshire in the Year 1578' *Miscellanies relating to Lancashire and Cheshire*, vol 4, RSLC 43, 1-24.

Jackson A J 1965 *Avro Aircraft since 1908*, London, Putnam.

Jackson A J 1995 *Avro Aircraft*, Stroud, Alan Sutton Publishing Ltd.

Jackson J W 1934-5 'The Prehistoric Archaeology of Lancashire and Cheshire' *TLCAS* 50, 65-106.

Jackson J W 1936 'Contributions to the Archaeology of the Manchester Region' *North Western Naturalist* 11, 110-19.

Jarvis R C 1947 'The Jacobite Risings and the Public Monies' *TLCAS* 59, 131-54.

Jarvis R C 1958 'The Mersey Bridges: 1745' *TLCAS* 68, 69-84.

Jeuda B 1983 *The Macclesfield, Bollington and Marple Railway: The Great Central and North Staffordshire Joint Railway*, Cheshire County Council.

Kay T 1896 'Remains of the Town Wall of Stockport' *TLCAS* 14, 55-61.

Keaveney E & Brown D L 1974 *The Ashton Canal: A History of the Manchester to Ashton-under-Lyne Canal*, privately published.

Kenyon D 1986 'Danish Settlement in Greater Manchester: The Place-name Evidence' *GMAJ* 2, 63-9.

Kenyon D 1988-9 'Notes on Lancashire Place-Names 2: The Later Names' *Journal of the English Place-name Society* 21, 23-53.

Kenyon D 1991 *The origins of Lancashire*, Manchester University Press.

Kenyon Mss – *The Manuscripts of Lord Kenyon*, Historical Manuscripts Commission, Fourteenth Report, Appendix part IV, 1894, HMSO.

Kermode J I & Phillips G B (eds) 1982 *Seventeenth-Century Lancashire: Essays presented to J.J. Bagley*, TLCAS 132.

Kerr J S, Renold C G & Thompson F C 1935 *The Iron, Steel and Engineering Industries of Manchester and District*, privately published for The Iron and Steel Institute.

Kerridge E 1985 *Textile Manufactures in Early Modern England*, Manchester University Press.

Kerry Revd C 1893 'A History of the Peak Forest' *DAJ* 15, 67-98.

Kidd A 1993 *Manchester*, Ryburn Publishing, Keele University Press.

Kirk N 1985 *The Growth of Working Class Reformism in Mid-Victorian England*, Croom Helm.

Lee A K 1979 *Mellor, Ludworth and Chisworth, 1650-1700*, unpublished Local History Certificate dissertation, University of Manchester Dept of Extra-Mural Studies.

Loverseed D E 1993a *A History of the Marple Gas Undertaking, 1845-1949*, North West Gas Historical Society.

Loverseed D E 1993b 'The 'Gas Question' in Marple 1887: Acquisition of the Marple Gas Company by the Marple (Cheshire) Local Board' *TLCAS* 8, 91-113.

Loverseed D E 1997 *The Green Giant: A History of the Stockport Gas Undertaking 1820-1949*, Woodsmoor, Stockport, DCS.

Lowe B 1972 *The Lancashire Textile Industry in the Sixteenth Century*, Chetham Society, 3rd series, 20.

Lowe K, Clark J & Collier R 1975-6 *Field Survey of the Westward-facing Slope of the Pennines; including Report of Trial Excavation*, unpublished report, University of Manchester Dept of Extra-Mural Studies.

MacGregor A J (ed) 1992 *The Alehouses and Alehouse-keepers of Cheshire 1629-1828*, Caupona Publications No 4.

McKenna S & Nunn C M (eds) 1992 *Stockport in the Mid-Seventeenth Century (1660-1669)*, Metropolitan Borough of Stockport for Stockport Historical Society.

McKnight P 1996 *Christys' Hat Works, Stockport: The site, buildings and industrial processes from 1742 to 1996*, unpublished thesis, Ironbridge Institute, University of Birmingham.

McLean I 1988 'The Lanky Cut' *SH* 5, 10.

McLean I 1993-4 'A Roman Puzzle' *SH* 2.12, 18-19.

Malet H 1977 *Bridgewater: The Canal Duke 1736-1803*, Manchester University Press.

Margary I D 1973 *Roman Roads in Britain*, 3rd edition, London, John Baker.

Marple Local History Society nd *The Oldknow Trail*.

Marple Local History Society 1993 *The History of Marple and District*, revised 5th edition.

Marriott Revd W 1810 *The Antiquities of Lyme and its Vicinity*, Stockport.

Marshall M 1975 *Stockport Corporation Tramways*, Manchester Transport Museum Society.

Mason J J 1981 'A Manufacturing and Bleaching Enterprise during the Industrial Revolution: The Sykeses of Edgeley' *Business History* 23, 59-83.

Million I R 1969 *A History of Didsbury*, Didsbury Civic Society & E J Morten.

Mills D 1976 *The Place-Names of Lancashire*, London, Batsford.

Mitchell F 1976-7 'The Tithe Maps and the Cheadle Cross' *Cheshire Sheaf*, 5th series, 27 no 67, 31 no 76.

Mitchell F (ed) 1978 *Minutes of the Select Vestry of Cheadle Bulkeley April 1827 to March 1829*, Greater Manchester County Record Office Publication No 1, Greater Manchester Council.

Mitchell F & Mitchell T 1980 *Gatley: A Pictorial History of The Parish of St. James The Apostle*, Gatley, The Vicar and Churchwardens of St. James Church.

Mitchell S I 1975 *Urban Markets and Retail Distribution, 1730-1815, with Particular Reference to Macclesfield, Stockport, and Chester*, unpublished DPhil thesis, Oxford University.

Mitchell S I 1980 'Retailing in Eighteenth- and Early Nineteenth-century Cheshire' *THSLC* 130, 36-60.

Mitchell S I 1982 'Food Shortages and Public Order in Cheshire, 1757-1812' *TLCAS* 81, 42-66.

Moorhouse F 1909 'On the Earthwork in Crow Holt Wood, near Bramhall Hall, Cheshire' *TLCAS* 27, 79-83.

Morgan P (ed) 1978a *Domesday Book: Cheshire*, Chichester, Phillimore.

Morgan P (ed) 1978b *Domesday Book: Derbyshire*, Chichester, Phillimore.

Morrill J S 1974 *Cheshire 1630-1660: County Government and Society during the English Revolution*, Oxford University Press.

Morrill J S 1975 'William Davenport and the 'silent majority' of early Stuart England' *JCAS* 58, 116-29.

Morris M (ed) 1983 *Medieval Manchester: A Regional Study*, The Archaeology of Greater Manchester vol 1, Greater Manchester Archaeological Unit.

Morris R H 1894 *Chester in the Plantagenet and Tudor Reigns*, privately published.

Moss F 1894 *A History of the Old Parish of Cheadle in Cheshire comprising the Townships of Cheadle Moseley, Cheadle Bulkeley and Handforth-cum-Bosden also an Account of the Hamlet of Gatley*, privately published (reprinted 1970, Didsbury, E J Morten).

Nelstrop W & Co Ltd 1970 *William Nelstrop & Co Ltd, Stockport, 150 Years: 1820-1970*, privately published.

Nevell M 1991 *Tameside 1066-1700*, Tameside Metropolitan Borough Council with the Greater Manchester Archaeological Unit.

Nevell M 1992a *Tameside Before 1066*, Tameside Metropolitan Borough Council with the Greater Manchester Archaeological Unit.

Nevell M 1992b 'A Romano-British Enclosure on Werneth Low, Tameside' *Archaeology North-West* 4, 19-22.

Nevell M 1993 *Tameside 1700-1930*, Tameside Metropolitan Borough Council with the Greater Manchester Archaeological Unit.

Nevell M 1994 *The People Who Made Tameside*, Tameside Metropolitan Borough Council with Greater Manchester Archaeological Contracts.

Nevell M 1996 'The 'Pot Shaft' Roman Coin Hoard: A Preliminary Note' *Archaeology North-West* 10, 96-8.

Newton Lady 1925 *Lyme Letters 1660-1760*, London, Heinemann.

Nicholls R 1992 *The Belle Vue Story*, Radcliffe, Neil Richardson.

Nicholson G 1990 *Surviving the Blitz*, Stockport Metropolitan Borough Museum and Art Gallery Service.

Nisbet S M 1991 'Newbridge Tunnel' *SH* 2.2, 12.

Norbury W 1888/9 'A Cheshire Farmer's Accounts' *CN&Q*, new series, 8 & 9.

O'Connell P 1988 *Greg's: the Story of the Albert Mills*, Congleton, Old Vicarage Publications.

Ogden M 1987 *A History of Stockport Breweries*, Swinton, Neil Richardson.

Oldham T 1995 *What Did They Leave? Some Mellor wills and inventories*, Marple Local History Society.

Oliver J S 1984 *Notes on Coal Mining in Bredbury*, unpublished typescript, SLHL.

Ormerod G (ed) 1844 *Tracts relating to Military Proceedings in Lancashire during the Great Civil War*, Chetham Society 2.

Ormerod G 1882 *The History of the County Palatine and City of Chester*, 2nd edition enlarged and revised by T Helsby, 3 vols.

Owen D 1977 *Canals to Manchester*, Manchester University Press.

Owen J nd Mss, vols 26 & 44, MCL.

Parkinson Revd R (ed) 1845 *The Life of Adam Martindale*, Chetham Society 4.

Pevsner N & Hubbard E 1971 *The Buildings of England: Cheshire*, Penguin Books.

Phelps J J 1909 'Catalogue of the Old Manchester and Salford Exhibition held at the Queen's Park Art Gallery Manchester 1909-10' *TLCAS* 27.

Phelps J J 1919 'Pre-Norman Crosses at Cheadle' *TLCAS* 37, 95-109.

Phillips A S 1987 'Money for Old Rope: Hemp growing in Stockport' *SH* 1, 16.

Phillips A S 1988a 'Bowkers, Brewsters and Websters' *SH* 4, 21.

Phillips A S 1988b *Notes on the Possible History of Staircase House*, unpublished report, SLHL.

Phillips C B & Smith J H (eds) 1985 *Stockport Probate Records 1578-1619*, RSLC 124.

Phillips C B & Smith J H (eds) 1992 *Stockport Probate Records 1620-1650*, RSLC 131.

Phillips C B & Smith J H 1994 *Lancashire and Cheshire from AD 1540*, London, Longman.

Piccope G J (ed) 1857 *Lancashire and Cheshire Wills and Inventories, the first portion*, Chetham Society 33.

Piccope G J (ed) 1860 *Lancashire and Cheshire Wills and Inventories, the second portion*, Chetham Society 51.

Pigot J & Co 1834 *National Commercial Directory for the counties of Chester, Cumberland, Durham, Lancaster*, Manchester.

Pipe Roll Society 1909, vol 30, *The Great Roll of the Pipe for the Twenty-Seventh Year of the Reign of King Henry the Second AD 1180-81*, London.

Pipe Roll Society 1910, vol 31, *The Great Roll of the Pipe for the Twenty-Eighth Year of the Reign of King Henry the Second AD 1181-82*, London.

Pipe Roll Society 1911, vol 32, *The Great Roll of the Pipe for the Twenty-Ninth Year of the Reign of King Henry the Second AD 1182-83*, London.

Port M H 1961 *Six Hundred New Churches: A Study of the Church Building Commission, 1818-1856, and its Church Building Activities*, London, SPCK.

Porter R E 1977 'The Marketing of Agricultural Produce in Cheshire during the 19th Century' *THSLC* 126, 139-55.

Powlesland D J 1974 *Stockport: An Archaeological Opportunity*, Historic Stockport Research Committee.

Pratt F nd *Canal Architecture in Britain*, British Waterways Board.

Preston R 1992 'Foggbrook mill, Offerton' *SH* 2.6, 24-5.

Radcliffe W 1828 *Origin of the New System of Manufacture Commonly Called Power-Loom Weaving*, Stockport (reprinted 1974, Clifton New Jersey, Augustus M Kelley Publishers).

Raines Revd F R (ed) 1845 *Notitia Cestriensis*, vol 1, Chetham Society 8.

Rands P 1989 'Rolling fields the price' *SH* 9, 25.

Reeves E L & Turner J A 1991 *Bredbury: A Nostalgic History*, Metropolitan Borough of Stockport Leisure Services Division.

Reid C A N 1974 *The Chartist Movement in Stockport*, unpublished MA thesis, University of Hull.

Reid T D W (ed) 1979 *Cheadle in 1851*, Metropolitan Borough of Stockport Recreation and Culture Division.

Reid T D W (ed) 1985 *Heaton Mersey, a Victorian Village, 1851-1881*, Stockport Historical Society with Metropolitan Borough of Stockport Leisure Services Division.

Reid T D W (ed) 1995 *Stockport's Hidden Army 1939-1945: Women in the Second World War and on the Home Front*, Stockport Libraries.

Reid T D W & Reid C A N 1979 'The 1842 "Plug Plot" in Stockport' *International Review of Social History* 24, 55-79.

Richards R 1947 *Old Cheshire Churches: A Survey of their History, Fabric and Furniture with Records of the Older Monuments*, London, Batsford.

Richardson A 1983 'Evidence of Roman Centuriation at Manchester' *Cheshire Archaeological Bulletin* 9, 9-17.

Richardson A 1986 'Further Evidence of Centuriation at Manchester' *The Manchester Geographer* 7, 44-50.

Richardson A 1987 'Some Evidence of Early Roman Activity on the South-west Pennine Flank' *Journal of the British Archaeological Association* 140, 18-35.

Robinson B R 1977 *Aviation in Manchester: A Short History*, Manchester Branch of the Royal Aeronautical Society.

Robson D 1966 *Some Aspects of Education in Cheshire in the Eighteenth Century*, Chetham Society, 3rd series, 13.

Rogers C D 1975 *The Lancashire Population Crisis of 1623*, University of Manchester Dept of Extra-Mural Studies.

Rose E A 1975 'Methodism in Cheshire to 1800' *TLCAS* 78, 22-37.

Rose E A 1982 'Methodism in South Lancashire to 1800' *TLCAS* 81, 67-91.

Rose M B 1986 *The Gregs of Quarry Bank Mill: The rise and decline of a family firm, 1750-1914*, Cambridge University Press.

Rylands J P (ed) 1880 *Lancashire Inquisitions Stuart Period, Part I, 1 to 11 James I*, RSLC 3.

Rylands J P (ed) 1887 *Lancashire Inquisitions Stuart Period, Part II, 12 to 19 James I*, RSLC 16.

Scard G 1981 *Squire and Tenant: Life in Rural Cheshire, 1760-1900*, A History of Cheshire vol 10, Cheshire Community Council.

Scholes J 1794 *Manchester and Salford Directory*, Manchester.

Scholes J 1797 *Manchester and Salford Directory*, 2nd edition, Manchester.

Seddon D 1995 'When the Eagle Landed' *SH* 3.6, 12-14.

Seddon P 1989 'The hall which nearly moved' *SH* 6, 20-1.

Seddon P 1990 'Cheshire Pilgrim' *SH* 11, 21-3.

Shenton W 1988 *Picture Palace to Super Cinema: A History of Stockport Cinemas*, Metropolitan Borough of Stockport Leisure Services Division.

Shercliff W H (ed) 1974 *Wythenshawe: A History of the Townships of Northenden, Northen Etchells and Baguley. Volume 1: to 1926*, Didsbury, E J Morten for Northenden Civic Society.

Shercliff W H 1976 *Gatley United Reformed Church 1777-1977*, Gatley United Reformed Church.

Shercliff W H 1985 'The Macclesfield Canal: Its Economic Importance to North East Cheshire' *TLCAS* 83, 86-124.

Shercliff W H 1987 *Nature's Joys are Free for All: A History of Countryside Recreation in North East Cheshire*, Poynton, privately published.

Shercliff W H, Kitching D A & Ryan J M 1990 *Poynton – a Coalmining Village: Social Life, Transport and Industry, 1700-1939*, revised edition, Poynton, privately published.

Shone W 1911 *Prehistoric Man in Cheshire*, London & Chester.

Shotter D 1990 *Roman Coins from North-West England*, Centre for North-West Regional Studies, Lancaster University.

Shotter D 1995 *Roman Coins from North-West England: First Supplement*, Centre for North-West Regional Studies, Lancaster University.

Simpson I 1990 'In the Days of Sail' *SH* 11, 8-9.

Singleton W A 1952 'Traditional House Types in Rural Lancashire and Cheshire' *THSLC* 104, 75-91.

Smiles S 1904 *Lives of the Engineers: Metcalfe – Telford*, London.

Smith A 1994 *Fearless, Dauntless, Ne'er Afraid: A History of Stockport Fire Brigade*, Stockport Libraries.

Smith C 1938 *Stockport in the Age of Reform, 1822-1870*, unpublished typescript, SLHL.

Smith L T (ed) 1910 *The Itinerary of John Leland in or about the years 1535-1543 Parts IX, X and XI*, London, G Bell & Sons.

Smith P J C 1988 *Flying Bombs over the Pennines: The story of the V-1 attack aimed at Manchester on December 24th 1944*, Radcliffe, Neil Richardson.

Smith P J C 1993 *The Invasion of 1745: The Drama in Lancashire and Cheshire*, Radcliffe, Neil Richardson.

Smith W J 1977 'The Staircase Cafe, Stockport: An Interim Report' *TLCAS* 79, 14-20.

Somerville R 1977 'Commons and Wastes in North-West Derbyshire – The High Peak 'New Lands'', *DAJ* 97, 16-22.

Speake R 1964 *The Story of Hazel Grove and Bramhall: A Local History*, Hayfield, Crescent Press.

Squire C 1976 *Cheadle Hulme: A Brief History*, Stockport Metropolitan Borough Recreation and Culture Division.

Steele I J D 1968 *A Study of the Education of the Working Class in Stockport during the Nineteenth Century*, unpublished MA thesis, University of Sheffield.

Stevenson I P & Gaunt G D 1971 *Geology of the Country around Chapel en le Frith*, Memoirs of the Geological Survey of Great Britain, London, HMSO.

Stewart-Brown R (ed) 1910 *Accounts of the Chamberlains and other Officers of the County of Chester 1301-1360*, RSLC 59.

Stewart-Brown R (ed) 1916 *Lancashire and Cheshire Cases in the Court of Star Chamber Part I*, RSLC 71.

Stewart-Brown R (ed) 1925 *Calendar of County Court, City Court and Eyre Rolls of Chester, 1259-1297*, Chetham Society, new series, 84.

Stewart-Brown R (ed) 1934 *Cheshire Inquisitions Post Mortem Stuart Period 1603-1660, Vol I, A-D*, RSLC 84.

Stockport Corporation 1935 *A Century of Local Government in Stockport*, Stockport Corporation.

Stockport History Trail nd, Stockport, Specialized Technical Services.

Stockport MBC 1992a *Bramall Hall*, Stockport Metropolitan Borough Museum and Art Gallery Service.

Stockport MBC 1992b *The Official Guide to Stockport*, Stockport MBC Marketing and Communications Unit.

Stubbs W (ed) 1867 *Gesta Regis Henrici Secundi Benedictii Abbatis*, vol 1, Roll Series 49.

Stubbs W (ed) 1872 *Memoriale fratris Walteri de Coventria*, vol 1, Roll Series 58.

Swindells G A 1972 *The Strines Journal, 1852-1860: An Appreciation*, Marple Antiquarian Society.

Swindells G A 1974a *A History of Marple*, Marple Antiquarian Society.

Swindells G A 1974b *History of Education in Marple 1603-1971*, Cheshire County Council & Marple Antiquarian Society.

Swindells G A & Western K (eds) 1980 *Marple in 1851 from the Census Returns*, Marple Antiquarian and Local History Society.

Sylvester D 1956 'The Open Fields of Cheshire' *THSLC* 108, 1-33.

Tait J 1904 *Mediaeval Manchester and the Beginnings of Lancashire*, Manchester University Press (reprinted 1991, Llanerch Publishers).

Tait J 1924 *Taxation in Salford Hundred 1524-1802*, Chetham Society, new series, 83.

Tate W E 1978 *A Domesday of English Enclosure Acts and Awards*, edited with an introduction by M E Turner, University of Reading.

Taylor B J, Price R H & Trotter F M 1963 *Geology of the Country around Stockport and Knutsford*, Memoirs of the Geological Survey of Great Britain, London, HMSO.

Taylor F 1950 'Hand-list of the Legh of Booths Charters in the John Rylands Library' *Bulletin of the John Rylands Library* 32, 229-300.

Taylor W M P 1974 *A History of the Stockport Court Leet*, revised edition, Stockport Museum Publication No 3, Stockport Library Museum and Art Gallery Service.

Thacker A T 1980 'The Chester Diocesan Records and the Local Historian' *THSLC* 130, 149-85.

Thelwall R E 1972 *The Andrews and Compstall their village*, Cheshire County Council Libraries and Museums & Marple Antiquarian Society.

Thorp J 1940 *A History of Local Government in Stockport between 1760 and 1820*, unpublished MA thesis, University of Manchester.

Tindall A S 1985 'Stockport: the development of the town' *GMAJ* 1, 69-73.

Trowsdale D H 1985 *The History of Hazel Grove and Bramhall*, revised edition, Shrewsbury, Baynham Edition.

Trunkfield R B nd *A Selection of Wills and Inventories of a Cheshire Parish, 1660-1760, Part 1, A-L*, unpublished typescript, SLHL.

Tunnicliff W 1787 *A Topographical Survey of the Counties of Stafford, Chester and Lancaster*, Nantwich.

Tupling G H 1945-6 'Lancashire Markets in the Sixteenth and Seventeenth Centuries, Part I' *TLCAS* 58, 1-34.

Tupling G H 1952-3 'The Turnpike Trusts of Lancashire' *Memoirs and Proceedings of the Manchester Literary and Philosophical Society* 94, 39-62.

Turnbull G 1979 *Traffic & Transport: An Economic History of Pickfords*, Allen & Unwin.

Turner N 1991 'Boom town, bad name' *SH* 2.2, 26.

Universal British Directory, vol 4, part 1, Facsimile Text Edition, 1993, King's Lynn, Michael Winton.

Unwin G with Hulme A & Taylor G 1968 *Samuel Oldknow and the Arkwrights: the Industrial Revolution at Stockport and Marple*, 2nd edition, Manchester University Press.

Ure A 1835 *The Philosophy of Manufactures*, 2nd edition, London.

Ure A 1836 *The Cotton Manufacture of Britain Systematically Investigated*, 2 vols, London (reprinted 1970, Johnson Reprint Corporation).

Urwick W (ed) 1864 *Historical Sketches of Nonconformity in The County Palatine of Chester*, London & Manchester.

Varley B 1957 *The History of Stockport Grammar School*, 2nd (enlarged) edition, Manchester University Press.

Wadsworth A P & Mann J de L (eds) 1931 *The Cotton Trade and Industrial Lancashire 1600-1780*, Manchester University Press.

Wadsworth D J 1982 *The Peak Forest Canal from Dukinfield to Hyde Bank: Construction, development of the area and industrial archaeology 1795 to 1900*, unpublished Local History Certificate dissertation, University of Manchester Dept of Extra-Mural Studies.

Wadsworth P 1990-1 'Strawberry Studio' *SH* 2.1, 21.

Wainwright J 1899 *Memories of Marple: Pictorial and Descriptive Reminiscences of a Lifetime in Marple* (reprinted 1989, MTD Rigg Publications).

Walker J S F & Tindall A S (eds) 1985 *Country Houses of Greater Manchester*, The Archaeology of Greater Manchester vol 2, Greater Manchester Archaeological Unit.

Walker R B 1966 'Religious Changes in Cheshire, 1750-1850' *Journal of Ecclesiastical History* 17, 77-94.

Walton J K 1987 *Lancashire: A Social History, 1558-1939*, Manchester University Press.

Wardle M & Bentham 1814 *The Commercial Directory of Manchester*.

Wark K R 1971 *Elizabethan Recusancy in Cheshire*, Chetham Society, 3rd series, 19.

Watkin W T 1883 *Roman Lancashire: or, a Description of Roman Remains in the County Palatine of Lancaster*, Liverpool.

Watkin W T 1886 *Roman Cheshire: a Description of Roman Remains in the County of Chester*, Liverpool (reprinted 1974, Wakefield, E P Publishing Ltd).

Watson Revd J nd *A Manuscript Collection towards a History of Cheshire*, Watson Mss, vol 1, SLHL (copy of original in the Bodleian Library).

Watson Revd J 1782 *Memoirs of the Ancient Earls of Warren and Surrey and the Descendants to the Present Time*, 2 vols, Warrington.

White F & Co 1860 *History, Gazetteer and Directory of Cheshire*, Sheffield.

Wilkinson D J 1982 'The Commission of the Peace in Lancashire, 1603-1642', in Kermode & Phillips (eds), 41-66.

Willan T S 1951 *The Navigation of the River Weaver in the Eighteenth Century*, Chetham Society, 3rd series, 3.

Willan T S 1980 *Elizabethan Manchester*, Chetham Society, 3rd series, 27.

Willan T S 1982 'Plague in Perspective: The Case of Manchester in 1605', in Kermode & Phillips (eds), 29-40.

Williams M with Farnie D A 1992 *Cotton Mills in Greater Manchester*, Carnegie Publishing Ltd.

Wilson J F 1991 *Lighting the Town: A Study of Management in the North-West Gas Industry*, London, Paul Chapman Publishing.

Winstanley I (ed) 1995 *Children in the Mines. The Children's Employment Commission of 1842. The Evidence: The Lancashire Coalfield*, Ashton in Makerfield, Picks Publishing, with The Lancashire Mining Museum, Salford.

Woodford Women's Institute nd *Scrapbook of Woodford*, privately published.

Worrall J 1884 *The Cotton Spinners and Manufacturers' Directory*, Oldham.

Worrall J Ltd 1939 *The Lancashire Textile Industry*, Oldham.

Yeatman J P 1892 'The Lost History of Peak Forest, the Hunting Ground of the Peverels' *DAJ* 14, 161-75.

Yeatman J P 1895a *The Feudal History of the County of Derby*, vol III, section V, privately published.

Yeatman J P 1895b *The Feudal History of the County of Derby*, vol III, section VI, privately published.

Youd D 1961 'The Common Fields of Lancashire' *THSLC* 113, 1-41.

Index

298

A NEW
and Accurate Map
of
the Environs
of
Stockport

By william Stopford

A SCALE OF | 2 MILES

N
W — E
S

LANCASHIRE

STOCKPORT

RIVER MERSEY

NORTHENDEN

Cheadle
Wood

Brink
Shaw

Shaw He

CHEADLE

Gatley Green

Edgley

Brook
Head

Bridge
Hall

ETCHELLS

Bates Le

Adfwood

ross
Green

Schools

Hill

Lady

Bridge

High Grove

eel
Hall

Pimm
Gate

Bramhall
Hall

Bradshaw
Hall

CHEADLE

Kell